Frommer's®
Vancouver & Victoria

My Vancouver & Victoria
by Donald Olson

I FEEL A FRESH SENSE OF ADVENTURE EVERY TIME I RETURN TO BUSY, buzzing Vancouver. The backdrop of mountains, forests, and sea adds an unusual perspective to an urban landscape filled with soaring glass towers and an architectural sensibility more European than American. Vancouver—dubbed "Hollywood North" by some—is a new city, with an odd, appealing mixture of pioneer spirit and up-to-the-minute trendiness. Explore its neighborhoods and markets, and you'll pick up a distinct international vibe. But cultures don't clash here, they co-exist—each one contributing to the city's cosmopolitan flavor.

Victoria is another story—once so dowdy and dull that local cynics dubbed it a place for the newly wed and the nearly dead. But in the past few decades, the quaint capital of British Columbia has dusted itself off and rediscovered what has always made it so desirable: nature on a grand scale, and a city whose faded charms were ripe for a makeover. Today, Victoria is cozy and relaxing, a mini-maritime delight. Whether you come to watch whales, paddle a kayak, take tea at the venerable Empress Hotel, or stroll the century-old paths of Butchart Gardens (one of the greatest gardens in North America), you'll find Victoria to be an uncommonly pleasant place to visit. The photos in these pages show Vancouver and the surrounding region at its best.

VANCOUVER AQUARIUM (left) An up-close and personal glimpse of a beluga whale in the icy-blue Arctic Canada exhibit at the Vancouver Aquarium Marine Science Center thrills landlubbers of all ages. For an extra fee, the aquarium also affords visitors the chance to help trainers feed the giant mammals throughout the day.

GASTOWN STEAM CLOCK (above) A quirky urban timepiece, the Steam Clock in Vancouver's historic Gastown gives a steamy rendition of the Westminster Chimes every 15 minutes, drawing its power from the underground steam-heat system. Vancouver's first neighborhood, established around "Gassy Jack's" saloon, Gastown is home to the city's oldest brick and cast-iron architecture and draws visitors to its art galleries, shops, pubs, clubs, and restaurants.

FIRST NATIONS TOTEM POLES (left): Distinctive First Nations artwork is a living tradition throughout British Columbia. A stunning array of totem poles can be found in Vancouver—this one is in Stanley Park. Originally home to the Musqueam and Squamish nations, the park now boasts one of the city's largest collections of totem poles.

KITSILANO BEACH IN SUMMER (below) On warm, sunny days, Vancouver turns into a beach town, Northwest-style. There are many beaches to choose from, but Kitsilano is one of the grooviest. If you get tired of the beach, the adjacent Boho Kits neighborhood is a joy to explore.

BUTCHART GARDENS IN SUMMER (above)
One of the great landscaping feats in
North America, the 20-hectare (50-
acre) Butchart Gardens—just north of
downtown Victoria—can be visited
year-round. Displaying more than a million plants throughout the year, the
gardens—still under the care of the
Butchart family a century after their
creation—are a national treasure.

COFFEE AT CAFFE ARTIGIANO (right) No
doubt about it: Vancouver's on a coffee
buzz. Cafes, coffeehouses, and caffeine are a way of life here. The art of
coffee has been perfected at Caffè
Artigiano, where your latte comes with
a design in the foam.

LIGHTHOUSE IN WEST VANCOUVER (above) On a rocky bluff overlooking the Strait of Georgia stands the Point Atkinson Lighthouse. Located in West Vancouver's Lighthouse Park, this iconic structure is just one of about 40 lighthouses that still survive along British Columbia's rugged and scenic coast.

GREAT BEAR RAINFOREST (right) Great Bear Rainforest on the western coast of Vancouver Island protects a magnificent swath of old-growth temperate rainforest, one of the last places in North America where several bear species—grizzly, black, and the rare Kermode, or spirit bear—thrive.

THE EMPRESS HOTEL Yes, it's touristy and expensive, but tea at the magnificent Empress is a must for visitors to Victoria. You'll be pleasantly pampered and shamelessly stuffed as an assortment of cakes, sandwiches, and scones with clotted cream appears—and disappears—at your table.

WHISTLER (above) For what many consider the best skiing in North America, take the spectacular scenic Sea-to-Sky highway to Whistler Resort, just 2 hours north of Vancouver. Chosen as the site of the 2010 Winter Olympics, Whistler is a world unto itself. In the winter, you can ski from your hotel right to the slopes; in summer, the ski slopes are converted into a world-class mountain bike course.

VANCOUVER ISLAND (right) "Super-natural" is one way to describe British Columbia, which draws visitors to its spectacular landscapes of sea, forest, and mountains. In Pacific Rim National Park, on the rugged west coast of Vancouver Island, hikers discover the beauty and wonders of a coastal rainforest.

DR. SUN YAT-SEN CLASSICAL CHINESE GARDEN (right) One of Vancouver's hidden treasures, the Dr. Sun Yat-sen Classical Chinese Garden reflects the timeless tranquillity and painstaking artistry found in Taoist-inspired Chinese gardens.

SCIENCE WORLD (below) This big, blinking geodesic dome on the eastern end of False Creek is the home of Science World at Telus World of Science, Vancouver's child-oriented science museum. Hands-on adventures—plus a giant-screen Omnimax theater—give young visitors a fresh look at the world around them and how it works.

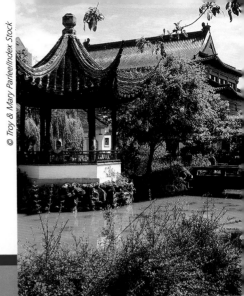

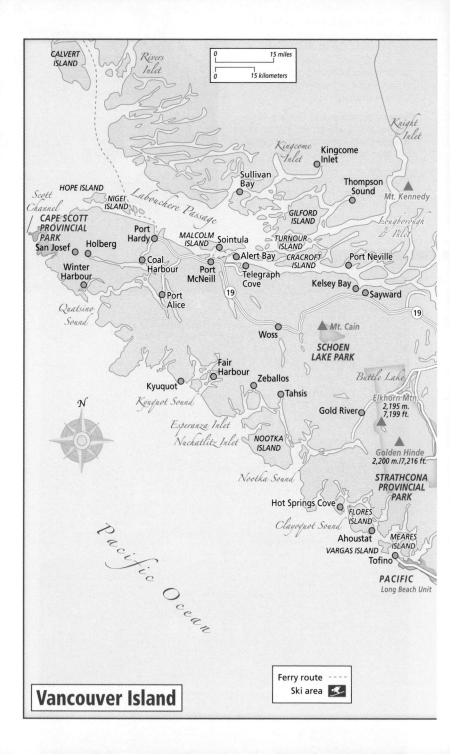

Vancouver Island

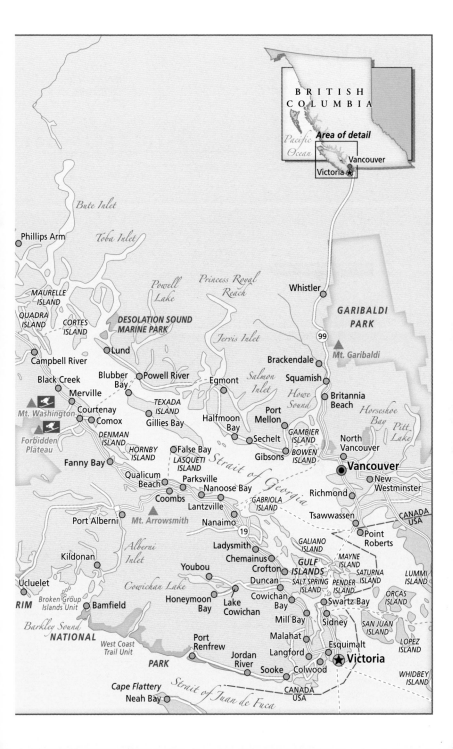

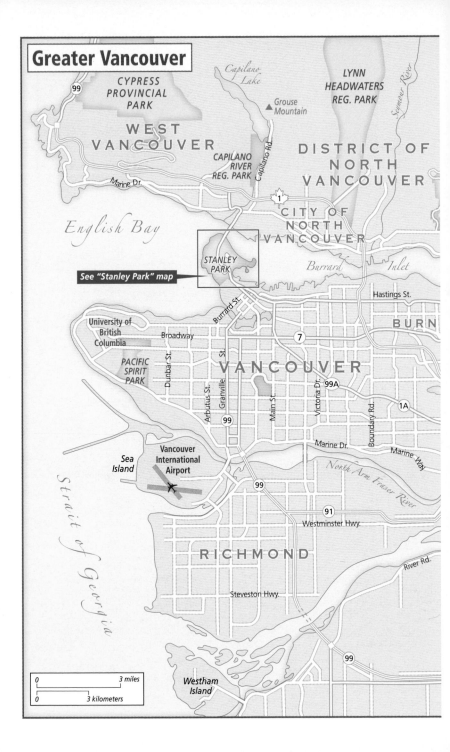

Greater Vancouver

99

CYPRESS
PROVINCIAL
PARK

Capilano Lake

Grouse Mountain

LYNN
HEADWATERS
REG. PARK

Seymour River

WEST VANCOUVER

CAPILANO
RIVER
REG. PARK

Capilano Rd.

Marine Dr.

DISTRICT OF NORTH VANCOUVER

1

English Bay

STANLEY
PARK

See "Stanley Park" map

CITY OF NORTH VANCOUVER

Burrard   *Inlet*

Hastings St.

Burrard St.

University of
British
Columbia

Broadway

BURN

PACIFIC
SPIRIT
PARK

Dunbar St.

Arbutus St.

Granville St.

VANCOUVER

Main St.

7

Victoria Dr.

99A

Boundary Rd.

1A

99

Marine Dr.

Marine Way

Sea Island

Vancouver
International
Airport

99

North Arm Fraser River

91

Westminster Hwy.

RICHMOND

River Rd.

Strait of Georgia

Steveston Hwy.

99

0 ———————— 3 miles

0 ———————— 3 kilometers

Westham Island

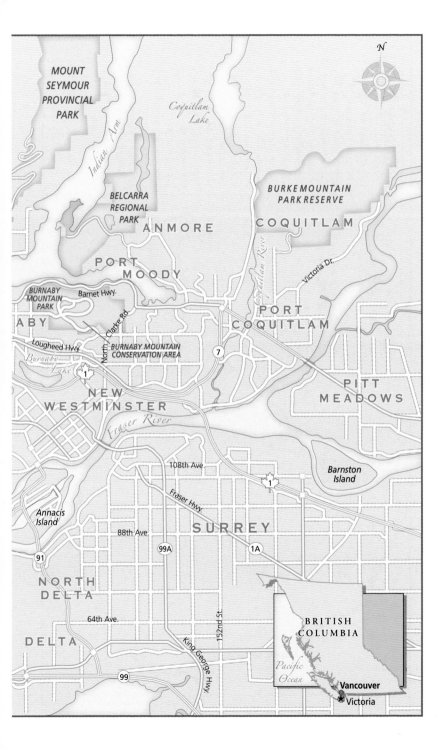

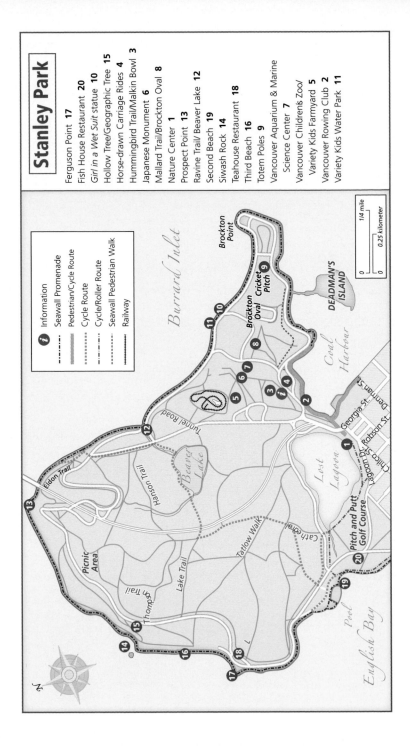

Stanley Park

Ferguson Point 17
Fish House Restaurant 20
Girl in a Wet Suit statue 10
Hollow Tree/Geographic Tree 15
Horse-drawn Carriage Rides 4
Hummingbird Trail/Malkin Bowl 3
Japanese Monument 6
Mallard Trail/Brockton Oval 8
Nature Center 1
Prospect Point 13
Ravine Trail/ Beaver Lake 12
Second Beach 19
Siwash Rock 14
Teahouse Restaurant 18
Third Beach 16
Totem Poles 9
Vancouver Aquarium & Marine
  Science Center 7
Vancouver Children's Zoo/
  Variety Kids Farmyard 5
Vancouver Rowing Club 2
Variety Kids Water Park 11

Legend:
- *i* Information
- Seawall Promenade
- Pedestrian/Cycle Route
- Cycle Route
- Cycle/Roller Route
- Seawall Pedestrian Walk
- Railway

0 1/4 mile
0 0.25 kilometer

Burrard Inlet

Brockton Point

Brockton Oval Cricket Pitch

DEADMAN'S ISLAND

Coal Harbour

Lost Lagoon

Tunnel Road

Beaver Lake

Hanson Trail

Eldon Trail

Cath Trail

Lake Trail

Tatlow Walk

Thompson Trail

Picnic Area

Pitch and Putt Golf Course

Georgia St.

Chilco St.

Lagoon Dr.

Robson St.

Denman St.

English Bay

N

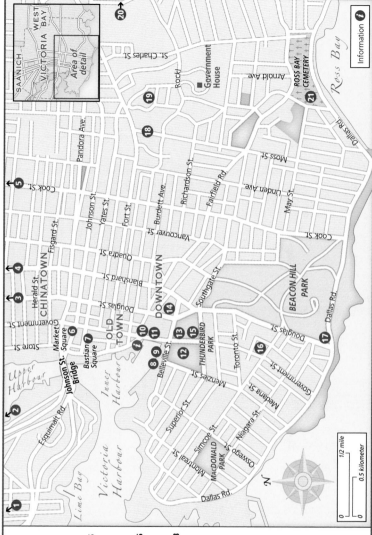

Downtown Victoria

Abkhazi Gardens **20**
Art Gallery of Greater Victoria **18**
British Columbia Aviation Museum **5**
Butchart Gardens **4**
Craigdarroch Castle **19**
Crystal Garden **14**
Dominion Astrophysical Laboratory **5**
Emily Carr House **16**
The Fairmont Empress **11**
Fort Rodd Hill & Fisgard Lighthouse **3**
Hatley Park Castle and Museum **1**
Helmcken House **15**
Maritime Museum of British
  Columbia **7**
Market Square **6**
Miniature World **10**
Mount Douglas Park **5**
Pacific Undersea Gardens **9**
Parliament Buildings
  (Provincial Legislature) **12**
Point Ellice House **2**
Ross Bay Cemetery **21**
Royal British Columbia Museum **13**
Royal London Wax Museum **8**
Trans-Canada Highway Mile 0 **17**

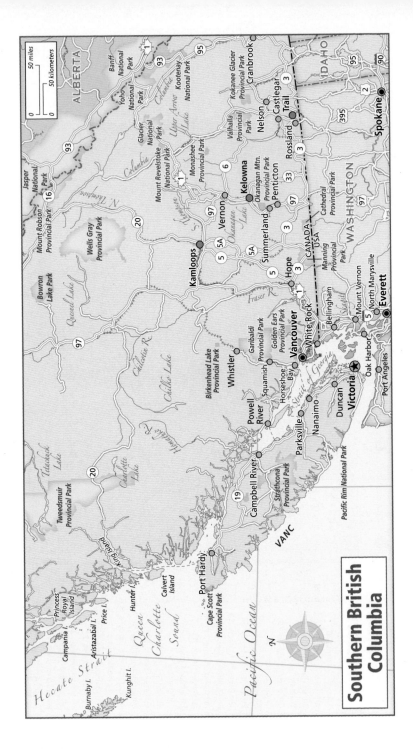

Southern British
Columbia

Frommer's®

Vancouver & Victoria

2008

by Donald Olson

with coverage of Whistler

Here's what the critics say about Frommer's:

"Amazingly easy to use. Very portable, very complete."

—*Booklist*

"Detailed, accurate, and easy-to-read information for all price ranges."

—*Glamour Magazine*

"Hotel information is close to encyclopedic."

—*Des Moines Sunday Register*

"Frommer's Guides have a way of giving you a real feel for a place."

—*Knight Ridder Newspapers*

Wiley Publishing, Inc.

Published by:

Wiley Publishing, Inc.

111 River St.
Hoboken, NJ 07030-5774

ISBN: 978-0-470-16563-8
Editor: Melinda Quintero
Production Editor: Lindsay Conner
Cartographer: Andrew Dolan
Photo Editor: Richard Fox
Anniversary Logo Design: Richard Pacifico
Production by Wiley Indianapolis Composition Services

Front cover photo: Detail of a First Nations' totem pole.
Back cover photo: False Creek Marina, with downtown Vancouver skyscrapers.

For information on our other products and services or to obtain technical support, please contact our Customer Care Department within the U.S. at 800/762-2974, outside the U.S. at 317/572-3993 or fax 317/572-4002.

Wiley also publishes its books in a variety of electronic formats. Some content that appears in print may not be available in electronic formats.

Manufactured in the United States of America

5 4 3 2 1

Contents

List of Maps

An Invitation to the Reader

In researching this book, we discovered many wonderful places—hotels, restaurants, shops, and more. We're sure you'll find others. Please tell us about them, so we can share the information with your fellow travelers in upcoming editions. If you were disappointed with a recommendation, we'd love to know that, too. Please write to:

Frommer's Vancouver & Victoria 2008
Wiley Publishing, Inc. • 111 River St. • Hoboken, NJ 07030-5774

An Additional Note

Please be advised that travel information is subject to change at any time—and this is especially true of prices. We therefore suggest that you write or call ahead for confirmation when making your travel plans. The authors, editors, and publisher cannot be held responsible for the experiences of readers while traveling. Your safety is important to us, however, so we encourage you to stay alert and be aware of your surroundings. Keep a close eye on cameras, purses, and wallets, all favorite targets of thieves and pickpockets.

About the Author

Donald Olson is a novelist, playwright, and travel writer. His newest novel, *Memoirs Are Made of This*, was published in the U.K. by Hodder-Headline in 2007 under the pen name Swan Adamson. Two earlier Swan Adamson novels, *My Three Husbands* and *Confessions of a Pregnant Princess*, were published in the U.S. and translated into French. Donald Olson's novel *The Confessions of Aubrey Beardsley*, was published in the United Kingdom by Bantam Press, and his play, *Beardsley*, was produced in London. His travel stories have appeared in *The New York Times*, *Travel + Leisure*, *Sunset*, *National Geographic*, and many other publications. His additional guidebooks *Best Day Trips from London*, *England For Dummies*, *Germany For Dummies*, and *London For Dummies* are all published by Wiley. *England For Dummies* won a 2002 Lowell Thomas Travel Writing Award for best guidebook.

Other Great Guides for Your Trip:

Frommer's British Columbia & the Canadian Rockies
Frommer's Canada

Frommer's Star Ratings, Icons & Abbreviations

Every hotel, restaurant, and attraction listing in this guide has been ranked for quality, value, service, amenities, and special features using a **star-rating system.** In country, state, and regional guides, we also rate towns and regions to help you narrow down your choices and budget your time accordingly. Hotels and restaurants are rated on a scale of zero (recommended) to three stars (exceptional). Attractions, shopping, nightlife, towns, and regions are rated according to the following scale: zero stars (recommended), one star (highly recommended), two stars (very highly recommended), and three stars (must-see).

In addition to the star-rating system, we also use **seven feature icons** that point you to the great deals, in-the-know advice, and unique experiences that separate travelers from tourists. Throughout the book, look for:

Finds	Special finds—those places only insiders know about
Fun Fact	Fun facts—details that make travelers more informed and their trips more fun
Kids	Best bets for kids and advice for the whole family
Moments	Special moments—those experiences that memories are made of
Overrated	Places or experiences not worth your time or money
Tips	Insider tips—great ways to save time and money
Value	Great values—where to get the best deals

The following **abbreviations** are used for credit cards:

AE	American Express	DISC	Discover	V	Visa
DC	Diners Club	MC	MasterCard		

Frommers.com

Now that you have the guidebook to a great trip, visit our website at **www.frommers.com** for additional travel information on more than 3,600 destinations. We update features regularly to give you instant access to the most current trip-planning information available. At Frommers.com, you'll find scoops on the best airfares, lodging rates, and car rental bargains. You can even book your travel online through our travel booking partners. Other popular features include:

- Online updates to our most popular guidebooks
- Vacation sweepstakes and contest giveaways
- Newsletter highlighting the hottest travel trends
- Online travel message boards with featured travel discussions

What's New in Vancouver & Victoria

Construction, construction, everywhere, both aboveground and beneath it. Why? Because in the summer of 2003, Vancouver was awarded hosting rights to the 2010 Olympic and Paralympic Winter Games. The excitement in and around the city (where the skating events and some skiing events will be held) and at Whistler Resort (where the skiing and most of the snow events will take place) is palpable. For more information, see "2010 Winter Olympics Update," below, or visit www.vancouver2010.com.

Prices are sure to rise for the Olympics, but for now, fabulous restaurants and accommodations in Vancouver and Victoria are still priced lower than those in Toronto, Montreal, or any major U.S. city. This is true even with the weakening value of the U.S. dollar.

VANCOUVER For the third year in a row, the readers of *Condé Nast Traveler* magazine voted Vancouver into the highest ranks of the category "Best City in the Americas" at their annual Readers' Choice Awards. The poll divides cities into five specific geographical divisions including the Americas, which covers Canada, Central America, and South America, and scores them on ambience, friendliness, culture and sites, restaurants, lodging, and shopping.

Transportation Parts of Vancouver are torn up for the construction of **Canada Line,** a new light-rail hookup from Vancouver International Airport. When it begins operation in 2009, visitors will be able to board the train at the airport and arrive downtown or in Yaletown in 22 minutes.

Travelers at **Vancouver International Airport (YVR)** can now enjoy a **first-class lounge** experience at one of two new Plaza Premium Lounges that have opened in the Domestic and International Terminals. The lounges are open to all passengers regardless of airline, travel class, or membership programs. The Domestic Terminal Lounge is located past the security checkpoint and features comfortable seating, runway views, business services, Wi-Fi, and refreshments for a nominal C$25 (US$21/ £11) entrance fee. The Plaza Premium Lounge at the International Terminal features all of the above, as well as napping stations and showers, for a C$30 (US$25/ £13) entrance fee. Lounges are open daily from 6am to 11:30pm. For more information visit www.plaza-ppl.com.

In May 2007, **Frontier Airlines** began a daily nonstop service between its Denver hub and Vancouver, the first U.S. low-cost carrier to serve Vancouver. The service also allows connection with Frontier's other routes serving 22 U.S. cities.

Accommodations The same *Condé Nast* readers' poll that voted Vancouver the best city in the Americas also recognized eight of Vancouver's hotels in the "Top 20 Canada Hotels" category. They include the **Pan Pacific Hotel Vancouver** (fifth), **Wedgewood Hotel** (sixth), **The Sutton Place Hotel** (seventh), **Opus Hotel** (ninth), **Four Seasons Hotel** (17th), and **The Fairmont Hotel Vancouver** (19th).

You'll find descriptions for all of them in chapter 5.

Situated in Vancouver's downtown, close to the Granville Street entertainment district, the new **Moda Hotel,** 900 Seymour St. (© **604/683-4251**), offers lots of style and excellent value. The hotel, located in a 1908 heritage building, recently opened its doors after receiving a significant makeover. Rooms feature a sleekly minimal European look. See p. 73.

Vancouver's newest hotel, the **Loden Vancouver,** opened in 2007. Located at Melville and Bute streets in downtown Vancouver, the 130-room luxury boutique hotel features a fitness center, spa, restaurant, and guest rooms with 42-inch flat-panel TVs, DVD players, iPod docking stations, cordless speaker phones, and high-speed wireless Internet access. See p. 69.

Dining   After 18 years, Chef Hidekazu Tojo relocated his highly acclaimed **Tojo's Restaurant** to a stunning new space at 1133 W. Broadway. Designed by sculptor and architect Colin Kwok, the 6,500-square-foot vaulted restaurant is a blend of Zen spatial dynamics, crisp modern forms, and an underlying Japanese sensibility that pervades everything, from the subtle colors to the custom-designed chairs. See p. 100.

In 2007, the always-fabulous **West,** 2881 Granville St. (© **604/738-8938**), won *Vancouver* magazine's prestigious Best Restaurant Award for the third year in a row. See p. 100.

Two new restaurants have opened in Gastown, adding to the area's mini-rejuvenation. Both are inexpensive and very welcome additions to the city's dining scene. **Salt,** in Blood Alley (© **604/633-1912**), is Vancouver's only charcuterie, serving cured meats and artisan cheeses. See p. 95. **Jules,** 216 Abbott St. (© **604/669-0033**), is a casual French bistro with a great fixed-price dinner. See p. 94.

Another new spot in Gastown, **Mink, A Chocolate Café,** 863 W. Hastings St. (© **604/633-2451**), caters to chocoholics with delicious chocolate drinks and hand-crafted bonbons. See p. 108.

Attractions & Sightseeing   Gale-force winds in December 2006 wreaked havoc on **Stanley Park,** toppling thousands of trees and damaging fully one-sixth of this beautiful urban forest park. For everyone who knows and loves Stanley Park, this was a heartbreaking event. Expect some hiking trails to be closed well into 2008.

Chef and Chauffeur (www.chefand chauffeur.com) has launched three tours of the Fraser Valley, located about an hour east of the city. The chauffeured tours visit a variety of wineries, farms, bakeries, and cheese makers. Optional dinner add-ons are available with a choice of remaining in the Fraser Valley or dining back in the city. See "Specialty Tours," p. 133, in chapter 7.

2010 Winter Olympics   A **countdown clock,** unveiled in 2007 at the Vancouver Art Gallery, ticks off the remaining days, hours, minutes, and seconds to the opening ceremony for both the 2010 Olympic and Paralympic Winter Games.

Construction of **The Richmond Oval,** where 12 speed-skating events will be held, began in November 2006. The facility will house a 400m track along with seating for 8,000 spectators. Post-Games, the Oval will become a multipurpose sports, recreation, and wellness facility. Along with an adjoining waterfront plaza and park, it will be the centerpiece of a major new City Centre community to be developed on 13 hectares (32 acres) along the banks of the Fraser River.

Construction is also underway on **Hillcrest/Nat Bailey Stadium Park.** Located about 15 minutes from downtown Vancouver, the facility will host the men's and women's curling competitions for the Games, as well as the wheelchair curling tournament for the Paralympic Games. The facility, scheduled for completion in 2008, will seat 6,000 during Olympic competitions. Post-Games, Hillcrest/Nat Bailey Stadium Park will become a community recreation center that will include an ice hockey rink, gymnasium, library, and a new aquatic center with a 50m (164-ft.) lap and leisure pool. The multipurpose center has been designed using leading environmental and business practices.

It's also been announced that the freestyle skiing site at West Vancouver's Cypress Mountain in **Cypress Provincial Park** (see chapter 7, p. 129) is now competition-ready, more than 3 years before the Games are to be held. The mountain, just 30 minutes from downtown, will serve as the venue for snowboarding, freestyle skiing, and the new ski cross events. In winter 2008, Cypress will open nine new runs for high-level intermediate/expert skiers and snowboarders, a 40% increase in the mountain's skiable terrain.

VICTORIA   Transportation   Delta Airlines now offers a direct flight to Victoria from Salt Lake City. Connecting flights from other destinations include Los Angeles, Phoenix, Miami, and others. The flights are operated by Delta Connection carriers Atlantic Southeast Airlines and SkyWest. For schedules and fares visit **www.delta.com**.

Accommodations In the seaside town of Sidney, about 20 minutes north of downtown Victoria, **Sidney Pier Hotel & Spa** (© **866/659-9445**) is a small, quiet, boutique-style luxury hotel perfect for a romantic getaway. It has the feel of a contemporary country inn or B&B. See p. 206.

SIDE TRIPS   Whistler The final okay has been given for the construction of the world's longest gondola, which will connect Whistler and Blackcomb mountains. Work won't be completed until 2009.

Howe Sound Seaplanes (© **866/882-3252**) now offers two daily flights from Victoria to the Whistler area. Passengers fly from Victoria's Inner Harbour via the Vancouver Airport to Squamish, located 30 minutes south of Whistler, where a courtesy shuttle transfers them to Whistler. The flight from Victoria to Vancouver is 35 minutes and from Vancouver to Squamish 30 minutes.

In preparation for the 2010 Winter Olympics, the **Sea-to-Sky Highway (Hwy. 99)** is being given a complete overhaul, and work will continue until 2009. To find out about potential delays due to construction, call © **877/474-3399** (toll-free in Canada) or 604/660-1008, or visit www.seatoskyimprovements.ca.

Whistler's newest hotel, **Adara Whistler Hotel,** 4122 Village Green (© **866/502-3272**), opened in June 2007, smack-dab in the center of Whistler Village. The location couldn't be better, and this upscale boutique hotel offers an array of special packages, including a romantic "Honeymooners Package" that flies you over to a nearby glacier for an unforgettable picnic lunch.

1

The Best of
Vancouver & Victoria

If you really want to understand **Vancouver,** stand at the edge of the Inner Harbour (the Canada Place cruise-ship terminal makes a good vantage point) and look around you. To the west you'll see Stanley Park, one of the world's largest urban parks, jutting out into the waters of Burrard Inlet. To the north, just across the inlet, rise snowcapped mountains. To the east, right along the water, is the low-rise brick-faced Old Town. And almost everything else you see lining the water's edge will be new glass-and-steel high-rise towers. As giant cruise ships glide in to berth, floatplanes buzz in and out, and your ears catch a medley of foreign tongues, you may wonder just where on earth you are. Vancouver is majestic and intimate, sophisticated and completely laid-back, a bustling, prosperous city that somehow, almost miraculously, manages to combine its contemporary, urban-centered consciousness with the free-spirited magnificence of nature on a grand scale.

Vancouver is probably one of the "newest" cities you'll ever visit, and certainly it's one of the most cosmopolitan. A youthfulness pervades, along with a certain Pacific Northwest chic (and cheek) that comes from being the backdrop in so many movies that Vancouver is sometimes called "Hollywood North" (as is Toronto, so maybe it's time to retire that rather tired phrase). I can guarantee you that part of your trip will be spent trying to figure out what makes it so unique. Nature figures big in that equation, but so does enlightened city planning and the diversity of cultures. Vancouver is a place where people *want* to live. It's a place that awakens dreams and desires.

The city's history is in its topography. Thousands of years ago, a giant glacier sliced along the foot of the coast range, carving out a deep trench and piling up a gigantic moraine of rock and sand. When the ice retreated, water from the Pacific flowed in and the moraine became a peninsula, flanked on one side by a deep natural harbor (today's Port of Vancouver on Burrard Inlet) and on the other by a river of glacial meltwater (today called the Fraser River). Vast forests of fir and cedar covered the land and wildlife flourished. The First Nations tribes that settled in the area developed rich cultures based on cedar and salmon.

Some 10,000 years later, a surveyor for the Canadian Pacific Railway (CPR) came by, took in the peninsula, the harbor, and the river, and decided he'd found the perfect spot for the CPR's new Pacific terminus. He kept it quiet, as smart railway men tended to do, until the company had bought up most of the land around town. In 1887 the railway moved in, set up shop, and the city of Vancouver was born.

Vancouverites have seemingly all fallen in love with the outdoors. And why shouldn't they? Every terrain needed for every kind of outdoor pursuit—hiking, in-line skating, mountainbiking, downhill and cross-country skiing, kayaking, windsurfing, rock climbing, parasailing, snowboarding—is right in their backyard: ocean, rivers, mountains, islands, sidewalks. The international resort town of Whistler (described in chapter 18), which will take center stage during the Winter Olympics in 2010, is just 2 hours north of downtown Vancouver.

When they're not skiing or kayaking, Vancouverites enjoy the best of their city's culinary offerings. In the past decade or so, Vancouver has become one of the top dining destinations in the world, bursting with an incredible variety of cuisines and making an international name for itself with its Pacific Northwest cooking. The new food mantra here is "buy locally, eat seasonally," which you'll find being practiced at many restaurants.

The rest of the world has taken notice of the blessed life people in these parts lead. Surveys generally list Vancouver as one of the 10 best cities in the world to live in. It's also one of the 10 best to visit, according to *Condé Nast Traveler,* and won that magazine's Readers' Choice Award in 2005 and 2006 as "Best City in the Americas." In 2003, the International Olympic Committee named Vancouver the host of the 2010 Olympic Winter Games. Heady stuff, particularly for a spot that less than 20 years ago was routinely derided as the world's biggest mill town.

Though some "heritage buildings" still remain in Vancouver, the face of the city you see today is undeniably new. Starting in the 1960s, misguided planners and developers seemed intent on demolishing every last vestige of the city's pioneer past, replacing old brick and wood buildings with an array of undistinguished concrete high-rises and blocky eyesores. Citizen outcry finally got the bulldozers to stop their rampage. Luckily, landscaping and gardening was an ingrained part of life in this mild climate, so plants, trees, and shrubs were not uprooted for endless parking lots. You may be amazed, in fact, by the amount of green, the number of fountains, and the overall lushness of neighborhoods like the West End, which also happens to be one of the most densely populated areas in the world. A building boom preceded Expo '86 (the last world's fair in North America) and followed it as well, spurred on by enormous amounts of cash pouring in from Hong Kong and Asia. The new residential towers, made of glass and steel, are much lighter looking than those from times past, and keep with the hip, international image that Vancouver is developing for itself.

If you miss the old in Vancouver, you'll find plenty of it in **Victoria,** some 80km (50 miles) across the Strait of Georgia on Vancouver Island. Victoria took the opposite approach from Vancouver and preserved nearly all its heritage buildings. As a result, British Columbia's capital, beautifully sited on its own Inner Harbour, is one of the most charming small cities you'll ever find (it has about 325,000 residents in the Greater Victoria area, compared to around two million in Vancouver). Since it's on an island, accessible only by ferry (the best way to go) or plane, a more leisurely sense of time prevails in Victoria. It's a perfect antidote for stressed-out mainlanders.

For years Victoria marketed itself quite successfully as a little bit of England on the North American continent. So successful was the colonial sales pitch, residents began to believe it themselves. They began growing elaborate rose gardens, which flourished in the mild Pacific climate, and they cultivated a taste for afternoon tea with jam and scones. They were islanders ruled by the mother island from which all culture emanated and was exported.

For decades this continued, until eventually the people of Victoria saw the glories all around them instead of those reflected from a dying empire. The town became a lot more interesting. It was discovered that not many residents of Victoria shared a taste for English cooking, so restaurants branched out into seafood, ethnic, and fusion cuisines. And lately, as visitors have shown more interest in exploring the natural world, Victoria has added whale-watching and mountainbiking trips to its traditional London-style double-decker bus tours. The result? Victoria is the only city in the world where you can zoom out on a boat in the morning to see a pod of killer whales and make it back in time for an expansive afternoon tea. Still, life is much quieter and 10 times more laid-back than Vancouver, but that's part of Victoria's charm. And if you add the Butchart Gardens, a truly world-class garden that celebrated its centenary in 2004, and the fabulous First Nations art collection in the Royal B.C. Museum, you've got all you need for a memorable vacation just a 90-minute ferry ride from the big city. If you want to explore more of Vancouver Island, head to Tofino and Pacific Rim National Park (described in chapter 18) on the Island's wild, wet, west coast.

1 The Most Unforgettable Travel Experiences: Vancouver

• **Taking a Carriage Ride through Stanley Park:** One of the largest urban parks in the world, and certainly one of the most beautiful, Stanley Park is nothing short of magnificent. Sample the highlights on a delightful 1-hour carriage ride that winds through the forest, along Burrard Inlet, past cricket fields, rose gardens, and the park's superlative collection of First Nations totem poles. See p. 116.

• **Wandering the West End:** Encompassing the über-shopping strip known as Robson Street, as well as cafe-lined Denman and a forest of high-rise apartments, the West End is the urban heart of Vancouver. Enjoy the lush trees lining the streets, the range of architecture, the diversity of cultures, the latest fashions and fashionistas, and neat little surprises on every side street. See Walking Tour 1, p. 145.

The Best Websites for Vancouver & Victoria

• **Entertainment Info** (www.ticketstonight.ca): This site is a great place for half-price night-of tickets and general entertainment information in the Vancouver area.

• **Pacific Rim Visitor Centre** (www.pacificrimvisitor.ca): This area-specific site is a great place to learn more about Vancouver Island's west coast.

• **Tourism B.C.** (www.hellobc.com): The official site of the provincial government tourism agency, this site provides good information on attractions, as well as higher-end accommodations.

• **Tourism Vancouver** (www.tourismvancouver.com): The official city tourism agency site provides a great overview of attractions, including an excellent calendar of events, plus a few last-minute deals on accommodations.

• **Tourism Victoria** (www.tourismvictoria.com): Victoria's official tourism site functions much the same as Vancouver's, with up-to-date, comprehensive information about what to do and see around the city.

• **Whistler Blackcomb Ski Resort** (www.whistlerblackcomb.com): This site offers a particularly helpful overview of activities and accommodations options available at North America's premier ski resort.

Southwestern British Columbia

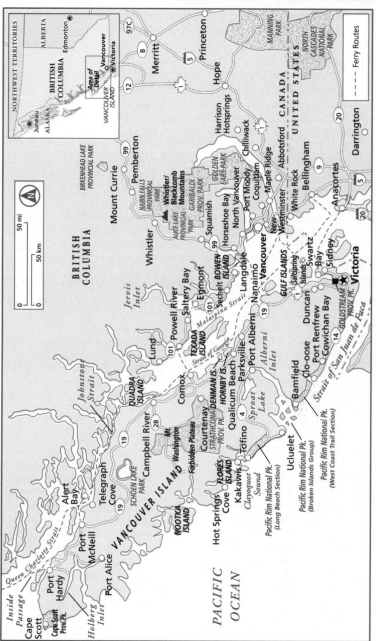

- - - - Ferry Routes

NORTHWEST TERRITORIES

ALASKA
Juneau

BRITISH COLUMBIA
Edmonton
ALBERTA

Area of Detail
Vancouver
Victoria
VANCOUVER ISLAND

BRITISH COLUMBIA

PACIFIC OCEAN

Inside Passage
Queen Charlotte Strait
Cape Scott
Cape Scott Prov. Pk.
Holberg Inlet
Port Hardy
Port McNeill
Port Alice
Alert Bay
Telegraph Cove
Johnstone Strait
SCHOEN LAKE PROV. PARK
Campbell River
Mt. Washington
Forbidden Plateau
STRATHCONA PROV. PK.
VANCOUVER ISLAND
NOOTKA ISLAND
Hot Springs Cove
FLORES ISLAND
Kakawis
Clayoquot Sound
Tofino
Pacific Rim National Park (Long Beach Section)
Ucluelet
Pacific Rim National Pk. (Broken Islands Group)
Bamfield
Pacific Rim National Pk. (West Coast Trail Section)
QUADRA ISLAND
Comox
Courtenay
Qualicum Beach
DENMAN IS.
HORNBY IS.
Parksville
Port Alberni
Sproat Lake
Alberni Inlet
Clo-oose
Port Renfrew
Cowichan Bay
GOLDSTREAM PROV. PK.
Duncan
Strait of San Juan de Fuca
Lund
TEXADA ISLAND
Powell River
Saltery Bay
Jervis Inlet
Egmont
Sechelt
Malaspina Strait
Strait of Georgia
Nanaimo
GULF ISLANDS
Saltspring Islands
Swartz Bay
Sidney
Victoria
BOWEN ISLAND
Langdale
Gibsons
Horseshoe Bay
North Vancouver
Vancouver
New Westminster
Port Moody
Coquitlam
Maple Ridge
White Rock
Abbotsford
Bellingham
Anacortes
Darrington
Squamish
Whistler
Whistler/Blackcomb Mountains
GARIBALDI PROV. PARK
ALICE LAKE PROVINCIAL PARK
NAIRN FALLS PROVINCIAL PARK
GOLDEN EARS PARK
Pemberton
Mount Currie
BIRKENHEAD LAKE PROVINCIAL PARK
Harrison Hotsprings
Chilliwack
Hope
Princeton
Merritt
Edmonton
Victoria
MANNING PARK
NORTH CASCADES NATIONAL PARK
CANADA
UNITED STATES

99
99
101
101
12
8
5
1
1
1
4
14
19
19
19
20
20
5
9
28
97C

A Short History of First Nations

When Captain Vancouver arrived in English Bay in 1792, more than 50 First Nations were living in what is now British Columbia, speaking about 30 languages from six distinct language families.

Exactly where each tribe lived, when they arrived, and how many members each had is all now a matter of some controversy, but evidence suggests that the area had been settled for some 10,000 years. One hundred percent of the province's land area is now claimed by one or more First Nations. Negotiations are proceeding slowly: One of the most important aspects of any claim is a band's oral tradition. The stories and legends about where a band came from, what lands it occupied, and how and where it gathered food are much more than just stories and legends; in certain circumstances they are considered the equivalent of legal documents, with their content and ownership a huge issue.

Living in the rainforest, all of these coastal peoples developed an extremely rich and complex culture, using cedar as their primary building material and, for food, harvesting marine resources such as herring, shellfish, and especially salmon. The richness of the local environment allowed these peoples ample surplus; their spare time was devoted to the creation of stories and art. Now undergoing a revival, coastal art, whether in wood, glass, or precious metals, usually depicts stylized figures from native mythology, including such universal figures as the Raven, or tribal totems such as the Bear, Frog, or Killer Whale.

The central ceremony of the coastal First Nations was and is the potlatch, a gathering of tribes held to mark a significant event such as the raising of a totem pole or the coming-of-age of a son or daughter. Invited tribes sing and dance traditional songs (which are considered to be their private intellectual property), while the host, both to thank his guests and to demonstrate his

- **Dining Out on Local Seafood:** Visitors are rightly amazed at the abundance of fresh-that-day seafood available in Vancouver's restaurants. This is a city where an appetizer of raw oysters often precedes a main course of wild salmon or halibut. See chapter 6.

- **Dining Out, Period:** The number of truly outstanding restaurants in Vancouver is astonishing. A meal at one of Vancouver's top restaurants will wake you up to the glories of the food scene here, and you'll find extraordinary tastes for every budget in chapter 6.

- **Visiting the Vancouver Aquarium:** It's a Jacques Cousteau special, live and right there in front of you. Fittingly enough, the aquarium has an excellent display on the Pacific Northwest, plus sea otters (cuter than they have any right to be), beluga whales, sea lions, and a Pacific white-sided dolphin. See p. 117.

- **Exploring Chinatown:** Fishmongers call out their wares before a shop filled with crabs, eels, geoducks, and bullfrogs, while farther down the street elderly Chinese women haggle over produce as their husbands hunt for deer antler or dried sea horse at a wealth, gives away presents. At the end of the 19th century, when First Nations culture—supported by a flood of wealth from the sea otter trade—reached unprecedented heights, potlatches could last for days, and chiefs would give away all they had.

The sea otter debacle aside (encouraged by American and British fur traders, coastal natives hunted sea otters to extinction along most of the coast), coastal indigenous peoples were exemplary environmental managers (many were instrumental in forming the blockades that prevented logging in Clayoquot Sound's old-growth forests in the 1980s and 1990s). Pre-contact, First Nations society was divided into a nobility of chiefly families, commoners, and slaves, the latter mostly war captives taken during raids.

In the years after contact, the coastal First Nations were decimated by diseases such as smallpox (it's estimated that some 10,000 people lived along the coastal waterways and all but 600 of them were killed by smallpox carried by white settlers), the loss of traditional fishing rights, the repression of traditional rituals such as the potlatch, and the forced assimilation into English-Canadian culture. In the decades after World War II, an entire generation of native children was forced into residential schools, where speaking native languages and learning native stories were forbidden. The 1970s saw the first steps toward a long and slow recovery. The term "First Nation" came into common usage in the '70s, replacing the word "Indian," which some regarded as derogatory. There is no legal definition of "First Nation," but the term "First Nations peoples" generally refers to all the indigenous peoples in Canada. Though still beset by problems, the First Nations communities are on their way back to becoming a powerful and important force on the B.C. coast.

traditional Chinese herbalist. When you're tired of looking and listening, head inside to any one of a dozen restaurants to sample succulent Cantonese cooking. See chapter 6 and Walking Tour 2, p. 150.

- **Marveling at First Nations Artwork in the Museum of Anthropology:** The building—by native son Arthur Erickson—is worth a visit in itself, but this is also one of the best places in the world to see and learn about West Coast First Nations art and culture. See p. 122.

- **Browsing the Public Market on Granville Island:** Down on False Creek, this former industrial site was long ago converted into a truly eye-popping and sense-staggering indoor public market. Hop on the miniferry at the foot of Davie Street in Yaletown, and in 10 minutes you'll be there. At the market you'll find incredible food and goodies; put together a picnic and sit outside by the wharf to people- or boat-watch as you nosh. See p. 120.

- **Kayaking on Indian Arm:** Vancouver is one of the few cities on the edge of a great wilderness, and one of the best ways to appreciate its splendor is by kayaking on the gorgeous Indian Arm. Rent a kayak or go with an outfitter—they may even serve you a gourmet meal of barbecued salmon. See "Outdoor Activities," p. 134, in chapter 7.

- **Discovering the Paintings of Emily Carr at the Vancouver Art Gallery:** It's always a thrill to discover a great artist, and Emily Carr's work hauntingly captures the primal appeal of B.C.'s rugged, rain- and wave-washed forests and shores. See p. 118.

- **Crossing the Capilano Suspension Bridge:** Stretched across a deep forested canyon, high above old trees and a rushing river, this famous pedestrian-only suspension bridge has been daring visitors to look down for more than 100 years. Now you can explore the giant forest trees, too, on a series of artfully constructed treewalks. See p. 125.

- **Watching the Sunset from a Waterside Patio:** Why else live in a city with such stunning views? Many places on False Creek, English Bay, and Coal Harbour have great waterside patios. See chapter 7.

2 The Most Unforgettable Travel Experiences: Victoria

- **Strolling Victoria's Inner Harbour:** Watch the boats and aquatic wildlife come and go while walking along a paved pathway that winds past manicured flower gardens. The best stretch runs south from the Inner Harbour near the century-old Provincial Legislature Buildings and The Fairmont Empress hotel. See p. 240 and Walking Tour 1 in chapter 15.

- **Savoring Afternoon Tea:** Yes, it's expensive and incredibly touristy, but it's also a complicated and ritual-laden art form that goes on for at least an hour. Besides, it's good. See p. 214.

- **Marveling at Butchart Gardens:** This world-class garden, 20 minutes north of downtown Victoria, is a must-see attraction. Gorgeous during the day and subtly illuminated on summer evenings, it takes on a whole new personality when the famous fireworks begin. Saturday nights in the summertime, you get both. See p. 222.

- **Touring the Royal B.C. Museum:** One of the best small museums in the world, the Royal B.C. does exactly

what a good regional museum should do—explain the region and its people. The First Nations galleries are breathtaking reminders of the richness of native culture. See p. 225.

- **Whale-Watching:** Of all the species of orcas (killer whales), those on the Washington and B.C. coasts are the only ones that live in large and complicated extended families. This makes Victoria a particularly good spot to whale-watch because the orcas travel in large, easy-to-find pods. There's something magical about being out on the water and seeing a pod of 15 animals surface just a few hundred feet away. See "Whale-Watching" in chapter 14, p. 239.

- **Touring by Miniferry:** Catch a Victoria Harbour Ferry, and take a 45-minute tour around the harbor past the floating neighborhood of West Bay or up the gorge, where tidal waterfalls reverse direction with the changing tide. Moonlight tours depart every evening at sunset. See "Getting Around" in chapter 11, and "Organized Tours" in chapter 14.

- **Biking the Dallas Road:** Where else can you find a bike path by an ocean with high mountain peaks for a backdrop? See p. 249.

3 The Most Unforgettable Travel Experiences beyond Vancouver & Victoria

- **Skiing and Mountainbiking at Whistler Blackcomb Resort:** The two best resorts in North America merged in 1997 for a total of more than 200 runs on two adjoining mountains. In the summer, the same slopes become a world-class mountainbiking network. See chapter 18.
- **Ziptrekking at Whistler:** Once you're strapped into your safety harness and hooked onto cables suspended hundreds of feet above a wild river, leap off, and away you go. Safe for everyone from 8 to 80, Ziptrek is an exhilarating adventure you'll never forget. See p. 279.
- **Looking for Bald Eagles in Squamish:** The bald eagle is the national symbol of the United States, but in winter, when the salmon are running, you can see more of these huge birds in Squamish than just about anywhere else in the world. See "Wildlife-Watching" in chapter 7, p. 141.
- **Discovering Pacific Rim National Park:** The drive to this rugged maritime park on Vancouver Island's west coast is stunning, and once there, you're in a world of old-growth temperate rainforests and surf-pounded beaches. It's a place where you can experience the primal glories of nature amid the pampering luxuries of a first-class resort. See chapter 18.

4 The Best Splurge Hotels: Vancouver

- **The Fairmont Hotel Vancouver** (900 W. Georgia St.; *©* **800/441-1414** or 604/684-3131; www.fairmont.com): A landmark in the heart of Vancouver, this grand hotel was built by the Canadian Pacific Railway and opened in 1939. The château-style exterior, the lobby, and even the rooms—now thoroughly restored—are built in a style and on a scale reminiscent of the great European railway hotels. See p. 68.
- **Opus Hotel** (322 Davie St.; *©* **866/ 642-6787** or 604/642-6787; www. opushotel.com): A contemporary boutique hotel that's cool without the attitude, Opus has an offbeat location in hip Yaletown, an array of room types, luscious room colors and finishes, and a luxurious but nontraditional aesthetic—plus good dining. See p. 69.
- **Pacific Palisades Hotel** (1277 Robson St.; *©* **800/663-1815** or 604/ 688-0461; www.pacificpalisadeshotel. com): Large rooms decorated in apple greens and lemon yellows; a lobby of bold, bright colors; a scene restaurant; and thoughtful freebies like the use of yoga gear make this West End high-rise one of the top choices for hip hotel aficionados. See p. 76.
- **Pan Pacific Hotel Vancouver** (300- 999 Canada Place; *©* **800/937-1515** or 604/662-8111; www.panpacific. com): Perched atop the Canada Place cruise-ship terminal and convention center, the Pan Pacific features rooms with stunning water, mountain, and city views; a great health club and spa; and first-class service. See p. 70.
- **Wedgewood Hotel** (845 Hornby St.; *©* **800/663-0666** or 604/689-7777;

www.wedgewoodhotel.com): The only boutique hotel in downtown, the Wedgewood is the most comfortably luxurious in that European style we love so much. Fabulous marble-clad bathrooms and a cozy bar/restaurant invite relaxing and romancing. See p. 71.

5 The Best Moderately Priced Hotels: Vancouver

• **Coast Plaza Hotel & Suites** (1763 Comox St.; ℂ 800/663-1144 or 604/688-7711; www.coasthotels.com): A former high-rise apartment building, the Coast offers large rooms with walk-out balconies and marvelous English Bay views, right in the heart of the West End. See p. 78.

• **West End Guest House** (1362 Haro St.; ℂ 888/546-3327 or 604/681-2889; www.westendguesthouse.com): Built in 1905 by two Vancouver photographers, this highly regarded B&B in the thick of the West End is filled with the artists' work as well as an impressive collection of Victorian antiques. See p. 79.

6 The Best Splurge Hotels: Victoria

• **The Aerie** (600 Ebedora Lane, Malahat; ℂ 800/518-1933 or 250/743-7115; www.aerie.bc.ca): A red-tiled villa high atop Mount Malahat, this luxury accommodation features hand-carved king-size beds, massive wood-burning fireplaces, Jacuzzis, and a famed restaurant. Private terraces offer views across forested mountains to a long coastal fjord. See p. 204.

• **Brentwood Bay Lodge & Spa** (849 Verdier Ave.; ℂ 888/544-2079 or 250/544-2079; www.brentwood baylodge.com): Every detail in the rooms and bathrooms is perfect at this small luxury resort overlooking a pristine fjord 20 minutes north of Victoria (plus the food is great). You can get treatments for two at the fabulous Essence of Life spa. See p. 204.

• **Delta Victoria Ocean Pointe Resort and Spa** (45 Songhees Rd.; ℂ 800/667-4677 or 250/360-2999; www.deltavictoria.com): The glass-fronted hotel lobby and harbor-facing rooms provide the best vantage point in Victoria for watching the lights of the legislature switch on. This comfortable hotel offers a host of services, including a calm, contemporary, Zen-like spa. See p. 192.

• **The Fairmont Empress** (721 Government St.; ℂ 800/441-1414 or 250/384-8111; www.fairmont.com/empress): Architect Francis Rattenbury's masterpiece, the landmark Empress on Victoria's Inner Harbour has charmed princes (and their princesses), potentates, movie stars, and the likes of you and me since 1908. The hotel's Willow Stream spa is a luxurious retreat. See p. 194.

• **Hotel Grand Pacific** (463 Belleville St.; ℂ 800/663-7550 or 250/386-0450; www.hotelgrandpacific.com): The rooms in this high-rise luxury hotel beside the harbor come with a full array of amenities, and the fully equipped fitness center offers aerobics classes, a 25m (82-ft.) ozonated indoor pool, a separate kids' pool, a weight room, sauna, whirlpool, and massage therapist. See p. 195.

• **Laurel Point Inn** (680 Montreal St.; ℂ 800/663-7667 or 250/386-8721; www.laurelpoint.com): With panoramic vistas of the harbor and an elegant, Japanese-influenced decor, this is the place for design junkies and aficionados. See p. 196.

• **Sooke Harbour House** (1528 Whiffen Spit Rd., Sooke; ✆ **800/889-9688** or 250/642-3421; www.sookeharbour house.com): In the little town of Sooke, just west of Victoria, this famed oceanside inn offers quiet West Coast elegance and an exceptional restaurant. See p. 206.

7 The Best Moderately Priced Hotels: Victoria

• **Admiral Inn** (257 Belleville St.; ✆ **888/823-6472** or 250/388-6267; www.admiral.bc.ca): Located on the edge of the Inner Harbour, the Admiral provides friendly service, free bikes, and the most reasonably priced harbor view around. See p. 197.

• **The Boathouse** (746 Sea Dr.; ✆ **866/654-9370** or 250/652-9370; www.members.shaw.ca/boathouse): If you're seeking tranquillity, privacy, and a memorable location, check out this one-room cottage created from a converted boathouse. Built in a secluded cove on Brentwood Bay, within rowing distance of Butchart Gardens, it features its own private dock and dinghy. See p. 204.

• **The Magnolia** (623 Courtney St.; ✆ **877/624-6654** or 250/381-0999; www.magnoliahotel.com): With its central location, elegant lobby, well-designed rooms, and large desks and dataports, The Magnolia is Victoria's best spot for business travelers and those who want understated luxury at a reasonable price. See p. 200.

• **Royal Scot Suite Hotel** (425 Quebec St.; ✆ **800/663-7515** or 250/388-5463; www.royalscot.com): This family-friendly hotel occupies a converted apartment building and offers spacious suites that'll make you and yours feel comfortably at home. The suites come with fully equipped kitchens, and a video arcade and playroom are in the basement. See p. 197.

• **Swans Suite Hotel** (506 Pandora Ave.; ✆ **800/668-7926** or 250/361-3310; www.swanshotel.com): In the heart of the Old Town and just a block from the harbor, this newly refurbished boutique hotel is right above Swans Pub, one of the most pleasant restaurant/brewpubs in the city. See p. 200.

8 The Most Unforgettable Dining Experiences: Vancouver

• **C** (1600 Howe St.; ✆ **604/681-1164**): The creativity of the chef, the quality of the ingredients, and the freshness of the seafood all combine to make this contemporary restaurant overlooking False Creek the best place in Vancouver for innovative seafood. See p. 86.

• **Cin Cin** (1154 Robson St.; ✆ **604/688-7338**): For maximum buzz, dine at this Robson Street star on a Friday or Saturday night. It's a lively people-watching spot where the Italian menu is divided into Old World and New, and *tutto* tastes terrific. See p. 95.

• **Coast** (1257 Hamilton St.; ✆ **604/685-5010**): "Catch it, cook it, eat it" is the motto of this superlative Yaletown restaurant. Fresh fish from around the world is cooked to elegant perfection in a beautiful space created with light wood and a dramatic center-island chef's kitchen. See p. 90.

• **Joe Fortes Seafood and Chop House** (777 Thurlow St.; ✆ **604/669-1940**): In the heart of the Robson shopping area, Joe Fortes has the best oyster bar in town and prepares its fresh fish the old-fashioned way, without a lot of culinary intervention. See p. 91.

- **Lumière** (2551 W. Broadway; ℂ 604/739-8185): Lumière has often won the top spot in the yearly Vancouver restaurant awards. It's expensive but worth it to be pampered by chef Rob Feenie, the darling of the Vancouver food world and an increasingly hot commodity in New York. See p. 100.
- **Raincity Grill** (1193 Denman St.; ℂ 604/685-7337): Vancouver is loco for local fish, meat, produce, and wine. Raincity was one of the first and continues to be one of the best purveyors of fresh, locally sourced ingredients all assembled into dishes

that show off the region's bounty, season by season. See p. 97.
- **Tojo's Restaurant** (1133 W. Broadway; ℂ 604/872-8050): The most sublime sushi in B.C., maybe in all of Canada. Just remember to take out an extra mortgage and practice your so-what-you're-a-movie-star-I-don't-care look. See p. 100.
- **West** (2881 Granville St.; ℂ 604/738-8938): For dazzling fine dining that utilizes the freshest local seasonal ingredients, you can't go wrong with this stellar restaurant in Kitsilano. It's the culinary highlight of the entire region. See p. 100.

9 The Most Unforgettable Dining Experiences: Victoria

- **The Aerie** (600 Ebedora Lane, Malahat; ℂ 800/518-1933 or 250/743-7115): Even if you're not staying at The Aerie, you might want to consider eating there, because chef Christophe Letard's cooking is as unmistakably French as his accent, and *très fantastique*. See p. 219.
- **SeaGrille** (Brentwood Bay Lodge, 849 Verdier Ave.; ℂ 888/544-2079 or 250/544-5100): The beautiful dining room of Brentwood Bay Lodge, about 20 minutes north of Victoria, serves a regionally inspired menu that changes daily according to what is fresh and in season. The wine list is exemplary, and so is the service. See p. 219.
- **Camille's** (45 Bastion Sq.; ℂ 250/381-3433): Enjoy a glass of fine wine as you savor the fresh, comforting Pacific Northwest cuisine at this

quiet, cozy, candlelit restaurant in downtown Victoria. See p. 214.
- **The Fairmont Empress** (721 Government St.; ℂ 250/384-8111): If you're doing the high tea thing only once, you may as well do it right, and there's no better place than Victoria's hotel crown jewel, where the tea is delicious and the service impeccable. See p. 214.
- **Sooke Harbour House** (1528 Whiffen Spit Rd., Sooke; ℂ 800/889-9688 or 250/642-3421): Quality, freshness, inventiveness, and incredible attention to detail make this fabled inn the most memorable dining experience in (well, near) Victoria. It serves the best gifts from the sea and its own garden, and eating here is always a culinary adventure, well worth the money and the trip. See p. 219.

10 The Best Things to Do for Free (or Almost): Vancouver

You'll find more suggestions for free things to do in "The Most Unforgettable Travel Experiences: Vancouver" section earlier in this chapter.

- **Walk the Stanley Park Seawall:** Or jog, blade, bike, skate, ride—whatever your favorite mode of transport is, use it, but by all means get out to enjoy this superlative and super-exhilarating path at the water's edge. See p. 116.

- **Watch the Fireworks Explode over English Bay:** Every August during the July/August HSBC Celebration of Light, three international fireworks companies compete by launching their best displays over English Bay. As many as 500,000 spectators cram the beaches around English Bay, while those with boats sail out to watch from the water. See p. 23.

- **Stroll the Beach:** It doesn't matter which beach, there's one for every taste. Wreck Beach below the University of British Columbia is for nudists, Spanish Banks is for dog walkers, Jericho Beach is for volleyballers, Kitsilano Beach is for serious suntanning,

and English Bay Beach is for serious people-watching. See p. 134.

- **Picnic at the Lighthouse:** Everyone has their favorite picnic spot—one of the beaches or up on the mountains. One of the prettiest picnic spots is Lighthouse Park on the North Shore. Not only do you get to look back over at Vancouver, but the walk down to the rocky waterline runs through a pristine, old-growth rainforest. See p. 128.

- **Hike the North Shore:** The forests of the North Shore are at the edge of a great wilderness and only 20 minutes from the city. Step into a world of muted light and soaring cathedral-like spaces beneath the tree canopy. See "Hiking" in chapter 7, p. 138.

11 The Best Things to Do for Free (or Almost): Victoria

You'll find more suggestions for free things to do in "The Most Unforgettable Travel Experiences: Victoria" section earlier in this chapter.

- **Climb Mount Douglas:** Actually, you don't even have to climb. Just drive up and walk around. The whole of the Saanich Peninsula lies at your feet. See p. 226.

- **Beachcomb:** Just find a beach, preferably a rocky one, and turn stuff over or poke through the tide pools.

The best beaches are along Highway 14A, starting with East Sooke Regional Park, and moving out to French Beach, China Beach, Mystic Beach, and, the very best of all, Botanical Beach Provincial Park, some 60km (37 miles) away by Port Renfrew. Remember to put the rocks back once you've had a peek. See "Beaches," "Especially for Kids," and "Watersports" in chapter 14.

2

Planning Your Trip to Vancouver & Victoria

Whether you're visiting Vancouver and Victoria for fun and frivolity, business or shopping, dining or dancing, beachcombing or backwoods trekking, here are some tips to help you plan your trip.

1 Visitor Information & Maps

VISITOR INFORMATION

Tourism Vancouver Touristinfo Centre, 200 Burrard St., Vancouver, B.C. V6C 3L6 (© **604/683-2000;** www.tourism vancouver.com), and **Tourism Victoria Visitor Centre,** 812 Wharf St., Victoria, B.C. V8W 1T3 (© **250/953-2033,** for hotel bookings only 800/663-3883 and 250/953-2022; www.tourismvictoria.com), can help you with everything from booking accommodations to making suggestions for what to see and do. Their websites are full of useful trip-planning information.

For additional information and city maps once you arrive, walk-in **Visitor Info Centres** are located just beyond the **US-BC Peace Arch border crossing** on Highway 99 in Surrey, B.C.; at the **Canada Place Cruise Ship Terminal;** and at **Vancouver International Airport** at the International Arrivals level.

If you're planning to spend time outside Vancouver and Victoria, you may also wish to contact the **Vancouver Coast and Mountains Tourism Region** (© **800/ 667-3306** or 604/739-9011; www.vcmbc. com). For travel information on Vancouver Island and the Gulf Islands, contact **Tourism Vancouver Island,** 203-335 Wesley St., Nanaimo, B.C. V9R 2T5 (© **250/754-3500;** www.seetheislands. com).

For information about travel and accommodations elsewhere in the province, contact **Tourism British Columbia,** 1803 Douglas St., Suite 300, Victoria, B.C. V8T 5C3 (© **800/ HELLO-BC** or 250/356-6363; www. hellobc.com).

For cultural information, check out *Vancouver* magazine's website at **www. vanmag.com**. The website www.alliance forarts.com also lists weekly art events in Vancouver.

2 Entry Requirements

If you're **driving** from Seattle, you'll enter British Columbia, Canada, at the Peace Arch crossing (open 24 hr.; often there's a 30-min. or longer wait) in Blaine, Washington. If you're **flying** directly into Vancouver International Airport or Victoria International Airport from another country, you'll go through immigration and Customs (passport control) in the terminal. Visitors arriving by **train, ferry,** or **cruise ship** from the U.S. have their entry documents checked before departure and upon arrival.

ENTRY DOCUMENTS FOR U.S. CITIZENS

There is a great deal of confusion regarding entry documents for U.S. citizens. The confusion stems from the **Western Hemisphere Travel Initiative** devised by the Bush Administration and the Department of Homeland Security. Under this legislation, **all U.S. citizens returning to the U.S. from Canada, Mexico, Bermuda, and the Caribbean are required to have a U.S. passport** (this includes children under the age of 18). The regulations took effect for air travelers in January 2007, and were to go into effect for land and sea travelers in January 2008. But the U.S. passport office was unable to keep up with the demand for passports (taking 10–12 weeks instead of 2–3 to issue the document) and implementation of the new border regulations was delayed until September 2007 for air travelers, and until mid-2008 for travelers entering Canada by land or sea.

In other words, if you are a U.S. citizen traveling to Canada by air any time in 2008, you must have a valid U.S. passport in order to get back into the U.S. And if you're traveling to Canada by land or sea (car or cruise ship), you must have a valid U.S. passport by mid-2008 (the date was not specified as of press time). Until that time, land and sea travelers can enter Canada and return to the U.S. by showing a government-issued photo ID (such as a driver's license) and proof of U.S. citizenship (such as a birth or naturalization certificate).

I urge all U.S. citizens traveling to and from Canada in 2008 to check the current entry requirements at the Web page of the U.S. State Department at **www.travel. state.gov**. You'll find current information on the **Canada Border Services Agency** website, **www.cbsa-asfc.gc.ca**.

U.S. citizens do not require visas to enter Canada.

Permanent U.S. residents who are not U.S. citizens should carry their passport and Resident Alien Card (U.S. form I-151 or I-551). Foreign students and other noncitizen U.S. residents should carry their passport, a Temporary Resident Card (form 1688) or Employment Authorization Card (1688A or 1688B), a visitor's visa, an I-94 arrival-departure record, a current I-20 copy of IAP-66 indicating student status, proof of sufficient funds for a temporary stay, and evidence of return transportation.

Visitors arriving by ferry from the U.S. must fill out International Crossing forms, which are collected before boarding.

ENTRY DOCUMENTS FOR COMMONWEALTH CITIZENS

Citizens of Great Britain, Australia, and New Zealand don't need visas to enter Canada, but they do need to show **proof of Commonwealth citizenship** (such as a **passport**), as well as evidence of funds sufficient for a temporary stay (credit cards work well here). Naturalized citizens should carry their naturalization certificates. Permanent residents of Commonwealth nations should carry their passports and resident status cards.

Foreign students and other residents should carry their passport, a Temporary Resident Card or Employment Authorization Card, a visitor's visa, an arrival-departure record, a current copy of student status, proof of sufficient funds for a temporary stay, and evidence of return transportation. *Note:* With changing security regulations, it is advisable for all travelers to check with the Canadian consulate before departure to find out the latest in travel document requirements. You will also find current information on the **Canada Border Services Agency** website, **www.cbsa-asfc.gc.ca**; follow the links under "FAQ."

For Residents of Australia: You can pick up a passport application from your local post office or any branch of Passports Australia, but you must schedule an interview at the passport office to present your application materials. Call the **Australian Passport Information Service** at © 131-232, or visit the government website at **www.passports.gov.au**.

For Residents of Ireland: You can apply for a 10-year passport at the **Passport Office,** Setanta Centre, Molesworth Street, Dublin 2 (© **01/671-1633;** www.irlgov.ie/iveagh). Those under age 18 and over 65 must apply for a 3-year passport. You can also apply at 1A South Mall, Cork (© **021/272-525**) or at most main post offices.

For Residents of New Zealand: You can pick up a passport application at any New Zealand Passports Office or download it from their website. Contact the **Passports Office** at © **0800/225-050** in New Zealand, or 04/474-8100, or log on to **www.passports.govt.nz**.

For Residents of the United Kingdom: To pick up an application for a standard 10-year passport (5-year passport for children under 16), visit your nearest passport office, major post office, or travel agency or contact the **United Kingdom Passport Service** at © **0870/521-0410** or search its website at **www.ukpa.gov.uk**.

CUSTOMS REGULATIONS

You'll pass through **Canadian Customs** (© **800/461-9999** in Canada, or 204/983-3500) upon arrival, and **U.S. Customs** (© **360/332-5771**), if you are traveling through the U.S., on your departure.

If you're **driving,** you'll go through Customs when you cross the border into Canada and show your passport.

Arriving by air, you'll go through Customs at the airport once you clear passport control. (Even if you don't have anything to declare, Customs officials randomly select a few passengers and search their luggage.)

Visitors arriving by **train, ferry,** or **cruise ship** from the U.S. pass through U.S. Customs before boarding and Canadian Customs upon arrival.

Your personal baggage can include the following: boats, motors, snowmobiles, camping and sports equipment, appliances, TV sets, musical instruments, personal computers, cameras, and other items of a personal or household nature. If you are bringing excess luggage, be sure to carry a detailed inventory list that includes the acquisition date, serial number, and cost or replacement value of each item. It sounds tedious, but it can speed things up at the border. Customs will help you fill out the forms that allow you to temporarily bring in your effects. This list will also be used by U.S. Customs to check off what you bring out. You will be charged Customs duties for anything left in Canada.

A few other things to keep in mind:

- If you're over 18, you're allowed to bring in 40 ounces of liquor and wine or 24 12-ounce cans or bottles of beer and ale, and 50 cigars, 400 cigarettes, or 14 ounces of manufactured tobacco per person. Any excess is subject to duty.
- Gifts not exceeding C$60 (US$51/£27) and not containing tobacco products, alcoholic beverages, or advertising material can be brought in duty-free. Meats, plants, and vegetables are subject to inspection on entry. There are restrictions, so contact the Canadian Consulate for more details if you want to bring produce into the country, or check the Canada Border Services Agency website, www.cbsa-asfc.gc.ca.
- If you plan to bring your dog or cat, you must provide proof of rabies inoculation during the preceding 36-month period. Other types of animals need special clearance and health certification. (Many birds, for instance, require 8 weeks in quarantine.)

If you need more information concerning items you wish to bring in and out of the country, contact **Canada Border Services** (✆ **800/461-9999** in Canada, or 204/983-3500; www.cbsa-asfc.gc.ca).

WHAT YOU CAN TAKE HOME FROM CANADA

Returning **U.S. citizens** who have been away for at least 48 hours are allowed to bring back, once every 30 days, US$800 (about C$950) worth of merchandise duty-free. You'll be charged a flat rate of 4% duty on the next US$1,000 (about C$1,200) worth of purchases. Be sure to have your receipts handy. On mailed gifts, the duty-free limit is US$200 (about C$240). With some exceptions, you cannot bring fresh fruits and vegetables into the U.S. For specifics on what you can bring back, download the free pamphlet *Know Before You Go* from **www.customs. gov**; click on "Travel," then click on "Know Before You Go Online Brochure." Or, contact the **U.S. Customs Service,** 1300 Pennsylvania Ave., NW, Washington, DC 20229 (✆ **877/287-8867**), and request the pamphlet.

The duty-free allowance amount in **Australia** is A$900, or A$450 for those under 18. Citizens 18 and older can bring in 250 cigarettes or 250 grams of loose tobacco, and 1,125 milliliters of alcohol. If you're returning with valuables you already own, such as foreign-made cameras, you should file form B263. *Know Before You Go* is a helpful brochure available from Australian consulates or Customs offices. For more information, call the **Australian**

Customs Service at ✆ **1300/363-263** (www.customs.gov.au).

The duty-free allowance for **New Zealand** is NZ$700. Citizens over 17 can bring in 200 cigarettes, 50 cigars, or 250 grams of tobacco (or a mixture of all three if their combined weight doesn't exceed 250 grams); plus 4.5 liters of wine and beer, or 1.125 liters of liquor. New Zealand currency does not carry import or export restrictions. Fill out a certificate of export, listing the valuables you are taking out of the country; that way, you can bring them back without paying duty. Most questions are answered in a free pamphlet available at New Zealand consulates and Customs offices: *New Zealand Customs Guide for Travellers, Notice no. 4.* For more information, contact **New Zealand Customs,** The Customhouse, 17–21 Whitmore St., Box 2218, Wellington (✆ **04/473-6099** or 0800/428-786; www.customs.govt.nz).

Citizens of the U.K. returning from Canada have a Customs allowance of 200 cigarettes; 50 cigars; 250 grams of smoking tobacco; 2 liters of still table wine; 1 liter of spirits or strong liqueurs (over 22% volume); 2 liters of fortified wine, sparkling wine, or other liqueurs; 60cc (ml) perfume; 250cc (ml) of toilet water; and £145 (about C$320) worth of all other goods, including gifts and souvenirs. People under 17 cannot have the tobacco or alcohol allowance. For more information, contact HM Customs & Excise at ✆ **0845/ 010-9000** (from outside the U.K., 020/ 8929-0152; www.hmce.gov.uk).

3 When to Go

WEATHER

A rainforest species like the western red cedar needs at least 30 inches of precipitation a year. Vancouver gets about 47 inches a year, a cause for celebration among the local cedar population. *Homo sapiens* simply learn to adjust.

Most of that precipitation arrives in the winter, when, with a 30-minute drive to the mountains, you can trade the rain for snow. Skiing and snowboarding are popular from mid-December until the mountain snowpack melts away in June.

Except in Whistler, hotels in the winter are quiet and the restaurants less busy.

Both Vancouver and Victoria enjoy moderately warm, sunny summers and mild, rainy winters. Victoria gets half as much rain as Vancouver, thanks to the sheltering Olympic Peninsula to the south and its own southeasterly position on huge Vancouver Island. The average annual rainfall in Vancouver is 47 inches; in Victoria, it's just 23 inches. You can find **weather statistics** for Vancouver at http://vancouver.weatherpage.ca.

Around mid-February, the winds begin to slacken, the sun shines a bit more, the buds on the cherry trees appear and early daffodils blossom. By March, azaleas, rhododendrons, and most other flowers are in bloom, and the sun is more frequent.

June sees more sun per summer day than farther south (mid-June sees 16 hr. of daylight). Only 10% of the annual rainfall occurs during the summer months, and the sun stays out through summer until the rains close in again in mid-October. These spring/summer/early autumn months are prime visiting time and when most visitors arrive. The first cruise ships start appearing in April.

Daily Mean Temperature & Total Precipitation for Vancouver, B.C.

	Jan	Feb	Mar	Apr	May	June	July	Aug	Sept	Oct	Nov	Dec
Temp (°F)	38	41	45	40	46	62	66	67	61	42	48	39
Temp (°C)	3	5	7	4	8	17	19	19	16	6	9	4
Precipitation (in.)	5.9	4.9	4.3	3	2.4	1.8	1.4	1.5	2.5	4.5	6.7	7
Precipitation (cm)	15	12.4	10.9	7.6	6.1	4.6	3.6	3.8	6.4	11.4	17	17.8

HOLIDAYS

The official British Columbia public holidays are as follows: New Year's Day (Jan 1); Good Friday, Easter, Easter Monday (Mar 21–24, 2008); Victoria Day (May 19, 2008); Canada Day (July 1); British Columbia Day (Aug 4, 2008); Labour Day (Sept 1, 2008); Thanksgiving (Oct 13, 2008); Remembrance Day (Nov 11); Christmas (Dec 25); and Boxing Day (Dec 26).

VANCOUVER & VICTORIA CALENDAR OF EVENTS

Festivals held in Vancouver and Victoria draw millions of visitors each year and reflect an extraordinary diversity of cultures and events. Things may seem a little quiet in the winter and early spring, but that's because most residents simply head for the ski slopes. Resorts such as **Whistler Blackcomb** (ℂ 800/944-7853; www.tourismwhistler.com) have events happening nearly every weekend. If no contact number or location is given for any of the events listed below, **Tourism Vancouver** (ℂ 604/683-2000; www.tourismvancouver.com) can provide further details.

VANCOUVER EVENTS
January

Polar Bear Swim, English Bay Beach. Thousands of hardy citizens show up in elaborate costumes to take a dip in the icy waters of English Bay. Call ℂ 604/665-3418 for more information, or visit www.city.vancouver.bc.ca. January 1.

Dine Out Vancouver. For a limited time every January, Vancouver's hottest restaurants offer three-course dinners between C$15 and C$35 (US$12–US$28/£7–£16) per person. For more information, contact Tourism Vancouver (ℂ 604/683-2000; www.tourismvancouver.com).

Annual Bald Eagle Count, Brackendale. Bald eagles gather en masse to feed on salmon every winter near

Brackendale. In January 1994, volunteers counted a world record of 3,700 eagles. The 2005 count wasn't too shabby either, with 1,975 raptors tallied. The count starts at the **Brackendale Art Gallery** (℃ **604/898-3333**). Meet at 9am at the Art Gallery for a guided tour. First Sunday in January.

International Bhangra Celebration, downtown. Vancouver's East Indian population of 60,000-plus celebrates with Bhangra, a lively form of folk music and dance that originates from the Punjab. Events include live music and dance demonstrations, workshops, and competitions at venues throughout downtown Vancouver. For more information, visit www.vibc.org. Mid-January.

PuSh International Performing Arts Festival, venues throughout Vancouver. An international performing arts festival featuring over 100 performances involving 18 works in the main program, and seven satellite shows by 23 companies at 16 venues. For more information visit www.pushfestival.ca. January 10 through February 4.

February

Chinese New Year, Chinatowns in Vancouver and Richmond. This is when the Chinese traditionally pay their debts and forgive old grievances to start the new lunar year with a clean slate. These Chinese communities launch a 2-week celebration, ringing in the new year with firecrackers, dancing dragon parades, and other festivities. Call ℃ **604/415-6322** for information, or visit www.vancouverchinesegarden. com. Dates vary yearly.

March

CelticFest, downtown. For 5 days in March, the sounds of fiddles, bagpipes, bodhrans, dancing feet, and voices resound throughout downtown Vancouver as the annual CelticFest

Vancouver brings visitors and locals together for a celebration of Celtic culture featuring hundreds of local and international artists at more than 60 events scheduled at dozens of popular venues and two outdoor stages along Granville Street. For information visit www.celticfestvancouver.com. March 14 to March 18.

Vancouver Playhouse International Wine Festival. This is a major wine-tasting event featuring the latest international vintages. For more information, call ℃ **604/873-3311,** or visit www. playhousewinefest.com. Late March or early April.

April

Baisakhi Day Parade. The Sikh Indian New Year is celebrated with a colorful parade around Ross Street near Marine Drive, and ends with a vegetarian feast at the temple. Contact **Khalsa Diwan Gurudwara Temple** (℃ **604/324-2010**) for more information. Mid-April.

Vancouver Sun Run. This is Canada's biggest 10K race, featuring more than 40,000 runners, joggers, and walkers who race through 10 scenic kilometers (6.2 miles). The run finishes at B.C. Place Stadium. Call ℃ **604/689-9441** for information, or register online at www.sunrun.com. April.

May

Vancouver International Marathon. Runners from around the world compete here. For information, call ℃ **604/ 872-2928,** or visit www.vanmarathon. com. First Sunday in May.

Cloverdale Rodeo, Cloverdale, Surrey. Professional cowboys from all over North America compete in roping, bull and bronco riding, barrel racing, and many other events. For information, call ℃ **604/576-9461,** or visit www. cloverdalerodeo.com. Mid-May.

International Children's Festival. Activities, plays, music, and crafts for children are featured at this annual event held in Vanier Park on False Creek. For information, call ✆ **604/ 708-5655,** or visit www.childrens festival.ca. Mid-May.

June

Vancouver Sun Garden Show. Presented at the **VanDusen Botanical Garden,** 5251 Oak St., at 37th Street (✆ **604/878-9274;** www.vandusen garden.org), this is Vancouver's premier flora gala. Early June.

Festival d'Eté Francophone de Vancouver/Francophone Summer Festival. This 4-day festival celebrating French music uses various venues and includes a street festival. Call ✆ **604/ 736-9806** for information, or check www.lecentreculturel.com. Mid-June.

Alcan Dragon Boat Festival. Traditional dragon-boat racing is a part of the city's cultural scene. Watch the races from False Creek's north shore, where more than 150 local and international teams compete. Four stages of music, dance, and Chinese acrobatics are presented at the **Plaza of Nations,** 750 Pacific Blvd. For more info, call ✆ **604/ 683-4707,** or visit www.adbf.com. Third week in June.

National Aboriginal Day Community Celebration. This event offers the public an opportunity to learn about Canada's First Nations cultures. Many events take place at the **Vancouver Aboriginal Friendship Centre,** 1607 E. Hastings at Commercial Street. Call ✆ **604/251-4844** for information. June 21.

Vancouver International Jazz Festival. More than 800 international jazz and blues players perform at 25 venues ranging from the Orpheum Theatre to the Roundhouse. Many are free performances. Call the **Jazz Hot Line**

(✆ **604/872-5200**), or visit www. coastaljazz.com for more information. Late June/early July.

Bard on the Beach Shakespeare Festival, Vanier Park. Three of Shakespeare's plays are performed in a tent overlooking English Bay. Call the box office (✆ **604/739-0559**), or check www. bardonthebeach.org. June to late September, Tuesday through Sunday.

July

Canada Day. Canada Place Pier hosts an all-day celebration that begins with the induction of new Canadian citizens. Music and dance are performed outdoors throughout the day. A 21-gun salute at noon, precision aerobatics teams in the afternoon, and a nighttime fireworks display on the harbor lead the festivities. Granville Island, Grouse Mountain, and other locations also host Canada Day events. For more information, call ✆ **604/647-7390,** or check www.canadadayatcanadaplace. com. July 1.

Steveston Salmon Festival, Steveston. Steveston celebrates Canada Day with a big parade, marching bands, clowns, a carnival, a traditional salmon bake, and more. Call ✆ **604/277-6812** for more info, or visit www.tourism richmond.com. July 1.

Ecomarine Kayak Marathon. Competitors race sea kayaks in Georgia Strait. The **Ecomarine Kayak Centre** (✆ **604/689-7575;** www.ecomarine. com), at Jericho Beach, hosts the race and can provide details. Mid-July.

Harrison Festival of the Arts, Harrison Hot Springs, lower mainland. This arts festival in the Fraser River valley, just east of Vancouver, attracts performing artists from around the world. Call ✆ **604/796-3664** for more information, or visit www.harrisonfestival. com. Mid-July.

Dancing on the Edge. Canadian and international dance groups perform modern and classic works at the **Firehall Arts Centre** and other venues. For information, call © **604/689-0929,** or visit www.dancingontheedge.org. Early to mid-July.

Vancouver Folk Music Festival. International folk music is performed outdoors at Jericho Beach Park. Contact the **Vancouver Folk Music Society** at © **604/602-9798** for more information, or visit www.thefestival.bc.ca. Second or third weekend in July.

Illuminares Lantern Festival, Trout Lake Park. This evening lantern procession circling Trout Lake is a phantasmagoric experience, complete with drums, costumes, fire-breathing apparitions, and lots of elaborate handcrafted lanterns. Various performances start at dusk. For info, call © **604/879-8611,** or visit www.publicdreams.org. Third or fourth Saturday in July.

Caribbean Days Festival, North Vancouver. The Trinidad and Tobago Cultural Society of B.C. hosts the city's premier Caribbean event at Waterfront Park in North Vancouver, featuring live music, authentic Caribbean food, arts, crafts, and a parade. For info, call © **604/512-2400,** or visit www.ttcsbc.com. Third or fourth weekend in July.

HSBC Celebration of Light. Three international fireworks companies compete for a coveted title by launching their best displays accompanied by music over English Bay Beach. Don't miss the big finale on the fourth evening. *Note:* Because of the crowds, some streets are closed to vehicles at night. Other prime viewing locations include Kitsilano Beach and Jericho Beach. Call © **604/641-1293** for information, or check www.celebration-of-light.com. End of July through first week of August.

August

Summer Dancing in Robson Square. Every Friday night in August, Robson Square in downtown Vancouver offers a free night of dancing under the stars. The evening starts with a free dance lesson given by a local instructor followed by showcase dancers and then a "general dance" where everyone (all ages and dance levels) is encouraged to join in. For more information visit www.dancesportbc.com.

Powell Street Festival. An annual fete of Japanese culture includes music, dance, food, and more. Contact the Powell Street Festival Society (© **604/739-9388;** http://powellstfestival.shinnova.com) for info. First weekend of August.

Gay Pride Parade, Vancouver. This huge and hugely popular gay- and lesbian-pride parade begins at noon and serves as the culmination of Pride Week. Celebrations at many local gay and lesbian nightclubs take place around town on the same long holiday weekend (B.C. Day weekend). For more info, contact the Pride Society (© **604/687-0955;** www.vancouverpride.ca). First Sunday in August.

Festival Vancouver. National and international artists perform orchestral, choral, opera, world music, chamber music, and jazz concerts in venues throughout Vancouver. For information, call © **604/688-1152,** or visit www.festivalvancouver.bc.ca. First 2 weeks in August.

Harmony Arts Festival, West Vancouver. This event highlights the talent of North Shore artists, offering free exhibitions, demonstrations, studio tours, theater, concerts, markets, and workshops. Call © **604/925-7268,** or visit www.harmonyarts.net for more information. First 2 weeks of August.

Abbottsford International Air Show, Abbottsford. Barnstorming stuntmen and precision military pilots fly everything from Sopwith Camels to Stealth Bombers. This is one of the biggest air shows in the world. Call © **604/852-8511,** or visit www.abbotsfordairshow.com for more info. Second weekend in August.

Pacific National Exhibition. The city's favorite fair includes one of North America's best all-wooden roller coasters. Special events include livestock demonstrations, logger competitions, fashion shows, and a midway. Call © **604/253-2311,** or visit www.pne.bc.ca for more details. Mid-August to Labour Day.

Vancouver Wooden Boat Festival, Granville Island. Call © **604/688-9622** for more info, or visit www.granvilleisland.com. Last weekend of August.

September

Vancouver Fringe Festival. The Fringe Festival is centered around Granville Island, Commercial Drive, and Yaletown's Roundhouse, and features more than 500 innovative and original shows performed by more than 100 groups from Canada and around the world. All plays cost less than C$15 (US$13/£7). Call © **604/257-0350,** or see www.vancouverfringe.com for more info. First and second week of September.

CanWest Comedy Fest. Comedians from Canada and the U.S. perform around town. Contact **Ticketmaster** for tickets at © **604/683-0883,** or check www.comedyfest.com for more information. Mid-September.

Mid-Autumn Moon Festival, Dr. Sun Yat-Sen Garden. This outdoor Chinese celebration includes a lantern festival, storytelling, music, and, of course, moon cakes. For info, call © **604/662-3207,** or visit www.vancouverchinesegarden.com. Early to mid-September,

according to the lunar cycle (15th day of the 8th month of the Chinese calendar).

Vancouver International Film Festival. This highly respected festival features 250 new works, revivals, and retrospectives, representing filmmakers from 40 countries (particularly Asia). Call © **604/685-0260,** or visit www.viff.org for details. Late September and first 2 weeks of October.

October

Vancouver International Writers and Readers Festival. Public readings by Canadian and international authors as well as writers' workshops take place on Granville Island and at other locations in the lower mainland. Call © **604/681-6330,** or check www.writersfest.bc.ca for details. Mid-October.

Parade of Lost Souls, Grandview Park. This bizarre and intriguing procession takes place around Commercial Drive to honor the dead and chase away bad luck. For more information, call © **604/879-8611,** or visit www.publicdreams.org. Last Saturday of October.

November

Remembrance Day. Celebrated throughout Canada, this day commemorates Canadian soldiers who gave their lives in war. Vintage military aircraft fly over Stanley Park and Canada Place, and, at noon, a 21-gun salute is fired from Deadman's Island. November 11.

Christmas Craft and Gift Market, VanDusen Botanical Garden. For info, call © **604/878-9274,** or check www.vandusengarden.org. November and December.

December

Carol Ship Parade of Lights Festival. Harbor cruise ships decorated with colorful Christmas lights sail around English Bay, while onboard guests sip cider and sing their way through the canon of Christmas carols. For more info, call ☏ **604/878-8999,** or check out www.carolships.org. Throughout December.

Festival of Lights. Throughout December, the VanDusen Botanical Garden is transformed into a magical holiday land with seasonal displays and more than 20,000 lights. Call ☏ **604/878-9274** for info, or visit www.vandusengarden.org.

Stanley Park Festival of Lights. Throughout December, the plaza in the middle of Stanley Park becomes a festive gathering point with more than a million twinkling lights transforming the surrounding forest and children's farmyard. The Stanley Park holiday train winds its way through the illuminated forest. For more information call ☏ **604/257-8400,** or visit www.vancouver.bc.ca/parks.

First Night. Vancouver closes its downtown streets for revelers in the city's New Year's Eve performing-arts festival and alcohol-free party. Events and venues change from year to year.

VICTORIA & SOUTHERN VANCOUVER ISLAND EVENTS
January

Annual Bald Eagle Count, Goldstream Provincial Park. More than 3,000 bald eagles take up residence to feed on the salmon, which begin to run in October. The eagle count usually takes place in mid- to late January, when the numbers peak. Throughout December and January, the park offers educational programs, displays, and guest speakers. Call ☏ **250/478-9414,** or visit www.goldstreampark.com for exact dates.

Robert Burns's Birthday. Celebrating the birthday of the great Scottish poet, events around Victoria and Vancouver include Scottish dancing, piping, and feasts of haggis. Most events take place in pubs. January 25.

February

Chinese New Year, Chinatown. See "Vancouver Events," earlier in this chapter. Late January or early February.

Trumpeter Swan Festival, Comox Valley. A weeklong festival celebrates these magnificent white birds that gather in the Comox Valley. Check dates with the Vancouver Island tourist office (☏ **250/754-3500**).

Flower Count. So many flowers bloom in Victoria and the surrounding area that the city holds an annual flower count. The third week in February is a great time to see the city as it comes alive with vibrant colors. Call ☏ **250/953-2033** for more info. Late February/early March.

March

Victoria Festival of Wine. Sample wines from British Columbia and around the world at this yearly festival. Food and music add to the enjoyment, as well as lectures and seminars for beginners and experts. For more information visit www.victoriafestivalofwine.com. Mid-March (dates vary yearly).

Pacific Rim Whale Festival, Tofino, Ucluelet, and Pacific Rim National Park. Every spring, more than 20,000 gray whales migrate past this coastline, attracting visitors to Vancouver Island's west coast beaches. The event features live crab races, storytelling, parades, art shows, guided whale-spotting hikes, and whale-watching boat excursions. Call ☏ **250/725-4426,** or visit www.pacificrimwhalefestival.org for more information. Mid-March to early April.

April

Annual Brant Wildlife Festival, Qualicum Beach. This 3-day celebration of the annual black brant migration to the area (20,000 birds) includes guided walks through old-growth forest and saltwater and freshwater marshes that are home to hundreds of bird species. For information, call © **250/752-9171,** or visit www.brantfestival.bc.ca. Early April.

May

Harbour Festival. This 10-day festival takes place in Victoria's downtown district and features heritage walks, entertainment, music, and more. For information, call © **250/953-2033,** or visit www.tourismvictoria.com. Last week of May.

Swiftsure Weekend. International sailing races make for spectacular scenery on the waters around Victoria. For information, call © **250/953-2033,** or visit www.tourismvictoria.com. End of May.

June

Jazz Fest International. Jazz, swing, bebop, fusion, and improv artists from across the globe perform at various venues around Victoria during this 10-day festival (© **250/388-4423;** www.jazzvictoria.ca). Late June/early July.

July

Canada Day. Victoria, the provincial capital, celebrates this national holiday with events centered on the Inner Harbour, including music, food, and fireworks. July 1.

Victoria Pride Celebration. Victoria's gay and lesbian community celebrates with a week of activities that culminates in a downtown parade and festival at Fisherman's Wharf Park. For more info visit **www.victoriapridesociety.org.** First week in July.

August

First Peoples Festival. This free event highlights the heritage of the Pacific Northwest First Nations with performances, carving demonstrations, and cultural displays at the Royal B.C. Museum (© **250/384-3211** or 250/953-3557). Second week in August.

Fringe Festival. Anything goes at this annual alternative theater festival. The festival is a summer's-end 12-day celebration of some of the most innovative theater offered anywhere in the country at eight locations throughout downtown Victoria. For more information call © **250/383-2663,** or visit www.intrepidtheatre.com. Late August/early September.

Classic Boat Festival. Boaters from around the world converge in Victoria's Inner Harbour for this annual Labour Day weekend celebration, which includes races, a parade of steam vessels, a cruise up the Gorge Waterway, and vessels open for tours. For more information call © **250/383-8306.** Last weekend in August.

September

The Great Canadian Beer Festival. Featuring samples from the province's best microbreweries, this event is held at the Victoria Conference Centre, 720 Douglas St. For more information call © **250/952-0360,** or visit www.gcbf.com. Early September.

October

Royal Victoria Marathon. This annual race attracts runners from around the world (half-marathon course available, too). Call © **250/658-4520,** or go to www.royalvictoria marathon.com for more info. Early October (Canadian Thanksgiving weekend).

November

Remembrance Day. See "Vancouver Events," earlier in this chapter. November 11.

December

Merrython Fun Run. This annual 8km (5.5-mile) race loops through Oak Bay and downtown Victoria. Call (© **250/953-2033**) for details. Early December.

First Night. See "Vancouver Events," earlier in this chapter. Call **Tourism** Victoria at ℂ **250/953-2033** for more details. December 31.

4 Getting to Vancouver

BY BUS

Greyhound Bus Lines (ℂ **800/231-2222** or 604/482-8747; www.greyhound.ca) offers daily bus service between Vancouver and all major Canadian cities, and between Vancouver and Seattle (at the border crossing, passengers disembark the bus and take their luggage through Customs). For information on Greyhound's cost-cutting **Canada Pass**, which allows for unlimited travel within Canada, and **Discovery Pass**, which allows for unlimited travel in the U.S. and Canada, consult their website. **Pacific Coach Lines** (ℂ **604/662-8074;** www.pacificcoach.com) provides service between Vancouver and Victoria (see "Getting to Victoria," below).

BY CAR

There are no major freeways within Vancouver, which makes it unique for a major North American city. You'll probably be driving into Vancouver along one of two routes. **U.S. Interstate 5** from Seattle becomes **Highway 99** when you cross the border at the Peace Arch. The 210km (130-mile) drive from Seattle takes about 2½ hours. On the Canadian side of the border, you'll drive through the cities of White Rock, Delta, and Richmond, pass under the Fraser River through the George Massey Tunnel, and cross the Oak Street Bridge. The highway ends there and becomes Oak Street, a busy urban thoroughfare heading toward downtown. Turn left at the first convenient major arterial (70th, 57th, 49th, 41st, 33rd, 16th, and 12th aves. will all serve) and proceed until you hit the next major street, which will be Granville Street. Turn right on Granville Street. This street heads directly into downtown Vancouver via the Granville Street Bridge.

Trans-Canada Highway 1 is a limited-access freeway that runs to Vancouver's eastern boundary, where it crosses the Second Narrows Bridge to North Vancouver. When traveling on Highway 1 from the east, exit at Cassiar Street and turn left at the first light onto Hastings Street (Hwy. 7A), which is adjacent to Exhibition Park. Follow Hastings Street 6.4km (4 miles) into downtown. When coming to Vancouver from parts north, take exit 13 (the sign says TAYLOR WAY, BRIDGE TO VANCOUVER) and cross the Lions Gate Bridge into Vancouver's West End.

BY PLANE

The Open Skies agreement between the U.S. and Canada has made flying to Vancouver easier than ever. Daily direct flights between major U.S. cities and Vancouver are offered by **Air Canada** (ℂ 888/247-2262; www.aircanada.com); **Alaska Airlines** (ℂ 800/252-7522; www.alaskaair.com); **American Airlines** (ℂ 800/433-7300; www.aa.com); **Continental** (ℂ 800/231-0856; www.continental.com); **Frontier Airlines** (ℂ 800/432-1359; www.frontierairlines.com): **Northwest Airlines** (ℂ 800/447-4747; www.nwa.com); and **United Airlines** (ℂ 800/241-6522; www.united.com). Direct flights on major carriers serve 33 cities in North America, including Denver, Phoenix, Dallas, New York, Houston, Minneapolis, Reno, and San Francisco; 12 cities in Asia; and 3 cities in Europe.

Domestic travelers within Canada have fewer options. **Air Canada** (ℂ **888/247-2262**) operates flights to Vancouver and Victoria from all major Canadian cities, connecting with some of the regional airlines. Cheaper and reaching farther all the time is the no-frills airline **WestJet**

(© 888/WEST-JET or 800/538-5696; www.westjet.com), which operates regular flights from Vancouver and Victoria to Prince George, Kelowna, Edmonton, Calgary, Toronto, Montreal, Ottawa, Halifax, and farther afield.

Direct flights between London and Vancouver are offered by **Air Canada** (© 0871/220-1111; www.aircanada.com) and the no-frills **Zoom** (© 866/359-9666 in North America, or 0870/213-266 in the U.K.; www.flyzoom.com). Other major carriers serving London (United, Continental, British Airways) make stops in the U.S. before continuing on to Vancouver.

Air Canada (© 0871/220-1111; www.aircanada.com) also flies to Vancouver from Sydney, Australia, and Auckland, New Zealand.

BY SHIP & FERRY

Vancouver is the major embarkation point for cruises going up British Columbia's Inland Passage to Alaska. The ships carry more than one million passengers annually on their nearly 350 Vancouver–Alaska cruises. In the summer, up to four cruise ships a day berth at **Canada Place** cruise-ship terminal (© 604/665-9085; www.portvancouver.com). A city landmark shaped like a cruise ship and topped by five eye-catching white Teflon sails, Canada Place Pier juts out into the Burrard Inlet at the base of Burrard Street right at the edge of the downtown financial district. It's an easy walk from the terminal to Gastown, downtown, or the West End. You'll also find taxis right outside, and the starting point for the Gray Line city sightseeing loop described under "Bus Tours" in chapter 7, p. 132.

The following cruises dock at Canada Place or the nearby Ballantyne Pier: **Princess Cruises** (© 800/PRINCESS; www.princess.com), **Holland America Line** (© 800/724-5425; www.hollandamerica.com), **Royal Caribbean** (© 800/398-9819; www.royalcaribbean.com),

Crystal Cruises (© 866/446-6625; www.crystalcruises.com), **Norwegian Cruise Line** (© 800/625-5306; www.norwegiancruiselines.com), **Radisson Seven Seas Cruises** (© 877/505-5370; www.rssc.com), and **Carnival** (© 866/386-7447; www.carnivalcruise.com). Public transit buses and taxis greet new arrivals, but you can also easily walk to many major hotels (the **Pan Pacific Hotel Vancouver,** perched directly atop the cruise-ship terminal, is the most convenient; see p. 70).

If you're arriving from Vancouver Island or Victoria, **B.C. Ferries** (© 888/223-3779 in B.C. only, or 250/386-3431; www.bcferries.com) has three daily routes. See "By Ship & Ferry," under "Getting to Victoria," below.

BY TRAIN

VIA Rail Canada, 1150 Station St., Vancouver (© 888/842-7245; www.viarail.com), connects with Amtrak at Winnipeg, Manitoba. From there you can transfer to The Canadian, the western transcontinental train that travels between Vancouver and Toronto, with stops in Kamloops, Jasper, Edmonton, Saskatoon, Winnipeg, and Sudbury Junction. Canadians, U.S. residents, and international travelers can purchase a 30-day, two-country **North America Railpass** for C$815 (US$693/£369) to C$1,149 (US$978/£517) at peak season, and use it for rail connections to Vancouver. For travel within Canada only, the 12-day **Canrailpass** (C$523/US$432/£235 off-peak; C$813/US$651/£366 peak) is available. Visit www.viarail.com for more information.

Amtrak (© 800/872-7245; www.amtrak.com) offers daily service from Seattle, though there's currently only one train in the morning; otherwise, the Seattle-Vancouver route is covered by an Amtrak bus. Amtrak also has a route from San Diego to Vancouver. It stops at all major U.S. West Coast cities, and takes a little under 2 days to complete the entire journey.

5 Getting to Victoria

BY BUS

Pacific Coach Lines (📞 **604/662-8074;** www.pacificcoach.com) provides service between Vancouver and Victoria with daily departures between 5:45am and 7:45pm. Pacific Coach Lines will pick up passengers from the Vancouver cruise-ship terminal and from most downtown hotels. They also offer an Island Excursion Program to Vancouver Island, departing downtown Vancouver at 9am on the HarbourLynx high-speed passenger ferry for Nanaimo. After a sightseeing tour and a day or overnight visit to Victoria, you return to Vancouver via B.C. Ferries. For more information, call 📞 **604/662-8074,** or visit www.pacificcoach.com.

BY PLANE

The **Victoria International Airport** (📞 **250/953-7500;** www.victoriaairport.com) is near the Sidney ferry terminal, 22km (14 miles) north of Victoria off the Patricia Bay Highway (Hwy. 17).

Air Canada (📞 **888/247-2262** or 800/661-3936; www.aircanada.com) and **Horizon Air** (📞 **800/547-9308;** www.horizonair.com) offer direct connections from Seattle, Vancouver, Portland, Calgary, Edmonton, Saskatoon, Winnipeg, and Toronto. Canada's low-cost airline **WestJet** (📞 **888/WEST-JET;** www.westjet.com) offers flights to Victoria from Kelowna, Calgary, Edmonton, and other destinations; WestJet service now extends to a few U.S. cities as well.

Delta Airlines (📞 **800/241-4141;** www.delta.com) offers a direct flight to Victoria from Salt Lake City. Connecting flights from Los Angeles, Phoenix, and Miami are also available. The flights are operated by Delta Connection, Atlantic Southeast Airlines, and SkyWest.

Commuter airlines, including floatplanes that land in Victoria's Inner Harbour, provide service to Victoria from Vancouver and destinations within B.C. They include **Air B.C.** (reached through Air Canada at 📞 **888/247-2262**); **Harbour Air Sea Planes** (📞 **604/274-1277** in Vancouver, or 250/384-2215 in Victoria; www.harbour-air.com); and **West Coast Air** (📞 **800/347-2222;** www.westcoastair.com).

In addition to serving B.C. destinations, **Kenmore Air** (📞 **800/543-9595;** www.kenmoreair.com) and **Helijet Airways** (📞 **800/665-4354;** www.helijet.com) offer 35-minute flights between Seattle and Victoria.

BY SHIP & FERRY

B.C. Ferries (📞 **888/223-3779** in B.C., or 250/386-3431; www.bcferries.com) has three routes from Vancouver to Vancouver Island and Victoria. Its large car-carrying ferries offer onboard restaurants, snack bars, gift shops, business-center desks with modem connections, and indoor lounges. In the summer, if you're driving, it's a good idea to reserve a space beforehand, especially on long weekends. Call B.C. Ferries reservations at 📞 **888/724-5223** (in B.C. only) or 604/444-2890.

The most direct B.C. Ferries route is the **Tsawwassen–Swartz Bay ferry,** which operates daily between 7am and 9pm (10pm on Sun). Ferries run every hour with extra sailings on holidays and in peak travel season. The crossing takes 95 minutes, but schedule an extra 2 hours for travel to and from both ferry terminals, including waiting time at the docks. Driving distance from Vancouver to Tsawwassen is about 20km (12 miles). Take Highway 99 south to Highway 17 and follow the signs to the ferry terminal.

Pacific Coach Lines (📞 **604/662-8074;** www.pacificcoach.com) provides regular bus service into Victoria for C$13 (US$11/£6) one-way, but you must book your seat on board the ferry and within

Tips **Commuter Whales**

For travelers pressed for time, **Prince of Whales** (© 888/383-4884; www.prince ofwhales.com) tours now offers a great way to spy on the whales that frequent the waters and straits near Vancouver Island, and maximize your travel time to Victoria. June to September, you can book a 4 hour whale watching tour that leaves from Vancouver's Burrard Inlet and docks right in front of the Fairmont Empress in Victoria. To return to Vancouver you can either book another tour, or book a seat on a floatplane, which will put you back in Vancouver in less than 45 minutes. The latter option even allows travelers to overnight in Victoria. One-way, whale watching fare is C$119 (US$100/£54); round trip C$199 (US$169/£90). Air transfer packages are C$239 (US$203/£108).

the first 20 minutes of the ferry ride (a Pacific Coast Lines desk is on board the ferry). You can take Pacific Coach Lines all the way from Vancouver to Victoria for C$73 (US$62/£33) round-trip, which includes the ferry ride.

Exiting the Swartz Bay ferry terminal by **car,** you'll be on Highway 17 (there is no other option), which leads directly into downtown Victoria where it becomes Douglas Street.

The **Vancouver-Nanaimo ferry** operates between Tsawwassen and Duke Point, just south of Nanaimo, about 100km (62 miles) north of Victoria. The 2-hour crossing runs eight times daily between 5:15am and 10:45pm.

The **Horseshoe Bay–Nanaimo ferry** has nine daily sailings, leaving Horseshoe Bay near West Vancouver (to reach Horseshoe Bay from Vancouver, take the Trans-Canada Highway/Hwy. 99 and Hwy. 1 west across the Lions Gate Bridge) and arriving 95 minutes later in Nanaimo. From the Nanaimo ferry terminal on Vancouver Island, passengers bound for Victoria board the E&N Railiner (see "By Train," below) or drive south to Victoria via the Island Highway (Hwy. 1).

Three different **U.S. ferry** services offer daily, year-round connections between Port Angeles, Bellingham, or Seattle, Washington, and Victoria. All of these ferries dock at Victoria's Inner Harbour near

the Empress Hotel and Parliament Buildings so you can walk right into town.

Black Ball Transport (© 250/386-2202 in Victoria, or 360/457-4491 in Port Angeles; www.cohoferry.com) operates between Port Angeles and Victoria. The crossing takes 1½ hours. There are four crossings per day in the summer (mid-June to Sept), and usually two sailings a day throughout the rest of the year (with a short 2-week closure in Jan).

Victoria Clipper (© 800/288-2535; www.victoriaclipper.com) operates a high-speed catamaran between Seattle and Victoria, with some sailings stopping in the San Juan Islands. It's a passenger-only service; sailing time is approximately 3 hours with daily runs from downtown Seattle and Victoria.

May 12 through September, the passenger-only MV *Victoria Star* operated by **Victoria San Juan Cruises** (© 800/443-4552 or 360/738-8099; www.whales. com) departs the Fairhaven Terminal in Bellingham, Washington, at 9am and arrives in Victoria at 2pm. It departs Victoria at 5pm, arriving in Bellingham at 8pm. This service offers special onboard salmon lunches and Victoria city tour add-ons and overnights.

Note: If you're riding the ferry between the U.S. and Canada, remember to bring your **passport,** as all passengers go through passport control and Customs on international ferry trips.

BY TRAIN

Travelers on the **Horseshoe Bay–Nanaimo ferry** (see "By Ship & Ferry," above) can board VIA Rail's **E&N Railiner** train at Nanaimo and wind down Vancouver Island's Cowichan River valley through Goldstream Provincial Park and to Victoria. The trip takes 2½ hours and ends at **E&N Station,** 450 Pandora Ave. (© **800/561-8630** in Canada), near the Johnson Street Bridge. For more information, contact **Via Rail Canada** (© **888/842-7245;** www.viarail.com).

6 Money & Costs

It's always advisable to bring money in a variety of forms on a vacation: a mix of cash, credit cards, and traveler's checks. You can exchange currency or withdraw Canadian dollars from an ATM upon arrival in Vancouver or Victoria. ATMs offer the best exchange rates. Avoid exchanging money at commercial exchange bureaus and hotels, which often have the highest transaction fees.

CURRENCY

The Canadian currency system is decimal and resembles both British and U.S. denominations. Canadian monetary units are dollars and cents, with dollar notes issued in different colors. The standard denominations are C$5, C$10, C$20, C$50, and C$100. The "loonie" (so named because of the loon on one side) is the C$1 coin that replaced the C$1 bill. A C$2 coin, called the "toonie" because it's worth two loonies, has replaced the C$2 bill. *Note:* If you're driving, it's a good idea to have a pocketful of toonies and loonies for parking meters.

Banks and other financial institutions offer a standard rate of exchange based on the daily world monetary rate (check **www.xe.com/ucc** for up-to-the-minute currency conversions). Avoid C$100 bills when exchanging money, as many stores refuse to accept these bills. The best exchange rates can be had by withdrawing funds from bank ATMs (cashpoints). Hotels will also gladly exchange your notes, but they usually give a slightly lower exchange rate. Almost all stores and restaurants accept American currency, and most will exchange amounts in excess of your dinner check or purchase. However, these establishments are allowed to set their own exchange percentages and generally offer the worst rates of all.

TRAVELER'S CHECKS

Traveler's checks in Canadian funds are universally accepted by banks (which charge a fee to cash them), larger stores, and hotels. If your traveler's checks are in a non-Canadian currency, you can exchange them for Canadian currency at any major bank.

ATM NETWORKS

The easiest and best way to get cash away from home is from an ATM. The **Cirrus** (© **800/424-7787;** www.mastercard.com) and **PLUS** (© **800/843-7587;** www.visa.com) networks span the globe; look at the back of your bank card to see which network you're on, then call or check online for ATM locations at your destination. Be sure you know your personal identification number (PIN) before you leave home, and be sure to find out your daily withdrawal limit before you depart. Many banks impose a fee every time a card is used at a different bank's ATM, and that fee can be higher for international transactions than for domestic ones. On top of this, the bank from which you withdraw cash may charge its own fee.

The Canadian Dollar & U.S. Dollar/U.K. Pound

The prices cited in this guide are given in Canadian and U.S. dollars and U.K. pounds sterling, with all amounts over US$10/£5 rounded to the nearest dollar. As of press time, the Canadian dollar was worth about 10% less than the U.S. dollar, although this will likely change. In this guide, C$1 is equal to US85¢/45p, which means that a C$200-a-night hotel room costs about US$170/£90, and a C$10 breakfast costs about US$8.50/£4.50. The actual exchange rate will fluctuate by a few pennies.

Here's a table of equivalents:

C$	US$	UK£	US$	C$	UK£
1.00	0.85	0.45	1.00	1.18	0.53
5.00	4.25	2.25	5.00	5.90	2.65
10.00	8.50	4.50	10.00	11.80	4.50
20.00	17.00	9.00	20.00	23.60	9.00
50.00	42.50	22.50	50.00	59.00	22.50
80.00	68.00	36.00	80.00	94.40	36.00
100.00	85.00	45.00	100.00	118.00	45.00

The 24-hour PLUS and Cirrus ATM systems are widely available throughout British Columbia. The systems convert Canadian withdrawals to your account's currency within 24 hours. Cirrus network cards work at ATMs at **BMO Bank of Montreal** (© 800/555-3000), **CIBC** (© 800/465-2422), **HSBC** (© 888/310-4722), **RBC Royal Bank** (© 800/769-2511), **TD Canada Trust** (© 866/567-8888), and at all other ATMs that display the Cirrus logo.

CREDIT & DEBIT CARDS

Major U.S. credit cards are widely accepted in British Columbia, especially American Express, MasterCard, and Visa.

British debit cards like Barclay's Visa are also accepted. Diners Club, Carte Blanche, Discover, JCB, and EnRoute are taken by some establishments, but not as many. The amount spent in Canadian dollars will automatically be converted by your issuing company to your currency when you're billed—generally at rates that are better than you'd receive for cash at a currency exchange. However, the bank may add a 3% "adjustment fee" to the converted purchase price. You can also obtain a PIN on your credit card and use it in some ATMs. You usually pay interest from the date of withdrawal and often pay a higher service fee than when using a regular ATM card.

7 Travel Insurance

The cost of travel insurance varies widely, depending on the destination, the cost and length of your trip, your age and health, and the type of trip you're taking, but expect to pay between 5% and 8% of the vacation itself. You can get estimates from various providers through **Insuremytrip. com.** Enter your trip cost and dates, your age, and other information, for prices from more than a dozen companies.

U.K. citizens and their families who make more than one trip abroad per year may find an annual travel insurance policy works out cheaper. Check **www.money supermarket.com**, which compares prices across a wide range of providers for single- and multitrip policies.

Most big travel agents offer their own insurance and will probably try to sell you their package when you book a holiday. Think before you sign. **Britain's Consumers' Association** recommends that you insist on seeing the policy and reading the fine print before buying travel insurance. **The Association of British Insurers** (℡ 020/7600-3333; www.abi.org.uk) gives advice by phone and publishes *Holiday Insurance,* a free guide to policy provisions and prices. You might also shop around for better deals: Try **Columbus Direct** (℡ 0870/033-9988; www.columbusdirect.net).

TRIP-CANCELLATION INSURANCE

Trip-cancellation insurance will help retrieve your money if you have to back out of a trip or depart early, or if your travel supplier goes bankrupt. Trip cancellation traditionally covers such events as sickness, natural disasters, and State Department advisories. The latest news in trip-cancellation insurance is the availability of **expanded hurricane coverage** and the **"any-reason"** cancellation coverage—which costs more but covers cancellations made for any reason. You won't get back 100% of your prepaid trip cost, but you'll be refunded a substantial portion. **TravelSafe** (℡ 888/885-7233; www.travelsafe.com) offers both types of coverage. Expedia also offers any-reason cancellation coverage for its air-hotel packages.

For details, contact one of the following recommended insurers: **Access America** (℡ 866/807-3982; www.accessamerica.com); **Travel Guard International** (℡ 800/826-4919; www.travelguard.com); **Travel Insured International**

(℡ 800/243-3174; www.travelinsured.com); and **Travelex Insurance Services** (℡ 888/457-4602; www.travelexinsurance.com).

MEDICAL INSURANCE

Most U.S. health plans (including Medicare and Medicaid) do not provide coverage outside of the U.S., and the ones that do often require you to pay for services upfront and reimburse you only after you return home.

As a safety net, you may want to buy travel medical insurance, particularly if you're traveling to a remote or high-risk area where emergency evacuation might be necessary. If you require additional medical insurance, try **MEDEX Assistance** (℡ 410/453-6300; www.medexassist.com) or **Travel Assistance International** (℡ 800/821-2828; www.travelassistance.com; for general information on services, call the company's **Worldwide Assistance Services, Inc.,** at ℡ 800/777-8710).

Canadians should check with their provincial health plan offices or call **Health Canada** (℡ 866/225-0709; www.hc-sc.gc.ca) to find out the extent of their coverage and what documentation and receipts they must take home in case they are treated overseas.

LOST-LUGGAGE INSURANCE

On international flights (including U.S. portions of international trips), baggage coverage is limited to approximately $9.07 per pound, up to approximately $635 per checked bag. If you plan to check items more valuable than what's covered by the standard liability, see if your homeowner's policy covers your valuables, get baggage insurance as part of your comprehensive travel-insurance package, or buy Travel Guard's "BagTrak" product.

If your luggage is lost, immediately file a lost-luggage claim at the airport, detailing the luggage contents. Most airlines require that you report delayed, damaged, or lost baggage within 4 hours of arrival. The airlines are required to deliver luggage, once found, directly to your house or destination free of charge.

AUTOMOBILE INSURANCE

Auto insurance is compulsory in British Columbia. Basic coverage consists of "no-fault" accident and C$200,000 (US$170,000/£90,000) third-party legal liability coverage. If you plan to drive in Canada, check with your insurance company to make sure that your policy meets this requirement. Always carry your insurance card, your vehicle registration, and your driver's license in case you get pulled over or have an accident. AAA also offers low-cost travel and auto insurance for its members. If you are a member and don't have adequate insurance, take advantage of this benefit.

Note: If you rent a car in British Columbia and plan to take it across the border into the U.S., let your rental agency know for insurance purposes.

8 Health

WHAT TO DO IF YOU GET SICK AWAY FROM HOME

If you become ill while traveling in Canada, you may have to pay all medical costs upfront and be reimbursed later. Medicare and Medicaid do not provide coverage for medical costs outside the U.S. Before leaving home, find out what medical services your health insurance covers. To protect yourself, consider buying medical travel insurance (see "Medical Insurance," under "Travel Insurance," above).

Very few health insurance plans pay for medical evacuation (which can cost $10,000 and up). A number of companies offer medical evacuation services anywhere in the world. If you're ever hospitalized more than 242km (150 miles) from home, **MedjetAssist** (© **800/527-7478;** www. medjetassistance.com) will pick you up and fly you to the hospital of your choice virtually anywhere in the world in a medically equipped and staffed aircraft 24 hours day,

7 days a week. Annual memberships are $225 individual, $350 family; you can also purchase short-term memberships.

I list **hospitals** and **emergency numbers** under "Fast Facts" for Vancouver (p. 60) and Victoria (p. 188).

If you suffer from a chronic illness, consult your doctor before your departure. Pack **prescription medications** in your carry-on luggage, and carry them in their original containers, with pharmacy labels—otherwise they won't make it through airport security. Carry the generic name of prescription medicines, in case a local pharmacist is unfamiliar with the brand name.

For conditions like epilepsy, diabetes, or heart problems, wear a **MedicAlert Identification Tag** (© **800/825-3785;** www.medicalert.org), which will immediately alert doctors to your condition and give them access to your records through MedicAlert's 24-hour hotline.

Healthy Travels to You

The following government websites offer up-to-date health-related travel advice.

- **Australia:** www.dfat.gov.au/travel
- **Canada:** www.hc-sc.gc.ca/index_e.html
- **U.K.:** www.dh.gov.uk/PolicyAndGuidance/HealthAdviceForTravellers
- **U.S.:** www.cdc.gov/travel

9 Safety

Overall, Vancouver is a safe city and Victoria is even safer. Violent-crime rates are quite low in both cities. However, property crimes and crimes of opportunity (such as items being stolen from unlocked cars) occur pretty frequently in Vancouver. Never leave valuable items on view in your parked car; put them in the trunk. Most hotels offer safe valet parking or parking in nearby lots.

Thanks to the mild climate and (controversially) lax laws, both Vancouver and Victoria have populations of transients living on the streets of certain neighborhoods. Vancouver's downtown East Side, between Gastown and Chinatown, is a troubled, drug-riddled neighborhood and should be avoided at night. In both Vancouver and Victoria, transients panhandle throughout downtown and tourist-heavy areas.

10 Specialized Travel Resources

TRAVELERS WITH DISABILITIES

Vancouver's mayor, Sam Sullivan, is keenly aware of accessibility issues, having been a quadriplegic since breaking his neck in a skiing accident at age 19. He's founded several nonprofit organizations dedicated to improving the quality of life for disabled people throughout North America. However, even before Sam Sullivan, Vancouver was working to improve accessibility.

According to *We're Accessible,* a newsletter for travelers with disabilities, Vancouver is **"the most accessible city in the world."** There are more than 14,000 sidewalk wheelchair ramps, and motorized wheelchairs are a common sight in the downtown area. The stairs along Robson Square have built-in ramps, and most major attractions and venues have ramps or level walkways for easy access. Most Vancouver hotels have at least partial wheelchair accessibility; many have specially equipped rooms for travelers with disabilities. Most SkyTrain stations and the SeaBus are wheelchair accessible, and most bus routes are lift-equipped. For further information about accessible public transportation, contact **Translink** (© **604/ 953-3333;** www.translink.bc.ca).

Many Vancouver hotels are also equipping rooms with visual smoke alarms and other facilities for hearing-impaired guests, while many crosswalks are now outfitted with beeping alerts to guide visually impaired pedestrians.

Victoria is similarly accessible. Nearly all Victoria hotels have rooms equipped to accommodate travelers with disabilities, and downtown sidewalks are equipped with ramps, though few intersections have beeping crosswalk signals for the visually impaired. The **Victoria Regional Transit System** (© **250/382-6161**) has a downloadable *Guide to Accessible Transit Services* on its website, **www.transitbc.com,** which includes information on which bus routes are equipped with lifts and/or low floors. The most notable spot in Victoria that isn't readily wheelchair accessible is the promenade along the water's edge in the Inner Harbour, which has only one rather challenging ramp near the Pacific Undersea Gardens.

The government of Canada hosts a comprehensive **Persons with Disabilities website** (www.accesstotravel.gc.ca) with resources for travelers with disabilities. In addition to information on public transit in cities across Canada, the site also lists accessible campsites, parks, coach lines, and a number of links to other services and associations of interest to travelers with disabilities. If you can't find what you need online, call © **800/ 465-7735.**

Outside of Canada, organizations that offer a vast range of resources and assistance to disabled travelers include **MossRehab** (© **800/CALL-MOSS;** www.moss resourcenet.org); the **American Foundation for the Blind (AFB)** (© **800/ 232-5463;** www.afb.org); and **SATH** (Society for Accessible Travel & Hospitality) (© **212/447-7284;** www.sath.org). **AirAmbulanceCard.com** is now partnered with SATH and allows you to preselect top-notch hospitals in case of an emergency.

Access-Able Travel Source (© **303/ 232-2979;** www.access-able.com) offers a comprehensive database on travel agents from around the world with experience in accessible travel; destination-specific access information; and links to such resources as service animals, equipment rentals, and access guides.

Many travel agencies offer customized tours and itineraries for travelers with disabilities. Among them are **Flying Wheels Travel** (© **507/451-5005;** www.flying wheelstravel.com); and **Accessible Journeys** (© **800/846-4537** or 610/521-0339; www.disabilitytravel.com).

Flying with Disability (www.flying-with-disability.org) is a comprehensive information source on airplane travel. **Avis Rent a Car** (© **888/879-4273**) has an "Avis Access" program that offers services for customers with special travel needs. These include specially outfitted vehicles with swivel seats, spinner knobs, and hand controls; mobility scooter rentals; and accessible bus service. Be sure to reserve well in advance.

Also check out the quarterly magazine *Emerging Horizons* (www.emerging horizons.com), available by subscription ($16.95 year in the U.S.; $21.95 outside the U.S.).

The "Accessible Travel" link at **Mobility-Advisor.com** (www.mobility-advisor. com) offers a variety of travel resources to disabled persons.

British travelers should contact **Holiday Care** (© **0845-124-9971** in the U.K.; www.holidaycare.org.uk) to access a wide range of travel information and resources for disabled and elderly people.

GAY & LESBIAN TRAVELERS

Since 2003, when the Province of British Columbia announced the legalization of same-sex marriage, Vancouver and Victoria have become favored sites for **gay and lesbian weddings.** (Same-sex marriage is now legal throughout Canada.) Information about the process is listed on the invaluable **www.gayvan.com** website.

What San Francisco is to the United States, **Vancouver** is to Canada—a hip, laid-back town with a large, thriving gay community. In fact, the largest gay population in Western Canada lives here, primarily in the **West End** and **Commercial Drive.** The club, bar, and party scene is chronicled in the biweekly gay and lesbian tabloid, *Xtra! West,* available at cafes, bars, and businesses throughout the West End. The **Gay Lesbian Transgendered Bisexual Community Centre,** 2-1170 Bute St. (© **604/684-5307;** www.lgtb centrevancouver.com), has all kinds of information on events and the current hot spots. Also check out the **Vancouver Pride Society** website (**www.vancouver pride.ca**) for upcoming special events, including the annual Vancouver Pride Parade in June, one of the largest gay pride events in North America. The **Out on Screen Film Festival** is held at the beginning of August; check **www.outon screen.com** for more details. You'll find hotels and restaurants in Vancouver to be very gay friendly. For nightlife options, see "Gay & Lesbian Bars," in chapter 10. The city's official tourism website, **www. tourismvancouver.com**, also has information for gay and lesbian travelers.

Also check out **Gay & Lesbian Ski Week** at Whistler, located 121km (75 miles) north of Vancouver; for information, go to **www.gaywhistler.com**.

The gay and lesbian scene in **Victoria** is small but active. Explore the gay and lesbian link under "Things to Do" at www.tourismvictoria.com, or go to the www.gayvictoria.ca website. At both sites you'll find information about special places to stay and dine, plus things to do. The **Victoria Pride Parade and Festival** is held every summer in early July. For nightlife options, see chapter 17.

The **International Gay and Lesbian Travel Association (IGLTA)** (© **800/ 448-8550** or 954/776-2626; www.iglta. org) is the trade association for the gay and lesbian travel industry, and offers an online directory of gay- and lesbian-friendly travel businesses and tour operators.

Gay.com Travel (© **800/929-2268** or 415/644-8044; www.gay.com/travel or www.outandabout.com), is an excellent online successor to the popular *Out & About* print magazine. It provides regularly updated information about gay-owned, gay-oriented, and gay-friendly lodging, dining, sightseeing, nightlife, and shopping establishments in every important destination worldwide. British travelers should click on the "Travel" link at **www.uk.gay.com** for advice and gay-friendly trip ideas.

SENIOR TRAVEL

Because B.C. has the mildest weather in all of Canada, Vancouver and Victoria have become havens for older and retired Canadians. Senior travelers often qualify for discounts at hotels and attractions throughout the area. Always ask; you'll be pleasantly surprised at the number of discounts available. **Discount transit passes** for persons over 65 (with proof of age) may be purchased at shops in Vancouver and Victoria that display a FAREDEALER sign (Safeway, 7-Eleven, and most newsstands). To locate a **FareDealer vendor,** contact B.C. Transit (© **604/521-0400;** www.transitbc.com).

If you're over 50, consider joining **AARP** (3200 E. Carson, Lakewood, CA 90712; © **800/424-3410;** www.aarp.org);

their card offers additional restaurant and travel bargains throughout North America.

FAMILY TRAVEL

Vancouver and Victoria are two of the most child-friendly, cosmopolitan cities in the world. Where else would you find a market especially for kids? In addition to the standard attractions and sights, you'll find a lot of free, adventurous, outdoor activities that both you and your kids will enjoy (see "Especially for Kids," in chapters 7 and 14). In both cities you'll find restaurants that aren't cafeteria-style or fast-food establishments, but are decidedly kid-friendly. Some hotels even offer milk and cookies for evening snacks, plus special menus and child-size terry robes.

To locate accommodations, restaurants, and attractions that are particularly kid-friendly, refer to the "Kids" icon throughout this guide.

Recommended family travel websites include **Family Travel Forum** (www.family travelforum.com), a comprehensive site that offers customized trip planning; **Family Travel Network** (www.familytravel network.com), an online magazine providing travel tips; and **Travelwithyourkids. com** (www.travelwithyourkids.com), a comprehensive site written by parents for parents offering sound advice for long-distance and international travel with children.

STUDENT TRAVEL

The southwestern corner of B.C. is definitely student-oriented territory. The University of British Columbia (UBC, with more than 30,000 students) in the Point Grey area, Burnaby's Simon Fraser University, and a number of smaller schools contribute to the enormous student population in **Vancouver.** Student travelers have a lot of free and inexpensive entertainment options, both day and night. The nightlife scene centers on **Yaletown,**

Granville Street, the West End, and Kitsilano. Pick up a copy of *Georgia Straight* to find out what's happening. Many attractions and theaters offer discounts if you have your student ID with you. While many establishments will accept a school ID, the surest way to obtain student discounts is with an International Student Identity Card (ISIC), which is available to any full-time high-school or college student from STA Travel (© 800/

781-4040; www.statravel.com), or from your local campus student society.

In Victoria, the University of Victoria (referred to locally as "U. Vic.") has a sprawling campus just east of downtown. The student population accounts for most, if not all, of Victoria's nightlife. Student discounts abound. Pick up a copy of Victoria's weekly paper, *Monday Magazine* (which comes out on Thurs), for current nightclub listings.

11 Sustainable Tourism/Ecotourism

In 2006, after years of protests and negotiations by First Nations tribes and environmentalists, Canada declared British Columbia's Great Bear Rainforest off-limits to loggers. This landmark decision preserves the largest remaining temperate coastal rainforest in the world, some 6 million hectares (15 million acres) that are home to rare white bears and has the highest concentration of grizzly bears in North America (p. 293). It must also be noted that much of British Columbia's economy is based on "resource extraction" of one kind or another, logging being the most prevalent.

Vancouver and Victoria are meccas of ecotourism in all its many guises. From patronizing restaurants that use only locally harvested foods and nonendangered fish to enjoying natural, nonpolluting fun by paddling kayaks and hiking through beautiful rainforests, the citizens of these two destinations definitely think green.

I list special low-impact walking tours and ecotours in and around Vancouver in chapter 7 under "Organized Tours" (p. 131) and "Outdoor Activities" (p. 134). For Victoria, turn to "Organized Tours" (p. 233) and "Outdoor Activities" (p. 235) in chapter 14. Ecotours of various sorts are also available in Whistler (see "What to See & Do Outdoors: Whistler's Raison d'Etre" in chapter 18, p. 274), and they're especially popular in and around Tofino

and the Pacific Rim National Park on the west coast of Vancouver Island (see "What to See & Do" in chapter 18, p. 290).

Each time you take a flight or drive a car, CO_2 is released into the atmosphere. You can help neutralize this danger to our planet through "carbon offsetting"— paying someone to reduce your CO_2 emissions by the same amount you've added. Carbon offsets can be purchased in the U.S. from companies such as Carbonfund.org (www.carbonfund.org) and TerraPass (www.terrapass.org), and from Climate Care (www.climatecare.org) in the U.K.

Responsible Travel (www.responsible travel.com) contains a great source of sustainable travel ideas run by a spokesperson for responsible tourism in the travel industry. Sustainable Travel International (www.sustainabletravelinternational.org) promotes responsible tourism practices and issues an annual Green Gear & Gift Guide.

You can find ecofriendly travel tips, statistics, and touring companies and associations—listed by destination under "Travel Choice"—at the TIES website, www.eco tourism.org. Also check out Conservation International (www.conservation.org)— which, with *National Geographic Traveler,* annually presents World Legacy Awards to those travel tour operators, businesses, organizations, and places that have made a

Frommers.com: The Complete Travel Resource

It should go without saying, but we highly recommend **Frommers.com,** voted Best Travel Site by *PC Magazine.* We think you'll find our expert advice and tips; independent reviews of hotels, restaurants, attractions, and preferred shopping and nightlife venues; vacation giveaways; and an online booking tool indispensable before, during, and after your travels. We publish the complete contents of over 128 travel guides in our **Destinations** section covering nearly 3,600 places worldwide to help you plan your trip. Each weekday, we publish original articles reporting on **Deals and News** via our free **Frommers. com Newsletter** to help you save time and money and travel smarter. We're betting you'll find our new **Events** listings (http://events.frommers.com) an invaluable resource; it's an up-to-the-minute roster of what's happening in cities everywhere—including concerts, festivals, lectures and more. We've also added weekly **Podcasts, interactive maps,** and hundreds of new images across the site. Check out our **Travel Talk** area featuring **Message Boards** where you can join in conversations with thousands of fellow Frommer's travelers and post your trip report once you return.

significant contribution to sustainable tourism. **Ecotravel.com** is part online magazine and part ecodirectory that lets you search for touring companies in several categories (water-based, land-based, spiritually oriented, and so on).

In the U.K., **Tourism Concern** (www.tourismconcern.org.uk) works to reduce social and environmental problems connected to tourism and find ways of improving tourism so that local benefits are increased.

The **Association of British Travel Agents (ABTA)** (www.abtamembers.org/responsibletourism) acts as a focal point for the U.K. travel industry and is one of the leading groups spearheading responsible tourism.

The **Association of Independent Tour Operators (AITO)** (www.aito.co.uk) is a group of interesting specialist operators leading the field in making vacations sustainable.

12 Staying Connected

TELEPHONES

Phones in British Columbia are identical to U.S. phones. The country code is the same as the U.S. code (1). Local calls normally cost C25¢ (US20¢/10p). Many hotels charge C$1 (US85¢/45p) or more per local call and much more for long-distance calls. You can save considerably by using a calling card or your cellphone. You can buy **prepaid phone cards** in various denominations at grocery and convenience stores.

To call Vancouver or Victoria:

1. If you're calling from outside North America, dial the international access code: 00 from the U.K., Ireland, or New Zealand; or 0011 from Australia. (Omit this step if you're calling from the U.S.)
2. Dial the country code 1.
3. For **Vancouver** or **Whistler,** dial the area code **604** and then the number. For **Victoria** or **Tofino,** dial the city code **250** and then the number.

Calling within Vancouver and Whistler: If you are in Vancouver or Whistler and want to call another number in Vancouver or Whistler, you must use the area code **604**, followed by the number.

Calling within Victoria: If you are in Victoria and calling another Victoria number you do not need to add the area code. If you are calling from Victoria to anywhere else on Vancouver Island, however, you must use the area code **250** before the number.

To make international calls: To call the U.S. or elsewhere in Canada dial 1, followed by the area code and phone number. To call the U.K., Ireland, Australia, or New Zealand, first dial 00 and then the country code (U.K. 44, Ireland 353, Australia 61, New Zealand 64), followed by the area code and number.

For directory assistance: For automated toll-free directory assistance within Canada (and the U.S.), dial ℂ **1-800-555-1212.** You can also dial **411** if you're looking for a number inside Canada. Dial **0** for numbers to all other countries. (You will incur a charge if you use the 411 and 0 directory assistance numbers.)

For operator assistance: If you need operator assistance making a call, dial 0.

Toll-free numbers: Numbers within Canada beginning with 800, 866, 877, and 888 are toll-free from the U.S., but calling a 1-800 number in the States from Canada is not toll-free. In fact, it costs the same as an overseas call.

CELLPHONES

The three letters that define much of the world's wireless capabilities are **GSM** (Global System for Mobile Communications), a big, seamless network that makes for easy cross-border cellphone use throughout Europe and dozens of other countries worldwide. In the U.S., T-Mobile, AT&T Wireless, and Cingular use this quasi-universal system; in Canada, Microcell and some Rogers customers are GSM, and all Europeans and most Australians use GSM. GSM phones function with a removable plastic SIM card, encoded with your phone number and account information. If your cellphone is on a GSM system, and you have a world-capable multiband phone such as many Sony Ericsson, Motorola, or Samsung models, you can make and receive calls across developed areas around much of the globe. Just call your wireless operator and ask for "international roaming" to be activated on your account.

You can **rent a cellphone** at a **Touristinfo Centre** at **Vancouver International Airport** (Touristinfo Centres are found in both the domestic and international terminals), or in the city at the **Vancouver Touristinfo Centre,** 200 Burrard St. (ℂ **604/683-2000**), for a minimum charge (at press time C$25/US$21/£11). For current rates and more information, contact the phone provider, **Cita Communications,** ℂ **888/593-2482;** www.cita.info.). There are currently no cellphone rental locations in Victoria; travelers to Vancouver Island generally rent and drop off their rented cellphones in Vancouver.

VOICE-OVER INERNET PROTOCOL (VOIP)

If you have Web access while traveling, you might consider a broadband-based telephone service (in technical terms, **Voice-over Internet protocol,** or **VoIP**) such as Skype (www.skype.com) or Vonage (www.vonage.com), which allows you to make free international calls if you use their services from your laptop or in a cybercafe. Check the sites for details and restrictions.

INTERNET/E-MAIL WITHOUT YOUR OWN COMPUTER

Almost all hotels in Vancouver and Victoria now provide some kind of free

> **Tips Hey, Google, did you get my text message?**
>
> It's bound to happen: The day you leave this guidebook back at the hotel for an unencumbered stroll through the West End, you'll forget the address of the lunch spot you had earmarked. If you're traveling with a mobile device, send a text message to © **466453 (GOOGLE)** for a lightning-fast response. For instance, type "banana leaf vancouver" and within 10 seconds you'll receive a text message with the address and phone number. This nifty trick works in a range of search categories: Look up weather ("weather whistler"), currency conversions ("10 usd in Canadian dollars"), and more. If your search results are off, be more specific ("the duff gay bar on granville"). For more tips and search options, see www.google.com/intl/en_us/mobile/sms/. Regular text message charges apply.

computer access, so you can at least check your e-mail. To find cybercafes in Vancouver and Victoria check **www.cybercaptive.com** and **www.cybercafe.com**.

Most major airports have **Internet kiosks** that provide basic Web access for a per-minute fee that's usually higher than cybercafe prices. Check out copy shops like **Kinko's** (FedEx Kinko's), which offers computer stations with fully loaded software (as well as Wi-Fi).

WITH YOUR OWN COMPUTER

More and more hotels, resorts, airports, cafes, and retailers are going **Wi-Fi** (wireless fidelity), becoming "hotspots" that offer free high-speed Wi-Fi access or charge a small fee for usage. To locate public Wi-Fi hotspots, go to **www.jiwire.com**; its Hotspot Finder holds the world's largest directory of public wireless hotspots. For dial-up access, most business-class hotels throughout the world offer dataports for laptop modems.

Wherever you go, bring a **connection kit** of the right power and phone adapters, a spare phone cord, and a spare Ethernet network cable—or find out whether your hotel supplies them to guests.

13 Packages for the Independent Traveler

Package tours are simply a way to buy the airfare, accommodations, and other elements of your trip (such as car rentals, airport transfers, and sometimes even activities) at the same time and often at discounted prices.

One good source of package deals is the airlines themselves. **Air Canada Vacations** (© 888/247-2262; www.aircanada vacations.ca) offers an array of package deals covering a whole series of travel bargains ranging from city packages to fly/drive tours, escorted tours, motor-home travel, and ski holidays. Other airlines with Canadian package holidays include **American Airlines** (© 800/321-2121; www.aavacations.com), Delta (© 800/221-6666; www.deltavacations.com), **Continental Airlines** (© 800/301-3800; www.coolvacations.com), and **United** (© 888/854-3899; www.united vacations.com).

Several big **online travel agencies**—Expedia, Travelocity, Orbitz, and Last minute.com—also do a brisk business in packages.

Travel packages are also listed in the travel section of your local Sunday newspaper. Or check ads in national travel magazines such as *Arthur Frommer's Budget Travel Magazine, Travel + Leisure, National Geographic Traveler,* and *Condé Nast Traveler.*

14 Escorted General-Interest Tours

Escorted tours are structured group tours, with a group leader. The price usually includes everything from airfare to hotels, meals, tours, admission costs, and local transportation.

Uniglobe Specialty Travel (© **800/455-0007** or 604/688-8816; www.discovercanada.com) in Vancouver offers multiday escorted tours of Vancouver and Victoria highlighting the major attractions in both cities. **Globus Tours** (© **866/755-8581;** www.globusjourneys.com), one of the largest tour companies in the U.S., provides escorted tours throughout Western Canada, including Vancouver and Victoria as part of a larger West Coast itinerary.

Despite the fact that escorted tours require big deposits and predetermine hotels, restaurants, and itineraries, many people derive security and peace of mind from the structure they offer. Escorted tours—whether they're navigated by bus, motorcoach, train, or boat—let travelers sit back and enjoy the trip without having to drive or worry about details. They take you to the maximum number of sights in the minimum amount of time with the least amount of hassle. They're particularly convenient for people with limited mobility and they can be a great way to make new friends.

On the downside, you'll have little opportunity for serendipitous interactions with locals. The tours can be jam-packed with activities, leaving little room for individual sightseeing, whim, or adventure—plus they often focus on the heavily touristed sites, so you miss out on many a lesser-known gem.

3

Suggested Vancouver & Victoria Itineraries

Vancouver and Victoria are preeminently maritime cities, and the visitor is always aware of water and the closeness of the immense Pacific. Vibrant Vancouver is (mostly) on the mainland, but charming Victoria occupies the southern tip of Vancouver Island, about 45km (28 miles) to the west. To get the most out of this glorious part of Canada, you'll need a car and you'll have to take a ferry to reach Victoria. In both Vancouver and Victoria, you can ditch your car and use public transportation or walk, but to enjoy the almost limitless sightseeing opportunities outside the cities, a car is essential.

1 The Best of Vancouver in 1 Day

This tour is meant to show off the city as a whole, giving you an overview of what makes it so appealing. Some places you'll explore on foot, and for others you'll drive to reach the destination. Nature, art, culture, and coffee are all part of today's itinerary. Start: Tourism Vancouver Touristinfo Centre, Burrard and Cordova streets.

❶ Canada Place
Start your day outside, on the upper (deck) level of the city's giant convention center and cruise-ship terminal, which juts out into Burrard Inlet across from the Touristinfo Centre. From here you'll get a good sense of Vancouver's natural and urban topography, with the North Coast Mountains rising up before you; low-rise, historic Gastown to the east; Stanley Park to the west; and a forest of glass residential towers in between. Canada Place is busiest in summer, when up to four giant cruise ships may dock in 1 day. For more on Canada Place, see Walking Tour 2, chapter 8, p. 150.

❷ Stanley Park ★★★
You can't really appreciate Stanley Park by driving through it in a car, so park your

vehicle and head in on foot via Lagoon Drive. Surrounded by a famed pedestrian seawall, this giant peninsular park invites hours of exploration. A 1-hour carriage ride (see "Specialty Tours," p. 133) is the perfect way to see the highlights. See p. 116.

❸ Vancouver Aquarium Marine Science Centre ★★
One of the best aquariums in North America is located right in Stanley Park. Don't miss the Arctic Canada exhibit with its beluga whales, and the Marine Mammal Deck, where you can see Pacific white-sided dolphins, sea otters, and other denizens of Pacific Northwest waters. See p. 117.

The Best of Vancouver in 1 & 2 Days

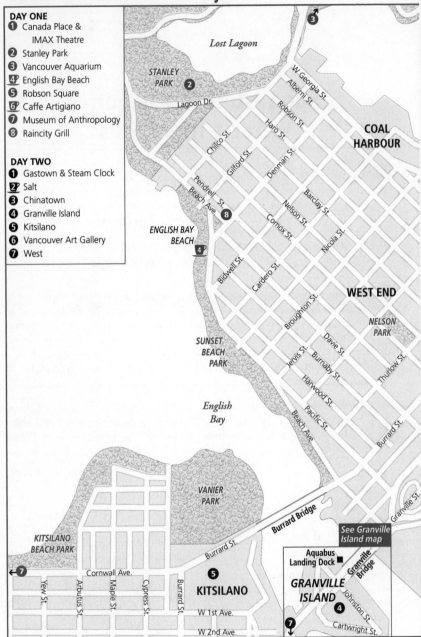

DAY ONE
1. Canada Place & IMAX Theatre
2. Stanley Park
3. Vancouver Aquarium
4. English Bay Beach
5. Robson Square
6. Caffe Artigiano
7. Museum of Anthropology
8. Raincity Grill

DAY TWO
1. Gastown & Steam Clock
2. Salt
3. Chinatown
4. Granville Island
5. Kitsilano
6. Vancouver Art Gallery
7. West

Lost Lagoon

STANLEY PARK 2

W Georgia St.
Alberni St.
Robson St.
Lagoon Dr.
Haro St.
Chilco St.
Gilford St.
Denman St.
Pendrell St.
Beach Ave.
Nelson St.
Comox St.
Barclay St.
Nicola St.

COAL HARBOUR

ENGLISH BAY BEACH

8

4

Bidwell St.
Cardero St.
Broughton St.

WEST END

NELSON PARK

SUNSET BEACH PARK

Davie St.
Jervis St.
Burnaby St.
Harwood St.
Pacific St.
Beach Ave.
Thurlow St.
Burrard St.

English Bay

VANIER PARK

Burrard Bridge

Granville St.

See Granville Island map

KITSILANO BEACH PARK

Aquabus Landing Dock

Granville Bridge

7

Cornwall Ave.

Yew St.
Arbutus St.
Maple St.
Cypress St.
Burrard St.

5

KITSILANO

GRANVILLE ISLAND

Johnston St.

4

W 1st Ave.

7

Cartwright St.

W 2nd Ave.

3

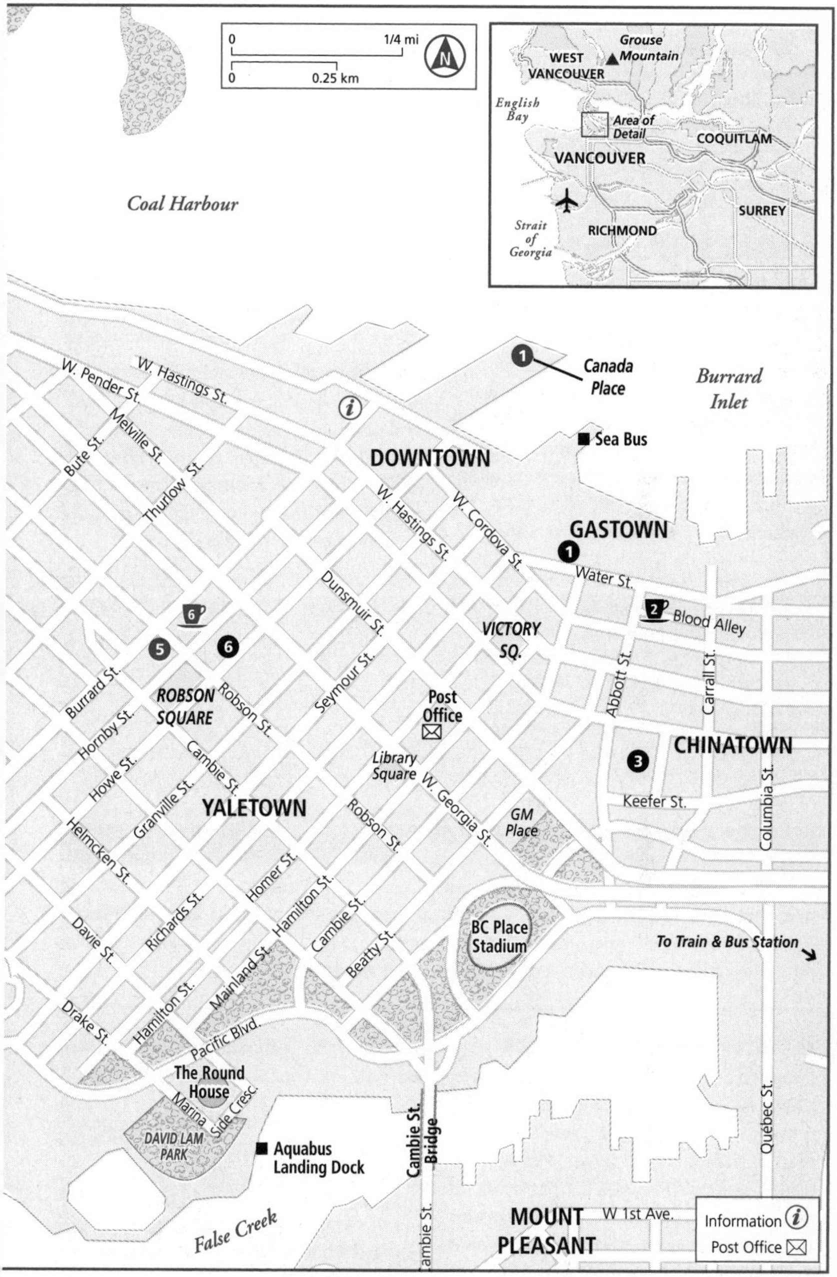
0
1/4 mi
0
0.25 km
N
WEST VANCOUVER
Grouse Mountain
English Bay
Area of Detail
COQUITLAM
VANCOUVER
SURREY
Strait of Georgia
RICHMOND
Coal Harbour
Canada Place
Burrard Inlet
Sea Bus
W. Hastings St.
W. Pender St.
Melville St.
Bute St.
Thurlow St.
DOWNTOWN
W. Hastings St.
W. Cordova St.
GASTOWN
Water St.
Dunsmuir St.
Blood Alley
VICTORY SQ.
Burrard St.
ROBSON SQUARE
Robson St.
Seymour St.
Post Office
Abbott St.
Carrall St.
Hornby St.
Howe St.
Cambie St.
Library Square
W. Georgia St.
CHINATOWN
Keefer St.
Columbia St.
Granville St.
YALETOWN
Robson St.
GM Place
Helmcken St.
Homer St.
Hamilton St.
Richards St.
Cambie St.
Davie St.
Beatty St.
BC Place Stadium
To Train & Bus Station
Mainland St.
Drake St.
Hamilton St.
Pacific Blvd.
The Round House
Marina Side Cresc.
DAVID LAM PARK
Aquabus Landing Dock
Cambie St. Bridge
Québec St.
False Creek
Cambie St.
MOUNT PLEASANT
W 1st Ave.
Information
Post Office

4 ENGLISH BAY BEACH ★

If the weather is warm, head to **English Bay Beach,** an all-seasons gathering spot on the south side of Stanley Park. You can pick up picnic eats or find takeout food on nearby Denman Street.

5 Robson Street & the West End

How you explore the West End is up to you. You can walk from English Bay Beach down Denman Street, and then turn south on Robson, taking in as much of the throbbing shopping and cafe scene as you want. It's also fun to explore the West End as a living neighborhood—the most densely populated in North America. For extra suggestions on exploring the West End, see Walking Tour 1 in chapter 8, p. 145.

6 CAFFÈ ARTIGIANO ★★

For the best latte in town, as well as grilled Italian sandwiches and snacks, stop in at this busy cafe right across from the Vancouver Art Gallery. The patio in front is perfect for people-watching. 763 Hornby St. ✆ 604/685-5333.

7 Museum of Anthropology ★★★

Hop in your car or on the bus for the 20-minute drive to the outstanding Museum of Anthropology at the University of British Columbia. Here, in one of North America's preeminent collections of First Nations art, you'll encounter powerful totem poles, spirit masks, and totemic objects. See p. 122.

8 Dinner

In the last decade, Vancouver has become one of the top dining cities in the world. For a romantic dinner that will introduce you to the best of Vancouver's "eat local" food philosophy, reserve a table at **Raincity Grill,** 1193 Denman St. (✆ **604/685-7337**), where the windows overlook English Bay, and the regional cuisine provides the perfect excuse to linger. See p. 97.

2 The Best of Vancouver in 2 Days

If you've already made your way through "The Best of Vancouver in 1 Day," you'll find that your second full-day tour takes in a roster of new sights and adventures. Today's itinerary will give you an entertaining handle on Vancouver's past, and introduce you to some of Vancouver's most appealing neighborhoods.

1 Gastown & the Steam Clock

Gastown is the oldest part of Vancouver, a low-rise brick district from the late 19th century, now making a comeback after years of neglect. Stroll down Water Street, timing your visit so you'll be in front of the famous steam clock when it steams and chimes at noon. You might also want to shop for a piece of First Nations art at one of Gastown's specialty galleries (see "First Nations Art & Crafts" in chapter 9,

p. 164). For a complete tour of Gastown, see Walking Tour 2, chapter 8, p. 150.

2 SALT ★

If it's lunchtime, head over to one of Gastown's smart new eateries. **Salt** (✆ **604/633-1912**), in Blood Alley, is Vancouver's only charcuterie, serving cured meats, soup, and artisan cheeses. See p. 95.

❸ Chinatown

Vancouver's Chinatown lies just east of Gastown, and you can walk there or drive. Though parts of Chinatown are touristy, the street markets are lively and authentic. Don't miss the **Dr. Sun Yat-Sen Classical Chinese Garden** ✿✿. For a complete tour of Chinatown, see Walking Tour 2, chapter 8, p. 150.

❹ Granville Island ✿✿✿

You can easily drive to Granville Island via the Granville Bridge, but it's more fun to hop on a miniferry from Yaletown Landing and take the 10-minute trip across False Creek. The **public market** ✿✿✿ is pure sensory overload, crammed with every kind of produce, seafood, and food product imaginable, while the area around it is a browser's heaven of shops, galleries, and outdoor-adventure outfitters. See p. 122. For a complete tour of Granville Island, see Walking Tour 3, chapter 8, p. 154.

❺ Kitsilano

You can drive or walk to Kitsilano, the funky upbeat neighborhood west of Granville Island. Check out the buffed beach scene at scenic Kitsilano Beach, facing English Bay. One of the world's largest freshwater pools is here if you want a summertime swim. For a complete walking tour of Kitsilano, see Walking Tour 3, chapter 8, p. 154.

❻ Vancouver Art Gallery ✿✿

You can drive or take a no. 4 or 7 bus on 4th Avenue for the 15-minute ride back to downtown Vancouver. Head for the Vancouver Art Gallery, and make your way specifically to the museum's collection of hauntingly atmospheric paintings by B.C. native Emily Carr. Her moodily expressive works sum up all that is grand and glorious in the Pacific Northwest landscape. See p. 118.

❼ Dinner

Cap off your day with a memorable meal at **West** ✿✿✿, 2881 Granville St. (© **604/738-8938**), a culinary high point of the city and winner of *Vancouver* magazine's Best Restaurant Award in 2007. See p. 100.

3 The Best of Victoria in 1 Day

Victoria is less than a quarter of the size of Vancouver, and you can easily hit the highlights in 1 day if you arrive on an early ferry. The scenic ferry ride—from Vancouver, Seattle, Anacortes, or Port Angeles—is part of the fun. Although it's easy to experience Victoria by foot, bike, and public transportation, having a car will help to maximize your sightseeing.

❶ Inner Harbour

Victoria's official facade, epitomized by a pair of landmark buildings designed by Francis Rattenbury, is reminiscent of an era that reveled in the idea of the British Empire. A stroll along the Inner Harbour takes you past the **Provincial Legislature** ✿, a massive stone edifice completed in 1898, and the famous Fairmont Empress hotel, which dates from 1908. Along the busy waterfront you'll also find information on whale-watching excursions, a popular Victoria pastime.

For a complete walking tour of the Inner Harbour, see Walking Tour 1 in chapter 15, p. 240.

❷ Royal B.C. Museum ✿✿✿

The highlight of this excellent museum is the First Peoples Gallery, an absorbing and thought-provoking showplace of First Nations art and culture. The other exhibits pale by comparison, but do have a look at the life-size woolly mastodon. See p. 225.

The Best of Victoria in 1 Day

1. Inner Harbour
2. Royal B.C. Museum
3. Fairmont Empress
4. Butchart Gardens
5. Il Terrazzo Ristorante

Upper Harbour
Store St.
Government St.
Herald St.
CHINATOWN
Esquimalt Rd.
Market Square
Johnson Bridge
Lime Bay
Bastion Square
Victoria Harbour
Inner Harbour
Wharf St.
OLD TOWN
Douglas St.
Blanshard St.
Quadra St.
Belleville St.
DOWNTOWN
Superior St.
Montreal St.
Simcoe St.
Menzies St.
THUNDERBIRD PARK
Southgate St.
Dallas Rd.
MacDONALD PARK
Oswego St.
Niagara St.
Toronto St.
Medana St.
Government St.
Douglas St.
BEACON HILL PARK
Dallas Rd.

Information (i)

SAANICH
WEST BAY
VICTORIA
Area of Detail

0 ___ 1/2 mi
0 ___ 0.5 km

---

3 THE FAIRMONT EMPRESS ★★
Tea at the **Empress** is a traditional affair that has remained a real treat despite its fame. Make it your main meal of the day (seatings at 12:30, 2, 2:30, and 5pm), and be sure to reserve in advance. 721 Government St. ℭ **250/384-8111**. See "Taking Afternoon Tea" in chapter 13, p. 214.

4 Butchart Gardens ★★★
This century-old garden is one of the gardening wonders of the world, meticulously planned and impeccably maintained. Though hordes of tourists can jam the paths in the summer months, time your visit for late afternoon, and you'll have more room, plus you can stay for the fabulous summer fireworks display. See p. 222.

5 Dinner
If there's time, have dinner at Victoria's best Italian restaurant, **Il Terrazzo Ristorante** (555 Johnson St., ℭ **250/361-0028**). See p. 215.

4 The Best of Vancouver, Victoria & Whistler in 1 Week

Lucky the traveler who gets to spend a whole week exploring this ruggedly beautiful part of the Pacific Northwest. If you don't arrive with a car, you can rent one in either Vancouver or Victoria. Most visitors travel to Victoria by car ferry, so it's important to know about ferry schedules and reservations. A week will allow you to savor the delights of both cities and go farther afield to explore Whistler, a year-round resort in the mountains north of Vancouver. The assumption here is that your week begins and ends in Vancouver, the major travel hub. For reference, see the map on the inside cover of this book.

Days ❶ & ❷: Vancouver ★★★

Start your week in Vancouver, following "The Best of Vancouver in 1 Day," and "The Best of Vancouver in 2 Days," above.

Day ❸: North Vancouver

Now that you've seen Vancouver's West End and West Side, use your third day to get out of the city. At **Capilano Suspension Bridge & Park** ★★ (p. 125), you can test your love-hate relationship with heights on the narrow, bouncy suspension footbridge that spans a scenic ravine, or you can hike under the canopies of the tallest trees on a series of tree bridges. Afterward, drive to the nearby **SkyRide gondola** and be transported to the summit of **Grouse Mountain Resort** ★, where you'll enjoy panoramic views of the entire region and can choose from different places to dine atop the mountain (p. 125). Capilano and Grouse Mountain have casual dining and picnic areas, or you can enjoy fine Pacific Northwest cuisine and a panoramic waterfront view at **The Beach House at Dundarave Pier** ★ (☎ 604/922-1414), a restored 1912 teahouse located on the water's edge.

Day ❹: Vancouver to Whistler ★★★

Take Georgia Street from downtown Vancouver and head west through Stanley Park, across the scenic Three Lions Bridge, and hook up with the **Sea-to-Sky Highway,** which winds along the edge of Howe Sound and climbs into the mountains. It should take you about 2 hours to

reach **Whistler Village.** Once you get to Whistler, ski (it is one of North America's greatest ski resorts, after all) . . . or mountainbike, or hike, or Ziptrek, or shop, or pamper yourself with a spa treatment. A casual and delicious lunch or dinner at **Chow Thyme Bistro** (☎ 604/932-9795) will set you up for whatever activities are on your agenda. You'll find a complete rundown of Whistler possibilities in chapter 18.

Day ❺: Whistler to Vancouver

Spend the night in Whistler. Before leaving the area, drive to **Nairn Falls Provincial Park** ★★, where the Green River shoots through basaltic rock formations and forms a series of thundering waterfalls (p. 277). The road back to Vancouver along the Sea-to-Sky Highway is just as spectacular in the reverse direction. Once back in Vancouver, enjoy fresh oysters and fish at **Blue Water Café and Raw Bar** ★★★ (☎ 604/688-8078) or **Coast** ★★★ (☎ 604/685-5010).

Day ❻: Vancouver to Victoria ★★★

Spend day 6 of your weeklong adventure in Victoria, preferably taking an early-morning ferry through the Gulf Islands. For your day in Victoria, see "The Best of Victoria in 1 Day," above.

Day ❼: Victoria to Vancouver

If time allows, make a trip from Victoria to **Pacific Rim National Park** ★★★, a temperate rainforest with old-growth trees and a wildly magnificent coastline on the west coast of Vancouver Island (a 4½-hr. drive or 45-min. flight). For a complete summary of what's there, including famous lodges and dining choices, see chapter 18. Otherwise, this is the day you return to Vancouver by ferry.

Back on the mainland, the Tsawassen ferry terminal is the closest to the Vancouver airport and hooks up with Interstate 5 south to Seattle or north to Vancouver. Or you can travel back via Port Angeles, a gateway to Washington's Olympic National Park, or Anacortes.

Getting to Know Vancouver

Getting lost as you wander around a fascinating new neighborhood is part of the fun of traveling. And getting lost in Vancouver, or at least losing your directional bearings, is possible, mostly because the main grid of streets doesn't run strictly north-south, but rather northwest to southeast like a parallelogram. If you do become directionally challenged, just look for the mountains. They are to the north, across a body of water called Burrard Inlet. If you're facing the mountains, east is to your right, west is to your left, and the back of your head is pointing south. That one tip will generally keep you pointed in the right direction, no matter where you are. You'll also find that Vancouverites are incredibly friendly: If you're scratching your head over a map, almost inevitably someone will ask if they can help. This chapter offers more detailed information on how to find your way around this scenic city.

1 Orientation

VANCOUVER AIRPORT

Vancouver International Airport (© **604/207-7077**; www.yvr.ca) is 13km (8 miles) south of downtown Vancouver on uninhabited Sea Island, bordered on three sides by Richmond and the Fraser River delta. It's the largest airport on Canada's west coast and one of the world's major airports, handling some 15 million passengers annually. The International Terminal features an extensive collection of First Nations sculptures and paintings set amid grand expanses of glass under soaring ceilings. Before you leave the International Terminal, catch a glimpse of Bill Reid's huge jade canoe sculpture, *The Spirit of Haida Gwaii.*

Tourist Information Centres (© **604/683-2000**), on Level 2 of the Main and International arrival terminals, are open daily from 8am to 11pm. **Parking** is available at the airport for both loading passengers and long-term stays. A **shuttle bus** links the Main and International terminals to the South Terminal, where smaller and private aircrafts are docked.

GETTING INTO TOWN FROM THE AIRPORT & VICE VERSA

The **YVR Airporter** (© **604/946-8866;** www.yvrairporter.com) provides **airport bus service** to downtown Vancouver's major hotels and cruise-ship terminal. It leaves from Level 2 of the Main Terminal every 15 minutes daily from 6:30am until midnight. Fares for the 30-minute ride across the Granville Street Bridge into downtown Vancouver are C$13 (US$11/£6) for adults (C$20/US$17/£9 round-trip); C$10 (US$8/£4.50) for seniors (C$20/US$17/£9 round-trip); C$6 (US$5/£2.70) for children (C$12/US$10/£5 round-trip); and C$26 (US$22/£12) for families (two adults, two children; C$40/US$34/£18 round-trip). Buses leave from selected downtown hotels every half-hour between 5:35am and 10:55pm. Scheduled pickups serve the bus station, cruise-ship terminal, Four Seasons, Hotel Vancouver, Georgian Court, Sutton Place, Landmark, and others. Ask the driver on the way in or ask your hotel concierge for the nearest pickup stop and time.

Getting to and from the airport with **public transit** is much slower and requires at least one transfer, but it costs less. Public buses are operated by **Translink** (© 604/ 953-3333; www.translink.bc.ca). If you wish to travel into town this way, catch bus no. 424 at Ground Level of the Domestic Terminal; it will take you to Airport Station. From there, bus no. 98B will take you into downtown Vancouver. B.C. Transit fares are C$3.25 (US$2.75/£1.50) during peak hours, and C$2.25 (US$1.90/£1) on weekends and after 6:30pm. You must have the exact fare because drivers do not make change. Transfers are free in any direction within a 90-minute period.

The average **taxi** fare from the airport to a downtown Vancouver hotel is approximately C$25 (US$21/£11) plus tip, but the fare can run up to C$40 (US$34/£18) if the cab gets stuck in traffic. **LimoJet** (© 604/273-1331; www.limojetgold.com) offers flat-rate stretch-limousine service at C$39 (US$33/£18) per trip (not per person) to the airport from any downtown location, plus tip, for up to three people (C$45/US$38/£20 for up to six passengers). The drivers accept all major credit cards; reserve in advance.

Most major **car-rental firms** have airport counters and shuttles. Drivers heading into Vancouver from the airport should take the Arthur Laing Bridge, which leads directly to Granville Street, the most direct route to downtown.

THE TRAIN & BUS STATION

All trains and Greyhound buses arrive at **Pacific Central Station,** 1150 Station St. (at Main St. and Terminal Ave.; © 800/872-7245), the main Vancouver railway station, located just south of Chinatown. You can reach downtown Vancouver from there by cab for about C$10 (US$8.50/£4.50). Plenty of taxis wait at the station entrance. One block from the station is the SkyTrain's Main Street Station (p. 58); within minutes, you'll be downtown. The Granville and Waterfront SkyTrain stations are two and four stops away, respectively.

VISITOR INFORMATION

TOURIST OFFICES & PUBLICATIONS The Vancouver Touristinfo Centre, 200 Burrard St. (© 604/683-2000; www.tourismvancouver.com), is your single best travel information source about Vancouver and the North Shore. An incredibly helpful and well-trained staff provides information, maps, and brochures, and can help you with all your travel needs, including hotel, cruise-ship, ferry, bus, and train reservations. The center also has a **half-price ticket office** (Tickets Tonight) for same-day shows and events. The Touristinfo Centre is open daily from 8:30am to 6pm.

If you're driving, a **Tourist Info Centre,** 356 Hwy. 99, Surrey, is located just north of the **US-BC Peace Arch border crossing.** Visitors arriving by ship will find a Tourist Info Centre at the **Canada Place Cruise Ship Terminal,** 999 Canada Place. Both of these are walk-in offices (no phone).

The free weekly tabloid *Georgia Straight* (© 604/730-7000; www.straight.com), found in cafes, bookshops, and restaurants, provides up-to-date schedules of concerts, lectures, art exhibits, plays, recitals, and other happenings. Not free but equally good—and with more attitude—is the glossy city magazine *Vancouver* (© 604/877-7732; www.vanmag.com), available on newsstands. The free guide called *Where*

Vancouver (© **604/736-5586;** www.where.ca) is available in many hotels and lists attractions, entertainment, upscale shopping, and fine dining. It also has good maps.

Two free monthly tabloids, *B.C. Parent* (© **604/221-0366;** www.bcparent.com) and *West Coast Families* (© **604/689-1331**), available at grocery stores and cafes around the city, are geared toward families with young children, listing many kid-friendly current events. Gay and lesbian travelers will want to pick up a copy of *Xtra! West* (© **604/684-9696**), a free biweekly tabloid available in cafes, bars, shops, and restaurants throughout the West End.

CITY LAYOUT

With four different bodies of water lapping at its edges and miles of shoreline, Vancouver's geography can seem a bit complicated. That's part of the city's maritime charm, of course, and visitors usually don't find it too difficult to get their bearings. **Downtown Vancouver** is on a peninsula: think of it as an upraised thumb on the mitten-shaped Vancouver mainland. **Stanley Park,** the **West End, Yaletown,** and Vancouver's business and financial center (downtown) are located on this thumb of land bordered to the north by Burrard Inlet, the city's main deepwater harbor and port, to the west by English Bay, and to the south by False Creek. Farther west beyond English Bay is the Pacific Ocean. Just south across False Creek is **Granville Island,** famous for its public market and the beach community of **Kitsilano.** This part of the city, called the **West Side,** covers the mainland, or the hand of the mitten. Its western shoreline looks out on the Strait of Georgia with the Pacific beyond, and the North Arm of the Fraser River demarcates it to the south. Pacific Spirit Park and the University of British Columbia (UBC), a locus for visitors because of its outstanding Museum of Anthropology, take up most of the western tip of the West Side; the rest is mostly residential, with a sprinkling of businesses along main arterial streets. Both the mainland and peninsula are covered by a simple rectilinear street pattern. North Vancouver is the mountain-backed area directly across Burrard Inlet from downtown.

MAIN ARTERIES & STREETS

On the downtown peninsula are four key **east-west streets** (to be more directionally exact, the streets run southeast to northwest). **Robson Street** starts at B.C. Place Stadium on Beatty Street, flows through the West End's more touristed shopping district, and ends at Stanley Park's Lost Lagoon on Lagoon Drive. **Georgia Street**—far more efficient for drivers than the pedestrian-oriented Robson—runs from the Georgia Viaduct on the eastern edge of downtown through Vancouver's commercial core, through Stanley Park, and over the Lions Gate Bridge to the North Shore. Three blocks north of Georgia is **Hastings Street,** which begins in the West End, runs east through downtown, and then skirts Gastown's southern border as it runs eastward to the Trans-Canada Highway. **Davie Street** starts at Pacific Boulevard near the Cambie Street Bridge, travels through Yaletown into the West End's more residential shopping district, and ends at English Bay Beach.

Three **north-south downtown streets** will get you everywhere you want to go in and out of downtown. Two blocks east of Stanley Park is **Denman Street,** which runs from West Georgia Street at Coal Harbour to Beach Avenue at English Bay Beach. This main West End thoroughfare is where locals dine out. It's also the shortest north-south route between the two ends of the Stanley Park Seawall.

Eight blocks east of Denman is **Burrard Street,** which starts near the Canada Place Pier and runs south through downtown, crosses the Burrard Street Bridge, and then

Greater Vancouver

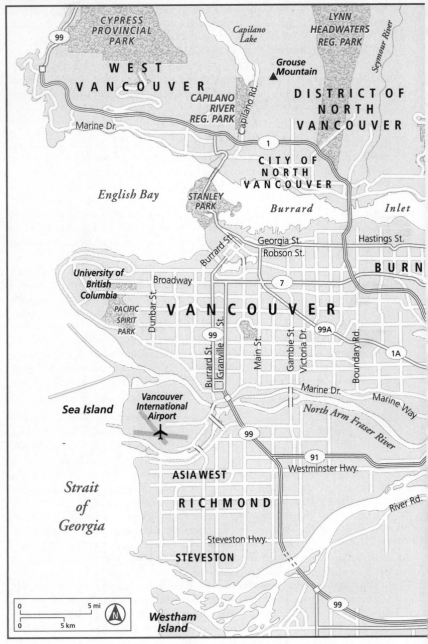

CYPRESS PROVINCIAL PARK

Capilano Lake

LYNN HEADWATERS REG. PARK

Seymour River

99

▲ Grouse Mountain

WEST VANCOUVER

CAPILANO RIVER REG. PARK

Capilano Rd.

DISTRICT OF NORTH VANCOUVER

Marine Dr.

1

CITY OF NORTH VANCOUVER

English Bay

STANLEY PARK

Burrard   Inlet

Georgia St.

Hastings St.

Burrard St.

Robson St.

University of British Columbia

Broadway

BURN

PACIFIC SPIRIT PARK

Dunbar St.

VANCOUVER

7

99A

Boundary Rd.

99

Granville St.

Main St.

Gambie St.

Victoria Dr.

1A

Burrard St.

Marine Dr.

Marine Way

Sea Island

Vancouver International Airport

North Arm Fraser River

99

Strait of Georgia

91

Westminster Hwy.

ASIA WEST

RICHMOND

River Rd.

Steveston Hwy.

STEVESTON

0   5 mi
0   5 km

N

99

Westham Island

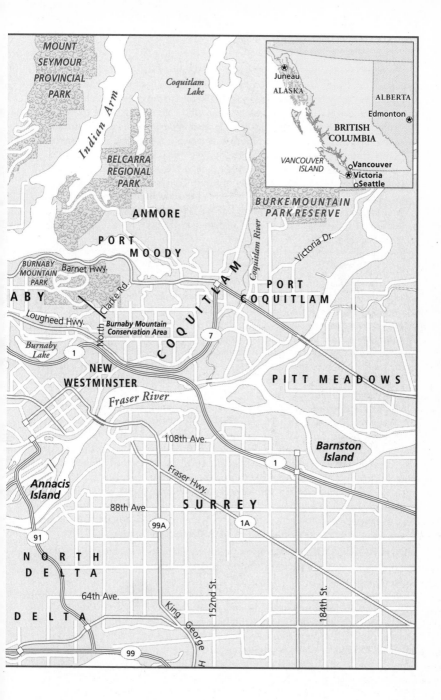

(Tips What's West

The thing to keep in mind when figuring out what's where in Vancouver, is that this is a city where property is king, and the word *west* has such positive connotations that folks have always gone to great lengths to associate it with their particular patch of real estate. Thus we have the **West End**, the **West Side**, and **West Vancouver**, which improbably enough is located immediately beside **North Vancouver**. It can be a bit confusing for newcomers, but fortunately each west has its own distinct character. The West End is a high-rise residential neighborhood on the downtown peninsula. The West Side is one-half of Vancouver, from Ontario Street west to the University of British Columbia. (The more working-class **East Side** covers the mainland portion of the city, from Ontario St. east to Boundary Rd.) Very tony West Vancouver is a city unto itself on the far side of Burrard Inlet. Together with its more middle-class neighbor, North Vancouver, it forms the **North Shore**.

---

forks. One branch, still **Burrard Street,** continues south and intersects West 4th Avenue and Broadway before ending at West 16th Avenue on the borders of the ritzy Shaughnessy neighborhood. The other branch becomes **Cornwall Avenue,** which heads west through Kitsilano, changing its name to **Point Grey Road** and then **NW Marine Drive** before entering the University of British Columbia campus.

Granville Street starts near the Waterfront Station on Burrard Inlet and runs the entire length of downtown, crosses the Granville Bridge to Vancouver's West Side, and carries on south across the breadth of the city before crossing the Arthur Laing Bridge to Vancouver International Airport.

On mainland Vancouver, the city's east-west roads are successively numbered from 1st Avenue at the downtown bridges to 77th Avenue by the banks of the Fraser River. The most important east-west route is **Broadway** (formerly 9th Ave.), which starts a few blocks from the University of British Columbia and extends across the length of the city to the border of neighboring Burnaby, where it becomes the **Lougheed Highway.** In Kitsilano, **W. 4th Avenue** is also an important east-west shopping and commercial corridor. Intersecting with Broadway at various points are a number of important north-south commercial streets, each defining a particular neighborhood. The most significant of these streets are (from west to east) **Macdonald Street** in Kitsilano, **Granville Street, Cambie Street, Main Street,** and **Commercial Drive.**

FINDING AN ADDRESS   In many Vancouver addresses, the suite or room number precedes the building number. For instance, 100-1250 Robson St. is Suite 100 at 1250 Robson St.

In downtown Vancouver, Chinatown's **Carrall Street** is the east-west axis from which streets are numbered and designated. Westward, numbers increase progressively to Stanley Park; eastward, numbers increase approaching Commercial Drive. For example, 400 W. Pender would be 4 blocks from Carrall Street heading toward downtown; 400 E. Pender would be 4 blocks on the opposite side of Carrall Street. Similarly, the low numbers on north-south streets start on the Canada Place Pier side and increase southward in increments of 100 per block (the 600 block of Thurlow St. is 2 blocks from the 800 block) toward False Creek and Granville Island.

Off the peninsula the system works the same, but **Ontario Street** is the east-west axis. Also, all east-west roads are avenues (for example, 4th Ave.), while streets (for example, Main St.) run exclusively north-south.

STREET MAPS   Tourist information centers (see "Visitor Information," above) and most hotels can provide you with a detailed downtown map. *Where Vancouver* (© 604/736-5586; www.where.ca), a free guide available at most hotels, has good maps. A good all-around metropolitan area map is the Rand McNally Vancouver city map. If you're an auto-club member, the Canadian Automobile Association (CAA) map is also good. It's not for sale, but is free to both AAA and CAA members, and is available at AAA offices across North America. **International Travel Maps and Books,** 539 W. Pender St. (© 604/687-3320), has the city's most extensive selection of Vancouver and British Columbia maps and specialty guidebooks.

2 Getting Around

BY PUBLIC TRANSPORTATION

Vancouver's public transportation system is the most extensive in Canada and includes service to all major tourist attractions, so it's not really necessary to have a car (especially if you're staying in the downtown area).

The **Translink** (otherwise known as B.C. Transit; © 604/521-0400; www.translink. bc.ca) system includes electric buses, the SeaBus catamaran ferry, and the light-rail Sky-Train. It's an ecologically friendly, highly reliable, inexpensive system that allows you to get everywhere, including the beaches and ski slopes. Regular service runs from 5am to 2am.

Schedules and routes are available online, at tourist information centers, at many major hotels, and on buses. Pick up a copy of *Discover Vancouver on Transit* at one of the tourist information centers (see "Visitor Information," above). This publication gives transit routes for many city neighborhoods, landmarks, and attractions. The back cover of this book has a downtown Vancouver transit map.

FARES   Fares are based on the number of zones traveled, and are the same for buses, the SeaBus, and the SkyTrain. One ticket allows you to transfer from one mode of transport to another, in any direction, within 90 minutes. A one-way, one-zone fare (everything in central Vancouver) costs C$2.25 (US$1.90/£1). A two-zone fare—C$3.25 (US$2.75/£1.45)—is required to travel to nearby suburbs such as Richmond or North Vancouver, and a three-zone fare—C$4.50 (US$3.80/£1.70)—is required for travel to the far-off edge city of Surrey. After 6:30pm on weekdays and all day on weekends and holidays, you can travel anywhere in all three zones for C$2.25 (US$1.90/£1). **DayPasses,** good on all public transit, cost C$8 (US$6.80/£3.60) for adults and C$6 (US$5/£2.70) for seniors, students, and children. They can be used for unlimited travel on weekdays or weekends and holidays.

Tip: Keep in mind that drivers do not make change, so you need the exact fare or a valid transit pass. Pay with cash or buy tickets and passes from ticket machines at stations, tourist information centers, both SeaBus terminals, and convenience stores, drugstores, and outlets displaying the FAREDEALER sign; most of these outlets also sell a transit map showing all routes for C$1.95 (US$1.60/90p).

BY BUS   Both diesel and electric-trolley buses service the city. Regular service on the busiest routes is every 12 minutes from 5am to 2am. Wheelchair-accessible buses and bus stops are identified by the international wheelchair symbol. Some key routes to keep in mind if you're touring the city by bus: **no. 5** (Robson St.), **no. 2** (Kitsilano Beach to downtown), **no. 50** (Granville Island), **no. 35** or **135** (to the Stanley Park bus loop), **no. 240** (North Vancouver), **no. 250** (West Vancouver–Horseshoe Bay), and buses **no. 4** or **10** (UBC–Exhibition Park via Granville St. downtown). From June until the end of September, the Vancouver Parks Board operates a **free bus through Stanley Park,** which stops at 14 points of interest. Call © **604/953-3333** for general public transportation information.

BY SKYTRAIN   The SkyTrain is a fast, light-rail service between downtown Vancouver and the suburbs. The **Expo Line** trains operate from Waterfront to King George station, running along a scenic 27km (17-mile) route from downtown Vancouver east to Surrey through Burnaby and New Westminster in 39 minutes. There are 20 stations along this route; four downtown stations are underground and marked at street level. The **Millennium Line,** which opened in fall 2002, makes the same stops from Waterfront to Columbia, then branches to Sapperton, Braid, Lougheed town center, and beyond to Commercial Drive. All stations except Granville are wheelchair accessible; trains arrive every 2 to 5 minutes.

BY SEABUS   The SS *Beaver* and SS *Otter* catamaran ferries take passengers, cyclists, and wheelchair riders on a scenic 12-minute commute across Burrard Inlet between downtown's Waterfront Station and North Vancouver's Lonsdale Quay. On weekdays, a SeaBus leaves each stop every 15 minutes from 6:15am to 6:30pm, then every 30 minutes until 1am. SeaBuses depart on Saturdays every half-hour from 6:30am to 12:30pm, then every 15 minutes until 7:15pm, then every half-hour until 1am. On Sundays and holidays, runs depart every half-hour from 8:30am to 11pm. Note that the crossing is a two-zone fare on weekdays until 6:30pm.

BY TAXI
Cab fares start at C$2.30 (US$1.95/£1) and increase at a rate of C$1.25 (US$1.10/ 55p) per kilometer, plus C30¢ (US25¢/15p) per minute at stoplights or in stalled traffic. In the downtown area, you can expect to travel for less than C$10 (US$8.50/ £4.50) plus tip. The typical fare for the 13km (8-mile) drive from downtown to the airport is C$25 (US$21/£11).

Taxis are easy to find in front of major hotels, but flagging one down can be tricky. Most drivers are usually on radio calls. But thanks to built-in satellite positioning systems, if you call for a taxi, it usually arrives faster than if you go out and hail one. Call for a pickup from **Black Top** (© **604/731-1111**), **Yellow Cab** (© **604/681-1111**), or **MacLure's** (© **604/731-9211**).

BY CAR
Vancouver's road system and traffic are easier to handle than those in many other cities, in large part because the city has no freeways. Traffic thus tends to move more slowly. If you're just sightseeing around town, public transit and cabs will easily see you through. However, if you're planning to visit the North Shore mountains or pursue other out-of-town activities, then a car is necessary. Gas is sold by the liter, averaging at press time around C$1.10 (US95¢/50p) per liter; a gallon of gas costs approximately C$4 (US$3.40/£1.80). *Note:* In Canada, speeds and distances are posted in kilometers. The speed limit in Vancouver is 50kmph (31 mph); highway speed limits vary from 90 to 110kmph (56–68 mph).

RENTAL CARS   Rates vary widely depending on demand, style of car, and special offers. If you're over 25 and have a major credit card, you can rent a vehicle from **Avis,** 757 Hornby St. (✆ **800/879-2847** or 604/606-2868); **Budget,** 501 W. Georgia St. (✆ **800/472-3325** or 604/668-7000); **Enterprise,** 585 Smithe St. (✆ **800/736-8222** or 604/688-5500); **Hertz Canada,** 1128 Seymour St. (✆ **800/263-0600** or 604/606-4711); **National/Tilden,** 1130 W. Georgia St. (✆ **800/387-4747** or 604/685-6111); or **Thrifty,** 1015 Burrard St. or 1400 Robson St. (✆ **800/847-4389** or 604/606-1666). These firms all have counters and shuttle service at the airport as well. To rent a recreational vehicle, contact **Go West Campers,** 1577 Lloyd Ave., North Vancouver (✆ **800/661-8813** or 604/987-5288; www.go-west.com).

PARKING   All major downtown hotels have guest parking, either in-house or at nearby lots. Rates vary from free to C$25 (US$21/£11) per day. Public parking is found at **Robson Square** (enter at Smithe and Howe sts.), the **Pacific Centre** (Howe and Dunsmuir sts.), and **The Bay** department store (Richards near Dunsmuir St.). You'll also find larger **parking lots** at the intersections of Thurlow and Georgia, Thurlow and Alberni, and Robson and Seymour streets.

Metered **street parking** may take a trip or three around the block to find a spot; the meters accept C$2 (US$1.70/90p) and C$1 (US85¢/45p) coins. Rules are posted and strictly enforced; generally, downtown and in the West End, metered parking is in effect 7 days a week. (**Note:** Drivers are given about a 2-min. grace period before their cars are towed away when the 3pm no-parking rule goes into effect on many major thoroughfares.) Unmetered parking on side streets is often subject to neighborhood residency requirements: Check the signs. If you park in such an area without the appropriate sticker on your windshield, you'll get ticketed and towed. If your car is towed away or you need a towing service and aren't a CAA or an AAA member, call **Unitow** (✆ **604/251-1255**) or **Busters** (✆ **604/685-8181**). If you are parking on the street, remove all valuables from your car; break-ins are not uncommon.

SPECIAL DRIVING RULES   Canadian driving rules are similar to those in the U.S. Stopping for pedestrians is required even outside crosswalks; seat belts are required. Children 4 years and under must be in a child seat; motorcyclists must wear helmets. It's legal to turn right at a red light after coming to a full stop unless posted otherwise. Though photo radar is no longer in use in B.C. (the new government got elected partially on its pledge to eliminate the hated system), photo-monitored intersections are alive and well. If you're caught racing through a red light, fines start at C$100 (US$85/£45). Unlike in the U.S., however, daytime headlights (dimmers) are mandatory.

AUTO CLUB   Members of the American Automobile Association (AAA) can get assistance from the **Canadian Automobile Association (CAA),** 999 W. Broadway, Vancouver (✆ **604/268-5600,** or for road service 604/293-2222; www.caa.ca).

BY BIKE

Vancouver is a biker's paradise. Along Robson and Denman streets near Stanley Park are plenty of places to rent bikes. (For specifics, see p. 136.) Paved paths crisscross through parks and along beaches, and new routes are constantly being added. Helmets are mandatory and riding on sidewalks is illegal except on designated bike paths.

You can take your bike on the SeaBus anytime at no extra charge. Bikes are not allowed in the George Massey Tunnel, but a tunnel shuttle operates four times daily from mid-May to September to transport you across the Fraser River. From May 1 to

Victoria Day (the third weekend of May), the service operates on weekends only. All of the West Vancouver blue buses (including the bus to the Horseshoe Bay ferry terminal) can carry two bikes, first-come, first-served, free of charge. In Vancouver, only a limited number of suburban bus routes allow bikes on board: no. 351 to White Rock, no. 601 to South Delta, no. 404 to the airport, and the no. 99 Express to UBC.

BY MINIFERRY

Crossing False Creek to Granville Island or beautiful Vanier Park on one of the zippy little miniferries is cheap and fun. These small, covered boats connect various points of interest; they are privately operated, so your public transit pass or ticket is not valid. It's well worth the extra money, though.

The **Aquabus** (© **604/689-5858**; www.aquabus.bc.ca) docks at the south foot of Hornby Street, the Arts Club on Granville Island, Yaletown at Davie Street, Science World, and Stamp's Landing. Ferries operate daily from 7am to 10:30pm (8:30pm in winter) and run every 15 minutes to half-hour from 10am to 5pm (later in May and June). One-way fares are C$2.50 to C$5 (US$2.10–US$4.25/£2.25–£1.10) for adults and C$1.25 to C$3 (US$1–US$2.50/60p–£1.35) for seniors and children. A day pass is C$12 (US$10/£5) for adults, C$11 (US$9/£4.95) for seniors, and C$8 (US$7/£3.60) for children. You can take a 25-minute scenic boat ride (one complete circuit) for C$6 (US$5/£2.70) adults, C$4 (US$3.40/£1.80) seniors and children.

FAST FACTS: Vancouver

Business Hours Vancouver **banks** are open Monday through Thursday from 10am to 5pm and Friday from 10am to 6pm. Some banks, like Canadian Trust, are also open on Saturday. **Stores** are generally open Monday through Saturday from 10am to 6pm. Last call at **restaurant bars** and **cocktail lounges** is 2am.

Child Care If you need to rent cribs, car seats, play pens, or other baby accessories, **Cribs and Carriages** (© **604/988-2742**; www.cribsandcarriages.com) delivers them right to your hotel.

Consulates The **U.S. Consulate** is at 1075 W. Pender St. (© **604/685-4311**). The **British Consulate** is at 800-1111 Melville St. (© **604/683-4421**). The **Australian Consulate** is at 1225-888 Dunsmuir St. (© **604/684-1177**). Check the Yellow Pages for other countries' consulates.

Currency Exchange Banks and ATMs have a better exchange rate than most foreign exchange bureaus. See "Money & Costs," in chapter 2, for more information.

Dentists Most major hotels have a dentist on call. **Vancouver Centre Dental Clinic,** Vancouver Centre Mall, 11-650 W. Georgia St. (© **604/682-1601**), is another option. You must make an appointment. The clinic is open Monday through Wednesday 8:30am to 6pm, Thursday 8:30am to 7pm, and Friday 9am to 6pm.

Doctors Hotels usually have a doctor on call. **Vancouver Medical Clinics,** Bentall Centre, 1055 Dunsmuir St. (© **604/683-8138**), is a drop-in clinic open Monday through Friday 8am to 4:45pm. Another drop-in medical center, **Carepoint**

Medical Centre, 1175 Denman St. (℃ **604/681-5338**), is open daily from 9am to 8pm (Mon–Wed until 9pm). See also "Emergencies," below.

Electricity As in the U.S., electric current is 110 volts AC (60 cycles).

Emergencies Dial ℃ **911** for fire, police, ambulance, and poison control. This is a free call.

Hospitals **St. Paul's Hospital,** 1081 Burrard St. (℃ **604/682-2344**), is the closest facility to downtown and the West End. West Side Vancouver hospitals include **Vancouver General Hospital Health and Sciences Centre,** 855 W. 12th Ave. (℃ **604/875-4111**), and **British Columbia's Children's Hospital,** 4480 Oak St. (℃ **604/875-3163**). In North Vancouver, there's **Lions Gate Hospital,** 231 E. 15th St. (℃ **604/988-3131**).

Hotlines Emergency numbers include **Crisis Centre** (℃ 604/872-3311), **Rape Crisis Centre** (℃ 604/255-6228), **Rape Relief** (℃ 604/872-8212), **Poison Control Centre** (℃ 604/682-2344), **Crime Stoppers** (℃ 604/669-8477), **SPCA** animal emergency (℃ 604/879-7343), **Vancouver Police** (℃ 604/717-3535), **Fire** (℃ 604/665-6000), and **Ambulance** (℃ 604/872-5151). See also "Emergencies," above.

Internet Access Free Internet access is available at the Vancouver **Public Library** Central Branch, 350 W. Georgia St. (℃ **604/331-3600**). **Cyber Space Internet Café,** 1741 Robson St. (℃ **604/684-6004**), and **Internet Coffee,** 1104 Davie St. (℃ **604/682-6668**), are both open until at least midnight.

Laundry & Dry Cleaning **Davie Laundromat,** 1061 Davie St. (℃ **604/682-2717**), offers self-service, drop-off service, and dry cleaning. **Laundry & Suntanning,** 781 Denman St. (℃ **604/689-9598**), doesn't have dry-cleaning services, but you can work on your tan while you wait. Also, almost all hotels have laundry service.

Liquor Laws The legal drinking age in British Columbia is 19. Spirits are sold only in government liquor stores, but beer and wine can be purchased from specially licensed, privately owned stores and pubs. Most LCBC (Liquor Control of British Columbia) stores are open Monday through Saturday from 10am to 6pm, but some are open until 11pm.

Lost Property The **Vancouver Police** have a lost property room (℃ **604/717-2726**), open 8:30am to 5pm Monday through Saturday. If you think you may have lost something on public transportation, call **Translink** (B.C. Transit) 8:30am to 5pm at ℃ **604/682-7887**.

Luggage Storage & Lockers Most downtown hotels will gladly hold your luggage before or after your stay. Lockers are available at the main Vancouver railway station (which is also the main bus depot), **Pacific Central Station,** 1150 Station St., near Main Street and Terminal Avenue south of Chinatown (℃ **604/661-0328**).

Mail Letters and postcards up to 30 grams cost C93¢ (US75¢/40p) to mail to the U.S. and C$1.78 (US$1.50/80p) for overseas airmail service; C52¢ (US45¢/25p) within Canada. You can buy stamps and mail parcels at the main post office (see "Post Office," below) or at any of the postal outlets inside drugstores and convenience stores. Look for a POSTAL SERVICES sign.

Newspapers & Magazines The two local papers are the ***Vancouver Sun*** (www.vancouversun.com), published Monday through Saturday, and the ***Province*** (www.canada.com/vancouver/theprovince), published Sunday through Friday mornings. The free weekly entertainment paper, the *Georgia Straight,* comes out on Thursday.

Pharmacies **Shopper's Drug Mart,** 1125 Davie St. (⟋ **604/685-6445**), is open 24 hours. Several Safeway supermarket pharmacies are open late; the one on Robson and Denman is open until midnight.

Police For emergencies, dial ⟋ **911.** This is a free call. Otherwise, the **Vancouver City Police** can be reached at ⟋ **604/717-3535.**

Post Office The **main post office,** 349 W. Georgia St. at Homer Street (⟋ **800/267-1177**) is open Monday through Friday from 8am to 5:30pm. You'll also find post office outlets in Shopper's Drug Mart and 7-Eleven stores with longer opening hours.

Restrooms Hotel lobbies are your best bet for downtown facilities. The shopping centers like Pacific Centre and Sinclair Centre, as well as the large department stores like The Bay, also have restrooms.

Smoking Smoking is prohibited in all public areas, including restaurants, bars, and clubs.

Taxes Hotel rooms are subject to a 10% tax. The **provincial sales tax (PST)** is 7% (excluding food, restaurant meals, and children's clothing). For specific questions, call the **B.C. Consumer Taxation Branch** (⟋ **604/660-0858;** www.sbr.gov.bc.ca/ctb). Most goods and services are subject to a 6% **federal goods and services tax (GST).** *Note:* The GST Visitors Rebate Program was eliminated in 2007, so it's no longer possible to get a rebate on goods and services purchased in Canada.

Time Zone Vancouver is in the Pacific time zone, as are Seattle, Portland, San Francisco, and Los Angeles. Daylight saving time applies the second Sunday in March to the first Sunday in November.

Tipping Tipping etiquette is the same as in the United States: 15% to 20% in restaurants, C$1 (US85¢/50p) per bag for bellboys and porters, and C$1 to C$4 (US85¢–US$3.40/50p–£1.80) per day for the hotel housekeeper. Taxi drivers get a sliding-scale tip—fares under C$4 deserve a C$1 (US85¢/50p) tip; for fares over C$5, tip 15%.

Weather Call ⟋ **604/664-9010** for weather updates. Each local ski resort has its own snow report line: **Cypress Ski area** ⟋ **604/419-7669; Whistler/Blackcomb** ⟋ **604/687-7507.**

5

Where to Stay in Vancouver

The Vancouver hotel business has seen a lot of activity in recent years. The building boom associated with Expo '86 was followed by a flush of new hotel construction and renovation in the late 1990s right up to 2003, when trendy Opus opened in Yaletown.

Most of the hotels are in the downtown area or in the West End. Central Vancouver is small and easily walkable, so in both of these neighborhoods you'll be close to major sights, services, and nightlife. Downtown—which includes Vancouver's financial district, the area around Canada Place convention center and cruise-ship terminal, and the central shopping-business area around Robson Square—is buzzing during the day but pretty quiet at night.

One thing to keep in mind when booking a room is that downtown hotels on south Granville Street (the Best Western Downtown Vancouver, Howard Johnson Hotel, and the Ramada Inn and Suites) offer a central location without the high price tag, but the area they're in is not very attractive and is a prime hangout for panhandlers. It's not dangerous, but you shouldn't book there unless you have a reasonable tolerance for the tattooed and pierced. This portion of Granville is also home to a large concentration of bars and

clubs. Be prepared for noisy revelry, especially on warm summer Friday and Saturday nights. This area is now on the path to gentrification, and in a couple of years will no doubt be considered trendy.

The West End is green, leafy, and residential, a neighborhood of high-rise apartment houses, beautifully landscaped streets, and in close proximity to Coal Harbour, Stanley Park, and the best beaches. While downtown gets quiet at night, the West End starts hopping; dozens of restaurants, cafes, and bars line Robson and Denman streets.

You'll also find a couple of hotels and some lovely B&Bs in great old houses on the West Side of Vancouver, the area south of False Creek on Granville Island and in the Kitsilano neighborhood. Staying in "Kits" can be fun because it's a complete neighborhood unto itself and has its own hangout spots on 4th Avenue and around Kits Beach.

Remember that quoted prices don't include the 10% **hotel room tax,** the 7% **provincial accommodations tax,** or the 6% **goods and services tax (GST).** And remember, too, that we list the rack rates: the rates you would receive if you walked in off the street and requested a room. By checking the hotel's website, you'll almost

---

(Tips Fido-Friendly Hotels

Vancouver is one of the dog-friendliest cities in the world. Nearly all downtown and West End hotels allow you to check in your canine companion, usually for an added daily charge of C$20 to C$25 (US$17–US$21/£9–11).

Bed & Breakfast Registries

If you prefer to stay in a B&B, the following agencies specialize in matching guests with establishments that best suit their needs:

- **Vancouver Bed & Breakfast,** 4390 Frances St., Burnaby, B.C. V5C ZR3 (© **604/298-8815**; fax 604/298-5917; www.vancouverbandb.bc.ca).
- **Canada-West Accommodations,** P.O. Box 86607, North Vancouver, B.C. V7L 4L2 (© **800/561-3223** or 604/990-6730; www.b-b.com).
- **Beachside Vancouver Bed & Breakfast Registry,** 1180 Renton Place, West Vancouver, B.C. V7S 2K7 (© **800/563-3311** or 604/922-7773; www.beach. bc.ca), specializes in high-end B&Bs in the Lower Mainland.

always be able to find lower rates, including special "romance packages" and weekend getaway specials.

RESERVATIONS Reservations are highly recommended June through September and during holidays. If you arrive without a reservation or have trouble finding a room, call the **Hello B.C./Super, Natural British Columbia** hotlines at © **800/ 435-5622** or 800/663-6000. You can also book a room by going to **Tourism Vancouver,** 200 Burrard St. (across from Canada Place), or by visiting their website **www.tourismvancouver.com**.

1 Best Vancouver Hotel Bets

For a quick overview of the city's best splurge and moderately priced hotels, see chapter 1, p. 11 and p. 12, respectively.

- **Best Historic Hotel: The Fairmont Hotel Vancouver,** 900 W. Georgia St. (© **800/ 441-1414** or 604/684-3131) harks back to a more gracious and traditional era. Even with all the modern amenities and services you could wish for, it wraps you up in old-fashioned charm and comfort. See p. 68.
- **Best for Business Travelers: The Westin Grand,** 433 Robson St. (© **800/937-8461** or 604/602-1999), in addition to having some of the nicest modern interior decor and marvelous day and nighttime views from rooms on its high floors, offers comfortable desks with dataports, high-speed and wireless Internet access, lots of electrical plugs, plus speakerphones, cordless phones, easy access to fax/laser printer/photocopiers, and in-room safes big enough for your laptop. See p. 71.
- **Best Boutique Hotel:** In trendy Yaletown, the stylish **Opus Hotel,** 322 Davie St. (© **866/642-6787** or 604/642-6787), a member of the Small Luxury Hotels of the World group, has an array of room types set in luscious colors, with superb beds, and an overall contemporary aesthetic that sets it apart. See p. 69.
- **Best for a Romantic Getaway:** The **Wedgewood Hotel,** 845 Hornby St. (© **800/ 663-0666** or 604/689-7777), the only boutique hotel downtown, has a comfy, romantic, European elegance that brings out the romance in everyone. See p. 71.
- **Best for Families:** The **Rosedale on Robson Suite Hotel,** 838 Hamilton at Robson Street (© **800/661-8870** or 604/689-8033), offers two-bedroom suites, a Treasure Chest in the lobby, and toys kids can enjoy in the pool. See p. 73.

- **Best Inexpensive Hotel:** With all the facilities of a convention center plus cheap, comfortable rooms, **The University of British Columbia Conference Centre,** 5961 Student Union Blvd. (© **604/822-1000**), is the best inexpensive choice in the city. See p. 81.
- **Best B&B:** Built in 1905 by two Vancouver photographers, the **West End Guest House,** 1362 Haro St. (© **888/546-3327** or 604/681-2889), is not only filled with the artists' work and a collection of Victorian antiques, but you also get fresh-baked brownies or cookies with your evening turndown service. See p. 79.
- **Best Location:** Everyone's definition of a great location is different, but the **Westin Bayshore Resort & Marina,** 1601 Bayshore Dr. (© **800/937-8461** or 604/682-3377), is just steps from Stanley Park and Denman Street, with easy access to the seawall and only 10 blocks from downtown. See p. 77.
- **Best Views:** So many Vancouver hotels have outstanding views that it's difficult to choose just one—so how about two? There's something special about the upper floors at the **Pan Pacific Hotel Vancouver,** 300–999 Canada Place (© **800/937-1515** in the U.S., or 604/662-8111), where the harborside rooms have un-impeded views of Coal Harbour, Stanley Park, the Lions Gate Bridge, and the North Shore's mountains. See p. 70. Just as spectacular, and with windows that you can open to savor the freshness of the air along with the magnificence of the water/mountain/park views, is the **Westin Bayshore Resort & Marina,** 1601 Bayshore Dr. (© **800/937-8461** or 604/682-3377). See p. 77.
- **Best Art:** Let's face it, the artwork in most hotel rooms tends to be embarrassing, forgettable, or both, but not at **The Listel Hotel,** 1300 Robson St. (© **800/663-5491** or 604/684-8461), where public spaces and rooms are adorned with art-work from Buschlen Mowatt Gallery, Vancouver's preeminent gallery for contem-porary art. See p. 75.
- **Best for Sports Fans:** The **Georgian Court Hotel,** 773 Beatty St. (© **800/663-1155** or 604/682-5555), has the closest beds to all the action. B.C. Place Stadium is right across the street, and GM Place is just a few blocks away. See p. 73.
- **Best Bathrooms:** Every large, marble-clad bathroom at the **Wedgewood Hotel,** 845 Hornby St. (© **800/663-0666** or 604/689-7777), has a deep, soaker tub and a separate, marble, walk-in Roman shower. See p. 71.
- **Best Spa:** The **Pan Pacific Hotel Vancouver,** 300–999 Canada Place (© **800/937-1515** in the U.S., or 604/662-8111), opened its new, luxurious Spa Utopia in 2005. See p. 70.

2 Downtown & Yaletown

All downtown hotels are within 5 to 10 minutes' walking distance of shops, restau-rants, and attractions. Hotels in this area lean more toward the luxurious than the modest, a state of affairs reflected in their prices.

VERY EXPENSIVE

Delta Vancouver Suites ★★ *Kids*   The Delta Vancouver Suites is a full-service, all-suites hotel with a special appeal to business travelers. It sits across the street from the Lookout! observation tower (p. 118), just minutes from Canada Place, Gastown, Chinatown, and Robson Square. The look throughout is high-end, with an attractive lobby connecting to a state-of-the-art conference facility. Renovated in 2006, each suite has a desk and mini-office/living area. Corner 09 rooms are long and narrow

Where to Stay in Downtown Vancouver

Barclay House Bed & Breakfast **7**
Best Western
  Downtown Vancouver **34**
Blue Horizon **11**
Buchan Hotel **1**
Camelot Inn **40**
Chocolate Lily **37**
Coast Plaza Hotel & Suites **4**
Days Inn Downtown **14**
Delta Vancouver Suites **16**
The Fairmont Hotel Vancouver **18**
Four Seasons Hotel **21**
Georgian Court Hotel **25**
Granville Island Hotel **41**
Hostelling International Vancouver
  Downtown Hostel **30**
Hostelling International Vancouver
  Jericho Beach Hostel **36**
Howard Johnson Hotel **33**
Inn at False Creek–Quality
  Hotel Downtown **31**
Kenya Court Ocean Front
  Guest House **38**
The Kingston Hotel **22**
Le Soleil Hotel & Suites **15**
The Listel Hotel **6**
Loden Vancouver **9**
Lonsdale Quay Hotel **12**
Metropolitan Hotel Vancouver **17**
Moda Hotel **23**
Opus Hotel **35**
Pacific Palisades Hotel **8**
Pan Pacific Hotel Vancouver **13**
Ramada Inn and Suites **32**
Rosedale on Robson Suite Hotel **27**
Sheraton Vancouver Wall
  Centre Hotel **28**
Sunset Inn & Suites **29**
The Sutton Place Hotel **19**
Sylvia Hotel **3**
The University of British Columbia
  Conference Centre **39**
Vancouver Marriott
  Pinnacle Hotel **10**
Wedgewood Hotel **20**
West End Guest House **5**
Westin Bayshore Resort
  & Marina **2**
The Westin Grand **24**
YWCA Hotel/Residence **25**

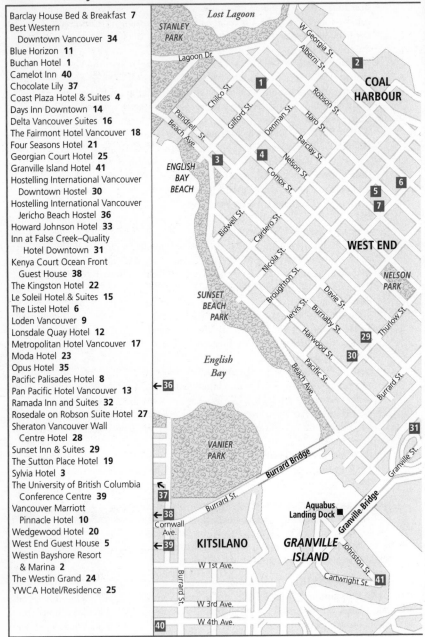

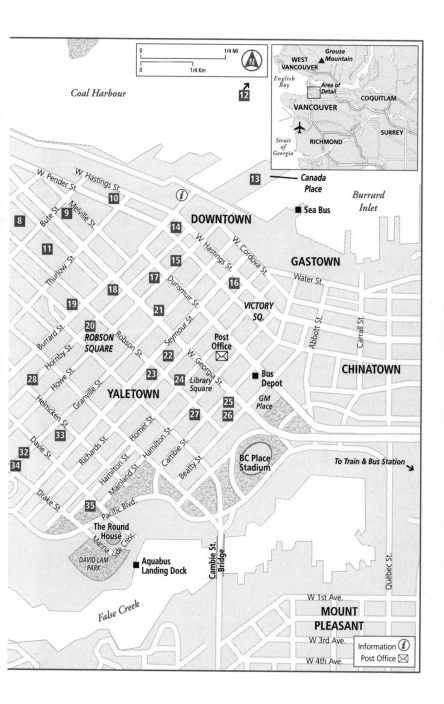

Coal Harbour

with a full wall of floor-to-ceiling glass. A C$55 (US$47/£25) upgrade to the Signature Club gets you a room on the top three floors and access to the Signature Lounge, which puts out a good continental breakfast and afternoon hors d'oeuvres (both included in the upgrade). All guests can use the heated indoor pool and fitness room. Kids are given a welcome pack on arrival.

550 W. Hastings St., Vancouver, B.C. V6B 1L6. ℭ 877/814-7706 or 604/689-8188. Fax 604/605-8881. www.deltahotels. com. 226 units. Oct 15–Apr C$349 (US$297/£157) double; May–Oct 14 C$409 (US$348/£184) double. Children under 18 stay free in parent's room. AE, DC, DISC, MC, V. Valet parking C$22 (US$18/£10). **Amenities:** Restaurant; bar; indoor pool; health club; spa services; concierge; business center; 24-hr. room service; massage; babysitting; laundry service; dry cleaning; nonsmoking rooms; executive-level rooms; rooms for those w/limited mobility. *In room:* A/C, TV w/pay movies and games, high-speed Internet, minibar, coffeemaker, hair dryer, iron/ironing board, safe.

The Fairmont Hotel Vancouver 🌑🌑

Thanks to a C$75-million (US$63-million/£34-million) renovation, the grande dame of Vancouver's hotels has been restored to its former glory. A landmark in the city since it first opened in 1939, and located directly across from busy Robson Square and the Vancouver Art Gallery, the hotel has been completely brought up to 21st-century standards but retains its very old-fashioned, traditional elegance. The rooms are spacious, quiet, and comfortable, if not particularly dynamic in layout or finish. The bathrooms gleam with marble floors and sinks, and you just don't find solid tubs like these anywhere anymore. The courtyard suites feature a large, luxuriously furnished living room, separated from the bedroom by glass French doors. A state-of-the-art spa features day packages and a la carte treatments including body scrubs and wraps.

900 W. Georgia St., Vancouver, B.C. V6C 2W6. ℭ 800/441-1414 or 604/684-3131. Fax 604/662-1929. www.fairmont. com. 556 units. High season C$349–C$535 (US$297–US$454/£157–£241) double; low season C$298–C$442 (US$253–US$376/£134–£199) double. Children under 18 stay free in parent's room. AE, DC, DISC, MC, V. Parking C$25 (US$21/£11). **Amenities:** 2 restaurants; bar; indoor pool; health club; spa; Jacuzzi; sauna; concierge; tour desk; car rental; business center; shopping arcade; salon; 24-hr. room service; massage; babysitting; laundry service; same-day dry cleaning; nonsmoking rooms; Fairmont Gold executive-level rooms; rooms for those w/limited mobility; rooms for hearing-impaired guests. *In room:* A/C, TV w/pay movies, dataport, minibar, coffeemaker, hair dryer, iron/ironing board.

Four Seasons Hotel 🌑🌑🌑 *Kids*

For nearly 30 years now, the Four Seasons has reigned as one of Vancouver's top hotels. The hotel is favored by international business travelers who expect impeccable service and a full array of services—everything from complimentary shoe shines to a car service. From the outside, this huge high-rise hotel across from the Vancouver Art Gallery is rather unappealing. But the elegant lobby opens up into a spacious garden terrace, and the appealingly large, light-filled rooms offer interesting views of downtown with glimpses of the mountains. The marble bathrooms are particularly well done. For a slightly larger room, reserve a deluxe corner room with wraparound floor-to-ceiling windows. One of the glories of this hotel is its health club with an enormous heated pool—half indoor, half outdoor—on a terrace right in the heart of downtown.

791 W. Georgia St., Vancouver, B.C. V6C 2T4. ℭ 800/332-3442 in the U.S., or 604/689-9333. Fax 604/844-6744. www.fourseasons.com/vancouver. 376 units. Nov–Apr C$230–C$520 (US$195–US$442/£103–£234) double; May–Oct C$350–C$790 (US$297–US$671/£157–£355) double. AE, DC, MC, V. Parking C$26 (US$21/£12). **Amenities:** 2 restaurants; bar; indoor and heated outdoor pool; exercise room; sauna; concierge; car rental; business center; shopping arcade; 24-hr. room service; massage; babysitting; laundry service; same-day dry cleaning; nonsmoking rooms; rooms for those w/limited mobility. *In room:* A/C, TV/VCR, Wi-Fi, minibar, hair dryer, iron/ironing board, safe.

Le Soleil Hotel & Suites 🌑

A boutique hotel midway between Robson Square and the financial district, Le Soleil tries hard to look like a glamorous French country manor with crystal chandeliers, plush carpeting, and gilded ceilings in the lobby.

Except for 10 doubles, all the units are suites; for maximum space, the corner suites are best. The problem with some of the units is that the sitting areas have no windows and consequently feel gloomy and confined, despite the Biedermeier-style furniture and richly colored wallpapers and fabrics. Where Le Soleil shines is in its personal service, but if you're looking for a luxury boutique hotel, the Wedgewood or the Opus (see below) are more appealing.

567 Hornby St., Vancouver, B.C. V6C 2E8. ℂ 877/632-3030 or 604/632-3000. Fax 604/632-3001. www.lesoleilhotel.com. 119 units. C$335–C$500 (US$285–US$425/£151–£225) double. AE, DC, MC, V. Valet parking C$22 (US$19/£10). **Amenities:** Restaurant; access to YWCA fitness facilities next door; concierge; business center; 24-hr. room service; laundry service; same-day dry cleaning; nonsmoking rooms. *In room:* A/C, TV w/pay movies, Wi-Fi, dataport, minibar, coffeemaker, hair dryer, iron/ironing board, safe.

Loden Vancouver ✶✶ *Finds*   Vancouver's newest downtown luxury boutique hotel opened in September 2007 at the edge of Coal Harbour's ritzy residential area. The chic, design-savvy rooms feature bold, striking patterns; plush fabrics in shades of taupe, cream, black, and soft blue; alabaster and Murano glass fixtures; and exotic woods. Enjoy the views north toward Burrard Inlet and the North Shore mountains through floor-to-ceiling windows. The bathrooms are similarly well designed. The hotel features all the amenities for a pampered stay.

1139 Melville St. (at Bute St.), Vancouver, B.C. V6B 2M4. ℂ 800/663-1155 or 604/682-5555. Fax 604/682-8830. www.lodenvancouver.com. 77 units. C$350–C$750 (US$297–US$637/£157–£337) double. AE, DC, MC, V. Parking C$25 (US$21/£11). **Amenities:** Restaurant; bar; health club; Jacuzzi; sauna; concierge; room service; babysitting; laundry service; dry cleaning; nonsmoking hotel. *In room:* A/C, TV/DVD, Wi-Fi, minibar, hair dryer, iron/ironing board, robes.

Metropolitan Hotel Vancouver ✶✶   Built in 1984 and centrally situated between the financial district and downtown shopping areas (Robson Square is a block away), the Metropolitan is geared toward business travelers and leisure travelers who want traditional luxury and full service. Guest rooms feature large, marble-tiled bathrooms with separate tub and shower, and wonderfully comfortable beds with Frette Italian linens. Over half of the rooms were refurbished in 2007 with new carpeting and furniture to add a splash of color to an otherwise muted color scheme; all units should be completed by 2008. Many units in the 18-story hotel have small balconies, but the views are not the hotel's selling point as the building is dwarfed by the Four Seasons across the street. Guests have use of a heated indoor pool and whirlpool, plus sauna and steam rooms. The hotel's restaurant, **Diva at the Met** (p. 87), is regarded as one of Vancouver's top restaurants.

645 Howe St., Vancouver, B.C. V6C 2Y9. ℂ 800/667-2300 or 604/687-1122. Fax 604/643-7267. www.metropolitan.com. 197 units. C$249–C$399 (US$212–US$339/£112–£180) double; C$249–C$699 (US$212–US$594/£112–£315) suite. Children under 18 stay free in parent's room. AE, DC, MC, V. Underground parking C$28 (US$24/£13). **Amenities:** Restaurant; bar; indoor pool; health club; Jacuzzi; concierge; business center; 24-hr. room service; laundry service; same-day dry cleaning; nonsmoking rooms; Wi-Fi in lobby and restaurant; squash court. *In room:* A/C, TV w/pay movies, Wi-Fi, CD player, iPod docking station, minibar, coffeemaker, hair dryer, iron/ironing board, safe.

Opus Hotel ✶✶✶   If you want to stay in a hip, happening, luxury hotel, try the Opus—in 2005, *Condé Nast Traveler* voted it one of the world's top 100 hotels. It's the only hotel in Yaletown, the trendiest area in the city for shopping, nightlife, and dining. Each room is furnished according to one of five "personalities," with its own layout, color, and flavor. Everything is done well here, and the luscious room colors are eye candy if you're tired of blah hotel interiors. The beds are wonderfully firm with feather duvets and top-quality linens. Bathrooms are fitted with high-design sinks, soaker tubs or roomy showers (or both), and feature L'Occitane toiletries. For the best views, book one of the corner suites on the seventh floor. The small exercise room has big windows for people-watching over the street while working out on the latest equipment. The hotel also has a business center available free for guests' use. The cool Opus Bar serves an international tapas menu, and on weekends becomes one of Yaletown's see-and-be-seen scenes (be forewarned: this area of Yaletown is Club Central, and can be noisy until the wee hours; book a Courtyard Room if you don't want to be disturbed). Opus's top-notch restaurant, **Elixir** (p. 90), serves modern French bistro food; if you just want a great latte and a croissant, pop into Café O, right off the lobby. A complimentary car service is available to take you to cruise-ship terminals or any downtown location. *Note:* Until mid-2008, part of Davie Street, right outside the hotel, is closed off for construction of the new Canada Line light-rail system. The highest prices below are for suites.

322 Davie St., Vancouver, B.C. V6B 5Z6. ℂ 866/642-6787 or 604/642-6787. Fax 604/642-6780. www.opushotel.com. 96 units. May–Oct C$429–C$569 (US$365–US$484/£193–£256) double, C$910–C$1,800 (US$773–US$1,530/£409–£810) suite; Nov–Apr C$349–C$489 (US$297–US$416/£157–£220) double, C$739–C$1,300 (US$628–US$585/£333–£585) suite. Children 17 and under stay free in parent's room. AE, DC, MC, V. Valet parking C$25 (US$21/£11). **Amenities:** Restaurant; bar; fitness center; concierge; complimentary car service; complimentary bicycles; 24-hr. room service; laundry service; dry cleaning; nonsmoking rooms. *In room:* A/C, TV w/pay movies, Wi-Fi, minibar, coffeemaker, hair dryer, iron/ironing board, safe, robes.

Pan Pacific Hotel Vancouver ★★★

Since its completion in 1986, this 23-story luxury hotel atop Canada Place, with its cruise-ship terminal and convention center, has become a key landmark on the Vancouver waterfront. Guest rooms begin on the ninth floor, above a huge lobby with a wall of glass overlooking the mountains and the harbor. Despite its size, the hotel excels in comfort and service, and it provides spectacular views (note, however, that construction of the massive new addition to Canada Place is going on just below the hotel on the west side). Book a deluxe Harbor and Mountain room, and you can wake to see the sun glinting off the North Shore mountains, floatplanes taking off from Burrard Inlet, and cruise ships arriving and departing just below your window. The rooms are spacious and comfortable, with large picture windows, contemporary furnishings, and a soothing palette of colors. Bathrooms are large and luxurious. Guests have free use of a heated outdoor pool and Jacuzzi overlooking the harbor. Spa Utopia offers men and women a full array of pampering treatments. Café Pacifica puts on one of the best breakfast buffets in Vancouver and is open for casual meals all day; the Five Sails Restaurant, open for dinner only, is the hotel's fine-dining option.

300-999 Canada Place, Vancouver, B.C. V6C 3B5. ℂ 800/937-1515 in the U.S., or 604/662-8111. Fax 604/685-8690. www.panpacific.com. 504 units. May–Oct C$490–C$640 (US$392–US$512/£221–£288) double, C$640–C$2,200 (US$512–US$1,760/£288–£990) suite; Nov–Apr C$390–C$480 (US$312–US$384/£176–£216) double, C$480–C$2,000 (US$384–US$1,600/£216–£900) suite. AE, DC, DISC, MC, V. Valet parking C$27 (US$22/£12). **Amenities:** 2 restaurants; bar; outdoor heated pool; health club; spa; Jacuzzi; sauna; concierge; business center; shopping arcade; 24-hr. room service; babysitting; laundry service; same-day dry cleaning; nonsmoking floors; squash court. *In room:* A/C, TV w/pay movies, high-speed Internet, minibar, coffeemaker, hair dryer, iron/ironing board, safe.

Sheraton Vancouver Wall Centre Hotel ★

The tallest—and with 736 rooms the largest—hotel in the city, the Wall Centre is hard to miss. The hotel occupies a curved spire of black glass and a second, earlier tower with a fountain-filled urban garden in between. It may remind you of a futuristic office park, a feeling that's unfortunately reinforced in the rooms, which have floor-to-ceiling polarized glass windows that look out onto great views but can't be opened, so it feels like you're always wearing sunglasses. This is upscale Sheraton at its best (or worst, if you hate huge hotels), and because of its size it caters to a lot of tour groups. The hotel features a vast lobby with some nice touches such as a gold-leaf staircase, custom-designed furniture, and handblown glass chandeliers. Rooms have a clean, contemporary look with blond-wood furnishings and nice bathrooms. Guests have the use of a 1,115-sq.-m (12,000-sq.-ft.) health club with an indoor pool and an ayurvedic wellness spa.

1088 Burrard St., Vancouver, B.C. V6Z 2R9. (C) 800/325-3535 or 604/331-1000. Fax 604/893-7200. www.sheraton wallcentre.com. 733 units. C$329–C$459 (US$280–US$390/£148–£207) double. AE, DC, MC, V. Valet parking C$26 (US$22/£12). **Amenities:** 2 restaurants; 2 bars; indoor pool; health club; spa; Jacuzzi; sauna; concierge; tour desk; business center; salon; 24-hr. room service; same-day laundry and dry cleaning; nonsmoking rooms; executive-level rooms. *In room:* A/C, TV w/pay movies, high-speed Internet, minibar, coffeemaker, hair dryer, iron/ironing board, safe.

The Sutton Place Hotel ★★   Don't let the bland, corporate-looking exterior fool you: This hotel has won many awards, and is one of only two AAA five-diamond hotels in Canada. Once you enter the lobby of this centrally located hotel, it's pure luxury, comparable to the Four Seasons (reviewed above). The lobby is elegantly decorated with marble, fresh flowers, chandeliers, and French-leaning European furnishings. The rooms here don't skimp on size or comfort, and are tastefully decorated in a traditional European style. The one- or two-bedroom junior suites have a small parlor. In larger suites, French doors separate the bedroom from the large sitting area. The European-style health club and spa has a big heated pool and sun deck. The Fleuri restaurant serves French Continental cuisine.

845 Burrard St., Vancouver, B.C. V6Z 2K6. (C) 800/961-7555 or 604/682-5511. Fax 604/682-5513. www.suttonplace. com. 397 units. May–Oct C$450 (US$382/£202) double, C$570 (US$484/£256) suite; Nov–Apr C$375 (US$319/£169) double, C$495 (US$421/£223) suite. AE, DC, DISC, MC, V. Underground self- or valet parking C$26 (US$22/£12). Bus: 22. **Amenities:** Restaurant; lounge (w/bistro fare); bakery-cafe; indoor pool; health club; full-service spa; Jacuzzi; sauna; complimentary bikes; children's program; concierge; business center; 24-hr. room service; laundry service; same-day dry-cleaning service; nonsmoking rooms. *In room:* A/C, TV w/pay movies, high-speed Internet, minibar, hair dryer, iron/ironing board, safe.

Wedgewood Hotel ★★★   If you're searching for a romantic, sophisticated hotel with superb service, spacious rooms, fine detailing, a good restaurant, a full-service spa, and a central downtown location, you can't do any better than the Wedgewood. One of the things that makes the award-winning Wedgewood so distinctive is that it's independently owned (by Greek-born Eleni Skalbania), and the owner's elegant personal touch is evident throughout. All 83 units are spacious and have balconies (the best views are those facing the Vancouver Art Gallery and Law Court; avoid the rooms that look out over the back of the hotel). Furnishings and antiques are of the highest quality, and the marble-clad bathrooms with deep soaker tubs and separate walk-in Roman showers are simply the best. Bacchus, the cozy hotel restaurant, serves a fairly traditional menu of fish, pasta, and meat. In 2006, *Travel + Leisure* readers ranked the Wedgewood one of the 500 best hotels in the world.

845 Hornby St., Vancouver, B.C. V6Z 1V1. (C) 800/663-0666 or 604/689-7777. Fax 604/608-5349. www.wedgewood hotel.com. 83 units. C$400–C$600 (US$340–US$510/£180–£270) double; C$500–C$1,500 (US$425–US$1,275/£225–£675) suite. AE, DC, MC, V. Valet parking C$20 (US$17/£9). **Amenities:** Restaurant; complimentary Wi-Fi; small weight room; spa; concierge; business center; 24-hr. room service; laundry service; dry cleaning; executive-level rooms. *In room:* A/C, TV/VCR w/pay movies, high-speed Internet, CD player, minibar, coffeemaker, hair dryer, iron/ironing board, safe.

The Westin Grand ★★★ *Kids*   It's such a pleasure to find a luxury-level hotel that's elegant instead of garish, and understated rather than pompous. Located across from Library Square, The Westin Grand offers high-end all-suite accommodations within easy walking distance of Yaletown, GM Place, and Robson shopping. The spacious suites are brightened by natural light pouring in through the floor-to-ceiling windows; if you can, spring for one of the deluxe 09 or 03 units, which have balconies. Sitting rooms come with a concealed kitchenette and loads of business-friendly amenities; bedrooms feature Westin's trademark *Heavenly* beds, with custom-designed Simmons mattresses (read: 900 coils), fine linens, and everything you need to be luxuriously cozy. The furnishings throughout are clean-lined and contemporary; bathrooms are roomy, most with separate tub and shower. Rooms for travelers with disabilities are available. Private workout equipment gets its own two rooms, and a great 24-hour on-site gym with an outdoor lap pool is on the top two floors. Kids get a special welcome kit, and the hotel's Aria restaurant has a kids' menu. Check the website for special deals; suites are often available for half the rack rate.

433 Robson St., Vancouver, B.C. V6B 6L9. ✆ 800/937-8461 or 604/602-1999. Fax 604/647-2502. www.westin grandvancouver.com. 207 suites. Oct 14–Apr 14 C$419–C$709 (US$356–US$603/£189–£319) suite; Apr 15–Oct 13 C$459–C$749 (US$390–US$637/£207–£337) suite. Up to 2 children under 17 stay free in parent's room. AE, DC, DISC, MC, V. Valet parking C$25 (US$21/£11). **Amenities:** Restaurant; outdoor pool; health club; Jacuzzi; sauna; children's welcome bag; concierge; business center; 24-hr. room service; in-room massage; babysitting; laundry service; same-day dry cleaning; nonsmoking hotel; executive-level rooms. *In room:* A/C, TV w/pay movies, Wi-Fi, kitchenette, minibar, coffeemaker, hair dryer, iron/ironing board, safe.

MODERATE

Best Western Downtown Vancouver   The 12-story Best Western is just a 5-block walk from the theater area on Granville Street at the south end of downtown. All rooms are comfortable, and some have harbor views. The corner rooms are a bit smaller than the rest, but they receive more light. This hotel is not overflowing with amenities, but the rooms are well furnished and the location is convenient. Rooms with a full kitchen are available for an additional C$20 to C$25 (US$15–US$19/£9–£11). Keep in mind, however, that while quite safe, this is still a very bohemian, nightlife-oriented, downtown neighborhood. You shouldn't book here unless you have a reasonable tolerance for the realities of street life. You'll save by booking on the website.

718 Drake St. (at Granville St.), Vancouver, B.C. V6Z 2W6. ✆ 888/669-9888 or 604/669-9888. Fax 604/669-3440. www.bestwesterndowntown.com. 143 units, 32 with full kitchen. C$189–C$209 (US$161–US$178/£85–£94) double. AE, DC, DISC, MC, V. Parking C$6 (US$5/£2.70). **Amenities:** Restaurant; rooftop exercise room; Jacuzzi; sauna; game room; tour desk; shuttle service to downtown; babysitting; laundry service; nonsmoking rooms; corporate rooms. *In room:* A/C, TV/VCR, dataport, coffeemaker, hair dryer, iron/ironing board, safe.

Days Inn Downtown   Situated in a heritage building dating from 1910, the well-maintained Days Inn Downtown is conveniently located in the heart of Vancouver's financial district and within easy walking distance of just about everything. All the rooms were refurbished in 2005, and the hotel is now completely nonsmoking. For travelers who don't need all the amenities of a large hotel, these small, newly refurbished rooms are comfortable and convenient, but if you check out other hotel websites, you might find a much nicer place for not much more money. Ten of the rooms have showers only. Request a water view or consider a harbor-facing suite; rooms facing east stare directly at the concrete walls of the building next door.

921 W. Pender St., Vancouver, B.C. V6C 1M2. ✆ 800/329-7466 or 604/681-4335. Fax 604/681-7808. www.daysinn vancouver.com. 85 units, 10 with shower only. C$149–C$219 (US$127–US$186/£67–£99) double. AE, DC, V. Valet parking C$10 (US$8/£4.50). **Amenities:** Restaurant; bar; concierge; laundry service; same-day dry cleaning; nonsmoking rooms. *In room:* A/C, TV w/pay movies, high-speed Internet, fridge, coffeemaker, hair dryer, iron/ironing board, safe.

Georgian Court Hotel *Value*   This modern, 14-story brick hotel dating from 1984 is extremely well located, just a block or two from B.C. Place Stadium, GM Place Stadium, the Queen Elizabeth Theatre, the Playhouse, and the Vancouver Public Library. You can walk to Robson Square in about 10 minutes. The guest rooms are relatively large, nicely decorated, and have good-size bathrooms. And while the big-time celebs are usually whisked off to the glamorous top hotels, their entourages often stay at the Georgian Court, as it provides all the amenities and business-friendly extras such as two phones in every room, brightly lit desks, and complimentary high-speed Internet access—a service that other hotels almost always charge for.

773 Beatty St., Vancouver, B.C. V6B 2M4. © 800/663-1155 or 604/682-5555. Fax 604/682-8830. www.georgian court.com. 180 units. May–Oct 15 C$199–C$249 (US$165–US$212/£90–£112) double; Oct 16–Apr C$150–C$195 (US$127–US$166/£68–£88) double. AE, DC, MC, V. Parking C$9 (US$8/£4). **Amenities:** Restaurant; bar; health club; Jacuzzi; sauna; concierge; business center; limited room service; babysitting; laundry service; dry cleaning; nonsmoking rooms. *In room:* A/C, TV, free high-speed Internet, minibar, hair dryer, iron/ironing board.

Inn at False Creek—Quality Hotel Downtown *Value* *Kids*   The Inn at False Creek went through a top-to-bottom refurbishment in 2007, making the rooms fresher and more contemporary. The upgraded decor, near-downtown (and Granville Island) location, and amenities make this a good choice for this price range, but street traffic is ever-present as the hotel sits next to the Granville Bridge on-ramp. Rooms are a good size, the tiled bathrooms have tubs and a shower, and the suites are great for families—some have full kitchens and narrow, glassed-in balconies. Rooms at the back are preferable but the traffic noise is minimized in the front by double-pane windows and blackout curtains. The Inn has a nice outdoor pool and patio (open summer only).

1335 Howe St. (at Drake St.), Vancouver, B.C. V6Z 1R7. © 800/663-8474 or 604/682-0229. Fax 604/662-7566. www.innatfalsecreek.com. 157 units. C$99–C$249 (US$84–US$212/£45–£112) double. AE, DC, DISC, MC, V. Parking C$10 (US$8/£4.50). **Amenities:** Restaurant; bar; outdoor pool; access to nearby health club; concierge; limited room service; babysitting; dry cleaning. *In room:* A/C, TV, free Wi-Fi, coffeemaker, hair dryer, iron/ironing board, safe.

Moda Hotel *Finds*   Situated downtown, across from the Orpheum Theatre and close to the clubs in the Granville Street entertainment district, the Moda offers lots of style and excellent value. The hotel, located in a 1908 heritage building, reopened its doors in 2007 after receiving a major makeover from Vancouver's acclaimed interior designer Alda Pereira. Rooms and suites feature a sleek, tailored, European look with dramatic colors, luxury beds and linens, flatscreen televisions, nice tiled bathrooms with a tub/shower, and double-glazed windows to dampen the traffic noise from Granville. The only thing the refurbers couldn't change was the slant in some of the old floors. For years, this hotel was called The Dufferin and catered to a mostly gay clientele; it's still gay-friendly, but anyone with a bit of adventure and a taste for something out of the ordinary will enjoy a stay here. Suites offer an extra half-bathroom, corner locations with more light, and upgraded amenities.

900 Seymour St., Vancouver, B.C. V6B 3L9. © 604/683-4251. Fax 604/683-4256. www.modahotel.ca. 57 units. C$119–C$229 (US$101–US$195/£54–£103) double; C$219–C$289 (US$186–US$246/£99–£130) suite. AE, DC, MC, V. **Amenities:** 2 restaurants, bar. *In room:* A/C, TV, high-speed Internet, hair dryer.

Rosedale on Robson Suite Hotel *Value* *Kids*   Directly across the street from Library Square, the Rosedale provides good value, particularly when it comes to amenities. All rooms are one- or two-bedroom suites, and feature separate living rooms with a pullout couch and full kitchenettes. Very family-friendly, the Rosedale offers designated two-bedroom family suites: The kids' bedrooms are furnished with two single beds. The lobby is oddly laid out and starting to look dated, but some of the upper-end suites have been refurbished. The small gym has an indoor pool with toys for the kids to enjoy. The hotel does a lot of business with tour groups, particularly Australians. Internet rates are considerably lower than the rack rates listed below.

838 Hamilton (at Robson St.), Vancouver, B.C. V6B 6A2. (C) **800/661-8870** or 604/689-8033. Fax 604/689-4426. www.rosedaleonrobson.com. 223 units. C$270–C$800 (US$216–US$680/£121–£360) suite. Additional adult C$20 (US$16/£9). Rates include continental breakfast. AE, DC, MC, V. Parking C$10 (US$8/£4.50). **Amenities:** Restaurant; indoor lap pool; exercise room; Jacuzzi; sauna; steam room; concierge; limited room service; babysitting; laundry service; dry cleaning; nonsmoking rooms; executive-level rooms. *In room:* A/C, TV w/pay movies, fax, dataport, kitchenette, coffeemaker, hair dryer, iron/ironing board.

INEXPENSIVE

Hostelling International Vancouver Downtown Hostel   Located in a converted nunnery, this modern curfew-free hostel offers a convenient base of operations for exploring downtown. The beach is a few blocks south; downtown is a 10-minute walk north. Most beds are in quad dorms, with a limited number of doubles and triples available. Except for two rooms with a private bathroom, all bathroom facilities are shared. Rooms and facilities are accessible for travelers with disabilities. There are common cooking facilities, as well as a rooftop patio and game room. The hostel is extremely busy in the summertime, so book ahead. Many organized activities such as ski packages and tours can be booked at the hostel. The hostel also provides a free shuttle service to the bus/train station and Jericho Beach.

1114 Burnaby St. (at Thurlow St.), Vancouver, B.C. V6E 1P1. (C) **888/203-4302** or 604/684-4565. Fax 604/684-4540. www.hihostels.ca. 68 units, 44 4-person shared dorm rooms, 24 double or triple private rooms. C$24–C$28 (US$20–US$24/£11–£13) dorm IYHA members; C$58–C$67 (US$49–US$57/£26–£30) double YHA members. Nonmembers additional C$4 (US$3.50/£1.80) per dorm bed; C$8 (US$7/£3.60) per person for private room. Rates include full breakfast. Annual adult membership C$35 (US$30/£16). MC, V. Limited free parking. **Amenities:** Bike rental; game room; activities desk; coin laundry; Wi-Fi. *In room:* No phone.

Howard Johnson Hotel *(Value)*   As yet another example of south Granville's ongoing gentrification, this formerly down-at-the-heels hotel was bought, gutted, renovated, and reopened with an eye to the budget-conscious traveler. The rooms are simply and adequately furnished; the suites have kitchenettes and sofa beds. To get any kind of view, request a unit facing Granville. The rooms are moderately larger and more comfortable than at the Ramada across the street. Keep in mind, however, that while quite safe, this is still a fringy downtown neighborhood where you'll see panhandlers and street kids.

1176 Granville St., Vancouver, B.C. V6Z 1L8. (C) **888/654-6336** or 604/688-8701. Fax 604/688-8335. www.hojo vancouver.com. 110 units. June–Sept C$149–C$179 (US$119–US$143/£67–£81) double, C$189–C$219 (US$151–US$175/£85–£99) suite; Oct–May C$79–C$159 (US$63–US$127/£36–£72) double, C$129–C$179 (US$103–US$143/£58–£81) suite. Children under 16 stay free in parent's room. In low season, rates include full breakfast. AE, DC, MC, V. Parking C$14 (US$11/£6.30). **Amenities:** Restaurant; bar; access to nearby health club; concierge; tour desk; laundry service; same-day dry cleaning; nonsmoking rooms. *In room:* A/C, TV w/pay movies, dataport, coffeemaker, hair dryer, iron/ironing board, safe.

The Kingston Hotel *(Value)*   An affordable downtown hotel is a rarity for Vancouver; but if you can do without the frills, The Kingston offers a clean, safe, inexpensive place to sleep and a complimentary continental breakfast to start your day. You won't find a better deal anywhere, and the premises have far more character than you'll find in a cookie-cutter motel. The Kingston is a Vancouver version of the kind of small budget B&B hotels found all over Europe. Just 9 of the 55 rooms have private bathrooms and TVs. The rest have hand basins and the use of shared showers and toilets on each floor.

In 2004, the hotel added a new lobby, breakfast room, pub-restaurant, and garden patio. The premises are well kept and the location is central so you can walk everywhere. The staff is friendly and helpful, and if you're just looking for a place to sleep and stow your bags, you'll be glad you found this place.

757 Richards St., Vancouver, B.C. V6B 3A6. © **888/713-3304** or 604/684-9024. Fax 604/684-9917. www.kingstonhotel vancouver.com. 55 units, 9 with private bathroom. C$65–C$75 (US$55–US$64/£24–£34) double with shared bathroom; C$85–C$145 (US$72–US$123/£38–£65) double with private bathroom. Additional person C$10 (US$8/£4.50). Rates include continental breakfast. AE, MC, V. Parking C$20 (US$17/£9) across the street. **Amenities:** Restaurant; bar; sauna; coin laundry; nonsmoking rooms. *In room:* TV (in units w/private bathrooms), no phone.

Ramada Inn and Suites   The Ramada, like the Howard Johnson across the street (reviewed above), was recently converted from a rooming house into a tourist hotel. The location is convenient for exploring downtown and Yaletown, as well as Granville Island or Kitsilano, but South Granville, though safe, is not a scenic or shopping area, so if urban grit is not your thing, don't book here. The motel-like rooms have dark-wood furniture and small desks. For any kind of view, ask for a room facing Granville; otherwise, you may be looking out at a wall. Suites feature a sofa bed, kitchenette, and small dining area, making them useful for families. Guests have full access to a nearby sports club. *Note:* Booking directly through the website below and using promotion code LENT will net you an additional 10% to 15% off the best rate of the day.

1221 Granville St., Vancouver, B.C. V6Z 1M6. © **888/835-0078** or 604/685-1111. Fax 604/685-0707. www.ramada vancouver.com. 116 units. C$89–C$259 (US$77–US$220/£40–£117) double. Children under 17 stay free in parent's room. AE, DC, DISC, MC, V. Valet parking C$15 (US$13/£7). **Amenities:** Restaurant; bar/lounge; access to nearby sports club; laundry service; nonsmoking rooms; free Wi-Fi. *In room:* A/C, TV w/pay movies, dataport, kitchenette (in suites), coffeemaker, hair dryer, iron/ironing board.

YWCA Hotel/Residence ✪ *Value*   This attractive 12-story residence next door to the Georgian Court Hotel is an excellent choice for travelers on limited budgets. Bedrooms are simply furnished; some have TVs. Quite a few reasonably priced restaurants and a number of grocery stores are nearby. Three communal kitchens are available for guests' use, and all rooms have minifridges. The Y has three TV lounges and free access to the best gym in town, the nearby coed YWCA Fitness Centre.

733 Beatty St., Vancouver, B.C. V6B 2M4. © **800/663-1424** or 604/895-5830. Fax 604/681-2550. www.ywcahotel.com. 155 units, 53 with private bathroom. C$59–C$77 (US$50–US$65/£27–£35) double with shared bathroom; C$76–C$137 (US$65–US$116/£34–£62) double with private bathroom. Weeklong discounts available. AE, MC, V. Parking C$10 (US$8/£4.50). **Amenities:** Access to YWCA facility; coin laundry; nonsmoking rooms. *In room:* A/C, TV, dataport, fridge, hair dryer.

3 The West End

A 10-minute walk from downtown, the West End's hotels are nestled amid the tree-lined, garden-filled residential streets bordering Stanley Park. Have no fear: You will not be out of the loop if you stay in the West End, though the area's relaxed, beachy ambience is very different from downtown. Within minutes you can be on Robson or Denman Street (both of them chockablock with shops and restaurants), at beautiful English Bay or Second Beach, or in Stanley Park. Though the area has fewer hotels than downtown, the choices are more diverse—and so are the people who live here.

EXPENSIVE
The Listel Hotel ✪✪ *Finds*   What makes The Listel unique is its artwork. Hallways and suites on the top two Gallery floors are decorated with original pieces from the

Buschlen Mowatt Gallery (Vancouver's preeminent international gallery) or, on the Museum floor, with First Nations artifacts from the UBC anthropology museum. The interior of this boutique hotel (much favored by business travelers) is luxurious without being flashy. All the rooms and bathrooms were refurbished in 2007. Rooms feature top-quality bedding and handsome furnishings. The roomy upper-floor suites facing Robson Street, with glimpses of the harbor and the mountains beyond, are the best bets. Each is individually decorated with handsome, handpicked pieces of furniture, and some have cozy window banquettes; you don't find this kind of personalized charm in many hotels. Some bathrooms are larger than others, with separate soaker tub and shower. Rooms at the back are quieter but face the alley and nearby apartment buildings. In the evenings, you can hear live jazz at O'Doul's, the hotel's restaurant and bar; during the Vancouver International Jazz Festival in late June, it's the scene of late-night jam sessions with world-renowned musicians. If you don't like jazz, go instead for the Eggs Benedict in the morning. The Listel also enjoys a killer location, right at the western end of the Robson Street shopping and restaurant strip. You can walk downtown or to Stanley Park in 10 minutes.

1300 Robson St., Vancouver, B.C. V6E 1C5. © **800/663-5491** or 604/684-8461. Fax 604/684-7092. www.thelistel hotel.com. 129 units. May–Sept C$260–C$320 (US$221–US$272/£117–£144) standard to gallery room double, C$520 (US$442/£234) suite; Oct–Apr C$180–C$240 (US$187–US$204/£81–£108) standard to gallery room double, C$340 (US$285/£153) suite. AE, DC, DISC, MC, V. Parking C$26 (US$22/£12). **Amenities:** Restaurant; bar; exercise room; whirlpool; concierge; limited room service; same-day laundry service and dry cleaning; executive-level rooms; free Internet access in lobby. *In room:* A/C, TV w/pay movies, high-speed Internet, Wi-Fi, iPod docking station, minibar, coffeemaker, hair dryer, iron/ironing board.

Pacific Palisades Hotel ✦✦✦ *(Kids) (Finds)* It's really hard not to like this place, and once you walk into the Pacific Palisades lobby, you know right away that this is not just another standard-issue hotel. The designer's theme throughout this Kimpton Group property is "South Park (Florida, not the TV series) meets Stanley Park." Sherbet yellows and apple greens, pastel-colored fabrics, bright splashes of color, and whimsical touches make the hotel bright and welcoming to the young and the young at heart (the ubiquitous rock music playing in the lobby can be upbeat or annoying, depending on your mood and musical tastes). Guest rooms, spread out over two towers dating from 1969, are spacious, airy, and equipped with kitchenettes (with minibar items priced at corner-store prices). The one-bedroom suites include large living/dining rooms and balconies. Other perks include the complimentary afternoon wine tasting in the attached art gallery, the complimentary yoga program (free mat, strap, block, and instruction video), the kid-friendly atmosphere (you can buy yo-yos in the minibar), the large indoor pool and fitness rooms, and the fact that pets stay free (a rarity in Vancouver, where there's usually a cleaning charge). Plus, you're right on trendsetting Robson Street, minutes from beaches, shopping, cafes, and restaurants. **Zin** (p. 98) is a cool spot for a drink and dinner; the hotel staff are warm, friendly, and helpful. And the hotel is "earth-conscious" and environmentally friendly as well.

1277 Robson St., Vancouver, B.C. V6E 1C4. © **800/663-1815** or 604/688-0461. Fax 604/688-4374. www.pacificpalisades hotel.com. 233 units. C$150–C$425 (US$127–US$361/£67–£191) double. AE, DC, DISC, MC, V. Valet parking C$26 (US$22/£12). **Amenities:** Restaurant; bar; indoor lap pool; health club; spa services; Jacuzzi; sauna; concierge; business center; limited room service; babysitting; coin laundry and laundry service; same-day dry cleaning; nonsmoking rooms; basketball court; yoga program. *In room:* A/C, TV, high-speed Internet, kitchenette, minibar, fridge, coffeemaker, hair dryer, iron/ironing board.

Vancouver Marriott Pinnacle Hotel   The high-rise Pinnacle gleams and glows between the West End and Coal Harbour, close to Stanley Park, the waterfront, and the cruise-ship terminal. The rooms are designed to maximize the light and the views, though the views are often partially obstructed by surrounding high-rises (you can pay to upgrade to a better view). The rooms in general are fine, fitted up with all the things business travelers expect, but the decor is remarkably bland for a new hotel. Bathrooms are fairly large and well designed with a tub and separate shower. If you can, score one of the -19 rooms (2019, 2119, 2219, and so forth); aside from being the largest rooms, these oval-shaped units also max out on windows and views.

1128 W. Hastings St., Vancouver, B.C. V6E 4R5. ℭ 800/207-4150 or 604/684-1128. Fax 604/298-1128. www. vancouvermarriottpinnacle.com. 434 units. Off season C$199 (US$169/£90) double; peak season C$289 (US$246/ £130) double. Children 18 and under stay free in parent's room. AE, DC, MC, V. Self-parking C$23 (US$20/£10); valet parking C$27 (US$22/£12). SkyTrain to Burrard Station. **Amenities:** Restaurant; bar; indoor lap pool; health club; Jacuzzi; sauna; concierge; business center; 24-hr. room service; laundry service; same-day dry cleaning; nonsmoking rooms; executive-level rooms. *In room:* A/C, TV w/pay movies, dataport, minibar, coffeemaker, hair dryer, iron/ironing board, safe.

Westin Bayshore Resort & Marina ⭒⭒⭒ *Kids*   This is Vancouver's only resort hotel with its own marina (should you arrive by private boat), and the views from all but a handful of its rooms are stunning. Perched on the water's edge overlooking Coal Harbour marina and Stanley Park on one side, and Burrard Inlet and the city on the other, the Bayshore is an easy stroll from Canada Place Pier, Robson Street, and downtown. Rooms in the original 1961 building have been refurbished with classic-looking decor and floor-to-ceiling windows that open wide. In the newer tower, the rooms are a bit larger and have narrow balconies. The bathrooms in both buildings are nicely finished but fairly small. The heated outdoor pool is reputedly the largest in North America; there's even a second indoor pool plus a full gym. Children receive their own welcome package. Like other Westins, the Bayshore is now completely nonsmoking and features the aptly named "Heavenly" beds, with down blankets, three layers of heavy cotton sheets, a down duvet, and dream-worthy pillows.

1601 Bayshore Dr., Vancouver, B.C. V6G 2V4. ℭ 800/937-8461 or 604/682-3377. Fax 604/687-3102. www.westin bayshore.com. 510 units. C$330–C$390 (US$280–US$331/£149–£176) double; C$550–C$695 (US$440–US$556/ £248–£313) suite. Children under 18 stay free in parent's room. AE, DC, MC, V. Self-parking C$20 (US$17/£9); valet parking C$23 (US$20/£10). **Amenities:** 2 restaurants; bar; 2 pools (both indoor and outdoor); health club; full-service spa; Jacuzzi; sauna; concierge; business center; shopping arcade; 24-hr. room service; babysitting; laundry service; same-day dry cleaning; nonsmoking hotel. *In room:* A/C, TV w/pay movies, high-speed Internet, minibar, coffeemaker, hair dryer, iron/ironing board, safe.

MODERATE

Barclay House Bed & Breakfast ⭒ *Finds*   The Barclay House is located on one of the West End's quiet maple-lined streets a block from historic Barclay Square. Built in 1904 by a local developer, this beautiful house can be a destination on its own. All rooms are beautifully furnished in Victorian style; a number of the pieces are family heirlooms. Modern conveniences such as CD players, TV/VCRs, and luxurious bathrooms blend in perfectly. The penthouse offers skylights, a fireplace, and a claw-foot tub; the south room contains a queen-size brass bed and an elegant sitting room. The parlors and dining rooms are perfect for lounging on a rainy afternoon or sipping a glass of complimentary sherry before dinner in the trendy West End. On a summer day, the front porch, with its wooden Adirondack chairs, is a cozy place to read.

1351 Barclay St., Vancouver, B.C. V6E 1H6. ℭ 800/971-1351 or 604/605-1351. Fax 604/605-1382. www.barclay house.com. 5 units. C$175–C$245 (US$149–US$208/£79–£110) double. MC, V. Free parking. **Amenities:** Access to nearby fitness center; concierge; nonsmoking rooms. *In room:* TV/VCR w/pay movies, Wi-Fi, CD player, video library, fridge, hair dryer, iron/ironing board.

Blue Horizon *(Value*   This 31-story high-rise built in the 1960s has a great location on Robson Street, just a block from the trendier Pacific Palisades and the tonier Listel Vancouver (see above for both). It's cheaper than those places and has views that are just as good if not better, but it lacks their charm and feels a bit like a high-rise motel. The rooms are fairly spacious, though, and every room is on a corner with wraparound windows, which maximizes the light and the view; every room has a small balcony, too. In 2000, the hotel renovated all its guest rooms, giving them a clean, contemporary look. Bathrooms are on the small side and have tubs with showers. Superior rooms and penthouse suites on the 15th to 30th floors offer breathtaking views looking north toward the mountains or west toward English Bay. If you're ecology minded, book a room on the "Green Floor," which features energy-efficient lighting, low-flow showerheads, and recycling bins. The entire hotel is nonsmoking.

1225 Robson St., Vancouver, B.C. V6E 1C3. ℂ **800/663-1333** or 604/688-1411. Fax 604/688-4461. www.bluehorizon hotel.com. 214 units. C$109–C$199 (US$93–US$169/£49–£90) double; C$119–C$219 (US$101–US$186/£54–£99) superior double; C$199–C$329 (US$169–US$280/£90–£148) penthouse suite. Children under 16 stay free in parent's room. AE, DC, MC, V. Self-parking C$14 (US$12/£6). **Amenities:** Restaurant; indoor pool; exercise room; Jacuzzi; sauna; concierge; same-day dry cleaning; nonsmoking hotel. *In room:* A/C, TV w/pay movies, free high-speed Internet, minibar, fridge, coffeemaker, hair dryer, iron/ironing board, safe.

Coast Plaza Hotel & Suites ⭐ *(Finds*   Built originally as an apartment building, this 35-story hotel atop Denman Place Mall attracts a wide variety of guests, from business travelers and tour groups to film and TV actors. They come for the large rooms, the affordable one- and two-bedroom suites, and the fabulous views of English Bay. The two-bedroom corner suites are bigger than most West End apartments, and afford spectacular panoramas. The spacious one-bedroom suites and standard rooms feature floor-to-ceiling windows and walk-out balconies; about half the units have full kitchens. Furnishings are plain and comfortable, if a little dated. While the hotel has a good-size heated pool, it's in the not-particularly-appealing basement.

1763 Comox St., Vancouver, B.C. V6G 1P6. ℂ **800/663-1144** or 604/688-7711. Fax 604/688-5934. www.coasthotels. com. 269 units. C$179–C$219 (US$143–US$175/£81–£99) double; C$219–C$299 (US$175–US$239/£99–£135) suite. AE, DC, DISC, MC, V. Valet parking C$8 (US$6/£4). **Amenities:** Restaurant; bar; indoor pool; complimentary access to Denman Fitness Centre in mall below; Jacuzzi; sauna; concierge; free downtown shuttle service; business center; shopping arcade; 24-hr. room service; babysitting; coin laundry; same-day dry cleaning; nonsmoking rooms. *In room:* A/C, TV, high-speed Internet, minibar, fridge, coffeemaker, hair dryer, iron/ironing board.

Sunset Inn & Suites ⭐ *(Value* *(Kids*   Just a couple of blocks from English Bay on the edge of the residential West End, the Sunset Inn offers roomy accommodations for a reasonable price. Units are either studios or one-bedroom apartments, and come with fully equipped kitchens and dining areas. Like many other hotels in this part of town, the Sunset Inn started life as an apartment building, meaning the rooms are larger than at your average hotel, and all have balconies. The view gets better on the higher floors, but the price remains the same, so book early and request an upper floor. For those traveling with children, the one-bedroom suites have a separate bedroom and a pullout couch in the living room. Most of the rooms have recently been redone to look upscale, but the finishes are faux and the furniture is oddly unyielding. Still, the beds are comfy, the staff is helpful and friendly, and the location is great for this price.

1111 Burnaby St., Vancouver, B.C. V6E 1P4. ℂ **800/786-1997** or 604/688-2474. Fax 604/669-3340. www.sunsetinn.com. 50 units. C$99–C$229 (US$84–US$200/£45–£103) studio; C$109–C$299 (US$97–US$254/£49–£135) 1-bedroom suite.

Additional person C$10 (US$8/£4.50). Children under 12 stay free in parent's room. Weekly rates available. AE, DC, MC, V. Free parking. **Amenities:** Small exercise room; coin laundry; nonsmoking rooms. *In room:* TV, free Wi-Fi, kitchen, coffeemaker, iron/ironing board.

West End Guest House ⚡ *(Finds* A heritage home built in 1906, the West End Guest House is a handsome example of what the neighborhood looked like before concrete towers and condos replaced the original Edwardian homes in the early 1950s. Decorated with early-20th-century antiques and a serious collection of vintage photographs of Vancouver taken by the original owners, this is a calm respite from the hustle and bustle of the West End. The seven guest rooms feature feather mattresses, down duvets, and your very own resident stuffed animal. The Grand Queen Suite, an attic-level bedroom with a brass bed, fireplace, sitting area, claw-foot bathtub, and skylights is the best and most spacious room; no. 7 is quite small. Owner Evan Penner pampers his guests with a scrumptious breakfast and serves iced tea and sherry in the afternoon (on the back second-floor balcony in the summer). Throughout the day, guests have access to a pantry stocked with home-baked munchies.

1362 Haro St., Vancouver, B.C. V6E 1G2. ℂ **888/546-3327** or 604/681-2889. Fax 604/688-8812. www.westend guesthouse.com. 9 units. C$89–C$295 (US$76–US$251/£40–£133) double. Rates include full breakfast. AE, DISC, MC, V. Free off-street parking. **Amenities:** Complimentary bikes; business center; laundry service. *In room:* TV/DVD, Wi-Fi, hair dryer.

INEXPENSIVE

Buchan Hotel *(Value* Built in 1926, this three-story building is tucked away on a quiet tree-lined residential street in the West End, less than 2 blocks from Stanley Park and Denman Street, and 15 minutes by foot from the business district. Like The Kingston (reviewed earlier in this chapter) downtown, this is a small European-style budget hotel that doesn't bother with frills or charming decor; unlike the Kingston, it isn't a B&B, so you won't get breakfast. The standard rooms are quite plain; be prepared for cramped quarters and tiny bathrooms, half of which are shared. The best rooms are the executive rooms: four nicely furnished front-corner rooms with private bathrooms. The hotel also has in-house bike and ski storage, and a reading lounge.

1906 Haro St., Vancouver, B.C. V6G 1H7. ℂ **800/668-6654** or 604/685-5354. Fax 604/685-5367. www.buchanhotel. com. 60 units, 30 with private bathroom. C$48–C$78 (US$41–US$66/£22–£35) double with shared bathroom; C$73–C$98 (US$62–US$83/£33–£49) double with private bathroom; C$110–C$135 (US$93–US$115/£49–£61) executive room. Children 12 and under stay free in parent's room. Weekly rates available. AE, DC, MC, V. Limited street parking available. **Amenities:** Lounge; coin laundry. *In room:* TV, hair dryer and iron available on request, no phone.

Sylvia Hotel *(Overrated* If the Sylvia were being built today, all its rooms facing onto English Bay would have balconies and probably be outfitted with luxurious appointments. But balconies were rarities back in 1912, when this venerable and much-used hotel appeared in the relatively unpopulated West End, so all you can do is stare out the windows at what is one of the loveliest views in town. Lots of folks love the Sylvia, mostly for its fabulous location, and many are eager to recommend it, but pretty as the old girl is from the outside, inside she's a bit of a wreck: Tatty carpeting lines the corridors, rooms sometimes smell musty, and in some the mismatched furniture hasn't been updated in decades. The public spaces are the ugliest you're likely to encounter in any Vancouver hotel, lost in a kind of garish 1950s lounge style that is so awful it isn't even camp. Still, you're not going to find waterfront accommodations anywhere else at Sylvia's prices. If you do stay, the best rooms are located on the higher floors facing English Bay. The suites have fully equipped kitchens and are large enough for families. The newer low-rise annex rooms are no better, and offer less atmosphere.

1154 Gilford St., Vancouver, B.C. V6G 2P6. ℂ **604/681-9321.** Fax 604/682-3551. www.sylviahotel.com. 118 units. May–Sept C$110–C$175 (US$93–US$149/£49–£79) double; Oct–Apr C$75–C$144 (US$64–US$122/£34–£65) double. Children under 18 stay free in parent's room. AE, DC, MC, V. Parking C$7 (US$6/£3). **Amenities:** Restaurant; bar; concierge; limited room service; dry cleaning; nonsmoking rooms. *In room:* TV, dataport, hair dryer.

4 The West Side

Right across False Creek from downtown and the West End is Vancouver's West Side, where you'll find cozy B&Bs and hotels. It's the perfect location if your agenda includes Granville Island; exploration of the laid-back Kitsilano neighborhood and Kits Beach; the Museum of Anthropology and famed gardens on the University of British Columbia campus; the sunken garden at Queen Elizabeth Park; or if you require close proximity to the airport without staying in an "airport hotel."

EXPENSIVE

Granville Island Hotel 𝒇 *Finds*   One of Vancouver's best-kept secrets, this hotel is tucked away on the edge of Granville Island in a unique waterfront setting, a short stroll from theaters, galleries, and the fabulous Granville Island public market. Rooms in the original wing are definitely fancier, so book these if you can, but the new wing is fine, too. Rooms are fairly spacious with traditional, unsurprising decor and large bathrooms with soaker tubs; some units have balconies and great views over False Creek. If you don't have a car, the only potential drawback to a stay here is the location. During the daytime when the False Creek ferries are running, it's a quick ferry ride to Yaletown or the West End. After 10pm, however, you're looking at a C$15-to-C$20 (US$13–US$17/£7–£9) cab ride or an hour walk. The Island after dark is reasonably happening, and the hotel's waterside restaurant and brewpub are good-weather hangout spots with outdoor seating.

1253 Johnston St., Vancouver, B.C. V6H 3R9. ℂ **800/663-1840** or 604/683-7373. Fax 604/683-3061. www.granville islandhotel.com. 85 units. Oct–Apr C$160 (US$136/£72) double, C$350 (US$297/£157) penthouse; May–Sept C$240 (US$204/£108) double, C$450 (US$382/£202) penthouse. AE, DC, DISC, MC, V. Parking C$8 (US$7/£3.60). **Amenities:** Restaurant; brewpub; access to nearby tennis courts; small fitness room w/Jacuzzi and sauna; concierge; tour desk; car-rental desk; business center; limited room service; massage; babysitting; laundry service; same-day dry cleaning; nonsmoking rooms. *In room:* A/C, TV w/pay movies, high-speed Internet, minibar, coffeemaker, hair dryer, iron/ironing board.

MODERATE

Camelot Inn 𝒇 *Finds*   This handsome 1906 house is one of the nicest and most romantic B&Bs in Vancouver. Surrounded by old trees, the Edwardian-era house is full of gorgeous period details (lots of wood) and decorated in an age-appropriate style. Plus, it's just 2 blocks from the nicest stretch of 4th Avenue in Kitsilano, and a 10-minute walk from Kits Beach. Three guest rooms are located on the second floor, and two lovely studios with separate entrances are tucked away in the back. The Camelot Room features a huge sleigh bed and large Jacuzzi tub beneath a leaded bay window. The somewhat smaller Eden Room sports a queen-size bed, antiques, and a bathroom with large soaker tub. The Camay Room, the smallest, is nice and bright and features a queen-size bed but only a large shower. All of the units are fitted out with kitchenettes. The Latvian-born innkeepers serve a very good breakfast (no breakfast is served in the winter, however). Unusual attention to detail is a hallmark of this find.

2212 Larch St., Vancouver, B.C. V6K 3P7. ℂ **604/739-6941.** www.camelotinnvancouver.com. 5 units. May–Sept C$159–C$189 (US$135–US$161/£72–£85) double; Oct–Apr C$120–C$140 (US$102–US$119/£54–£63) double. Summer rates include full breakfast. MC, V. Street parking. *In room:* TV, kitchenette, no phone.

Chocolate Lily *★* *(Finds)* *(Kids)*   If you're looking for a self-catering place, this attractive, Craftsman-style house, just minutes from all the splash of Kits Beach and the dash of Kits shopping, is a real find. You don't need a car; public transportation can get you downtown in minutes. The two self-contained suites have private entrances and patios and are both small but carefully designed (a sofa in each makes into an extra bed) and furnished in a comfortable Northwest style. Both units have kitchenettes; the rear unit has only a shower. Breakfast is not served, but you're given a basket of fruit and baked goods upon arrival. In high season a 3-day minimum stay is required; special rates apply for longer stays.

1353 Maple St., Vancouver, B.C. V6M 1G6. *(C)* 866/903-9363 or 604/731-9363. www.chocolatelily.com. 2 self-catered suites. C$95–C$165 (US$81–US$140/£43–£74). MC, V. Free parking. *In room:* TV, DVD player (in 1 unit), high-speed Internet, kitchenette w/microwave, coffeemaker, toaster-oven.

Kenya Court Ocean Front Guest House *(Finds)*   With no distinguishing sign outside, from the street this unusual B&B simply looks like the three-story 1926 apartment house that it is. But press button no. 5, and your hosts will welcome you into their unusual and surprisingly pleasant establishment, where you'll find five furnished apartments rented on a B&B basis. Not only is the house in a fantastic location—directly across the street from Kits Beach, one of the most popular spots in Vancouver—but every unit has a view of English Bay, downtown Vancouver, and the Coast Mountains. The ground floor has a newly refurbished and very nice little studio with a Murphy bed; the other units are much larger, with a living room, bathroom, separate bedroom (or two), and full kitchen. In the mornings, you climb up a spiral staircase for breakfast, which is served in a glass-walled solarium on the roof. One thing to keep in mind: In the summer, Kits Beach and Cornwall Avenue running past it are very busy; this can be either a plus or a minus, depending on your point of view.

2230 Cornwall Ave., Vancouver, B.C. V6K 1B5. *(C)* 604/738-7085. h&dwilliams@telus.net. 5 units. C$150–C$175 (US$127–US$149/£68–£79) double. No credit cards. Free garage or street parking. **Amenities:** Outdoor pool; tennis court and jogging trails nearby; beach across the street. *In room:* TV, kitchenette, fridge, coffeemaker, hair dryer, iron/ironing board.

INEXPENSIVE

Hostelling International Vancouver Jericho Beach Hostel   Located in a former military barracks, this hostel (open May–Sept only) is surrounded by an expansive lawn adjacent to Jericho Beach. Individuals, families with children over age 5, and groups are welcome. The 10 private rooms can accommodate up to six people. These particular accommodations go fast, so if you want one, call far in advance. The dormitory-style arrangements are well maintained and supervised. Linens are provided. Basic, inexpensive food is served in the cafe, or you can cook for yourself in the shared kitchen. The hostel's program director operates tours and activities.

1515 Discovery St., Vancouver, B.C. V6R 4K5. *(C)* 888/203-4303 or 604/224-3208. Fax 604/224-4852. www.hihostels.ca. 286 beds in 14 dorms; 10 private family units. No private bathrooms. C$20–C$22 (US$17–US$19/£9–£10) dorm IYHA members, C$24–C$26 (US$20–US$22/£11–£12) dorm nonmembers; C$60 (US$51/£27) private room members, C$67 (US$57/£30) private room nonmembers. MC, V. Parking C$5 (US$4.25/£2.25). Bus: 4. Children under 5 not allowed. **Amenities:** Cafe; bike rental; activities desk; coin laundry; nonsmoking rooms. *In Room:* No phone.

The University of British Columbia Conference Centre *★* *(Value)*   The University of British Columbia Conference Centre is in a pretty, forested setting on the tip of Point Grey, convenient to Kitsilano and the university itself. If you don't have a car, it's a half-hour bus ride from downtown. Although the on-campus accommodations are actually student dorms most of the year, rooms are usually available. The rooms are nice, but don't expect luxury. The 17-story Walter Gage Residence offers comfortable accommodations, many on the upper floors with sweeping views of the city and ocean. One-bedroom suites come equipped with private bathrooms, kitchenettes, TVs, and phones. Each studio has a twin bed; each one-bedroom features a queen-size bed; the six-bedroom Tower—a particularly good deal for families—features one double bed and five twin beds. The West Coast Suites, renovated in 2007, are the most appealing, and have a very reasonable price.

5961 Student Union Blvd., Vancouver, B.C. V6T 2C9. ⓒ 604/822-1000. Fax 604/822-1001. www.ubcconferences.com. About 1,900 units. Gage Towers units available May 10–Aug 26; Pacific Spirit Hostel units available May 15–Aug 19; West Coast Suite units (adjacent to the Gage Residence) available year-round. Gage Towers: C$39 (US$33/£18) single with shared bathroom; C$89 (US$67/£40) studio, C$119 (US$101/£54) 1-bedroom suite. Pacific Spirit Hostel: C$28 (US$24/£13) single; C$56 (US$48/£25) double; C$99 (US$84/£45) studio suite with private bathroom. West Coast Suites: C$159 (US$135/£72) suite. AE, MC, V. Parking C$5 (US$4/£2.25). Bus: 4, 17, or 99. **Amenities** (nearby on campus): Restaurant; cafeteria; pub; access to campus Olympic-size swimming pool; tennis courts; weight room; sauna for C$5 (US$3.75/£2.25) per person; video arcade; laundry. A public golf course is nearby. *In room:* A/C, TV, hair dryer.

5 The North Shore (North Vancouver & West Vancouver)

The North Shore cities of North and West Vancouver are pleasant, lush, and much less hurried than Vancouver. Staying here also offers easy access to the North Shore mountains, including hiking trails, the Capilano Suspension Bridge, and the ski slopes on Mount Seymour, Grouse Mountain, and Cypress Bowl. The disadvantage is that if you want to take your car into Vancouver, there are only two bridges, and during rush hour they're painfully slow. The passenger-only SeaBus, however, is quick and scenic.

MODERATE

Lonsdale Quay Hotel Directly across the Burrard Inlet from the Canada Place Pier, this hotel sits at the water's edge above the Lonsdale Quay Market at the SeaBus terminal. An escalator rises from the midst of the market's food, crafts, and souvenir stalls to the hotel's front desk on the third floor. Some rooms have unique harbor and city views, but others have wedge-shaped concrete balconies and feel closed in. This is a good location if you're exploring North Vancouver: The hotel is only 15 minutes by bus or car from Grouse Mountain Ski Resort and Capilano Regional Park.

123 Carrie Cates Court, North Vancouver, B.C. V7M 3K7. ⓒ 800/836-6111 or 604/986-6111. Fax 604/986-8782. www.lonsdalequayhotel.com. 70 units. C$90–C$169 (US$76–US$144/£40–£77) double. Senior discount available. AE, DC, DISC, MC, V. Parking C$7 (US$6/£3); free on weekends and holidays. SeaBus: Lonsdale Quay. **Amenities:** 2 restaurants; small exercise room; spa; bike rental; concierge; limited room service; babysitting; laundry service; same-day dry cleaning. *In room:* A/C, TV, dataport, minibar, coffeemaker, hair dryer, iron/ironing board.

6

Where to Dine in Vancouver

Foodies, take note: Vancouver is one of North America's top dining cities, right up there with New York, San Francisco, London, and any other food capital you can think of. Estimates are that the city has anywhere from *2,000 to 5,000* restaurants. What's undeniably true is that Vancouverites dine out more than residents of any other Canadian city. Outstanding meals are available in all price ranges and in many different cuisines, with a preponderance of informal Chinese, Japanese, Vietnamese, and Thai restaurants. Sushi lovers will be in heaven here as superlative sushi is available all over town for a fraction of what you'd pay elsewhere. For Pacific Northwest cuisine, Vancouver's top restaurants can compete with the very best when it comes to preparation, taste, and presentation.

For discerning travelers who love to dine out and dine well, Vancouver is a delightful discovery. Most of the top restaurants offer tasting menus, and if you're into food, I recommend that you try them. In particular, the tasting menus at West, C, Raincity Grill, and Cin Cin will give you a brilliant sampling of the best, freshest, and most creative cooking in Vancouver. Keep in mind, too, that Vancouver is perhaps the West Coast's preeminent city for seafood. You can dine on fresh oysters and superbly prepared local fish for less than you'd pay in any other city.

"Buy local, eat seasonal" is the mantra of all the best restaurateurs in Vancouver, and they take justifiable pride in the bounty of local produce, game, and seafood available to them. More restaurants in Vancouver are shifting to seasonal, even monthly, menus, giving their chefs greater freedom.

Be sure to try a British Columbian wine; the sommeliers at the top restaurants will be able to recommend one or do wine pairings with your meal. B.C. wines are now winning international acclaim and rival vintages from California, Australia, France, and Germany. The big wine-producing areas are in the Okanagan Valley (in southern B.C.'s dry interior) and on southern Vancouver Island. (If you have a few extra days, both areas are worth a visit.)

Restaurant meals in British Columbia carry no provincial tax, but venues add the **6% goods and services tax (GST).** Restaurant hours vary. Lunch is typically served from noon to 1 or 2pm; Vancouverites begin dining around 6:30pm, later in summer. Reservations are recommended at most restaurants and are essential at the city's top tables.

1 Best Vancouver Dining Bets

For a quick overview of the city's top restaurants, see "The Most Unforgettable Dining Experiences: Vancouver," in chapter 1, p. 13.

- **Best Spot for a Romantic Dinner: Raincity Grill,** 1193 Denman St. (© 604/ 685-7337), with its low ceiling, crisp linens, windows overlooking English Bay, and fabulous food, is a place that makes you want to linger. See p. 97.
- **Best Pacific Northwest Cuisine: West,** 2881 Granville St. (© 604/738-8938), is the best—for an all-round, upscale, Pacific Northwest dining experience. But don't just take my word for it. This storied West Side eatery has won *Vancouver* magazine's "Best Restaurant" award for 3 years running. See p. 100.
- **Best Spot for a Celebration: Cin Cin,** 1154 Robson St. (© 604/688-7338), serves superlative Italian cuisine in one of the city's loveliest and most comfortable dining rooms; the covered, heated patio is wonderful, too. See p. 95.
- **Best View:** For a combination of top-notch food and a killer view of mountains, Burrard Inlet, and Stanley Park, try **Lift,** 333 Menchions Mews (© 604/689-5438). See p. 96.
- **Best for Kids: Romano's Macaroni Grill,** 1523 Davie St. (© 604/689-4334), has a popular kids' menu, highchairs, and a great old mansion to explore—kids love it. See p. 98.
- **Best Chinese Cuisine:** The best Vancouver Chinese remains **Sun Sui Wah,** 3888 Main St. (© 604/872-8822). It's definitely worth the trip. See p. 105.
- **Best French Cuisine:** For several years, **Lumière,** 2551 W. Broadway (© 604/ 739-8185), has won the top spot in the yearly Vancouver restaurant awards. See p. 100.
- **Best Tapas: Bin 941 Tapas Parlour,** 941 Davie St. (© 604/683-1246), was serving tapas before the trend hit, and this tiny hangout still does it best. See p. 92.
- **Best Newcomer:** It's a tossup between **Jules,** 216 Abbott St. (© 604/669-0033), a casual French bistro, and **Salt,** Blood Alley (© 604/633-1912), a casual charcuterie. Both are in Gastown, both are inexpensive, both are worth trying. See p. 94 and 95.
- **Best Italian:** At the wonderful **Cin Cin,** 1154 Robson St. (© 604/688-7338), the menu emphasizes seasonal delights cooked in a wood-fired oven, and everything tastes divine. See p. 95.
- **Best Japanese:** If you're looking for the best sushi and sashimi in Vancouver, **Tojo's Restaurant,** 1133 W. Broadway (© 604/872-8050) is the place to go. It's expensive, but you'll be treated to the freshest fish and most exquisitely prepared seafood delicacies in B.C. See p. 100.
- **Best Late-Night Dining:** A scene-stealer with its opulent Silk Road decor and cuisine, **Sanafir,** 1026 Granville St. (© 604/678-1049), is a great place to drink and dine into the wee hours. See p. 93.
- **Best Outdoor Dining:** For unsurpassed ocean views, reserve a table under the trees at **Sequoia Grill at the Teahouse in Stanley Park,** Ferguson Point (close to Third Beach; © 604/669-3281). This patio also doubles as the **best place to watch the sunset.** See p. 97.
- **Best Oysters: Joe Fortes Seafood and Chop House,** 777 Thurlow St. (© 604/ 669-1940), has become a Vancouver institution, and if you order one of the seafood towers, you'll see why. Or try a few freshly shucked oysters before your grilled salmon or halibut, and you'll go away happy. See p. 91.
- **Best Vegetarian: Annapurna,** 1812 W. 4th Ave. (© 604/736-5959), has flavorful food, a cozy little room, and the most reasonable wines in town. Who says you have to sacrifice when you're a veggie eater? See p. 104.

2 Restaurants by Cuisine

AMERICAN
Sophie's Cosmic Café (West Side, $, p. 105)
The Tomahawk Restaurant (North Shore, $, p. 107)

BARBECUE
Memphis Blues Barbeque House 🍴 (West Side, $$, p. 101)

BELGIAN
Chambar Belgian Restaurant 🍴🍴 (Yaletown, $$$, p. 90)

CARIBBEAN
The Reef (East Side, $$, p. 105)

CASUAL
Bin 941 Tapas Parlour 🍴 (Downtown, $$, p. 92)
Café Zen (West Side, $$, p. 101)
The Locus Café (East Side, $$, p. 105)
The SandBar (Granville Island, $$, p. 102)

CHARCUTERIE
Salt 🍴 (Gastown, $, p. 95)

CHINESE/DIM SUM
Park Lock Seafood Restaurant (Chinatown, $$, p. 94)
Pink Pearl 🍴 (Chinatown, $$, p. 94)
Sha-Lin Noodle House (West Side, $, p. 104)
Sun Sui Wah 🍴🍴 (East Side, $$$, p. 105)

COFFEE/TEA
Caffè Artigiano 🍴🍴 (Downtown, West End, $, p. 107)
Epicurean Delicatessen Caffè (Kitsilano, $, p. 108)
The Fish House in Stanley Park 🍴🍴 (West End, $$$, p. 96)
Mink, A Chocolate Cafe 🍴 (Gastown, $$$, p. 108)

Moonstruck Tea House (West End, $, p. 108)
T (West Side, $, p. 108)

DESSERTS
La Casa Gelato 🍴 (East Side, $, p. 108)

FAMILY STYLE
Old Spaghetti Factory (Gastown, $, p. 95)
Romano's Macaroni Grill (West End, $$, p. 98)
Sophie's Cosmic Café (West Side, $, p. 105)
The Tomahawk Restaurant (North Shore, $, p. 107)

FRENCH
Elixir 🍴🍴 (Yaletown, $$$, p. 90)
Jules 🍴 (Gastown, $, p. 94)
Le Gavroche 🍴🍴 (West End, $$$, p. 96)
Lumière 🍴🍴🍴 (West Side, $$$$, p. 100)
Nu (Yaletown, $$$, p. 92)
The Smoking Dog 🍴 (Kitsilano, $$, p. 102)
West 🍴🍴🍴 (West Side, $$$$, p. 100)

FUSION
Fiddlehead Joe's (Yaletown, $$, p. 92)
glowbal grill & satay bar 🍴🍴 (Yaletown, $$$, p. 91)
Zin (West End, $$, p. 98)

GREEK
Stephos (West End, $, p. 99)

INDIAN
Annapurna 🍴 (West Side, $, p. 104)
Rangoli (West Side, $, p. 104)
Vij 🍴🍴🍴 (West Side, $$, p. 103)

INTERNATIONAL
Coast 🍴🍴🍴 (Yaletown, $$$, p. 90)
Sanafir 🍴🍴 (Downtown, $$, p. 93)

Key to Abbreviations: $$$$ = Very Expensive $$$ = Expensive $$ = Moderate $ = Inexpensive

ITALIAN

Amarcord ✸ (Yaletown, $$$, p. 87)

Cin Cin ✸✸✸ (West End, $$$, p. 95)

Gusto ✸ (North Shore, $$$, p. 106)

Il Giardino di Umberto Ristorante ✸✸ (Yaletown, $$$, p. 91)

Old Spaghetti Factory (Gastown, $, p. 95)

Romano's Macaroni Grill (West End, $$, p. 98)

JAPANESE

Gyoza King (West End, $, p. 99)

Hapa Izakaya ✸ (West End, $$, p. 97)

Ichiban-ya (West End, $$, p. 98)

Tanpopo (West End, $$, p. 98)

Tojo's Restaurant ✸✸✸ (West Side, $$$$, p. 100)

MALAYSIAN

Banana Leaf ✸ (West End, $, p. 99)

PACIFIC NORTHWEST

Aurora Bistro ✸✸ (West Side, $$, p. 101)

The Beach House at Dundarave Pier ✸ (North Shore, $$$, p. 106)

C ✸✸✸ (Yaletown, $$$$, see below)

Diva at the Met ✸✸ (Downtown, $$$$, p. 87)

Feenie's ✸ (West Side, $$, p. 101)

The Fish House in Stanley Park ✸✸ (West End, $$$, p. 96)

Lift ✸✸ (West End, $$$, p. 96)

Raincity Grill ✸✸✸ (West End, $$$, p. 97)

The Salmon House on the Hill ✸ (North Shore, $$$, p. 106)

Sequoia Grill at the Teahouse in Stanley Park (West End, $$$, p. 97)

West ✸✸✸ (West Side, $$$$, p. 100)

PIZZA

Incendio ✸ (Gastown, $, p. 94)

SEAFOOD

Blue Water Cafe and Raw Bar ✸✸✸ (Yaletown, $$$, p. 87)

C ✸✸✸ (Yaletown, $$$$, see below)

The Cannery ✸ (Gastown, $$$, p. 93)

Coast ✸✸✸ (Yaletown, $$$, p. 90)

The Fish House in Stanley Park ✸✸ (West End, $$$, p. 96)

Joe Fortes Seafood and Chop House ✸✸✸ (Downtown, $$$, p. 91)

The Salmon House on the Hill ✸ (North Shore, $$$, p. 106)

Sun Sui Wah ✸✸ (East Side, $$$, p. 105)

SOUTHWESTERN

The Locus Café (East Side, $$, p. 105)

TAPAS

Bin 941 Tapas Parlour ✸ (Downtown, $$, p. 92)

Zin (West End, $$, p. 98)

THAI

Simply Thai ✸ (Yaletown, $$, p. 93)

VEGETARIAN

Annapurna ✸ (West Side, $, p. 104)

The Naam Restaurant ✸ (West Side, $, p. 104)

VIETNAMESE

Phnom Penh Restaurant ✸ (Chinatown, $, p. 95)

3 Downtown & Yaletown

VERY EXPENSIVE

C ✸✸✸ SEAFOOD/PACIFIC NORTHWEST   Since opening in 1997, the popularity of this trendsetter hasn't flagged for a moment, and at the 2006 *Vancouver* magazine restaurant awards, it snagged "Best Seafood" and "Best Chef" honors. The waterside location on False Creek is sublime, opening out to a passing parade of boats on the water and people on the seawall; the dining room is a cool white space with painted steel and lots of glass. Ingredients make all the difference here: The chef and his highly knowledgeable staff can tell you not only where every product comes from, but also the name of the boat or farm. Expect exquisite surprises and imaginative preparations: For appetizers, fresh B.C. oysters with a tongue-tickling saffron anise cream and juices of jalapeño and cucumber, or watercress salad with sablefish and scallop sausage. Mains are artfully created: grilled ultrarare albacore tuna sits atop creamy couscous with charred lemon and caper condiments. Give chef Robert Clark a chance to show off, and order the nine-course sampling menu as you watch the sun set over the marina. Excellent wine pairings, too.

1600 Howe St. ✆ 604/681-1164. www.crestaurant.com. Reservations recommended. Main courses C$35–C$48 (US$30–US$41/£16–£22); sampling menu C$120 (US$102/£54). AE, DC, MC, V. Dinner daily 5:30–11pm; lunch Mon–Fri 11:30am–2:30pm (May to Labour Day). Valet parking C$7 (US$6/£3.15). Bus: 1 or 2.

Diva at the Met ✿✿ PACIFIC NORTHWEST   Diva's triple-tiered dining room with a giant wall of glass brick in the rear makes for an elegant dining experience. This is arguably the best hotel restaurant in Vancouver, yet it has a life of its own and attracts savvy diners who appreciate attentive service and dependably marvelous food. The menu draws from the best of fresh seasonal ingredients and takes a light, international approach to spices and seasonings. If you're looking for something to write home about, try the sumptuous six-course tasting menu. Depending on the season, it might include New Zealand abalone on ice, pan-seared Quebec foie gras, shark's fin and Dungeness crab soup, Nova Scotia lobster with sweet-and-sour sauce, sautéed crispy rack of lamb, and a sweet yam pancake with maple vanilla ice cream. Diva's wine list is regularly rated one of the best in town.

In the Metropolitan Hotel (p. 69), 645 Howe St. ✆ 604/602-7788. www.metropolitan.com/diva. Reservations recommended. Dinner main courses C$24–C$42 (US$20–US$36/£11–£19), lunch C$16–C$25 (US$14–US$21/£7–£11); tasting menu C$99 (US$84/£45). AE, DC, DISC, MC, V. Daily 6:30am–1am. Bus: 4 or 7.

EXPENSIVE

Amarcord ✿ NORTHERN ITALIAN   Traditional northern Italian cuisine (in this case, from Emilia-Romagna) doesn't get much respect these days, but the food at Amarcord is so good that it's worth rediscovering the joys of freshly made pasta or risotto teamed with a lovingly prepared sauce. Think gnocchi with Italian sausage, fresh tomato, and basil, or linguine with mussels, scallops, and tiger prawns. Wines hail from Tuscany and California. The atmosphere is formal without being fussy. Service is knowledgeable and very friendly.

104-1168 Hamilton St. ✆ 604/681-6500. www.amarcord.ca. Reservations recommended. Main courses C$17–C$32 (US$14–US$27/£8–£14). AE, DC, MC, V. Mon–Fri 11:30am–2:30pm; daily 5–10pm. Closed on holidays. Bus: 2.

Blue Water Cafe and Raw Bar ✿✿✿ SEAFOOD   Blue Water Cafe in Yaletown has become one of Vancouver's hottest restaurants. If you had to describe this busy, buzzy place in one word, it would be *fresh,* as in fresh, seasonal seafood; only the best from sustainable and wild fisheries makes it onto the menu. If you love sushi, the raw bar under the direction of Yoshihio Tabo offers up some of the city's best sushi and sashimi. Frank Pabst, the restaurant's executive chef, creates his dishes in another large open kitchen. For starters, try a medley of Kushi oysters with various toppings, a sushi platter, or smoked sockeye salmon terrine with salmon caviar, crème fraîche, and red-onion relish. Main courses depend on whatever is in season: It might be spring salmon, halibut, Dungeness crab, and flying squid served with couscous, chickpeas,

Where to Dine in Downtown Vancouver

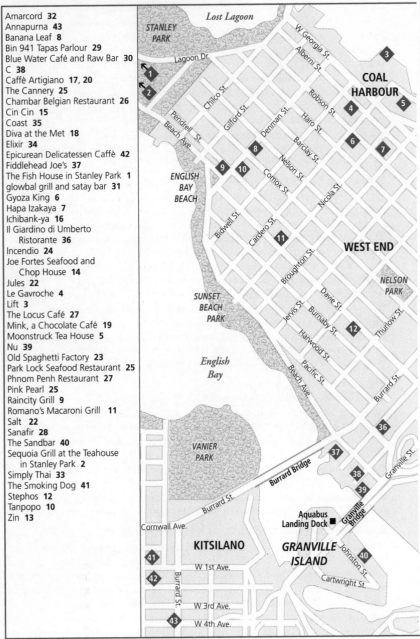

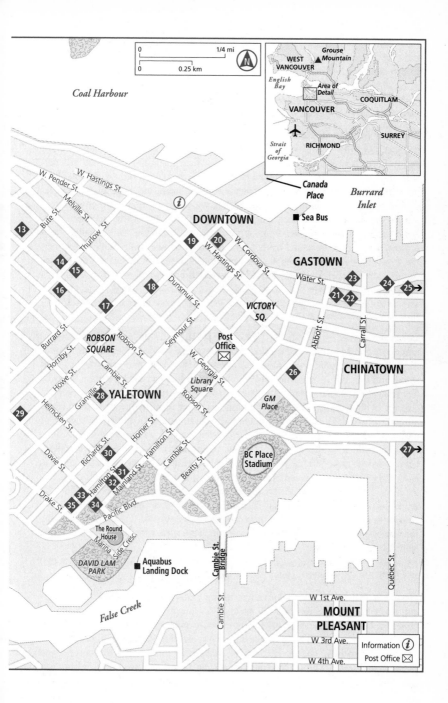

green onions, tomatoes, and harissa vinaigrette, or B.C. sablefish caramelized with soy and sake. The desserts are fabulous, everything from homemade sorbet to warm dark Cuban chocolate cake. A masterful wine list and an experienced sommelier assure fine wine pairings.

1095 Hamilton St. (at Helmcken). (✆ 604/688-8078. www.bluewatercafe.net. Reservations recommended. Main courses C$30–C$46 (US$25–US$39/£14–£20). AE, DC, MC, V. Daily 5pm–midnight. Valet parking C$8 ($7/£4). Bus: 2.

Chambar Belgian Restaurant 𝄞𝄞 BELGIAN   One of Vancouver's favorite restaurants, Chambar occupies an intriguing space in a kind of no man's land on lower Beatty Street between Yaletown and Gastown. Michelin-trained chef Nico Scheuerman and his wife, Karri, have worked hard to make the place a success, and plenty of plaudits have come their way. The menu features small and large plates. Smaller choices might include mussels cooked in white wine, bacon, and cream (or with fresh tomatoes); halibut and candied ginger beignet; or green and white asparagus salad. Main courses feature market-fresh options such as *waterzooi* (bouillabaisse) with prawns, scallops, mussels, and halibut, or a tagine of braised lamb shank with honey. For dessert, try the classic Belgian chocolate mousse or the hot mocha soufflé. Chambar specializes in Belgian beers, some 25 varieties in bottles and on tap.

562 Beatty St. (✆ 604/879-7119. www.chambar.com. Reservations recommended. Small plates C$10–C$20 (US$8–US$17/£4.50–£9); main courses C$23–C$28 (US$20–US$24/£10–£13); 3-course set menu C$50 (US$42/£23). AE, MC, V. Daily 5:30–11pm. Bus: 5 or 17.

Coast 𝄞𝄞𝄞 *(Finds* SEAFOOD/INTERNATIONAL   This dashing Yaletown restaurant opened in May 2004 and quickly became a culinary and people-watching spot of note. The dining room is a handsomely designed affair with two levels, lots of light wood, and a special "community table" around an induction cooking surface, so lucky diners can watch chef Jeremy Atkins prepare their culinary teasers. The concept at Coast is to offer an extensive variety of fresh (and nonendangered) seafood from coasts around the world. For starters you might have Ahi tuna sashimi and avocado salad, or a wild, white sea tiger prawn cocktail. Then, from the grill, you could order Hawaiian Ahi tuna, wild B.C. salmon, Indian Ocean tiger prawns, or hand-harvested scallops from Newfoundland. Other temptations might include Alaskan king crab gnocchi, garlic tiger prawns and capellini pasta, and (always) Liverpool-style fish and chips. Or, for a reasonably priced splash, try the signature seafood platter (C$68/US$58/£31) with lobster, mussels, crab roll, crab cocktail, prawns, oysters, and smoked salmon. The cooking is just right for every dish, never overdone or underdone, never overwhelming the fish, and a joy for the taste buds. Accompany your meal with a recommended wine from Coast's large cellar.

1257 Hamilton St. (✆ 604/685-5010. www.coastrestaurant.ca. Reservations recommended. Main courses C$18–C$33 (US$15–US$28/£8–£15). AE, DC, MC, V. Daily 4:30–11pm. Bus: 1 or 22.

Elixir 𝄞𝄞 FRENCH   Elixir, located in the hip Opus Hotel, actually has three different dining areas: the velvet room, an enclosed space with dark-wood paneling and red velvet banquettes; the brighter garden room, more appropriate for an informal breakfast or brunch; and an adjacent dining area that looks like a Left Bank bistro. A horseshoe bar unites them, and the menu is the same in all three—modern brasserie food prepared with excellent local ingredients, utilizing a medley of spices culled from former French colonies the world over. For appetizers, think spiced beef tartare with french fries; for salads, warm frisée and bacon with a soft poached egg; for soups,

French onion; and for main courses, roasted sablefish with a confit of porcini mushrooms or spice-crusted venison loin with a cassonade of cranberries, parsnip purée, and bitter chocolate sauce. A selection of local artisan cheeses is a perfect way to end your meal, but the pastry chef excels, too. The wine list covers a wide swath of the world. Late in the evening, the restaurant becomes more like a Yaletown lounge and offers the same kind of small plates found in the Opus Bar.

In the Opus Hotel (p. 69), 350 Davie St. ⓒ 604/642-0577. www.elixir-opusbar.com. Reservations recommended. Main courses C$17–C$40 (US$15–US$34/£8–£18). AE, DC, MC, V. Mon–Wed 6:30am–2:30pm and 5–11pm; Thurs–Fri 6:30am–2:30pm and 5pm–12:30am; Sat 6:30–11:30am, 10:30am–2:30pm (brunch), and 5pm–12:30am; Sun 6:30–11:30am, 10:30am–2:30pm (brunch), and 5–11pm. Closed holidays. Bus: 1 or 22.

glowbal grill & satay bar 𝒜𝒜 FUSION   Glowbal occupies a top spot in the trendy Yaletown dining scene, so if you're looking for an evening of good food served in a loud, buzzy atmosphere, try this place. The dining room—divvied up into a long elevated bar, a rank of semisecluded dining tables, a file of glowing dining cubes, and an open kitchen—maximizes the noise and drama all around. Have one of their famous martinis as you peruse the menu, and sample some of the delicious satays as an appetizer. Glowbal started the Vancouver craze for these succulent skewers of grilled meat or fish served with a dipping sauce. Or perhaps start with some wild mushroom ravioli or a Caprese salad with tomatoes and buffalo mozzarella. Then, if you're in the mood for seafood, go with whatever is fresh: It may be wild salmon served with bok choy and lobster mashed potatoes, or tea-smoked cod filet. Upscale comfort-food options include a fabulous spaghetti with truffles and Kobe meatballs. Service is fun and friendly, the wine list exemplary. As the evening rolls on, the in-crowd rolls into Afterglow, the small lounge behind the dining room. If you want to try the food but avoid the scene, go for lunch Monday to Friday.

1079 Mainland St. ⓒ 604/602-0835. www.glowbalgrill.com. Reservations recommended. Main courses lunch C$9–C$17 (US$8–US$14/£4–£8), dinner C$17–C$32 (US$14–US$27/£8–£14). AE, DC, MC, V. Daily 11:30am–midnight. Bus: 2.

Il Giardino di Umberto Ristorante 𝒜𝒜 ITALIAN   Restaurant magnate Umberto Menghi started this small restaurant, tucked away in a yellow heritage house at the bottom of Hornby Street, about 3 decades ago. Today, it still serves some of the best Italian fare in town, and has one of the prettiest garden patios. A larger restaurant now adjoins the original house, opening up into a spacious and bright dining room that re-creates the ambience of an Italian villa. The menu leans toward Tuscany, with dishes that emphasize pasta and game. Entrees usually include classics such as *osso buco* with saffron risotto, and that Roman favorite, spaghetti carbonara. A daily list of specials makes the most of seasonal fresh ingredients, often offering outstanding seafood dishes. The wine list is comprehensive and well chosen.

1382 Hornby St. (between Pacific and Drake). ⓒ 604/669-2422. Fax 604/669-9723. www.umberto.com. Reservations recommended. Main courses C$15–C$35 (US$13–US$30/£7–£16). AE, DC, MC, V. Mon–Fri 11:30am–3pm and 6–11pm; Sat 6–11pm. Closed holidays. Bus: 1 or 22.

Joe Fortes Seafood and Chop House 𝒜𝒜𝒜 SEAFOOD   Named after the burly Caribbean seaman who became English Bay's first lifeguard, Joe Fortes is the best place to come if you're hankering for top-of-the-line fresh seafood served the "old-fashioned" way, without a lot of modern culinary intrusions. The downstairs dining room evokes a kind of turn-of-the-20th-century saloon elegance, but if the weather's fine, try for a table on the rooftop patio. Stick with the seafood because it's what they do best. The waiters will inform you what's just come in and where it's from. Although Joe's is adding more fusion elements to boost the novelty, you can ask for your fish selection to be simply grilled or sautéed. My personal recommendation is that you sample the seasonal oysters (Joe Fortes has the best oyster bar in Vancouver) and/or order the trio of grilled fresh fish or the famous seafood tower, which comes with an iced assortment of marinated mussels, poached shrimp, grilled and chilled scallops, marinated calamari, tuna sashimi, Manila clams, Dungeness crab, and local beach oysters. Heavy on the white, the wine list is gargantuan and includes some wonderful pinots from the Okanagan Valley.

777 Thurlow St. (at Robson). ℭ 604/669-1940. www.joefortes.ca. Reservations recommended. Main courses C$27–C$45 (US$23–US$38/£12–£20). AE, DC, DISC, MC, V. Daily 11am–10:30pm (brunch Sat–Sun 11am–4pm). Bus: 5.

Nu FRENCH   Nu means "naked" in French, but it's not clear how that applies to this stylish new Yaletown hot spot. The same can be said for the 1970s airport lounge decor. You're never quite sure if you're in a lounge or a dining room; Nu is both, obviously. But if the weather's nice, go out to the patio overlooking False Creek, because that's much more comfortable, and it's a great spot to enjoy a good lunch or a glass of wine and a snack, such as fresh oysters or *pommes frites* with mayo or foie gras gravy. More substantial fare includes flatiron steak, seared salmon, or caramelized lamb shanks. C (p. 86) is just steps away, and a better choice for a splurge dinner with a view; the same team runs both.

1661 Granville St. ℭ **604/646-4668.** www.whatisnu.com. Reservations recommended. Main courses C$10–C$40 (US$8–US$34/£4.50–£18). AE, DC, MC, V. Mon–Fri 11am–1am; Sat 10:30am–1am; Sun 10:30am–midnight. Bus: 1 or 2.

MODERATE

Bin 941 Tapas Parlour ⚘ TAPAS/CASUAL   Still booming after 8 years, Bin 941 remains the place for trendy tapas dining, and in 2006 won "Best Tapas" at the *Vancouver* magazine restaurant awards. True, the music's too loud and the room's too small, but the food that alights on the bar and eight tiny tables is delicious and fun, and the wine list is great. Look especially for local seafood offerings such as scallops and tiger prawns tournedos. In this sliver of a bistro sharing is unavoidable, so come prepared for socializing. A second Bin, dubbed Bin 942, opened at 1521 W. Broadway (ℭ **604/673-1246**). The tables start to fill up at 6:30pm at both spots, and by 8pm, the hip and hungry have already formed a long and eager line.

941 Davie St. ℭ **604/683-1246.** www.bin941.com. Reservations not accepted. All plates are C$15 (US$13/£7). MC, V. Daily 5pm–1:30am. Bus: 4, 5, or 8.

Fiddlehead Joe's FUSION   Overlooking a marina and the busy entrance to False Creek, just east of the Burrard Bridge, this casual eatery has one of the few outdoor dining patios on the Vancouver seawall. The patio is heated, and that's where you want to sit, enjoying a casual lunch or the busy brunch on Saturday and Sunday. The scene is as much a part of this place as the fusion-style food. During the day, when Fiddlehead Joe's is a cafe, you can sit and people-watch with coffee, a sandwich, dessert, or a glass of wine. More serious dining begins in the evening, when you can order small, medium, or large plates. Stick to the simpler dishes here. Large plates include dishes such as almond-crusted duck breast, pan-fried trout, and grilled rib-eye steak. The popular brunch includes skillet frittatas, corned beef hash with poached eggs and hollandaise sauce, and puff pastries filled with scallops, shrimp, and portobello mushrooms.

1A-1012 Beach Ave. (on the Seawall). ℭ 604/688-1980. www.fiddleheadjoeseatery.com. Reservations recommended for brunch. Main courses C$15–C$25 (US$13–US$21/£7–£11). AE, MC, V. Mon 5–11pm; Tues–Fri 11am–1am; Sat 10am–1am; Sun 10am–midnight. Bus: 1 or 22.

Sanafir 🍴🍴 *(Finds)* INTERNATIONAL   Influenced by the exotic dining and decor found along the Silk Road, Sanafir creates an opulent and fun dining experience that doesn't cost a fortune. The first-floor dining room is loud and buzzily exciting, but parties can also drink and dine upstairs while reclining on pillows beneath sexy harem-style draperies. The tapas-style plates come in three of five possible Silk Road variations: Asian, Mediterranean, Middle Eastern, Indian, or North African. And the trio of tastes costs only C$14 (US$12/£6). Say you order the scallops, your three-dish tapas plate might contain a seared Indian five-spice scallop with mango chutney, sautéed scallops wrapped in lettuce with a hoison glaze, and a gently poached scallop over a kasha and sumac salad in a fennel-scented phyllo cup. Larger chef's specials are also available, such as the superrich oxtail cappelletti with white truffle cream, Parmigiano-Reggiano, and shaved black truffle. The showoff interior and the quality of the food makes this a destination restaurant worth trying. There's no sign, but look for the most glamorous place on gentrifying Granville Street, and you'll be there.

1026 Granville St. (at Nelson). ⓒ 604/678-1049. www.sanafir.ca. Reservations recommended. Tapas C$14 (US$12/ £6); chef's specials C$17 (US$14/£8). AE, DC, MC, V. Daily 5pm–midnight. Bus: 4 or 7.

Simply Thai 🍴 THAI   At this small Thai restaurant in the trendy heart of Yaletown, you can watch chef and owner Siriwan in the open kitchen as she cooks up a combination of northern and southern Thai dishes with some fusion sensations. The appetizers are perfect finger foods: *gai satay* features succulent pieces of grilled chicken breast marinated in coconut milk and spices, and covered in a peanut sauce, while the delicious *cho muang* consists of violet-colored dumplings stuffed with minced chicken. Main courses run the gamut of Thai cuisine: noodle dishes and coconut curries with beef, chicken, or pork, as well as a good number of vegetarian options. Don't miss the *tom kha gai*, a deceptively simple-looking coconut soup with chicken, mushrooms, and lemon grass. Siriwan creates a richly fragrant broth that balances the delicate flavors of the lemon grass and other spices with thick coconut milk. The set menu is a good way to sample a bit of everything.

1211 Hamilton St. ⓒ 604/642-0123. www.simplythairestaurant.com. Reservations recommended on weekends. Main courses C$13–C$26 (US$11–US$22/£6–£12); set menu C$40 (US$34/£18). AE, DC, MC, V. Mon–Fri 11:30am–3pm and 5–10:30pm; Sat–Sun 5–10:30pm. Bus: 2.

4 Gastown & Chinatown

EXPENSIVE

The Cannery 🍴 SEAFOOD   At least some of the pleasure of eating at The Cannery comes from the adventure of finding the place. (Drive or take a cab because it's impossible to get there on foot or by public transportation.) Hop the railroad tracks, thread your way past a harbor security checkpoint, pass container terminals and fish-packing plants, and there it is—a timber-framed rectangular building hanging out over the waters of Burrard Inlet. The interior, with its exposed beams and seafaring memorabilia, adds to the charm, but many come here for the view, one of the best in Vancouver. You'll find good, solid, traditional seafood, and ever-changing specials. Famous dishes include salmon Wellington (salmon, shrimp, and mushrooms baked in a puff pastry), smoked Alaskan black cod, and roasted mussels. Meat lovers can get a grilled New York steak or Alberta beef tenderloin. Chef Frederic Couton has been getting more inventive lately, but when an institution founded in 1971 is still going strong, no one's ever *too* keen to rock the boat. The wine list is stellar, and the desserts are wonderfully inventive.

2205 Commissioner St. (near Victoria Dr). ℂ **877/254-9606** or 604/254-9606. www.canneryseafood.com. Reservations recommended. Main courses C$23–C$40 (US$15–US$34/£10–£18). AE, DC, DISC, MC, V. Mon–Fri 11:30am–2:30pm and 5:30–9pm; Sat 5–9:30pm; Sun 5–9pm. Closed Dec 24–26. From downtown, head east on Hastings St., turn left on Victoria Dr. (2 blocks past Commercial Dr.), then right on Commissioner St.

MODERATE

Park Lock Seafood Restaurant (Kids) CHINESE/DIM SUM If you've never done dim sum, this large, second-floor dining room in the heart of Chinatown is a good place to give it a try, even though you'll have to listen to schlocky Western music while you dine. From 8am to 3pm daily, waitresses wheel little carts loaded with Chinese delicacies past the tables. When you see something you like, just point and ask for it. The final bill is based upon how many little plates are left on your table. Dishes include spring rolls, *hargow* (shrimp dumplings), *shumai* (steamed shrimp, beef, or pork dumplings), prawns wrapped in fresh white noodles, small steamed buns, sticky rice cooked in banana leaves, curried squid, and lots more. Parties of four or more are best—that way you get to try each other's food.

544 Main St. (at E. Pender St., on the 2nd floor). ℂ **604/688-1581.** Reservations recommended. Main courses C$10–C$25 (US$8–US$21/£4.50–£11); dim sum dishes C$3–C$7 (US$2.50–US$6/£1.50–£3.25). AE, MC, V. Mon–Thurs 7:30am–4pm; Fri–Sun 7:30am–4pm and 5–9:30pm. Bus: 19 or 22.

Pink Pearl ★ (Kids) CHINESE/DIM SUM Opened in 1981, the Pink Pearl remains Vancouver's best spot for dim sum. The sheer volume and bustle here are astonishing, and at peak times you may have to wait up to (or only, depending on your patience level) 15 minutes for a table. Dozens of waiters parade a cavalcade of trolleys stacked high with baskets, steamers, and bowl of dumplings, spring rolls, shrimp balls, chicken feet, and even more obscure and delightful offerings. At the tables, extended Chinese families banter, joke, and feast; towers of empty plates pile up in the middle, a tribute to the appetites of the brunchers, as well as the growing bill. Fortunately, dim sum is still a steal, perhaps the best and most fun way to sample Cantonese cooking.

1132 E. Hastings St. ℂ **604/253-4316.** www.pinkpearl.com. Main courses C$11–C$35 (US$9–US$30/£5–£16); dim sum C$3–C$7 (US$2.50–US$6/£1.50–£3.25). AE, DC, MC, V. Sun–Thurs 9am–10pm; Fri–Sat 9am–11pm (dim sum served 9am–2:30pm). Bus: 10.

INEXPENSIVE

Incendio ★ (Finds) PIZZA If you're looking for something casual and local that won't be full of other tourists reading downtown maps, this little Gastown hideaway is just the spot. The 22 pizza combinations are served on fresh, crispy crusts baked in an old wood-fired oven; pastas are homemade. The wine list is decent; the beer list is inspired. And they even have a patio. Much to the delight of Kitsilano residents, a second location with a slightly larger menu opened next to the 5th Avenue movie theater at 2118 Burrard (ℂ **604/736-2220**).

103 Columbia St. ℂ **604/688-8694.** Main courses C$11–C$24 (US$9–US$20/£5–£11). AE, MC, V. Mon–Thurs 11:30am–3pm and 5–10pm; Fri 11:30am–3pm and 5–11pm; Sat 5–11pm; Sun 4:30–10pm. Closed Dec 23–Jan 3. Bus: 1 or 8.

Jules ★ (Finds) FRENCH Jules, which opened in February 2007, is one of those places that is hard not to like. Like Salt (reviewed below), this casual French bistro is part of a mini-Renaissance putting new life into Gastown. Jules can be really loud, but the staff is friendly and the food is honest, unpretentious, and very reasonably priced. The menu's limited to just a few standard bistro items, all of them well prepared: steak frites (rib-eye or hanger steak with french fries), cassoulet, braised lamb shank, steamed mussels, or a vegetarian shepherd's pie. You can start with classics like French onion soup, escargots in garlic and herb butter, or country-style pâté.

216 Abbott St. ℂ **604/669-0033**. Main courses C$15–C$21 (US$13/£7–US$18/£7–£9); 3-course fixed-price dinner C$21 (US$18/£9). AE, MC, V. Tues–Sat 11am–2:30pm and 5–10pm. Bus: 1 or 8.

Old Spaghetti Factory *(Kids* *(Value* FAMILY STYLE/ITALIAN   The Old Spaghetti Factory has a convenient location in the Gastown heritage district and is a great place to take kids thanks to their selection of half-size, half-price pasta dishes, including spaghetti with meatballs. For the older and more adventurous are more complicated pastas with clam or Alfredo sauce, as well as veal and steak. All entrees come with a green salad, sourdough bread, coffee or tea, and spumoni ice cream. A small list of wines is offered, plus beer and chocolate milk.

53 Water St. ℂ **604/684-1288**. www.oldspaghettifactory.ca. Main courses C$9–C$15 (US$8–US$13/£4–£7). AE, MC, V. Mon–Thurs 11am–10pm; Fri–Sat 11am–11pm; Sun 11am–9pm. Bus: 50.

Phnom Penh Restaurant ✿ VIETNAMESE   This family-run restaurant, serving Vietnamese and Cambodian cuisine, is a perennial contender for, and occasional recipient of, the *Vancouver* magazine award for the city's best Asian restaurant. Khmer dolls are suspended in glass cases, and the subdued lighting is a welcome departure from the harsh glare often found in inexpensive Chinatown restaurants. Try the hot-and-sour soup, loaded with prawns and lemon grass. The deep-fried garlic squid served with rice is also delicious. For dessert, the fruit-and-rice pudding is an exotic treat.

244 E. Georgia St., near Main St. ℂ **604/682-5777**. Dishes C$6–C$11 (US$5–US$9/£2.75–£5). AE, MC. Daily 10am–10pm. Bus: 8 or 19.

Salt ✿ CHARCUTERIE   The location of this new dining spot might put some visitors off, and single women will probably be uncomfortable walking along the horribly named Blood Alley alone at night. And that's really a shame, because Salt is unique, and a wonderful place to get a good, inexpensive meal. The room is long and minimalistically modern, with communal spruce dining tables. Salt has no kitchen per se as it serves only cured meats and artisan cheeses plus a daily soup, a couple of salads, and grilled meat and cheese sandwiches. For the tasting plate you mix and match three of the meats and cheeses listed on the blackboard. To drink, choose from a selection of beers, and several good wines and whiskeys, or opt for a wine flight. As Blood Alley has no street numbers, look for the salt shaker flag over the doorway. Try it for lunch if you're in Gastown.

Blood Alley, Gastown. ℂ **604/633-1912**. Tasting plates C$15 (US$13/£7); soup C$6 (US$5/£2.75). AE, MC, V. Daily noon–midnight. Bus: 1 or 8.

5 The West End

EXPENSIVE

Cin Cin ✿✿✿ MODERN ITALIAN   Vancouverites in need of great Italian food frequent this award-winning, second-story restaurant on Robson Street. The spacious dining room, done in a rustic Italian-villa style, surrounds an open kitchen built around a huge wood-fired oven and grill; the heated terrace is an equally pleasant dining and people-watching spot. The food at Cin Cin is exemplary, and if you're in the mood to sample a bit of everything, I'd recommend the fabulous five-course tasting menu. The dishes change monthly, but the tasting menu might begin with fresh buffalo mozzarella with rosso bruno tomatoes, go on to tortelli pasta stuffed with ricotta

and chard, followed by wood-roasted fish and shellfish in fennel broth, and then venison loin served with chestnut and sweet garlic tortellini, after which a chestnut crème
brûlée arrives. Mouthwatering a la carte possibilities include taglierini pasta with
wood-roasted lobster, mushroom-dusted sablefish cooked in the wood-fired oven, Ahi
tuna and beef tenderloin from the wood grill, and a delicious pizza with prosciutto,
asparagus, fontina cheese, roasted garlic, and rosemary. The award-winning wine list
is extensive, as is the selection of wines by the glass. Service is exemplary.

1154 Robson St. *C* 604/688-7338. www.cincin.net. Reservations recommended. Main courses C$19–C$44
(US$16–US$37/£8–£20); tasting menu C$78 (US$67/£35). AE, DC, MC, V. Mon–Fri 11:30am–2:30pm and 5–11pm;
Sat–Sun 5–11pm. Bus: 5 or 22.

The Fish House in Stanley Park *※※* SEAFOOD/PACIFIC NORTHWEST/TEA
Reminiscent of a more genteel era, this green clapboard clubhouse from 1929 is surrounded by green lawns and ancient cedar trees, and looks out over English Bay (in
the summer, try for a table on the veranda). Inside, you'll find a warm, comfortable
atmosphere and wonderfully friendly service. Enjoy a traditional afternoon tea, Sunday brunch, or a memorable lunch or dinner of fresh B.C. oysters and shellfish, fresh
seasonal fish, and signature dishes such as maple-glazed salmon, flaming prawns (done
at your table with ouzo), and a seafood cornucopia. The wine list is admirable; the
desserts sumptuous. Guests have been enjoying chef Karen Barnaby's cooking since
1993; in addition to her signature standbys, she often creates special theme menus and
offers a reasonably priced three-course set dinner menu every month.

8901 Stanley Park Dr. *C* 877/681-7275 or 604/681-7275. www.fishhousestanleypark.com. Reservations recommended. Main courses C$17–C$30 (US$14–US$26/£8–£13); 3-course set menu C$30 (US$26/£13); afternoon tea C$24
(US$20/£11). AE, DC, DISC, MC, V. Mon–Sat 11:30am–10pm; Sun 11am–10pm; afternoon tea daily 2–4pm. Closed Dec
24–26. Bus: 1, 35, or 135.

Le Gavroche *※※* FRENCH   This charmingly intimate French restaurant located
in a century-old house has always been a place for special occasions and celebrations,
and with food and wine of this caliber, there's a lot to celebrate. The food is classical
French—but with inventive overtones and underpinnings. Try one of the tasting
menus with wine pairings, and you won't regret a mouthful. Start with Kobe beef tar-
tar and buffalo carpaccio, followed by a classic Caesar salad mixed at your table (Le
Gavroche is known for its personal attention). Then, try duck Magret with a white
peach reduction, a venison chop with strawberry ketchup, or mustard-crusted rack of
lamb. Seafood and vegetarian choices are available as well. Finish your feast with a
Grand Marnier soufflé or the incomparable "Lili" cake.

1616 Alberni St. *C* 604/685-3924. www.legavroche.ca. Reservations recommended. Main courses C$29–C$45
(US$25–US$38/£13–£20); set menus C$45–C$65 (US$38–US$55/£20–£29). AE, DC, MC, V. Mon–Fri 11:30am–
2:30pm and 5:30–10pm; Sat–Sun 5:30–10pm. Bus: 5.

Lift *※※* *Finds* PACIFIC NORTHWEST   Built on pilings right on Coal Harbour,
Lift offers gorgeous mountain, water, and city views. Chef Dave Jorgenson's contemporary West Coast cuisine comes with a French twist and is equal to the sexy setting.
The interior is luxe, with an illuminated onyx bar and different seating areas for drinking, eating, or both, as well as a rooftop patio. After 5pm, the restaurant serves "whet
plates" (larger than an appetizer, but smaller than an entree), such as mussels with mer-
guez sausage, panko-crusted calamari, or grilled lamb loin. Main courses include Ahi
tuna, spiced paella, or the wonderful Duck Two Ways. The Sunday brunch is hopping,

too, and reasonably priced. The wine list here is good, but don't expect to find any bargain delights to accompany your meal.

333 Menchions Mews (behind Westin Bayshore Resort). © **604/689-5438.** www.liftbarandgrill.com. Reservations recommended. Whet plates C$11–C$20 (US$9–US$17/£5–£9); main courses C$23–C$33 (US$20–US$30/£10–£15). AE, DC, MC, V. Mon–Fri 11:30am–midnight; Sat–Sun 11am–midnight; Sun brunch 11am–2:30pm. Bus: 240.

Raincity Grill ✿✿✿ PACIFIC NORTHWEST   This top-starred restaurant is a gem—painstaking in preparation, arty in presentation, and yet completely unfussy in atmosphere. Raincity Grill was one of the very first restaurants in Vancouver to embrace the "buy locally, eat seasonally" concept, and in 2006, it won the *Vancouver* magazine award for "Best Regional Restaurant." The menu focuses on seafood, game, poultry, and organic vegetables, all of it from British Columbia and the Pacific Northwest. The room is long, low, and intimate—perfect for romantic dining. To sample a bit of everything, I recommend the seasonal tasting menu, a bargain at C$60 (US$51/£27), or C$89 (US$76/£40) with wine pairings. One recent tasting menu included organic chicken leg with Yukon potato confit; roasted Berkshire pork belly with sunroot and candied kabocha squash; duck breast with braised endive, beets, and celeriac; and fennel seed and honey panna cotta—all of it made with ingredients found within 161km (100 miles) of the restaurant. The wine list is huge and, in keeping with the restaurant's philosophy, sticks pretty close to home. From May through Labour Day, Raincity opens a takeout window on Denham Street, where you can get a gourmet sandwich, salad, and sweet to go for C$10 (US$8/£4.50).

1193 Denman St. © **604/685-7337.** www.raincitygrill.com. Reservations recommended. Main courses C$17–C$33 (US$14–US$28/£8–£15). AE, DC, MC, V. Mon–Fri 11:30am–2:30pm and 5–10:30pm; Sat–Sun 10:30am–3pm (brunch) and 5–10:30pm. Bus: 1 or 5.

Sequoia Grill at the Teahouse in Stanley Park PACIFIC NORTHWEST   Perched on Ferguson Point in Stanley Park overlooking English Bay, the Sequoia Grill is one of Vancouver's most venerable seaside landmarks. The view is perhaps more memorable than the food, and after the sun fades, the lights cast a magical glow on the trees and garden. Try for a seat on the outdoor patio or at a window-side table in the conservatory. The restaurant was taken over and redone in 2004 to make it more contemporary in cuisine and ambience. The new menu sticks with safe tourist choices and a selection of what trendy Vancouverites are eating these days. Appetizers include wok-fried squid with Thai chiles and oyster sauce, and mushrooms stuffed with crab, shrimp, and cream cheese. Main courses are divided between seafood and meat, with pasta and risotto thrown in for good measure.

Ferguson Point, Stanley Park. © **604/669-3281.** www.vancouverdine.com. Reservations recommended. Small plates C$7–C$16 (US$6–US$14/£3–£7); main courses C$18–C$39 (US$15–US$33/£8–£18). AE, DC, MC, V. Mon–Fri 11:30am–9:45pm; Sat 11:30am–9:45pm (brunch 11:30am–2:30pm); Sun 10:30am–9:45pm (brunch 10:30am–2:30pm); small plates daily 2:30–5:30pm; dinner daily 5:30–9:45pm.

MODERATE

Hapa Izakaya ✿ JAPANESE   Dinner comes at almost disco decibels in Robson Street's hottest Japanese "eat-drink place" (the literal meaning of Izakaya), where chefs call out orders, servers shout acknowledgments, and the maitre d' and owner keep up a running volley to staff about the (often sizable) wait at the door. The menu features inventive nontraditional dishes such as bacon-wrapped asparagus, *negitori* (spicy tuna roll), and fresh tuna belly chopped with spring onions and served with bite-size bits of garlic bread. Inventive appetizers and meat dishes and a scrumptious Korean hot pot are also on the menu, for the non–raw fish eaters in your party. The crowd is about a third expat Japanese, a third Chinese (both local and expat), and a third well-informed Westerners. The service is fast and obliging, and the price per dish is very reasonable. A second location is in Kitsilano at 1516 Yew St. (© **604/738-4272**).

1479 Robson St. © **604/689-4272**. www.hapaizakaya.com. No reservations accepted 6–8pm. Main courses C$8–C$14 (US$7–US$12/£4–£6). AE, MC, V. Sun–Thurs 5:30pm–midnight; Fri–Sat 5:30pm–1am. Bus: 5.

Ichiban-ya JAPANESE   In contrast to Hapa (see above), this small basement sushi bar (with a rather dramatic red and black interior) has served old-fashioned, straight-up sushi for more than 2 decades. The quality is high and the salmon, tuna, halibut, and other diverse sea creatures come nice and fresh. Options for non-sushiphiles include tempura and teriyaki.

770 Thurlow St. © **604/682-6262**. www.ichiban-ya.com. Reservations accepted. Main courses C$7–C$17 (US$6–US$14/£3.25–£8). AE, DC, MC, V. Daily 11:30am–midnight. Bus: 5.

Romano's Macaroni Grill _Kids_ FAMILY STYLE/ITALIAN   It's almost worth eating here just to see the interior. Housed in a stone mansion built in 1900 by sugar baron B. T. Rogers, Romano's is a fun and casual chain restaurant with an Italian-influenced menu. This isn't high-concept Italian; the food is simple, understandable, and reliably good. The pastas are definitely favorites. The children's menu features lasagna, mac and cheese, spaghetti with meatball, and tasty pizzas. In the summer it's fun to dine outside on the beautiful garden patio, but the stunning interior, filled with handcrafted wood detailing and stained glass, is pretty amazing.

1523 Davie St. © **604/689-4334**. www.macgrillbc.com. Reservations recommended. Main courses C$15–C$23 (US$13–US$20/£7–£10); children's courses C$4.95 (US$4/£2.25). AE, DC, MC, V. Mon–Thurs noon–10pm; Fri–Sat noon–11pm. Bus: 5.

Tanpopo _Value_ JAPANESE   Occupying the second floor of a corner building on Denman Street, Tanpopo has a partial view of English Bay, a large patio, and a huge menu of hot and cold Japanese dishes. But the line of people waiting 30 minutes or more every night for a table are here for the all-you-can-eat sushi. The unlimited fare includes the standards—makis, tuna and salmon sashimi, California and B.C. rolls—as well as cooked items such as tonkatsu, tempura, chicken kara-age, and broiled oysters. The quality is okay, a bit above average for an all-you-can-eat place. A couple of secrets to getting seated: You might try to call ahead, but they only take an arbitrary percentage of reservations for dinner each day. Otherwise, ask to sit at the sushi bar.

1122 Denman St. © **604/681-7777**. Reservations recommended for groups. Main courses C$7–C$20 (US$6–US$17/£3.25–£9); all-you-can-eat sushi C$25 (US$21/£11) for dinner, C$14 (US$12/£6) for lunch. AE, DC, MC, V. Daily 11:30am–10pm. Bus: 5.

Zin FUSION/TAPAS   Come to Zin's for a restaurant meal (breakfast, lunch, or dinner) or tapas made with fresh local ingredients and a global accent. The interior glows with candlelight and deep reddish hues offset by comfy loungeable sofas and chairs on one side, and dining booths on the other. Small plates are priced in the C$7-to-C$16 (US$6–US$14/£4–£7) range. Dishes include Asian-inspired specialties such as coconut crab cakes and lobster and coriander spring rolls, but you can also snack on truffled popcorn or goat cheese fondue. For your main course, try steak and fries, wild salmon laksa, pan-seared halibut, butter curry scallops, or a vegetarian biryani. The result, whether you're dining on entrees or sharing small plates, is a fun, casual experience with cuisine that's more varied and less expensive than any of the glorified pub-food outlets on

Robson. Zin's offers a large selection of martinis, wines by the glass, and the best selection of zinfandel in town. The restaurant is in the Pacific Palisades Hotel (see chapter 5, p. 76) but managed separately.

In the Pacific Palisades Hotel, 1277 Robson St. ℂ 604/408-1700. www.zin-restaurant.com. Main courses C$17–C$28 (US$14–US$24/£8–£13). AE, DC, MC, V. Mon–Thurs 7am–midnight; Fri 7am–1am; Sat 8am–1am; Sun 8am–midnight.

INEXPENSIVE

Banana Leaf ℱ MALAYSIAN   One of the city's best spots for Malaysian food, Banana Leaf is just a hop and a skip from English Bay. The menu includes inventive specials such as mango and okra salad, delicious south Asian mainstays such as *gado gado* (a salad with hot peanut sauce), *mee goreng* (fried noodles with vegetables topped by a fried egg) and occasional variations such as an assam curry (seafood in hot-and-sour curry sauce), with okra and tomato. For dessert, don't pass up on *pisang goring*— fried banana with ice cream. The small room is tastefully decorated in dark tropical woods; the rather unadventurous wine list features a small selection of inexpensive reds and whites. Service is very friendly. A second location is located at 820 W. Broadway (ℂ 604/731-6333); same prices and hours apply.

1096 Denman St. ℂ 604/683-3333. www.bananaleaf-vancouver.com. Main courses C$10–C$20 (US$8–US$17/£4.50–£9). AE, MC, V. Sun–Thurs 11:30am–10pm; Fri–Sat 11:30am–11pm. Bus: 5.

Gyoza King JAPANESE   Gyoza King features an entire menu of *gyoza*—succulent Japanese dumplings filled with prawns, pork, vegetables, and other combinations—as well as Japanese noodles and staples like *katsu-don* (pork cutlet over rice) and *o-den* (a rich, hearty soup). This is the gathering spot for hordes of young Japanese visitors looking for reasonably priced eats that approximate home cooking. (The menu was revised and the prices went up considerably in 2007.) Seating is divided among Western-style tables, the bar (where you can watch the chef in action), and the Japanese-style low table, which is reserved for larger groups if the restaurant is busy. The staff is very courteous and happy to explain the dishes.

1508 Robson St. ℂ 604/669-8278. Main courses C$15–C$30 (US$13–US$26/£7–£13). AE, MC, V. Mon–Fri 5:30pm–2am; Sat 11:30am–2am; Sun 11:30am–midnight. Bus: 5.

Stephos ⟨Value⟩ GREEK   A fixture on the Davie Street dining scene, Stephos has been packing them in since Zorba was a boy. The cuisine is Greek at its simplest and cheapest. Customers line up outside for a seat amid Greek travel posters, potted ivy, and whitewashed walls (the average wait is about 10–15 min., but it could be as long as 30 min., as once you're inside, the staff will never rush you out the door). Order some pita and dip (hummus, spicy eggplant, or garlic spread) while you peruse the menu. An interesting appetizer is the *avgolemono* soup, a delicately flavored chicken broth with egg and lemon, accompanied by a plate of piping hot pita bread. When choosing a main course, keep in mind that portions are huge. The roasted lamb, lamb chops, fried calamari, and a variety of souvlakia are served with rice, roast potatoes, and Greek salad. The beef, lamb, or chicken pita come in slightly smaller portions served with fries and *tzatziki* (a sauce made from yogurt, cucumber, and garlic).

1124 Davie St. ℂ 604/683-2555. Reservations accepted for parties of 5 or more. Main courses C$6–C$11 (US$5–US$9/£3–£5). AE, MC, V. Daily 11am–11:30pm. Bus: 5.

6 The West Side

VERY EXPENSIVE

Lumière ★★★ FRENCH   The success of this French dining experiment in the heart of Kitsilano has turned chef Rob Feenie into a star. His preparation and presentation are immaculately French, while ingredients are resolutely local, making for interesting surprises—fresh local ginger with the veal, or raspberries in the foie gras. Lumière's tasting menus are a series of delightful plates that change with the season, perfectly matched to a local wine (not included in the fixed price) and gorgeously presented. Diners can choose from three different menus: the signature tasting menu, a meat-and-seafood Chef's menu, or a vegetarian menu. At the adjoining **Lumière Tasting Bar,** patrons can sample smaller dishes for $14 (US$12/£6) a plate, or enjoy an inventive cocktail at the sophisticated bar. The intrepid Feenie is also the force behind the more casual **Feenie's,** right next door (see review below).

2551 W. Broadway. © **604/739-8185.** www.lumiere.ca. Reservations required for restaurant, not accepted for bar. Tasting menus C$125–C$160 (US$106–US$136/£56–£72). AE, DC, MC, V. Restaurant Tues–Sun 5:30–9:30pm; tasting bar Tues–Sun 5:30–11pm. Bus: 9 or 10.

Tojo's Restaurant ★★★ JAPANESE   Tojo's is considered Vancouver's top Japanese restaurant, the place where celebs come to dine on the best sushi in town. It's expensive, but the food is absolutely fresh, inventive, and boy is it good. In 2007, the restaurant relocated to a stunning new 604-sq.-m (6,500-sq.-ft.) space designed by sculptor/architect Colin Kwok. The main area wraps around Chef Tojo and his sushi chefs with a giant curved maple sake bar and an adjoining sushi bar. Tojo's ever-changing menu offers such specialties as sea urchin on the half shell, herring roe, lobster claws, tuna, crab, and barbecue eel. Go for the Chef's Arrangement—tell them how much you're willing to spend (per person), and let the good times roll.

1133 W. Broadway. © **604/872-8050.** www.tojos.com. Reservations required. Main courses C$16–C$30 (US$14–US$25/£7–£13); sushi/sashimi C$8–C$28 (US$7–US$24/£4–£13); Chef's Arrangement C$50–C$100 (US$42–US$85/£22–£45). AE, DC, MC, V. Mon–Sat 5–10pm. Closed Christmas week. Bus: 9.

West ★★★ FRENCH/PACIFIC NORTHWEST   I wasn't surprised when West won the Best Restaurant Award from *Vancouver* magazine in 2005, 2006, and 2007. Every meal I've had here has been memorable. This is a restaurant where details matter, high standards reign, and cooking is a fine art. And yet it's not stuffy or stiff. You'll want to dress up, though, and linger over your food, prepared by executive chef David Hawksworth. The credo at West is deceptively simple: "True to our region, true to the seasons." That means fresh, organic, locally harvested seafood, game, and produce are transformed into extraordinary creations. The menu changes three to four times a week, but first courses might include caramelized scallops with apple curry vinaigrette or a ravioli of quail; for a main course you might find fennel and pepper crusted yellowfin tuna with watermelon radish and miso mustard; honey and clove braised pork cheeks; or lamb with wild mushrooms and sage and confit garlic gnocchi. For the ultimate dining experience, try one of the seasonal tasting menus—a multicourse progression through the best the restaurant has to offer. An early bird menu is served until 6pm; a carefully chosen wine list includes a selection of affordable wines by the glass and half-bottle. If you're really into cooking, reserve one of the two "chef tables" adjacent to Chef Hawksworth's bustling kitchen.

2881 Granville St. ℂ **604/738-8938**. www.westrestaurant.com. Reservations recommended. Main courses C$17–C$44 (US$15–US$37/£16–£20); tasting menus C$78–C$129 (US$66–US$110/£35–£58); early prix-fixe menu until 6pm C$45 (US$38/£20). AE, DC, MC, V. Mon–Fri 11:30am–2:30pm and 5:30–11pm; Sat–Sun 5:30–11pm. Bus: 8.

MODERATE

Aurora Bistro ℱℱ PACIFIC NORTHWEST   How nice to discover a top-notch restaurant with fine food and great service at reasonable prices. Others obviously feel the same way, for in 2006, Aurora was chosen as one of Vancouver's top five restaurants by *Vancouver* magazine. Aurora opened in 2003 with a "back-to-the-basics" philosophy, allowing ingredients to speak for themselves rather than masking them with complicated sauces or combining too many tastes. You might want to start with a country-style pork pâté or blue cheese tart, and then try sweet potato gnocchi or root beer–braised bison short ribs. What you find on the menu will be seasonal and sustainable. All wines are from B.C. A pleasant, lower-key experience in Vancouver's overheated restaurant scene.

2420 Main St. ℂ **604/873-9944**. www.aurorabistro.ca. Reservations recommended. Main courses C$25–C$27 (US$21–US$23/£11–£12). MC, V. Daily 5:30–10:30pm. Bus: 3, 8, or 19.

Café Zen CASUAL   A huge brunch menu, fast and efficient service, reasonable prices, and great eggs Benedict (plus the best French toast in Vancouver) turn this little cafe into a packed dining room by 10am on weekends, when guests spill out the doorway and up the long, steep sidewalk. Sandal-clad traffic from Kits Beach (next door) heads here for breakfast and lunch during the week.

1631 Yew St. (at York). ℂ **604/731-4018**. Main courses C$6–C$12 (US$5–US$10/£2.70–£5). MC, V. Daily 7am–4pm. Bus: 2, 4, 7, or 22.

Feenie's ℱ PACIFIC NORTHWEST   Feenie's opened in 2003 right next door to Rob Feenie's other restaurant, Lumière (p. 100). It became an instant hit with those who wanted to feel close to the celebrated chef without having to buy an eight-course meal. In this bright, relentlessly hip dining room, you can order something as simple as a gourmet hamburger or hot dog, or pastas, fresh fish, and various meat dishes. The bar, painted a glowing magenta-red, serves up special martinis and drinks du jour. The fixed-price lunch and dinner menus are a good value.

2563 W. Broadway. ℂ **604/739-7115**. www.feenies.com. Reservations recommended. Main courses C$12–C$21 (US$10–US$18/£5–£9); 3-course menu lunch C$25 (US$20/£11), dinner C$35 (US$28/£16). AE, DC, MC, V. Mon–Fri 11:30am–2:30pm and 5:30–10pm; Sat–Sun 10am–2pm (brunch) and 5:30–10pm. Closed Jan 1–15. Bus: 4 or 7.

Memphis Blues Barbeque House ℱ *Finds* BARBECUE   At the busy intersection of Granville and Broadway, this hole-in-the-wall barbecue pit has made a name for itself with corn-pone, southern-boy barbecue. With *real* southern barbecue—as the owners will endlessly remind you—the meat has to be smoked for hours over a low-heat, hardwood fire. Ribs come out tender enough to pull apart with your fingers (which is how food is eaten here; the cutlery is mostly for show), yet still sweet and firm. The beef brisket is cooked long enough that the fat is all rendered out, while the lean flesh remains juicy and tender. The pork butt is slow cooked until you can pull it apart with a fork. Those three meats (plus catfish and Cornish game hen) are essentially what's offered here. Put that meat on greens, and you've got a southern salad. Put it on bread, and it becomes a sandwich. Serve it on a plate with beans and a potato, and it becomes an entree. Wines are sold by the glass and bottle, but what you want is the ice-cold, home-brewed beer. A second location has opened at 1342 Commercial Dr. (ℂ **604/215-2565**); same hours apply.

Where to Dine in Kitsilano & the West Side

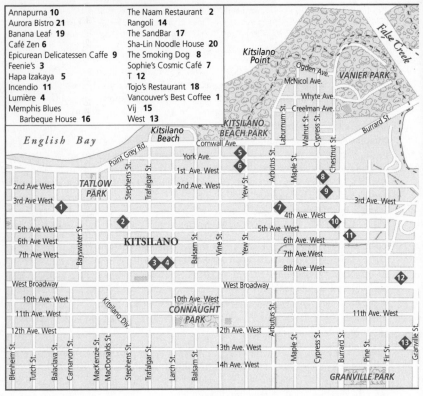

Annapurna **10**
Aurora Bistro **21**
Banana Leaf **19**
Café Zen **6**
Epicurean Delicatessen Caffe **9**
Feenie's **3**
Hapa Izakaya **5**
Incendio **11**
Lumière **4**
Memphis Blues
   Barbeque House **16**

The Naam Restaurant **2**
Rangoli **14**
The SandBar **17**
Sha-Lin Noodle House **20**
The Smoking Dog **8**
Sophie's Cosmic Café **7**
T **12**
Tojo's Restaurant **18**
Vancouver's Best Coffee **1**
Vij **15**
West **13**

1465 W. Broadway. ℂ **604/738-6806.** www.memphisbluesbbq.com. Main courses C$7–C$10 (US$6–US$8/£3.15–£4.50); complete meals C$14–C$33 (US$12–US$28/£6–£15). AE, DC, MC, V. Mon–Thurs 11am–10pm; Fri 11am–midnight; Sat noon–midnight; Sun noon–10pm. Bus: 4, 7, or 10.

The SandBar CASUAL   On Fridays and Saturdays, the bar and patio here fill up with 20-something singles and an assortment of baby boomers; a DJ spins at 9pm. Those who aren't ready to tear into the pickup scene can sink their teeth into a number of fairly decent tapas and entrees. Shrimp and pork dumplings, lettuce wraps, pad thai, and wok dishes provide the Asian component of a menu that spans the globe. Main courses range from cedar-planked grilled salmon to daily pasta and pizza specials. In summer, the third floor patio is fabulous for lazing about in the sunshine.

1535 Johnston St., Granville Island. ℂ **604/669-9030.** www.mysandbar.com. Reservations not accepted for patio. Main courses C$12–C$27 (US$10–US$23/£5–£12); tapas C$6–C$13 (US$5–US$11/£2.70–£6). AE, MC, V. Sun–Thurs 11:30am–10pm; Fri–Sat 11:30am–11pm. Bus: 50 to Granville Island.

The Smoking Dog ✪ FRENCH   To date, the little Kitsilano neighborhood of Yorkville Mews has remained a local secret, perhaps because the few tourists who do venture into this delightful 1-block stretch are immediately confronted with a confusing variety of choices. However, the choice is easy—this bistro with international French-fusion overtones beats all the others when it comes to food. The menu features

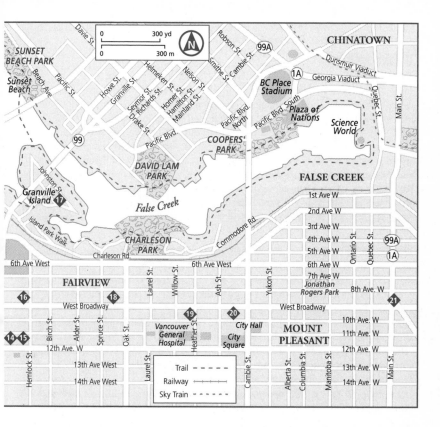

striploin steak with bordelaise sauce, pesto-crusted red snapper, steamed mussels and fries, sandwiches, and pasta. If weather permits, take a seat on the heated patio and enjoy the bustling street life. Enjoy live jazz Wednesday, Friday, and Saturday nights.

1889 W. 1st Ave. ⓒ **604/732-8811.** www.thesmokingdog.com. Main courses C$13–C$19 (US$11–US$16/£6–£9). AE, DC, MC, V. Mon–Fri 11:30am–10:30pm; Sat 5:30–9:30pm. Bus: 2 or 22.

Vij ✦✦✦ INDIAN   Vij doesn't take reservations, as is apparent by the line outside every night, but patrons huddled under the neon sign don't seem to mind since they're treated to tea and *papadums* (a thin bread made from lentils). Inside, the decor is as warm and subtle as the seasonings, which are all roasted, hand-ground, and used with studied delicacy. The menu changes monthly, though some of the more popular entrees remain constants. Recent offerings included pan-fried coriander quail cakes, lemon-ghee marinated grilled chicken breast, and beef shortribs in a cinnamon and red-wine curry. Vegetarian selections abound, including curried vegetable rice pilaf with cilantro cream sauce, and Indian lentils with naan and *raita* (yogurt-mint sauce). The wine and beer list is short but carefully selected. And for teetotalers, Vij has developed a souped-up version of the traditional Indian chai, the chaiuccino. Vij recently opened Rangoli (see below), right next door, for lunch and takeout.

1480 W. 11th Ave. ⓒ **604/736-6664.** www.vijs.ca. Reservations not accepted. Main courses C$20–C$26 (US$17–US$21/£9–£11). AE, DC, MC, V. Daily 5:30–10pm. Closed Dec 24–Jan 8. Bus: 8 or 10.

INEXPENSIVE

Annapurna 🎤 *Value* INDIAN/VEGETARIAN   A Kitsilano favorite, Annapurna's small dining room is hung with dozens of white, red, yellow, and orange rice-paper lamps that emanate a soft, warm glow. The menu is all vegetarian, but with the amazing combinations of Indian spices, herbs, and local vegetables, the dishes are rich and satisfying. Appetizers include samosas, *pakoras,* and lentil dumplings soaked in tangy yogurt with chutney. A variety of breads, such as *paratha,* naan, and *chapatis,* are served piping hot. Entrees such as *aloo-ghobi* (potato curry with cauliflower, onions, and cilantro) or *navrattan korma* (seasonal vegetables simmered in poppy-seed paste, flavored with saffron, aniseed, and sliced almonds) can be prepared from mild to screaming hot. The wine list is small but very reasonably priced.

1812 W. 4th Ave. ⓒ **604/736-5959.** Main courses C$11–C$13 (US$9–US$10/£5–£9). AE, MC, V. Daily 11:30am–10pm. Bus: 4 or 7.

The Naam Restaurant 🎤 *Kids* VEGETARIAN   Back in the '60s, when Kitsilano was Canada's hippie haven, the Naam was tie-dye central. Things have changed since then, but Vancouver's oldest vegetarian and natural-food restaurant still retains a pleasant granola feel, and it's open 24/7. The decor is simple, earnest, and welcoming, and includes well-worn wooden tables and chairs, plants, an assortment of local art, a nice garden patio, and live music every night. The brazenly healthy fare ranges from all-vegetarian burgers, enchiladas, and burritos to tofu teriyaki, Thai noodles, and a variety of pita pizzas. The sesame spice fries are a Vancouver institution. And though The Naam is not quite vegan, they do offer specialties like the macrobiotic Dragon Bowl of brown rice, tofu, sprouts, and steamed vegetables.

2724 W. 4th Ave. ⓒ **604/738-7151.** www.thenaam.com. Reservations accepted on weekdays only. Main courses C$5–C$12 (US$4–US$10/£2.25–£5). AE, MC, V. Daily 24 hr. Live music every night 7–10pm. Bus: 4 or 22.

Rangoli INDIAN   Vij, reviewed above, takes Indian cuisine to inventive new heights and tastes. But Vij is only open for dinner, so right next door you can get lunch and takeout versions of Vij's curries and other specialties. Try lamb stewed in Vij's masala, spicy pulled pork, or beef in garlic and green onion curry. A sweet and savory snacks menu is offered from 4 to 8pm: Rice and *paneer* cakes with fresh mango salsa, vegetable samosas, and warm mango custard are some of the offerings. Rangoli has a hip, simple-looking interior with just a few tables and a lot of stainless steel.

1488 W. 11th Ave. ⓒ **604/736-5711.** www.vijsrangoli.ca. Reservations not accepted. Main courses C$8–C$13 (US$7–US$11/£3.60–£6). AE, DC, MC, V. Daily 11am–8pm. Bus: 8 or 10.

Sha-Lin Noodle House *Kids* CHINESE/DIM SUM   Ever wonder how fresh your noodles really are? At Sha-Lin, you can watch the noodle chef make them right before your eyes. Unique for Vancouver, Sha-Lin is one of the few places where each order of noodles is made from scratch. The chefs mix, knead, toss, stretch, and compress the dough until it almost magically gives way to thin strands. Two or three dishes make a satisfying meal for two; choose from a wide variety of meat and vegetable dishes. For a little entertainment, order the special tea, and watch the server pour it from a meter-long (3-ft.) pot originally designed to allow male servants to maintain a polite distance from an 18th-century Chinese empress.

548 W. Broadway. ✆ **604/873-1816.** Main courses C$5–C$11 (US$4–US$9/£2.25–£5). No credit cards. Lunch Wed–Mon 11:30am–3pm; dinner daily 5:30–9:30pm. Bus: 9.

Sophie's Cosmic Café *(Kids)* FAMILY STYLE/AMERICAN   For a fabulous home-cooked, diner-style breakfast in a laid-back but buzzy atmosphere, come to this Kitsilano landmark. On Sunday morning get here early, or you may have to wait a half-hour or more to get in. You can also have a good, filling lunch or dinner here. Every available space in Sophie's is crammed with toys and knickknacks from the 1950s and 1960s so, understandably, children are inordinately fond of the place. Crayons and coloring paper are always on hand. The menu is simple and includes pastas, burgers and fries, great milkshakes, and a few classic Mexican and "international" dishes, but it's the breakfast menu that draws the crowds.

2095 W. 4th Ave. ✆ **604/732-6810.** www.sophiescosmiccafe.com. Main courses C$5–C$17 (US$4.25–US$14/£2.25–£8). MC, V. Daily 8am–9:30pm. Bus: 4 or 7.

7 The East Side

Many of these "east side" restaurants are on Main Street, which is on the borderlands between upscale west and working-class east. Main thus has some funky urban authenticity to go with its ever-increasing trendiness.

EXPENSIVE

Sun Sui Wah *(★★)* CHINESE/DIM SUM/SEAFOOD   One of the most elegant and sophisticated Chinese restaurants in town, the award-winning Sun Sui Wah is well known for its seafood. Fresh and varied, the catch of the day can include fresh crab, geoduck, scallops, oyster, prawns, and more. Pick your meal from the tank, or order from the menu if you'd rather not meet your food eye-to-eye before it's cooked. Dim sum is a treat, with the emphasis on seafood. Choices abound for meat lovers and vegetarians, though they will miss out on one of the best seafood feasts in town.

3888 Main St. ✆ **604/872-8822.** www.sunsuiwah.com. Main courses C$11–C$50 (US$10–US$42/£5–£22). AE, DC, MC, V. Daily dim sum 10:30am–3pm; dinner 5–10:30pm. Bus: 3.

MODERATE

The Locus Café CASUAL/SOUTHWESTERN   Even if you arrive by your lonesome, you'll soon have plenty of friends because The Locus is a cheek-by-jowl kind of place, filled with a friendly, funky crowd of artsy Mount Pleasant types. The big bar is overhung with "swamp-gothic" lacquer trees and surrounded by a tier of stools with booths and tiny tables. The cuisine originated in the American Southwest and picked up an edge along the way, as demonstrated in the roasted half-chicken with a cumin-coriander crust and sambuca citrus demi-glace. Keep an eye out for fish specials, such as grilled tomba tuna with a grapefruit and mango glaze. The pan-seared calamari makes a perfect appetizer. Bowen Island brewery provides the beer, so quality's high. Your only real problem is catching the eye of the busy bartender.

4121 Main St. ✆ **604/708-4121.** Reservations recommended. Main courses C$9–C$15 (US$8–US$13/£4–£7). MC, V. Mon–Sat 11am–1:30am; Sun 11am–midnight. Bus: 3.

The Reef *(Value)* CARIBBEAN   The "JERK" in the phone number refers to a spicy marinade of bay leaves, scotch bonnets, allspice, garlic, soya, green onions, vinegar, and cloves. The Reef serves a number of jerk dishes, including their signature quarter jerk chicken breast. Other dishes are equally delightful, including a tropical salad of fresh mango, red onions, and tomatoes; shrimp with coconut milk and lime juice; grilled blue marlin; and Trenton spiced ribs. With a glass of wine from the thoughtfully selected list you have good dining at a bargain price. Afternoons, the tiny patio is drenched in sunlight, while in the evenings a DJ spins the sounds of the Islands.

4172 Main St. ℂ **604/874-JERK.** www.thereefrestaurant.com. Main courses C$9–C$17 (US$8–US$14/£4–£8). AE, DC, MC, V. Sun–Wed 11am–midnight; Thurs–Sat 11am–1am. Bus: 3.

8 The North Shore
EXPENSIVE
The Beach House at Dundarave Pier ❀ PACIFIC NORTHWEST   The Beach House offers a panoramic view of English Bay from its waterfront location. Diners on the heated patio get more sunshine, but they miss out on the rich interior of this restored 1912 teahouse. The food is consistently good—innovative, but not so experimental that it leaves the staid West Van burghers gasping for breath. Appetizers include soft-shell crab tempura with salt-and-fire jelly; spicy calamari with ginger; and a salad of crab, shrimp, avocado, and tomato. Entrees have included espresso-crusted pork tenderloin with risotto, pan-fried halibut with artichoke purée, and grilled prawns and scallops. The wine list is award-winning.

150 25th St., West Vancouver. ℂ **604/922-1414.** www.atthebeachhouse.com. Reservations recommended. Main courses C$18–C$36 (US$15–US$31/£8–£16). AE, DC, MC, V. Daily 11am–10pm. Bus: 255 to Ambleside Pier.

Gusto ❀ ITALIAN   West Vancouverites have always had numerous fine-dining options, but for folks in more working-class North Vancouver (to the east of Lions Gate Bridge), times were always tougher. That is until the father-and-son Corsi team opened Gusto just steps from the Lonsdale Quay SeaBus Terminal. The menu focuses on the cuisine of central Italy. To start, try the fresh mozzarella wrapped in prosciutto and radicchio and drizzled with cherry vinaigrette, or the grilled calamari in a tomato coulis. Signature main courses include pistachio-crusted sea bass; duck breast with Frangelico, toasted pine nuts, and grilled orange; and spaghetti quattro, a spicy concoction of minced chicken, black beans, garlic, and chile. The wine list leans heavily toward Italy, offering a good selection of chianti and other table wines.

1 Lonsdale Ave., North Vancouver. ℂ **604/924-4444.** www.quattrorestaurants.com. Reservations recommended. Main courses C$12–C$32 (US$10–US$27/£5–£14). AE, DC, MC, V. Mon–Fri 11:30am–2pm and 5–10pm; Sat–Sun 5–10pm. SeaBus to Lonsdale Quay.

The Salmon House on the Hill ❀ PACIFIC NORTHWEST/SEAFOOD   High above West Vancouver, The Salmon House offers a spectacular view of the city and Burrard Inlet. The rough-hewn cedar walls are adorned with a growing collection of indigenous West Coast art. An alder wood–fired grill dominates the kitchen, lending a delicious flavor to many of the dishes. Start with the Salmon House Sampler, featuring smoked and candied salmon accompanied by fresh salsas, chutneys, and relishes. Entrees include a seared Ahi tuna with a tomato, soy, and cumin barbecue sauce, and alder-grilled B.C. salmon with leeks and rémoulade sauce. Desserts bear little resemblance to early First Nations cuisine: Belgian chocolate mousse and orange crème caramel. The wine list earned an award of excellence from *Wine Spectator*.

2229 Folkstone Way, West Vancouver. ℂ **604/926-3212.** www.salmonhouse.com. Reservations recommended for dinner. Main courses C$13–C$31 (US$11–US$26/£6–£14). AE, DC, MC, V. Mon–Sat 11:30am–2:30pm and 5–10pm; Sun 11am–2:30pm (brunch) and 5–10pm. Bus: 251 to Queens St.

INEXPENSIVE

The Tomahawk Restaurant *Finds* FAMILY STYLE/AMERICAN   This is a typical American-style diner with one critical difference that makes it worth a visit: The Tomahawk is packed with native knickknacks and gewgaws and some truly first-class First Nations art. It all started back in the 1930s when proprietor Chick Chamberlain began accepting carvings from Burrard Band First Nations in lieu of payment. Over the years, the collection just kept growing. So how's the food? Good, in a burgers-and-fries kind of way. Portions are large, burgers are tasty, and milkshakes come so thick the spoon stands up straight like a totem pole.

1550 Philip Ave., North Vancouver. ✆ **604/988-2612.** www.tomahawkrestaurant.com. Reservations not accepted. Main courses C$4.50–C$17 (US$4–US$14/£2–£16). AE, DC, MC, V. Sun–Thurs 8am–9pm; Fri–Sat 8am–10pm. Bus: 239 to Philip Ave.

9 Coffee, Tea, Sweets & Ice Cream

Caffè Artigiano ★★ *Finds*   Absolutely the best lattes in town, in my opinion. The trick is to start with the perfect beans, brew the coffee to an exact temperature, give the steamed milk the respect it deserves, and pour it out ever so slowly, forming a leaf- or heart-shaped pattern in your cup. This is latte-making as an art form. Pop in for a light lunch or pastry, too. The original location at 1101 W. Pender (at Thurlow) in the financial district is less intimate than the digs on Hornby, right across from the Vancouver Art Gallery; the Hornby location has a little outdoor patio perfect for people-watching. A new location is at 740 W. Hastings.

763 Hornby St. ✆ **604/685-5333.** www.caffeartigiano.com. Sweets and sandwiches C$3–C$8 (US$2.50–US$7/£1.35–£3.60). AE, MC, V. Mon–Sat 6:30am–9:30pm; Sun 6:30am–7pm (other locations not open evenings, West Pender not open Sun). Bus: 22.

Caffeine Nation

"I've never seen so much coffee in all my life. The whole town is on a caffeine jag," said Bette Midler, when she performed in Vancouver.

Though the population had been softened up to the idea by a generation of Italian immigrants, the recent fine-coffee explosion started first in Seattle, Vancouver's sister city to the south. The city now has more than 60 of the Seattle-based **Starbucks,** as well as **Blenz, Roastmasters,** and other chain cafes. The Starbucks franchises facing each other on Robson and Thurlow are famed for the movie stars who drop in and the regular crowd of bikers who sit sipping lattes on their hogs. The city's best java joint—fittingly enough—is **Vancouver's Best Coffee,** 2959 W. 4th Ave. (✆ **604/739-2136),** on a slightly funky section of West 4th Avenue at Bayswater.

Nearly as good and far more politically correct is **Joe's Cafe,** 1150 Commercial Dr. (✆ **604/255-1046;** www.joescafebar.com), in the heart of the immigrant- and activist-laden Commercial Drive area, where lesbian activists, Marxist intellectuals, Guatemalan immigrants, and little old Portuguese men all sit and sip their cappuccinos together peacefully.

For the best lattes, see the review above for Caffè Artigiano.

Tea for You?

Everyone knows Vancouver runs on coffee, but now drinking tea has become the latest craze. The quality of tea depends on its growing region, soil, weather, harvesting season and ways of processing. You can see (and taste) the difference at **T**, a tasting boutique located on the West Side at 1568 West Broadway (between Granville and Fir; ⓒ **604/730-8390**; www.tealeaves.com), where over 100 varieties and blends of tea from the four corners of the world are available. Visitors can sample whole leaf, premium leaf iced, and whole leaf pyramid teabags. The boutique also sells spa kits including the popular Jetlag AM and PM packs. **Moonstruck Tea House,** 1590 Coal Harbour Quay (ⓒ **504/602-6609**; www.moonstruckteahouse.com), located across from the Westin Bayshore Resort right on the water, has a vast selection of teas, edible flowers and herbs direct from China's best tea farms. Moonstruck also offers Chinese tea ceremonies for two to four people.

Epicurean Delicatessen Caffè *Finds*   The Epicurean brews a mean espresso, a real Italian *caffè* in Kitsilano. Locals and visitors flock to this tiny neighborhood deli, packing the sidewalk spots on nice days or the cozy small tables inside when the weather turns gray. Italian sweets, biscotti, and sorbet go well with any of the coffees, but for a savory treat, have a peek at the glass display case in the back. Freshly made antipasti, cold cuts, salads, panini sandwiches, and risotto are just some of the delectables available for lunch or takeout. Eat-in guests can sip a glass of wine with the fab food. The menu changes regularly, as the owners try out new recipes.

1898 W. 1st Ave. ⓒ **604/731-5370.** Fax 604/731-5369. Everything under C$10 (US$8/£4.50). MC, V. Daily 8am–9pm. Bus: 22 to Cornwall and Cypress.

La Casa Gelato *Finds*   No self-respecting ice-cream fiend could possibly pass up a visit to La Casa Gelato. Trust me; it's worth the trek out to this obscure industrial area near Commercial Drive, where ice-cream lovers gather for a taste of one or more of the 198 flavors in store. Of course you don't get that many flavors by simply serving up chocolate, vanilla, and strawberry. How about garlic, lavender, durian, basil, or hot chile ice cream, or pear with Gorgonzola sorbet? You're entitled to at least several samples before committing to one or two flavors, so go ahead and be adventurous.

1033 Venables St. ⓒ **604/251-3211.** www.lacasagelato.com. Everything under C$6.50 (US$5.50/£3). MC, V. Daily 10am–11pm. Bus: 10 to Commercial and Venables.

Mink, A Chocolate Cafe *Finds*   Baristas can make a fabulous cup of coffee, but chocolate—both hot and cold—is what Mink is all about. This unique chocolate cafe serves exceptionally fine chocolate beverages made with special spices and ingredients (like chipotle). Their little handcrafted (made in Vancouver) chocolate bars are heavenly, and the bonbons . . . well, try one and you'll know what I mean.

863 W. Hastings St. (at Hornby, on west side of Terminal City Club). ⓒ **604/633-2451.** www.minkchocolates.com. Coffee and chocolate drinks C$3.75–C$5.95 (US$3.20–US$5/£1.75–£2.70); chocolates C$1.50–C$5.25 (US$1.25–US$4.50/£1–£3.60). MC, V. Mon–Fri 8am–6pm; Sat–Sun 10am–6pm. Bus: 10, 16, or 20.

7

Exploring Vancouver

A city perched on the edge of a great wilderness, Vancouver offers unmatched opportunities for exploring the outdoors. But within the city limits, Vancouver is intensely urban, with buzzy sidewalk cafes and busy shopping streets. The forest of high-rises ringing the central part of the city reminds some visitors of New York or Shanghai, and Chinatown inevitably invites comparisons to San Francisco. But comparisons with other places begin to pall as you come to realize that Vancouver is entirely its own creation: a young, self-confident, sparklingly beautiful city like no other place on earth.

1 Neighborhoods to Explore

The best way to get to know a city is to explore its different neighborhoods. Here's a quick guide on where to go and what to look for in Vancouver. For more in-depth explorations, turn to the neighborhood walking tours in chapter 8.

DOWNTOWN

Most of Vancouver's commercial and office space is found in a square patch starting at Nelson Street and heading north to the harbor, with Homer Street and Burrard Street forming the east and west boundaries respectively. Many of the city's best hotels are also found in this area, clustering near Robson Square and the water's edge. **Canada Place,** on the waterfront facing Burrard Inlet, is the city's huge convention center and cruise-ship terminal. The most interesting avenues for visitors are Georgia, Robson, and Granville streets. **Georgia Street**—in addition to being the prime address for class-A commercial property—is where you'll find the Vancouver Art Gallery (p. 118), the Coliseum-shaped Vancouver Public Library (p. 155), and the Pacific Centre regional shopping mall. **Robson Street** is Trend Central, crammed with designer boutiques, restaurants, and cafes. Rapidly gentrifying **Granville Street** is the home of bars, clubs, theaters, pubs, and restaurants (along with one or two remaining porn shops to add that key touch of seedy authenticity).

THE WEST END

This was Vancouver's first upscale neighborhood, settled in the 1890s by the city's budding class of merchant princes. By the 1930s, most of the grand Edwardian homes had become rooming houses, and in the late 1950s some of the Edwardians came down and high-rise apartments went up. The resulting neighborhood owes more to the verticality of Manhattan than to the sprawling cities of the west, though the lush landscaping, gardens, and gorgeous beaches along English Bay and Stanley Park are pure Northwest. All the necessities of life are contained within the West End's border, especially on **Denman** and **Robson streets:** great cafes, good nightclubs, many and varied bookshops, and some of the city's best restaurants. That's part of what makes it such a sought-after

Downtown Vancouver Attractions

Canada Place **8**
Dr. Sun Yat-sen Classical
  Chinese Garden **10**
H.R. MacMillan Space Centre **4**
Lookout! Harbour Centre
  Tower **7**
Museum of Anthropology **3**
Science World at Telus World
  of Science **11**
Steam Clock **9**
UBC Botanical Garden &
  Nitobe Japanese Garden **3**
Vancouver Aquarium Marine
  Science Centre **1**
Vancouver Art Gallery **5**
Vancouver Centennial
  Police Museum **10**
Vancouver Maritime Museum **2**
Vancouver Museum **4**
Vancouver Public Library **6**

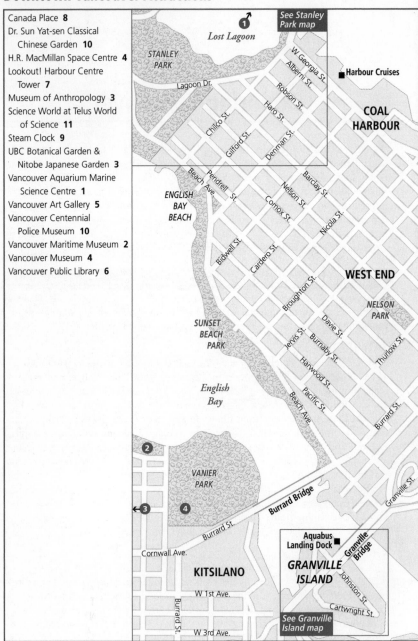

See Stanley
Park map

Lost Lagoon

STANLEY
PARK

Lagoon Dr.

W. Georgia St.

Alberni St.

Robson St.

Haro St.

Chilco St.

Gilford St.

Denman St.

■ Harbour Cruises

COAL
HARBOUR

Beach Ave.

Pendrell St.

Barclay St.

Nelson St.

Comox St.

Nicola St.

ENGLISH
BAY
BEACH

Bidwell St.

Cardero St.

Broughton St.

WEST END

NELSON
PARK

SUNSET
BEACH
PARK

Davie St.

Jervis St.

Burnaby St.

Harwood St.

Thurlow St.

English
Bay

Pacific St.

Beach Ave.

Burrard St.

②

VANIER
PARK

←③

④

Burrard Bridge

Granville St.

Burrard St.

Cornwall Ave.

KITSILANO

W 1st Ave.

Burrard St.

W 3rd Ave.

Aquabus
Landing Dock ■

Granville
Bridge

GRANVILLE
ISLAND

Johnston St.

Cartwright St.

See Granville
Island map

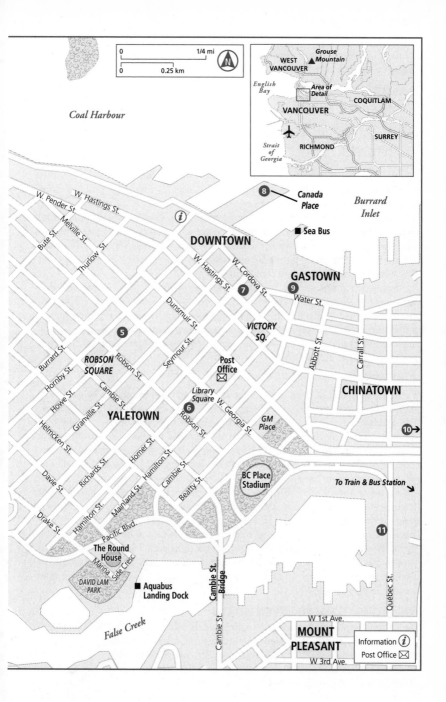

Coal Harbour

WEST VANCOUVER ▲ Grouse Mountain

English Bay

Area of Detail

VANCOUVER **COQUITLAM**

Strait of Georgia ✈

RICHMOND **SURREY**

0   1/4 mi
0   0.25 km

W. Hastings St.

W. Pender St.

Melville St.

Bute St.

Thurlow St.

Thurlow St.

8 Canada Place

Burrard Inlet

ⓘ

■ Sea Bus

DOWNTOWN

W. Hastings St.

W. Cordova St.

GASTOWN

Dunsmuir St.

7 **9** Water St.

VICTORY SQ.

5

Burrard St.

Hornby St.

Howe St.

ROBSON SQUARE

Robson St.

Cambie St.

Granville St.

Seymour St.

Abbott St.

Carrall St.

CHINATOWN

Post Office ⊠

YALETOWN

Library Square

6

Robson St.

W. Georgia St.

GM Place

10→

Helmcken St.

Davie St.

Richards St.

Homer St.

Hamilton St.

Mainland St.

Cambie St.

Beatty St.

To Train & Bus Station ↘

Drake St.

Hamilton St.

Pacific Blvd.

BC Place Stadium

11

Marinaside Cresc.

The Round House

DAVID LAM PARK

■ Aquabus Landing Dock

Cambie St. Bridge

Cambie St.

Québec St.

False Creek

W 1st Ave.

MOUNT PLEASANT

Information ⓘ
Post Office ⊠

W 3rd Ave.

address, but it's also the little things, like the street trees, the mix of high-rise condos and sturdy old Edwardians, and the way that, in the midst of such an urban setting, you now and again stumble on a view of the ocean or the mountains.

GASTOWN

The oldest section of Vancouver, Gastown has a charm that shines through the souvenir shops and panhandlers. It can be seedy—druggies and winos hang out around its fringes—but it's recently become home to some great new restaurants and stores. It's worth visiting, though, because it's the only section of the city that has the feel of an old Victorian town—the buildings stand shoulder to shoulder, and cobblestones line the streets. The current Gastown was built from scratch just a few months after an 1886 fire wiped out the entire city. (Photographs of the time show proper-looking men in black coats selling real estate out of tents erected on the still-smoking ashes.) Also, rents in Gastown have stayed low, so it's still the place to look for a new and experimental art gallery, a young fashion designer setting up shop, or a piece of beautiful, hand-carved First Nations art in one of the galleries along **Water** and **Hastings streets.** It's also the setting for the famous Steam Clock on Water Street (see "Gastown & Chinatown" walking tour in chapter 8).

Alcohol has always been a big part of Gastown's history. The neighborhood is named for a saloonkeeper—Gassy Jack Deighton—who, according to local legend, talked the local mill hands into building a saloon as Vancouver's first structure in return for all the whiskey they could drink. Nowadays, Gastown is still liberally endowed with pubs and clubs—it's one of two or three areas where Vancouverites congregate when the sun goes down.

CHINATOWN

Even though much of Vancouver's huge Asian population has moved out to Richmond, Chinatown remains a kick because it hasn't become overtly touristy. The low-rise buildings in this lively community are painted in bright colors, and sidewalk markets abound. For the tens of thousands of Cantonese-speaking Canadians who live in the surrounding neighborhoods, Chinatown is simply the place they go to shop. And for many others who have moved to more outlying neighborhoods, it's still one of the best places to come and eat. One of North America's more populous Chinatowns, the area was settled about the same time as the rest of Vancouver, by migrant laborers brought in to build the Canadian Pacific Railway. Many white settlers resented the Chinese labor, and race riots periodically broke out. At one point, Vancouver's Chinatown was surrounded with Belfast-like security walls. By the 1940s and 1950s, however, the area was mostly threatened with neglect. The 1970s saw a serious plan to tear the whole neighborhood down and put in a freeway, but a huge protest stopped that, and now the area's future seems secure. For visitors, the fun is to simply wander, look, and taste.

YALETOWN & FALSE CREEK NORTH

Vancouver's former meatpacking and warehouse district, Yaletown has been converted to an area of apartment lofts, nightclubs, restaurants, high-end furniture shops, and a fledgling multimedia biz. It's a relatively tiny area, and the main streets of interest are **Mainland, Hamilton,** and **Davie.** For visitors, it features some interesting cafes and patios, some high-end shops, and a kind of gritty urban feel. This old-time authenticity provides an essential anchor to the brand-new bevy of towers that have risen in the past 10 years on **Pacific Boulevard** along the north edge of False Creek. Officially (and unimaginatively) called False Creek North, the area is more often referred to as "the Concorde lands" after the developer, or "the Expo lands" after the world's fair held in 1986 on the land where the towers now stand. Where the shiny newness of Concorde can prove a little disconcerting, gritty Yaletown provides the antidote. And vice versa. The two neighborhoods are slowly melding into one wonderful whole.

GRANVILLE ISLAND

Part crafts fair, part farmers market, part artist's workshop, part mall, and part industrial site, Granville Island seems to have it all. Some 20 years ago, the federal government decided to try its hand at a bit of urban renewal, so they took this piece of industrial waterfront and redeveloped it into . . . well, it's hard to describe. But everything you could name is here: theaters, pubs, restaurants, artists' studios, bookstores, crafts shops, an art school, a hotel, a cement plant, and lots and lots of people. One of the most enjoyable ways to experience the Granville Island atmosphere is to head down to the **Granville Island Public Market,** grab a latte (and perhaps a piece of cake or pie to boot), then wander outside to enjoy the view of the boats, the buskers, and the children endlessly chasing flocks of squawking seagulls.

KITSILANO

Hard to believe, but in the 1960s Kitsilano was a neighborhood that had fallen on hard times. Nobody respectable wanted to live there—the 1920s homes had all been converted to cheap rooming houses—so hippies moved in. The neighborhood became Canada's Haight-Ashbury, with coffeehouses, head shops, and lots of incense and long hair. Once the boomer generation stopped raging against the machine, they realized that Kitsilano—right next to the beach, but not quite downtown—was a very groovy place to live indeed, and a fine place to own property. Real estate began an upward trend that has never stopped, and "Kits" became thoroughly yuppified. Nowadays, it's a fun place to wander. You will discover great bookstores and trendy furniture and housewares shops, lots of consignment clothing stores, snowboard shops, coffee everywhere, and lots of places to eat (every third storefront is a restaurant). The best parts of Kitsilano are the stretch of **West 4th Avenue** between Burrard and Balsam streets, and **West Broadway** between Macdonald and Alma streets. Oh, and **Kits Beach,** of course, with that fabulous heated saltwater swimming pool.

COMMERCIAL DRIVE

Known as "The Drive" to Vancouverites, Commercial Drive is the 12-block section from Venables Street to East 6th Avenue. The Drive has a less glitzy, more down-to-earth, fading counterculture feel to it. It's an old immigrant neighborhood that, like everyplace else in Vancouver, has been rediscovered. The first wave of Italians left old-fashioned, delightfully tacky cafes such as **Calabria,** 1745 Commercial Dr. (© **604/253-7017**), and **Caffe Amici,** 1344 Commercial Dr. (© **604/255-2611**). More recent waves of Portuguese, Hondurans, and Guatemalans have also left their mark. And lately, lesbians, vegans, and artists have moved in—the kind of folks who love to live in this kind of milieu. Shops and restaurants reflect the mix. Think Italian cafe next to the Marxist bookstore across from the vegan deli selling yeast-free Tuscan bread. After the relentless see-and-be-seen scene in the West End, it's nice to come out to The Drive for a bit of unpretentious fun.

SHAUGHNESSY

Distances within the Shaughnessy neighborhood aren't conducive for a comfortable stroll, but Shaughnessy is a great place to drive or bike, especially in the spring when trees and gardens are blossoming. Designed in the 1920s as an enclave for Vancouver's budding elite, this is Vancouver's Westmount or Nob Hill. Thanks to the stranglehold Shaughnessy exerts on local politics—every second mayor hails from this neighborhood—traffic flow is carefully diverted away from the area, and it takes a little bit of driving around to find your way in. It's an effort worth making, however, if only to see the stately homes and monstrous mansions, many of which are now featured in film shoots or rented by Hollywood movie stars while they're in town filming. This is also home to many old Vancouver families with a pioneer past. To find the neighborhood, look on the map for the area of curvy and convoluted streets between Cypress and Oak streets and 12th and 32nd avenues. The center of opulence is the Crescent, an elliptical street to the southwest of Granville and 16th Avenue.

RICHMOND

Twenty years ago, Richmond was mostly farmland with a bit of sleepy suburb. Now it's Asia West, an agglomeration of shopping malls geared to the new—read: rich, educated, and successful—Chinese immigrant. The residential areas of the city are not worth visiting (unless tract homes are your thing), but malls like the **Aberdeen Mall** or the **Yao Han Centre** are something else. It's like getting into your car in Vancouver and getting out in Singapore.

STEVESTON

Steveston, located at the southwest corner of Richmond by the mouth of the Fraser River, once existed for nothing but salmon. Fishermen set out from its port to catch the migrating sockeye, and returned to have the catch cleaned and canned. Huge processing plants covered its waterfront, where thousands of workers gutted millions of fish. Much of that history is reprised in the **Gulf of Georgia Cannery National Historic Site,** near the wharf at Bayview Street and 4th Avenue (© **604/664-9009**). Since the fishery was automated long ago, Steveston's waterfront has been fixed up. There are public fish sales, charter trips up the river or out to the Fraser delta, first-rate restaurants, fish and chips, and, above all, a laid-back, small-town atmosphere.

PUNJABI MARKET

India imported. Most of the businesses on this 4-block stretch of Main Street, from 48th up to 52nd Avenue, are run by and cater to Indo-Canadians, primarily Punjabis. The area is best seen during business hours, when the fragrant scent of spices wafts out from food stalls, and the sound of Hindi pop songs blares from hidden speakers. Young brides hunt through sari shops or seek out suitable material in discount textile outlets. **Frontier Cloth House,** 6695 Main St. (© **604/325-4424**), specializes in richly colored silk saris, shawls, fabrics, and costume jewelry.

2 The Top Attractions

DOWNTOWN & THE WEST END

Canada Place ⑅⑅   If you've never been to Vancouver, this is a good place to orient yourself and see some of what makes B.C.'s largest city so special. (Or you may arrive here on a cruise ship, in which case this will be your first introduction to Vancouver.) With its five tall Teflon sails and bowsprit jutting out into Burrard Inlet, Canada Place is meant to resemble a giant sailing ship. Inside it's a convention center on one level and a giant cruise-ship terminal below, with the Pan Pacific Hotel (p. 70) perched on top. Around the perimeter is a promenade with plaques at regular intervals explaining the

Stanley Park

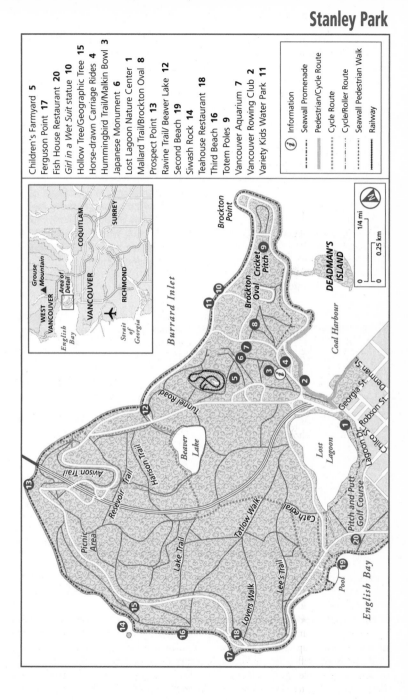

Children's Farmyard **5**
Ferguson Point **17**
Fish House Restaurant **20**
Girl in a Wet Suit statue **10**
Hollow Tree/Geographic Tree **15**
Horse-drawn Carriage Rides **4**
Hummingbird Trail/Malkin Bowl **3**
Japanese Monument **6**
Lost Lagoon Nature Center **1**
Mallard Trail/Brockton Oval **8**
Prospect Point **13**
Ravine Trail/ Beaver Lake **12**
Second Beach **19**
Siwash Rock **14**
Teahouse Restaurant **18**
Third Beach **16**
Totem Poles **9**
Vancouver Aquarium **7**
Vancouver Rowing Club **2**
Variety Kids Water Park **11**

(i) Information
--·--·-- Seawall Promenade
───── Pedestrian/Cycle Route
········· Cycle Route
─·─·─· Cycle/Roller Route
·········· Seawall Pedestrian Walk
▪▪▪▪▪▪▪▪ Railway

Stanley (Fun) Park

Stanley Park is the scene of several yearly events that have become part of the collective consciousness of Vancouverites. Every December, the Miniature Railway becomes the **Bright Nights Christmas Train** and runs through a forest illuminated with thousands of festive lights. In October, the train is transformed into the **Halloween Ghost Train,** with actors portraying vampires and ghouls scaring delighted passengers as the train puffs through the forest. From June to August, **Dance at Dusk** takes place Monday through Wednesday (on good-weather evenings) at 7 to 9:30pm, near Ceperley Playground's red fire engine. No partner is required, all ages are welcome, instruction is provided, and it's free. Summer is also the time to enjoy **Theatre Under the Stars,** a Stanley Park tradition at the Malkin Bowl since 1934. In mid-July thousands of Vancouverites participate in the **Walk With the Dragon** festival, following a giant Chinese dragon along the entire length of the seawall. See the Stanley Park website (www.city.vancouver.bc.ca/parks) for dates and details.

sights and providing historical tidbits. A huge expansion to add more convention space and additional docking facilities is currently underway. You can walk all the way around on a pedestrian promenade that offers wonderful views across Burrard Inlet to the North Shore peaks and toward nearby Stanley Park. Continue around the promenade, and you'll get great city views and be able to see the older, low-rise buildings of Gastown, where Vancouver began. Bus sightseeing tours begin here, there's a giant-screen **Imax Theatre** (© **604/682-IMAX**), and the Tourism Vancouver Touristinfo Centre is right across the street. Walking Tour 2 in chapter 8 begins at Canada Place and takes you into nearby Gastown and Chinatown.

Canada Place at the end of Burrard St. Promenade daily 24 hr. Bus: 1 or 5.

Stanley Park 🌟🌟🌟 *Kids*   The green jewel of Vancouver, Stanley Park is a 400-hectare (1,000-acre) rainforest jutting out into the ocean from the edge of the busy West End. Exploring the second-largest urban forest in Canada is one of Vancouver's quintessential experiences. However, portions of Stanley Park were damaged by a windstorm (see the box "Stanley Park Damaged by Windstorm," below) that felled some 5,000 to 10,000 trees and left big gaps in the forest canopy.

The park, created in 1888, is still filled with towering western red cedar and Douglas fir, manicured lawns, flower gardens, placid lagoons, and countless shaded walking trails that meander through it all. The famed **seawall** 🌟🌟🌟 runs along the waterside edge of the park, allowing cyclists and pedestrians to experience the magical interface of forest, sea, and sky. One of the most popular free attractions in the park is the **collection of totem poles** 🌟🌟🌟 at Brockton Point, most of them carved in the 1980s to replace the original ones that were placed in the park in the 1920s and 1930s. The area around the totem poles features open-air displays on the Coast Salish First Nations and a small gift shop/visitor information center.

The park is home to lots of wildlife, including beavers, coyotes, bald eagles, blue herons, cormorants, trumpeter swans, brant geese, ducks, raccoons, skunks, and gray squirrels imported from New York's Central Park decades ago and now quite at home in the Pacific Northwest. (No, there are no bears.) For directions and maps, brochures, and exhibits on the nature and ecology of Stanley Park, visit the **Lost Lagoon Nature House** (© **604/257-8544;** open 10am–7pm July 1 to Labour Day, weekends only outside this period; free admission). On Sundays they offer Discovery Walks of the park. Equally nature-focused but with way more wow is the **Vancouver Aquarium** ⚡⚡ (see below). The **Stanley Park's Children's Farm** (© **604/257-8530**) is a petting zoo with peacocks, rabbits, calves, donkeys, and Shetland ponies. Next to the petting zoo is **Stanley Park's Miniature Railway** ⚡ (© **604/257-8531**), a diminutive steam locomotive that pulls passenger cars on a circuit through the woods.

Swimmers head to **Third Beach** and **Second Beach** (p. 134), the latter with an outdoor pool beside English Bay. For kids there's a free **Spray Park** near Lumberman's Arch, where they can run and splash through various water-spewing fountains. Perhaps the best way to explore the park is to rent a bike (p. 136) or in-line skates, and set off along the seawall. If you decide to walk, remember the free shuttle bus that circles the park every 15 minutes, allowing passengers to alight and descend at most of the park's many attractions, as well as the wonderful **horse-drawn carriage ride** ⚡⚡ that begins near Lost Lagoon (see above). Of the three restaurants located in the park, the best is **The Fish House in Stanley Park** (p. 96), where you can have lunch, afternoon tea, or dinner.

For a complete listing of attractions, operating hours, admission fees, and a poststorm restoration report, check the website.

Stanley Park. © **604/257-8400.** www.city.vancouver.bc.ca/parks. Free admission; charge for individual attractions. Parking: entire day C$5 (US$4.25/£2.25) summer, C$3 (US$2.50/£1.35) winter. Park does not close. Bus: 23, 35, or 135; free "Around the Park" shuttle bus circles the park at 15-min. intervals June 13–Sept 23 (visitors can get off and on at 14 points of interest).

Vancouver Aquarium Marine Science Centre ⚡⚡ *Kids*   One of North America's largest and best, the Vancouver Aquarium houses more than 8,000 marine species. In the icy-blue Arctic Canada exhibit, you can see beluga whales whistling and blowing water at unwary onlookers. Human-size freshwater fish inhabit the Amazon rainforest gallery, while overhead, an hourly rainstorm is unleashed in an atrium that houses three-toed sloths, brilliant blue and green poison tree frogs, and piranhas. Regal angelfish glide through a re-creation of Indonesia's Bunaken National Park coral reef,

---

Stanley Park Damaged by Windstorm

In the early morning hours of December 15, 2006, a major windstorm struck Stanley Park and left, after 2 short hours of gale-force winds, a level of devastation that had not been seen since Hurricane Frieda in 1962. The gusting winds blew down an estimated 5,000 to 10,000 trees, mostly on the west side, leveling more than 41 hectares (100 acres) of the park's 243 hectares (600 acres) of forest. Large waves and falling trees also damaged sections of the seawall. Restoration costs have been put at C$12 million (US$10.2 million/£5.4 million). Obviously, cleanup efforts are going to take some time, and it will be decades before Stanley Park's forest regenerates to anything like what it was. In the meantime, Stanley Park is still a place you will want to visit—all of the attractions, such as the totem poles and the horse-drawn carriage rides, are still accessible. You may, however, find that some hiking trails in the wilder sections of the park, and portions of the seawall are still closed.

360 Degrees of Vancouver

The most popular (and most touristed) spot from which to view Vancouver's sky-line and surrounding topography is high atop the space needle observation deck at the **Lookout!, Harbour Centre Tower** ☆, 555 W. Hastings St. (ⓒ **604/689-0421**). It's a great place for first-time visitors who want a panorama of the city. The glass-encased Skylift whisks you up 166m (545 ft.) to the rooftop deck in less than a minute. The 360-degree view is remarkable (yes, that is Mt. Baker looming above the southeastern horizon), but the signage could be a lot better. Skylift admission is C$13 (US$11/£6) for adults, C$11 (US$9/£5) for seniors, C$9 (US$8/£4) for students and youth 11 to 17, C$6 (US$5/£2.70) children 4 to 10, and free for children under 4. It's open daily in summer from 8:30am to 10:30pm and in win-ter from 9am to 9pm, and tickets are valid for the entire day.

and blacktip reef sharks menacingly scour the Tropical Gallery's waters. (Call for the shark and sea otter feeding times.) The Pacific Canada exhibit is dedicated to sea life indigenous to B.C. waters, including the Pacific salmon and the giant Pacific octopus. On the Marine Mammal Deck are sea otters, Steller sea lions, beluga whales, and a Pacific white-sided dolphin. During regularly scheduled shows, the aquarium staff explains marine mammal behavior while working with these impressive creatures.

For a substantial extra fee (C$150/US$127/£67 per person; C$210/US$178/£94 adult and one child age 8–12), you can have a behind-the-scenes Beluga Encounter, helping to feed these giant white cetaceans, then head up to the Marine Mammal deck to take part in the belugas' regular training session. Beluga encounters are available daily from 9 to 10:30am, with extra encounters on weekends between 2 and 4pm. On the more reasonably priced Trainer Tours (C$25–C$35/US$21–US$30/£11–£16 per person; C$40–C$50/US$34–US$42/£18–£22 adult and one child age 8–12), you go on a 45-minute behind-the-scenes tour, helping an aquarium trainer prepare the daily rations and then feeding the sea otters or harbor seals. Trainer tours are available daily but times vary. Call ⓒ **800/931-1186** to reserve all of these programs ahead of time. Children must be 8 or older to participate. *Note:* If you have smaller children, I rec-ommend the sea otters; Steller sea lions are enormous and sometimes ill-tempered.

Stanley Park. ⓒ **604/659-FISH**. www.vanaqua.org. Admission C$20 (US$17/£9) adults; C$15 (US$13/£7) seniors, students, and youths 13–18; C$12 (US$10/£6) children 4–12; free for children 3 and under. Summer daily 9:30am–7pm; winter daily 10am–5:30pm. Bus: 135; "Around the Park" shuttle bus June–Sept only. Parking C$6 (US$5/£2.70) summer, C$3 (US$2.50/£1.35) winter.

Vancouver Art Gallery ☆☆   Designed as a courthouse by B.C.'s leading early-20th-century architect Francis Rattenbury (the architect of Victoria's Empress Hotel and the Parliament buildings), and renovated into an art gallery by B.C.'s leading late-20th-century architect Arthur Erickson, the VAG is an excellent stop to see what sets Canadian and West Coast art apart from the rest of the world. Along with an impres-sive collection of paintings by B.C. native **Emily Carr** ☆☆☆ are examples of a unique Canadian art style created during the 1920s by members of the "Group of Seven," which included Vancouver painter Fred Varley. The VAG also hosts rotating exhibits of contemporary sculpture, graphics, photography, and video art from around the world. Geared to younger audiences, the Annex Gallery offers rotating presentations of visually exciting educational exhibits.

CLOSED
due to
accidental demolition

WEGEN BISSIGEN
EICHHÖRNCHEN GESCHLOSSEN

CERRADO
CABRAS

Κλειστό
Μετεωρίτες

プール も
POOL CLOSED
ELECTRIC EELS
閉鎖中

Hotel
closed for
facelifting

FERMÉ POUR
RAISON
DE GRÈVE
DES BONNES

FECHADO!
POR CAUSA DE
ATAQUES DOS CROCODILOS

— I don't speak sign language.

A hotel can close for all kinds of reasons.

Our Guarantee ensures that if your hotel's undergoing construction, we'll let you know in advance. In fact, we cover your entire travel experience. See www.travelocity.com/guarantee for details.

travelocity
You'll never roam alone.

750 Hornby St. ℂ **604/662-4719** or 604/662-4700. www.vanartgallery.bc.ca. Admission C$20 (US$17/£9) adults; C$15 (US$13/£7) seniors; C$14 (US$12/£6) students; C$6.50 (US$5/£3) children 5–12; C$49 (US$42/£22) family; Tues 5–9pm by donation. Daily 10am–5:30pm (Tues, Thurs until 9pm). SkyTrain: Granville. Bus: 3.

GASTOWN & CHINATOWN

Dr. Sun Yat-Sen Classical Chinese Garden ★★   This small reproduction of a Classical Chinese scholar's garden truly is a remarkable place, but to get the full effect, it's best to take the free guided tour. Untrained eyes will only

Countdown Clock

The giant Omega countdown clock installed in 2007 at the Vancouver Art Gallery counts down the remaining days, hours, minutes, and seconds to the Opening Ceremony for both the 2010 Olympic and Paralympic Winter Games. The clock represents Canadian and West Coast themes and has become a signature landmark in Vancouver.

see a pretty pond surrounded by bamboo and oddly shaped rocks. The engaging guides, however, can explain this unique urban garden's Taoist yin-yang design principle, in which harmony is achieved through dynamic opposition. To foster opposition (and thus harmony) in the garden, Chinese designers place contrasting elements in juxtaposition: Soft-moving water flows across solid stone; smooth, swaying bamboo grows around gnarled immovable rocks; dark pebbles are placed next to light pebbles in the paving. Moving with the guide, you discover the symbolism of intricate carvings and marvel at the subtle, ever-changing views from covered serpentine corridors. This is one of two Classical Chinese gardens in North America (the other is in Portland, Oregon) created by master artisans from Suzhou, the garden city of China.

578 Carrall St. ℂ **604/689-7133**. www.vancouverchinesegarden.com. C$8.75 (US$7/£4) adults; C$7 (US$6/£3.15) seniors and students; free for children 5 and under; C$20 (US$17/£9) family pass. Free guided tour included. May–June 14 and Sept daily 10am–6pm; June 15–Aug daily 9:30am–7pm; Oct–Apr Tues–Sun 10am–4:30pm. Bus: 19 or 22.

Vancouver Centennial Police Museum   If you have a real fascination with crime or an interest in the history of the Vancouver police department, this museum will occupy an hour of your time; if not, I wouldn't recommend a visit. It's a well-meaning, old-fashioned place housed in the old Vancouver Coroner's Court (where actor Errol Flynn was autopsied in 1959 after dropping dead in the arms of a 17-year-old girl) and dedicated to memorializing some of the best cops and worst crimes in the city's short but colorful history. The confiscated illegal-weapons display is hair-raising, along with the morgue, a simulated autopsy room (with pieces of damaged body parts in specimen bottles), and forensics lab (sleuths of all ages can partake in the Forensic Science program on Sun noon–4pm). More fun and a lot more fascinating is the 2-hour **Sins of the City Walking Tour** ★, which departs from the museum Tuesdays at 10am and Saturdays at 4pm (late May to late Sept) and covers (or uncovers) the history of vice in a 10-block area around the museum. Tour cost is C$12 (US$10/£5) for adults, C$10 (US$8/£4.50) seniors and students; it's essential to make reservations 1 day ahead. If you take the walking tour, you can visit the museum for free.

240 E. Cordova St. ℂ **604/665-3346**. www.vancouverpolicemuseum.ca. Admission C$7 (US$5.50/£3.15) adults; C$5 (US$4.25/£1.90) seniors, students, youths 7–13; C$20 (US$17/£9) families. Mon–Sat 9am–5pm. Bus: 4 or 7.

THE WEST SIDE

Granville Island ★★★ (Kids)   Almost a city within a city, Granville Island is a good place to browse away a morning, an afternoon, or a whole day. You can wander

In a Summer Garden

Every Friday evening at 7:30pm from mid-July through the first weekend in September, the Dr. Sun Yat-Sen Classical Chinese Garden is the scene of musical performances and dances. The eclectic repertoire includes classical, Asian, world, Gypsy jazz, Slavic soul, and fusion music. Shows cost C$15 (US$13/£7). Visit the website for a full listing of concerts.

through a busy public market jammed with food stalls, shop for crafts, pick up some fresh seafood, enjoy a great dinner, watch the latest theater performance, rent a yacht, stroll along the waterfront, or simply run through the sprinkler on a hot summer day; it's all there and more. If you only have a short period of time, make sure you spend at least part of it in the **Granville Island Public Market** ☆☆☆, one of the best all-around markets in North America.

Once a declining industrial site, Granville Island started transforming in the late 1970s when the government encouraged new, people-friendly developments. Maintaining its original industrial look, the former warehouses and factories now house galleries, artist studios, restaurants, and theaters; the cement plant on the waterfront is the only industrial tenant left. Access to Granville Island is by Aquabus from the West End, Yaletown, or Kitsilano (see "By Miniferry," in chapter 4; the Aquabus drops you at the public market) or by foot, bike, or car across the bridge at Anderson Street (access from W. 2nd Ave.). Avoid driving over on weekends and holidays—you'll spend more time trying to find a parking place than in the galleries. Check the website for upcoming events or stop by the information center, behind the Kids Market. *Note:* Also see Walking Tour 3 in chapter 8 (p. 154).

If you can't bear to leave the island, consider staying at the **Granville Island Hotel** (p. 80). One of the best-kept secrets in town, this hotel is reasonably priced, has a fabulous waterfront location, and is steps from all the island has to offer. Even if you don't stay, it's worth stopping by the hotel's brewpub restaurant, the Dockside Brewery Company, for a brew with a view.

Located on the south shore of False Creek, under the Granville St. Bridge. For studio and gallery hours and other information about Granville Island, contact the information center at ℂ 604/666-5784. www.granville-island.net. Public market daily 9am–7pm. For information on getting to Granville Island, see "By Miniferry," in chapter 4. Bus: 50.

H. R. MacMillan Space Centre ☆ *Kids* In the same building as the Vancouver Museum, the space center and observatory has hands-on displays and exhibits that will delight budding astronomy buffs and their parents (or older space buffs and their children). Displays are highly interactive: In the Cosmic Courtyard, you can try designing a spacecraft or maneuvering a lunar robot. Or, punch a button and get a video explanation of the *Apollo 17* manned-satellite engine that stands before you. The exciting **Virtual Voyages Simulator** ☆☆ takes you on a voyage to Mars—it's a thrilling experience for adults and kids. In the GroundStation Canada Theatre, video presentations explore Canada's contributions to the space program and space in general. The StarTheatre shows movies—many of them for children—on an overhead dome. The Planetarium Star Theatre features exciting laser shows in the evening.

1100 Chestnut St., in Vanier Park. ℂ 604/738-7827. www.spacecentre.ca. Admission C$15 (US$13/£7) adults; C$11 (US$9/£5) seniors, students, youths 11–18; C$11 (US$9/£5) children 5–10; C$7 (US$6/£3.15) children under 5; C$45

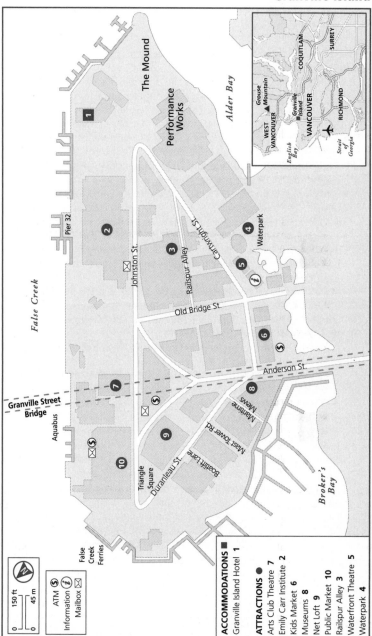

Granville Island

The Mound

Performance Works

Alder Bay

Pier 32

Johnston St.

Cartwright St.

Railspur Alley

Waterpark

Old Bridge St.

Anderson St.

Maritime Mews

Granville Street Bridge

Aquabus

Mast Tower Rd.

Boatlift Lane

Triangle Square

Duranleau St.

Broker's Bay

False Creek

False Creek Ferries

150 ft

45 m

ATM $
Information (i)
Mailbox ⊠

ACCOMMODATIONS ■
Granville Island Hotel **1**

ATTRACTIONS ●
Arts Club Theatre **7**
Emily Carr Institute **2**
Kids Market **6**
Museums **8**
Net Loft **9**
Public Market **10**
Railspur Alley **3**
Waterfront Theatre **5**
Waterpark **4**

WEST VANCOUVER
Grouse Mountain
COQUITLAM
SURREY
Granville Island
VANCOUVER
English Bay
RICHMOND
Strait of Georgia

Granville's Greatest Hits

Even though the bustling **Public Market** ☆☆☆ makes a fine destination in itself, Granville Island offers much more. To really get a feel for this neighborhood, stroll along the side streets and explore the alleys and lanes away from the main entrance. Check out the recommended attractions below.

- RailSpur Alley's 12 artist studios are perfect for browsing; stop in at **Al'Arte Silk** in the Alley Gallery (1369 RailSpur Alley; ℂ **604/879-7235**) to see some of the beautifully hand-painted wearable silk art; check out the wares at **Artisan Sake** (1339 Railspur Alley; ℂ **604/685-7253**), Canada's first boutique premium sake winery; or pause at the **Railspur Alley Café and Bistro** (1363 RailSpur Alley; ℂ **604/669-0724**) for a latte and pastry.

- Art exhibits in the North Building at the **Emily Carr Institute of Art + Design** (1399 Johnston St.; ℂ **604/844-3800**; www.eciad.ca) showcase the works of the institute's grads and students. You may be looking at the next Andy Warhol. Media and Concourse Galleries are free and open daily 10am to 5pm; the Charles H. Scott Gallery, showing exhibits of international work, is open Monday to Friday noon to 5pm, Saturday and Sunday 10am to 5pm.

- In summer, check the **Performance Works** (ℂ **604/687-3020**; www.gi culturalsociety.org) schedule for free outdoor Shakespearean plays, or see what's at the **Arts Club Theatre** (ℂ **604/687-1644**; www.artsclub.com) or **Waterfront Theatre** (ℂ **604/685-1731**).

- Paddle off into the sunset by renting a kayak from one of the marinas on the west side of the island. Beginners can take lessons or head out on a guided tour. **Ecomarine Ocean Kayak Centre** (ℂ **604/689-7575**; www. ecomarine.com) has everything to get you started. A 3-hour kayak lesson for C$69 (US$59/£31) teaches you the basic strokes. Or explore the waters of False Creek and English Bay on a 2½-hour tour with a guide for C$54 (US$46/£24). Experienced paddlers can rent single or double kayaks (C$45/ US$38/£20 single kayak; C$85/US$72/£38 double kayak for 2 hr.).

- Granville Island is one big playground. On a rainy day, duck into the **Kids Only Market** (daily 10am–6pm) to check out toys, kites, clothes, art supplies, and an indoor play area, or visit the **Granville Island Museum** (ℂ **604/ 683-1939**) to admire its collection of model boats and miniature trains. The museum is open Tuesday to Sunday from 10am to 5:30pm; admission is C$7.50 (US$6.50/£3.40) adults, C$6 (US$5/£2.70) seniors and students, free for children 4 and under. On warm days, the free **waterpark** is the place to be. Open daily (weather permitting) from 10am to 6pm, late May until Labour Day.

(US$38/£20) families (up to 5, maximum 2 adults). Evening laser shows C$11 (US$9/£5) each. Tues–Sun 10am–5pm; evening laser shows Thurs 9:30pm, Fri–Sat 9:30pm and 10:45pm. Closed Dec 25. Bus: 22.

Museum of Anthropology ☆☆☆   This isn't just any old museum. In 1976, architect Arthur Erickson created a classic native post-and-beam-style structure out of poured concrete and glass to house one of the world's finest collections of West Coast native art.

Enter through doors that resemble a huge, carved, bent-cedar box. Artifacts from different coastal communities flank the ramp leading to the Great Hall's **collection of totem poles.** Haida artist Bill Reid's cedar bear and sea wolf sculptures sit at the Cross Roads; Reid's masterpiece, ***The Raven and the First Men,*** is worth the price of admission all by itself. The huge carving in glowing yellow cedar depicts a Haida creation myth, in which Raven—the trickster—coaxes humanity out into the world from its birthplace in a clamshell. Some of Reid's fabulous jewelry creations in gold and silver are also on display.

The **Masterpiece Gallery**'s argillite sculptures, beaded jewelry, and hand-carved ceremonial masks lead the way to the Visible Storage Galleries, where more than 15,000 artifacts are arranged by culture. You can open the glass-topped drawers to view small treasures and stroll past larger pieces housed in tall glass cases.

Also at the museum is the somewhat incongruous Koerner Ceramics Gallery, a collection of European ceramics that—while interesting—is really only there because old man Koerner had the money to endow the wing to hold his collection.

After visiting the galleries, take a walk around the grounds behind the museum. Overlooking Point Grey are two **longhouses** built according to the Haida tribal style, resting on the traditional north-south axis. Ten hand-carved totem poles stand in attendance along with contemporary carvings on the longhouse facades. ***Note:*** You might want to combine your visit to the Museum of Anthropology with the nearby UBC Botanical Garden and Nitobe Japanese Garden (see below).

6393 NW Marine Dr. (at Gate 4). ☎ 604/822-5087. www.moa.ubc.ca. Admission C$9 (US$8/£4) adults; C$7 (US$6/£3.15) seniors, students, children 6–18; free for children under 6; free Tues 5–9pm. Summer Wed–Mon 10am–5pm, Tues 10am–9pm; winter Wed–Sun 11am–5pm, Tues 11am–9pm. Closed Dec 25–26. Bus: 4 or 99 (10-min. walk from UBC bus loop).

Science World at Telus World of Science ★ (Kids)

Science World is impossible to miss: It's the big blinking geodesic dome (built for Expo '86 and now partnered with Telus, a telephone company, hence the branded name) on the eastern end of False Creek. Inside, it's a hands-on scientific discovery center where you and your kids can light up a plasma ball, walk through a 160-sq.-m (1,722-sq.-ft.) maze, wander through the interior of a camera, create a cyclone, watch a zucchini explode as it's charged with 80,000 volts, stand inside a beaver lodge, play in wrist-deep magnetic liquids, create music with a giant synthesizer, and watch mind-blowing three-dimensional slide and laser shows as well as other optical effects. Science World is loaded with first-rate adventures for kids from toddler age to early teens; you'll want to spend at least a couple of hours here. Throughout the day, special shows, many with nature themes, are presented in the OMNIMAX Theatre—a huge projecting screen equipped with surround sound.

1455 Quebec St. ☎ 604/443-7443. www.scienceworld.ca. Admission C$16 (US$14/£7) adults; C$13 (US$11/£6) seniors, students, C$11 (US$9/£4) children 4–17; free for children under 4; C$54 (US$46/£24) family pass for 6 related people. Combination tickets additional C$5 (US$4.25/£2.25) for OMNIMAX film. Sept–June Mon–Fri 10am–5pm, Sat–Sun 10am–6pm; July–Aug daily 10am–6pm; holidays 10am–6pm. SkyTrain: Main St.–Science World.

Steam Clock (Kids)

The Steam Clock in Gastown is a favorite photo op for tourists, but you're not missing much if you miss it. Built by horologist Raymond Saunders in 1977 (based on an 1875 design), it's the only steam clock in the world, powered by steam from an underground system of pipes that supply heat to many downtown buildings. The clock is supposed to sound its whistles (playing "The Westminster Chimes") every quarter-hour as the steam shoots out from vents at the top. Sometimes, however, it simply steams with no musical accompaniment. It's a stop on my Gastown and Chinatown Walking Tour 2, chapter 8.

Gastown, at the intersection of Water and Cambie sts. Free.

UBC Botanical Garden & Nitobe Japanese Garden ✿

Serious plant lovers will love the University of British Columbia. The prime attraction on campus, besides the must-see Museum of Anthropology (see p. 122), is the 28-hectare (69-acre) **UBC Botanical Garden,** home to more than 10,000 species of trees, shrubs, and flowers grouped into a B.C. native garden, a physic (or medicinal) garden, a food garden, and several others. You can also peruse the excellent plant and seed store (*Note:* You can't bring plants in soil across the U.S. border, or back into most countries, including the U.K.). Give yourself at least an hour if you want to explore this garden; an audio guide is available for C$4 (US$3.40/£1.80). Nearby is the **Nitobe Memorial Garden,** a beautiful traditional Japanese garden considered among the top five Japanese gardens in North America and one of the most authentic Tea and Stroll Gardens outside of Japan. Cherry blossoms peak in April and May, the irises bloom in June, and autumn brings colorful leaf displays. Both gardens are free from mid-October to mid-March.

Botanical Garden: 6804 SW Marine Dr., Gate 8. ℭ 604/822-4208. www.ubcbotanicalgarden.org. Admission C$7 (US$6/£3.15) adults; C$5 (US$3.50/£2.25) seniors, C$3 (US$2.50/£1.35) students, youth; free for children under 6. Nitobe Japanese Garden: 6565 NW Marine Dr., Gate 4. ℭ 604/822-6038. www.nitobe.org. Admission C$5 (US$3.50/£2.25) adults, C$3 (US$2.50/£1.35) seniors, C$2.50 (US$2.10/£1.10) students. Dual pass for both gardens C$10 (US$7/£4.50). Mid-Mar to mid-Oct daily 10am–6pm; mid-Oct to mid-Mar daily 10am–5pm. Botanical Garden closed late Dec to early Jan.

Vancouver Maritime Museum *Kids*

This is a well-meaning but dull museum unless you're a real nautical nut. The museum's main attraction is the 1920s RCMP Arctic patrol vessel *St. Roch,* the first ship to find the Northwest Passage, preserved with most of its original stores and equipment onboard. Tours of the *St. Roch* are popular with kids—they get to clamber around the boat poking and prodding stuff.

The other half of the museum displays model ships, maps, prints, and a number of permanent exhibits. If the weather is pleasant, walk across the front lawn at the edge of False Creek to Heritage Harbour, where the museum keeps a collection of vintage boats. You can also catch the miniferry there to Granville Island or the West End.

1905 Ogden Ave., in Vanier Park. ℭ 604/257-8300. www.vancouvermaritimemuseum.com. Admission C$10 (US$8/£4.50) adults, C$7.50 (US$6/£3.40) seniors and youths 6–19, free for children under 6, C$25 (US$21/£11) families. Daily 10am–5pm (closed Mon Labour Day to last Mon in May). Bus: 22, then walk 4 blocks north on Cypress St. Boat: False Creek ferries dock at Heritage Harbour.

Vancouver Museum

Located in the same building as the H. R. MacMillan Space Centre (see p. 120), the Vancouver Museum is dedicated to the city's history, from its days as a native settlement and European outpost to its 20th-century maturation into a modern urban center. The exhibits have been remounted and revitalized to make them more interesting to the casual visitor. Of most importance here is the wonderful collection of First Nations art and artifacts. Hilarious, campy fun abounds in the 1950s Room, where a period film chronicles "Dorothy's All-Electric Home." Next to this is another fun, and socially intriguing, room devoted to Vancouver's years as a hippie capital, with film clips, commentary, and a replica hippie apartment.

1100 Chestnut St. ℭ 604/736-4431. www.vanmuseum.bc.ca. Admission C$10 (US$8/£4.50) adults, C$8 (US$7/£3.60) seniors, C$6 (US$5/£2.25) youths 4–19. Daily 10am–5pm (Thurs 10am–9pm). Closed Mon Sept–Apr. Bus: 22, then walk 3 blocks south on Cornwall Ave. Boat: Granville Island Ferry to Heritage Harbour.

NORTH VANCOUVER & WEST VANCOUVER

Capilano Suspension Bridge & Park 🐾   Vancouver's first and oldest tourist trap (built in 1889), this attraction still works—mostly because there's still something inherently thrilling about walking across a narrow, shaky walkway 69m (226 ft.) above a canyon floor, held up by nothing but a pair of tiny cables. Set in a beautiful 8-hectare (20-acre) park about 15 minutes from downtown, the suspension bridge itself is a 135m-long (443-ft.) cedar-plank and steel-cable footbridge, which sways gently above the Capilano River. Visitors nervously cross above kayakers and salmon shooting the rapids far below. A new attraction called **"Treetops Adventure"** features more bridges and walkways, only these are attached to giant tree trunks 24m (79 ft.) above the rainforest floor.

In addition to the bridge is a **carving center** where native carvers demonstrate their skill; an exhibit describing the region's natural history; guides in period costume who recount Vancouver's frontier days; and a pair of overpriced and poorly serviced restaurants. Though overall it's quite well done, it's hard to justify the exorbitant entrance fee, and the summer crowds can be off-putting. If the admission price is a roadblock, you can have a similar experience at the nearby Lynn Canyon Suspension Bridge, which is almost as high, set in a far larger forest, almost untouristed, and absolutely free (see "The *Other* Suspension Bridge," p. 128).

3735 Capilano Rd., North Vancouver. 🕐 604/985-7474. www.capbridge.com. Admission winter/summer C$24–C$27 (US$20–US$23/£11–£12) adults, C$22–C$25 (US$19–US$12/£10–£11) seniors, C$19–C$21 (US$16–US$18/£8–£9) students, C$14–C$16 (US$12–US$14/£6–£7) youths 13–16, C$7.50–C$8.50 (US$6.50–US$7/£3.40–£3.80) children 6–12, free for children under 6. Hours change monthly; generally, May–Sept daily 8:30am–dusk, Oct–Apr daily 9am–5pm. Closed Dec 25. Bus: 246 from downtown Vancouver, 236 from Lonsdale Quay SeaBus terminal. Car: Hwy. 99 north across Lions Gate Bridge to exit #14 on Capilano Rd.

Grouse Mountain 🐾🐾 *(Kids)*   Once a local ski hill, Grouse Mountain has developed into a year-round mountain recreation park that claims to be the number-one attraction in Vancouver. It's fun if you're sports minded or like the outdoors; if not, you might find it disappointing. Located only a 15-minute drive from downtown, the **SkyRide gondola** 🐾🐾 transports you to the mountain's 1,110m (3,642-ft.) summit. (Hikers can take a near vertical trail called the Grouse Grind. See "Doin' the Grouse Grind" box, below.) On a clear day, the **view** 🐾🐾🐾 from the top is the best around: you can see the city and the entire lower mainland, from far up the Fraser Valley east across the Gulf of Georgia to Vancouver Island. In the lodge, **Theater in the Sky** 🐾 shows wildlife movies. Outside, in the winter, you can ski and snowboard (26 runs, 13 runs for night skiing/snowboarding; drop-in ski lessons available), go snowshoeing, skate on the highest outdoor rink in Canada, take a brief "sleigh ride" (behind a huge

---

Doin' the Grouse Grind

The "Grouse Grind" trail, a popular 2.9km (1.8-mile) trail commonly referred to by locals as "Mother Nature's Stairmaster," generally opens late spring or early summer. Over 110,000 hikers per year take on the challenge of the rugged terrain and steep climb. By the time you reach the plateau, your ascent will have gained 853m (2,800 ft.). Average completion time is usually 1½ hours, with the fastest completion time just over 26 minutes. The best part is that once you reach the top, you can then take the tram back down for just C$5 (US$4/£2.25).

snow-cat), and the kids can play in a special snow park. In warmer weather, you can wander forest trails, take a scenic chair ride, enjoy a lumberjack show or Birds in Motion demonstrations, visit the Refuge for Endangered Wildlife, or ride on the mountainbike trails. Most of these activities are included in the rather exorbitant price of your Skyride ticket; you have to pay extra for a lift ticket and equipment rentals. Additional activities include helicopter tours and tandem paragliding. Casual and fine-dining options, and a Starbucks, are in the lodge.

6400 Nancy Greene Way, North Vancouver. (©) 604/984-0661. www.grousemountain.com. SkyRide C$30 (US$25/£13) adults, C$28 (US$24/£13) seniors, C$17 (US$14/£8) youths 13–18, C$11 (US$9/£5) children 5–12, free children 4 and under. Full day ski-lift tickets C$45 (US$38/£20) adults, C$35 (US$28/£16) senior and youth, C$20 (US$17/£9) children, C$125 (US$106/£56) family (2 adults, 2 children under 18). SkyRide free with advance Observatory Restaurant reservation. Daily 9am–10pm. Bus: 232, then transfer to bus no. 236. SeaBus: Lonsdale Quay, then transfer to bus no. 236. Car: Hwy. 99 north across Lions Gate Bridge, take North Vancouver exit to Marine Drive, then up Capilano Road for 5km (3 miles). Parking C$3 (US$2.50/£1.35) for 2 hr. in lots below SkyRide.

3 Vancouver's Plazas & Parks

OUTDOOR PLAZA

Unlike many cities, Vancouver's great urban gathering places stand not at the center but on the periphery, on two opposite sides of the **seawall** that runs around Stanley Park: **English Bay,** on the south side of Denman Street, and **Coal Harbour,** on the northern, Burrard Inlet side, are where Vancouverites go to stroll and be seen. On warm sunny days, these two areas are packed. Another waterside gathering spot is **Canada Place** (p. 114), built for Expo '86 and now being enlarged. Built in the shape of a cruise ship and serving as the city's cruise-ship terminal (as well as a huge convention center with a giant hotel on top for good measure), it has wide walkways all around it that are super for strolling and offers fabulous views of the mountains.

Designed by architect Arthur Erickson to be Vancouver's central plaza, **Robson Square**—downtown, between Hornby and Howe streets from Robson to Smithe streets—has never really worked. The square, which anchors the north end of the Provincial Law Courts complex designed by Erickson in 1972, suffers from a basic design flaw: It's sunk one story below street level, making it difficult to see and to access. The Law Courts complex, which sits on a higher level, raised above the street, is beautifully executed with shrubbery, cherry trees, sculptures, and a triple-tiered waterfall, but Robson Square below is about as appealing as a drained swimming pool. Just opposite Robson Square, however, the steps of the **Vancouver Art Gallery** are a great people place, filled with loungers, political agitators, and old men playing chess. It just goes to show that grandiose urban theory and urban design, especially back in the 1970s, doesn't always take the human element into account.

Library Square—a few blocks east from Robson Square at the corner of Robson and Homer streets—is an example of a new urban space that does work. It's been popular with locals since it opened in 1995. People sit on the steps, bask in the sunshine, read, harangue passersby with half-baked political ideas, and generally seem to enjoy themselves.

PARKS & GARDENS

Park and garden lovers are in heaven in Vancouver. The wet, mild climate is ideal for gardening, and come spring the city blazes with blossoming cherry trees, rhododendrons, camellias, azaleas, and spring bulbs. And roses in summer. Gardens are everywhere. For general information about Vancouver's parks, call (©) **604/257-8400,** or try www.parks.vancouver.bc.ca. For information on **Stanley Park** ✸✸✸, the queen of them all, see p. 116.

On the West Side you'll find the magnificent **UBC Botanical Garden,** one of the largest living botany collections on the West Coast, and the sublime **Nitobe Japanese Garden** ✸; for descriptions of both, see p. 124.

In Chinatown, the **Dr. Sun Yat-Sen Classical Chinese Garden** ✸✸ (p. 119) is a small, tranquil oasis in the heart of the city, built by artisans from Suzhou, China; right next to it, accessed via the Chinese Cultural Centre on Pender Street, is the pretty (and free) **Dr. Sun Yat-Sen Park,** with a pond, walkways, and plantings.

On the West Side, **Queen Elizabeth Park**—at Cambie Street and W. 33rd Avenue—sits atop a 150m-high (492-ft.) extinct volcano and is the highest urban vantage point south of downtown, offering panoramic views in all directions (although leafy deciduous trees now block some of the best views). Along with the rose garden in Stanley Park, it's Vancouver's most popular location for wedding-photo sessions, with well-manicured gardens and a profusion of colorful flora. There are areas for lawn bowling, tennis, pitch-and-putt golf, and picnicking. The **Bloedel Conservatory** (✆ **604/257-8584**) stands next to the park's huge sunken garden, an amazing reclamation of an abandoned rock quarry. A 42m-high (138-ft.) domed structure, the conservatory houses a tropical rainforest with more than 100 plant species as well as free-flying tropical birds. Admission to the conservatory is C$4.50 (US$4/£2) for adults, with discounts for seniors and children. Take bus no. 15 to reach the park.

VanDusen Botanical Gardens, 5251 Oak St., at West 37th Avenue (✆ **604/878-9274;** www.vandusengarden.org), is located just a few blocks from Queen Elizabeth Park and the Bloedel Conservatory. In contrast to the flower fetish displayed by Victoria's famous Butchart Gardens (see chapter 14, "Exploring Victoria"), Vancouver's 22-hectare (54-acre) botanical garden concentrates on whole ecosystems. From trees hundreds of feet high down to the little lichens on the smallest of damp stones, the gardeners at VanDusen attempt to re-create the plant life of a number of different environments. Depending on which trail you take, you may find yourself wandering through the Southern Hemisphere section, the Sino-Himalayan garden, or the Northern California sequoia garden. Should all this tree gazing finally pall, head for the farthest corner of the garden, where you'll find a devilishly difficult Elizabethan garden maze. Admission April through September C$8.25 (US$7/£4) adults, C$6 (US$5/£2.70) seniors, C$6.25 (US$5/£2.80) youth 13 to 18, C$4.25 (US$3.60/£1.90) children 6 to 12, C$19 (US$16/£9) families, free for children under 6. Admission is about C$2 less from October through March. Open daily 10am to dusk. Take bus no. 17. *Note:* Be aware that the garden lost hundreds of trees in the December 2006 windstorm that also devastated Stanley Park.

Adjoining UBC on the city's west side at Point Grey, **Pacific Spirit Regional Park,** called the **Endowment Lands** by longtime Vancouver residents, is the largest green space in Vancouver. Comprising 754 hectares (1,863 acres) of temperate rainforest, marshes, and beaches, the park includes nearly 35km (22 miles) of trails ideal for hiking, riding, mountainbiking, and beachcombing.

Across the Lions Gate Bridge, six provincial parks delight outdoor enthusiasts year-round. Good in winter or for those averse to strenuous climbing is the publicly maintained **Capilano River Regional Park,** 4500 Capilano Rd. (✆ **604/666-1790**), surrounding the Capilano Suspension Bridge & Park (p. 125). Hikers can follow a gentle trail by the river for 7km (4.3 miles) down the well-maintained **Capilano trails**

Finds **The *Other* Suspension Bridge**

Lynn Canyon Park, in North Vancouver between Grouse Mountain and Mount Seymour Provincial Park on Lynn Valley Road, offers a free alternative to the Capilano Suspension Bridge. True, the **Lynn Canyon Suspension Bridge** ✦ is both shorter and a little lower than Capilano (p. 125), but the waterfall and swirling whirlpools in the canyon below add both beauty and a certain fear-inducing fascination. Plus, it's free.

The park is located is a gorgeous 247-hectare (610-acre) rainforest of cedar and Douglas fir, laced throughout with walking trails. It's also home to an **Ecology Centre** (3663 Park Rd.; ✆ **604/981-3103**), which presents natural history films, tours, and displays that explain the local ecology. Staff members lead frequent walking tours. The center is open daily from 10am to 5pm (Sat–Sun Oct–May noon–4pm). The park itself is open from 7am to 7pm in spring and fall, 7am to 9pm in summer, and 7am to dusk in winter; it's closed December 25 and 26 and January 1. To get there, take the SeaBus to Lonsdale Quay, then transfer to bus no. 229; by car, take the Trans-Canada Highway (Hwy. 1) to the Lynn Valley Road exit (about a 20-min. drive from downtown), and follow Lynn Valley Road to Peters Road, where you turn right. The park's cafe serves sit-down and takeout meals.

Six kilometers (3¾ miles) up Lynn Valley Road from the highway is the **Lynn Headwaters Regional Park** (✆ **604/985-1690** for trail conditions), one of the best places close to the city to experience the breathtaking nature of the Northwest. Until the mid-1980s, this was inaccessible wilderness and bear habitat. The park and the bears are now managed by the Greater Vancouver Regional Parks Department. Some of the 12 marked trails of various levels of difficulty meander by the riverbank, while others climb steeply up to various North Shore peaks, and one trail leads to a series of cascading waterfalls.

to the Burrard Inlet and the Lions Gate Bridge, or about a mile upstream to **Cleveland Dam,** a launching point for white-water kayakers and canoeists.

The **Capilano Salmon Hatchery,** on Capilano Road (✆ **604/666-1790**), is on the river's east bank about .5km (⅓ mile) below the Cleveland Dam. Approximately two million Coho and Chinook salmon are hatched annually in glass-fronted tanks connected to the river by a series of channels. You can observe the hatching fry (baby fish) before they depart for open waters, as well as the mature salmon that return to the Capilano River to spawn (Sept–Dec are best viewing times). Admission is free, and the hatchery is open daily from 8am to 7pm (until 4pm in the winter). Drive across Lions Gate Bridge and follow the signs to North Vancouver and the Capilano Suspension Bridge. Or take the SeaBus to Lonsdale Quay and transfer to bus no. 236; the trip takes less than 45 minutes.

Eight kilometers (5 miles) west of Lions Gate Bridge on Marine Drive West, West Vancouver, is **Lighthouse Park** ✦. This 74-hectare (183-acre) rugged-terrain forest has 13km (8 miles) of groomed trails and—because it has never been clear-cut—some of the largest and oldest trees in the Vancouver area. One of the paths leads to the 18m

(59-ft.) **Point Atkinson Lighthouse,** on a rocky bluff overlooking the Strait of Georgia and a fabulous view of Vancouver. It's an easy trip on bus no. 250. For information about other West Vancouver parks, call © **604/925-7200** weekdays.

Driving up-up-up the mountain from **Lighthouse Park** will eventually get you to the top of **Cypress Provincial Park.** Stop halfway at the scenic viewpoint for a sweeping vista of the Vancouver skyline, the harbor, the Gulf Islands, and Washington State's Mount Baker, which peers above the eastern horizon. The park is 12km (7½ miles) north of Cypress Bowl Road and the Highway 99 junction in West Vancouver. Cypress Provincial Park has an intricate network of trails maintained for hiking during the summer and autumn and for downhill and cross-country skiing during the winter.

Rising 1,430m (4,692 ft.) above Indian Arm, **Mount Seymour Provincial Park,** 1700 Mt. Seymour Rd., North Vancouver (© **604/986-2261**), offers another view of the area's Coast Mountains range. The road to this park roams through stands of Douglas fir, red cedar, and hemlock. Higher than Grouse Mountain, Mount Seymour has a spectacular view of Washington State's Mount Baker on clear days. It has challenging hiking trails that go straight to the summit, where you can see Indian Arm, Vancouver's bustling commercial port, the city skyline, the Strait of Georgia, and Vancouver Island. The trails are open all summer for hiking; during the winter, the paths are maintained for skiing, snowboarding, and snowshoeing. Mount Seymour is open daily from 7am to 10pm.

HISTORIC LANDMARKS & ATTRACTIONS

The **Burnaby Village Museum,** 6501 Deer Lake Ave., Burnaby (© **604/293-6501;** www.burnabyvillagemuseum.ca), is a 3.5-hectare (8¾-acre) re-creation of the town as it might have appeared in the 1920s. You can walk along boardwalk streets among costumed townspeople, shop in a general store, ride a vintage carousel, peek into an authentic one-room schoolhouse, and visit a vintage ice-cream parlor that's been in the same location since the turn of the 20th century. At Christmastime, the whole village is aglow in lights and Victorian decorations. Admission is C$10 (US$8/£4.50) for adults; C$7.50 (US$6.50/£3.40) for seniors, students, and youths 13 to 18; C$5 (US$4.25/£2.25) for children 6 to 12; and free for children under 6. It's open daily early May through early September from 11am to 4:30pm; November 24 through December 12 noon to 5pm; December 13 through January 1 from noon to 8pm; closed December 24 and 25. From the Metrotown Skystation take bus no. 110 to Deer Lake.

The **Fort Langley National Historic Site,** 23433 Mavis Ave., Fort Langley (© **604/513-4777;** www.pc.gc.ca/fortlangley), is the birthplace of British Columbia. In 1827, the Hudson's Bay Company established this settlement to supply its provincial posts. Costumed craftspeople demonstrate blacksmithing, coopering, and woodworking, bringing this landmark back to life. It's open year-round, daily from 10am to 5pm March through October; call or visit the website for winter hours. Admission is C$7.25 (US$6.20/£3.25) for adults, C$6 (US$5/£2.70) for seniors, C$3.50 (US$3/£1.60) for children 6 to 16, and free for children under 6; a family pass is C$18 (US$15/£8). To get there, take the SkyTrain to Surrey Central Station and transfer to bus no. 501. *Note:* The main street of Fort Langley Village, Glover Road, is packed with antiques shops, a bookstore, and cafes, and it's only a 2-minute stroll away.

See also **Gulf of Georgia Cannery National Historic Site,** described under the Steveston section in "Neighborhoods to Explore" on p. 114.

4 Especially for Kids

Pick up copies of the free monthly newspapers *B.C. Parent,* 4479 W. 10th Ave., Vancouver, B.C. V6R 4P2 (© **604/221-0366;** www.bcparent.com); and *West Coast Families,* 8-1551 Johnston St., Vancouver, B.C. V6H 3R9 (© **604/689-1331;** www. westcoastfamilies.com). *West Coast Families'* centerfold, "Fun in the City," and event calendar list all current events, including **CN IMAX** shows at Canada Place Pier, **OMNIMAX** (© **604/443-7443**) shows at Science World at Telus World of Science (p. 123), and free children's programs. Both publications, and Tourism Vancouver's **Kids' Guide,** are available at Granville Island's Kids Market and at neighborhood community centers throughout the city.

To give kids an overview of the city, take the fun trolley tour offered by **Vancouver Trolley Company** (© **888/451-5581** or 604/801-5515; www.vancouvertrolley.com). Gas-powered trolleys run through Downtown, Chinatown, the West End, and Stanley Park (for more info, see "Organized Tours," below).

Stanley Park ★★★ (p. 116) offers a number of attractions for children, including a fabulous and free **Spray Park** near Lumberman's Arch. **Stanley Park's Children's Farm** (© **604/257-8531**) has peacocks, rabbits, calves, donkeys, and Shetland ponies. Next to the petting zoo is Stanley Park's **Miniature Railway** ★ (© **604/257-8531**), a diminutive steam locomotive with passenger cars that runs on a circuit through the woods. The zoo and railway are open from 11am to 4pm daily June through early September, plus Christmas week and on weekends October through March depending on weather. Admission for the petting zoo or the miniature railroad is C$5.50 (US$4.70/£2.50) for adults, C$3.75 (US$3.20/£1.70) for seniors, C$4 (US$3.40/£1.80) for youths 13 to 18, and C$2.75 (US$2.40/£1.25) for kids 2 to 12. **Second Beach** on the park's western rim has a playground, a snack bar, and an immense heated oceanside **pool** ★ (© **604/257-8371**), open from May through September. Admission is C$4.85 (US$4/£2.20) for adults, C$3.40 (US$3/£1.50) for seniors, C$3.65 (US$3.10/£1.65) for youths 13 to 18, and C$2.45 (US$2/£1.10) for children 6 to 12. Kids will also be impressed with the collection of giant **totem poles** ★★★ in Stanley Park, and the entire family will enjoy the **horse-drawn carriage rides** ★★★ that begin near Lost Lagoon (p. 117).

Also in Stanley Park, the **Vancouver Aquarium Marine Science Centre** ★★ (p. 117) has sea otters, sea lions, whales, and numerous other marine creatures, as well as many exhibits and special programs geared toward children.

Right in town, **Science World at Telus World of Science** (p. 123) is a terrific interactive kids' museum where budding scientists can get their hands into everything.

A trip to **Granville Island** ★★★ will delight kids, and there are a couple of specific places kids really enjoy. Granville Island's **Kids Market,** 1496 Cartwright St. (© **604/ 689-8447**), is open daily from 10am to 6pm. Playrooms and shops filled with toys, books, records, clothes, and food are all child-oriented. At **Granville Island's Water Park and Adventure Playground,** 1496 Cartwright St., kids can really let loose with movable water guns and sprinklers. They can also have fun on the water slides or in the wading pool. The facilities are open during the summer daily (weather permitting) from 10am to 6pm. Admission is free; changing facilities are nearby at the False Creek Community Centre (© **604/257-8195**).

Across Burrard Inlet on the North Shore, **Maplewood Farm,** 405 Seymour River Place, North Vancouver (© **604/929-5610;** www.maplewoodfarm.bc.ca), has more than 200 barnyard animals (from cows to chickens) living on its 2-hectare (5-acre) farm, which is open daily year-round. A few working farms once operated in the area but were put out of business by competition from the huge agricultural concerns in Fraser River valley. The parks department rescued this one and converted it into an attraction. The ticket booth (a former breeding kennel) sells birdseed for feeding the ducks and other fowl. The farm also offers pony rides. Special events include the summertime Sheep Fair, the mid-September Farm Fair, 101 Pumpkins Day in late October, and the Country Christmas weekend. The farm is open daily April through mid-September (closed Mon the rest of the year) from 10am to 4pm. Admission is C$4.75 (US$4/£2.15) for adults, C$2.75 (US$2.40/£1.25) for seniors and children. Take bus no. 210 and transfer to the no. 211 or 212.

Greater Vancouver Zoo, 5048 264th St., Aldergrove (© **604/856-6825;** www. greatervancouverzoo.com), located 48km (30 miles) east of downtown Vancouver (about a 45-min. drive), is a lush 48-hectare (119-acre) reserve filled with lions, tigers, ostriches, buffalo, elk, antelope, zebras, giraffes, a rhino, and camels; 124 species in all. The zoo also has food service and a playground. It's open daily 9am to 4pm from October through March; 9am to 7pm from April through September. Admission is C$16 (US$14/£7) for adults, C$13 (US$11/£6) for seniors and children 3 to 15, and free for children under 3. Take the Trans-Canada Highway to Aldergrove, exit 73; parking is C$3 (US$2.50/£1.35) per day.

Walk high above the rushing waters at the **Capilano Suspension Bridge & Park** (p. 125) and the **Lynn Canyon Suspension Bridge** (p. 128). In winter, **Mount Seymour Provincial Park** (p. 140) and **Grouse Mountain Resort** (p. 140) offer ski programs for kids and adults; in summer, both are great for hikes.

A 45-minute drive north of Vancouver, the **B.C. Museum of Mining,** Highway 99, Britannia Beach (© **800/896-4044;** www.bcmuseumofmining.org), is impossible to miss. Located at the head of Howe Sound, it's marked by a 235-ton truck parked in front. During the summer it offers guided tours of the old copper mine, demonstrations of mining techniques, and even a gold-panning area where anyone can try straining gravel for the precious metal. It's open daily from the first Sunday in May to Thanksgiving from 9am to 5:30pm; the rest of the year it's closed on weekends. Call ahead for the tour schedule; allow about 1½ to 2 hours. Admission is C$15 (US$12/£7) for adults; C$12 (US$10/£5.50) for seniors, students, and youths; and C$50 (US$42/£22) for families; it's free for children under 5.

A whale-watching excursion is one of the most exciting adventures you can give a kid. See "Wildlife-Watching" later in this chapter for information.

5 Organized Tours

If you don't have the time to arrange your own sightseeing tour, let the experts take you around Vancouver. They will escort you in a bus, trolley, double-decker bus, seaplane, helicopter, boat, ferry, taxi, vintage car, or horse-driven carriage. Please note that the 6% General Services Tax (GST) may be applied to the tour prices listed below.

AIR TOURS

Baxter Aviation Adventure Tours ✭✭✭ (1075 West Waterfront; © **800/661-5599** or 604/683-6525; www.baxterair.com), operates daily floatplane flights from its downtown Vancouver terminal next to Canada Place cruise-ship terminal. Floatplanes are single-prop, six-seater planes that take off and land on water. The 20-minute "Vancouver Scenic" tour (C$95/US$81/£43 per person) flies over Stanley Park and all around the metro region, giving you an unparalleled bird's-eye view of the magnificent terrain;

the 5-hour "Whistler Mountain Resort" tour (C$379/US$322/£171 per person for groups of four) includes a 3-hour stopover. Other tours will take you to Victoria, glacial lakes, and prime fly-fishing and whale-watching spots. The 6-hour "Victoria and Butchart Gardens" tour (C$419/US$346/£189 per person for a group of four) flies you across the Strait of Georgia to Vancouver Island, where you have a 4-hour stopover.

Harbour Air (© 800/665-0212 or 604/274-1277; www.harbour-air.com) is on Coal Harbour just west of the Canada Place Pier. Thirty-minute seaplane flights over downtown Vancouver, Stanley Park, and the North Shore are C$99 (US$84/£45) per person. Longer tours to alpine lakes, glaciers, and nearby islands, as well as regularly scheduled flights to Victoria, Nanaimo, and Prince Rupert, are also available.

From April through September, **Helijet Charters** (© 800/987-4354 or 604/270-1484; www.helijet.com), offers a variety of daily tours that depart from their terminal next to Canada Place and their helipad on top of Grouse Mountain. The "Coastal Scenic Tour" is a 20-minute tour of the city, Stanley Park, and North Shore mountains for C$159 (US$135/£72) per person.

BOAT TOURS

Harbour Cruises, Harbour Ferries, no. 1, north foot of Denman Street (© 604/688-7246; www.boatcruises.com), will take you on a 2½-hour **Sunset Dinner Cruise,** including a buffet meal and onboard entertainment; cost for adults, seniors, and students is C$70 (US$59/£32), C$60 (US$51/£27) for children 2 to 11. The cruise leaves at 7pm May through October. The 4-hour Indian Arm **Luncheon Cruise** (May–Sept) includes a salmon or chicken lunch, with departure at 11am. Cost for adults, seniors, and children is C$62 (US$52/£28).

Harbour Cruises also conducts a 75-minute narrated **Harbour Tour** aboard the MPV *Constitution,* an authentic 19th-century stern-wheeler with a smokestack. Tours depart at 11:30am, 1pm, and 2:30pm daily from early May to late September and once a day at 2:30pm mid-April through early May and late September through October (dates vary yearly). Fares are C$25 (US$21/£11) for adults, C$21 (US$18/£10) for seniors and youths 12 to 17, C$10 (US$8/£4.50) for children 5 to 11, and free for children under 5. This tour allows you to see harbor facilities and gets you out onto Burrard Inlet, but the narration, read from a script, is rather dull and unengaging.

Accent Cruises, 1676 Duranleau St. (© 800/993-6257 or 604/688-8072; www.champagnecruises.com), offers a 2½-hour Sunset Cruise departing Granville Island weekends May through October at 5:45pm. Cost for adults is C$60 (US$51/£27) with dinner, C$25 (US$21/£11) for the cruise only.

Paddlewheeler River Adventures, New Westminster Quay, New Westminster (© 604/525-4465; www.vancouverpaddlewheeler.com), operates Fraser River tours from New Westminster aboard the 19th-century vessel SS *Native.* The company offers a 3-hour **Dine and Dance** cruise Saturday evenings at 7pm, and a **Family Dine and Dance** cruise on Sunday at 5pm. Ticket prices are C$30 (US$25/£13) for adults, C$27 (US$23/£13) seniors, C$15 (US$13/£7) for children 6 to 12; food and beverages can be purchased on board. More interesting but not regularly scheduled are lunch cruises and day trips to historic Fort Langley; call or visit the website for dates.

BUS TOURS

Gray Line of Vancouver, 255 E. 1st Ave. (© 800/667-0882 or 604/879-3363; www.grayline.ca), offers a wide array of tour options. The **"Deluxe City Tour"** is a 4-hour excursion through Stanley Park, Gastown, Chinatown, Canada Place, Queen

Elizabeth Park, Robson Street, Granville Island, Shaughnessy, and English Bay Beach. Offered year-round, the tour is C$62 (US$53/£28) for adults, C$56 (US$48/£26) for seniors and students, and C$42 (US$36/£19) for children 2 to 11. Departing at 8:45am (and 1:30pm in summer), the bus picks you up from downtown hotels approximately 30 minutes before departure. The daily **"Mountains and Vistas Tour"** takes you up to Grouse Mountain and the Capilano Suspension Bridge. Departing at 1:30pm, it costs C$93 (US$79/£42) for adults, C$84 (US$71/£38) for seniors and students, and C$62 (US$53/£28) for children 6 to 11, including admission and the SkyRide funicular up to Grouse Mountain Resort. Other options are day, overnight, multinight, and helicopter tours of Vancouver, Victoria, and Whistler, and dinner cruises. Gray Line also runs a fleet of double-decker buses on a "hop-on, hop-off" **sightseeing loop around the city** (C$35/US$30/£16 adults; C$19/US$16/£9 children); buses depart from Canada Place daily between 8:30am and 6pm.

Vancouver Trolley Company, 875 Terminal Ave., Vancouver (© **888/451-5581** or 604/801-5515; www.vancouvertrolley.com), operates gas-powered trolleys on a route through downtown, Chinatown, the West End, and Stanley Park. Between 9am and 6pm in summer (4:30pm in winter), passengers can get on and off at any of the 23 stops, explore, and catch another scheduled trolley. Onboard, drivers provide detailed commentary. Purchase tickets from the driver for C$33 (US$28/£16) for adults and C$19 (US$16/£9) for children 4 to 12 (or at the Gastown ticket booth at 157 Water St.).

FIRST NATIONS TOURS

The Tsleil-Waututh Nation of North Vancouver offers a number of cultural and eco-tours that provide an introduction to both First Nations culture and the stunning Indian Arm fjord. Their company, **Takaya Tours,** 3093 Ghum-Lye Dr., North Vancouver (© **604/940-7410;** www.takayatours.com), offers a bevy of outdoor tours such as tours in traditional northwest canoes, plant nature walks, and full moon paddles, at prices running from C$25 to C$140 (US$21–US$119/£12–£63).

SPECIALTY TOURS

AAA Horse & Carriage Ltd., Stanley Park (© **604/681-5115;** www.stanleypark. com), carries on a century-old tradition of **horse-drawn carriage rides through Stanley Park** ✫✫✫. Tours depart every 20 minutes mid-March through October from the lower aquarium parking lot on Park Drive near the Georgia Street park entrance. Tours last an hour and cover portions of the park that many locals have never seen. Rates are C$25 (US$21/£11) for adults, C$24 (US$21/£11) for seniors and students, C$15 (US$12/£7) for children 3 to 12.

Playing off Vancouver's growing reputation as a culinary tourism destination, **Chef and Chauffeur,** 103-4900 Cartier St. (© **604/267-1000;** www.chefandchauffeur. com), has launched several tours of the Fraser Valley, located an hour east of the city. Participants start the day with coffee, fresh orange juice and cinnamon buns while their guide maps out the day's adventures. The tours, in a luxury SUV, visit a variety of wineries, farms, bakeries, and cheese makers. Optional dinner add-ons are available with a choice of remaining in the Fraser Valley or dining back in the city. Day tours range from C$395 to C$695 (US$336–US$591/£178–£313).

Early Motion Tours, 1-1380 Thurlow St. (© **604/687-5088**), offers private sightseeing tours around Vancouver aboard a restored 1930 Model A Ford Phaeton convertible that holds up to four passengers plus the driver. Reservations are required.

Limousine rates apply: C$100 (US$85/£45) per hour for up to four people with a 1-hour minimum. The office is open daily from 7:30am to 8pm.

WALKING TOURS

Walkabout Historic Vancouver (© 604/720-0006; www.walkabouthistoricvancouver.com) offers 2-hour walking tours through Vancouver and Granville Island historic sites, complete with guides dressed as 19th-century schoolmarms. Tours depart daily at 10am and 2pm February through November, and by request during other months. Tours are wheelchair accessible. The cost is C$25 (US$21/£12) per person.

During the summer months (June–Aug), the **Architectural Institute of B.C.** (© 604/638-8588, ext. 306; www.aibc.ca) offers a number of **architectural walking tours** ★★★ of downtown Vancouver neighborhoods, including Chinatown, for only C$5 (US$4/£2.50) per person. The 2-hour tours run Tuesday through Saturday and depart at 1pm from the AIBC Architecture Centre, 440 Cambie St. Call or visit the website for details and to book.

The **Vancouver Centennial Police Museum** offers an entertaining "Sins of the City" walking tour; see the museum description (p. 119) for details.

Or, devise your own walking tour with brochures from the Tourism Vancouver **Touristinfo Centre** at 200 Burrard St. (p. 52).

6 Outdoor Activities

Vancouver is definitely an outdoors-oriented city and just about every imaginable sport has an outlet within the city limits. Downhill and cross-country skiing, snowshoeing, sea kayaking, fly-fishing, hiking, paragliding, and mountainbiking are just a few of the options. Activities in the vicinity include rock climbing, river rafting, and heli-skiing. If you don't find your favorite sport listed here, take a look at chapter 18; also check out "Parks & Gardens" earlier in this chapter on p. 126.

An excellent resource for outdoor enthusiasts is **Mountain Equipment Co-op,** 130 W. Broadway (© 604/872-7858; www.mec.ca). The MEC's retail store has a knowledgeable staff, the co-op publishes an annual mail-order catalog, and you can find useful outdoor activities information on the website.

BEACHES

Only 10% of Vancouver's annual rainfall occurs during June, July, and August; 60 days of summer sunshine is not uncommon, although the Pacific never really warms up enough for a comfortable swim. Still, **English Bay Beach** ★★, at the end of Davie Street off Denman Street and Beach Avenue, is a great place to see sunsets. The bathhouse dates to the turn of the 20th century, and a huge playground slide is mounted on a raft just off the beach every summer.

On **Stanley Park**'s western rim, **Second Beach** ★ is a short stroll north from English Bay Beach. A playground, a snack bar, and an immense heated oceanside **pool** ★ (© 604/257-8370), open from May through September, makes this a convenient and fun spot for families. Admission to the pool is C$4.85 (US$4/£2.25) for adults, C$3.40 (US$2.80/£1.50) for seniors, C$3.65 (US$3/£1.50) for youth 13 to 18, and C$2.45 (US$2/£1.10) for children 6 to 12. Farther along the seawall, due north of Stanley Park Drive, lies secluded **Third Beach.** Locals tote along grills and coolers to this spot, a popular place for summer-evening barbecues and sunset watching.

South of English Bay Beach, near the Burrard Street Bridge, is **Sunset Beach** ⚝. Running along False Creek, it's actually a picturesque strip of sandy beaches filled with enormous driftwood logs that serve as windbreaks and provide a little privacy for sunbathers and picnickers. A snack bar, a soccer field, and a long, gently sloping grassy hill are available for people who prefer lawn to sand.

On the West Side, **Kitsilano Beach** ⚝⚝⚝, along Arbutus Drive near Ogden Street, is affectionately called Kits Beach. It's an easy walk from the Maritime Museum and the False Creek ferry dock. If you want to do a saltwater swim but can't handle the cold, head to the huge (135m/443-ft.) heated (77°F/25°C) **Kitsilano Pool** ⚝⚝. Admission is the same as for Second Beach Pool, above.

Farther west on the other side of Pioneer Park is **Jericho Beach** (Alma St. off Point Grey Rd.), another local after-work and weekend social spot. **Locarno Beach,** off Discovery Street and NW Marine Drive, and **Spanish Banks,** NW Marine Drive, wrap around the northern point of the UBC campus and University Hill. (Be forewarned that beachside restrooms and concessions on the promontory end abruptly at Locarno Beach.) Below UBC's Museum of Anthropology is **Point Grey Beach,** a restored harbor defense site. The next beach is **Wreck Beach** ⚝⚝⚝—Canada's largest nude beach. You get down to Wreck Beach by taking the very steep Trail 6 on the UBC campus near Gate 6 down to the water's edge. Extremely popular with locals, and maintained by its own preservation society, Wreck Beach is also the city's most pristine and least-developed sandy stretch, bordered on three sides by towering trees.

At the northern foot of the Lions Gate Bridge, **Ambleside Park** is a popular North Shore spot. The quarter-mile beach faces the Burrard Inlet.

For information on any of Vancouver's many beaches, call ℂ **604/738-8535** (summer only).

BOATING

With thousands of miles of protected shoreline along B.C.'s West Coast, boaters enjoy some of the finest cruising grounds in the world. You can rent powerboats for a few hours or up to several weeks at **Bonnie Lee Boat Rentals,** 1676 Duranleau St., Granville Island (ℂ **866/933-7447** or 604/290-7441; www.bonnielee.com). Rates for a 5.8m (19-ft.) sport boat with 115-horsepower motor begin at C$55 (US$47/£25) per hour (plus C$7/US$6/£3.15 insurance fee and fuel), or C$350 (US$297/£158) for an 8-hour package. **Jerry's Boat Rentals,** Granville Island (ℂ **604/644-3256**), is steps away and offers similar deals. **Delta Charters,** 3500 Cessna Dr., Richmond (ℂ **800/661-7762** or 604/273-4211; www.deltacharters.com), has weekly and monthly rates for skippered boats that sleep four.

CANOEING & KAYAKING

Both placid, urban False Creek and the incredibly beautiful 30km (19-mile) North Vancouver fjord known as Indian Arm have launching points that can be reached by car or bus. Prices range from about C$40 (US$34/£18) per 2-hour minimum rental to C$70 (US$59/£32) per 5-hour day for single kayaks and about C$60 (US$51/£27) for canoe rentals. Customized tours range from C$75 to C$150 (US$64–US$127/£34–£67) per person.

Ecomarine Ocean Kayak Centre, 1668 Duranleau St., Granville Island (ℂ **888/425-2925** or 604/689-7575; www.ecomarine.com), has 2-hour, daily and weekly kayak rentals, as well as courses and organized tours. The company also has an office at the **Jericho Sailing Centre,** 1300 Discovery St., at Jericho Beach (ℂ **604/222-3565;**

www.jsca.bc.ca). In North Vancouver, **Deep Cove Canoe and Kayak Rentals,** 2156 Banbury Rd. (at the foot of Gallant St.), Deep Cove (℗ **604/929-2268;** www.deep covekayak.com), is an easy starting point for anyone planning an Indian Arm run. It offers hourly and daily rentals of canoes and kayaks, as well as lessons and customized tours.

Lotus Land Tours, 2005-1251 Cardero St. (℗ **800/528-3531** or 604/684-4922; www.lotuslandtours.com), runs guided kayak tours on Indian Arm that come with hotel pickup, a barbecue salmon lunch, and incredible scenery. The wide, stable kayaks are perfect for first-time paddlers. One-day tours cost C$155 (US$132/£70) for adults, C$114 (US$97/£51) for children.

See also **Takaya Tours,** an excellent First Nations eco-outfitter (p. 133).

CYCLING & MOUNTAINBIKING

Cycling in Vancouver is fun, amazingly scenic, and very popular. Cycling maps are available at most bicycle retailers and rental outlets. Some West End hotels offer guests bike storage and rentals. Hourly rentals run around C$5 (US$4/£2.50) for a one-speed "Cruiser" to C$10 (US$8/£4.50) for a top-of-the-line mountainbike; C$15 to C$40 (US$13–US$34/£7–£18) for a day, helmets and locks included. Popular shops that rent city and mountainbikes, child trailers, child seats, and in-line skates (protective gear included) include **Spokes Bicycle Rentals & Espresso Bar,** 1798 W. Georgia St. (℗ **604/688-5141;** www.spokesbicyclerentals.com), at the corner of Denman Street at the entrance to Stanley Park; **Alley Cat Rentals,** 1779 Robson St., in the alley (℗ **604/684-5117**); and **Bayshore Bicycle and Rollerblade Rentals,** 745 Denman St. (℗ **604/688-2453;** www.bayshorebikerentals.ca). *Note:* Be advised that wearing a helmet is mandatory, and one will be included in your bike rental.

The most popular cycling path in the city runs along the **seawall** ✦✦✦ around the perimeter of Stanley Park, although portions of this might be closed in 2008 because of the restoration work following the December 2006 windstorm. Offering magnificent views of the city, the Burrard Inlet, the mountains, and English Bay, this flat, 10km (6¼-mile) pathway attracts year-round bicyclists, in-line skaters, and pedestrians. (*Note:* Runners and cyclists have separate lanes on developed park and beach paths.) Another popular route is the **seaside bicycle route,** a 15km (9⅓-mile) ride that begins at English Bay and continues around False Creek to the University of British Columbia. Some of this route follows city streets that are well marked with cycle-path signs; the sights include the Plaza of Nations, Science World, Granville Island, the Pacific Space Centre, the Kitsilano Pool and the Jericho Sailing Centre, and the University of British Columbia, home to the UBC Botanical Garden, Nitobe Japanese Garden (p. 124), and the lush Pacific Spirit Park (p. 127).

Serious mountainbikers also have a wealth of world-class options within a short drive from downtown Vancouver. The trails on **Grouse Mountain** (p. 125) are some of the lower mainland's best. The very steep **Good Samaritan Trail** on **Mount Seymour** connects to the Baden-Powell Trail and the Bridle Path near Mount Seymour Road. Local mountainbikers love the cross-country ski trails on **Hollyburn Mountain** in **Cypress Provincial Park,** just northeast of Vancouver on the road to Whistler on Highway 99. Closer to downtown, both **Pacific Spirit Park** and **Burnaby Mountain** offer excellent beginner and intermediate off-road trails.

ECOTOURS

Lotus Land Tours, 2005-1251 Cardero St. (© **800/528-3531** or 604/684-4922; www. lotuslandtours.com), runs guided kayak tours on Indian Arm (see "Canoeing & Kayaking," above). From late November to the end of January, this small local company also offers unique float trips on the Squamish River to see the large concentration of bald eagles up close. **Rockwood Adventures** (© **888/236-6606** or 604/980-7749; www. rockwoodadventures.com) has 4-hour **guided walks of the North Shore rainforest** ⚡, complete with a trained naturalist, stops in Capilano Canyon and at the Lynn Canyon Suspension Bridge (p. 128), and lunch. Cost is C$75 (US$64/£34) for adults, C$66 (US$56/£30) for seniors and students, and C$60 (US$51/£27) for children 6 to 11.

FISHING

Five species of salmon, rainbow and Dolly Varden trout, steelhead, and sturgeon abound in the local waters around Vancouver. To fish, anglers over the age of 16 need a **nonresident saltwater or freshwater license.** Licenses are available province-wide from more than 500 vendors, including tackle shops, sporting goods stores, resorts, service stations, marinas, charter boat operators, and department stores. Saltwater (tidal waters) fishing licenses cost C$7.50 (US$6/£34) for 1 day, C$20 (US$17/£9) for 3 days, and C$33 (US$28/£15) for 5 days. Fly-fishing in national and provincial parks requires special permits, which you can get at any park site for a nominal fee. Permits are valid at all Canadian parks.

The B.C. *Tidal Waters Sport Fishing Guide* and *B.C. Sport Fishing Regulations Synopsis for Non-Tidal Waters,* and the *B.C. Fishing Directory and Atlas,* available at many tackle shops, are good sources of information. The *Vancouver Sun* prints a daily **fishing report** in the B section that details which fish are in season and where they can be found. Another good source of general information is the **Fisheries and Ocean Canada** website (www.pac.dfo-mpo.gc.ca).

Hanson's Fishing Outfitters, 102-580 Hornby St. (© **604/684-8988;** www.hansons-outfitters.com), and **Granville Island Boat Rentals,** 1696 Duranleau St. (© **604/682-6287**), are outstanding outfitters. **Bonnie Lee Fishing Charters Ltd.,** 1676 Duranleau St., Granville Island © **604/290-7447;** www.bonnielee.com), is another reputable outfitter and also sells fishing licenses.

GOLF

With five public 18-hole courses, half a dozen pitch-and-putt courses in the city, and dozens more nearby, golfers are never far from their love. For discounts and short-notice tee times at more than 30 Vancouver-area courses, contact the **A-1 Last Minute Golf Hot Line** (© **800/684-6344** or 604/878-1833; www.lastminutegolfbc.com).

A number of excellent public golf courses, maintained by the **Vancouver Board of Parks and Recreation** (© **604/280-1818** to book tee times; www.city.vancouver.bc.ca/ parks), can be found throughout the city. **Langara Golf Course,** 6706 Alberta St., around 49th Avenue and Cambie Street (© **604/713-1816**), built in 1926 and recently renovated and redesigned, is one of the most popular golf courses in the province. Depending on the course, summer greens fees range from C$24 to C$55 (US$20–US$47/£11–£25) for an adult, with discounts for seniors, youths, and off-season tee times.

The public **University Golf Club,** 5185 University Blvd. (© **604/224-1818;** www. universitygolf.com), is a great 6,560-yard, par-71 course with a clubhouse, pro shop, locker rooms, bar and grill, and sports lounge.

Leading private clubs are situated on the North Shore and in Vancouver. Check with your club at home to see if you have reciprocal visiting memberships with one of the following: **Capilano Golf and Country Club,** 420 Southborough Dr., West Vancouver (✆ **604/922-9331;** www.capilanogolf.com); **Marine Drive Golf Club,** West 57th Avenue and SW Marine Drive (✆ **604/261-8111;** www.marine-drive. com); **Seymour Golf and Country Club,** 3723 Mt. Seymour Pkwy., North Vancouver (✆ **604/929-2611;** www.seymourgolf.com); **Point Grey Golf and Country Club,** 3350 SW Marine Dr. (✆ **604/261-3108;** www.pointgreygolf.com); and **Shaughnessy Golf and Country Club,** 4300 SW Marine Dr. (✆ **604/266-4141;** www. shaughnessy.org). Greens fees range from C$42 to C$75 (US$36–US$64/£19–£34).

HIKING

Great trails for hikers of all levels run through Vancouver's dramatic environs. Good trail maps are available from **International Travel Maps and Books,** 539 Pender St. (✆ **604/687-3320;** www.itmb.com), which also stocks guidebooks and topographical maps. You can pick up a local trail guide at any bookstore.

If you're looking for a challenge without a longtime commitment, hike the aptly named **Grouse Grind** from the bottom of **Grouse Mountain** (p. 125) to the top; then buy a one-way ticket down on the Grouse Mountain SkyRide gondola.

For a bit more scenery with a bit less effort, take the Grouse Mountain SkyRide up to the **Grouse chalet** and start your hike at an altitude of 1,100m (3,609 ft.). The trail north of **Goat Mountain** is well marked and takes approximately 6 hours round-trip, though you may want to build in some extra time to linger on the top of Goat and take in the spectacular 360-degree views of Vancouver, Vancouver Island, and the snowcapped peaks of the Coast Mountains.

Lynn Canyon Park, Lynn Headwaters Regional Park, Capilano River Regional Park, Mount Seymour Provincial Park, Pacific Spirit Park, and **Cypress Provincial Park** (see "The Top Attractions" and "Parks & Gardens," earlier in this chapter) have good, easy-to-challenging trails that wind up through stands of Douglas fir and cedar and contain a few serious switchbacks. Pay attention to the trail warnings posted at the parks (some have bear habitats), and always remember to sign in with the park service at the start of your chosen trail.

A little farther outside the city, the 6- to 10-hour hike to **Black Tusk** is one of the finest day hikes in North America. The trail head is located in **Garibaldi Provincial Park** (✆ **604/898-3678**), located 13km (8 miles) north of Squamish, which is 97km (60 miles) north of Vancouver along Highway 99 on the road to Whistler. The park has five access points; Black Tusk/Garibaldi Lake is the second marked turnoff; it takes about an hour to get there. The trail switchbacks up 1,000m (3,281 ft.) in about 6km (3.7 miles), then levels onto a rolling alpine plateau with fabulous views. The best time to make this climb is from July to October.

ICE-SKATING

The highest ice-skating rink in Canada is located on **Grouse Mountain;** see the Grouse Mountain description under "The Top Attractions," earlier in this chapter. In the city, the **West End Community Centre,** 870 Denman St. (✆ **604/257-8333**), rents skates at its enclosed rink, open October through March. Another option is the **Kitsilano Ice Rink,** 2690 Larch St. (✆ **604/257-6983;** www.vancouverparks.ca), open from October to June. The enormous **Burnaby 8 Rinks Ice Sports Centre,** 6501 Sprott, Burnaby (✆ **604/291-0626**), is the Vancouver Canucks' official practice facility. It has eight rinks, is open year-round, and offers lessons and rentals. Call ahead to check hours for public skating at all these rinks.

IN-LINE SKATING

All over Vancouver you'll find lots of locals rolling along beach paths, streets, park paths, and promenades. If you didn't bring a pair of blades, try **Bayshore Bicycle and Rollerblade Rentals,** 745 Denman St. (© **604/688-2453;** www.bayshorebikerentals. com). Rentals run C$5 (US$4.25/£2.25) per hour or C$20 (US$17/£9) for 8 hours. For information on in-line skating lessons and group events, visit www.rollerblade vancouver.com.

JOGGING

Local runners traverse the **Stanley Park seawall** ★★★ and the paths around **Lost Lagoon** and **Beaver Lake.** If you're a dawn or dusk runner, take note that this is one of the world's safer city parks. However, if you're alone, don't tempt fate—stick to open and lighted areas. Other prime jogging areas are **Kitsilano Beach, Jericho Beach,** and **Spanish Banks** (see "Beaches," earlier in this chapter); all of them offer flat running paths along the ocean. You can also take the seawall path from English Bay Beach south along **False Creek.** If you feel like doing a little racing, competitions take place throughout the year; ask for information at any runners' outfitters such as **Forerunners,** 3504 W. 4th Ave. (© **604/732-4535**), or **Running Room,** 679 Denman St. (corner of Georgia; © **604/684-9771**). Check www.runningroom.com for information on clinics and events around Vancouver and British Columbia.

The **Sun Run** in April and the **Vancouver International Marathon** in May attract runners from around the world. Contact the **Vancouver International Marathon Society,** 1601 Bayshore Dr., in the Westin Bayshore Hotel (© **604/872-2928;** www. vanmarathon.bc.ca), or the **Vancouver Sun Run,** 655 Burrard St. (© **604/689-9441;** www.sunrun.com), for information.

PARAGLIDING

In North Vancouver, **First Flight Paragliding** (© **604/988-1111;** www.first-flight.ca) offers tandem flights June through September from the peak of Grouse Mountain at C$190 (US$161/£86) for 1 hour; lift ticket to the summit of Grouse Mountain not included. The actual flight takes approximately 20 minutes.

SAILING

Trying to navigate a sailboat in the unfamiliar straits around Vancouver is unwise and unsafe unless you enroll in a local sailing course before attempting it. Knowing the tides, currents, and channels is essential, and you won't be able to rent a sailboat without this basic navigational and safety knowledge. Multiday instruction packages sometimes include guided Gulf Island cruises.

Cooper Boating Centre, 1620 Duranleau St. (© **604/687-4110;** www.cooper boating.com), offers chartered cruises, boat rentals, and sailing instruction.

SKIING & SNOWBOARDING

World-class skiing lies outside the city at the **Whistler Blackcomb Ski Resort,** 110km (68 miles) north of Vancouver (see chapter 18). However, you don't have to leave the city to get in a few runs. It seldom snows in the city's downtown and central areas, but Vancouverites can ski before work and after dinner at the three ski resorts in the North Shore mountains. In 2010, these local mountains will play host to the freestyle and snowboard events in the Winter Olympics.

   Grouse Mountain Resort, 6400 Nancy Greene Way, North Vancouver (© **604/ 984-0661,** snow report 604/986-6262; www.grousemountain.com), is about 3km (1¾ miles) from the Lions Gate Bridge and overlooks the Burrard Inlet and Vancouver sky-line (p. 125). Four chairs, two beginner tows, and two T-bars take you to 24 alpine runs. The resort has night skiing, special events, instruction, and a spectacular view, as well as a 90m (295-ft.) half-pipe for snowboarders. All skill levels are covered, with two beginner trails, three blue trails, and five black-diamond runs, including Coffin and Inferno, which follow the east slopes down from 1,230 to 750m (4,035–2,461 ft.). Rental packages and a full range of facilities are available. Lift tickets good for all-day skiing are C$45 (US$38/£21) for adults, C$35 (US$30/£16) for seniors and youths, and C$20 (US$17/£9) for children 5 to 12; free for children under 4. Lift prices do not include your gondola ride to the summit.

   Mount Seymour Provincial Park, 1700 Mt. Seymour Rd., North Vancouver (© **604/986-2261,** snow report 604/986-3999; www.mountseymour.com), has the area's highest base elevation; it's accessible via four chairs and a tow. Lift tickets are C$39 (US$33/£18) all day for adults, C$27 (US$23/£12) for seniors, C$32 (US$27/ £15) for youths 12 to 19, and C$16 (US$14/£7) for children 6 to 11. Nighttime skiing from 4 to 10pm costs less. In addition to day and night skiing, the facility offers snowboarding, snowshoeing, and tobogganing along its 22 runs, as well as 26km (16 miles) of cross-country trails. The resort specializes in teaching first-timers. Camps for children and teenagers, and adult clinics, are available throughout the winter. Mount Seymour has one of Western Canada's largest equipment rental shops, which will keep your measurements on file for return visits. Shuttle service is available during ski season from various locations on the North Shore, including the Lonsdale Quay SeaBus. For more information, call © **604/953-3333.**

   Cypress Bowl, 1610 Mt. Seymour Rd. (© **604/926-5612,** snow report 604/419-7669; www.cypressmountain.com), has the area's longest vertical drop (525m/1,722 ft.), challenging ski and snowboard runs, and 16km (10 miles) of track-set cross-country ski trails (including 5km/3.1 miles set aside for night skiing). Full-day lift tickets are C$43 to C$47 (US$37–US$40/£20–£22) for adults, with reduced rates for youths, seniors, and children. Cross-country full-day passes are C$16 (US$14/£7) for adults, with reduced rates for youths, seniors, and children. Snowshoe tours and excellent introductory ski packages are available. *Note:* Cypress will be home to the 2010 Olympics freestyle skiing (moguls and aerials), snowboarding (half pipe and parallel giant slalom), and brand-new ski cross events. In winter 2008 Cypress will open nine new runs for intermediate and expert skiers and snowboarders, accessed by a new quad chairlift. A new day lodge is under construction and is set to open for the winter 2008/ 2009 season.

SWIMMING & WATERSPORTS

Vancouver's midsummer saltwater temperature rarely exceeds 18°C (65°F). If you've really got a hankering to have a saltwater swim, try the **heated outdoor pools** at both **Kitsilano Beach** 🌀🌀🌀 and **Second Beach** 🌀 (see "Beaches," earlier this chapter). You can also take to the water at public aquatic centers.

   The **Vancouver Aquatic Centre,** 1050 Beach Ave., at the foot of Thurlow Street (© **604/665-3424**), has a heated, 50m (164-ft.) Olympic pool, saunas, whirlpools, weight rooms, diving tanks, locker rooms, showers, child care, and a tot pool. Adult admission is C$4.85 (US$4/£2.25), C$2.45 (US$2.10/£1.10) children 2 to 12. The new, coed **YWCA Fitness Centre,** 535 Hornby St. (© **604/895-5777;** www.ywcavan. org), in the heart of downtown, has a 6-lane, 25m (82-ft.), ozonated (much milder than chlorinated) pool, steam room, whirlpool, conditioning gym, and aerobic studios. A day pass is C$16 (US$14/£7) for adults. UBC's **Aquatic Centre,** 6121 University Blvd. (© **604/822-4522;** www.aquatics.ubc.ca), located next door to the Student Union Building and the bus loop, sets aside time for public use. Adult admission is C$4.75 (US$4/£2.20), C$3.75 (US$3.20/£2) for youths and students, and C$2.75 (US$2.20/£1.25) for seniors and children 3 to 12.

TENNIS

The city maintains 180 outdoor hard courts that have a 1-hour limit and accommodate patrons on a first-come, first-served basis from 8am until dusk. Local courtesy dictates that if people are waiting, you surrender the court on the hour. (Heavy usage times are evenings and weekends.) With the exception of the Beach Avenue courts, which charge a nominal fee in summer, all city courts are free.

Stanley Park has four courts near Lost Lagoon and 17 courts near the Beach Avenue entrance, next to the Fish House Restaurant. During the summer season (May–Sept), six courts are taken over for pay tennis and can be pre-booked by calling © **604/605-8224. Queen Elizabeth Park**'s 18 courts service the central Vancouver area, and **Kitsilano Beach Park**'s ✦ 10 courts service the beach area between Vanier Park and the UBC campus.

Play at night on the **Langara Campus** of Vancouver Community College, on West 49th Avenue between Main and Cambie streets. The **UBC Coast Club,** on Thunderbird Boulevard (© **604/822-2505;** www.tennis.ubc.ca), has 10 outdoor and four indoor courts. Indoor courts are C$12 to C$22 (US$10–US$19/£4.50–£10) an hour, depending on the time; outdoor courts are C$5 (US$4.25/£2.25) per person.

WHITE-WATER RAFTING

A 2½-hour drive from Vancouver, on the wild Nahatlatch River, **Reo Rafting,** 845 Spence Way, Anmore (© **800/736-7238** or 604/461-7238; www.reorafting.com), offers some of the best guided white-water trips in the province, at a very reasonable price. One-day packages—including lunch, all your gear, and 4 to 5 hours on the river—start at C$109 (US$93/£50) for adults. Multiday trips and group packages are available, and they can provide transportation from Vancouver.

Only a 1½-hour drive from the city is **Chilliwack River Rafting** (© **800/410-7238;** www.chilliwackriverrafting.com), which offers half-day trips on the Chilliwack River and in the even hairier Chilliwack Canyon. The cost is C$89 (US$76/£40) for adults and C$69 (US$59/£31) for children.

WILDLIFE-WATCHING

Vancouver is an internationally famous stop for naturalists, ecotourists, pods of orca whales, and thousands of migratory birds; so bring your camera, binoculars, and bird-spotting books. Salmon, bald eagles, herons, beavers, and numerous rare, indigenous marine and waterfowl species live in the metropolitan area.

Orcas, or killer whales, are the largest mammals to be seen in Vancouver's waters. Three pods (families), numbering about 80 whales, return to this area every year to feed on the salmon that spawn in the Fraser River starting in May and continuing into

October. The eldest female leads the group; the head of one pod is thought to have been born in 1911. From April through October, daily excursions offered by **Vancouver Whale Watch,** 12240 2nd Ave., Richmond (© **604/274-9565;** www.vancouver whalewatch.com), focus on the majestic whales plus Dall's porpoises, sea lions, seals, eagles, herons, and other wildlife. The cost is C$105 (US$89/£48) per person. The same adult rates apply at **Steveston Seabreeze Adventures,** 12551 No. 1 Rd., Richmond (© **604/272-7200;** www.seabreezeadventures.ca), but the price for seniors is C$89 (US$76/£36) and for children it's C$59 (US$50/£27). Both companies offer a shuttle service from downtown Vancouver.

Thousands of migratory birds following the Pacific flyway rest and feed in the Fraser River delta south of Vancouver, especially at the 340-hectare (840-acre) **George C. Reifel Bird Sanctuary,** 5191 Robertson Rd., Westham Island (© **604/946-6980;** www.reifelbirdsanctuary.com), which was created by a former bootlegger and wetland-bird lover. Many other waterfowl species have made this a permanent habitat. More than 263 species have been spotted, including a Temminck's stint, a spotted redshank, bald eagles, Siberian (trumpeter) swans, peregrine falcons, blue herons, owls, and coots. The **Snow Goose Festival,** celebrating the annual arrival of the huge, snowy white flocks, is held here during the first weekend of November. The snow geese stay in the area until mid-December. (High tide, when the birds are less concealed by the marsh grasses, is the best time to visit.) An observation tower, 3km (2 miles) of paths, free birdseed, and picnic tables make this wetland reserve an ideal outing spot from October to April, when the birds are wintering in abundance. The sanctuary is wheelchair accessible and open daily from 9am to 4pm. Admission is C$4 (US$3.40/£1.80) for adults and C$2 (US$1.70/£1) for seniors and children.

The **Richmond Nature Park,** 11851 Westminster Hwy. (© **604/718-6188**), was established to preserve the Lulu Island wetlands bog. It features a Nature House with educational displays and a boardwalk-encircled duck pond. On Sunday afternoons, knowledgeable guides give free tours. Admission is by donation.

To hook up with local Vancouver birders, try the **Vancouver Natural History Society** (© **604/737-3074;** www.naturalhistory.bc.ca/VNHS). This all-volunteer organization runs birding field trips most weekends; many are free.

During the winter, thousands of bald eagles—in fact, the largest number in North America—line the banks of the **Squamish, Cheakamus,** and **Mamquam** rivers to feed on spawning salmon. To get there by car, take the scenic **Sea-to-Sky Highway** (Hwy. 99) from downtown Vancouver to Squamish and Brackendale; the trip takes about an hour. The route winds along the craggy tree-lined coast of Howe Sound through the town of Britannia Beach and past two beautiful natural monuments: Shannon Falls and the continent's tallest monolithic rock face, the Stawamus Chief. Alternatively, you can take a **Greyhound** bus from Vancouver's Pacific Central Station, 1150 Station St. (© **604/482-8747;** www.greyhound.ca); trip time is 1¼ hours. Contact **Squamish & Howe Sound Visitor Info Centre** (© **604/892-9244;** www. squamishchamber.bc.ca) for more information.

The annual summer salmon runs attract more than bald eagles. Tourists also flock to coastal streams and rivers to watch the waters turn red with leaping coho and sockeye. The salmon are plentiful at the **Capilano Salmon Hatchery** (p. 128), **Goldstream Provincial Park** out on Vancouver Island, and numerous other fresh waters.

Stanley Park and **Pacific Spirit Park** are both home to heron rookeries. You can see these large birds nesting just outside the Vancouver Aquarium. Ravens, dozens of species of waterfowl, raccoons, skunks, beavers, gray squirrels (imported from New York's Central Park decades ago), and even coyotes are also full-time residents. The **Stanley Park Ecological Society** (© 604/257-8544) runs regular nature walks in the park. Call or check their website (www.stanleyparkecology.ca) for more information, or drop by the **Lost Lagoon Nature House** in Stanley Park (p. 117).

WINDSURFING

Windsurfing is not allowed at the mouth of False Creek near Granville Island, but you can bring a board to **Jericho** and **English Bay beaches** ★★ or rent one there. Equipment sales, rentals (including wet suits), and instruction can be found at **Windsure Windsurfing School,** 1300 Discovery St., at Jericho Beach (© 604/224-0615; www.windsure.com). Rentals start at about C$18 (US$15/£8) per hour, wet suit and life jacket included.

7 Spectator Sports

You can get schedules for all major events at Tourism Vancouver's **Travelinfo Centre,** 200 Burrard St. (© 604/683-2000; www.tourismvancouver.com). You can also get information and purchase tickets from Ticketmaster at the **Vancouver Ticket Centre,** 1304 Hornby St. (© 604/280-4444; www.ticketmaster.ca), or from 40 outlets in the Greater Vancouver area. Popular events such as Canucks games and the Vancouver Indy sell out weeks or months in advance, so be sure to book ahead.

FOOTBALL

The Canadian Football League's **B.C. Lions** (© 604/589-7627; www.bclions.com) play their home and Grey Cup championship games (in good seasons) in the 60,000-seat **B.C. Place Stadium,** 777 Pacific Blvd. S. (at Beatty and Robson sts.). Canadian football differs from its American cousin: It's a three-down offense game on a field that's 10 yards longer and wider. Some of the plays you see will have American fans leaping out of their seats in surprise. Tickets for individual games are available from Ticketmaster (© 604/280-4639; www.ticketmaster.ca); prices run C$27 to C$70 (US$23–US$59/£12–£31).

HOCKEY

The National Hockey League's **Vancouver Canucks** play at **General Motors Place** (otherwise known as GM Place, or the Garage), 800 Griffith's Way (© 604/899-4600; event hotline 604/899-7444; www.canucks.com). Tickets are C$33 to C$94 (US$28–US$80/£15–£42) and while difficult to obtain because the season tends to sell out in advance, some individual seats are made available for every home game.

HORSE RACING

Thoroughbreds run at **Hastings Park Racecourse,** Exhibition Park, East Hastings and Cassiar streets (© 604/254-1631; www.hastingspark.com), from mid-April to October. Post time varies; call ahead or check the website for the latest schedule if you want to place a wager. The racecourse has a decent restaurant, so you can make a full afternoon or evening of dining and racing.

RUNNING

The **Vancouver Sun Run** in April and the **Vancouver International Marathon** (Canada's largest) in May attract thousands of runners from around the world and even more spectators. Contact the **Vancouver International Marathon Society** (© **604/872-2928;** www.vanmarathon.bc.ca), or the **Vancouver Sun Run,** 655 Burrard St. (© **604/689-9441;** www.sunrun.com), for information.

SOCCER

The American Professional Soccer League's **Vancouver Whitecaps** (© **604/899-9283**) play at Swangard Stadium (© **604/435-7121;** www.whitecapssoccer.com) in Burnaby. Admission is normally C$21 to C$42 (US$18–US$36/£10–£19).

8

Vancouver Strolls

Down below's Stanley Park. On the side of the trees there's a beach. You can't see it [points over to left]. Steveston's over there. [points to left] Coast Guard station. There's the Yacht Club, and beyond it, the docks. Then over on the other side of the inlet, there's Grouse Mountain. It's about 4,000 feet high. There's a restaurant on top of it. Nice restaurant.

—from the screenplay for *Playback,* by Raymond Chandler

Chandler's detective Philip Marlow was one of Hollywood's most popular creations, but studio executives so hated his set-in-Vancouver screenplay that it never made it into celluloid. That was back in the days before Vancouver came to be called "Hollywood North" because of all the films that are shot here. Chandler's geography in the above excerpt was a bit off, but that's quite understandable, since it can be a little difficult to orient yourself in this city surrounded by water. If you have directional problems, just remember that the grid of streets basically runs northwest to southeast rather than straight north-south, and that the mountains (which you can't always see) are north. The best way to get acquainted with this unique city is to explore its various neighborhoods on foot. The tours below provide a good overall introduction.

WALKING TOUR 1   DOWNTOWN & THE WEST END

Start:	The Fairmont Hotel Vancouver.
Finish:	Cathedral Place.
Time:	2 to 3 hours, not including museum, shopping, and eating stops.
Best Time:	Daytime, particularly during the week when the Law Courts building is open.
Worst Time:	Late in the evening when the shops and offices have closed.

Vancouver's West End is said to be the densest residential district west of Manhattan. I don't know if that's true or not, but what I do know is that urban density has never been more beautifully planned or landscaped than in Vancouver. Every Edwardian house and every high-rise residential tower in the West End is surrounded by lush, beautiful plantings of trees, shrubs, and flowers. This appealingly green idea of the urban working *with* nature instead of against it carries over into Vancouver's commercial downtown, where the placement and orientation of buildings has been carefully controlled to preserve view corridors to the mountains and bodies of water. Remember to look up as you wander downtown—more often than not, you'll be rewarded with a peekaboo view of a North Shore peak.

An appropriate place to begin this tour is:

❶ The Fairmont Hotel Vancouver

At 900 W. Georgia St. (© **604/684-3131**) and dating from 1939, this hotel is owned by the Canadian Pacific Railway (CPR), just as the city itself was for many, many years. In return for agreeing in 1885 to make Vancouver its western terminus, the CPR was given 2,400 hectares (5,931 acres) of prime real estate—nearly the whole of today's downtown. The Hotel Vancouver is built in the CPR's signature château style, with a verdigris-green copper roof. It's worth stepping inside to see the grand, old-fashioned ambience of the lobby.

Leaving by the Burrard Street exit, turn left. When you reach the corner, turn right, cross Burrard Street, and you're on:

❷ Robson Street

The shops on this corner get more foot traffic than any others in Canada. Things were different back in the 1950s, when so many German delis and restaurants opened up that for a time the street was nicknamed "Robsonstrasse." Beginning in the 1980s, the older businesses were replaced with high-end clothiers and new restaurants and gift shops with signs in Japanese. Whether you're into shopping or not, Robson Street is a great place to walk and people-watch. The street has an international cosmopolitan feel to it, and chances are you'll hear Cantonese, Croatian, Japanese, and other tongues as you stroll.

Two blocks farther down Robson at Bute Street, turn left and walk 1 block through a minipark to Barclay Street, and you've entered:

❸ The West End

Beginning in about 1959, this down-at-its-heels neighborhood of once-grand Edwardian houses was transformed by the advent of the concrete high-rise. By 1970, most of the Edwardian houses had been replaced by apartment towers, and the West End was on its way to becoming one of the densest—and simultaneously one of the most livable—inner cities on the continent. The minipark at Bute and Barclay is one of the things that makes the neighborhood so successful: Traffic is kept to a minimum on the tree-lined West End streets, so that residents—though they live in the city center—can enjoy a neighborhood almost as quiet as that in a small town. Beautiful landscaping, and plenty of it, adds to the area's appealing allure.

Turn right and walk 3 blocks down Barclay Street to Nicola Street. Along the way you'll see some of the elements that make the West End such a sought-after enclave: the gardens, street trees, and the range and variety of buildings—including a few surviving Edwardians, like the Arts and Crafts house at 1351 Barclay, and the pair of houses at the corner of Barclay and Nicola streets, otherwise known as:

❹ Barclay Square

This beautifully preserved bit of 19th-century Vancouver consists of Barclay Manor, built in the Queen Anne style in 1890, and Roedde House, a rare domestic design by British Columbia's leading 19th-century institutional architect, Francis Rattenbury. **Roedde House,** 1415 Barclay St. (© **604/684-7040;** www.roeddehouse.org), is now a museum, open for guided tours Wednesday through Friday 2 to 4pm; admission C$5 (US$4/£2.25). On Sundays, tea and cookies are served and the admission price is C$1 (US85¢/45p) more.

Turn left and walk south down Nicola Street for 1 block—past Fire Station No. 6—then turn right and go 1 block on Nelson, then left again onto Cardero Street, passing by the tiny Cardero Grocery at 1078 Cardero St. All the grocery needs of the West End were once supplied by little corner stores like this one. Turn right and walk 2 blocks on Comox Street to reach Denman Street, the perfect place to:

TAKE A BREAK
If Robson Street is the place Vancouverites go for hyperactive shopping sprees, Denman is where they go to sit back, sip a latte, and watch their fellow citizens stroll past. **Urban Rush,** 1040 Denman St. (© **604/685-2996**), is a fine spot

Walking Tour 1: Downtown & the West End

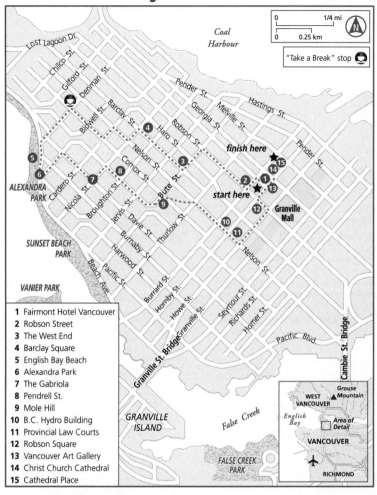

0   1/4 mi
0   0.25 km

"Take a Break" stop

Coal Harbour

finish here

start here

Granville Mall

ALEXANDRA PARK

SUNSET BEACH PARK

VANIER PARK

GRANVILLE ISLAND

False Creek

FALSE CREEK PARK

1 Fairmont Hotel Vancouver
2 Robson Street
3 The West End
4 Barclay Square
5 English Bay Beach
6 Alexandra Park
7 The Gabriola
8 Pendrell St.
9 Mole Hill
10 B.C. Hydro Building
11 Provincial Law Courts
12 Robson Square
13 Vancouver Art Gallery
14 Christ Church Cathedral
15 Cathedral Place

WEST VANCOUVER   ▲ Grouse Mountain
English Bay   Area of Detail
VANCOUVER
RICHMOND

for coffee and baked goods, particularly if you can nab a table on their outdoor terrace. One block down on the opposite side of the street, **Delany's on Denman**, 1105 Denman St. (✆ 604/662-3344), is a favorite coffee hangout for members of the West End's sizable gay community. Everyone's welcome, of course, and the pies and cakes at this little cafe are great.

When you're ready to continue the walking tour, go 2 blocks farther down Denman Street and you're at:

5 English Bay Beach

This is the place to be when the sun is setting, or on one of those crystal-clear days when the mountains of Vancouver Island can be seen looming in the distance—or any day at all, really, so long as the sun is shining. Every January 1, shivering Vancouverites in fancy costumes surround the bathhouse here at the very foot of

Denman Street (entrance at beach level) to take part in the annual Polar Bear Swim.

Walk southeastward (left, as you're facing the water) on Beach Avenue, and you come to a tiny green space with a band shell known as:

❻ Alexandra Park

Back around the turn of the 20th century, a big Bahamian immigrant named Joe Fortes used to make his home in a cottage near this spot, that is, when he wasn't down on the beach teaching local kids to swim. In recognition of his many years of free service, the city finally appointed Fortes its first lifeguard. Later, a marble water fountain was erected in his memory by the Beach Avenue entrance to the park.

When you're finished looking around the park, head up Bidwell Street 2 blocks to Davie Street, cross the street, turn right, walk 2 blocks farther on Davie Street, and on your left at no. 1531 you'll see:

❼ The Gabriola

This was the finest mansion in the West End when it was built in 1900 for sugar magnate B. T. Rogers. Its name comes from the rough sandstone cladding, quarried on Gabriola Island in the Strait of Georgia. Unfortunately for Rogers, the Shaughnessy neighborhood soon opened up across False Creek, and the West End just wasn't a place a millionaire could afford to be seen anymore. By 1925, the mansion had been sold off and subdivided into apartments. Since 1975, it's been a restaurant of one sort or another—currently Romano's Macaroni Grill (reviewed in chapter 6). The wrought-iron tables in the garden are nice spots to sit on a summer day.

Cut through the garden and walk up through the Nicola Street minipark, turning right on:

❽ Pendrell Street

A few interesting bits of architecture reside on this street. One block farther, at the corner of Broughton Street, is the **Thomas Fee house,** 1119 Broughton St.,

where one of the city's leading turn-of-the-20th-century developer-architects made his home. Farther along, at the southeast corner of Pendrell and Jervis streets, is **St. Paul's Episcopal Church,** a 1905 Gothic Revival church built entirely of wood. A block away at 1254 Pendrell is the **Pendrellis**—a piece of architecture so unbelievably awful, one gets a perverse delight just looking at it. Built as a seniors' home at the height of the 1970s craze for concrete, the multistory tower is one great concrete block, with nary a window in sight.

At Bute Street, turn left and walk 1 block to Comox Street, and you're at:

❾ Mole Hill

These 11 preserved Edwardian homes provide a rare view of what the West End looked like in, say, 1925. That they exist at all is more or less a fluke. The city bought the buildings in the 1970s but continued renting them out, thinking one day to tear them down for a park. By the 1990s, however, heritage had become important. The residents of the houses waged a sophisticated political campaign, renaming the area Mole Hill and bringing in nationally known architectural experts to plead the case for preservation. The city soon gave in.

Cut across the park to Nelson Street and continue down Nelson Street past Thurlow Street to 970 Burrard St., where stands:

❿ The B.C. Hydro Building

Built in 1958 by architect Ned Pratt, it was one of the first modernist structures erected in Canada, and has since become a beloved Vancouver landmark, thanks in no small part to its elegant shape and attention to detail. Note how the windows, the doors, and even the tiles in the lobby and forecourt echo the six-sided lozenge shape of the original structure. In the mid-'90s, the building was converted to condominiums and rechristened The Electra.

From here, continue on Nelson Street, crossing Burrard Street and Hornby Street to:

⑪ The Provincial Law Courts

Internationally recognized architect Arthur Erickson has had an undeniable impact on his native city of Vancouver. His 1973 Law Courts complex covers three full city blocks, including the Erickson-renovated Vancouver Art Gallery at its north end. Linking the two is Robson Square, which Erickson—and everyone else—envisioned as the city's main civic plaza. As with so many Erickson designs, this one has elements of brilliance—the boldness of the vision itself, the tiered fountains (behind them are the offices of the Crown attorney—the Canadian equivalent of a district attorney), the cathedral-like space of the courthouse atrium—but, raised above street level, the entire ensemble is removed from all the life around it. To reach the courthouse, take the concrete stairway up and follow the elevated pedestrian concourse. The courthouse, with its giant glass-covered atrium, is worth a visit.

When you've seen the Law Courts, backtrack along the concourse, and you'll end up at:

⑫ Robson Square

As a civic plaza, Robson Square should be grand, but in fact it's pretty underwhelming. Its basic problem is that it has been sunk 6m (20 ft.) below street level, so it's never exactly appealing or inviting to passersby. Although there's a pleasant cafe in the square and a UBC bookstore, Robson square lacks the throngs of people that add the essential ingredient—life—to a civic plaza. But just look across the street, and you'll see all the life that Robson Square lacks.

Directly across from Robson Square at 750 Hornby St. is the:

⑬ Vancouver Art Gallery

On sunny days, people bask like seals on the steps of the old courthouse-turned-art-gallery, a great gathering place and the perfect spot to see jugglers and buskers,

pick up a game of outdoor speed chess, or listen to an activist haranguing the world at large about the topic du jour.

Designed as a courthouse by Francis Rattenbury (architect of Roedde House, described above, and the Legislature Buildings and Fairmont Empress hotel in Victoria) and renovated into an art gallery by Arthur Erickson, the Vancouver Art Gallery (p. 118) is home to a tremendous collection of works by iconic West Coast painter Emily Carr, as well as rotating exhibits ranging from native masks to video installations. Film buffs may remember the entrance steps and inside lobby from the movie *The Accused.*

To continue the tour, go around the gallery and proceed down Hornby Street. Note the fountain on the Art Gallery's front lawn. It was installed by a very unpopular provincial government as a way—according to some—of forever blocking protesters from gathering on what was then the courthouse lawn. In 2007, the 2010 Winter Olympics countdown clock was placed here.

Cross Georgia Street and have a glance inside the **Hong Kong Bank building,** 885 W. Georgia St., where a massive pendulum designed by artist Alan Storey slowly swings back and forth.

Cross Hornby and continue west on Georgia Street to 690 Burrard, where stands:

⑭ Christ Church Cathedral

A Gothic Revival sandstone church with a steep gabled roof, buttresses, and arched stained-glass windows, the Anglican Christ Church Cathedral was completed in 1895. It was nearly demolished in the 1930s, when developers offered a lot of money to the church for the land. A local reporter uncovered the clergy's plot to raze the landmark in exchange for a big profit, and publicized it while negotiations were in the final stages. The public outcry marked the first shift in local sentiment toward the preservation of heritage sites.

Backtrack east to Hornby, turn left, walk half a block, and climb the few steps into:

⑮ Cathedral Place

Often overlooked by Vancouverites, peaceful Cathedral Place is a charming example of an urban park. The building behind it, at 639 Hornby, is a postmodern structure with small Art Deco parts melded onto a basically Gothic edifice. Some of the panels on its front were salvaged from the Georgia Medical-Dental building, a much-loved skyscraper that used to stand on this site. As for the Cathedral Place courtyard itself, it has the formality and calm of a French garden, the perfect spot to sit and enjoy a bit of peace.

WALKING TOUR 2   GASTOWN & CHINATOWN

Start:	Canada Place.
Finish:	Maple Tree Square.
Time:	2 to 4 hours, not including shopping, eating, and sightseeing stops.
Best Time:	Any day during business hours, but Chinatown is particularly active in the mornings. If you arrive between noon and 2pm, you can enjoy dim sum at many of the restaurants.
Worst Time:	Chinatown's dead after 6pm, except on weekends in the summer, when they close a few streets to traffic and hold a traditional Asian night market from 6:30 to 11pm.

Chinatown and Gastown are two of Vancouver's most fascinating neighborhoods. Gastown has history and the kind of old-fashioned architecture that no longer exists downtown or in the West End. Chinatown has brightly colored facades, street markets, and the buzz of modern-day Cantonese commerce. One small travel advisory, however: The two neighborhoods border on Vancouver's Downtown Eastside, a skid row area troubled by alcoholism and drug use. While there's actually little danger for outsiders, there is a good chance you'll cross paths with a down-and-outer here and there, particularly around Pigeon Park at the corner of Carrall and Hastings streets. The tour route has been designed to avoid these areas.

Begin the tour at:

❶ Canada Place

With its five tall Teflon sails and bowsprit jutting out into Burrard Inlet, Canada Place is meant to resemble a giant sailing ship. Inside it's a convention center and giant cruise-ship terminal, with the Pan Pacific Hotel (p. 70) perched on top. Around the perimeter is a promenade with plaques at regular intervals explaining the sights or providing historical tidbits. During the summer months, this area is jammed with tourists and passengers arriving and departing from Alaskan cruises; the rest of the year you'll have it pretty much to yourself. A huge expansion to add more convention space and additional docking facilities is currently underway.

To follow the promenade, start by the fountain flying the flags of Canada's provinces and territories, and head north along the walkway. On the roof at the far end of the pier, a pair of leaping bronze lions point up and out toward a pair of peaks on the North Shore called the Lions, so-named for their supposed resemblance to the Landseer Lions in Trafalgar Square, but really because the local morality squad wanted to eliminate forever the name given to the peaks by the rough-minded early settlers—Sheila's Paps. Continue around the promenade, and you'll turn and look back toward the city: The line of low-rise older buildings just beyond the railway tracks is Gastown.

Walking Tour 2: Gastown & Chinatown

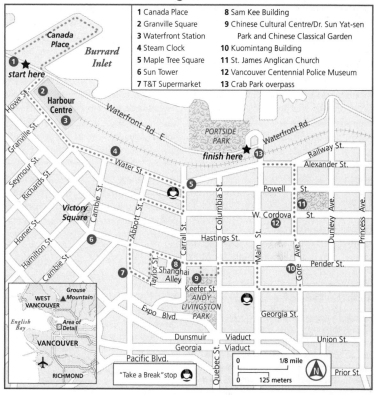

1 Canada Place
2 Granville Square
3 Waterfront Station
4 Steam Clock
5 Maple Tree Square
6 Sun Tower
7 T&T Supermarket
8 Sam Kee Building
9 Chinese Cultural Centre/Dr. Sun Yat-sen
   Park and Chinese Classical Garden
10 Kuomintang Building
11 St. James Anglican Church
12 Vancouver Centennial Police Museum
13 Crab Park overpass

Canada Place

Burrard Inlet

1 ★ start here

2

Harbour Centre

3

Waterfront Rd. E.

PORTSIDE PARK

Waterfront Rd.

finish here ★ 13

Railway St.

Alexander St.

Water St.

4

5

Powell St.

Columbia St.

W. Cordova St.

12

11

Dunlevy Ave.

Princess Ave.

Victory Square

6

Abbott St.

Carrall St.

Hastings St.

Main St.

Gore Ave.

7

8 Shanghai Alley

9

Taylor St.

Keefer St.

ANDY LIVINGSTON PARK

Expo Blvd.

Pender St.

10

Georgia St.

Grouse Mountain

WEST VANCOUVER

English Bay

Area of Detail

VANCOUVER

RICHMOND

Dunsmuir Viaduct

Georgia Viaduct

Union St.

Pacific Blvd.

Quebec St.

"Take a Break" stop

0   1/8 mile
0   125 meters

Prior St.

To continue the tour, walk back toward shore along the promenade, go down the steps, turn left, and curve along the sidewalk until you pass the Aqua Riva restaurant. Then turn left and go up the steps to an elevated plaza. You're now at:

② Granville Square

Had some ill-advised politicians and developers had their way, all of Gastown and Chinatown would have been re-placed by towers like the one you see here at 200 Granville. In 1970, the plans were drawn up and the bulldozers were set to move when a coalition of hippies, her-itage lovers, and Chinatown merchants took to the barricades in revolt. This undistinguished building was the only one ever built, and the plan was aban-doned soon afterward.

At the east end of the plaza a doorway leads into:

③ Waterfront Station

Though this Beaux Arts edifice at 601 W. Cordova St. was converted into the SeaBus terminal in the 1970s (SkyTrain was added in 1986), the building was originally the CPR's Vancouver passenger-rail terminal. Look up high on the walls, and you'll see oil paintings depicting scenes you might encounter if you took the train across Canada (much easier then than now). On the main floor is a Star-bucks and some tourist shops. This is also where you can catch the SeaBus over to Lonsdale Quay in North Vancouver.

Leave by the front doors, turn left, and proceed to cobblestoned Water Street,

Gastown's main thoroughfare. **The Landing,** at 375 Water St., is home to some high-end retail stores and offices. Like most of Gastown's buildings, the Landing was built in the boom years between the Great Fire of 1886 and World War I. Klondike gold fueled much of the construction. As you walk along, note the **Magasin Building** at 322 Water St. Each of the column capitals bears the bronze head of a Gastown notable, among them Ray Saunders, the man who designed the:

❹ Steam Clock

A quirky urban timepiece, the Steam Clock at Water and Cambie streets gives a steamy rendition of the Westminster Chimes every 15 minutes, drawing its power from the city's underground steam-heat system. A plaque on the base of the clock explains the mechanics of it all. (Note: The chimes can be erratic.)

Continue down Water Street, past Hill's Native Art (165 Water St.), where Bill Clinton picked up a little bear statuette as a gift for you-know-who. At Abbot Street, cross over to the south side and continue on Water Street until you come to the Gaoler's Mews building (12 Water St.). Duck in through the passageway and:

TAKE A BREAK
The name **Gaoler's Mews** refers to Vancouver's very first jail, which was built on this site. When that burned to the ground in the 1886 fire, the jail was replaced by a fire hall. The current structure was built as a parking garage but was renovated in the 1970s into a remarkably pleasant complex joined to a common courtyard/atrium. It's now being overhauled once again, and when it's complete, this place will command the highest real estate prices in Gastown. Meanwhile, you'll find excellent beer and good food at the **Irish Heather,** 217 Carrall St. (© **604/688-9779**), accessible either via its back solarium—facing onto the mews—or by going out through the far passageway onto Carrall Street. You have to go this way eventually in order to reach:

❺ Maple Tree Square

A historic spot, Maple Tree Square is where Vancouver first began. The statue by the maple tree (not the original tree, but a replacement planted in the same spot) is of Gassy Jack Deighton, a riverboat captain and innkeeper who erected Vancouver's first significant structure—a saloon—in 1867. Deighton got the nickname Gassy because of his propensity to jaw on at length (gassing, as it was known) about whatever topic happened to spring to mind. In 1870, when the town was officially incorporated as Granville, it was home to exactly six businesses: a hotel, two stores, and three saloons. Most folks called it Gastown, after Jack. More recent history: On August 7, 1971, some 1,500 hippies gathered in the square for the Grasstown Smoke-in & Street Jamboree. There were riots, arrests, and lots of stoned people.

Continue south on Carrall Street to West Cordova, turn right, and walk 1 block to Abbot Street. Turn left and walk 2 blocks down Abbot, crossing West Hastings Street and stopping at West Pender Street, where you get a great view of the:

❻ Sun Tower

At 500 Beatty St., it was the tallest building in the British Empire when it was built in 1911 to house the publishing empire of Louis D. Taylor, publisher of *Vancouver World.* Not only was the building tall, it was also slightly scandalous, thanks to the nine half-nude caryatids that gracefully support the cornice halfway up the building. Three years after the building opened, Louis D. was forced to sell it.

Cross West Pender Street and continue on Abbot Street until you come to the entrance at 179 Keefer Place of:

❼ T&T Supermarket

Think you know supermarkets? Unless your hometown is Hong Kong or Singapore, you haven't seen one like this. Just have a gander at the seafood display inside the doors: king crab, scallops, three different kinds of oysters, lobster, and geoducks. Farther in is a host of other wondrous products, including strange Asian fruits like rambutan, lychee, and the pungent durian. Browse, maybe pick up something you don't recognize, and have an impromptu picnic in nearby Andy Livingstone Park.

Outside, walk 1 block east on Keefer Street to Taylor Street. Andy Livingstone Park is farther ahead to your right, but to continue the tour, turn left on Taylor Street and walk 1 block north to Pender Street. Turn right on Pender, and walk 1 block. Now you're in one of North America's most populous Chinatowns. Our first Chinatown stop, at 8 W. Pender St., is the:

8 Sam Kee Building

The world's thinnest office building—just shy of 1.5m deep (4 ft. 11 in. to be exact)—was Sam Kee's way of thumbing his nose at both the city and his greedy next-door neighbor. In 1912, the city expropriated most of Kee's land in order to widen Pender Street, but refused to compensate him for the tiny leftover strip. Kee's neighbor, meanwhile, hoped to pick up the leftover sliver dirt-cheap. The building was Kee's response. Huge bay windows helped maximize the available space, as did the extension of the basement well out underneath the sidewalk (note the glass blocks in the pavement).

Just behind the Sam Kee Building is the forlorn-looking **Shanghai Alley,** which just 40 years ago was jampacked with stores, restaurants, a pawnshop, a theater, rooming houses, and a public bath. (**Canton Alley,** on your right between E. Pender and E. Hastings sts., still gives an idea of what these teeming alleyways looked like a few decades ago, but it's now an unsavory hangout for drug users.) More interesting is the **Chinese Freemason's building,** just across the street at 1 W. Pender. The building

could be a metaphor for the Chinese experience in Canada. On predominantly Anglo Carrall Street, the building is the picture of Victorian conformity. On the Pender Street side, on the other hand, the structure is exuberantly Chinese.

Walk 1 block farther (east) on Pender Street and you'll come to the:

9 Chinese Cultural Centre/ Dr. Sun Yat-Sen Park & Chinese Classical Garden

A modern building with an impressive traditional gate, the cultural center provides services and programs for the neighborhood's thousands of Chinese-speaking residents. Straight ahead as you enter the courtyard, a door set within a wall leads into the **Dr. Sun Yat-Sen Park,** a small urban park with a pond, walkways, and a nice gift shop, **Silk Road Art Trading Co.,** 561 Columbia St. (© **604/683-8707**), which sells scaled-down replicas of the ancient terra-cotta warriors unearthed in the tomb of Chinese Emperor Qon Shi Huang. Admission to the park is free.

Adjoining the park, and accessible through another small doorway to the right of it, is the **Dr. Sun Yat-Sen Classical Chinese Garden** (p. 119). Modeled after a Ming period (1368–1644) scholar's retreat in the Chinese city of Suzhou, this garden is definitely worth a visit. Dr. Sun Yat-Sen (1866–1925), for whom the park and garden are named, is known as the father of modern China.

Exit the Chinese Classical Garden by the gate on the east side, turn left on Columbia Street, and you'll find the **Chinese Cultural Centre Museum and Archives** at 555 Columbia St.

From here, continue on Columbia Street up to Pender, turn right and continue east, peeking in here and there to explore Chinese herbalist shops like Vitality Enterprises at 126 E. Pender. At Main Street, turn right and walk south 1 block to Keefer Street and:

TAKE A BREAK
Though it's Canada's largest Chinese restaurant, **Floata Seafood Restaurant**, 180 Keefer St. (© 604/602-0368), isn't easy to find. In classic Hong Kong restaurant style, it's on the third floor of a bright red shopping plaza/parking garage. Time your arrival for mid-morning dim sum (a kind of moving Chinese smorgasbord) if you can. Alternatively, you might want to check out the recommended Chinatown restaurants in chapter 6.

To continue the tour, stroll east on Keefer Street, lined with sidewalk markets selling fresh fish, fruit, and vegetables. Turn left on Gore Street, and walk 1 block north to Pender Street. On your left, at 296 E. Pender St., is the:

⑩ Kuomintang Building

Though often a mystery to outsiders, politics was and remains an important part of life in Chinatown. Vancouver was long a stronghold of the Chinese Nationalist Party, or Kuomintang (KMT), whose founder, Dr. Sun Yat-Sen, stayed in Vancouver for a time raising funds. In 1920, the party erected this building to serve as its western Canadian headquarters. When the rival Chinese Communist party emerged victorious from the Chinese civil war in 1949, KMT leader Chiang Kai-shek retreated to Taiwan. Note the Taiwanese flags on the roof.

Return to Gore Street and turn left (north) for 2 blocks. At the corner of Gore and Cordova streets (303 E. Cordova St.) stands:

⑪ St. James Anglican Church

Just before getting this commission, architect Adrian Gilbert Scott had designed a cathedral in Cairo—and it shows.

One block west on Cordova brings you to the:

⑫ Vancouver Centennial Police Museum

Located in the former Coroner's Court at 240 E. Cordova, the **Vancouver Centennial Police Museum** (p. 119) is worth a visit if you're in a macabre mood. Among other displays, the museum has the autopsy report of Errol Flynn, who died in Vancouver in 1959 in the arms of his 17-year-old girlfriend.

Back on Gore Street, walk north 2 blocks to Alexander Street. Turn left, and walk 1 block west on Alexander to the:

⑬ Crab Park Overpass

City Hall calls it Portside Park, and that's how it appears on the map, but to everyone else it's Crab Park. It was created after long and vigorous lobbying by eastside activists, who reasoned that poor downtown residents had as much right to beach access as anyone else. The park is pleasant enough, though not worth the trouble of walking all the way up and over the overpass. What is worthwhile, however, is walking halfway up to where two stone Chinese lions stand guard. From here, you can look back at Canada Place—where the tour started—or at the container port and fish plant to your right.

To bring the tour to an end, return to Alexander Street and walk 2 blocks west back to Maple Tree Square (stop 5).

WALKING TOUR 3	YALETOWN, GRANVILLE ISLAND & KITSILANO

Start:	The Vancouver Public Library Central Branch at Horner and Georgia streets.
Finish:	The Capers Building, 285 W. 4th Ave. (at Vine), in Kitsilano.
Time:	2 to 4 hours, not including shopping, eating, and sightseeing stops.
Best Time:	Any time during business hours.
Worst Time:	After 6pm, when Granville Island's shops have closed.

This tour takes you through three of Vancouver's most interesting neighborhoods: the trendy warehouse-turned-retail/restaurant district of Yaletown, the industrial-area-turned-public-market called Granville Island, and the laid-back enclave of Kitsilano. The tour includes a brief ferry ride and a stroll along the waterfront and beach.

We begin at:

❶ Vancouver Public Library

Designed by architect Moshe Safdie, the library, 350 W. Georgia St. (ⓒ **604/331-3600**), was enormously controversial when it opened in 1995. Though Safdie denied that the ancient Roman coliseum served as inspiration, the coliseum is exactly what comes to mind when you first see the exterior of this postmodern building. Architectural critics pooh-poohed it as derivative and ignorant of West Coast architectural traditions, but for the public it was love at first sight. The steps out front have become a popular public gathering place, the lofty atrium inside a favored hangout spot and "study-date" locale. Go inside the atrium and then into the high-tech library itself: It's light, airy, and wonderfully accessible.

From the library, walk south down Homer Street and turn left on Nelson Street. At Hamilton Street you're in:

❷ Yaletown

Vancouver's former meatpacking warehouse district, Yaletown was where roughneck miners from Yale (up the Fraser Valley) used to come to drink and brawl. The city considered leveling the area in the 1970s until someone noticed that the raised loading docks would make great outdoor terraces and the low brick buildings themselves could be renovated into commercial space. Though it's taken years for the neighborhood to really catch on, the result is a funky upscale district of furniture shops, restaurants, multimedia companies, "New York–style" lofts, and lots and lots of clubs. Hamilton Street and Mainland Street are the trendiest arteries in Yaletown. Note the metal canopies over

the loading docks on many buildings—they used to keep shipping goods dry; now they do the same for tourists and latte-sipping computer programmers.

Walk down Mainland and turn left at Davie. Continue southeast down Davie Street, turn right on Pacific Boulevard, and across the street you'll see:

❸ The Roundhouse

The Roundhouse is so named because that's exactly what this brick-and-timber frame building was, back when this land was the CPR's switching yard. The structure has since been converted into a community center. It's worth ducking inside to have a look at the locomotive that pulled the first passenger train into Vancouver, way back in 1887; you can also see the locomotive from the street, through a giant glass window.

Follow Davie Street south to the False Creek waterfront and the:

❹ Yaletown Landing (at the Foot of Davie St.)

The forest of high-rises ringing the north shore of False Creek, where you're now standing, is the creation of one company—Concorde Pacific, owned by Hong Kong billionaire Li Ka Shing. Formerly a railway switching yard, the area was transformed for the Expo '86 World's Fair. When the fair came to an end, the provincial government sold the land to Li Ka Shing for a song on the understanding he would build condominiums. And did he ever.

At the landing site, note the large art piece, *Street Light*, designed by Bernie Miller and Alan Tregebov and installed in 1997. The large panels, each of which depicts a seminal event in False Creek's history, have been arranged so that on the anniversary of that event, the sun will shine directly through the panel, casting a shadowed image on the street.

From here, at the end of the dock, catch the **Aquabus miniferry** (© **604/ 689-5858**) for Granville Island, right across False Creek. The little boats leave about every 15 minutes through the day; the fare is C$2.50 (US$2.25/£1.20) for adults.

The Aquabus will scoot you across False Creek harbor in about 5 minutes and let you off at:

❺ Granville Island Ferry Dock

To be topographically honest, Granville Island (p. 120) is not really an island; it's more of a protuberance. But it contains a fascinating collection of shops, restaurants, theaters, artists' workshops, housing, a hotel, and still-functioning heavy industry—one of the few successful examples of 1970s urban renewal. The **Granville Island Information Centre,** 1592 Johnston St. (© **604/666-5784**), near the Public Market, has excellent free maps, but they're not really necessary—the place is so compact, the best thing to do is simply wander and explore.

Right at the top of the Aquabus dock is an entrance into the:

❻ Granville Island Public Market

This is an amazing place that sells just about anything and everything that's edible. The market is a wonderful place to stop and:

 TAKE A BREAK
If it's edible, the **Granville Island Public Market** probably has it, from chocolate and fresh salmon to fresh bread and strawberries picked that morning out in the Fraser Valley. Those with an immediate hunger gravitate to the far side of the market, where **A La Mode** (© **604/685-8335**) sells lattes and fabulous rhubarb-strawberry pie. The most fun way to

---

feed yourself, however, is to roam the market stalls for sandwiches, sausages, or picnic supplies—artichoke hearts, artisan cheese, cold smoked salmon, Indian candy, pepper pâté, freshly baked bread—then head outside for an alfresco feast at one of the tables on the dock overlooking False Creek. The views are great, the fresh air invigorating, and, if you've brought small children along, it's the perfect place to play that endlessly fascinating (to kids) game of Catch the Seagull.

From Triangle Square, the small plaza in front of the public market, head south (left) on Duranleau Street, where you'll pass enticing shops and marine charter services. At Anderson Street turn right and right again on waterside Island Park Walk, following it north to the:

❼ Government Fish Dock

Want to buy fresh from the boat? This is the place to do it. Find fresh salmon in season (summer and early fall), prawns, scallops, and other shellfish much of the rest of the year. Sales take place every day in high season and on weekend mornings the rest of the year. Hours and availability, of course, depend on the catch.

Continue on the seaside walkway, and eventually you pass beneath the:

❽ Burrard Bridge

In 1927, the city fathers commissioned noted urban planner Harland Bartholomew to provide some guidance on how to expand their rather raw seaport city. One of Bartholomew's first injunctions: Build beautiful bridges. The Burrard Bridge is the result, an elegant steel span with two castles guarding the approaches at either end.

Walk beneath the bridge and continue along the waterside pedestrian path in Vanier Park to:

❾ Heritage Harbour

Many older wooden boats find shelter here, including the seiner BCP45 shown on the back of the old Canadian $5 bill. Those interested in a shortcut can pick up a ferry (**False Creek Ferries;** © **604/684-7781**) at this point and ride back to Granville Island (stop 5) or over to the West End. On

Walking Tour 3: Yaletown, Granville Island & Kitsilano

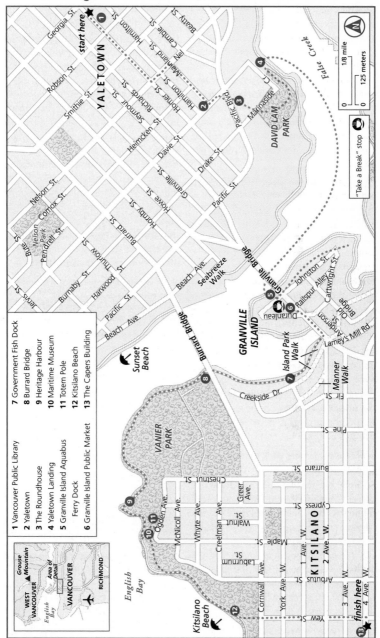

Legend:

1 Vancouver Public Library
2 Yaletown
3 The Roundhouse
4 Yaletown Landing
5 Granville Island Aquabus Ferry Dock
6 Granville Island Public Market
7 Government Fish Dock
8 Burrard Bridge
9 Heritage Harbour
10 Maritime Museum
11 Totem Pole
12 Kitsilano Beach
13 The Capers Building

"Take a Break" stop

1/8 mile
125 meters

YALETOWN

start here

DAVID LAM PARK

False Creek

GRANVILLE ISLAND

VANIER PARK

English Bay

Sunset Beach

Kitsilano Beach

KITSILANO

finish here

WEST VANCOUVER
Grouse Mountain
Area of Detail
VANCOUVER
RICHMOND
English Bay

weekdays and in the off season, the ferries run less frequently. Hours and fares are posted on the sign at the end of the dock.

If you're continuing the walk, proceed west along the shoreline. To your left stands artist Chung Hung's massive iron sculpture *Gate to the Northwest Passage.* Just beyond that, the conical building is the **Vancouver Museum,** 1100 Chestnut St. (℃ **604/736-4431;** p. 124) and **H. R. MacMillan Space Centre** (℃ **604/738-STAR;** p. 120). The low building next to that is the **Vancouver Archives,** 1150 Chestnut (℃ **604/736-8561**), home to some truly fascinating panoramic photographs of Vancouver back in the early days.

Continue on the waterside path until you come to the:

⑩ Maritime Museum

For centuries, the quest of every European explorer was to find the Northwest Passage, the seagoing shortcut to the riches of the East. The little ship housed inside the Maritime Museum, 1905 Ogden Ave. (℃ **604/257-8300**), is the one that finally did it. Tours of the RCMP vessel, the *St. Roch,* are available at regular intervals throughout the day (p. 124). Out back of the museum, the junk on the lawn by the north side all comes from various ships wrecked on the B.C. coast.

In front of the museum, you'll see the:

⑪ Totem Pole

Carved by the exceptional Kwakiutl carver Mungo Martin (who also did many of the poles displayed in the Museum of Anthropology and in Stanley Park), the 10 figures on this 30m-tall (98-ft.) pole each represent an ancestor of the 10 Kwakiutl clans. An identical pole was presented to Queen Elizabeth in 1958 to mark B.C.'s centenary. It now stands in Windsor Great Park in England.

Continue on the waterside pathway to:

⑫ Kitsilano Beach

Vancouver is blessed with beaches. From here, they stretch almost unbroken to the University of British Columbia, 10km (6¼ miles) west on the tip of the Point Grey peninsula. Each beach has its own distinct personality. Below UBC, Wreck Beach is a semiwild strand for nudists and nature lovers. Beaches in between cater to dogs, picnicking families, and hikers. Kitsilano Beach (Kits Beach for short) is home to a spandex-and-testosterone set that loves a fast and furious game on the volleyball courts. But relaxers love Kits, too. The logs lined up on the beach make it a fine place to lay out a blanket and laze the day away. Small children love to play on the nearby swings, while older kids favor the lifeguarded swimming area or the world's largest outdoor saltwater swimming pool. On a clear day, the views of the mountains are tremendous.

About midway down Kits Beach, a sidewalk veers left and takes you up to Yew Street. Follow Yew uphill to 4th Avenue and turn right. At 2285 W. 4th Ave. you'll find:

⑬ The Capers Building

Back in the 1960s, Kitsilano was Canada's Hippie Central, a Haight-Ashbury–like enclave of head shops, communes, and coffeehouses. In the early 1970s, Vancouver's supersquare mayor, Tom Campbell, went so far as to propose rounding up all the tie-dyed long-hairs and shipping them off to a detention center. As the years passed, the hippies' waistlines and wallets got thicker, run-down communes and boardinghouses were renovated or replaced with new apartments and condos, and the shops came to reflect Kitsilano's new affluence, though still with a touch of counterculture.

The retail/office/apartment building at 2285 W. 4th Ave. was built according to an innovative energy-efficient design, and now serves as home to an excellent bookstore called **Duthie's,** and to **Capers,** an organic supermarket.

The walk ends here. You may want to explore the shopping opportunities along 4th Avenue. Or you can catch a no. 4 or 7 bus to take you back to downtown Vancouver.

Vancouver Shopping

Blessed with a climate that seems semi-tropical in comparison to the rest of Canada, Vancouverites never really developed a taste for indoor malls. Instead, most residents shop on the street. Below are a few thoughts on where to start exploring.

1 The Shopping Scene

Outside of malls, stores in Vancouver are generally open Monday through Saturday from 9am to 6pm. A few exceptions: Stores on Robson Street stay open later (usually until 9pm), while stores in Kitsilano open later (around 10am). On Sunday most stores are open 11am to 6pm, but a few remain closed all day. Malls such as the Pacific Centre are open from 9am to 7pm Monday through Wednesday, 9am to 9pm Thursday through Saturday, and 10am to 6pm on Sunday. During Christmas shopping season, stores extend their hours from 9am to 9pm 7 days a week.

ROBSON STREET   It's been said that the corner of Robson and Burrard gets more foot traffic than any other corner in Canada. It's a busy, colorful parade of humanity, with many students, visitors, and residents from Asia (hence the sushi bars and shops with Japanese signs), most with money. Over the past few years, rents have risen so much that Robson Street now mostly offers upscale chain shops and international designer boutiques, though here and there a few local stores survive. Look for high-end clothing and accessories, with a focus on young designer fashions.

SOUTH GRANVILLE   The 10-block stretch of Granville Street—from 6th Avenue up to 16th Avenue—is where Vancouver's old-money enclave of Shaughnessy comes to shop. Classic and expensive clothiers, housewares, and furniture boutiques predominate. This is also the heart of the gallery district.

WATER STREET & GASTOWN   Though a little too heavy on the souvenir shops, Water Street and Gastown are by no means just a tacky tourist enclave. Look for antiques and cutting-edge furniture, galleries of First Nations art, funky basement retro shops, and up-to-the-minute fashions by local designers.

MAIN STREET   Antiques, and lots of 'em. From about 19th up to 27th, Main Street is chockablock with antiques shops. Rather than outbid each other, the stores have evolved so that each covers a particular niche, from Art Deco to country kitchen to fine Second Empire. It's fun to browse, and if your eyes start to glaze over at the thought of yet another divan, the area also has cafes, bookshops, and clothing stores.

GRANVILLE ISLAND   A rehabilitated industrial site beneath the Granville Street Bridge, the Public Market is one of the best places to pick up salmon and other seafood. It's also a great place to browse for crafts and gifts. You can also observe potters, silversmiths, and glass blowers as they work their magic. Particularly interesting is Kids Market, a kind of minimall for children, featuring play areas and services for the not-yet-10 demographic. See the Granville Island listing (p. 113).

ASIA WEST   If you've never been to Hong Kong, or are just itching to get back, this new commercial area on Richmond's No. 3 Road between Capstan and Alderbridge roads is the place to shop. Stores in four new malls—the Yaohan Centre, President Plaza, Aberdeen Centre, and Parker Place—cater to Vancouver's Asian community by bringing in goods directly from the Far East. If the prices seem a bit high, a simple inquiry is often enough to bring them plummeting by as much as 80%.

PUNJABI MARKET   Just like an imported India, the 4 blocks of Main Street, on either side of 49th Avenue, contain the whole of the subcontinent, shrunk down to a manageable parcel. Look for fragrant spice stalls, sari shops, and textile outlets selling luxurious fabrics—at bargain-basement prices.

2 Shopping A to Z

ANTIQUES

Bakers Dozen Antiques   This charming shop specializes in antique toys, model ships and boats, folk art, and unusual 19th- and early-20th-century furniture. 3520 Main St. ⓒ 604/879-3348.

Mihrab *(Finds)*   Part museum and part subcontinental yard sale, Mihrab specializes in one-of-a-kind Indian antiques for the house and garden. Think intricately carved teak archways or tiny jewel-like door pulls, all selected by partners Lou Johnson and Kerry Lane on frequent trips to the subcontinent. 2229 Granville St. ⓒ **604/879-6105.**

Uno Langmann Limited   Catering to upscale shoppers, Uno Langmann specializes in European and North American paintings, furniture, silver, and objects d'art from the 18th through early 20th centuries. 2117 Granville St. ⓒ **604/736-8825.** www.langmann.com.

Vancouver Antique Centre   Housed in a heritage commercial building, this maze contains about a dozen separate shops on two levels, specializing in everything from china, glass, and jewelry to military objects, sports, toys, retro '50s and '60s collectibles, home furnishings, and watches. Neighboring buildings house even more shops. 422 Richards St. ⓒ **604/684-9822.**

BOOKS

Blackberry Books   Although this small Granville Island store tends toward general interest, they have a healthy selection of books about art, architecture, and cuisine. They're right across from the public market. 1663 Duranleau St. ⓒ **604/685-4113** or 604/685-6188. www.bbooks.ca.

Chapters   Chapters chain bookstores are pleasant and well planned, with little nooks, comfy benches, and a huge stock of titles. 788 Robson St. ⓒ **604/682-4066.** Also at 2505 Granville St. (ⓒ **604/731-7822).** www.chapters.ca.

Duthie Books Fourth Avenue   This well-known local bookstore on Granville Island has been in business since 1957. It's a good place to find local authors and stocks an excellent inventory of Canadian and international titles. 2239 W. 4th Ave., Kitsilano. ⓒ **604/732-5344.** www.duthiebooks.com.

International Travel Maps and Books *(Finds)*   This store has the best selection of travel books, maps, charts, and globes in town, plus an impressive selection of special-interest British Columbia guides. This is the hiker's best source for detailed topographic

charts of the entire province. 539 West Pender St. ℂ **604/687-3320.** Also at 530 W. Broadway
(ℂ **604/879-3621).** www.itmb.com.

Kidsbooks *(Kids* The largest and most interesting selection of children's literature in
the city also has an amazing collection of puppets and holds regular readings. 3083 W.
Broadway. ℂ **604/738-5335.** Also 3040 Edgemont Blvd., North Vancouver (ℂ **604/986-6190).** www.
kidsbooks.ca.

CAMERAS

Dunne & Rundle foto source   Dunne & Rundle is conveniently located downtown, can handle repairs for most major brands, and sells parts, accessories, and film.
891 Granville St. ℂ **604/681-9254.** www.dunneandrundle.com.

Lens & Shutter   Located near the food court of the downtown Pacific Centre Mall,
Lens & Shutter provides film and camera advice, sells and repairs cameras, and devel-
ops photos. 8700 W. Georgia St. (in Pacific Centre). ℂ **604/684-4422.** Also 2912 W. Broadway
(ℂ **604/736-3461).** www.lensandshutter.com.

CERAMICS, CHINA, SILVER & CRYSTAL

Gallery of B.C. Ceramics   This Granville Island gallery is owned and operated by
the Potters Guild of British Columbia and features a collection of sculptural and functional ceramic works from 100 B.C. potters. Gallery hours change seasonally, so
phone ahead to confirm hours of operation. Closed on Mondays in January and February. 1359 Cartwright St. ℂ **604/669-5645.** www.bcpotters.com.

Martha Sturdy Originals *(Finds* Local designer Martha Sturdy—once best known
for her collectible, usable, handblown glassware trimmed in gold leaf—is now creating a critically acclaimed line of cast-resin housewares, as well as limited-edition
couches and chairs. Expensive, but, if you've got the dough, the furniture is well worth
it. 3039 Granville St. ℂ **604/737-0037.** www.marthasturdy.com.

CHINESE GOODS

Silk Road Art Trading Co. *(Finds* This store, with an entrance on Columbia Street
and another within Dr. Sun Yat-Sen Park in the Chinese Cultural Centre, sells reproductions of Chinese art objects, including the ancient terra-cotta warriors unearthed
in a Chinese emperor's tomb. 561 Columbia St. ℂ **604/683-8707.**

T&T Supermarket *(Finds* This store has racks and racks of goods you won't find at
home (unless your home is China), but the real entertainment is the seafood and produce, where strange and ungainly comestibles lurk: fire-dragon fruit, lily root, and
enoki mushrooms. 181 Keefer St. ℂ **604/899-8836.** www.tnt-supermarket.com.

Ten Ren Tea & Ginseng Co.   Whether you prefer the pungent aroma of Chinese
black tea or the exotic fragrance of chrysanthemum, jasmine, or ginger flower, you
must try the numerous varieties of drinking and medicinal teas in this Chinatown
shop. It also carries Korean, American, and Siberian ginseng for a lot less than you
might pay elsewhere. 550 Main St. ℂ **604/684-1566.**

Tung Fong Hung Foods Co. *(Finds* If you've never been to a Chinese herbalist, this
is the one to try: jars, bins, and boxes full of such things as dried sea horse, thinly sliced
deer antler, and bird's nest. It's fun to explore and potentially good for what ails you.
Chinese remedies can have side effects, however, so before ingesting anything unfamiliar, consult the on-site herbalist. 536 Main St. ℂ **604/688-0883.**

A Special Vancouver Experience: Asian Night Markets

Whether you're hoping to sample steamed dumplings, pick up a tin of oolong tea, or just poke around a fascinating scene, visiting one of Vancouver's Asian night markets is great fun. Throughout the summer, both Pender and Keefer streets in historic Chinatown are closed to make room for the **Chinatown Night Market** (www.vcma.shawbiz.ca). Styled after Asian marketplaces where shopping is personal and haggling is the name of the game, stalls and tables are loaded with bargain-priced merchandise, including CDs, garments, novelties, watches, food, and accessories. Enjoy horse-drawn carriage rides on Fridays, entertainment shows on Saturdays, and family fun and games on Sundays. The market runs every Friday, Saturday, and Sunday, May 18 to September 9, from 6:30 to 11pm. In Held in Richmond, about 30 minutes from downtown Vancouver, the **Richmond Night Market** (www.richmondnightmarket.com) is an all-out event that feels like a summer festival with up to 15,000 visitors in 1 night. Over 300 booths sell merchandise from all over the world, and over 50 food vendors cook up a storm to please both curious and hungry samplers. Entertainment is also a big part of the market with various performers during the evening. The market runs from May 18 through October 8 every Friday, Saturday, and Sunday.

CIGARS & TOBACCO

Americans remember: If they're Cuban, you have to light up on this side of the border.

La Casa del Habano   Directly across from Planet Hollywood on Robson Street, Casa del Habano has Vancouver's largest walk-in humidor. Cigars range in price from a few dollars to more than a hundred. 980 Robson St. *C* **604/609-0511.**

Vancouver Cigar Company   The selection here is reputed to be the city's most extensive, featuring brands such as Cohiba, Monte Cristo, Macanudo, Hoyo de Monterrey, Romeo y Julieta, Partagas, Ashton, and A. Fuente. The shop also carries a complete line of accessories. 1093 Hamilton St. *C* **604/685-0445.** www.vancouvercigar.com.

DEPARTMENT STORES

The Bay (Hudson's Bay Company)   From the establishment of its early trading posts during the 1670s to its modern coast-to-coast department-store chain, The Bay has built its reputation on quality goods. You can still buy a Hudson's Bay woolen "point" blanket (the colorful stripes originally represented how many beaver pelts each blanket was worth in trade), but you'll also find Tommy Hilfiger, Polo, DKNY, and more. 674 Granville St. *C* **604/681-6211.** www.hbc.com.

Hills of Kerrisdale *(Value*   This neighborhood department store in central Vancouver is a city landmark. Carrying full lines of quality men's, women's, and children's clothes, as well as furnishings and sporting goods, it's a destination for locals because the prices are often lower than those in the downtown core. 2125 W. 41st Ave. *C* **604/266-9177.** www.hillsofkerrisdale.com.

DISCOUNT SHOPPING

The strip of West 4th Avenue between Cypress and Yew streets has recently emerged as consignment-clothing central. New shops open regularly.

In-Again Clothing *(Value)*   This shop has a good variety of seasonal consignment clothing, and the selection keeps up with fashion trends. Don't miss the collection of purses, scarves, and belts. 1962 W. 4th Ave. (C) **604/738-2782.**

Second Suit for Men & Women *(Value)*   This resale- and sample-clothing store has the best in men's and women's fashions, including Hugo Boss, Armani, Donna Karan, Nautica, Calvin Klein, and Alfred Sung. The inventory changes rapidly. 2036 W. 4th Ave. (C) **604/732-0338.**

FASHIONS
FOR CHILDREN

Isola Bella *(Kids)*   This store imports an exclusive collection of rather expensive, high-fashion newborn and children's clothing from designers like Babar, Milou, Petit Bateau, and Paul Smith. 5692 Yew St. (C) **604/266-8808.** www.isolabella.ca.

Please Mum *(Kids)*   This Kitsilano store sells attractive Canadian-made toddler's and children's cotton clothing. 2951 W. Broadway. (C) **604/732-4574.** www.pleasemum.com.

FOR MEN & WOMEN

Vancouver has the Pacific Northwest's best collection of clothes from Paris, London, Milan, and Rome, in addition to a great assortment of locally made, cutting-edge fashions. It seems that almost every week a new designer boutique opens in Yaletown, Kitsilano, or Kerrisdale. International designer outlets include **Chanel Boutique,** 900 W. Hastings St. ((C) 604/682-0522); **Salvatore Ferragamo,** 918 Robson St. ((C) 604/669-4495); **Gianni Versace Boutique,** 757 W. Hastings St. ((C) 604/683-1131); **Polo/Ralph Lauren,** the Landing, 375 Water St. ((C) 604/682-7656); and **Plaza Escada,** Sinclair Centre, 757 W. Hastings St. ((C) 604/688-8558).

Dorothy Grant *(Finds)*   Designed to look like a Pacific Northwest longhouse, this shop is where First Nations designer Dorothy Grant exhibits her unique designs as well as her husband's (acclaimed artist Robert Davidson) collection of exquisitely detailed Haida motifs, which she appliqués on coats, leather vests, jackets, caps, and accessories. The clothes are gorgeous and collectible. She also carries contemporary Haida art and jewelry. 1656 W. 75th St. (corner of Granville St., near Vancouver International Airport). (C) **604/681-0201.** www.dorothygrant.com.

Dream 311   Big-name designs can be found anywhere, but this little shop is one of the few places to show early collections—clothing and jewelry—of local designers. 311 W. Cordova. (C) **604/683-7326.**

Leone   Shop where the stars shop. Versace, Donna Karan, Byblos, Armani, and fabulous Italian and French accessories are sold in this very elegant building; valet parking provided, and private after-hours shopping by appointment for VIPs. Sinclair Centre, 757 W. Hastings St. ℰ 604/683-1133. www.leone.ca.

Obakki Visit this great new fashion boutique in Gastown for original garments created by talented new Canadian designers; high-quality fabrics and attention to design are the hallmarks. 44 Water St. ℰ **604/669-9727.** www.obakki.com.

Roots Canada Proudly Canadian, this chain features sturdy casual clothing, including leather jackets and bags, footwear, outerwear, and athletic wear for the whole family. 1001 Robson (corner of Burrard). ℰ **604/683-4305.** www.roots.com.

Swimco Located near Kitsilano Beach, this store sells a large variety of bikinis and bathing suits in the latest styles for men, women, and children. 2166 W. 4th Ave. ℰ **604/ 732-7946.** www.swimco.com.

Venus & Mars *(Finds* Add some drama to your life. This Gastown boutique features Vancouver designer Sanné Lambert's work, specializing in one-of-a-kind handmade gowns and velvet robes. Some plus sizes also available. 315 Cambie St. ℰ **604/687-1908.** www.venusandmars.biz.

Zonda Nellis Design Ltd. *(Finds* Rich colors and intricate patterns highlight this Vancouver designer's imaginative hand-woven separates, pleated silks, sweaters, vests, and soft knits. Nellis has also introduced a new line of hand-painted silks and sumptuous, sheer, hand-painted evening wear. 2203 Granville St. ℰ **604/736-5668.** www.zondanellis.com.

VINTAGE CLOTHING
Deluxe Junk Co. The name fits—there's tons of junk here. However, some real bargains have been known to pop up among the polyester jackets and worn-out dress shirts. 310 W. Cordova St. ℰ **604/685-4871.** www.deluxejunk.com.

Legends Retro-Fashion Specializing in unique retro clothing, Legends is well known among vintage purists for its cache of one-of-a-kind pieces. Most of the clothes, such as evening dresses, shoes, kid gloves, and other accessories, are in immaculate condition. Closed Monday and Tuesday. 4366 Main St. ℰ **604/875-0621.**

True Value Vintage Clothing This underground shop has a collection of funky fashions from the 1930s through the 1990s, including tons of fake furs, leather jackets, denim, soccer jerseys, vintage bathing suits, formal wear, smoking jackets, sweaters, and accessories. 710 Robson St. ℰ **604/685-5403.**

FIRST NATIONS ART & CRAFTS
You'll find First Nations art all over the city. You don't have to purchase a pricey antique to acquire original Coast Salish or Haida work. As the experts at the **Museum of Anthropology** explain, if an item is crafted by any of the indigenous Pacific Northwest artisans, it's a real First Nations piece of art. The culture is ancient yet still very much alive. Galleries will tell you about the artist, and explain how to identify and care for these beautifully carved, worked, and woven pieces. Bold, traditional, and innovative geometric designs, intricate carvings, strong primary colors, and rich wood tones are just a few of the elements you'll find in First Nations crafts.

Even if you're not in the market, go gallery-hopping to see works by Haida artists **Bill Reid** (the province's best-known native artist) and **Richard Davidson,** and by Kwakwaka'wakw artist and photographer **David Neel.**

Coastal Peoples Fine Arts Gallery This Yaletown boutique offers an extensive collection of fine First Nations jewelry. The motifs—Bear, Salmon, Whale, Raven, and others—are drawn from local myths and translated into 14-karat or 18-karat gold and sterling silver creations. Inuit sculptures and items made of glass or wood are also worth a look. Custom orders can be filled quickly and shipped worldwide. 1024 Mainland St. ℂ 604/685-9298. www.coastalpeoples.com.

Hill's Native Art ✮   In a re-creation of a trading post interior, this shop, established in 1946 and claiming to be North America's largest Northwest coast native art gallery, sells ceremonial masks, Cowichan sweaters, moccasins, wood sculptures, totem poles, silk-screen prints, soapstone sculptures, and gold, silver, and argillite jewelry. 165 Water St. ℂ 604/685-4249. www.hillsnativeart.com.

Images for a Canadian Heritage ✮ *Finds*   This store and the Inuit Gallery of Vancouver (see below) are government-licensed First Nations art galleries, featuring traditional and contemporary works such as native designs on glass totems and copperplates. With a museum-worthy collection, this shop deserves a visit whether you're buying or not. 164 Water St. (at Cambie St.). ℂ 604/685-7046. www.imagesforcanada.com.

Inuit Gallery of Vancouver   This store is home to one of Canada's foremost collections of Inuit and First Nations art. Prices are for serious buyers, but it's worth a visit. 206 Cambie St. ℂ 604/688-7323. www.inuit.com.

Khot-La-Cha Salish Handicrafts *Finds*   Hand-tanned moose-hide crafts, woodcarvings, Cowichan sweaters, porcupine-quill jewelry, and bone, silver, gold, and turquoise accessories are just a few of the selections at this Coast Salish crafts shop. 270 Whonoak St., North Vancouver. ℂ 604/987-3339. Turn south on Capilano Rd. (off Marine Dr.) and make the first left (Whonoak is parallel to Capilano Rd.). www.khot-la-cha.com.

Lattimer Gallery *Finds*   This beautiful gallery showcases museum-quality Pacific Northwest First Nations art, including ceremonial masks, totem poles, limited-edition silk-screen prints, argillite sculptures, and expensive gold and silver jewelry. 1590 2nd Ave. ℂ 604/732-4556. www.lattimergallery.com.

Marion Scott Gallery   For 30 years, this gallery has been well regarded for its Inuit and First Nations art collections. 481 Howe St. ℂ 604/685-1934. www.marionscottgallery.com.

Museum of Anthropology   Works by contemporary First Nations artisans as well as books about the culture and publications on identifying and caring for Pacific Northwest crafts. University of British Columbia, 6393 NW Marine Dr. ℂ 604/822-5087. www.moa.ubc.ca.

FOOD

You'll find **salmon** everywhere in Vancouver. Many shops package whole, fresh salmon with ice packs for visitors to take home. Shops also carry delectable smoked salmon in travel-safe, vacuum-packed containers. Some offer decorative cedar gift boxes; most offer overnight air transport. Try other salmon treats such as salmon jerky and Indian candy (chunks of marinated smoked salmon), which are available at public markets such as **Granville Island Public Market** and **Lonsdale Quay Market.**

Chocolate Arts *Finds*   The works at this chocolatier are made with exquisite craftsmanship. Seasonal treats include pumpkin truffles around Halloween or eggnog truffles for Christmas. They even make chocolate toolboxes filled with tiny chocolate tools. Look for the all-chocolate diorama in the window—it changes every month or so. 2037 W. 4th Ave. ℂ 604/739-0475. www.chocolatearts.com.

The Lobsterman   Live lobsters, Dungeness crabs, oysters, mussels, clams, geoducks, and scallops are just a few of the varieties of seafood swimming in the saltwater tanks at this Granville Island fish store. The staff steams the food fresh on the spot, free. Salmon and other seafood can also be packed for air travel. 1807 Mast Tower Rd. ✆ 604/687-4531. www.lobsterman.com.

Murchie's Tea & Coffee This Vancouver institution has been the city's main tea and coffee purveyor for more than a century. You'll find everything from Jamaican Blue Mountain and Kona coffees to Lapsang Souchong and Kemun teas. The knowledgeable staff will help you decide which flavors and blends fit your taste. A fine selection of bone china and crystal serving ware as well as coffeemakers and teapots are also on sale. 970 Robson St. ✆ 604/669-0783. www.murchies.com.

Salmon Village If you want some salmon to take home, Salmon Village has a good selection to choose from. Smoked salmon or jerky are vacuum sealed for travel, and fresh salmon can be packed in an ice box or (for a price) shipped to you anywhere on the planet. 779 Thurlow St. ✆ 604/685-3378. www.salmonvillage.com.

South China Seas Trading Company The South Seas have always been a source of intrigue. This shop re-creates a bit of that wonder, with a remarkable collection of rare spices and hard-to-find sauces. Look for fresh Kaffir lime leaves, Thai basil, young ginger, sweet Thai chile sauce, and occasional exotic produce like mangosteens and rambutans. Pick up recipes and ideas from the knowledgeable staff. Granville Island Public Market. ✆ 604/681-5402. www.southchinaseas.ca.

GALLERIES

On the first Thursday of every month, many galleries host free openings from 5 to 8pm. Check the *Georgia Straight* or *Vancouver* magazine for listings, or visit **www.art-bc.com** for more details on Vancouver's art scene.

Buschlen Mowatt This is the city's leading "establishment" gallery. Look for paintings, sculptures, and prints from well-known Canadian and international artists. 111-1445 W. Georgia St. ✆ 604/682-1234. www.buschlenmowatt.com.

Diane Farris Gallery Contemporary painting and sculpture from up-and-coming and established artists. 1590 W. 7th Ave. ✆ 604/737-2629. www.dianefarrisgallery.com.

Monte Clark Gallery *Value* This cutting-edge gallery—in the otherwise slightly staid confines of south Granville's gallery row—is one of the best spots to look for that rising superstar without the rising prices. 2339 Granville St. ✆ 604/730-5000. www.monteclarkgallery.com.

HOME FURNISHINGS & ACCESSORIES

Farfalla *Finds* Newly relocated in 2007 to the Koret Lofts in Gastown, Farfalla features a choice array of products rarely found outside their country of origin, including Artel glass from Prague, Santa Maria Novella toiletries from Florence, Lomonosov tea ware from St. Petersburg, and various lines from the Weavers Guild of Europe. They do custom monogramming and even have a tearoom where they serve Hediard tea from Paris. 57 E. Cordova St. (near Carrall). ✆ 604/215-8704. www.monogrammafarfalla.com.

Inform Interiors *Finds* Chances are you won't be lugging a sofa back home, but this classy interior design store in Gastown has contemporary lighting, home accessories, and design books in addition to furniture. Their new bed and bath store is right across the street at 50 Water St. 97 Water St. ✆ 604/682-3868. www.informinteriors.com.

JEWELRY

Costen Catbalue *(Finds)*   One-of-a-kind pieces in platinum and gold are made on the premises here by a team of four goldsmiths and artists Mary Ann Buis and Andrew Costen. The two artists' styles complement each other; Buis favors contemporary and clean lines, and Costen's designs tend toward a more ornate Renaissance style. 1832 W. 1st Ave. (C) **604/734-3259**. www.costencatbalue.com.

Forge & Form   Master Granville Island metal designers Dietje Hagedoorn and Jürgen Schönheit specialize in customized gold and silver jewelry. Renowned for their gold and silver bow ties, they also create unique "tension set" rings, which hold a stone in place without a setting. Their studio (open by appointment) is located just past the False Creek Community Centre. 1334 Cartwright St. (C) **604/684-6298**.

Karl Stittgen and Goldsmiths *(Finds)*   Karl Stittgen's gold pins, pendants, rings, and other accessories demonstrate his eye for crisp design and fine craftsmanship. Each work is a miniature architectural wonder. 2203 Granville St. (C) **604/737-0029**.

The Raven and the Bear   If you've never seen West Coast native jewelry, it's worth making a trip here. Deeply inscribed with stylized creatures from Northwest mythology, these rings, bangles, and earrings are unforgettable. (See also "First Nations Art & Crafts," above.) 1528 Duranleau St. (C) **604/669-3990**.

MALLS & SHOPPING CENTERS

Pacific Centre Mall   This 3-block complex contains 200 shops and services, including Godiva, Benetton, Crabtree & Evelyn, and Eddie Bauer. 700 W. Georgia St. (at Howe). (C) **604/688-7236**. www.pacificcentre.ca.

Park Royal Shopping Centre   Park Royal consists of two malls that face each other on Marine Drive, just west of the Lions Gate Bridge. GAP, Coast Mountain Sports, Cypress Mountain Sports, Future Shop, Marks & Spencer, Disney, Eaton's, The Bay, Eddie Bauer, and a public market are just a few of the 250 stores in the center. Cinemas, bowling lanes, a golf driving range, community and special events, and a food court are next door. 2002 Park Royal St. (at foot of Lions Gate Bridge), West Vancouver. (C) **604/925-9576**. www.shopparkroyal.com.

Sinclair Centre   The Sinclair Centre incorporates four Vancouver landmarks: the Post Office (1910), the Winch Building (1911), the Customs Examining Warehouse (1913), and the Federal Building (1937). Now restored, they house elite shops like Armani and Leone, as well as smaller boutiques, art galleries, and a food court. 757 W. Hastings St. (C) **604/659-1009**. www.sinclaircentre.com.

Vancouver Centre   Here you'll find The Bay, restaurants, a food fair, a pair of Famous Players cinemas showing first-run movies, and more than 115 specialty stores (including high-fashion hair salon Suki's and the electronics and pharmacy outlet London Drugs). The complex is connected underground to the adjoining Pacific Centre Mall (see above). 650 W. Georgia St. (at Granville). (C) **604/684-7537**.

MARKETS

Chinatown Night Market *(Value)*   Across Asia, prime shopping time comes only after the sun has gone down and the temperature has dropped to something bearable. Friday and Saturday nights May through September, merchants in Chinatown bring the tradition to Canada by closing two separate blocks to traffic and covering them with booths, tables, and food stalls offering all manner of things, useful and otherwise.

Come down, grab a juicy satay skewer, sip the juice from a freshly cracked coconut, and see what's up. 200 Keefer St. and 200 E. Pender St. Phone the Vancouver Tourism Touristinfo Centre at ✆ **604/683-2000** for dates and times. www.vcma.shawbiz.ca.

Granville Island Public Market ✫✫✫   This 4,645-sq.-m (49,998-sq.-ft.) public market features produce, meats, fish, wines, cheeses, arts and crafts, and lots of unique fast-food counters offering a little of everything. The market is open daily 9am to 6pm. From mid-June to September, the Farmers' Truck Market operates here Thursday from 9am to 6pm. For more information, see p. 156. 1669 Johnston St. ✆ **604/666-6477.** www.granvilleisland.com.

Lonsdale Quay Market *(Kids)*   Located at the SeaBus terminal, this public market is filled with produce, meats, fish, specialty fashions, gift and book shops, food counters, coffee bars, a hotel, and Kids' Alley (a section dedicated to children's shops and a play area). 123 Carrie Cates Court, North Vancouver. ✆ **604/985-6261.** www.lonsdalequay.com.

New Westminster Quay Public Market   A smaller version of the Granville Island Public Market, this market is located 25 minutes away by SkyTrain from downtown Vancouver. Here you'll find a variety of gift shops, specialty stores, a food court, a delicatessen, and produce stands. Once you're finished browsing, make sure to have a gander at the neighboring Fraser River. A walkway extends along the river and allows great views of the waterfront, the busy boat traffic, and the occasional seal or sea lion. 810 Quayside, New Westminster. ✆ **604/520-3881.**

Vancouver Flea Market *(Value)*   Near the train/bus terminal, Vancouver's largest flea market is filled with more than 350 stalls. Go early, or the savvy shoppers will have already cleaned out the gems. Open weekends and holidays 9am to 5pm. 703 Terminal Ave. ✆ **604/685-0666.**

MUSIC

Virgin Megastore   With more than 150,000 titles housed in a three-story, 3,902-sq.-m (42,001-sq.-ft.) space, this is Canada's largest music and entertainment store. 788 Burrard St. (at Robson St.). ✆ **604/669-2289.** www.virginmega.com.

Zulu Records *(Finds)*   Zulu Records specializes in alternative music, local and import, new and used. You'll also find a good selection of vinyl and magazines. The staff is happy to make recommendations and bring you up to speed on what's hot in the local music scene. 1972 W. 4th Ave. ✆ **604/738-3232.** www.zulurecords.com.

SHOES

David Gordon   Vancouver's oldest Western boot, hat, and accessories store is far from stodgy. Boots include an extensive selection of Tony Lama, Boulet, Durango, HH Brown, and Dan Post. You'll also find Vans, Doc Martens, and a lineup of other funky footwear that attracts skateboarders and club kids. 822 Granville St. ✆ **604/685-3784.**

John Fluevog Boots & Shoes Ltd.   This native Vancouverite has a growing international cult following of designers and models clamoring for his under-C$200 (US$150/£90) urban and funky creations. You'll find outrageous platforms and clogs, Angelic Sole work boots, and a few bizarre experiments for the daring footwear fetishist. You may even meet the designer, who often spends his time at this flagship store. 837 Granville St. ✆ **604/688-2828.** www.fluevog.com.

SPECIALTY

Buddha Supply Centre *(Finds* Want money to burn? At Chinese funerals, people burn *joss*—paper replicas of earthly belongings—to help make the afterlife for the deceased more comfortable. This shop has more than 500 combustible products to choose from, including $1-million notes (drawn on the bank of hell), luxury penthouse condos, and that all-important cellphone. 4158 Main St. (*C*) 604/873-8169.

Escents Beautifully displayed, the large collection of soaps, bath oils, shampoos, and other body products here come in a variety of scents, such as the fresh ginger-citrus twist or the relaxing lavender sea. Locally produced and made with minimal packaging, the all-natural, environmentally friendly products come in convenient sizes and prices and can be individually blended to fit your mood. Additional stores at 2579 W. Broadway and 1744 Commercial Dr. 28D-701 W. Georgia St. (*C*) 604/687-4700. www.escentsaromatherapy.com.

Lush Lush has the look of an old-fashioned deli with big wheels of cheese, slabs of sweets, and vats of dips and sauces, but all those displays are really soaps (custom cut from a block), shampoos, skin treatments, massage oils, and bath bombs made from all-natural ingredients. 1025 Robson St. (*C*) 604/687-5874. www.lushcanada.com.

The Market Kitchen Store This store has everything you'd like to have (or could even imagine) on your kitchen counters or in your drawers—gourmet kitchen accessories, baking utensils, gadgets, and the like. 2-1666 Johnston (Net Loft, Granville Island). (*C*) 604/681-7399.

The Ocean Floor If you want to bring home a few gifts from the sea, then select from this Granville Island shop's collection of seashells, ship models, lamps, chimes, coral, shell jewelry, stained glass, and marine brass. 1522 Duranleau St., Granville Island. (*C*) 604/681-5014.

Three Dog Bakery Beagle Bagels, Scottie Biscotti, or Gracie's Rollovers. Canines will have a hard time deciding on a favorite treat from this gone-to-the-dogs bakery. The store also has leashes, collars, greeting cards, and other dog paraphernalia. 2186 W. 4th Ave. (*C*) 604/737-3647. www.threedog.com.

SPORTING GOODS

A 2-block area near the Mountain Equipment Co-op (see below) has become Outdoor Central, with at least a half-dozen stores such as **Altus Mountain Gear** (137 W. Broadway; (*C*) 604/876-2525; www.altusmountaingear.com); **Great Outdoors Equipment** (222 W. Broadway; (*C*) 604/872-8872); and **AJ Brooks** (147 W. Broadway; (*C*) 604/874-1117; www.ajbrooks.com). Just a block north on 8th Avenue, you'll find **Taiga** (380 W. 8th Ave.; (*C*) 604/875-8388; www.taigaworks.ca), which carries inexpensive fleece and other quality outdoor gear.

In the past few years, the corner of 4th Avenue and Burrard Street has become the spot for high-quality snow/skate/surfboard gear as well as the place to see top-level boarders and their groupies hanging out. Shops here include **Pacific Boarder** (1793 W. 4th Ave.; (*C*) 604/734-7245; www.pacificboarder.com), and the particularly noteworthy **West Beach** (1766 W. 4th Ave.; (*C*) 604/731-6449; www.westbeach.com), which sometimes hosts pro-skate demos on the half-pipe at the back of the store. **Thriller** (3467 Main St.; (*C*) 604/736-5651; www.thrillershop.com), is another well-known shop carrying independent labels and accessories for surfers and boarders real and wannabe.

Comor Sports   "Go play outside" is Comor's motto, and they certainly have the goods to get you out there. Pick up some skateboard garb, swimwear, hiking shoes, in-line skates, skis, boards, and snow toys. 1090 W. Georgia St. © 604/899-2111. www.comorsports.com.

Mountain Equipment Co-op   A true West Coast institution and an outdoor-lover's dream come true, this block-long store houses the best selection of top-quality outdoor equipment: rain gear, clothing, hiking shoes, climbing gear, backpacks, sleeping bags, tents, and more. Memorize the MEC label; you're sure to see it later—at the beach, the bar, or the concert hall. 130 W. Broadway (between Manitoba and Columbia). © 604/872-7858. www.mec.ca.

TOYS

The Games People (Kids)   The Games People carries a huge selection of board games, strategy games, role-playing games, puzzles, models, toys, hobby materials, and other amusements. It's difficult to walk past this store—whether you're an adult or a kid. 157 Water St. © 604/685-5825.

Kids Market (Kids)   Probably the only mall in North America dedicated to kids, the Kids Market on Granville Island features a Lilliputian entryway; toy, craft, and book stores; play areas; and services for the younger set, including a "fun hairdresser." 1496 Cartwright St. (on Granville Island). © 604/689-8447. www.kidsmarket.ca.

Kites on Clouds (Kids)   This little Gastown shop has every type of kite. Prices range from C$10 to C$20 (US$7.50–US$15/£4.50–£9) for nylon or Mylar dragon kites to around C$200 (US$150/£90) for more elaborate ghost clippers and nylon hang-glider kites. The Courtyard, 131 Water St. © 604/669-5677.

WINE

Ten years of restructuring, reblending, and careful tending by French and German master vintners have won the province's vineyards world recognition. When buying B.C. wine, look for the VQA (Vintner Quality Alliance) seal on the label; it's a guarantee that all grapes used are grown in British Columbia and meet European standards for growing and processing.

   Summerhill, Cedar Creek, Mission Hill, and **Okanagan Vineyards** are just a few of the more than 50 local estates producing hearty cabernet sauvignons, honey-rich ice wines, and oaky merlots. These wines can be found at any government-owned **LCB** liquor store, such as the one at 1716 Robson St. (© 604/660-4576) and at some privately owned wine stores.

Marquis Wine Cellars   If you're looking for a particular B.C. vintage, try this place first. The owner and staff of this West End wine shop are dedicated to educating their patrons about wines. They conduct evening wine tastings, featuring selections from their special purchases. They also publish monthly newsletters. In addition to carrying a full range of British Columbian wines, the shop also has a large international selection. 1034 Davie St. © 604/684-0445. www.marquis-wines.com.

The Okanagan Estate Wine Cellar   This department store annex, located in the Vancouver Centre mall Market Square, offers a great selection of British Columbian wines by the bottle and the case. The Bay, 674 Granville St. © 604/681-6211.

10

Vancouver After Dark

Vancouver is a fly-by-the-seat-of-your-pants kind of town. With so much to see and do—and with the outdoors always beckoning—Vancouverites often wait until the day or the hour before a show to plunk their cash down for a ticket. It drives promoters crazy. Entertainment options run the gamut, from cutting-edge theater companies and a top-notch opera to symphony, folk, and jazz festivals that draw people from up and down the coast. And then there are the bars, pubs, clubs, and cafes—lots of them—for every taste, budget, and fetish. Dining out at a fine restaurant is also considered an evening out; at a restaurant like C or West (both reviewed in chapter 6), the presentation is theater on a plate; in a restaurant-lounge like the new Sanafir, the theatricality of the decor will wow you.

For the best overview of Vancouver's nightlife, pick up a copy of the weekly *Georgia Straight* (www.georgiastraight.com). The Thursday edition of the *Vancouver Sun* contains the weekly entertainment section *Queue*. The monthly *Vancouver* magazine (www.vanmag.com) is filled with listings and strong views about what's really hot in the city. Or, get a copy of *Xtra! West* (www.xtra.ca), the free gay and lesbian biweekly tabloid, available in shops and restaurants throughout the West End.

The **Alliance for Arts and Culture,** 100-938 Howe St. (© **604/681-3535;** www.allianceforarts.com), is a great information source for all performing arts, literary events, and art films. The office is open Monday through Friday from 9am to 5pm.

Ticketmaster (Vancouver Ticket Centre), 1304 Hornby St. (© **604/280-4444;** www.ticketmaster.ca), has 40 outlets in the Vancouver area.

Half-price tickets for same-day shows and events are available at the **Tickets Tonight** (www.ticketstonight.ca) kiosk (open Tues–Sat 11am–6pm) in the **Vancouver Touristinfo Centre,** 200 Burrard St. (© **604/684-2787** for recorded events info). The Touristinfo Centre is open from May to Labour Day daily from 8am to 6pm; the rest of the year, it's open Monday through Saturday from 8:30am to 5pm.

1 The Performing Arts

Three major theaters in Vancouver regularly host touring performances. The **Orpheum Theatre,** 801 Granville St. (© **604/665-3050;** www.city.vancouver.bc.ca/theatres), is a 1927 theater that originally hosted the Chicago-based Orpheum vaudeville circuit. The theater now hosts the Vancouver Symphony and pop, rock, and variety shows. The Queen Elizabeth Theatre and the Vancouver Playhouse comprise the **Queen Elizabeth Complex,** 600 Hamilton St., between Georgia and Dunsmuir streets (© **604/665-3050;** www.city.vancouver.bc.ca/theatres), home to the Vancouver Opera and Ballet British Columbia. The 670-seat Vancouver Playhouse presents chamber-music performances and recitals. Located in a converted turn-of-the-20th-century church, the

Finds Art on the Edge

For more original performance fare, don't miss **The Fringe—Vancouver's Theatre Festival** (© 604/257-0350; www.vancouverfringe.com). Centered on Granville Island, the Fringe Festival features more than 500 innovative and original shows each September, all costing under C$20 (US$17/£9).

Vancouver East Cultural Centre (the "Cultch" to locals), 1895 Venables St. (© 604/251-1363; www.vecc.bc.ca), coordinates an impressive program that includes avant-garde theater productions, performances by international musical groups, and children's programs.

On the UBC campus, the **Chan Centre for the Performing Arts,** 6265 Crescent Rd. (© 604/822-2697; www.chancentre.com), showcases the work of the UBC music and acting students and hosts a winter concert series. Designed by local architectural luminary, Bing Thom, the Chan Centre's crystal-clear acoustics are the best in town.

THEATER

An annual summertime Shakespeare series, **Bard on the Beach,** is presented in Vanier Park (© 604/737-0625; www.bardonthebeach.org). You can also bring a picnic dinner to Stanley Park and watch **Theatre Under the Stars** (see below), which features popular musicals and light comedies.

Arts Club Theatre Company   The 425-seat **Granville Island Stage** presents dramas, comedies, and musicals, with post-performance entertainment in the Backstage Lounge. The Arts Club **Revue Stage** is an intimate, cabaret-style showcase for small productions, improvisation nights, and musical revues. The Art Deco **Stanley Industrial Alliance Theatre** plays host to longer-running plays and musicals. The box office is open 9am to 7pm. Granville Island Stage, 1585 Johnston St., and the Stanley Industrial Alliance Theatre, 2750 Granville St. © 604/687-1644. www.artsclub.com. Tickets C$25–C$45 (US$21–US$38/£12–£21).

Frederic Wood Theatre *Value*   Some students at UBC are actors in training, and their productions are extremely high caliber. For the price, they're a steal. Presentations range from classic dramatic works to new plays by Canadian playwrights. All shows start at 7:30pm. There are no performances during the summer. Gate 4, University of British Columbia. © 604/822-2678. www.theatre.ubc.ca. Tickets C$20 (US$17/£10) adult; C$14 (US$12/£6) seniors, C$12 (US$10/£6).

Theatre Under the Stars   From mid-July to mid-August, old-time favorite musicals like *The King and I, West Side Story,* and *Grease* are performed outdoors by a mixed cast of amateur and professional actors. Bring a blanket (it gets cold once the sun sets) and a picnic for a relaxing evening. Malkin Bowl, Stanley Park. © 604/257-0366 or 604/687-0174. www.tuts.bc.ca. Tickets C$30 (US$25/£14) adults; C$25 (US$21/£11) seniors and youth; C$20 (US$17/£9) children 6–10; C$85 (US$72/£39) family (2 adults and 2 children).

Vancouver Playhouse   Now in its third decade, the company at the Vancouver Playhouse presents a program of six plays each season, usually a mix of the internationally known, nationally recognized, and locally promising. You can buy tickets through **Ticketmaster** (© 604/280-4444; www.ticketmaster.ca). 600 Hamilton, between Georgia and Hamilton sts. in the Queen Elizabeth complex. © 604/665-3050. www.city.vancouver.bc.ca/theatres. Tickets usually C$25–C$55 (US$21–US$47/£11–£25).

CLASSICAL MUSIC & OPERA

Vancouver Bach Choir *KK*   Vancouver's international, award-winning amateur choir, a 150-voice ensemble, presents five major concerts a year at the Orpheum Theatre. Specializing in symphonic choral music, the choir's singalong performance of Handel's *Messiah* during the Christmas season is a favorite. Tickets are available through Ticketmaster at © **604/280-4444** or www.ticketmaster.ca. 805-235 Keith Rd., West Vancouver. © **604/921-8012**. www.vancouverbachchoir.com. Tickets C$20–C$35 (US$17–US$30/£9–£16) depending on the performance.

Vancouver Cantata Singers *K*   This semiprofessional, 40-person choir specializes in early music. The company performs works by Bach, Brahms, Monteverdi, Stravinsky, and Handel, as well as Eastern European choral music. The season normally includes three programs: in October, December, and March, all at various locations. Tickets are available through Ticketmaster (© **604/280-4444;** www.ticketmaster.ca) or at the door. 5115 Keith Rd., West Vancouver. © **604/921-8588**. www.vancouvercantatasingers.com. Tickets C$10–C$30 (US$8–US$26/£4.50–£14).

Vancouver Chamber Choir *KKK*   Western Canada's only professional choral ensemble presents an annual concert series at the Orpheum Theatre, the Chan Centre, and Ryerson United Church. Under conductor John Washburn, the choir has gained an international reputation. Tickets available through Ticketmaster at © **604/280-4444** or www.ticketmaster.ca. 1254 W. 7th Ave. © **604/738-6822**. www.vancouverchamberchoir.com. Tickets C$15–C$35 (US$13–US$30/£7–£16) adults, C$13–C$25 (US$10–US$20/£6–£11) seniors and students.

Vancouver Opera *KKK*   I've always been impressed with the quality of the stagings and performances at the Vancouver Opera. The company produces both concert versions and fully staged operas, often sung by international stars. The season runs October through May, with most performances in the Queen Elizabeth Theatre. 500-845 Cambie St. © **604/683-0222**. www.vanopera.bc.ca. Tickets usually C$24–C$130 (US$25–US$110/£11–£58).

Vancouver Symphony *KKK*   At its home in the Orpheum Theatre during the fall, winter, and spring, Vancouver's excellent orchestra, under the baton of maestro Branwell Tovey, presents a variety of year-round concerts. The box office is open from 6pm until showtime. 601 Smithe St. © **604/876-3434** for ticket information. www.vancouversymphony.ca. Tickets C$20–C$75 (US$17–US$64/£9–£34), discounts available for seniors and students.

DANCE

The new **Scotiabank Dance Centre,** 677 Davie St., provides a focal point for the Vancouver dance community. Renovated by Arthur Erickson, the former bank building now offers studio and rehearsal space to more than 30 dance companies, and is open to the general public for events, workshops, and classes. For more information, call © **604/606-6400,** or check www.thedancecentre.ca.

For fans of modern dance, the time to be here is early July, when the **Dancing on the Edge Festival** (© **604/689-0691;** www.dancingontheedge.org) presents 60 to 80 original pieces over a 10-day period. For more information about other festivals and dance companies around the city, contact the **Dance Centre** at © **604/606-6400** or www.thedancecentre.ca.

Ballet British Columbia *K*   This established company strives to present innovative works, such as those by choreographers John Cranko and William Forsythe, along with more traditional productions by visiting companies, such as the American Ballet

Theatre and the Moscow Classical Ballet. Performances are usually at the Queen Elizabeth Theatre, at 600 Hamilton St. 1101 W. Broadway. ✆ **604/732-5003**. www.balletbc.com. Tickets C$25–C$50 (US$21–US$42/£11–£23).

2 Laughter & Music

COMEDY CLUB/IMPROV SHOW

Vancouver TheatreSports League ✪✪   Part comedy, part theater, and partly a take-no-prisoner's test of an actor's ability to think extemporaneously, TheatreSports involves actors taking suggestions from the audience and spinning them into short skits or full plays, often with hilarious results. Since moving to the Arts Club Stage, Vancouver's TheatreSports leaguers have had to rein in their normally raunchy instincts for the more family-friendly audience—except, that is, for Friday and Saturday at 11:45pm, when the Red-Hot Improv show takes the audience into the R-rated realm. Shows are Wednesday and Thursday at 7:30pm and Friday and Saturday at 8, 10, and 11:45pm. New Revue Stage, 1601 Johnston St., Granville Island. ✆ **604/687-1644**. www. vtsl.com. Tickets C$10–C$18 (US$8–US$15/£4.50–£8).

STRICTLY LIVE

The **Vancouver International Jazz Festival** (✆ 604/872-5200; www.coastaljazz.com) takes over many venues and outdoor stages around town every June. The festival includes a number of free concerts.

The **Vancouver Folk Festival** (✆ 800/986-8363 or 604/602-9798; www.thefestival. bc.ca) is one of the big ones on the West Coast. It takes place outdoors in July on the beach at Jericho Park.

The Commodore Ballroom ✪   Every town should have one, but sadly very few do: a huge old-time dance hall, complete with a suspended hardwood dance floor. And though the room and floor date back to the Jazz Age, the lineup nowadays includes many of the best modern bands coming through town (and also groups like the Harlem Gospel Choir). In fact, the Commodore is one of the best places to catch a midsize band—and thanks to a renovation, the room looks better than ever. Purchase tickets through Ticketmaster (✆ **604/280-4444**; www.ticketmaster.ca). 868 Granville St. ✆ **604/739-7469**. Tickets C$5–C$50 (US$4–US$42/£2.25–£22).

O'Doul's Restaurant & Bar ✪✪   Every night, the restaurant for the lovely Listel Hotel (p. 75) becomes the venue for Vancouver's top jazz performers. You can dine on West Coast cuisine by candlelight or enjoy a drink while listening to the mellow sounds. During the Vancouver International Jazz Festival in late June, O'Doul's becomes the scene of late-night jam sessions with world-renowned musicians. 1300 Robson St. (at Jervis). ✆ **604/661-1400**. www.odoulsrestaurant.com.

The Roxy   Live bands play every day of the week in this no-holds-barred club, which also features bartenders with Tom Cruise *Cocktail*-style moves. Theme parties (often with vacation giveaways)—Extreme Karaoke, '80s only, Sunday Country Night (with two-step)—and other events add to the entertainment and the uninhibited and sometimes pretty raucous scene. On weekends, the lines are long, the patrons often soused. Dress code: no bags, no backpacks, no track suits, no ripped jeans; everything else is okay. 932 Granville St. ✆ **604/684-7699**. www.roxyvan.com. Cover C$5–C$15 (US$4–US$13/£2.15–£7).

The WISE Club *(Finds)* In the far-off reaches of East Vancouver (okay, Commercial Dr. area), The WISE Club was unplugged long before MTV ever thought of reaching for the power cord. Bands are local and international, and the room's a lot of fun—like a church basement or community center with alcohol. 1882 Adanac St. (C) **604/254-5858.** www.wisehall.ca. Cover depends on show; C$15 (US$13/£7) for most bands.

Yale Hotel This century-old tavern on the far south end of Granville is Vancouver's one-and-only home of the blues. Visiting heavyweights have included Stevie Ray Vaughan and Jeff Healey. When outside talent's not available, the Yale features the homegrown, including Long John Baldry and local bluesman Jim Byrne. Shows are Monday through Saturday at 9:30pm. On Saturday and Sunday is an open-stage blues jam from 3 to 7pm. 1300 Granville St. (C) **604/681-9253.** www.theyale.ca. Cover Thurs–Sat C$5–C$15 (US$4–US$12/£2.25–£7).

3 Bars, Pubs & Other Watering Holes

Vancouver has loosened up a great deal in the last few years. Until recently, patrons in a restaurant could drink only if they were eating or *had the intention of eating.* Nowadays, Vancouver drinkers can stand tall and order that beer with no fear of being forced to purchase a token cookie or french fry. Even better, bars can now regularly stay open until 2am, and as late as 4am in peak summer months.

That said, officialdom in the city still doesn't love the late-night crowd. They seem to look on drinkers and revelers as an unfortunate byproduct of urbanism, and bars as a necessary evil. City policy has been to concentrate the city's pubs and clubs into two ghettos—er, *entertainment zones*—one along **Granville Street** and the other along **Water and Pender streets** in Gastown. **Yaletown** has recently become a third, more upscale, bar/lounge/club zone. Pubs and clubs can be found in other places, and many are listed below, but if you just want to wander out for a serendipitous pub-crawl, the Granville or Water Street strips are best. Speaking generally, Granville Street tends more to Top 40 discos and upscale lounges, while down in Gastown, it's dark cellars spinning hip-hop and house. Yaletown is the newest late-night entertainment/drinking area, a place where martinis reign and some of the restaurants turn into cocktail lounges at 11pm.

BARS MASQUERADING AS RESTAURANTS

One holdover from the bad old days of the liquor license drought is the relatively large number of restaurants that look suspiciously like pubs. You can order food in these places. Indeed, it used to be a condition of drinking (wink, wink), but most patrons stick to a liquid diet.

The Alibi Room This high-end, trendy restaurant/bar has new owners and a new chef creating Modern British Pub-style cuisine, but there's still a DJ and a dance floor. Located on the eastern edge of Gastown. 157 Alexander St. at Main (C) **604/623-3383.** www.alibi.ca.

The Atlantic Trap and Gill Regulars in this sea shanty of a pub know the words to every song sung by the Irish and East Coast bands that appear onstage Thursday and Saturday night. 612 Davie St. at Seymour. (C) **604/806-6393.** www.trapandgill.com.

The Jupiter Cafe *(Finds)* Located just off busy Davie Street in the West End, The Jupiter Cafe combines a postapocalyptic industrial look with lounge chic. Black ceilings, exposed pipes, and roof struts mix surprisingly well with chandeliers, velvet curtains, and plush chairs. More important, the Jupiter is open late (until 4am some nights). True, it can be a challenge to flag down your waiter, but that gives you more time to scope out the crowd: gay and straight, funky and preppy, casual and dressed to kill. A huge outdoor patio provides a pleasant refuge from the street, but on colder nights, it's the exclusive domain of die-hard smokers. The menu—burgers, pastas, and pizzas—is largely decorative. 1216 Bute St. at Davie. ⓒ 604/609-6665. www.jupitercafe.com.

Monsoon Restaurant   What this slim little bistro in the otherwise sleepy (but starting-to-wake-up) section of Main and Broadway does really well is beer and fusion-induced tapas, accompanied by a buzzing atmosphere generated by interesting and sometimes beautiful people. The kitchen is open noon until 11pm on weekdays, later on weekends. 2526 Main St. at Broadway. ⓒ 604/879-4001.

Urban Well   The taut and tanned from nearby Kits Beach drop into the Well as the sun goes down, and often don't emerge until the next day. Monday and Tuesday features stand-up comedy, while a DJ keeps things groovy the rest of the week. 1516 Yew St. ⓒ 604/737-7770. www.urbanwell.com.

ACTUAL BARS

The Irish Heather   A bright, pleasant Irish pub in the dark heart of Gastown, the Heather boasts numerous nooks and crannies, some of the best beer in town, and a menu that does a lot with the traditional Emerald Isle spud. The clientele is from all over the map, from artsy types to urban pioneers. 217 Carrall St. ⓒ 604/688-9779. www.irishheather.com.

The Lennox Pub   Part of the renewal of Granville Street, this new pub fills a big void in the neighborhood; it's a comfortable spot for a drink without having to deal with lines or ordering food. The beer list is extensive, featuring such hard-to-find favorites as Belgian Kriek, Hoegaarden, and Leffe, along with a great selection of single-malt Scotches, too. The menu covers all the pub-food basics. 800 Granville St. ⓒ 604/408-0881.

A SPORTS BAR

The Shark Club Bar and Grill   The city's premier sports bar, The Shark Club—in the Sandman Inn—features lots of wood and brass, TVs everywhere, and on weekend evenings, lots of young women who don't look terribly interested in sports. 180 W. Georgia St. at Beatty. ⓒ 604/687-4275. www.sharkclubs.com. Cover Fri–Sat C$6–C$8 (US$3.20–US$4.80/ £2.70–£3.60).

BARS WITH VIEWS

You're in Vancouver. Odds are you're aware that this is a city renowned for its views. The entire population could make more money living in a dull flat place like Toronto, but they stay here because of the addicting scenery. As long as that's your raison d'être, you may as well drink in style at one of the places below. Also check out the view at the new restaurant, **Lift** (p. 96); it's in the same Coal Harbour vicinity as Cardero's (see next review).

Cardero's Marine Pub   On the water at the foot of Cardero Street, this Coal Harbour pub and restaurant offers a great view of Stanley Park, the harbor, and the North Shore. Overhead heaters take away the chill when the sun goes down. 1583 Coal Harbour Quay. ⓒ 604/669-7666.

Cloud Nine   As this sleek hotel-top lounge rotates 6 degrees a minute, your vantage point circles from volcanic Mount Baker, the Fraser estuary, and English Bay to Stanley Park, the towers of downtown, the harbor, and East Vancouver. 1400 Robson St. (42nd floor of the Empire Landmark Hotel). ⓒ 604/662-8328. Cover Fri–Sat after 8:30pm C$5 (US$4/£2.25).

The Dockside Brewing Company   The Dockside is located in the Granville Island Hotel (reviewed in chapter 5) and looks out across False Creek to Yaletown and Burnaby Mountain far in the distance. The grub's not much to write about, but the beer is among the best in town—brewed-on-the-premises lagers, ales, and porters. Even with the overhead gas heaters on chillier evenings, it's a good idea not to arrive too late: An hour or two after the sun goes down, the mostly 30-something patrons remember that they have homes to go to. 1253 Johnson St. © 604/685-7070. www.dockside brewing.com.

The Flying Beaver Bar *(Finds*   Located beneath the flyway of Vancouver International, the Beaver offers nonflyers great views of incoming jets, along with mountains, bush planes, river craft, and truly fine beer. 4760 Inglis Dr., Richmond. © 604/273-0278.

LOUNGES

Afterglow   Intimate couches and a soft soundtrack (which gets cranked up to deafening decibels as the evening wears on) make for candlelit foreplay to a meal at glowbal grill (p. 91); you can also stay in the low-slung love seats for a long evening's cuddle. 350 Davie St. © 604/642-0577.

The Arts Club Backstage Lounge   The Arts Club Lounge has a fabulous location under the Granville Bridge by the water on the edge of False Creek. The crowd is a mix of tourists and art school students from neighboring Emily Carr College. A live band plays on Friday and Saturday evenings. Most other times, if the sun's out, the waterfront patio is packed. 1585 Johnston St., Granville Island. © 604/687-1354. www.artsclub.com.

Bacchus Lounge ✦   This luxuriously comfy hot spot in the tony Wedgewood Hotel (p. 71) stages a powerhouse cocktail hour for mostly well-to-do professionals, then becomes an irony-free piano bar. 845 Hornby St., in the Wedgewood Hotel. © 604/608-5319. www.wedgewoodhotel.com.

George Ultra Lounge ✦   Small, loud, crowded, and hedonistic. Look for local glitterati and primo cocktails from the mixologist who started Vancouver's high-end cocktail trend. 1137 Hamilton St. © 604/628-5555. www.georgelounge.com.

Ginger Sixty-Two   Ginger Sixty-Two is one of the most successful newcomers to a yuppifying Granville Street. A mix of lounge, restaurant, and club, it's the darling of the fashion industry trendsetters who love to be spotted here. The room is funky warehouse-chic-meets-adult-rec-room, decorated in red, orange, and gold. Comfy crash pads are strategically placed throughout the room, and plenty of pillows help prop up those less-than-young in the joints. 1219 Granville St. © 604/688-5494. www.ginger62.com.

Gotham Cocktail Bar   A clear case of the law of unintended consequences: The lounge adjoining this new steakhouse was designed for a male clientele—thick leather benches and a mural of sensuous women in Jazz Age fashions. Men do show up—well-off suits in their 30s and 40s particularly—but they're often a minority amid the great gaggles of women, all seemingly 30-somethings with romantic aspirations. 615 Seymour St. between Dunsmuir and Georgia. © 604/605-8282. www.gothamsteakhouse.com.

Opus Bar ✦   Supertrendy decor, great drinks, and a succulent small-plates menu, has helped the Opus Bar in the cool Opus Hotel (p. 69) become a Yaletown hot spot for a pre-dinner martini or an extended evening schmooze. In the Opus Hotel, 50 Davie St. © 604/642-0577. www.elixir-opusbar.com.

BREWPUBS

Don't forget **The Dockside Brewing Company,** 1253 Johnson St. (© **604/685-7070**), in the Granville Island Hotel, listed under "Bars with Views," above.

Steamworks Pub & Brewery   Winding your way from room to room in this Gastown brewery is almost as much fun as drinking. Upstairs, by the doors, it's a London city pub where stockbrokers ogle every new female entrant. Farther in by the staircase, it's a refined old-world club, with wood paneling, leather chairs, and great glass windows overlooking the harbor. Down in the basement, it's a Bavarian drinking hall with long lines of benches, set up parallel to the enormous copper vats. Fortunately, the beer's good. Choose from a dozen in-house beers. 375 Water St. © **604/689-2739.** www.steamworks.com.

Yaletown Brewing Company   Every Sunday, all pints of brewed-on-the-premises beer are C$3.75 (US$3/£1.75) and pizzas are half-price. The excellent beer is complemented by an extremely cozy room, a great summertime patio, and a good appetizer menu. 1111 Mainland St. at Helmcken. © **604/681-2739.** www.markjamesgroup.com.

4 Dance Clubs

Generally clubs are open until 2am every day but Sunday, when they close at midnight. In the summer months (mid-June through Labour Day), opening hours are extended to 4am. The city's clubs and discos are concentrated around two "entertainment zones," downtown around Granville Street, and along Water and Pender streets in Gastown.

Au Bar   An address is unnecessary for Au Bar; the long Seymour Street line of those not-quite-beautiful-enough for expedited entry immediately gives it away. Inside, this downtown bar is packed with beautiful people milling from bar to dance floor to bar (there are two) and back again. Observing them is like watching a nature documentary on the Discovery Channel: Doelike women prance and jiggle while predatory men roam in packs, flexing pecs and biceps. 674 Seymour St. © **604/648-2227.** www.aubarnightclub.com. Cover C$5–C$8 (US$4–US$7/£2.25–£3.60).

Balthazar   A funky Spanish Revival building with a seedy past as a bordello, Balthazar offers martinis, wine, and tapas until the wee hours (2am), plus two small dance floors each with its own DJ. One spins house, the other roams all over. The crowd in this West End lounge is a little older and dresses the part. 1215 Bidwell St. at Davie. © **604/689-8822.** www.balthazarvancouver.com.

Caprice   Upstairs, it's The Lounge, with dark wood, a fireplace, a big-screen TV showing old Audrey Hepburn movies, and roll-top doors opening on a Granville Street patio. Downstairs, it's The Nightclub, a large room with a funky semicircular glowing blue bar, big comfy wall banquettes, a secluded circular passion pit in one corner, and a medium-size dance floor. Earlier in the week the DJ spins house, but on weekends, when the older, richer 25-and-overs come out to play, the cover goes up and the DJ retreats to the safety of Top 40. 965 Granville St. © **604/681-2114.** www.capricenightclub. com. Cover Tues–Thurs C$6 (US$5/£2.75), Fri–Sat C$10 (US$8/£4.50).

The Cellar   The Cellar inhabits that netherworld between dance club, bar, meat market, and personals ads. Dance club characteristics include a cover charge, small dance floor, and a DJ who mostly spins Top 40. But Cellar patrons are far less interested in groovin' than they are in meeting other Cellar dwellers, a process facilitated by a wall-length message board upon which pickup lines are posted. 1006 Granville St. ℂ **604/605-4350**. www.cellarvan.com. Cover C$5–C$8 (US$4–US$7/£2/25–£3.75).

Crush Champagne Lounge Wine snobs will feel right at home at the Crush Champagne Lounge; unique for a dance club, this venue has a professional sommelier on staff to help you make your wine selection. The drink list also includes a large selection of sexy champagne cocktails and by-the-glass bubblies. The lounge has a small dance floor and the music is mellow R&B, soul, classic lounge, and jazz. It's not just fancy drinks, this crowd likes to dress up for the occasion; no fleece or Gore-Tex in sight. 1180 Granville St. at Davie in the Howard Johnson Hotel. ℂ **604/684-0355**. www.crushlounge.ca. Cover C$5 (US$4/£2.25).

The Plaza Club This former movie theater makes a great nightclub with its high ceilings and spacious dance floor. Lineups start early at this popular club, which features different club nights (hip-hop, reggae) and DJs spinning Top 40 tunes on Friday and Saturday. 881 Granville St. ℂ **604/646-0064**. www.plazaclub.net. Cover C$4–C$8 (US$3–US$7/£1.80–£3.60).

The Red Room This basement warren has two bars, numerous intimate cubby holes, and a DJ that does progressive house and hip-hop, plus a live band sometimes on the weekend. And if that weren't enough, there's also a pool. 398 Richards St. ℂ **604/687-1307**. Cover C$7–C$15 (US$6–US$13/£3.15–£7).

Richard's on Richards For years, this club was a notorious pickup spot. Things have mellowed since then, but as the line of limos out front on busy nights attests, Dick's is still hot. Inside are two floors, four bars, a laser light system, and lots of DJ'ed dance tunes and concerts. 1036 Richards St. ℂ **604/687-6794**. www.richardsonrichards.com. Cover Fri–Sat C$8 (US$7/£3.60) for the club, C$10–C$30 (US$8–US$25/£4.50–£14) for concerts.

Shine This downstairs cellar in Gastown plays house and hip-hop, with occasional forays into other genres such as reggae. 364 Water St. ℂ **604/408-4321**. www.shinenightclub.com. Cover C$5–C$10 (US$4–US$8/£2.25–£4.50).

Sonar Loud bass. Flashing lights. The endlessly thrumming rhythms of house. It's a combination that's best with the aid of psychedelic substances. Of course, the Sonar crowd already knows that. 66 Water St. ℂ **604/683-6695**. www.sonar.bc.ca. Cover varies C$5–C$10 (US$4–US$8/£2.25–£4.50).

The Stone Temple Here, frat boys from America are tickled pink that the drinking age in B.C. is only 19. And dude, the beer's so cheap! Opens at 9pm. 1082 Granville St. ℂ **604/488-1333**. www.stonetemplenightclub.com. Cover weeknights C$5 (US$4/£2.25), weekends C$10 (US$8/£4.50).

Tonic Squeeze past the well-endowed door bunnies, and you're in a narrow room with a soaring ceiling, oversize paintings of hard liquor bottles, and an impressive-looking disco ball. The crowd is post-university but as yet unmated. Music is Latin, Brazilian, and Top 40 mix on weekends. 919 Granville St. ℂ **604/669-0469**. www.thetonicclub.com. Cover C$6–C$10 (US$5–US$8/£2.75–£4.50).

Voda Nightclub Voda attracts folks young, old, and in-between, with the only real common denominator being cash. The intriguing interior is a mix of waterfalls, rocks, and raw concrete—like a beautiful piece of 1950s modernism. The small dance floor basks in the warm light from the hundreds of candles everywhere. Monday night is old-fashioned R&B and funk; Tuesday is reserved for bands playing Latin or reggae;

Thursday nights are martini-elegant and a mix of DJs; and bands fill out the rest of the week with lots of hip-hop and R&B. 783 Homer St. in the Westin Grand Hotel. (C) **604/684-3003.** Cover C$5–C$8 (US$4–US$7/£2.25–£3.75).

5 Gay & Lesbian Bars

B.C.'s enlightened attitude—remember, same-sex couples can wed in Canada—has had a curious effect on Vancouver's queer dance-club scene: it's so laid-back and attitude-free that it's often hard to tell straight from gay, male go-go dancers and naked men in showers notwithstanding. The "Gay Village" is in the West End, particularly on Davie and Denman streets. Many clubs feature theme nights and dance parties, drag shows are ever popular, and every year in early August, as Gay Pride nears, the scene goes into overdrive. The **Gay Lesbian Transgendered Bisexual Community Centre,** 2-1170 Bute St. ((C) **604/684-5307;** www.lgtbcentrevancouver.com), has information on the current hot spots, but it's easier just to pick up a free copy of *Xtra West!,* available in most downtown cafes.

The Duff The Dufferin Pub, attached to what was for years the gay Dufferin Hotel (now the Moda Hotel, p. 73), was a city institution. Other drag shows might be raunchier, but none had the style of The Duff. With the hotel makeover in 2007, The Duff was downsized and, as of press time, no one was quite sure of The Duff's fate. So this one is a maybe. 900 Seymour St. (C) **604/683-4251.** www.the-duff.com.

The Fountain Head Pub Reflecting the graying and—gasp!—mellowing of Vancouver's boomer-age gay crowd, the hottest hangout for gays is The Fountain Head, a pub located in the heart of the city's gay ghetto on Davie Street. The Head offers excellent microbrewed draft, good pub munchies, and a pleasant humming atmosphere until the morning's wee hours. 1025 Davie St. (C) **604/687-2222.** www.thefountainheadpub.com.

Lotus Hotel Once among the most disreputable of Gastown gay bars, this aging hotel was given a face-lift and is now home to three bars and lounges, all with a largely but not exclusively gay clientele. Downstairs, the Lotus Lounge is one of the hottest house music venues in town, particularly on Straight Up Fridays with an all-female DJ team on the turntables. Lick, on the main floor, is a lesbian bar. The third venue, also on the main floor, is Honey, a comfortable lounge where a mixed crowd gathers for cocktails or beers. On most nights, the DJs keep the music on a mellow, conversational level. However, on Saturdays, decibels go up significantly when the Queen Bee review, a New York–style cabaret drag show, fills the house. 455 Abbott St. (C) **604/685-7777.** Cover Milk and Lotus C$5–C$12 (US$4–US$10/£2.25–£6) some nights, Honey only on Sat C$7 (US$6/£3.25).

Numbers A multilevel dance club with five floors and three bars, Numbers hasn't changed much over the years. Extroverts hog the dance floor while admirers look on from the bar above. Great sound and lights. On the second floor, carpets, wood paneling, pool tables, darts, and a lower volume of music give it a neighborhood pub feel. 1042 Davie St. (C) **604/685-4077.** www.numbers.ca. Cover Fri–Sat C$3 (US$2.50/£1.25).

The Odyssey Odyssey is the hottest and hippest gay/mixed dance bar in town (alley entrance is for men; women go in by the front door). The medium-size dance space is packed. Shows vary depending on the night. Saturday it's Fallen Angel go-go dancers, and Sunday it's the Feather Boa drag show. And on Thursday, it's "Shower Power"—yes, that is a naked man in the shower above the dance floor. 1251 Howe St. (C) **604/689-5256.** www.theodysseynightclub.com. Cover Thurs–Tues C$3–C$5 (US$2.50–US$4/£1.35–£2.25).

6 Cinema

Thanks to the number of resident moviemakers (both studio and independent), Vancouver is becoming quite a film town. First-run theaters show the same Hollywood junk seen everywhere in the world, but for those with something more adventurous in mind, plenty of options can be found.

Attendance at the **Vancouver International Film Festival** (*✆* **604/685-0260;** www.viff.org) reaches more than 100,000, not including the celebs who drop in. At this highly respected October event, more than 250 new films are shown, representing filmmakers from 40 countries. Asian films are particularly well represented.

SPECIALTY THEATERS

Since 1972, the **Pacific Cinematheque,** 1131 Howe St. (*✆* **604/688-FILM;** www.cinematheque.bc.ca), has featured classic and contemporary films from around the world. Screenings are organized into themes, such as "Jean Luc Godard's Early Efforts," film noir, or the "Hong Kong Action Flick: A Retrospective." Schedules are available in hipper cafes, record shops, and video stores around town, and on the website. Admission is C$9.50 (US$8/£4.25) for adults, C$8 (US$7/£4) for seniors and students; double features cost C$2 (US$1.75/£1) extra. Annual membership, required to purchase tickets, is C$3 (US$2.50/£1.35).

At the **CN IMAX,** Canada Place (*✆* **604/682-IMAX**), a gargantuan screen features large-format flicks about denizens of the animal kingdom (sharks, wolves, elephants, extreme athletes). A similar large screen at the **Alcan OMNIMAX,** Science World (*✆* **604/443-7443**), features flicks about empty, wide-open spaces, colorful coral reefs, and the like. See the Canada Place and Science World at Telus World of Science listings under "The Top Attractions" in chapter 7, p. 114.

Way off in the strip-mall lands of farthest Kingsway stands the **Raja,** 3215 Kingsway (*✆* **604/436-1545;** www.rajacinema.com), a modest single-screen movie house dedicated to bringing in the best flicks from Bombay, the world's moviemaking capital. Expect unbelievable plots mixed with big-production musical numbers. Some have English subtitles, though strictly speaking they're not necessary. If Kingsway is too far off, another Raja is on 639 Commercial Dr. (*✆* **604/253-0402**).

11

Getting to Know Victoria

To realize Victoria, you must take all that the eye admires most in Bournemouth, Torquay, the Isle of Wight, the Happy Valley at Hong Kong, the Doon, Sorrento and Camps Bay; add reminisces of the Thousand Islands, and arrange the whole round the Bay of Naples, with some Himalayas in the background.

—Rudyard Kipling, after visiting the city around 1908

Okay, so he was a writer and prone to exaggeration, but Rudyard Kipling wasn't too far off the mark. If you want to experience Victoria as Kipling saw it, head over to the Bengal Lounge in The Fairmont Empress, sink into a leather armchair, and order a drink. Overhead, breezes gently waft down from the old ceiling fans, while the light from the roaring fire sparkles off the glass eyeballs of the poor Bengal tiger mounted above the mantelpiece. In this time-warped atmosphere, you might think you're in colonial India or some outpost of the empire on the edge of an unknown territory . . . Except that your drink might be a fluorescent blue martini, the music from the sound system is mellow jazz, and the coats piled up on a nearby armchair are made of Gore-Tex and fleece instead of wool or oilskin.

And that's Victoria, or at least one part of it: a little patch of the former British Empire wading into the shoals of a highly internationalized 21st century, and doing it with an appealing vitality that tweaks nostalgia for the past with a thoroughly modern sensibility. Even though they're in *British* Columbia, some people traveling here don't "get" the British part. Just what is this tie that Victoria has to England?

First of all, the entire region was once claimed by the British (among others), and came under British rule in the mid–19th century, when the Strait of Juan de Fuca became one of the new dividing lines between the U.S. and Canada. Victoria really *was* a British colony, Which goes a long way to explain why a statue of Queen Victoria, the city's namesake, stands in front of the Provincial Legislature building (which some still insist on calling "Parliament"). With colonyhood (and a big gold rush) came colonists, who imported British customs and brought a kind of domesticating Old World sensibility to their wild, New World home. They thought they were bringing civilization, but that wasn't how the First Nations tribes that had been in the area for at least 8,000 years saw it.

British patriotism and customs might have faded away altogether except that in the 1920s, Victoria's population began to drop as business shifted over to Vancouver. Local merchants panicked. And it was then that San Francisco–born George Warren of the Victoria Publicity Bureau put forward his proposal: Sell the Olde England angle.

Warren had never been to England and had no idea what it looked like, but to him, Victoria seemed "English." To the city's merchants, Warren's scheme seemed like just the thing, and for three-plus generations it served the city well. While other places (including Vancouver) were leveling their "old" downtowns in the name of urban renewal, Victoria nurtured and preserved its heritage buildings, adding gardens and city parks. Eventually it possessed that rarest of commodities for a North American city—a lively, walkable, historic city center.

True, the "let's pretend we're in England" mindset meant ignoring certain details. Whales sometimes swam into the Inner Harbour; snowcapped mountain peaks loomed just across the water from Ross Bay; and trees in the surrounding forests towered far higher than Big Ben. So be it. It worked, and it didn't turn into Disneyland in the process.

As in Vancouver, you'll be amazed at how nice the people of Victoria are. Of course, you'd be nice, too, if you lived in such a pleasant place surrounded by such generous doses of natural beauty. Victoria, after all, with a population of about 325,000, occupies just a tiny corner of an island one-fifth the size of England but far more wild—so wild, in fact, that parts of it still have no roads and the only way to get around is by boat or on foot.

Speaking of boats: As an essential ingredient in Victoria's generous allotment of maritime charm, they also help to explain why the people who live and work here live such a leisurely pace. The modern anxiety that comes from clogged traffic arteries and bumper-to-bumper commutes simply does not exist in Victoria. Instead of road rage, Victoria residents have "ferry stress." In order to get on or off their island, they have to take a ferry (or a floatplane). And gliding through the waters of the Pacific Northwest, with mountains gleaming and orcas (maybe) splashing, is not the same as driving along a freeway. Getting to Victoria is half the fun, especially if you take one of the ferries that wind through the beautiful Gulf Islands. During your stay, you'll be pleasantly aware of all kinds of marine activity. In the summer, of course, Victoria is a major port of call for cruise ships.

The city is one thing, its location something else. Only in the past decade or so has Victoria finally begun to understand its stunning physical surroundings. Whale-watching is now a major industry; kayak tours are becoming ever more popular; mountainbikes have taken to competing for road space with the bright-red double-decker tour buses; ecotourism is big; and "outdoor adventures" are available in just about every form you can think of. Your trip will be even more memorable if you move a bit beyond Tourist Central (the Inner Harbour area) and put yourself in touch with Mother Nature.

Afterward, you can sip a lovely cream tea or a fluorescent blue martini.

1 Orientation

Victoria is on the southeastern tip of Vancouver Island, which lies southwest of the city of Vancouver across the Strait of Georgia and Haro Strait. It's 72km (45 miles) south of the 49th parallel, the border between most of Canada and the contiguous United States. B.C.'s island capital looks south across the Strait of Juan de Fuca to Port Angeles, Washington, and Washington state's snowcapped Olympic peninsula. Anacortes, Washington, is almost due west. Many people arrive in Victoria by ferry (see "Getting to Victoria," in chapter 2): the ferry from Port Angeles is the only one that arrives in the Inner Harbour downtown; the ferries from Vancouver and Anacortes arrive in Swartz Bay or Sidney, about 20 minutes north of Victoria.

Once you've arrived, head for the Inner Harbour, right in the heart of the city. A waterfront causeway runs along it in front of The Fairmont Empress hotel, one of Victoria's most picturesque spots. Just a few steps away are the Royal British Columbia Museum, Pacific Undersea Gardens, Thunderbird Park's totem poles, Chinatown, downtown and Old Town's shopping streets and restaurants, and Beacon Hill Park.

GETTING INTO TOWN FROM VICTORIA AIRPORT & VICE VERSA

Several **car-rental** firms have desks at the airport, including **Avis** (© **800/879-2847** or 250/656-6033; www.avis.com), **Budget** (© **800/668-9833** or 250/953-5300; www.budgetvictoria.com), **Hertz** (© **800/654-3131** or 250/656-2312; www.hertz.com), and **National** (© **800/227-7368** or 250/656-2541; www.nationalcar.com). If you're driving from the airport, take Highway 17 south to Victoria; it becomes Douglas Street as you enter downtown.

The **Akal Airporter shuttle bus** (© **250/386-2525;** www.victoriaairporter.com) makes the trip downtown in about a half-hour. Buses leave every 30 minutes daily from 4:30am to midnight; the fare is C$15 (US$13/£7) one-way; C$10 (US$8/£4.50) per person for groups of three or more. Drop-offs are made at most hotels and bed-and-breakfasts, and pickups can be arranged as well. A limited number of hotel courtesy buses also serve the airport. A cab ride into downtown Victoria costs about C$45 (US$38/£20) plus tip. **Empress Cabs** and **Blue Bird Cabs** (p. 188) make airport runs.

VISITOR INFORMATION

TOURIST OFFICES & MAGAZINES **Tourism Victoria Visitor Centre,** 812 Wharf St. (© **250/953-2033;** www.tourismvictoria.com), is located on the Inner Harbour, across from The Fairmont Empress hotel. If you didn't reserve a room before you arrived, you can go to this office or call its **reservations hotline** (© **800/663-3883;** daily 9am–5pm) for last-minute bookings at hotels, inns, and B&Bs. The center is open daily September through June 5 from 9am to 5pm, and June 6 through August from 9am to 8:30pm.

If you want to explore the rest of the 459km-long (285-mile) Vancouver Island (it's roughly the size of Holland), this office will help put you on the right track; you'll find a list of all the **regional tourism offices** on Vancouver Island at **www.islands.bc.ca**.

For details on the after-dark scene, pick up a copy of *Monday Magazine* (www.mondaymag.com/monday), available free in cafes around the city. *Monday Magazine* not only is an excellent guide to Victoria's nightlife but also has driven at least one mayor from office with its award-winning muckraking journalism. The online version has detailed entertainment listings.

CITY LAYOUT

Victoria was born at the edge of the Inner Harbour in the 1840s and spread outward from there. The areas of most interest to visitors, including **downtown** and **Old Town,** lie along the eastern edge of the **Inner Harbour.** (North of the Johnson St. Bridge is the **Upper Harbour,** which is largely industrial but taking on new life as old buildings are redeveloped.) A little farther east, the **Ross Bay** and **Oak Bay** residential areas around Dallas Road and Beach Drive reach the beaches along the open waters of the Strait of Juan de Fuca.

Victoria's central landmark is **The Fairmont Empress** hotel on Government Street, right across from the Inner Harbour. If you turn your back to the hotel, downtown and Old Town are on your right, while the provincial **Legislative Buildings** and the

Royal B.C. Museum are on your immediate left. Next to them is the dock for the Seattle–Port Angeles ferries, and beyond that the residential community of James Bay, the first neighborhood in the city to be developed.

MAIN ARTERIES & STREETS   Three main north-south arteries intersect just about every destination you may want to reach in Victoria.

Government Street goes through Victoria's main downtown shopping-and-dining district. Wharf Street, edging the harbor, merges with Government Street at The Fairmont Empress. Douglas Street, running parallel to Government Street, is the main business thoroughfare as well as the road to Nanaimo and the rest of the island. It's also Trans-Canada Highway 1. The "Mile 0" marker sits at the corner of Douglas and Dallas Road. Also running parallel to Government and Douglas streets is Blanshard Street (Hwy. 17), the route to the Saanich Peninsula, including the Sidney-Vancouver ferry terminal, and Butchart Gardens.

Important east-west streets include the following: Johnson Street lies at the northern end of downtown and the Old Town, where the small E&N Station sits opposite Swans Hotel at the corner of Wharf Street. The Johnson Street Bridge is the demarcation line between the Upper Harbour and the Inner Harbour. Belleville Street is the Inner Harbour's southern edge. The Legislative Buildings and the ferry terminal are here. Belleville Street loops around westward toward Victoria Harbour before heading south, becoming Dallas Road. Dallas Road follows the water's edge past residential areas and beaches before it winds northward up to Oak Bay.

FINDING AN ADDRESS   Victoria addresses are written like those in Vancouver: The suite or room number precedes the building number. For instance, 100-1250 Government St. refers to suite 100 at 1250 Government St.

Victoria's streets are numbered from the city's southwest corner and increase in increments of 100 per block as you go north and east. (1000 Douglas St., for example, is 2 blocks north of 800 Douglas St.) Addresses for all the east-west streets (Fort, Yates, Johnson, and so on) downtown start at 500 at Wharf Street; thus, all buildings between Wharf and Government streets fall between 500 and 599, while all buildings between Government and Douglas streets fall between 600 and 699, and so on.

STREET MAPS   Street maps are available free at the Tourism Victoria Visitor Centre (see "Visitor Information," above). The best map of the surrounding area is the B.C. Provincial Parks map of Vancouver Island, also available at the Info Centre.

NEIGHBORHOODS IN BRIEF

DOWNTOWN & OLD TOWN   These areas have been the city's social and commercial focal points since the mid-1800s, when settlers first arrived by ship. This is also the area of the city most popular with visitors, filled with shops, museums, heritage buildings, and lots of restaurants. The area's fascinating Barbary Coast history—which includes rum smuggling, opium manufacturing, gold prospecting, whaling, fur trading, and shipping—is reflected in the hundreds of heritage buildings, once home to chandleries, warehouses, factories, whorehouses, and gambling dens.

The two neighborhoods are usually listed together because it's difficult to say where one leaves off and the other begins. The Old Town consists of the pre-1900 commercial sections of the city that grew up around the original Fort Victoria at View and Government streets. Roughly speaking, it extends from Fort Street north to Pandora and from Wharf Street east to Douglas. Downtown is everything outside of that, from the Inner Harbour to Quadra Street in the east and from Belleville Street in the south up to Herald Street at the northern edge of downtown.

CHINATOWN   Victoria's Chinatown is tiny—only 2 square blocks—but venerable. In fact, it's the oldest Chinese community in North America. Its many interesting historic sites include Fan Tan Alley, Canada's narrowest commercial street, where legal opium manufacturing took place in the hidden courtyard buildings flanking the 1.2m-wide (4-ft.) way.

JAMES BAY, ROSS BAY & OAK BAY   When Victoria was a busy port and trading post, the local aristocracy would retire to homes in these neighborhoods to escape the hustle-bustle in the city center below. Today, they remain beautiful residential communities. Houses perch on hills overlooking the straits or nestle amid lushly landscaped gardens. Golf courses, marinas, and a few cozy inns edge the waters, where you can stroll the beaches or go for a dip if you don't mind a chill.

2 Getting Around

Strolling along the Inner Harbour's pedestrian walkways and streets is very pleasant. The terrain is predominantly flat and, with few exceptions, Victoria's main points of interest are accessible in less than 30 minutes on foot.

BY PUBLIC TRANSPORTATION

BY BUS   The **Victoria Regional Transit System (B.C. Transit)** (© **250/382-6161;** www.bctransit.com) operates 40 bus routes through greater Victoria as well as the nearby towns of Sooke and Sidney. Buses run to both the Butchart Gardens and the Vancouver Ferry Terminal at Sidney. Regular service on the main routes runs daily from 6am to just past midnight.

Schedules and route maps are available at the Tourism Victoria Visitor Centre (see "Visitor Information," above), where you can pick up a copy of the *Victoria Rider's Guide* or *Discover Vancouver on Transit: Including Victoria*. Popular Victoria bus routes include **no. 2** (Oak Bay), **no. 5** (downtown, James Bay, Beacon Hill Park), **no. 14** (Victoria Art Gallery, Craigdarroch Castle, University of Victoria), **no. 61** (Sooke), **no. 70** (Sidney, Swartz Bay), and **no. 75** (Butchart Gardens).

Fares are calculated on a per-zone basis. One-way single-zone fares are C$2.25 (US$1.90/£1) for adults and students and C$1.40 (US$1.20/£.70) for seniors and children 5 to 13; two zones cost C$3 (US$2.50/£1.40) and C$2.25 (US$1.90/£1), respectively. Transfers are good for travel in one direction only, with no stopovers. A **DayPass,** C$7 (US$6/£3.20) for adults and students, and C$5 (US$4.25/£2) for seniors and children 5 to 13, covers unlimited travel (all zones) throughout the day. You can buy passes at the Tourism Victoria Visitor Centre (see "Visitor Information," above), convenience stores, and ticket outlets throughout Victoria displaying the FAREDEALER sign.

BY FERRY   Crossing the Inner, Upper, and Victoria harbors by one of the blue 12-passenger **Victoria Harbour Ferries** (© **250/708-0201;** www.victoriaharbourferry.com) is cheap and fun. May through September, the ferries to The Fairmont Empress, Coast Harbourside Hotel, and Ocean Pointe Resort hotel run about every 15 minutes daily from 9am to 9pm. In March, April, and October, ferry service runs daily 11am to 5pm. November through February, the ferries run only on sunny weekends 11am to 5pm. The cost per hop is C$4 (US$3.40/£1.80) for adults and C$2 (US$1.70/£1) for children.

(Moments The Ferry Ballet

Starting at 9:45am every Sunday during summer, the ferries gather in front of The Fairmont Empress to perform a **ferry "ballet"**—it looks a bit like the hippo dance in Disney's *Fantasia*.

Instead of just taking the ferry for a short hop across, try the 45-minute **Harbour tour** 👣 or the 55-minute **Gorge tour** 👣; both cost C$20 (US$17/£9) adults, C$18 (US$15/£8) seniors, and C$10 (US$8/£4.50) children under 12.

BY CAR

You can easily explore the downtown area of Victoria on foot. If you're planning out-of-town activities, you can rent a car in town or bring your own on one of the car-passenger ferries from Vancouver, Port Angeles, or Anacortes. Traffic is light in Victoria, largely because the downtown core is so walkable.

RENTALS   Car-rental agencies in Victoria include the following: **Avis,** 1001 Douglas St. (© **800/879-2847** or 250/386-8468; www.avis.com; bus no. 5 to Broughton St.); **Budget,** 757 Douglas St. (© **800/668-9833** or 250/953-5300; www.budgetvictoria. com); **Hertz,** 655 Douglas St., in the Queen Victoria Inn (© **800/654-3131** or 250/ 360-2822; www.hertz.com); and **National,** 767 Douglas St. (© **800/227-7368** or 250/ 386-1213; www.nationalvictoria.com). These latter three can be reached on the no. 5 bus to the Convention Centre.

PARKING   Metered **street parking** is available in the downtown area, but be sure to feed the meter because rules are strictly enforced. Unmetered parking on side streets is rare. All major downtown hotels have guest parking, with rates from free to C$20 (US$17/£11) per day. Parking lots can be found at **View Street** between Douglas and Blanshard streets, **Johnson Street** off Blanshard Street, **Yates Street** north of Bastion Square, and **the Bay** on Fisgard at Blanshard Street.

DRIVING RULES   Canadian driving rules are similar to regulations in the U.S. Seat belts must be worn, children under 5 must be in child restraints, and motorcyclists must wear helmets. It's legal to turn right on a red light after you've come to a full stop. Unlike in the U.S., daytime headlights are mandatory. Some of the best places on Vancouver Island can be reached only via gravel logging roads, on which logging trucks have absolute right of way. If you're on a logging road and see a logging truck coming from either direction, pull over to the side of the road and stop to let it pass.

AUTO CLUB   Members of the **American Automobile Association (AAA)** can get emergency assistance from the **British Columbia Automobile Association (BCAA;** © **604/293-2222)** by calling © **800/222-4357** (or the number listed on the back of your AAA membership card).

BY BIKE

Biking is the easiest way to get around the downtown and beach areas. The city has numerous bike lanes and paved paths in parks and along beaches. Helmets are mandatory, and riding on sidewalks is illegal, except where bike paths are indicated. You can rent bikes starting at C$7 (US$6/£3.20) per hour and C$24 (US$20/£11) per day (lock and helmet included) from **Cycle B.C.,** 747 Douglas St. (© **866/380-2453** or 250/380-2453; www.cyclebc.ca).

BY TAXI

Within the downtown area, you can expect to travel for less than C$10 (US$8/£4.50), plus tip. It's best to call for a cab; you won't have much luck if you try to flag one down on the street. Drivers don't always stop, especially when it's raining. Call for a pickup from **Empress Cabs** (© 250/381-2222) or **Blue Bird Cabs** (© 250/382-4235).

BY PEDDLE-CAB

You get to sit while an avid bicyclist with thighs of steel peddles you anywhere you want to go for C$1 (US85¢/50p) per minute (C$2/US$1.70/£1 per min. if there are four of you). You'll see these two- and four-seater bike cabs along the Inner Harbour at the base of Bastion Square, or you can call **Kabuki Kabs** (© 250/385-4243; www.kabukikabs.com) for 24-hour service.

FAST FACTS: Victoria

Area Code The telephone area code for all of Vancouver Island, including Victoria and most of British Columbia, is **250**. For the greater Vancouver area, including Squamish and Whistler, it's **604**. If you're calling a Victoria number within Victoria, you don't need to dial the area code.

Business Hours Victoria **banks** are open Monday through Thursday 10am to 3pm and Friday 10am to 6pm. **Stores** are generally open Monday through Saturday 10am to 6pm. Some establishments are open later, as well as on Sundays, in summer. Last call at the city's **bars** and **cocktail lounges** is 2am.

Consulates All the consulates are in Vancouver. See "Fast Facts: Vancouver," in chapter 4.

Currency Exchange The best exchange rates in town can be found at banks and by using ATMs. **Royal Bank,** 1079 Douglas St. at Fort Street, is in the heart of downtown. Take bus no. 5 to Fort Street.

Dentist Most major hotels have a dentist on call. **Cresta Dental Centre,** 3170 Tillicum Rd., at Burnside Street in the Tillicum Mall (© 250/384-7711; bus no. 10), is open Monday through Friday 8am to 9pm, Saturday 9am to 5:30pm, and Sunday 11am to 5pm.

Doctor Hotels usually have doctors on call. The **Tillicum Mall Medical Clinic,** 3170 Tillicum at Burnside Street (© 250/381-8112; bus no. 10 to Tillicum Mall), accepts walk-in patients daily 9am to 9pm.

Electricity The same 110 volts AC (60 cycles) applies as in the U.S.

Emergencies Dial © **911** for fire, police, ambulance, and poison control. This is a free call.

Hospitals Local hospitals include the **Royal Jubilee Hospital,** 1900 Fort St. (© 250/370-8000, emergency 250/370-8212), and the **Victoria General Hospital,** 1 Hospital Way (© 250/727-4212, emergency 250/727-4181). You can get to both hospitals on bus no. 14.

Internet Access In the heart of Old Town, **Stain Internet Café,** 609 Yates St. (© 250/382-3352), is open daily 10am to 2am (C$2.50/US$2.10/£1.20 per half-hour). Closer to the Legislature, try **James Bay Coffee and Books,** 143 Menzies

St. (© **250/386-4700**), open daily 7:30am to 10pm (C$1/US85¢/45p per 10 min.). Most hotels have Internet access, as does the Victoria Public Library; see below.

Library The **Greater Victoria Public Library** (© **250/382-7241**; bus no. 5 to Broughton St.) is at 735 Broughton St., near the corner of Fort and Douglas streets.

Luggage Storage & Lockers Most hotels will store bags for guests who are about to check in or who have just checked out. Otherwise, coin lockers are available outside the bus station (behind The Fairmont Empress). Take bus no. 5 to the Convention Centre.

Pharmacies **Shopper's Drug Mart,** 1222 Douglas St. (© **250/381-4321**; bus no. 5 to View St.), is open Monday through Friday 7am to 8pm, Saturday 9am to 7pm, and Sunday 9am to 6pm.

Police Dial © **911.** This is a free call. The **Victoria City Police** can also be reached by calling © **250/995-7654.**

Post Office The **main post office** is at 714 Yates St. (© **250/953-1352;** bus no. 5 to Yates St.). There are also postal outlets in **Shopper's Drug Mart** (see "Pharmacies," above) and in other stores displaying the CANADA POST postal outlet sign. Supermarkets and many souvenir and gift shops also sell stamps.

Smoking Smoking is prohibited in any public areas, including restaurants, bars, and clubs.

12

Where to Stay in Victoria

Victoria has been welcoming visitors for more than a century, so it knows how to do so with style. You'll find a wide choice of fine accommodations in all price ranges, most in the Old Town, in downtown, or around the Inner Harbour and within easy walking distance of the city's main attractions (except for Butchart Gardens). But you don't have to limit yourself to Victoria proper. A 20-minute or half-hour drive north, east, or west takes you to all manner of marvelous resorts and inns, some on the ocean, some next to quiet bays and harbors, and some perched on mountaintops. You'll find information on the hotel choices in Brentwood Bay, Sooke, Sidney, Bear Mountain, and Malahat in the "Outside the Central Area" section, later in this chapter.

Spas are now an almost essential part of big hotels in Victoria—so much so that the Inner Harbour has been dubbed Spa Harbour, with major spas at the Delta Ocean Pointe, The Fairmont Empress, and the Hotel Grand Pacific. You can get fine spa treatments at all three and also at Brentwood Bay Lodge, Westin Bear Mountain Golf Resort & Spa, and the new

Sidney Pier Hotel & Spa; at the Laurel Point Inn, the spa services are all in-room. Check the hotel websites for special spa/accommodations packages.

Speaking of websites, it's always a good idea to check them out because you'll usually find much cheaper promotional rates or seasonal rates than the rack rates listed here.

You'll save big time if you schedule your holiday from October to May. When the high summer season starts in June, rates tend to skyrocket, especially at the finer resort hotels.

Reservations are essential in Victoria June through September. If you arrive without a reservation and have trouble finding a room, **Tourism Victoria** (🕿 **800/663-3883** or 250/953-2022) can make reservations for you at hotels, inns, and B&Bs. It deals only with establishments that pay a fee to list with them; fortunately, most do.

Prices quoted here don't include the 10% **hotel room tax,** the 7% **provincial accommodations tax,** or the 6% **goods and services tax (GST).**

1 Best Victoria Hotel Bets

For a quick overview of the best splurge and moderately priced hotels in Victoria, see chapter 1, p. 12 and p. 13, respectively.

- **Best Historic Hotel:** She's a grande dame, no doubt about it, and she sits on Victoria's Inner Harbour like an Empress on her throne. For sheer showoffy splendor **The Fairmont Empress,** 721 Government St. (🕿 **800/441-1414** or 250/384-8111), has no peers. See p. 194.

- **Best for Business Travelers: The Magnolia,** 623 Courtney St. (© **877/624-6654** or 250/381-0999), sits in a convenient location right downtown and features business-friendly amenities. The views are nothing to write home about, but the rooms are comfortable and the bathrooms surprisingly luxe. See p. 200.
- **Best Place to Pretend You Died & Went to Hollywood:** Perched above a fjord, **The Aerie,** 600 Ebedora Lane, Malahat (© **800/518-1933** or 250/743-7115), is famed for its over-the-top splendor. Some find it a bit too too-too, but others love it for just that reason. The restaurant is one of Vancouver Island's best, and the possibilities for pampering are endless. See p. 204.
- **Best Hotel Lobby:** The two-story, plate-glass windows in the lobby of the **Delta Victoria Ocean Pointe Resort and Spa,** 45 Songhees Rd. (© **800/667-4677** or 250/360-2999), provide the best vantage in Victoria for watching the lights on the Legislature switch on. There are also comfy chairs and fireplaces to sit and get warm. See p. 192.
- **Best for Families:** Honest, thrifty, and down-to-earth, the **Royal Scot Suite Hotel,** 425 Quebec St. (© **800/663-7515** or 250/388-5463), is great if you have kids in tow thanks to the in-suite kitchens and communal pool, game room, and arcade. See p. 197.
- **Best B&B:** With rooms double the size of those in other B&Bs and every possible need taken care of, the friendly innkeepers at **The Haterleigh Heritage Inn,** 243 Kingston St. (© **866/234-2244** or 250/384-9995), do themselves proud. See p. 195.
- **Best Small Hotel:** The tastefully indulgent **Abigail's Hotel,** 906 McClure St. (© **866/347-5054** or 250/388-5363), has sumptuous sleeping chambers and warm, welcoming hosts. See p. 199.
- **Best Moderately Priced Hotel:** The **Admiral Inn,** 257 Belleville St. (© **888/823-6472** or ©/fax 250/388-6267), deserves a salute. The rooms are motel-like but the location, just steps from the Inner Harbour, inspires loyalty. See p. 197.
- **Best Inexpensive Hotel:** While the rooms in the main hotel are just okay, the next-door suites and cottage operated by **The James Bay Inn,** 270 Government St. (© **800/836-2649** or 250/384-7151), are a veritable steal. See p. 198.
- **Most Romantic Hotel: Brentwood Bay Lodge & Spa,** 849 Verdier Ave. (© **888/544-2079** or 250/544-2079), is a small luxury resort overlooking a pristine fjord. Every detail in the rooms and bathrooms is perfect, from fabrics to fireplace. See p. 204.
- **Most Environmentally Conscious Hotel: Sooke Harbour House,** 1528 Whiffen Spit Rd., Sooke (© **800/889-9688** or 250/642-3421), wins hands down in the go-green department: It has its own bioreactor to reprocess wastewater, which is then used to water its gardens, and it has a green parking lot. Incidentally, this hotel also has the **best hotel restaurant,** and the **best oceanside location.** See p. 206.
- **Best Alternative Accommodations: The Boathouse,** 746 Sea Dr. (© **866/654-9370** or 250/652-9370), is a real (converted) boathouse, with a private dock and a rowing dinghy. Built in a secluded cove, the tiny cottage is a perfect spot for those seeking privacy and a glorious outlook right on the water. See p. 204.
- **Best Location: Swans Suite Hotel,** 506 Pandora Ave. (© **800/668-7926** or 250/361-3310), is chock-full of heritage, history, and original art, and it's above **Swans Pub,** Victoria's best brewpub. See p. 200.

- **Best Spa:** There are two in the city and two about a 20-minute drive from downtown that qualify in this category. **Delta Victoria Ocean Pointe Resort and Spa,** 45 Songhees Rd. (℗ **800/667-4677** or 250/360-2999), is a calm, contemporary, Zen-like facility; see below. More traditional, and completely luxurious, is the Willow Stream spa at **The Fairmont Empress,** 721 Government St. (℗ **800/ 441-1414** or 250/384-8111); see p. 194. The Essence of Life spa at **Brentwood Bay Lodge & Spa,** 849 Verdier Ave. (℗ **888/544-2079** or 250/544-2079), has the most impressive hydrobath in British Columbia, and offers massage treatments for couples; see p. 204. Nonsurgical skin treatments (such as Botox and microdermabrasion) are available at the new Santé Spa at Bear Mountain in the **Westin Bear Mountain Victoria Golf Resort & Spa,** 1376 Lynburne Place (℗ **888/533-2327** or 250/391-7160); see p. 207. All four spas offer complete skin and body treatments, aesthetics, and aromatherapy treatments to pamper the body and spirit.
- **Best Fitness Center and Pool:** In town, the fitness center at the **Hotel Grand Pacific,** 463 Belleville St. (℗ **800/663-7550** or 250/386-0450), offers aerobics classes, a 25m (82-ft.) ozonated indoor pool, a separate kids' pool, and a weight room; the hotel's sauna, whirlpool, and massage therapist can help ease the pain from all that exercise; see p. 195. You'll find the best fitness center and outdoor pool on Vancouver Island at the new **Westin Bear Mountain Victoria Golf Resort & Spa,** 1376 Lynburne Place (℗ **888/533-2327** or 250/391-7160), about 20 minutes from downtown. See p. 207.
- **Best New Hotel: Sidney Pier Hotel & Spa,** 9805 Seaport Place (℗ **866/ 659-9445**), which opened in May 2007 in the seaside town of Sidney, about 20 minutes north of Victoria, is stylish and comfortable, with oceanview rooms and a smart restaurant. See p. 206.
- **Best View:** Score a newly redesigned and redecorated suite in the South Wing of the **Laurel Point Inn,** 680 Montreal St. (℗ **800/663-7667** or 250/386-8721), facing the harbor and you may never want to leave. Outside of town, **The Aerie,** 600 Ebedora Lane, Malahat (℗ **800/518-1933** or 250/743-7115), offers private terraces with views across tree-clad mountains to a long blue coastal fjord. See p. 196 and 204, respectively.

2 The Inner Harbour & Nearby

VERY EXPENSIVE

Delta Victoria Ocean Pointe Resort and Spa *ꝏꝏ (Kids)*   The "OPR," located across the Johnson Street Bridge on the Inner Harbour's north shore, is a big, bright, modern hotel with commanding views of downtown, the Legislature, The Fairmont Empress, and the busy harbor itself. You'll see this view as you enter the grand lobby with its two-story-tall windows. The rooms here are nice and big, and so are the bathrooms. The decor, like the hotel itself, is a blend of contemporary and traditional; the beds, with duvets and fine linens, are really comfortable. The prime-view rooms face the Inner Harbour; rooms with a "working harbor" view look out over a less interesting industrial mixed-use scene. A few extra dollars buys a few extra perks, like breakfast and evening hors d'oeuvres in the third-floor Signature Lounge. All guests have use of the big indoor pool, a really good whirlpool, and a fully equipped gym with racquetball and tennis courts. Lots of guests come for the new spa, one of the best in Victoria. Like all the Delta hotels, OPR is very kid-friendly: Kids receive a free welcome kit, and they'll love the pool.

Where to Stay in Victoria

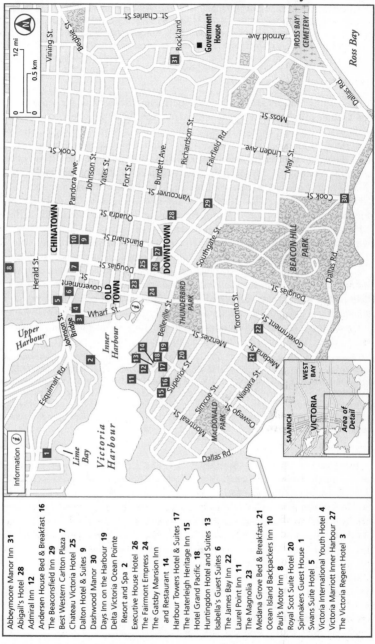

Abbeymoore Manor Inn **31**
Abigail's Hotel **28**
Admiral Inn **12**
Andersen House Bed & Breakfast **16**
The Beaconsfield Inn **29**
Best Western Carlton Plaza **7**
Chateau Victoria Hotel **25**
Dalton Hotel & Suites **9**
Dashwood Manor **30**
Days Inn on the Harbour **19**
Delta Victoria Ocean Pointe
    Resort and Spa **2**
Executive House Hotel **26**
The Fairmont Empress **24**
The Gatsby Mansion Inn
    and Restaurant **14**
Harbour Towers Hotel & Suites **17**
The Haterleigh Heritage Inn **15**
Hotel Grand Pacific **18**
Huntingdon Hotel and Suites **13**
Isabella's Guest Suites **6**
The James Bay Inn **22**
Laurel Point Inn **11**
The Magnolia **23**
Medana Grove Bed & Breakfast **21**
Ocean Island Backpackers Inn **10**
Paul's Motor Inn **8**
Royal Scot Suite Hotel **20**
Spinnakers Guest House **1**
Swans Suite Hotel **5**
Victoria International Youth Hotel **4**
Victoria Marriott Inner Harbour **27**
The Victoria Regent Hotel **3**

45 Songhees Rd., Victoria, B.C. V9A 6T3. ⓒ 800/667-4677 or 250/360-2999. Fax 250/360-1041. www.deltavictoria. com. 242 units. C$119–C$499 (US$101–US$424/£54–£225) double; C$349–C$999 (US$297–US$849/£157–£450) suite. Children under 17 stay free in parent's room. AE, DC, MC, V. Underground valet parking C$14 (US$12/£6). Bus: 24 to Colville. **Amenities:** Restaurant/lounge; indoor pool; outdoor tennis courts; health club; full-service spa; Jacuzzi; sauna; concierge; 24-hr. business center; 24-hr. room service; babysitting; same-day dry cleaning; nonsmoking rooms; executive-level rooms; rooms for those w/limited mobility. *In room:* A/C, TV/VCR w/pay movies, Internet, minibar, coffeemaker, hair dryer, iron/ironing board, safe.

The Fairmont Empress 𝒜𝒜   Francis Rattenbury's 1908 harborside creation is the most famous landmark on the Victoria waterfront. When you see it, you'll instantly want to stay here. Think twice, however, before throwing down the plastic. The hotel's 256 standard rooms (called Fairmont rooms) cost more and offer less than you can find elsewhere in the city: They're small rooms with smaller bathrooms, and offer little in the way of view. For some, the hotel's fabulous location and the building itself, as well as its first-class amenities—large pool, good weight room, luxurious Willow Stream spa, lounge, restaurant, tea lobby, and so on—or just the aura of being in the Empress, makes up for this lack of personal space. The 80 Deluxe rooms are bigger, with high ceilings and—for 60 of them anyway—a view of the harbor. They come with a small sitting area, a writing desk, and the same small, functional bathroom. The 12 Signature rooms are corner rooms with a big desk, queen-size bed, small seating area, and yes, the same small, functional bathroom. At the top of the heap are the Fairmont Gold rooms with high, arched ceilings, wide windows, king-size beds, a big desk, a CD player, and—finally—bathrooms with a (one-person) soaker tub and shower. If you can afford a Fairmont Gold or a Signature room—go for it. If you can't, it may be better to admire the Empress from afar. Or just come here for afternoon tea (see "Taking Afternoon Tea," in chapter 13).

721 Government St., Victoria, B.C. V8W 1W5. ⓒ 800/441-1414 or 250/384-8111. Fax 250/381-4334. www.fairmont. com/empress. 477 units. C$179–C$569 (US$152–US$484/£81–£257) double; C$319–C$1,519 (US$271–US$1,291/£144–£684) suite. AE, DC, DISC, MC, V. Underground valet parking C$19 (US$16/£9). Bus: 5. **Amenities:** 2 restaurants; bar/lounge; tearoom; indoor pool; high-quality health club; spa; Jacuzzi; sauna; concierge; business center; shopping arcade; limited room service; in-room massage; babysitting; laundry service; same-day dry cleaning; nonsmoking rooms; executive-level rooms; rooms for those w/limited mobility. *In room:* TV w/pay movies, Internet, hair dryer, iron/ironing board.

EXPENSIVE
Andersen House Bed & Breakfast 𝒜   The art and furnishings in Andersen House are drawn from the whole of the old British Empire and a good section of the modern world beyond. The 1891 house has the high ceilings, stained-glass windows, and ornate fireplaces typical of the Queen Anne style, but the art and decorations are far more eclectic. Each room has a unique style: The sun-drenched Casablanca room on the top floor, for example, boasts Persian rugs, a four-poster queen-size bed, and a boxed window seat. All rooms have private entrances and come with books, CD players and CDs, and complimentary high-speed wireless Internet access; all feature soaker tubs or two-person Jacuzzis.

301 Kingston St., Victoria, B.C. V8V 1V5. ⓒ 877/264-9988 or 250/388-4565. Fax 250/388-4502. www.andersenhouse. com. 4 units. C$125–C$275 (US$106–US$234/£56–£123) double. Rates include breakfast. MC, V. Free off-street parking. Bus: 30 to Superior and Oswego sts. Children under 12 not accepted. **Amenities:** Jacuzzi; nonsmoking rooms. *In room:* TV/VCR, free Wi-Fi, coffeemaker, hair dryer, iron/ironing board.

Harbour Towers Hotel & Suites 𝒜 *Kids*   Though this 12-story tower by the Inner Harbour has a few standard rooms, the one- and two-bedroom suites with fully equipped kitchens are a better value. In recent years, the hotel has added some great

The Best Bed & Breakfast Registry

If you prefer to stay at a B&B other than those listed in this chapter, the following agency specializes in matching guests to the B&Bs that best suit their needs:

- **Canada-West Accommodations Bed & Breakfast Registry,** P.O. Box 86607, North Vancouver, B.C. V7L 4L2 (© **800/561-3223** or 604/990-6730; www. b-b.com).

features, such as an impressively upscale lobby, a day spa, and an improved fitness center with indoor pool. The rooms also received a complete overhaul, but the traditional-looking decor, though comfy, is fairly uninspired, and plastic plants look decidedly weird in verdant Victoria. Most units feature floor-to-ceiling windows opening onto private balconies; some of the suites are bi-level. The harbor views are quite spectacular and worth reserving. The best rooms are the 12th-floor deluxe penthouse suites with enormous bathrooms, Jacuzzi tubs, and fireplaces. The larger suites are great for families, and the gym has a glass-walled kids' play area, so you can keep your eyes on the little ones while working out.

345 Quebec St., Victoria, B.C. V8V 1W4. © **800/663-5896** or 250/385-2405. Fax 250/360-2313. www.harbour towers.com. 195 units. C$94–C$388 (US$79–US$325/£42–£175) double; C$119–C$378 (US$101–US$321/£54–£170) suite; C$250–C$800 (US$212–US$680/£112–£360) penthouse suite. Additional person C$19 (US$16/£9). Children 16 and under stay free in parent's room. AE, DC, MC, V. Underground parking C$7 (US$6/£3.20). Bus: 30 or 31 to Superior and Oswego sts. **Amenities:** Restaurant; bar; indoor pool; health club; spa; Jacuzzi; sauna; business center; limited room service; babysitting; laundry service; same-day dry cleaning. *In room:* TV w/pay movies, free high-speed Internet, coffeemaker, hair dryer, iron/ironing board.

The Haterleigh Heritage Inn ☞
Haterleigh innkeeper Paul Kelly is a font of information, on Victoria in general and on this lovingly restored 1901 home in particular. With his wife, Elizabeth, he runs this exceptional B&B that captures the essence of Victoria's romance with a combination of antique furniture, original stained-glass windows, and attentive personal service. The rooms feature high arched ceilings, large windows, sitting areas, and large bathrooms, some with hand-painted tiles and Jacuzzi tubs. On the top floor, the cozy Angel's Reach room features a big four-poster bed. The second-floor Secret Garden room has a small balcony with views of the Olympic mountain range. The Day Dreams room downstairs is the dedicated honeymoon suite. A full gourmet breakfast with organic produce is served family-style at 8:30am, and complimentary sherry is available in the drawing room each evening.

243 Kingston St., Victoria, B.C. V8V 1V5. © **866/234-2244** or 250/384-9995. Fax 250/384-1935. www.haterleigh.com. 7 units. C$135–C$340 (US$115–US$289/£61–£153) double. Rates include full breakfast. MC, V. Free parking. Bus: 30 to Superior and Montreal sts. **Amenities:** Jacuzzi; free Internet. *In room:* Hair dryer.

Hotel Grand Pacific ☞☞☞
On Victoria's bustling Inner Harbour, directly across the street from the Port Angeles–Victoria ferry dock, the Grand Pacific is more luxurious than the Delta Ocean Pointe, and has rooms that are generally more spacious than those at The Fairmont Empress. Like those other two hotels on the Inner Harbour, the Grand Pacific has its own spa; its health club is better than the others, and features a huge ozonated indoor pool. All rooms have balconies and are attractively

and comfortably furnished. Standard rooms face the Olympic Mountains and Ogden Point or, for a bit more money, the Inner Harbour; bathrooms are on the small side. Suites provide the best views, overlooking the harbor and the Empress. The fabulous luxury suites feature huge bathrooms, fireplaces, and several balconies. Fine dining options include the informal Pacific Restaurant and **The Mark** (p. 211).

463 Belleville St., Victoria, B.C. V8V 1X3. ✆ **800/663-7550** or 250/386-0450. Fax 250/380-4473. www.hotel grandpacific.com. 304 units. C$152–C$286 (US$129–US$243/£68–£129) double; C$212–C$390 (US$180–US$331/ £95–£176) suite. Additional person C$30 (US$25/£14). AE, DC, DISC, MC, V. Self-parking free; valet parking C$10 (US$8/£4.50). Bus: 30 to Superior and Oswego sts. **Amenities:** 2 restaurants; cafe; bar; indoor pool; superior health club; full-service spa; Jacuzzi; concierge; tour desk; business center; 24-hr. room service; massage; babysitting; laundry service; same-day dry cleaning; nonsmoking rooms; squash courts. *In room:* A/C, TV w/pay movies, Internet, minibar, coffeemaker, hair dryer, iron/ironing board, safe.

Laurel Point Inn ★★★   The three stars are for the newly refurbished and utterly gorgeous South Wing suites featuring stylish, contemporary furnishings, Asian artwork, balconies overlooking a Japanese garden, shoji-style sliding doors, and luxurious marble bathrooms with deep soaker tubs and glassed-in showers (you may want to move into one of the bathrooms). This art-filled, resort-style hotel occupies a prettily landscaped promontory jutting out into the Inner Harbour, and consists of the original north wing and the newer south wing designed by noted Vancouver architect Arthur Erickson in 1989. The overall design reflects the elegant simplicity of Japanese artistic principals and is a refreshing change from the chintz and florals found in so many Victoria hotels. Rooms in the older north wing are fine—with good beds, pocket balconies (every room in the hotel has a water view), and nice bathrooms— but the south wing is where you want to be. A complete menu of in-room spa services is available. The hotel is in the process of a total remodel to be completed in 2008.

680 Montreal St., Victoria, B.C. V8V 1Z8. ✆ **800/663-7667** or 250/386-8721. Fax 250/386-9547. www.laurelpoint.com. 200 units. C$124–C$264 (US$105–US$224/£56–£119) double; C$204–C$394 (US$173–US$335/£92–£177) suite. Additional adult C$15 (US$13/£7). Children under 18 stay free in parent's room. AE, DC, DISC, MC, V. Free secure parking. Bus: 30 to Montreal and Superior sts. **Amenities:** Restaurant; bar; indoor pool; whirlpool; complimentary access to YMCA facilities; concierge; business center; 24-hr. room service; babysitting; same-day dry cleaning; free lobby Wi-Fi; nonsmoking hotel; rooms for those w/limited mobility. *In room:* A/C, TV, free high-speed Internet, free local calls, coffeemaker, hair dryer, iron/ironing board, safe.

MODERATE

The Gatsby Mansion Inn and Restaurant   Built in 1897, this white clapboard Victorian across from the Seattle–Port Angeles ferry terminal has been faithfully restored and now serves as a B&B-style inn. With its hand-painted ceramic-tiled fireplace, rich wood paneling, stained-glass windows, frescoed ceilings, and crystal chandeliers, it evokes a turn-of-the-last-century elegance. The spacious rooms feature down duvets, fine linen, and lots of Victorian antiques. Some rooms have views of the Inner Harbour, while others have private parlors. There's now an on-site spa. It's a pretty property, but because it's part of the larger Huntingdon hotel complex (see next listing), it lacks that owner-operated B&B feel.

309 Belleville St., Victoria, B.C. V8V 1X2. ✆ **800/563-9656** or 250/388-9191. Fax 250/382-7666. www.bellevillepark. com. 20 units. C$159–C$319 (US$119–US$239/£72–£144) double. Rates include breakfast. AE, DC, MC, V. Free parking. Bus: 30 or 31 to Belleville and Government sts. **Amenities:** Restaurant; spa; Jacuzzi; sauna; bike rental; limited room service; massage; laundry service. *In room:* TV w/pay movies, coffeemaker, hair dryer.

Huntingdon Hotel and Suites *(Value (Kids*   Set within a stone's throw of the Inner Harbour, the Ramada and the adjacent Gatsby Mansion Inn (owned by the same company) are set on a landscaped block with a courtyard, cafes, and shops. Built in 1981, the three-story Ramada is a pleasant low-key hotel that's particularly good if you're traveling with children. The standard rooms are fairly large, and all rooms come equipped with fridges. The prime rooms are the split-level gallery rooms or lofts on the third floor, which have a sitting room with TV, a pullout double bed on the ground floor, and a master bedroom (and second TV) upstairs; all sleep four comfortably; some even accommodate six. Some units have fully equipped kitchens, but you have to pay an additional C$10 (US$8/£4.50) charge to use them.

330 Quebec St., Victoria, B.C. V8V 1W3. © **800/663-7557** or 250/381-3456. Fax 250/382-7666. www.belleville park.com. 116 units. C$89–C$189 (US$71–US$151/£40–£85) double; C$109–C$249 (US$87–US$199/£49–£112) suite. AE, DC, MC, V. Parking C$5 (US$4/£2.25). Bus: 5, 28, or 30. **Amenities:** Restaurant; bar; Jacuzzi; sauna; limited room service; laundry; dry cleaning; nonsmoking rooms. *In room:* A/C (3rd-floor gallery suites only), TV, Internet, kitchen (in some units), fridge, coffeemaker, hair dryer, iron/ironing board.

Royal Scot Suite Hotel *Value* *Kids*   A block from the Inner Harbour, the Royal Scot provides friendly service and good value, particularly if you opt for a studio or one-bedroom suite. It was constructed as an apartment building, so the rooms are larger than average. Each studio suite has a divider separating the bedroom from the living room. One-bedroom suites have separate bedrooms with king-size, queen-size, or twin beds. All suites have lots of closet space, fully equipped kitchens, complimentary refreshments, and sofa beds in the living rooms. The decor is comfortable but uninspired, and bathrooms tend to be on the small side. In summer, the Royal Scot fills up with families. Kids make heavy use of the pool, game room, and the video arcade, which is tucked away out of earshot of other guests. In winter, the hotel is favored by retirees from the prairie provinces escaping subzero weather.

425 Quebec St., Victoria, B.C. V8V 1W7. © **800/663-7515** or 250/388-5463. Fax 250/388-5452. www.royalscot.com. 176 units. C$155–C$229 (US$132–US$195/£70–£103) double; C$185–C$415 (US$157–US$352/£83–£187) suite. AE, DC, MC, V. Free parking. Bus: 5 to Belleville and Government sts. **Amenities:** Restaurant; indoor pool; exercise room; Jacuzzi; sauna; game room; shuttle service to downtown; limited room service; laundry service; nonsmoking rooms. *In room:* TV, Internet, kitchen, coffeemaker, hair dryer, iron/ironing board.

Spinnakers Guest House *★* *Value*   This bed-and-breakfast-style guesthouse offers good accommodations at a moderate price. The two separate buildings are owned and operated by the same local entrepreneur who runs Spinnakers Brewpub. The 1884 heritage building on Catherine Street is the more luxurious. Rooms here feature queen-size beds, lovely furnishings, in-room Jacuzzis, fireplaces, high ceilings, and lots of natural light. The four Garden Suites units on Mary Street are really self-contained apartments, with separate bedrooms and full kitchens, perfect for longer stays or for families. Guests at both buildings get an in-room breakfast. The waterfront location is a 10- to 20-minute walk from downtown; the harbor ferry stops nearby.

308 Catherine St., Victoria, B.C. V9A 3S3. © **877/838-2739** or 250/384-2739. Fax 250/384-3246. www.spinnakers. com. 11 units. C$129–C$249 (US$110–US$212/£58–£112) double. Rates include breakfast. AE, DC, MC, V. Free parking. Bus: 24 to Catherine St. **Amenities:** Nonsmoking rooms. *In room:* Kitchen (some units), fireplace (some units), Jacuzzi.

INEXPENSIVE

Admiral Inn *Value* *Kids*   The family-operated Admiral is in a three-story building on the Inner Harbour, near the Washington-bound ferry terminal and close to restaurants and shopping. The combination of clean comfortable rooms and reasonable rates attracts young couples, families, seniors, and other travelers in search of a harbor view at a price that doesn't break the bank. The rooms are pleasant and comfortably furnished, a bit motel-like, with small bathrooms and balconies or terraces. The more expensive rooms come with a kitchenette with a small fridge and stove. The suites come with full kitchens. Some units can sleep up to six (on two double beds and a double sofa bed). The owners provide sightseeing advice as well as extras like free bicycles, free local calls, and an Internet terminal in the lobby.

257 Belleville St., Victoria, B.C. V8V 1X1. © **888/823-6472** or ©/fax 250/388-6267. www.admiral.bc.ca. 29 units. C$99–C$219 (US$84–US$186/£45–£99) double; C$129–C$249 (US$110–C$212/£58–£112) suite. Additional person C$10 (US$8/£4.50). Children under 12 stay free in parent's room. Rates include continental breakfast. AE, DC, MC, V. Free parking. Bus: 5 to Belleville and Government sts. **Amenities:** Complimentary bikes; coin laundry; dry cleaning; nonsmoking rooms; complimentary Internet access. *In room:* A/C, TV, kitchen/kitchenette (in some units), fridge, coffeemaker, hair dryer, iron/ironing board.

Days Inn on the Harbour   This hotel across from the MV *Coho* ferry terminal on the Inner Harbour has small, motel-like rooms that aren't very distinguished but at least put you in a great location. Half the rooms face the Inner Harbour; the other half have views of the nearby residential area. View rooms cost a little more. The rooms come with queen-size, king-size, or two double beds, and are outfitted with standard furnishings and step-up bathtubs. Eighteen rooms are equipped with kitchenettes. A small outdoor pool is in back and a patio overlooking the harbor is in front.

427 Belleville St., Victoria, B.C. V8V 1X3. © **800/665-3024** or ©/fax 250/386-3451. www.daysinnvictoria.com. 71 units. C$99–C$203 (US$84–US$173/£45–£91) double. Additional person C$10 (US$8/£4.50). Children under 12 stay free in parent's room. AE, DC, MC, V. Free parking. Bus: 5 to Belleville and Government sts. **Amenities:** Restaurant; bar; seasonal heated outdoor pool; Jacuzzi; laundry service; nonsmoking floors. *In room:* TV, kitchenettes (in some units), coffeemaker, hair dryer, safe.

The James Bay Inn *⟨Value⟩*   The Inner Harbour/James Bay area isn't especially blessed with cheap digs, but this Edwardian manor on the edge of Beacon Hill Park is one of the few. Built in 1907, it still offers one of the best accommodations deals downtown. The standard rooms in the main building of this four-story walk-up are somewhat small and very simply furnished. The real bargains: the adjacent cottage and four suites located next door in a renovated heritage property. The two studios are on the small side but come with a separate full-size kitchen; the larger one-bedroom suites also feature a full kitchen, a bedroom with queen-size bed, and a separate living room area. Furnishings and decorations are comfortable and pleasantly done. The cottage is a fully furnished, two-bedroom house cater-cornered to The James Bay Inn. With space for eight people and a peak-season price of C$240 (US$204/£108), it's a steal.

270 Government St., Victoria, B.C. V8V 2L2. © **800/836-2649** or 250/384-7151. Fax 250/385-2311. www.james bayinn.bc.ca. 45 units. C$79–C$172 (US$67–US$146/£36–£77) double; C$105–C$230 (US$89–US$196/£47–£104) suite; C$145–C$240 (US$123–US$204/£65–£108) cottage. AE, MC, V. Free limited parking. Bus: 5 or 30 to Niagara St. **Amenities:** Restaurant; bar; tour desk; nonsmoking rooms. *In room:* TV, dataport, hair dryer, iron/ironing board.

Medana Grove Bed & Breakfast   Just a few blocks from the Inner Harbour, this 1908 home is tucked away on a quiet residential street in the James Bay district. The front parlor and dining room on the main floor of this small and cheerfully unpretentious bed-and-breakfast are nicely restored with stained-glass windows, a fireplace, and hardwood floors. The three guest rooms are plainly furnished but provide comfortable accommodations. The smallest bedroom, with a queen-size bed, is located on the ground floor, across from the parlor. The other two rooms are on the second floor, up a steep and very narrow staircase. The one overlooking the front of the house accommodates three people with one double and one single bed. The other, with a king-size bed, looks out toward the garden. Smoking and pets aren't permitted, though the innkeepers themselves have two charming and very friendly Samoyed dogs. A C$10 (US$8/£4.50) surcharge is added for single-night bookings in summer.

162 Medana St., Victoria, B.C. V8V 2H5. © **800/269-1188** or 250/389-0437. Fax 250/389-0425. www.medana grove.com. 3 units. C$95–C$145 (US$81–US$123/£43–£65) double. Rates include full breakfast. MC, V. Street parking. Bus: 11 to Simcoe at Menzies. **Amenities:** Computer w/Internet free for guests' use. *In Room:* TV, no phone.

3 Downtown, Old Town & Nearby

EXPENSIVE

Abigail's Hotel 🏵🏵   A Tudor-style mansion in a residential neighborhood just east of downtown, Abigail's began life in the 1920s as a luxury apartment house before being converted to a boutique hotel. If you like small, personalized bed-and-breakfast hotels, you'll enjoy this impeccably maintained property. Everything is done well here, and the quality is high throughout. In the original building, some of the 16 rooms are bright and sunny and beautifully furnished, with pedestal sinks and goose-down duvets. Others feature soaker tubs and double-sided fireplaces, so you can relax in the tub by the light of the fire. The six Celebration Suites in the Coach House are even more luxurious. Recent renovations added Italian marble bathrooms, new furniture, and a new spa. Abigail's chef prepares a multicourse gourmet breakfast served in the sunny breakfast room, on the patio, or in your room.

906 McClure St., Victoria, B.C. V8V 3E7. © **866/347-5054** or 250/388-5363. Fax 250/388-7787. www.abigailshotel. com. 23 units. C$139–C$450 (US$118–US$382/£63–£202) double. Rates include full breakfast. AE, MC, V. Free parking. Bus: 1 to Cook and McClure sts. Children under 10 not accepted. **Amenities:** Concierge; dry cleaning; afternoon appetizers. *In room:* A/C, TV (in some rooms), high-speed Internet, Wi-Fi, hair dryer, iron/ironing board, Jacuzzi (in some rooms), fireplace (in some rooms).

The Beaconsfield Inn 🏵   Built in 1905, this elegantly restored Edwardian mansion is located just a few blocks from Beacon Hill park and the Inner Harbour. Commissioned by local industrial baron R. P. Rithet as a wedding gift for his daughter Gertrude, it seems only fitting that it survives today as a charming retreat favored by newlyweds and other incurable romantics. The inn features fir paneling, mahogany floors, antique furnishings, and stained-glass windows. The nine guest rooms are lavishly decorated and filled with fresh flowers from the garden. Some suites also have skylights and French doors that open onto the garden. For couples who want to get away from it all, book the cozy Beaconsfield Suite. Located on the third floor, this attic room has a four-poster canopy bed, a sitting area in front of a wood-burning fireplace, a jetted tub, and a window seat. A full hot breakfast is served in the sunroom or the dining room, and afternoon tea is served in the library. Children, pets, and smoking are not permitted.

998 Humboldt St., Victoria, B.C. V8V 2Z8. © **888/884-4044** or 250/384-4044. Fax 250/384-4052. www.beaconsfield inn.com. 9 units. C$109–C$299 (US$93–US$254/£50–£135) double. Full breakfast, afternoon tea, and sherry hour included. AE, MC, V. Free parking. Bus: 1 or 2 to Humboldt and Quadra sts. Children 12 and older permitted. **Amenities:** Access to nearby health club; Jacuzzi. *In room:* Hair dryer, fireplace, no phone.

Isabella's Guest Suites 🏵 *(Finds*   Two suites located above Willy's bakery provide affordable, fun, and surprisingly stylish accommodations in the heart of the city. The front suite is a large, elegantly furnished studio with a bed/sitting room that opens into a dining room and full kitchen. Bright colors and cheerful accents, upscale rustic furniture, high ceilings, large windows, and plenty of space make this a great home base for exploring Victoria. The second unit, a one-bedroom suite, overlooks the alley and patio of Il Terrazzo restaurant (reviewed in chapter 13). The living room is painted in bright red, which goes surprisingly well with the wood floors and funky furniture. Both units have king-size beds and are nonsmoking. Breakfast is included and served at the bakery. Parking is free, and you have your own front door.

537 Johnson St., Victoria, B.C. V8W 1M2. ℂ 250/595-3815. Fax 250/381-8415. www.isabellasbb.com. 2 units. C$150–C$195 (US$127–US$166/£68–£88) double. Rates include continental breakfast. Free parking. Bus: 5. *In room:* A/C, TV, full kitchen, hair dryer, iron/ironing board.

The Magnolia 𝖆𝖆 A boutique hotel in the center of Victoria, The Magnolia was completed in 1999 and offers a taste of luxury at a reasonable price. The small lobby, with a fireplace, chandelier, and overstuffed chairs, has a clubby Edwardian look. The room decor manages to be classic without feeling frumpy, with high-quality linen, down duvets, and quality furnishings. The spacious marble bathrooms are perhaps the best in Victoria, with walk-in showers and deep soaker tubs. The windows extend floor to ceiling, letting in lots of light, but the hotel really does not have any great views. The needs of business travelers are kept in mind: Work desks are large and well-lit, with dataports and high-speed Internet access. Local calls are complimentary. The Diamond Suites on the sixth and seventh floors feature a sitting room with fireplace. The hotel has a good restaurant, a fine microbrewery, and a full-service Aveda spa. If you want a small downtown hotel with personalized service and fine finishes, this is a good choice.

623 Courtney St., Victoria, B.C. V8W 1B8. ℂ 877/624-6654 or 250/381-0999. Fax 250/381-0988. www.magnolia hotel.com. 63 units. C$169–C$329 (US$143–US$280/£76–£148) double. Rates include continental breakfast. AE, DC, MC, V. Valet parking C$15 (US$13/£7). Bus: 5. **Amenities:** Restaurant; bar; access to nearby health club; spa; concierge; limited room service; laundry service; same-day dry cleaning; executive-level rooms. *In room:* A/C, TV w/pay movies, high-speed Internet, minibar, fridge, coffeemaker, hair dryer, iron/ironing board.

Swans Suite Hotel 𝖆𝖆 *Kids* In 1988, this heritage building was turned into a hotel, restaurant, brewpub, and nightclub. Located near the Johnson Street Bridge, it's now one of Old Town's best-loved buildings, and just minutes from Bastion Square, Chinatown, and downtown. Like any good boutique hotel, Swans is small, friendly, and charming. The suites are large and many are split-level, featuring open lofts and huge exposed beams. All come with fully equipped kitchens, dining areas, living rooms, queen-size beds, and original artwork. The two-bedroom suites are like little town houses; they're great for families, accommodating up to six comfortably. Want a room with your own totem pole? The sumptuous 279-sq.-m (3,003-sq.-ft.) penthouse suite comes with a collection of original Pacific Northwest art, a state-of-the-art kitchen, dining room, a spacious bedroom and guest room, and a deck with panoramic city/harbor views and a hot tub that seats 10. Swan's Brew Pub is one of the most popular in the city and features nightly live entertainment. The one drawback to this otherwise fine hotel is that a homeless shelter is located across the street where drop-outs and druggies may hang around.

506 Pandora St., Victoria, B.C. V8W 1N6. ℂ 800/668-7926 or 250/361-3310. Fax 250/361-3491. www.swanshotel.com. 30 units. C$179–C$199 (US$152–US$169/£81–£90) studio; C$219–C$359 (US$186–US$305/£99–£162) suite; C$895 (US$681/£403) penthouse. Children under 12 stay free in parent's room. AE, DC, DISC, MC, V. Parking C$12 (US$10/£5). Bus: 23 or 24 to Pandora Ave. **Amenities:** Restaurant; brewpub; limited room service; laundry room; same-day dry cleaning. *In room:* TV, Wi-Fi, kitchen, coffeemaker, hair dryer, iron/ironing board.

The Victoria Regent Hotel *Kids* An outside upgrade freshened the exterior of this hotel, which sits right on the Inner Harbour, closer to the water than any other hotel in Victoria. Rooms are fairly large and comfortable, though the decor is not always very inspired. The 10 large one-bedroom suites feature king-size beds, good views and small balconies, and standard serviceable bathrooms. The 36 two-bedroom suites have larger bathrooms and great views of the harbor (you're right on it). All the suites have full kitchens, so the hotel is popular with snowbirds in winter and families year-round.

1234 Wharf St., Victoria, B.C. V8W 3H9. (℗) **800/663-7472** or 250/386-2211. Fax 250/386-2622. www.victoriaregent. com. 48 units. C$199 (US$169/£90) double; C$269–C$699 (US$229–US$594/£121–£315) suite. Rates include continental breakfast. Additional person C$20 (US$17/£9). Children under 16 stay free in parent's room. AE, DC, DISC, MC, V. Free underground parking. Bus: 6, 24, or 25 to Wharf St. **Amenities:** Restaurant; access to nearby health club; concierge; babysitting; laundry service; same-day dry cleaning; rooms for those w/limited mobility. *In room:* TV/VCR, high-speed Internet, CD player, minibar, coffeemaker, hair dryer, iron/ironing board.

MODERATE

Abbeymoore Manor Inn ⚜ *Finds* This impressive 1912 mansion is in Rockland, an area of "Old Victoria" where grand homes were built by Victoria's elite. It's one of the best B&Bs you'll find, with large, attractive rooms, lots of period antiques and finishes, and an overall charm that's hard to beat. All the rooms are individually decorated and have private bathrooms and beds fitted with fine linens. Two ground-floor garden suites have separate entrances and fully equipped kitchens; the penthouse suite has views of the ocean. A delicious gourmet breakfast is served, and complimentary beverages are available throughout the day.

1470 Rockland Ave., Victoria, B.C. V8S 1W2. (℗) **888/801-1811** or 250/370-1470. Fax 250/370-1470. www.abbeymoore. com. 7 units. C$99–C$199 (US$84–US$169/£45–£90) double; C$129–C$229 (US$110–US$195/£58–£103) suite. Additional person C$40 (US$34/£18). Rates include full breakfast. MC, V. Free street parking. **Amenities:** Computer; Wi-Fi. *In room:* TV, CD player.

Best Western Carlton Plaza *Kids* In the heart of Victoria's shopping and entertainment district, the Best Western Carlton is ideally located for those who like to step right into the hustle and bustle of downtown. Rooms are comfortably furnished. Almost half the units come with a fully equipped kitchen, and even the standard rooms are pretty large. Perfect for families, the junior suites have two double beds, a sitting area with a pullout couch, a dining room table, and full kitchen. One-bedroom suites are also available; a number of these are wheelchair accessible. The Best Western prides itself on being a child-friendly hotel, and young guests are greeted with a goody bag, treats and toys, and a special room-service delivery of milk and cookies. Even the family dog is welcomed with a bag of home-baked biscuits upon arrival.

642 Johnson St., Victoria, B.C. V8W 1M6. (℗) **800/663-7241** or 250/388-5513. Fax 250/388-5343. www.bestwestern carltonplazahotel.com. 103 units. C$89–C$190 (US$76–US$161/£40–£86) double; C$260 (US$221/£117) suite. Additional person C$20 (US$16/£9). Children 17 and under stay free in parent's room. AE, MC, V. Free parking. Bus: 5 to Douglas and Johnson sts. **Amenities:** Restaurant; exercise room; children's programs; concierge; salon; limited room service; laundry service; coin laundry; nonsmoking rooms; lobby Wi-Fi; rooms for those w/limited mobility. *In room:* A/C, TV w/pay movies, coffeemaker, hair dryer, iron/ironing board.

Chateau Victoria Hotel *Value* This 18-story hotel was built in 1975 as a high-rise apartment building, so the hotel's rooms and one-bedroom suites are unusually spacious; many suites have kitchenettes, and all have balconies. The one-bedroom suites were renovated in 2006 and there have been some decor changes throughout, making this a good value for your money (including free local phone calls and complimentary high-speed Internet access). Prices are higher for the 5th through 15th floors, where the views are better; if you can, get one of the corner 09 rooms with windows on two sides. The Vista 18 Rooftop Lounge offers one of the best views of downtown Victoria.

740 Burdett Ave., Victoria, B.C. V8W 1B2. (℗) **800/663-5891** or 250/382-4221. Fax 250/380-1950. www.chateauvictoria. com. 177 units. C$86–C$162 (US$73–US$138/£39–£73) double; C$99–C$212 (US$79–US$180/£45–£95) suite. Children

under 18 stay free in parent's room. AE, DC, DISC, MC, V. Free parking. Bus: 2 to Burdett Ave. **Amenities:** Rooftop restaurant; bar; indoor pool; small exercise room; Jacuzzi; concierge; limited room service; babysitting; laundry service; same-day dry cleaning; nonsmoking rooms. *In room:* A/C, TV w/pay movies, free Internet, coffeemaker, hair dryer, iron/ironing board.

Dashwood Manor   This lovely old Elizabethan-style, half-timbered manor sits in a great location on the edge of Beacon Hill Park, just across Dallas Road from the beach and the Strait of Juan de Fuca. The place has recently been upgraded into a comfortable and rather distinctive all-suites hotel. The rooms are large and bright, with carefully chosen furniture and wood-paneled walls. Bathrooms have been updated with new tile and fixtures, including deep-jetted tubs, and several of the rooms have large Jacuzzis. Every suite has a kitchen, well stocked for do-it-yourself breakfast. Most of the rooms offer excellent views; some have balconies. Complimentary sherry, port, and wine are laid out in the lobby in the evenings.

1 Cook St., Victoria, B.C. V8V 3W6. (© **800/667-5517** or 250/385-5517. Fax 250/383-1760. www.dashwoodmanor.com. 14 units. C$105–C$265 (US$89–US$225/£47–£114) suite. Additional person C$45 (US$38/£20). AE, DC, MC, V. Free parking. Bus: 5 to Dallas Rd. and Cook St. **Amenities:** Nonsmoking rooms. *In room:* TV, kitchen, fridge, coffeemaker, hair dryer, iron/ironing board.

Executive House Hotel *(Kids)*   You can't miss the Executive House, a concrete highrise looming above The Fairmont Empress on Old Town's east side. Inside, the rooms are better than average in size, and—as in the adjacent and very similar Chateau Victoria (see above)—some intelligent thought has gone into their layout. A recent renovation freshened up the decor and furnishings. Bathrooms are small and functional. Each penthouse-level suite has a Jacuzzi in its own little atrium, a fireplace, a garden terrace with a panoramic view, a dining table, and a fully equipped kitchen.

777 Douglas St., Victoria, B.C. V8W 2B5. (© **800/663-7001** or 250/388-5111. Fax 250/385-1323. www.executive house.com. 181 units. C$75–C$210 (US$64–US$178/£34–£95) double; C$95–C$395 (US$81–US$334/£43–£178) suite; C$395–C$895 (US$316–US$716/£158–£402) penthouse rooms and suites. Additional person C$15 (US$12/ £7). Children under 16 stay free in parent's room. AE, DC, DISC, MC, V. Parking C$3 (US$2.40/£1.35) per night. Bus: 2 to the Convention Center. **Amenities:** 2 restaurants; 3 bars; exercise room; spa; concierge; limited room service; babysitting; same-day laundry service and dry cleaning; nonsmoking rooms; executive-level rooms. *In room:* TV w/pay movies, dataport, fridge, coffeemaker, hair dryer, iron/ironing board, safe.

Victoria Marriott Inner Harbour   The Marriott is a high-rise hotel behind the old Crystal Gardens (a former indoor swimming pool and tourist attraction). Inside, you'll find lots of marble in the lobby, and all the usual Marriott amenities, including an added-price concierge level that offers a pleasant lounge with breakfast and evening hors d'oeuvres. What you won't find is a whole lot of personality. The rooms are nice enough, especially the concierge-level suites on the 16th floor, but they're decorated in an indefinable style that's meant to look traditional but doesn't convey much beyond a cookie-cutter corporate aesthetic. The hotel has a good workout room and a nice big indoor pool. If you're a fan of Marriott, you'll find it all to your liking. If not, I'd suggest you look for a place with a bit more individuality, like Swans Suite Hotel or the Laurel Point Inn (both reviewed earlier in this chapter).

728 Humboldt St., Victoria, B.C. V8W 3Z5. (© **877/333-8338** or 250/480-3800. Fax 250/480-3838. www.victoria marriott.com. 236 units. C$149–C$259 (US$127–US$220/£67–£117) double. AE, DC, MC, V. Valet or self-parking C$12 (US$10/£5) per day. Bus: 2 to the Convention Center. **Amenities:** Restaurant; lounge; indoor pool; health club; Jacuzzi; 24-hr. room service; babysitting; laundry service; same-day dry cleaning; nonsmoking rooms; executive-level rooms; concierge-level rooms. *In room:* A/C, TV, Internet, minibar, coffeemaker, hair dryer, iron/ironing board, safe.

INEXPENSIVE

Dalton Hotel & Suites *(Value)*   Victoria's oldest hotel (built in 1876), formerly known as the Dominion, has changed its name and is undergoing some much-needed renovations. The hotel is never going to be glamorous, but the rooms have been considerably upgraded and are a good value for the location. Keep in mind that this is an old building; some rooms look out into window wells; and the furnishings, though new, can be on the dark and drab side (supposedly the color schemes are going to be enlivened in the near future). Some larger suites with fireplaces face into the interior courtyard and feature small wrought-iron balconies.

759 Yates St., Victoria, B.C. V8W 1L6. ✆ **800/663-6101** or 250/384-4136. www.daltonhotel.ca. 101 units. C$79–C$139 (US$67–US$118/£36–£63) double; C$179–C$219 (US$152–US$186/£144–£99) suite. AE, MC, V. Parking C$9 (US$8/£4). Bus: 10, 11, or 14 to Yates St. **Amenities:** Coffee shop; same-day laundry and dry-cleaning service; nonsmoking hotel. *In room:* TV (in some rooms), free Wi-Fi, coffeemaker, hair dryer, fireplace (in some suites).

Ocean Island Backpackers Inn ✪ *(Value)*   This is one of the best spots in Victoria for pleasant and inexpensive lodging, and it's located right downtown, just a few blocks from Bastion Square and the Inner Harbour. All sorts of travelers make their way to this hostel (an alternative to the Hostelling International network), from families with children to on-the-go seniors and young adults with global wanderlust. The big, comfy lounge/common area always has all kinds of stuff going on, including live music and open-mic evenings. You can buy cheap meals and snacks, use the kitchen, or kick back with a beer or glass of wine. In addition to the dorm rooms are 60 private rooms, in various configurations, including some with their own bathrooms. The staff here goes out of its way to help guests make the most of their time in Victoria and on Vancouver Island, including arranging day trips to out-of-the-ordinary places.

791 Pandora Ave., Victoria, B.C. V8W 1N9. ✆ **250/385-1785.** Fax 250/385-1780. www.oceanisland.com. 50 units. C$19–C$24 (US$16–US$20/£9–£11) dorm bed; C$25–C$68 (US$21–US$58/£11–£31) private room (some with private bathroom). MC, V. Parking C$5 (US$4.25/£2.25). Bus: 70 to Pandora Ave. and Douglas St. **Amenities:** Restaurant; lounge; tour desk; coin laundry; coin Internet; Wi-Fi; free bike/luggage storage. *In room:* TV (in some rooms), Wi-Fi.

Paul's Motor Inn *(Value)*   Sometimes nothing but an inexpensive motor inn or motel will do, and that's where Paul's comes in. It's been around for ages, it's very well maintained, and it's within walking distance to downtown. The rooms are pleasant for what they are, and much nicer than those in many motel chains. The staff here is friendly and helpful and there's an above-average restaurant. Clean and cheerful all around.

1900 Douglas St., Victoria, B.C. V8T 4R8. ✆ **866/333-7285.** www.paulsmotorinn.com. 78 units. C$59–C$104 (US$50–US$88/£27–£47) double. AE, DC, DISC, MC, V. Free parking. Bus: 30 to Douglas and Chatham sts. **Amenities:** Restaurant; coin laundry; fax/copying services. *In room:* TV, Internet, fridge, coffeemaker.

Victoria International Youth Hostel   The location is perfect—right in the heart of Old Town. In addition, this hostel has all the usual accouterments, including two kitchens (stocked with utensils), a dining room, a TV lounge, a game room, a common room, a library, laundry facilities, an indoor bicycle lockup, 24-hour security, and hot showers. The dorms are on the large side (16 people to a room), showers are shared and segregated by gender, and a couple of family rooms are available (one of which has a private toilet). There's an extensive ride board, and the collection of outfitter and tour information rivals that of the tourism office. The front door is locked at 2:30am, but you can make arrangements to get in later.

516 Yates St., Victoria, B.C. V8W 1K8. 🕐 888/883-0099 or 250/385-4511. Fax 250/385-3232. www.hihostels.ca. 104 beds. International Youth Hostel members C$18–C$21 (US$15–US$18/£8–£9) dorm bed, C$40–C$52 (US$34–US$44/£18–£23) private room; nonmembers pay C$3 (US$2.50/£1.40) extra for dorm bed, C$8 (US$7/£3.60) extra for private room. Wheelchair-accessible unit available. MC, V. Parking on street. Bus: 70 from Swartz Bay ferry terminal. **Amenities:** Lounge; game room; laundry facilities; kitchens, free Wi-Fi.

4 Outside the Central Area

EXPENSIVE

The Aerie On a forested mountain slope high above a fjord about half an hour from town, this Mediterranean-inspired villa enjoys a spectacular view. A member of the prestigious Relais & Châteaux association, The Aerie is one of the most luxurious retreats you'll find on Vancouver Island, though some may find the European-inspired decor and design a bit over-the-top. Accommodations are in three separate buildings, including the newly completed Villa Cielo, which offers the most amazing views of all. All rooms include big comfortable beds with top-quality linen, and all but the lowest-priced Deluxe rooms include a soaker tub for two (sometimes right in the middle of the room). As you move into the master and residence suites, you get private decks and fireplaces. An on-site full-service spa offers a variety of aesthetic treatments. Dining is an integral part of the experience, and **The Aerie restaurant** (p. 219) is among the best on the island. A full breakfast is included in the room rate.

600 Ebedora Lane (P.O. Box 108), Malahat, B.C. V0R 2L0. 🕐 800/518-1933 or 250/743-7115. Fax 250/743-4766. www.aerie.bc.ca. 29 units. C$195–C$295 (US$166–US$251/£88–£133) double; C$300–C$565 (US$255–US$480/£135–£268) suite. Rates include breakfast. AE, DC, MC, V. Free parking. Take Hwy. 1 north, turn left at the Spectacle Lake turnoff, take the first right, and follow the winding driveway. **Amenities:** Restaurant; bar; small indoor pool; tennis courts; small weight room; full spa; indoor and outdoor Jacuzzis; concierge; 24-hr. room service; laundry service; dry cleaning; all nonsmoking rooms. In room: A/C, TV, free Wi-Fi, minibar, coffeemaker, hair dryer, iron/ironing board.

The Boathouse *Finds* Vancouver Island has nothing else like it, and I can almost guarantee you'll fall in love with this tiny, secluded cottage—a former boathouse—set on pilings over Saanich Inlet on Brentwood Bay. The only passersby you're likely to encounter are seals, bald eagles, otters, herons, and raccoons, plus the occasional floatplane flying in. The converted boathouse is at the end of a very long flight of stairs behind the owner's home (if you have mobility issues, this is not the place for you). Outside is a waterside porch you may never want to leave; inside are a queen-size bed, a dining table, a kitchen area with a small refrigerator and toaster oven, an electric heater, and a reading alcove with a stunning view all the way up Finlayson Arm. Toilet and shower facilities are in a separate bathhouse, 17 steps back uphill. All the makings for a delicious continental breakfast are provided. Just below the boathouse is a floating dock—which doubles as a great sun deck—with a small dinghy reserved exclusively for guests' use. What could be more stylish, fun, and ecologically sound than rowing up to the dock at Butchart Gardens? Open March through September.

746 Sea Dr., Brentwood Bay, Victoria, B.C. VM8 1B1. 🕐 866/654-9370 or 250/652-9370. www.members.shaw.ca/boathouse. 1 unit. C$215 (US$183/£97) double with continental breakfast; C$195 (US$165/£88) double without breakfast. 2-night minimum. AE, MC, V. Free parking. Closed Oct–Feb. Bus: 75 to Wallace Dr. and Benvenuto Ave. No children under 18. In room: Fridge, coffeemaker, hair dryer, iron/ironing board.

Brentwood Bay Lodge & Spa *Finds* Located on a pristine inlet about 20 minutes north of downtown Victoria, just minutes from Butchart Gardens, this contemporary timber-and-glass lodge offers the best of everything, including a fabulous spa, boat shuttle to Butchart Gardens, and all manner of ecoadventures, including kayaking, scuba diving, fishing, and boat trips through the surrounding waters. This is a place where every detail has been carefully considered and beautifully rendered. The rooms are gloriously outfitted with handcrafted furnishings, gas fireplaces, luxurious bathrooms with soaker tubs and body massage showers, balconies, and king-size beds fitted with the highest quality Italian linens. The **SeaGrille** dining room (p. 219) offers seasonal menus focusing on foraged and organic local ingredients, plus a wine-tasting bar with a selection of fine wines from the resort's award-winning cellar. You can also dine in the casual Marine Pub. The hotel has its own marina and is a licensed PADI (Professional Association of Diving Instructors) dive center—the fjord on which it sits is considered one of the best diving spots in the world. The Essence of Life spa offers fresh Pacific seaweed, herb, ocean salt, and other treatments in a tranquil environment. Breakfast is delivered to your room.

849 Verdier Ave. on Brentwood Bay, Victoria, B.C. V8M 1C5. © 888/544-2079 or 250/544-2079. Fax 250/544-2069. www.brentwoodbaylodge.com. 33 units. C$179–C$419 (US$152–US$356/£81–£189) double; C$369–C$699 (US$314–US$594/£166–£315) suite. Rates include continental breakfast. AE, DC, MC, V. Free parking. Take Pat Bay Hwy. north to Keating Crossroads, turn left (west) to Saanich Rd., turn right (south) to Verdier Ave. **Amenities:** Restaurant; pub; heated outdoor pool; full-service spa; Jacuzzi; concierge; 24-hr. room service; laundry service; dry cleaning. *In room:* A/C, TV/DVD, free Wi-Fi, minibar, coffeemaker, hair dryer, iron/ironing board, entertainment system, fireplace, hot tub (in suites).

Miraloma on the Cove ★★ *(Finds* If you're looking for a small, quiet, luxury boutique hotel off the beaten tourist track, consider the Miraloma in Sidney. The building, with a three-story central atrium lobby area, is fairly new and was completely refurbished in 2005. The spacious, well-decorated rooms come with sumptuous beds, large bathrooms (heated floors and towel racks, separate showers, and soaker tubs), gas fireplaces, and a high-end kitchen or kitchenette; all but two have balconies. Surrounded by a pretty garden, the hotel is next door to a historic home that once served as the lieutenant governor's getaway residence, and a 5-minute walk to Van Isle marina. The Swartz Bay–Vancouver ferry terminals are 10 minutes to the north, Victoria is 20 minutes to the south, or you can bike into the seaside town of Sidney (known for its bookstores) on one of the hotel's complimentary bikes.

2326 Harbour Rd., Sidney, B.C. V8L 2P8. © 877/956-6622 or 250/656-6622. Fax 250/656-1212. www.miraloma.ca. 22 units. C$119–C$400 (US$101–US$340/£54–£180) double; C$169–C$638 (US$144–US$542/£76–£287) suite. Rates include buffet continental breakfast. AE, MC, V. Free parking. **Amenities:** Small fitness center; outdoor hot tub; non-smoking hotel. *In room:* TV/DVD, high-speed Internet, CD player, kitchen, fridge, coffeemaker, hair dryer, iron/ironing board, washer-dryer (in suites).

Poets Cove Resort & Spa ★★ To reach Pender Island, one of the Gulf Islands between the mainland and Vancouver Island, you have to take a ferry or water taxi from Sidney, north of Victoria. It's worth the trip, because staying at Poets Cove, the most luxurious resort and spa in the Gulf Islands, makes for a great romantic getaway. Overlooking Bedwell Harbour and its own marina (many guests arrive on their own boats), it opened in 2004 as a 22-room lodge with a cluster of seaside cottages, all built with a contemporary Craftsman-style Pacific Northwest look and ambience. All the accommodations feature ocean or forest-and-water views, fireplaces, big bathtubs for soaking, and all the amenities of an upscale resort. The lodge rooms are snug and charming, with great bathrooms, private balconies, and harbor views. Cottages and villas have two or three bedrooms, gourmet kitchens, and usually come with a patio or outdoor hot tub. You can dine on fresh Pacific Northwest cuisine at the Aurora Restaurant in the lodge, or enjoy snacks and comfort food in the lounge. Sussurus Spa offers a full complement of relaxation and aesthetic treatments, including spa treatments for couples.

9801 Spalding Rd., Pender Island, B.C. V0N 2M3. ℂ 888/512-7638 or 250/629-2100. www.poetscove.com. 22 lodge units, 15 cottages, 9 villas. C$159–C$179 (US$135–US$152/£72–£81) double in lodge; C$319–C$439 (US$271–US$373/£144–£198) villa; C$339–C$609 (US$288–US$176/£153–£274) cottage. AE, DC, MC, V. Free parking. Ferry from Sidney to Pender Island (www.bcferries.com); take Island Hwy. from ferry terminal. **Amenities:** Restaurant; lounge; 2 heated outdoor pools and hot tubs (seasonal); fitness center; spa; concierge; complimentary shuttle service; laundry service. *In room:* TV/DVD/CD entertainment systems, coffeemaker, hair dryer, iron/ironing board, fireplace; in cottages and villas: kitchen, patio (most units), outdoor hot tub (some units).

Sidney Pier Hotel & Spa ★★ *Finds* *Kids*   When this seaside boutique hotel opened in May 2007, it brought a splash of stylish (but low-key) glamour to Sidney's waterfront (the Vancouver and Anacortes ferry terminals are less than 5 min. away and there's a marina for private boats). Using calm colors, local materials, and lots of glass, the hotel's interior spaces reflect the surrounding maritime environment, while its street-side cafe and inviting bar and restaurant, both spilling out onto patios in good weather, are nicely incorporated into Sidney's urban/ocean scene. The guest rooms are well designed and comfortable, with calm, minimalist interiors and a refreshing lack of froufrou. Most of the rooms have ocean views; the suites have balconies, fireplaces, and connect with adjoining rooms, making them very family-friendly. Bathrooms are equally well designed, some with showers only, others with soaker tubs and walk-in showers. Haro's, the hotel's restaurant, serves deliciously fresh area specialties, including salads, fish, and lamb. And to top it all off is Haven Spa, where all manner of rejuvenating and refreshing treatments are available, including seaweed wraps, massages, facials, and manicures. A winner all-around.

9805 Seaport Place, Sidney, B.C. V8L 4X3. ℂ 866/659-9445 or 250/659-9445. Fax 250/655-0715. www.sidneypier.com. 55 units. C$109–C$299 (US$93–US$254/£49–£135) double; C$209–C$459 (US$178–US$207/£94–£207) suite. AE, MC, V. From Victoria, drive north on Hwy. 17/Patricia Bay Hwy. to Sidney, turn right/east on Beacon Ave. and continue toward waterfront, turn left/north on Seaport Place. **Amenities:** Restaurant; bar; fitness center; on-site spa; nonsmoking hotel. *In room:* TV/DVD, high-speed Internet, kitchen (in suites), coffeemaker, hair dryer, iron/ironing board, bathrobes, fireplace (in suites).

Sooke Harbour House ★★★   This quirkily distinctive inn and restaurant, located right on the ocean at the end of a sand spit about 30km (19 miles) west of Victoria, has earned an international reputation (voted second-best country inn *in the world* by *Gourmet Magazine* in 2000) thanks to the care lavished on the guests by owners Frederique and Sinclair Philip and their attentive staff. Frederique looks after the sumptuous rooms, each furnished and decorated according to a particular Northwest theme. The Herb Garden room, looking out over the hotel's magnificent seaside gardens of fragrant herbs and edible flowers, is done in pale shades of mint and parsley. The large split-level Thunderbird room is a celebration of First Nations culture, with books, carvings, totems, and masks. Thanks to some clever architecture, all the rooms are awash in natural light and have fabulous ocean views. In addition, all have wood-burning fireplaces and sitting areas, all but one have sun decks, and most have Jacuzzis or soaker tubs. The other half of the Harbour House's reputation comes from the outstanding restaurant (p. 219). Breakfast (served in your room) and a picnic lunch is included in the room rate. This is the most environmentally conscious hotel on Vancouver Island, with its own bioreactor to process waste water for reuse in the gardens, and biopermeable parking areas.

1528 Whiffen Spit Rd., Sooke, B.C. V0S 1N0. ℂ 800/889-9688 or 250/642-3421. Fax 250/642-6988. www.sooke harbourhouse.com. 28 units. C$175–C$575 (US$149–US$489/£79–£259) double. Rates include full breakfast and picnic lunch (no picnic lunch weekdays Nov–Apr). MC, V. Free parking. Take the Island Hwy. (Hwy. 1) to the Sooke/Colwood turnoff (junction Hwy. 14); follow Hwy. 14 to Sooke; about 1.6km (1 mile) past the town's only traffic light, turn left onto Whiffen Spit Rd. **Amenities:** Restaurant; sauna; nearby golf course; access to nearby health club; spa; limited room service; babysitting; laundry service; nonsmoking rooms. *In room:* Wi-Fi, CD player, minibar, fridge, coffeemaker, hair dryer, iron/ironing board, fireplace.

Westin Bear Mountain Victoria Golf Resort & Spa ★★★   Destined to become

a major destination for golfers, this new (opened in June 2006) resort hotel overlooks an 18-hole mountaintop golf course designed by Jack Nicklaus and his son. Part of a new, high-end resort-community development covering some 486 hectares (1,200 acres), the hotel is big and handsomely crafted, with fine natural finishes of wood and stone and the overall ambience of a giant West Coast mountain lodge. Rooms (in two separate buildings) are spacious, well designed, and furnished in a way that's both luxurious and comfortable; each has a balcony where you can enjoy mountain views and the sound of wind in the trees. The extralarge bathrooms feature soaker tubs and separate showers. Housed in a separate building, the gym is the best on Vancouver Island, and the spa offers medically supervised dermatology services. Dining options include the Copper River Grille, open for breakfast, lunch, and dinner, and the more exclusive Panache, serving both traditional and fusion-inspired fare, including fresh seafood and local produce.

1376 Lynburne Place, Victoria, B.C. V9B 6S1. ✆ **888/533-2327** or 250/391-7160. Fax 250/391-3792. www.bear mountain.ca. 156 units. Spring/summer: C$199–C$349 (US$169–US$297/£90–£157) double, C$269–C$419 (US$229–US$356/£121–£189) 1-bedroom suite; fall/winter: C$179–C$349 (US$152–US$297/£81–£157) double, C$249–C$419 (US$212–US$356/£112–£181) 1-bedroom suite. AE, MC, V. Valet parking C$15 (US$13/£7). Take the Island Hwy. (Hwy. 1) to exit 14, then follow Millstream Rd. to Bear Mountain Pkwy. and follow the signs. **Amenities:** Restaurant; sports bar; world-class golf course; health club w/outdoor pool; full-service spa; 24-hr. room service; babysitting; laundry service; dry-cleaning; nonsmoking hotel. *In room:* TV w/pay movies, high-speed Internet, kitchen, fridge, coffeemaker, hair dryer, iron/ironing board, gas fireplace.

MODERATE

Birds of a Feather Oceanfront Bed & Breakfast   Located on an oceanfront

lagoon 20 minutes west of Victoria, this quiet, ecofriendly B&B run by Annette Moen and Dieter Gerhard is super for bird-watchers and nature lovers. The lagoon is on the Pacific Flyway and attracts thousands of migratory birds and other wildlife. The three guest rooms, in their own separate wing, are furnished with Arts and Crafts–inspired beds and comfy leather chairs; they all have a good-size bathroom, kitchen, gas fireplace, and patio area with views of the water. The Honeymoon Suite is flooded with light on two sides; the family room has two levels with a spiral staircase.

206 Portsmouth Dr., Victoria, B.C. V9C 1R9. ✆ **800/730-4790** or 250/391-8889. www.birdsofafeather.ca. 3 units. C$145–C$210 (US$123–US$178/£65–£99) double. Rates include full breakfast. AE, MC, V. From Victoria take Hwy. 1 to exit 10 (Colwood/View Royal), turn left at Knob Hill St., left on Ocean Blvd, right on Lagoon Rd. right on Heatherbell, right on Portsmouth Dr. **Amenities:** Complimentary bikes, canoes, kayaks; nonsmoking B&B. *In room:* TV/DVD, Wi-Fi, kitchen w/fridge, microwave, tea/coffeemaker, hair dryer, fireplace, bathrobes.

The Gazebo   Built in 1971 in the style of a country manor, the main house of this

B&B features two guest rooms with private entrances and a separate cottage. The decor throughout is comfortably elegant with many nice features. The property is surrounded by tall trees and pretty landscaping. Butchart Gardens is minutes away.

5460 Old West Saanich Rd., Victoria, B.C. V9E 2A7. ✆ **877/211-2288** or 250/727-2420. Fax 250/727-6605. www. gazebo-victoria.com. 3 units; C$145–C$210 (US$123–US$178/£65–£99) double. Rates include full breakfast. AE, MC, V. From Victoria take Hwy. 17A (West Saanich Rd.) north for 3.2km/2 miles, turn right onto Old West Saanich Rd. and follow it for 3km/1½ miles. **Amenities:** Infrared sauna. *In room:* TV/DVD, CD player, high-speed Internet, fridge, tea/coffeemaker, hair dryer, fireplace, whirlpool, bathrobes.

INEXPENSIVE

Point-No-Point Resort ✦ *Finds*   Away from it all in your own little cabin, you'll have 16 hectares (40 acres) of wilderness around you and a wide rugged beach in front of you, with nothing to do but laze away the day in your hot tub. Or stroll along the beach. Or roam in the forest. Or look at an eagle. Since 1950, this oceanfront resort has been welcoming guests, first to a pair of tiny cabins, now to 25. Cabins vary depending on when they were built. All have fireplaces, full kitchens, and bathrooms; newer ones have hot tubs on their private decks. Lunch and afternoon tea are available daily in the small, sunny central dining room. Dinner is served Wednesday through Sunday. The dining room tables are conveniently equipped with binoculars, so you won't miss a bald eagle as you dine.

1505 West Coast Hwy. (Hwy. 14), Sooke, B.C. V0S 1N0. ℂ 250/646-2020. Fax 250/646-2294. www.pointnopoint resort.com. 25 units. C$130–C$260 (US$110–US$221/£59–£117). AE, MC, V. Free parking. No public transit. Take Hwy. 14 to exit 10 (Sooke); resort is 20 min. past Sooke. **Amenities:** Jacuzzi. *In room:* Kitchen, no phone.

University of Victoria Housing, Food, and Conference Services *Value*   One of the best deals going is found at the University of Victoria, when classes aren't in session and summer visitors are welcomed. All rooms have single or twin beds and basic furnishings; bathrooms, pay phones, and TV lounges are on every floor. Linens, towels, and soap are provided. The suites are an extremely good value—each has four bedrooms, a kitchen, a living room, and 1½ bathrooms. For C$5 (US$3.75/£2.25) extra per day, you can make use of the many on-campus athletic facilities. Each of the 28 buildings has a coin laundry. The disadvantage, of course, is that the U. Vic. campus is a painfully long way from everywhere—the city center is about a half-hour drive away.

P.O. Box 1700, Sinclair at Finerty Rd., Victoria, B.C. V8W 2Y2. ℂ 250/721-8395. Fax 250/721-8930. www.hfcs. uvic.ca. 898 units. May–Aug C$48 (US$41/£22) single; C$58 (US$49/£26) double; C$185 (US$157/£83) suite (sleeps 4 people). Rates include full breakfast and taxes. MC, V. Parking C$5 (US$4/£2.25). Closed Sept–Apr. Bus: 4 or 14 to University of Victoria. **Amenities:** Indoor pool; access to athletic facilities; coin laundry; nonsmoking rooms.

13

Where to Dine in Victoria

Though early Victoria settlers were intent on re-creating a little patch of the Old Country on their wild western island, the one thing they were never tempted to import was British cooking. Instead, following the Canadian norm, each immigrant group imported its own cuisine, so that now Victoria is a cornucopia of culinary styles from around the world. With more than 700 restaurants in the area, something is available for every taste and wallet.

Note that the touristy restaurants along Wharf Street serve mediocre food for folks they know they'll never have to see again. The canny visitor knows to head inland (even a block is enough), where the proportion of tourists to locals drops sharply and the quality jumps by leaps and bounds.

The dining scene in Victoria isn't nearly as sophisticated as Vancouver's, but more and more attention is being paid to the glories of fresh local produce. Good wines are now produced in the Cowichan Valley, and cheesemakers on Salt Spring Island are producing some delicious cheeses.

The one aspect of English cuisine Victoria *did* import was the delicious custom of afternoon tea. American visitors in particular should give it a try. For the best places, see "Taking Afternoon Tea," later in this chapter.

Most restaurants close at 10pm. Reservations are strongly recommended for prime sunset seating during summer, especially on Friday and Saturday. No provincial tax is added to restaurant meals in British Columbia, just the **6% goods and services tax (GST).**

Note: Because Victoria is so compact, most of the restaurants listed in this chapter are in Old Town and no more than a 10-minute walk from most hotels. Thus, in this chapter, I've listed public transit information only for those spots that are a bit farther out.

1 Best Victoria Dining Bets

For a quick overview of the city's top restaurants, see "The Most Unforgettable Dining Experiences: Victoria" in chapter 1, p. 14.

- **Best Spot for a Romantic Dinner: Camille's,** 45 Bastion Sq. (© **250/381-3433**), offers a quiet, intimate, candlelit room and a wine list with a bottle or glass for every occasion. See p. 214.
- **Best French Cuisine:** At **The Aerie,** 600 Ebedora Lane, Malahat (© **800/518-1933** or 250/743-7115), chef Christophe Letard's cooking is as unmistakably French as his accent. See p. 219.
- **Best Italian Cuisine: Il Terrazzo Ristorante,** 555 Johnson St., off Waddington Alley (© **250/361-0028**), gets points for its excellent northern Italian cooking and lovely patio. See p. 215.

- **Best Pacific Northwest:** Much of the menu at **Sooke Harbour House,** 1528 Whiffen Spit Rd., Sooke (© **800/889-9688** or 250/642-3421), is picked fresh from the adjacent garden, a treasure-trove of edible beauty. You'll find unique seasonal flavors, inventive cooking, and a superlative wine cellar. See p. 219.
- **Best Local Crowd: Café Brio,** 944 Fort St. (© **250/383-0009**), one of Victoria's top dining spots, celebrated its 10th anniversary in 2007 and remains a local fave. See p. 213.
- **Best Brewpub Restaurant: Canoe,** 450 Swift St. (© **250/361-1940**), is casual but upscale, has great beer, good food, and the option of dining indoors or out. See p. 213.
- **Best for Kids: rebar,** 50 Bastion Sq. (© **250/361-9223**), offers large portions, terrific quality, and a funky laid-back atmosphere. See p. 218.
- **Best Burgers & Beer: Six Mile Pub,** 494 Island Hwy., View Royal (© **250/478-3121**), offers 10 house brews, juicy burgers (even veggie burgers), and loads of British pub-style atmosphere. See p. 219.
- **Best Afternoon or High Tea:** How can you brag about your trip to Victoria if you don't include tea at **The Fairmont Empress,** 721 Government St. (© **250/384-8111**)? It's more than a tradition—it's a legendary experience, and the closest you'll come to reliving a bygone era. See p. 214.

2 Restaurants by Cuisine

BAKERY
Ottavio ✦ (Oak Bay, $, p. 217)
Q V Bakery & Café (Downtown, $, p. 218)
Willy's (Old Town, $, p. 217)

BISTRO
Med Grill@Mosaic (Downtown, $, p. 218)

CARIBBEAN
The Reef (Downtown, $$, p. 216)

CHINESE
J&J Wonton Noodle House ✦ (Downtown, $, p. 217)

DELI
Sam's Deli (Downtown, $, p. 218)

FISH & CHIPS
Barb's Place (Inner Harbour, $, p. 213)

FRENCH
The Aerie ✦✦✦ (Greater Victoria, $$$$, p. 219)
Brasserie L'Ecole ✦✦ (Old Town, $$$, p. 213)

INDIAN
Da Tandoor (Downtown, $$, p. 216)

ITALIAN
Café Brio ✦✦✦ (Downtown, $$$, p. 213)
Il Terrazzo Ristorante ✦✦ (Downtown, $$$, p. 215)
Pagliacci's (Downtown, $$, p. 216)
Zambri's ✦ (Downtown, $$, p. 216)

PACIFIC NORTHWEST
Café Brio ✦✦✦ (Downtown, $$$, p. 213)
Camille's ✦✦✦ (Downtown, $$$, p. 214)
Canoe ✦ (Inner Harbour, $$, p. 213)
The Mark ✦✦ (Inner Harbour, $$$, p. 211)
SeaGrille ✦ (Greater Victoria, $$$$, p. 219)
Sooke Harbour House ✦✦✦ (Greater Victoria, $$$$, p. 219)
Spinnakers Brewpub (Inner Harbour, $$, p. 213)

Key to Abbreviations: $$$$ = Very Expensive $$$ = Expensive $$ = Moderate $ = Inexpensive

PUB GRUB
Canoe ☆ (Inner Harbour, $$, p. 213)
Six Mile Pub (Greater Victoria, $, p. 219)
Spinnakers Brewpub (Inner Harbour, $$, p. 213)

SEAFOOD
The Blue Crab Bar and Grill ☆ (Inner Harbour, $$$, see below)

TAPAS
The Tapa Bar (Old Town, $$, p. 216)
Med Grill@Mosaic (Downtown, $, p. 218)

TEA
Abkhazi Garden (Greater Victoria, $, p. 215)

Butchart Gardens Dining Room Restaurant ☆☆☆ (Greater Victoria, $$$, p. 215)
The Fairmont Empress ☆☆☆ (Downtown, $$$$, p. 214)
Point Ellice House (Greater Victoria, $$, p. 214)
White Heather Tea Room ☆☆ (Greater Victoria, $, p. 215)

THAI
Siam Thai Restaurant (Downtown, $, p. 218)

VEGETARIAN
Green Cuisine (Downtown, $, p. 217)
rebar (Downtown, $, p. 218)

3 The Inner Harbour

EXPENSIVE

The Blue Crab Bar and Grill ☆ SEAFOOD   One of Victoria's best bets for seafood, The Blue Crab combines excellent fresh ingredients and straightforward preparation. It also has a great view—floatplanes slip in and out while you're dining, little ferries chug across the harbor, and the sun sets slowly over the Sooke Hills. Like other top-end restaurants in town, the Crab sources much of its ingredients locally, but you might also find scallops from Alaska or lamb from New Zealand. For lunch or dinner you can tuck-in to tasty offerings such as seafood chowder or a smoked salmon and crab sandwich. The award-winning wine list (*Wine Spectator* Award of Excellence from 2003–05) features midrange and top-end vintages, drawn mostly from B.C., Washington, and California. The service is deft and obliging.

In the Coast Hotel, 146 Kingston St. ☎ **250/480-1999.** www.bluecrab.ca. Reservations recommended. Main courses C$25–C$34 (US$21–US$29/£11–£15). AE, DC, MC, V. Daily 6:30am–10pm (dinner from 5pm). Bus: 30 to Erie St. or harbor miniferry to Coast Hotel.

The Mark ☆☆ PACIFIC NORTHWEST   The fine dining room at the Hotel Grand Pacific is a small, candlelit haven. Here you can enjoy highly personalized service, delicious food prepared with locally grown ingredients, and fine wines chosen by an astute sommelier. To sample the best of everything, try the six-course seafood tasting menu, priced at C$70 (US$59/£31), or C$112 (US$95/£50) with wine pairings. The menu might start with smoked oyster bisque, followed by a Dungeness crab and tomato salad, spiced scallops and octopus confit, a palate-cleansing rhubarb and gin ice, albacore tuna sashimi, and three different kinds of chocolate. The a la carte menu features meat dishes such as smoked tenderloin and venison striploin. The hotel's casual **Pacific Restaurant** is also a good choice for lunch or dinner, with nicely done dishes such as West Coast seafood linguine, vegetarian pizzas, and high-quality steak and lamb. The Pacific has a great outdoor patio overlooking the harbor.

In the Hotel Grand Pacific (p. 195), 463 Belleville St. ☎ **250/386-0450.** www.themark.ca. Reservations required for The Mark, recommended for Pacific Restaurant. The Mark main courses C$29–C$48 (US$25–US$41/£13–£22); Pacific

Where to Dine in Victoria

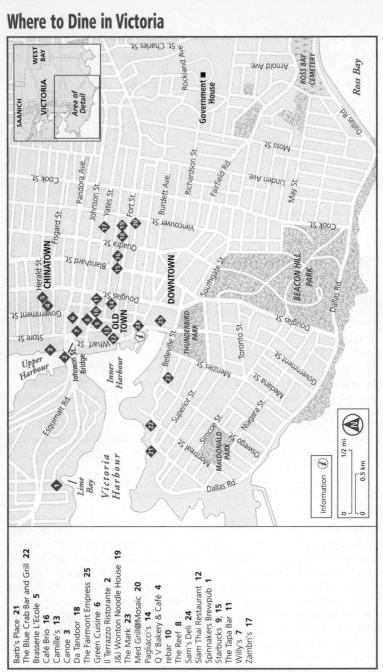

Barb's Place **21**
The Blue Crab Bar and Grill **22**
Brasserie L'Ecole **5**
Café Brio **16**
Camille's **13**
Canoe **3**
Da Tandoor **18**
The Fairmont Empress **25**
Green Cuisine **6**
Il Terrazzo Ristorante **2**
J&J Wonton Noodle House **19**
The Mark **23**
Med Grill@Mosaic **20**
Pagliacci's **14**
Q V Bakery & Café **4**
rebar **10**
The Reef **8**
Sam's Deli **24**
Siam Thai Restaurant **12**
Spinnakers Brewpub **1**
Starbucks **9, 15**
The Tapa Bar **11**
Willy's **7**
Zambri's **17**

Restaurant main courses C$16–C$30 (US$14–US$25/£6–£14). AE, DC, MC, V. The Mark daily 5–9:30pm; Pacific Restaurant daily 6:30am–10pm.

MODERATE

Canoe ✪ PUB GRUB/PACIFIC NORTHWEST What was once a Victorian power station is now one of Victoria's loveliest and liveliest brewpub restaurants, with an outdoor patio overlooking the harbor toward the Johnson Street Bridge and an industrial-inspired interior with massive masonry walls and heavy timber crossbeams. Canoe is popular because it basically has something for every palate and everything is very tasty. The kitchen offers intriguing variations on standard pub fare and bar snacks, including thin-crust pizzas (but with grilled lamb or chile prawns) and classic burgers. Head upstairs for finer fare such as premium top sirloin steak or seafood curry masala. The beer is excellent, and the award-winning wine list is small but select.

450 Swift St. ✆ **250/361-1940.** www.canoebrewpub.com. Reservations recommended for weekend dinner and Sun brunch. Main courses C$11–C$32 (US$9–US$27/£5–£14); pub fare and bar snacks C$6–C$17 (US$5–US$14/£2.75–£8). AE, MC, V. Daily 11am–midnight.

Spinnakers Brewpub PUB GRUB/PACIFIC NORTHWEST Spinnakers beer has always been extraordinary—rich ales, stouts, and lagers are all craft-brewed on the premises. The cuisine has changed over the years and evolved into above-average gas-tro-pub fare with some adventurous fresh West Coast seafood, all served in a fun, bustling pub atmosphere with great Inner Harbour views. It's hard to go wrong with the burgers, steamed mussels, or fish and chips.

308 Catherine St. ✆ **250/384-2739.** www.spinnakers.com. Main courses C$10–C$21 (US$8–US$18/£4–£8). AE, MC, V. Daily 11am–11pm.

INEXPENSIVE

Barb's Place *Kids* FISH & CHIPS The best "chippie" in town, Barb serves lightly breaded halibut and hand-hewn chips, plus a good seafood chowder, seafood special-ties, and burgers from a stand (picnic tables are nearby) at Fisherman's Wharf.

310 Erie St. ✆ **250/384-6515.** www.barbsplace.ca. Menu items C$6–C$17 (US$5–US$14/£2.70–£8). MC, V. Daily 10am–sunset.

4 Downtown & Old Town

EXPENSIVE

Brasserie L'Ecole ✪✪ FRENCH In the overheated world of food fashion, it's so refreshing to find simple French bistro fare deftly prepared and served at amazingly reasonable prices. Honesty is what's on offer at this warm, comfortable restaurant, the brainchild of longtime Victoria chef Sean Brenner. L'Ecole's menu changes daily, depending entirely on what comes in fresh from Victoria's hinterland farms. Prepa-ration is simple, no big reductions or complicated *jus,* just shellfish, local fish, meats with red-wine sauces, and fresh vegetables with vinaigrettes. The wine list is small, with no hugely expensive vintages, but has good straightforward wine to match the excellent food. Very satisfying in every way.

1715 Government St. ✆ **250/475-6262.** www.lecole.ca. Reservations recommended. Main courses C$19 (US$16/£9). AE, MC, V. Tues–Sat 5:30–11pm.

Café Brio ✪✪✪ PACIFIC NORTHWEST/ITALIAN Having just celebrated its 10th anniversary, Café Brio remains one of Victoria's best and buzziest spots for casual but top-flight dining. The Tuscan-influenced cuisine strongly reflects the seasons, fresh

Moments **Taking Afternoon Tea**

Far from a simple cup of hot water with a Lipton teabag beside it, a proper afternoon tea is both a meal and a ritual.

Any number of places in Victoria serve afternoon tea; some refer to it as high tea. Both come with sandwiches, berries, and tarts, but high tea usually includes some more substantial savory fare such as a meat-and-vegetable-filled turnover. Though the caloric intake can be hefty, it's really more about the ritual than the potential weight gain. For that reason, you don't want to go to any old teahouse. Note that in summer it's a good idea to book *at least* a week ahead.

If you want, and can afford, the best experience, head to **The Fairmont Empress** ✿✿✿, 721 Government St. (p. 194; ✆ 250/384-8111; bus no. 5 to the Convention Centre), where tea is served in the Tea Lobby, a busy and beautifully ornate room at the front of the hotel. Price depends on the time and season, and runs from C$38 to C$55 (US$32–US$47/£17–£25). For that, you'll be pampered with fresh berries and cream; sandwiches of smoked salmon, cucumber, and carrot and ginger; and scones with strawberry preserves and thick Jersey cream. Even the tea is a special house blend. When you leave, you'll receive a gift of 10 bags to brew at home. Seatings are every 15 minutes four times a day starting at noon, 1:30, 3, and 4:30pm; reservations are essential.

More affordable, less crowded, and just as historic is tea on the lawn of **Point Ellice House**, 2616 Pleasant St. (✆ 250/380-6506; www.pointellicehouse. ca), where the cream of Victoria society used to gather in the early 1900s. On the Gorge waterway, Point Ellice is just a 5-minute trip by ferry from the Inner

local meats and produce, and Pacific seafood. The menu changes daily, but appetizers always include locally harvested oysters, a wonderful house-made paprika sausage, and a delicious charcuterie plate (the chef makes all his charcuterie on the premises). For entrees, choose from handmade pasta (such as fresh herb-ricotta agnolotti) or roasted or poached wild fish. The wine list is excellent, with an impressive selection of B.C. and international reds and whites. The service is deft, friendly, and knowledgeable, and the kitchen stays open as long as guests keep ordering. An all-around winner.

944 Fort St. ✆ 250/383-0009. www.cafe-brio.com. Reservations recommended. Main courses C$17–C$30 (US$14–US$25/£8–£13). AE, MC, V. Daily 5:30–9:30pm.

Camille's ✿✿✿ PACIFIC NORTHWEST The most romantic of Victoria's restaurants, Camille's is also one of the very best. Tucked away in two rooms beneath the old Law Chambers, its decor contrasts white linen with century-old exposed brick, stained-glass lamps, and candlelight. Chef and owner David Mincey was one of the founders of a Vancouver Island farm cooperative that brings local farmers together with local restaurants, so you're usually dining on foods found within a 100-mile radius of the restaurant. The ever-changing menu displays Mincey's love for cheeky invention and the seasonal bounty of Vancouver Island. To sample a bit of everything

Harbour, or take bus no. 14 to Pleasant Street. Afternoon tea costs C$22 (US$18/£10) and includes a half-hour tour of the mansion and gardens, plus the opportunity to play a game of croquet. Open daily 10am to 4pm (tea served 11am–4pm) May through the first Monday of September; phone ahead for Christmas hours.

If you want your tea in a historic garden setting, head over to **Abkhazi Garden,** 1964 Fairfield Rd. (© **250/598-8096;** by car or bus no. 1 from downtown), where tea is served daily in the small, modernist house built by Russian Prince and Princess Abkhazi; see p. 221 for a description of the garden.

Set in impeccably maintained gardens, "Afternoon Tea at the Gardens" at the **Butchart Gardens Dining Room Restaurant** ✿✿✿, 800 Benvenuto Ave. (© **250/652-4422;** www.butchartgardens.com; bus no. 75), is a memorable experience. Sitting inside the Butchart mansion and looking out over the flowers, you can savor this fine tradition for C$25 (US$21/£11) per person. Tea is served daily noon to 5pm year-round; reservations recommended. Call ahead for winter hours.

What the **White Heather Tea Room** ✿✿, 1885 Oak Bay Rd. (© **250/595-8020**), lacks in old-time atmosphere it makes up for with the sheer quality and value of the tea, and the charm of proprietress and tea mistress Agnes. Of all the numerous options on offer, all of them are less expensive than a similar experience at The Empress. For those feeling not so peckish, try the Wee Tea at C$12 (US$10/£5). For those a little hungrier, the Not So Wee Tea at C$16 (US$14/£7). For the borderline starving is the Big Muckle Great Tea for Two at C$37 (US$31/£17). Open Tuesday through Saturday 10am to 5pm.

try the five-course tasting menu, a fantastic bargain at C$50 (US$42/£22), or C$75 (US$64/£34) with wine pairings. The reasonable and extensive wine list comes with liner notes that are amusing and informative. A meal here is a quiet, memorable occasion abetted by the professionalism of the staff.

45 Bastion Sq. © 250/381-3433. www.camillesrestaurant.com. Reservations recommended. Main courses C$24–C$34 (US$21–US$29/£11–£15). AE, MC, V. Tues–Sun 5:30–10pm.

Il Terrazzo Ristorante ✿✿ ITALIAN   This charming spot in a converted heritage building off Waddington Alley is always a top contender for Victoria's best Italian restaurant. You can be assured of a good meal here. The northern Italian cooking includes wood-oven-roasted meats, fish, and pizzas, as well as homemade pastas. An emphasis on fresh produce and local seafood sets the tone for the menu, with appetizers such as artichokes stuffed with salmon and crabmeat drizzled with a light lemon-cream sauce, and entrees like salmon crusted with almond and black pepper and baked in the wood-burning oven, or a fabulous rack of lamb. The mood is bustling and upbeat, complete with an atmospheric courtyard furnished with flowers, marble tables, wrought-iron chairs, and heaters. The wine list is enormous, with some 1,200 vintages. Service is friendly and helpful.

555 Johnson St., off Waddington Alley. ⓒ 250/361-0028. www.ilterrazzo.com. Reservations recommended. Main courses C$19–C$37 (US$16–US$31/£9–£17). AE, MC, V. Mon–Sat 11:30am–3pm (Oct–Apr no lunch on Sat); daily 5–10pm. Bus: 5.

MODERATE

Da Tandoor INDIAN   The best of Victoria's several Indian restaurants, Da Tandoor hides itself behind an unprepossessing facade on the outer edge of Fort Street's antiques row, near Café Brio, Med Grill, and J&J Wonton Noodle House. The cuisine is well worth the 10-minute walk from downtown. Tandoori chicken, seafood, and lamb and fish curries are the house specialties; but the extensive menu also includes masalas, vindaloos, and goshts, and classic appetizers like samosas and papadums. If you get inspired to try it at home, the restaurant sells a wide variety of spices and chutneys. Decor is nothing special, and service can sometimes be slow.

1010 Fort St. ⓒ **250/384-6333.** Reservations recommended. Main courses C$10–C$30 (US$8–US$25/£4.50–£13). MC, V. Sun–Thurs 5–9pm; Fri–Sat 5–10pm.

Pagliacci's ITALIAN   Victoria's night owls used to come here when Pagliacci's was one of the few places to offer late-night dining. Though the city's evening scene has improved since expatriate New Yorker Howie Siegal opened the restaurant in 1979, Pagliacci's can still boast an un-Victoria kind of big city buzz and energy. Tables jostle against one another as guests ogle each other's food and eavesdrop on conversations. The menu is southern Italian—veal parmigiana, tortellini, and 19 or 20 other a la carte pastas, all fresh and made by hand, many quite inventive. Live jazz, swing, blues, or Celtic music starts at 8:30pm, Sunday through Wednesday. Howie hosts a very good brunch, also on Sunday.

1011 Broad St. ⓒ **250/386-1662.** Reservations not accepted. Main courses C$12–C$26 (US$10–US$22/£5–£12); Sun brunch C$10–C$15 (US$8–US$13/£4.50–£7). AE, MC, V. Mon–Thurs 11:30am–10pm; Fri–Sat 11:30am–11pm; Sun 10am–10pm.

The Reef CARIBBEAN   An outgrowth of the Vancouver restaurant (p. 105), this Island Reef offers the same menu, the centerpiece of which is jerk—a spicy Caribbean marinade. The Reef serves up a number of jerk dishes, including their signature quarter jerk chicken breast. Other dishes are equally good, including shrimp with coconut milk and lime juice, and grilled blue marlin. In the evenings, a DJ spins tunes, and The Reef turns into its own little island lounge.

533 Yates St. ⓒ **250/388-5375.** www.thereefrestaurant.com. Main courses C$9–C$17 (US$8–US$14/£4–£8). MC, V. Mon–Wed 11am–11pm; Thurs 11am–midnight; Fri–Sat 11am–1am.

The Tapa Bar *Finds* TAPAS   The perfect meal for the commitment-shy, tapas are small and flavorful plates that you combine together to make a meal. Tapas to be sampled in this warm and welcoming spot include fried calamari, hearts of palm, and grilled portobello mushrooms. However, don't pass up on the *gambas al ajillo*—shrimp in a rich broth of garlic. The martini list is likely longer than the list of wines, but between the two there's plenty to keep the room buzzing until the witching hour.

620 Trounce Alley. ⓒ **250/383-0013.** Tapas plates C$7–C$15 (US$6–US$13/£3.25–£7). AE, MC, V. Mon–Thurs 11:30am–11pm; Fri–Sat 11:30am–midnight; Sun 11am–10pm.

Zambri's *Finds* ITALIAN   This little deli-restaurant in a strip mall off Yates Street has earned numerous accolades for its honest and fresh Italian cuisine served in an unpretentious, no-nonsense style. The lunch menu, served cafeteria-style, includes daily pasta specials and a handful of entrees such as fresh rockfish or salmon. In the

Finding High-Octane Coffee

Good coffee is one of the great joys of life. Fortunately, Victoria's tea-party Englishness hasn't stopped it from buzzing into the same coffee-cuckooness that's engulfed Vancouver and the rest of the Pacific Northwest. Some to savor:

- **Starbucks** has any number of outposts here. The one at the corner of Fort and Blanshard streets (© **250/383-6208**) is fairly central, open 6am to 11pm Sunday through Thursday, and 6am to midnight Friday and Saturday; bus no. 5 to Fort Street. They have another central location at 1234 Government St. (© **250/920-7203**), open Monday through Friday 6:30am to 9pm, Saturday 7:30am to 10pm, and Sunday 8:30am to 7pm; bus no. 5 to View Street.

- On a sunny day, head for **Willy's,** 537 Johnson St. (© **250/381-8414**). Order your brew from the counter, and take a seat on the patio. This bakery serves up excellent sweets and great hot breakfasts. It's open Monday to Friday 7am to 5pm, Saturday 8am to 5pm, and Sunday 8:30am to 4:30pm; bus no. 25.

- Out in Oak Bay, **Ottavio** ★, 2272 Oak Bay Ave. (© **250/592-4080;** www. ottaviovictoria.com), is a charming cafe, bakery, and deli with great Italian pastries, snacks, and coffee. It's open Tuesday to Saturday from 8am to 6pm, and Sunday from 10am to 6pm. Take bus no. 2 Oak Bay to Oak Bay Avenue and Monterey Street.

evenings, the atmosphere is slightly more formal with table service and a regularly changing a la carte menu. Menu items veer from penne with sausage and tomato to pasta with chicken liver pâté or peas and Gorgonzola. Many diners come for the three-course dinner (C$40–C$45/US$34–US$38/£18–£20).

110-911 Yates St. © **250/360-1171.** Reservations not accepted. Lunch C$8–C$14 (US$7–US$12/£3.60–£6); dinner main courses C$22–C$25 (US$19–US$21/£10–£11). MC, V. Tues–Sat 11:30am–2:30pm and 5–9pm.

INEXPENSIVE

Green Cuisine *Value* VEGETARIAN   In addition to being undeniably healthy, Victoria's only fully vegan eatery offers remarkably tasty choices, with a self-serve salad bar, hot buffet, dessert bar, and full bakery. Available dishes range from pasta primavera salad to pumpkin tofu cheesecake, not to mention a wide selection of freshly baked breads (made with natural sweeteners and fresh-ground organic flour). Green Cuisine also has a large selection of freshly squeezed organic juices, smoothies, and shakes, as well as organic coffees and teas.

560 Johnson St., in Market Sq. © **250/385-1809.** www.greencuisine.com. Main courses C$4–C$10 (US$3.40–US$8/ £1.80–£4.50). AE, MC, V. Daily 10am–8pm (Sun 10am–5pm in winter).

J&J Wonton Noodle House ★ *Finds* CHINESE   This place doesn't go overboard on the atmosphere (it's perfectly pleasant), and you won't find better noodles anywhere in Victoria. The kitchen is glassed in so you can watch the chefs spinning out noodles. Lunch specials—which feature different fresh seafood every day—are good and cheap, so expect a line of locals at the door. If you miss the specials, noodle soups, chow mein, and other dishes are also quick, delicious, and inexpensive. Dinner is pricier.

1012 Fort St. ℂ 250/383-0680. www.jjnoodlehouse.com. Main courses C$11–C$16 (US$9–US$14/£5–£7); lunch specials C$6–C$13 (US$5–US$11/£2.75–£6). MC, V. Tues–Sat 11am–2pm and 4:30–8:30pm. Bus: 5.

Med Grill@Mosaic *(Finds* TAPAS/BISTRO   This tasty bistro and tapas bar has a light, contemporary interior with lots of wood and huge windows, and a late-night happy hour (nightly 9–10pm) with tasty bar fare for less than C$10 (US$8/£4.50), including bacon-wrapped prawns, thin-crust pizzas, and crab and shrimp cakes. A Tuscan Table three-course dinner is served nightly for under C$20 (US$17/£9). You'll also find soup, salad, sandwiches, pasta, and entrees of fresh salmon, pork tenderloin, or oven-roasted chicken.

1063 Fort St. ℂ 250/381-3417. Main courses C$10–C$22 (US$8–US$19/£4.50–£10); bar menu C$5–C$10 (US$4–US$8/£2.25–£4.50). AE, MC, V. Daily 11am–10pm. Bus: 5.

Q V Bakery & Café BAKERY   The main attraction of the simple food here on the edge of downtown isn't so much its quality—though the coffee, muffins, cookies, and light meals like lasagnas and salads are all good—as its availability. On weekends, Q V is open 24 hours, which in Victoria is enough to make it very special indeed.

1701 Government St. ℂ 250/384-8831. Main courses C$4–C$10 (US$3.50–US$8/£2–£4.50). MC, V. Sun–Thurs 6am–3am; Fri–Sat 24 hr.

rebar *(Kids* VEGETARIAN   Even if you're not hungry, it's worth dropping in here for a juice blend—say grapefruit, banana, melon, and pear with bee pollen or blue-green algae for added oomph. If you're hungry, rejoice: rebar is the city's premier purveyor of vegetarian comfort food. Disturbingly wholesome as that may sound, rebar is not only tasty, but fun, and a great spot to take the kids for brunch or breakfast. The room—in the basement of an 1890s heritage building—is bright and funky, with loads of cake tins glued to the walls. The service is friendly and casual. The food tends toward the simple and wholesome, including quesadillas, omelets, and crisp salads. Juices are still the crown jewels, with more than 80 blends on the menu.

50 Bastion Sq. ℂ 250/361-9223. www.rebarmodernfood.com. Main courses C$7.50–C$16 (US$6–US$14/£3.40–£7). AE, MC, V. Mon–Thurs 8:30am–9pm; Fri–Sat 8:30am–10pm; Sun 8:30am–3:30pm. Reduced hours in the winter. Bus: 5.

Sam's Deli DELI   If you don't like lines, avoid the lunch hour, for Sam's is *the* lunchtime soup-and-sandwich spot in Victoria. Sandwiches come in all tastes and sizes (mostly large), but the shrimp and avocado is the one to get. The homemade soups are excellent, as is the chili. And Sam's is right across the street from the harbor, making it unbeatably convenient.

805 Government St. ℂ 250/382-8424. www.samsdeli.com. Main courses C$4–C$10 (US$3.50–US$8/£2–£4.50). MC, V. Summer Mon–Fri 7:30am–10pm, Sat–Sun 8am–10pm; winter Mon–Fri 7:30am–5pm.

Siam Thai Restaurant *(Value* THAI   Tucked away in a vintage building just half a block or so from the waterfront, this little local favorite offers good-quality Thai cooking. Menu items are starred from mild to spicy (one to four peppers), so there's no risk of having your tongue scorched, and include many signature Thai dishes such as pad thai noodles and a variety of curries (red, yellow, and green). Most items can be adapted to accommodate vegetarians. The lunch specials are a great deal.

512 Fort St. ℂ 250/383-9911. www.siamthai.ca. Main courses C$10–C$20 (US$8–US$16/£4.50–£9); lunch specials C$7–C$11 (US$5–US$9/£3.15–£5). MC, V. Mon–Fri 11:30am–2pm and 4:30–9:30pm; Sat noon–2pm and 5pm–closing. Bus: 5.

5 Outside the Central Area

VERY EXPENSIVE

The Aerie 𝕗𝕗𝕗 FRENCH   The dining room of this hotel enjoys a breathtaking view over Finlayson Inlet, the Strait of Juan de Fuca, and, on a clear day, the Olympic Mountains. The room itself is decorated with a 14-carat gold-leaf ceiling, crystal chandeliers, and a large open-hearth fireplace. As for the food—well, eating at this award-winning restaurant is definitely a culinary event. Chef Christophe Letard combines West Coast freshness with unmistakably French accents. A recent tasting menu included sautéed spot prawns from Finlayson Arm, steamed halibut pavé, and Cowichan Valley duck breast. Excellent wine pairings, featuring local vintages, and impeccable service help to make meals even more memorable.

In The Aerie hotel (p. 204), 600 Ebedora Lane, Malahat. 𝄐 800/518-1933 or 250/743-7115. www.aerie.bc.ca. Reservations required. Main courses C$36–C$42 (US$21–US$36/£16–£19); tasting menu C$100 (US$85/£45). AE, DC, MC, V. Daily noon–3pm and 5:30–8:30pm (Sun brunch noon–2pm). Take Hwy. 1 to the Spectacle Lake turnoff; take the first right and follow the winding driveway.

SeaGrille 𝕗 PACIFIC NORTHWEST   The dining room of beautiful Brentwood Bay Lodge (p. 204), about a 20-minute drive north of Victoria, is all warm wood with giant windows overlooking Saanich Inlet. The food prepared here emphasizes fresh, seasonal seafood such as seared B.C. salmon or halibut and king crab risotto. You could also choose from steaks, chops, and chicken breast, plus a vegetarian special or order from the more casual pub menu, which includes thin-crust pizzas and staples such as fish and chips and a halibut burger.

In Brentwood Bay Lodge and Spa, 849 Verdier Ave., Brentwood Bay. 𝄐 888/544-2079 or 250/544-5100. www.brentwoodbaylodge.com. Reservations recommended. Main courses C$11–C$34 (US$9–US$29/£5–£15). AE, DC, MC, V. Daily 5–10pm. From Victoria, take Pat Bay Hwy. north to Keating Crossroads, turn left (west) to Saanich Rd., turn right (south) to Verdier Ave.

Sooke Harbour House 𝕗𝕗𝕗 PACIFIC NORTHWEST   The dining room of this celebrated restaurant/hotel offers spectacular waterfront views of Sooke Harbour, a relaxed atmosphere, and some of Canada's best and most inventive food. Dishes on the daily-changing, seasonally adjusted menu are prepared with care, imagination, and flair. Ingredients are resolutely local (many come from the inn's own organic garden or from the ocean at the Harbour House's doorstep). Depending on the season, dishes might include grilled flounder with hazelnut, arugula and cheese pesto or grilled pork tenderloin with a red-wine meat stock reduction and dried cherry and thyme compote. The presentation is always interesting, and the staff is knowledgeable and professional. The wine cellar is one of the best in Canada, and the pairings are particularly well chosen. Instead of the four-course set menu, for the most memorable meal, and the best of everything, order the Gastronomical Menu.

In the Sooke Harbour House Hotel (p. 206), 1528 Whiffen Spit Rd., Sooke. 𝄐 800/889-9688 or 250/642-3421. www.sookeharbourhouse.com. Reservations required. Set menus C$75–C$100 (US$64–US$85/£34–£45). MC, V. Daily 5:30–9pm. Take the Island Hwy. to the Sooke/Colwood turnoff (Junction Hwy. 14); continue on Hwy. 14 to Sooke; about 2km (1 mile) past the town's only traffic light, turn left onto Whiffen Spit Rd.

INEXPENSIVE

Six Mile Pub PUB FARE   In an 1855 building, this pub has a rich history. Originally named the Parson's Bridge Hotel (after the man who built Parson's Bridge, which opened the Sooke area to vehicle traffic), it was filled with sailors when the Esquimalt Naval Base opened nearby in 1864. When Victoria elected to continue Prohibition until 1952, the

Six Mile Pub became the hub for provincial bootleggers. Loyal locals still come for the atmosphere and the dinner specials. You can enjoy the warm ambience of the fireside room, or sit on the outdoor patio. Start with one of the 10 house brews on tap, then enjoy a hearty Cornish pasty (pronounced *pass*-tee, filled with mystery meat, peas, potatoes, and carrots in a pastry envelope), steak-and-mushroom pie, or juicy prime rib. If meat isn't part of your diet, try a veggie burger. They've recently gone "international," too, and serve various tapas, pot stickers, and more adventuresome seafood dishes. Just don't bring the kids—you must be at least 19 years old to enter.

494 Island Hwy., View Royal. ℰ 250/478-3121. www.sixmilepub.com. Main courses C$7–C$14 (US$6–US$12/£3.20–£6). MC, V. Mon–Thurs 11am–11pm; Fri–Sat 11am–1am; Sun 10am–11pm.

14

Exploring Victoria

Victoria's top draws are its waterfront—the beautiful view created by The Fairmont Empress and the Legislature buildings on the edge of the Inner Harbour—and its historic Old Town. Two world-class attractions are the Butchart Gardens, about a 20-minute drive from downtown, and the Royal B.C. Museum on the Inner Harbour.

So attractive is this small city, though, that folks sometimes forget what a beautiful and wild part of the world it's set in. If you have time, step out of town and see some nature: Sail out to see killer whales, beachcomb for crabs, kayak along the ocean shorelines, or hike into the hills for fabulous views and scenery.

1 Seeing the Sights

THE TOP ATTRACTIONS

Abkhazi Garden ✦ *(Finds)* It's a bit out-of-the-way, about 5 minutes east of downtown by car, but if you're a nature lover, you'll love discovering this .4-hectare (1-acre) jewel box of a garden and the romantic story behind its creation. The wealthy Marjorie (Peggy) Pemberton-Carter met Russian Prince Nicholas Abkhazi in Paris in the 1920s, but they didn't meet again until 1946, by which time both had endured incarceration in prisoner-of-war camps (she in Shanghai as a British national, he in Germany). They wed, moved to Victoria, and set about creating a landscape garden that takes full advantage of a dramatic site that contains quiet woodland, rocky slopes, and lovely vistas. The rhododendron woodland includes treelike plants more than 100 years old. The modernist summerhouse the Abkhazis built first has been lovingly restored, as has the small, charming house where they eventually lived. The house is used as a tearoom and gift shop. Allow 1 hour.

1964 Fairfield Rd. (€) 250/598-8096. www.abkhazi.com. Admission C$10 (US$8/£4.50) adults, C$7.50 (US$6/£3.40) seniors and students, free for children under 12, C$35 (US$30/£16) families. Daily 11am–5pm; tearoom daily 11:30am–4pm. Bus: 1 to Fairfield Rd. and Foul Bay.

Art Gallery of Greater Victoria Housed in a combination of contemporary exhibition space and a historic 19th-century mansion called Gyppeswick, the Art Gallery of Greater Victoria features a permanent collection of more than 15,000 objets d'art, drawn from Asia, Europe, and North America, though the gallery's primary emphasis is on Canada and Japan. The permanent **Emily Carr exhibit** ✦ integrates Carr's writings, works from the gallery collection, and images from the British Columbia provincial archives to create a compelling portrait of this preeminent Victoria artist. Allow 1½ hours.

1040 Moss St. (€) 250/384-4101. www.aggv.bc.ca. Admission C$12 (US$10/£5) adults, C$10 (US$8/£4.50) seniors and students, C$2 (US$1.75/£1) children 6–17. Daily 10am–5pm (Thurs until 9pm). Closed holidays. Bus: 11, 14, or 22.

British Columbia Aviation Museum ✦   Located adjacent to Victoria International Airport, this small hangar is crammed with a score of original, rebuilt, and replica airplanes. The collection ranges from the first Canadian-designed craft ever to fly (a bizarre kitelike contraption) to slightly more modern water bombers and helicopters. Thursdays you can watch the all-volunteer crew in the restoration hangar working to bring these old crafts back to life.

1910 Norseman Rd., Sidney. ✆ 250/655-3300. www.bcam.net. Admission C$7 (US$6/£3.20) adults, C$5 (US$4/£2.25) seniors, C$3 (US$2.50/£1.35) students, free for children under 12. Summer daily 10am–4pm; winter daily 11am–3pm. Closed Dec 25, Jan 1. Bus: Airport.

Butchart Gardens ✦✦✦   These internationally acclaimed gardens were created after Robert Butchart exhausted the limestone quarry near his Tod Inlet home, about 22km (14 miles) from Victoria. His wife, Jenny, gradually landscaped the deserted eyesore into the resplendent Sunken Garden, opening it for public display in 1904. Over the years, a Rose Garden, Italian Garden, and Japanese Garden were added. As the fame of the 20-hectare (49-acre) gardens grew, the Butcharts also transformed their house into an attraction. The gardens—still in the family—now display more than a million plants throughout the year. On one stroll, passing through all the gardens, you'll be amazed at the gardeners' painstaking care and the beauty of the plantings.

On summer evenings, the gardens are illuminated with a variety of softly colored lights. June through September, musical entertainment is provided free Monday through Saturday evenings. You can even watch **fireworks displays** ✦✦✦ on Saturdays in July and August. A very good lunch, dinner, and afternoon tea are offered in the Dining Room Restaurant in the historic residence; afternoon and high teas are also served in the Italian Garden (reservations recommended). Allow 2 to 3 hours; in peak summer months you'll encounter less congestion in the garden if you come very early or after 3pm.

800 Benvenuto Ave., Brentwood Bay. ✆ 866/652-4422 or 250/652-4422; dining reservations 250/652-8222. www. butchartgardens.com. Admission June 15–Sept C$25 (US$21/£11) adults, C$13 (US$11/£6) youths 13–17, C$3 (US$2/£1.35) children 5–12, free for children under 5; admission prices reduced rest of the year. Open daily 9am–sundown (call or visit website for seasonal closing times); visitors can remain in gardens for 1 hr. after gate closes. Bus: 75 or the Gray Line shuttle from the Victoria Bus Station (runs late Apr to Sept); C$14 (US$12/£6) round-trip. For shuttle departure times, call ✆ 800/663-8390 or 250/388-6539. Take Blanshard St. (Hwy. 17) north toward the ferry terminal in Saanich, then turn left on Keating Crossroads, which leads directly to the gardens—about 20 min. from downtown Victoria; it's impossible to miss if you follow the trail of billboards.

Craigdarroch Castle ✦   What do you do when you've clawed, scraped, and bullied your way up from indentured servant to coal baron and richest man in British Columbia? You build a castle, of course, to show the other buggers what you're worth. Located in the highlands above Oak Bay, Robert Dunsmuir's home, built in the 1880s, is a stunner. The four-story, 39-room Highland-style castle is topped with stone turrets and chimneys, and filled with the opulent Victorian splendor such as detailed woodwork, Persian carpets, stained-glass windows, paintings, and sculptures. The nonprofit society that runs Craigdarroch does an excellent job showcasing the castle. You're provided with a self-tour booklet; several volunteer docents are happy to provide further information. The castle also hosts many events throughout the year, including theater performances, concerts, and dinner tours. Allow 30 minutes to 1 hour for castle tour. After visiting Craigdarroch, you might want to visit Hatley Park, the castle built by Dunsmuir's son in 1910 (see description below).

1050 Joan Crescent (off Fort St.). ✆ 250/592-5323. www.craigdarrochcastle.com. Admission C$12 (US$10/£5) adults, C$11 (US$9/£5) seniors, C$3.75 (US$3/£1.70) children 5–12, free for children under 5. June 15 to Labour Day

Art Gallery of Greater Victoria **14**

Craigdarroch Castle **15**

Emily Carr House **12**

The Fairmont Empress **8**

Helmcken House **11**

Maritime Museum of
British Columbia **2**

Market Square **1**

Miniature World **5**

Pacific Undersea Gardens **7**

Parliament Buildings
(Provincial Legislature) **9**

Pioneer Square **3**

Ross Bay Cemetery **16**

Royal British Columbia Museum **10**

Royal London Wax Museum **6**

Trans-Canada Highway Mile 0 **13**

Victoria Bug Zoo **4**

daily 9am–7pm; day after Labour Day to June 14 daily 10am–4:30pm. Closed Dec 25, 26, and Jan 1. Bus: 11 to Joan Crescent. Take Fort St. out of downtown, just past Cook, and turn right on Joan Crescent.

Fort Rodd Hill & Fisgard Lighthouse   Perched on an outcrop of volcanic rock, the **Fisgard Lighthouse** has guided ships toward Victoria's sheltered harbor since 1873. The light no longer has a keeper (the beacon has long been automated), but the site itself has been restored to its 1873 appearance. Two floors of exhibits in the light keeper's house recount stories of the lighthouse, its keepers, and the terrible shipwrecks that gave this coastline its ominous moniker "the graveyard of the Pacific."

Adjoining the lighthouse, **Fort Rodd Hill** is a preserved 1890s coastal artillery fort sporting camouflaged searchlights, underground magazines, and its original guns. Audiovisual exhibits bring the fort to life with the voices and faces of the men who served at the outpost. Displays of artifacts, room re-creations, and historic film footage add to the experience. Both attractions are National Historic Sites. Allow 1 to 2 hours.

603 Fort Rodd Hill Rd. ⓒ 250/478-5849. www.parkscanada.ca/fortroddhill. Admission C$4 (US$3.40/£1.80) adults, C$3.50 (US$3/£1.60) seniors, C$2 (US$1.80/£1) children 6–16, free for children under 6, C$10 (US$8/£4.50) families. Feb 15–Oct daily 10am–5:30pm; Nov–Feb 14 daily 9am–4:30pm. No public transit. Head north on Douglas St. until it turns into Hwy. 1. Stay on Hwy. 1 for 5km (3 miles), then take the Colwood exit (exit 10). Follow Hwy. 1A for 2km (1¼ miles), then turn left at the 3rd traffic light onto Ocean Blvd; follow the signs to the site.

Hatley Park National Historic Site ⭐   Craigdarroch Castle (see above) was built during the 1880s to serve as Scottish coal-mining magnate Robert Dunsmuir's home. In 1908, Dunsmuir's son James, after a bitter inheritance battle with his mother, built his own palatial manse, Hatley Castle, on a 226-hectare (565-acre) waterfront estate about 25 minutes from Victoria. The younger Dunsmuir reportedly commissioned architect Samuel Maclure with the words, "Money doesn't matter, just build what I want." The bill came to more than C$1 million (equivalent to about US$40 million/£21 million today). The impressive castle, built of local stone in a hybrid Norman-Tudor fantasy style, belongs to Royal Roads University but is open to visitors on guided tours from mid-May to Labour Day (the not-very-interesting museum down in the basement is open year-round). As you're shown around the castle, you have to use your imagination, since all the furniture was sold in 1937 (much of it is now in Craigdarroch Castle) and the rooms are either empty or filled with office modules and equipment. The paneling and wood floors are truly remarkable, though. The surrounding estate features several lovely heritage gardens, including the tranquil Japanese Garden, designed almost a century ago by the Japanese architect Isaburo Kishida, who also designed the Japanese Gardens at Butchart Gardens. Allow 1 to 2 hours; I'd recommend that you take the 1-hour tour.

Royal Roads University, 200 Sooke Rd., Colwood. ⓒ 250/391-2511. www.hatleypark.ca. 1-hr. castle tour and garden access C$17 (US$10/£5) adults, C$16 (US$14/£7) seniors, C$11 (US$9/£5) youth 13–17, C$9 (US$8/£4) children 6–12. Gardens only C$9 (US$8/£4) adults, C$8 (US$7/£3.50) seniors, C$6 (US$5/£2.75) youth 13–17, C$27 (US$23/£12) family (2 adults, 3 children). Mid-May to Aug castle tours daily 10am–4pm (Sat–Sun until 3:15pm), museum and gardens 10am–8pm; Sept–Apr gardens and museum daily 10am–5pm. From Victoria, take Government St. north for about 2km (1¼ miles), turn left onto Gorge Rd. (Hwy. 1A) and follow about 20km (12 miles); turn left onto Sooke Rd. (Hwy. 14A) and look for signs to Royal Roads University or Hatley Park National Historic Site.

Maritime Museum of British Columbia   Housed in the former provincial courthouse, this museum is dedicated to recalling B.C.'s rich maritime heritage. The displays do a good job of illustrating maritime history, from the early explorers to the grand ocean liners. An impressive collection of ship models and paraphernalia—uniforms, weapons, gear—is complemented by photographs and journals. The museum also shows films in its Vice Admiralty Theatre. Allow 1 hour.

28 Bastion Sq. © 250/385-4222. www.mmbc.bc.ca. Admission C$8 (US$7/£3.60) adults, C$5 (US$4/£2.25) seniors and students, C$3 (US$2.50/£1.35) children 6–11, free for children under 6; C$20 (US$17/£9) families. Daily 9:30am–4:30pm (until 5pm June 15–Sept 15). Closed Dec 25. Bus: 5 to View St.

Miniature World *(Kids)*   It sounds cheesy—hundreds of dolls, miniatures, and scenes from old fairy tales, but Miniature World, inside The Fairmont Empress (the entrance is around the corner), is actually kinda cool, and kids ages 5 to 11 love it. You walk in, and you're plunged into darkness, except for a moon, some planets, and a tiny spaceship flying up to rendezvous with an orbiting mother ship. This is the most up-to-date display. Farther in are re-creations of battle scenes, a miniature Canadian Pacific Railway running all the way across a miniature Canada, and a three-ring circus and midway. Better yet, most of these displays do something: The train moves at the punch of a button, and the circus rides whirl around and light up as simulated darkness falls. Allow 30 minutes to an hour to see it all.

649 Humboldt St. © 250/385-9731. www.miniatureworld.com. Admission C$9 (US$8/£4) adults, C$8 (US$7/£3.60) youths, C$7 (US$6/£3.15) children 4–12, free for children under 4. Summer daily 8:30am–9pm; fall/winter daily 9am–5pm; spring daily 9am–7pm. Bus: 5, 27, 28, or 30.

Pacific Undersea Gardens   Savvy locals aren't very keen on the sight of this conspicuous white structure floating in the Inner Harbour, and those with some knowledge of Vancouver Island's marine environment will tell you that many of the creatures on display here are not indigenous to these waters. But your kids might enjoy a visit— or they might not, since the place is dark and kind of scary for little ones. A gently sloping walkway leads down to a glass-enclosed viewing area. Every hour, on the hour, is an underwater show in which a diver catches and—thanks to a microphone hookup—explains a variety of undersea fauna. One of the star attractions is a remarkably photogenic octopus (reputedly the largest in captivity). Injured seals and orphaned seal pups are cared for in holding pens alongside the observatory as part of a provincial marine-mammal rescue program. Allow 1 hour.

490 Belleville St. © 250/382-5717. www.pacificunderseagardens.com. Admission C$9.50 (US$8/£4.30) adults, C$8.50 (US$7/£3.80) seniors, C$7.50 (US$6/£3.40) youths 12–17, C$5.50 (US$4/£2.50) children 5–11, free for children under 5. Sept–Mar daily 10am–5pm; Apr–May daily 10am–6pm; June–Aug daily 9am–8pm. Bus: 5, 27, 28, or 30.

Parliament Buildings (Provincial Legislature) 𝖆𝖆   Designed by a 25-year-old Francis Rattenbury and built between 1893 and 1898 at a cost of nearly C$1 million (US$850,000), the Parliament Buildings (also called the Legislature) are an architectural gem. The 40-minute tour comes across at times like an eighth-grade civics lesson, but it's worth it to see the fine mosaics, marble, woodwork, and stained glass.

501 Belleville St. © 250/387-3046. www.legis.gov.bc.ca. Free admission. Late May to Labour Day daily 9am–5pm; Sept to late May Mon–Fri 9am–5pm. Tours offered every 20–30 min. in summer; in winter call ahead for the public tour schedules as times vary due to school group bookings. Bus: 5, 27, 28, or 30.

Royal B.C. Museum 𝖆𝖆𝖆 *(Kids)*   One of the world's best regional museums, the Royal B.C. has a mandate to present the land and the people of coastal British Columbia. The second-floor **Natural History Gallery** showcases the coastal flora, fauna, and geography from the Ice Age to the present; it includes dioramas of a temperate rainforest, a seacoast, and (particularly appealing to kids) a life-size woolly mastodon. The third-floor **Modern History Gallery** presents the recent past, including historically faithful re-creations of Victoria's downtown and Chinatown. On the same floor, the **First Peoples Gallery** 𝖆𝖆𝖆 is an incredible showpiece of First Nations art and culture with rare artifacts used in day-to-day native life, a full-size re-creation of a longhouse,

On the Lookout: Victoria's Best Views

In town, the best view of The Fairmont Empress and the Legislature comes from walking along the pedestrian path in front of the **Delta Ocean Pointe Resort,** off the Johnson Street Bridge. In summer, sit and enjoy a coffee or glass of wine with the view from the patio.

When the fishing fleets come in early in the morning, head over to **Fisherman's Wharf,** at St. Lawrence and Erie streets, to watch as the fishermen unload their catches. Later on, you can enjoy the sunset from the wharf along the eastern edge of the Inner Harbour or from the 18th floor of the **Vista 18 Restaurant,** 740 Burdett Ave. (© **250/382-9258**).

Just south of downtown, you can see across the Strait of Juan de Fuca and the San Juan Islands to the mountains of the Olympic Peninsula from the **Ogden Point** breakwater, the top of the hill in **Beacon Hill Park,** or the walking path above the beach along **Dallas Road.** Farther afield, **Fort Rodd Hill** and **Fisgard Lighthouse** offer equally good views of the mountains, as well as a view of the ships in Esquimalt Harbour.

Mount Douglas ⊛, a 15-minute drive north of the city on Shelbourne Street, affords a panoramic view of the entire Saanich Peninsula, with a parking lot just a 2-minute walk from the summit. To the east, **Mount Work** offers an equally good view, but the walk up takes about 45 minutes. At the top of Little Saanich Mountain (about 16km/10 miles north of Victoria) stands the **Dominion Astrophysical Observatory,** 5071 W. Saanich Rd. (© **250/363-8262**), and its new **Centre of the Universe** interpretive center, which offers guided tours and activities for C$9 (US$7.20/£4) adults, C$8 (US$6.40/£3.60) seniors and students, C$5 (US$4/£2.25) youths 6 to 18, and C$23 (US$18/£10) families. The interpretive center is open Tuesday through Friday from 10am to 4:30pm and Saturday from 10am to 5:30pm November to March. The observatory stays open later in the year, with evening prices C$12 (US$9.60/£5.40) adults, C$10 (US$8/£5) seniors and students, and C$7 (US$5.60/£3.15) youths 6 to 18.

and a hauntingly wonderful gallery with totem poles, masks, and artifacts. The museum also has an **IMAX theater** showing an ever-changing variety of large-screen movies. On the way out (or in), be sure to stop by **Thunderbird Park,** beside the museum, where a cedar longhouse (Mungo Martin House, named after a famous Kwakiutl artist) houses a workshop where native carvers work on new totem poles. To see and experience everything takes 3 to 4 hours.

675 Belleville St. © **888/447-7977** or 250/387-3701. www.royalbcmuseum.bc.ca. Admission C$14 (US$12/£6) adults; C$9.50 (US$8/£4.25) seniors, students, youths; free for children under 6; C$35 (US$30/£16) families. IMAX C$11 (US$9/£4.50) adults, C$9.50 (US$8/£4.25) students, C$8.25 (US$7/£3.70) children 6–18, C$5 (US$4.25/£2.25) children. Daily 9am–5pm (June–Sept Fri–Sat 9am–10pm); IMAX daily 9am–8pm. Closed Dec 25 and Jan 1. Bus: 5, 28, or 30.

Royal London Wax Museum *(Overrated)*   I've never understood why one of Victoria's most beautiful classical buildings, right on the waterfront, had to be used for a wax museum. And a pretty cheesy one at that. Inside, you can see the same dusty royal family and other figures ranging from Buddha to Goldie Hawn (the most recent addition, probably because she has a house in B.C.). It's doubtful even your kids will much enjoy it, except, of course, for the gory Chamber of Horrors (which might put off some kids). An hour is more than enough.

470 Belleville St. ℂ **877/929-3228** or 250/388-4461. www.waxmuseum.bc.ca. Admission C$10 (US$8/£4.50) adults, C$9 (US$8/£4) seniors, C$7 (US$6/£3.20) students 13 and older, C$5 (US$4/£2.25) children 6–12, free for children under 6. Daily 9:30am–5pm. Bus: 5, 27, 28, or 30.

Victoria Butterfly Gardens 𝕂 *Kids*   This is a great spot for kids, nature buffs, or anyone who just likes butterflies. An ID chart allows you to identify the hundreds of exotic, colorful butterflies fluttering freely through this lush tropical greenhouse. Species range from the tiny Central American Julia (a brilliant orange butterfly about 3 in. across) to the Southeast Asian Giant Atlas Moth (mottled brown and red, with a wingspan approaching a foot). Naturalists are on hand to explain butterfly biology, and a display allows you to see the beautiful creatures emerge from their cocoons. Allow 1 hour. *Note:* The gardens are closed from November through February.

1461 Benvenuto Ave. (P.O. Box 190), Brentwood Bay. ℂ **877/722-0272** or 250/652-3822. www.butterflygardens.com. Admission C$11 (US$9/£4.50) adults; C$10 (US$8/£4.50) seniors, students; C$5.75 (US$5/£2.60) children 5–12; free for children under 5. Mar to mid-May daily 9:30am–4:30pm; mid-May to early-Sept daily 9am–5:30pm; Mid-Sept–Oct daily 9:30am–4:30pm. Closed Nov–Feb. Bus: 75.

ARCHITECTURAL HIGHLIGHTS & HISTORIC HOMES

First a trading post, and then a gold-rush town, a naval base, and a sleepy provincial capital, Victoria bears architectural witness to all these eras. What Vancouver mostly demolished, Victoria saved, so you really do have a feast of heritage buildings to enjoy. The best of Victoria's buildings date from the pre–World War I years, when gold poured in from the Fraser and Klondike rivers, fueling a building boom responsible for most of downtown.

Finds **Emily Carr—Visionary from Victoria**

Victoria was the birthplace of one of British Columbia's most distinguished early residents, the painter and writer Emily Carr (1871–1945). Though trained in the classical European tradition, Carr developed her own style in response to the powerful landscapes of the Canadian west coast. Eschewing both marriage and stability, she spent her life traveling the coast, drawing inspiration from the land, seascapes and native peoples for her vivid and striking works. In addition to visiting the great collection of Carr's paintings at the **Art Gallery of Greater Victoria** (p. 221), you can visit the **Emily Carr House** 𝕂, 207 Government St. (ℂ **250/383-5843**; www.emilycarr.com), where she was born. The house has been restored to the condition it would have been in when Carr lived there. In addition, many of the rooms have been hung with reproductions of her art or quotations from her writings. June through Labour Day, the house is open daily 11am to 4pm; May and September it's open the same hours but closed Sunday and Monday. On Fridays and Saturdays from June through August, a local actress portrays Emily Carr and regales visitors with Carr family stories. Admission is C$5 (US$4/£2.25); C$10 (US$8/£4.50) for special events. The **Vancouver Art Gallery** (see chapter 7, p. 118) also has a major collection of Carr's hauntingly evocative paintings.

Tips   Another Victoria Teahouse

On a promontory above the Gorge Waterway, the completely restored **Point Ellice House** ☆, 2616 Pleasant St. (© **250/380-6506**), was the summer gathering place for much of Victoria's elite. From mid-May to mid-September, it's open for 30-minute guided tours daily from noon to 5pm; admission is the same as for Carr House, above. Point Ellice is also one of the better spots for afternoon tea (p. 214). The easiest way to reach the house is by harbor ferry from in front of The Fairmont Empress for C$4 (US$3.20/£1.80) one-way.

Perhaps the most intriguing downtown edifice isn't a building but a work of art. The walls of **Fort Victoria,** which once spanned much of downtown, have been demarcated in the sidewalk with bricks bearing the names of original settlers and traders. Look on the sidewalk on the corner of Government and Fort streets.

Most of the retail establishments in Victoria's Old Town area are housed in 19th-century shipping warehouses that have been carefully restored as part of a heritage-reclamation program. You can take a **self-guided tour** of the buildings, most of which were erected between the 1870s and 1890s; their history is recounted on easy-to-read outdoor plaques. The majority of the restored buildings are between Douglas and Government streets from Wharf Street to Johnson Street. The most impressive structure once housed a number of shipping offices and warehouses, and is now the home of a 45-shop complex known as **Market Square,** 560 Johnson St./255 Market Sq. (© **250/386-2441**).

Some of the British immigrants who settled Vancouver Island during the 19th century built magnificent estates and mansions. In addition to architect Francis Rattenbury's crowning turn-of-the-20th-century achievements—the provincial **Legislature Buildings,** 501 Belleville St. (completed in 1898), and the opulent **Fairmont Empress,** 721 Government St. (completed in 1908)—you'll find a number of other magnificent historic architectural sites.

Helmcken House, 610 Elliot St. Sq. (© **250/356-7226**), is the oldest house in B.C. still standing on its original site. Dr. John Sebastian Helmcken, a surgeon with the Hudson's Bay Company, set up house here in 1852 when he married the daughter of Governor Sir James Douglas. Originally a three-room log cabin, the house was built by Helmcken and expanded as both the prosperity and size of the family grew. It still contains its original furnishings, imported from England. Helmcken went on to become a statesman and helped negotiate the entry of British Columbia as a province into Canada. Helmcken House is open daily May through September from 10am to 5pm. Admission is C$5 (US$4/£2.25) for adults, C$4 (US$3.50/£1.80) for seniors and students, and C$3 (US$2.50/£1.35) for children.

CEMETERIES

Ross Bay Cemetery, 1495 Fairfield St. at Dallas Road, has to be one of the finest locations in all creation to spend eternity. Luminaries interred here include the first governor of the island, James Douglas; frontier judge Matthew Begbie; and West Coast painter Emily Carr. *An Historic Guide to Ross Bay Cemetery,* available in Munro's

Books (p. 252) as well as other bookstores, gives details on people buried here and directions to grave sites.

Pioneer Square, on the corner of Meares and Quadra streets beside Christ Church, is one of British Columbia's oldest cemeteries. Hudson's Bay Company fur traders, ship captains, sailors, fishermen, and crew members from British Royal Navy vessels lie beneath the worn sandstone markers.

Contact the **Old Cemeteries Society** (© 250/598-8870; www.oldcem.bc.ca) for more information on tours of both of these graveyards.

NEIGHBORHOODS OF NOTE

From the time the Hudson's Bay Company settled here in the mid-1800s, the historic **Old Town** was the center of the city's bustling business in shipping, fur trading, and legal opium manufacturing. Market Square and the surrounding warehouses once brimmed with exports like tinned salmon, furs, and timber bound for England and the United States. Now part of the downtown core, this is still a terrific place to find British, Scottish, and Irish imports (a surprising number of these shops date back to the early 1900s), souvenirs of all sorts, and even outdoor equipment for modern-day adventurers. Just a block north on Fisgard Street is **Chinatown.** Founded in 1858, it's the oldest Chinatown in Canada.

The **James Bay** area on the southern shores of the Inner Harbour is a quiet, middle-class, residential community. As you walk through its tree-lined streets, you'll find many older private homes that have maintained their original Victorian flavor.

Beautiful residential communities such as **Ross Bay** and **Oak Bay** have a more modern West Coast appearance, with houses and apartments perched on hills overlooking the beaches amid lush, landscaped gardens. Private marinas in these areas are filled with perfectly maintained sailing craft.

PARKS & GARDENS

With the mildest climate in Canada, Victoria's gardens are in bloom year-round. In addition to the world-renowned **Butchart Gardens** ❀❀❀ (p. 222) the **Abkhazi Garden** ❀ (p. 221), and the gardens at **Hatley Park National Historic Site** ❀ (p. 224), several city parks attract strollers and picnickers whenever the weather is pleasant. The 61-hectare (151-acre) **Beacon Hill Park** ❀ stretches from Southgate Street to Dallas Road between Douglas and Cook streets. In 1882, the Hudson's Bay Company gave this property to the city. Stands of indigenous Garry oaks (found only on Vancouver, Hornby, and Salt Spring islands) and manicured lawns are interspersed with floral gardens and ponds. Hike up Beacon Hill to get a clear view of the Strait of Georgia, Haro Strait, and Washington's Olympic Mountains. The children's farm (see "Especially for Kids," p. 232), aviary, tennis courts, lawn-bowling green, putting green, cricket pitch, wading pool, playground, and picnic area make this a wonderful place to spend a few hours with the family. The **Trans-Canada Highway's "Mile 0" marker** stands at the edge of the park on Dallas Road. Beacon Hill Park celebrated its 125th anniversary in 2007.

Just outside downtown, **Mount Douglas Park** has great views of the area, several hiking trails, and—down at the waterline—a picnic/play area with a trail leading to a good walking beach.

About 45 minutes southwest of town, **East Sooke Park** ❀ is a 1,400-hectare (3,459-acre) microcosm of the West Coast wilderness: jagged seacoast, native petroglyphs, and

A Provincial Park, a Native Village & a Few Wineries

A short drive north from Victoria along the Island Highway takes you to three spots well worth a visit: Goldstream Provincial Park, the Quw'utsun' (Cowichan) Cultural Centre, and the Cowichan Valley wineries. The drive—along the ocean, up over the Malahat mountains, and then through the beautiful Cowichan Valley—is short enough to complete in one fairly leisurely day.

GOLDSTREAM PROVINCIAL PARK   This quiet little valley overflowed with prospectors during the 1860s gold-rush days. Trails take you past abandoned mine shafts and tunnels as well as 600-year-old stands of towering Douglas fir, lodgepole pine, red cedar, indigenous yew, and arbutus trees. The **Gold Mine Trail** leads to Niagara Creek and the abandoned mine that was operated by Lt. Peter Leech, a royal engineer who discovered gold in the creek in 1858. **The Goldstream Trail** leads to the salmon spawning areas. (You might also catch sight of mink and river otters racing along this path.)

For general information on Goldstream Provincial Park and all other provincial parks on the South Island, contact **B.C. Parks** at ✆ **250/391-2300,** or check www.bcparks.ca. Throughout the year, Goldstream Park's **Freeman King Visitor Centre** (✆ **250/478-9414**) offers guided walks, talks, displays, and programs geared toward kids but interesting for adults, too. Open daily 9am to 4pm. Take Highway 1 about 30 minutes north of Victoria. Note that B.C. government cutbacks have significantly reduced the number of events and services in most provincial parks. There is now a C$3 (US$2.40/£1.80) day-use parking fee at Goldstream.

Three species of salmon (chum, chinook, and steelhead) make **annual salmon runs** up the Goldstream River during October, November, December, and February. You can easily observe this natural wonder along the riverbanks. Contact the park's visitor center for details.

QUW'UTSUN' CULTURAL AND CONFERENCE CENTRE ✪   The main reason for visiting the town of Duncan is to see the Quw'utsun' Cultural and Conference Centre, 200 Cowichan Way (✆ **877/746-8119** or 250/746-8119; www.quwutsun.ca). Created by the Cowichan People, the center brings First Nations culture to visitors in a way that's commercially successful yet still respectful of native traditions.

Longhouses along the crystal-clear Cowichan River give you an idea of the lodgings and ceremonial structures built by the aboriginal tribes who have lived in the area for thousands of years. Totem poles placed throughout the grounds represent traditional stories and legends. Though you can visit and take a self-guided tour year-round, it's best to tour the 2.4-hectare (6-acre) site with one of the native guides in July or August when there are ceremonial midday dances beside the river and a salmon barbecue (Tues–Sat at 1pm). Master and apprentice carvers create poles, masks, and feasting bowls in workshops open to the public; the traditional Cowichan art of knitting sweaters is also demonstrated. Original tools, clothing, and pictures are on display and a film presents an oral history of the Cowichan culture. A large gift shop in the complex sells native-made carvings, crafts, jewelry, clothing, silk-screened prints, and other items. The center and gift shops are open daily May through September 9am to 5pm (until 4pm on weekends); closed weekends October through March. Admission is C$13 (US$11/£6) for adults, C$11 (US$9/£5) for seniors and youths 12 to 18, C$2 (US$1.80/£1) for children 6 to 11, and C$25 (US$21/£11) for families. (Salmon barbecue and dance performance costs C$35/US$30/£16 for adults, C$33/US$28/£15 for seniors and students, and C$24/US$20/£11 for children.) You can enjoy authentic native foods (salmon, oysters, venison) at the **River Walk Café,** open for lunch Monday through Saturday 11am to 4pm. All in all, a unique experience.

The **Duncan-Cowichan Visitor Info Centre** is at 381A Trans-Canada Hwy. (in the Overwaitea Mall), Duncan, B.C. V9L 3R5 (© **250/746-4636**). During July and August, it's open daily from 9am to 6pm; September through June, hours are Monday through Saturday 9am to 3pm.

THE COWICHAN VALLEY WINERIES The Cowichan Valley is a gorgeous agricultural area a couple of hours' drive from Victoria. Area wineries and the seaside town of Cowichan Bay are worth a stop.

The vintners of Cowichan Valley have gained a solid reputation for producing fine wines. Several of the wineries offer 1-hour tours—a great introduction for novices. They usually include a tasting of the vintner's art as well as a chance to purchase bottles or cases of your favorites. (Great gift idea because you will not find any of these wines outside British Columbia.)

Cherry Point Vineyards, 840 Cherry Point Rd., Cowichan (© **250/743-1272;** www.cherrypointvineyards.com), looks like a slice of California's Napa Valley. The wine-tasting room and gift shop is open daily 10am to 5pm. You can have lunch at the on-site Bistro (main courses about C$15/US$13/£7). **Blue Grouse Vineyards,** 4365 Blue Grouse Rd., Mill Bay (© **250/743-3834;** www.bluegrouse vineyards.com), is a smaller winery that began as a hobby. April through September, it's open for tastings and on-site purchases Wednesday through Sunday 11am to 5pm (Wed–Sat the rest of the year). **Merridale Cidery,** located just south of Cowichan Bay at 1230 Merridale Rd. (© **800/998-9908** in B.C. only, or 250/743-4293; www.merridalecider.com), is worth a stop to taste their artisan ciders; you can have lunch at their bistro, La Pommeraie. Open daily 10:30am to 5:30pm (phone ahead to confirm open hours).

Cowichan Bay (off Hwy. 1, south of Duncan) is a pleasant half-hour drive from the wine country. Just southeast of Duncan, Cowichan Bay is a pretty little seaside town with a view of the ocean and a few attractions. The **Cowichan Bay Maritime Centre,** 1761 Cowichan Bay Rd., Cowichan Bay (© **250/746-4955;** www.classicboats.org), is a unique museum where the boats are displayed in special pods seen from atop an old, picturesque pier that stretches out into the bay. It's open daily 9am to dusk; admission is by donation.

Finds **Strolling the Governor's Gardens**

Government House, the official residence of the lieutenant governor, is at 1401 Rockland Ave., in the Fairfield residential district. Around back, the hillside of Garry oaks is one of the last places to see what the area's natural fauna looked like before European settlers arrived. The rose garden at the front is quite sumptuous.

hiking trails up to a 270m (886-ft.) hilltop. Access is via the Old Island Highway and East Sooke Road.

2 Especially for Kids

Victoria offers unique opportunities for kids to view creatures from whales and giant butterflies to sea anemones and hermit crabs. The oldest of petting zoos is the **Beacon Hill Children's Farm,** Circle Drive, Beacon Hill Park (© **250/381-2532;** www.beacon hillpark.ca), where kids can ride ponies; pet goats, rabbits, and other barnyard animals; and cool off in the wading pool. May to Labour Day, the farm is open daily 10am to 5pm (11am–4pm in the fall, 10am–4pm in the spring). Admission is by donation.

To see and touch (or be touched by) even smaller creatures, visit the **Victoria Butterfly Gardens** (p. 227). Closer to town is the **Victoria Bug Zoo,** 631 Courtney St. (© **250/384-BUGS;** www.bugzoo.bc.ca), home to praying mantises, stick insects, and giant African cockroaches. Admission is C$8 (US$7/£3.60) for adults, C$6 (US$5/£2.70) for seniors, C$7 (US$6/£3.15) for students, C$5 (US$4/£2.25) for children 3 to 16, and free for children under 3; open Monday through Saturday 9:30am to 5pm, Sundays 11am to 5:30pm.

The **Pacific Undersea Gardens** (p. 225) is a face-to-face introduction to some of the sea creatures of the Pacific coast. Better still, take the kids out to explore any of the tide pools on the coast. **Botanical Beach Provincial Park** *✾✾✾*, near Port Renfrew, is excellent, though the 60km (37-mile) drive west along Highway 14A may make it a bit far for some. Closer to town, try **French Beach** *✾* or **China Beach** *✾* (also along Hwy. 14A), or even the beach in **Mount Douglas Park.** The trick is to find a good spot, bend down over a tide pool, and look—or else pick up a rock to see crabs scuttle away. Remember to put the rocks back where you found them.

In **Goldstream Provincial Park** (p. 230), the Visitor Centre (© **250/478-9414**) has nature programs and activities geared especially for children. The **Swan Lake Christmas Hill Nature Sanctuary,** 3873 Swan Lake Rd. (© **250/479-0211;** www.swanlake.bc.ca), offers a number of nature-themed drop-in programs over the summer, including Insectmania and Reptile Day.

Back in the city, the **Royal B.C. Museum** *✾✾✾* (p. 225) has many displays geared toward kids, including a rather dramatic and amazing life-size reconstruction of a woolly mastodon.

Miniature World (p. 225), with its huge collection of dolls and dollhouses, model trains, and diminutive circus displays, is a favorite with kids of all ages.

Located in Elk and Beaver Lake Regional Park (p. 235), **Beaver Lake** is a great freshwater spot where kids can enjoy a day of watersports and swimming in safe, lifeguard-attended waters.

On truly hot days, head for the waterslides at **All Fun Recreation Park,** 2207 Mill-stream Rd. (© **250/474-3184;** www.allfun.bc.ca). From mid-June to Labour Day, it's open daily 11am to 7pm. The cost is C$20 (US$17/£9) for sliders 11 years and older; C$15 (US$13/£7) for those 4 to 10 years old; it's free for children under 4. Cost for observers (including use of the hot tub, minigolf, and beach volleyball courts) is C$6 (US$5/£2.70). The park also has go-carts and batting cages.

3 Organized Tours

BUS TOURS

Gray Line of Victoria, 700 Douglas St. (© **800/663-8390** or 250/388-6539; www.grayline.ca), conducts a number of tours of Victoria and Butchart Gardens. The 1½-hour "Grand City Tour" costs C$21 (US$17/£9) for adults and C$10 (US$9/£4.50) for children ages 5 to 11. There are daily departures throughout the year, usually at 12:30 and 2:30pm. For other tours, check the website.

SPECIALTY TOURS

Victoria Harbour Ferries, 922 Old Esquimalt Rd. (© **250/708-0201;** www.victoria harbourferry.com), offers a terrific 45-minute **harbor tour** ⚓ for C$20 (US$17/£9) adults, C$18 (US$16/£7) seniors, and C$10 (US$8/£4.50) for children under 12. Harbor tours depart from seven stops around the Inner Harbour every 15 or 20 min-utes daily 10am to 5:30 (May–Sept daily 9am–8pm). If you wish to stop for food or a stroll, you can get a token good for reboarding at any time during the same day. A 50-minute **Gorge Tour** ⚓ takes you to the gorge opposite the Johnson Street Bridge, where tidal falls reverse with each change of the tide. The price is the same as for the harbor tour; June through September, gorge tours depart from the dock in front of The Fairmont Empress every half-hour 9am to 8:15pm; at other times the tours oper-ate less frequently, depending on the weather. The ferries are 12-person, fully enclosed boats, and every seat is a window seat.

Heritage Tours and Daimler Limousine Service, 713 Bexhill Rd. (© **250/474-4332;** www.islandnet.com/~daimler), guides you through the city, Butchart Gardens, and Craigdarroch Castle in a six-passenger British Daimler limousine. Rates start at C$75 (US$63/£34) for the Daimler per hour per vehicle (not per person). Also avail-able are stretch limos that seat 8 to 10 people, starting at C$85 (US$72/£38) per hour per vehicle.

The bicycle-rickshaws operated by **Kabuki Kabs,** 613 Herald St. (© **250/385-4243;** www.kabukikabs.com), can usually be found on the causeway in front of The Fairmont Empress or hailed in the downtown area. Prices for a tour are C$1 (US85¢/45p) per minute for a two-person cab.

Tallyho Horse-Drawn Tours, 2044 Milton St. (© **250/383-5067;** www.tallyho tours.com), has conducted tours of Victoria in horse-drawn carriages and trolleys since 1903. Horse-drawn trolley and carriage excursions start at the corner of Belleville and Menzies streets. Fares for the trolley are C$15 (US$13/£7) for adults, C$11 (US$9/£5) for students, C$8 (US$7/£3.60) for children 17 and under. Trolley tours operate daily every 30 minutes 9am to 3pm during summer. An assortment of private carriage tours (maximum six people) are available throughout the year and in the summer from 10am to 10pm; cost runs from C$40 (US$34/£18) for 15 minutes, or C$200 (US$170/£90) for 1½ hours.

To get a bird's-eye view of Victoria, take a 30-minute tour with **Harbour Air Seaplanes,** 1234 Wharf St. (*©* **800/665-0212** or 250/384-2215; www.harbour-air.com). Rates are C$99 (US$84/£45) per person. For a romantic evening, try the "Fly and Dine" to Butchart Gardens deal; C$215 (US$183/£97) per person includes the flight to the gardens, admission, dinner, and a limousine ride back to Victoria.

Fresh Air Tours Ltd. (*©* **877/868-7790;** www.freshairtours.com) offers year-round scenic sightseeing minicoach and cycling tours to Victoria's highlights, wineries, Butchart Gardens, the town of Sidney, Salt Spring Island, All Fun Recreation Park waterslides, and seasonal tours such as the Halloween pumpkin patch and Christmas lights. The company provides complimentary hotel pickup and drop-off; on cycling tours, bicycles, helmets, and support van are provided.

WALKING TOURS

Chapter 15 has two self-guided walking tours around Victoria. If you'd prefer to have a guide, **Victoria Bobby Walking Tours** (*©* 250/995-0233; www.walkvictoria.com) offers a leisurely story-filled walk around Old Town with a former English bobby as guide. Tours depart at 11am daily, May through September 15, from the Visitor Centre on the Inner Harbour; cost is C$15 (US$13/£7) per person.

Discover the Past (*©* **250/384-6698;** www.discoverthepast.com) organizes interesting walks year-round. In the summer, **Ghostly Walks** explores Victoria's haunted Old Town, Chinatown, and historic waterfront; tours depart from the front of the Visitor Info Centre on Friday and Saturday at 7:30pm from October through May, and nightly at 7:30 and 9:30pm from June through September. The cost is C$12 (US$10/£5) adults, C$10 (US$8/£4.50) seniors and students, C$8 (US$7/£3.60) children 6 to 10, and C$30 (US$25/£13) for families. Check the website for other walks.

The name says it all for **Walkabout Historical Tours** (*©* **250/592-9255;** www. walkabouts.ca). Charming guides lead tours of The Fairmont Empress, Victoria's Chinatown, Antique Row, and Old Town Victoria, or will help you with your own itinerary. The Empress Tour costs C$10 (US$8/£4.50) and begins at 10am daily in the Empress Tea Lobby. Other tours have different prices and starting points.

The **Victoria Heritage Foundation,** No. 1 Centennial Square (*©* **250/383-4546;** vhf@pinc.com), offers the excellent free pamphlet *James Bay Heritage Walking Tour.* The well-researched pamphlet (also available at the Visitor Info Centre) describes a self-guided walking tour through the historic James Bay neighborhood.

Finds Victoria's Cemetery Tours

The **Old Cemetery Society of Victoria** (*©* 250/598-8870; www.oldcem.bc.ca) runs regular cemetery tours throughout the year. Particularly popular are the **Lantern Tours of the Old Burying Ground** *☆*, which begin at the Cherry Bank Hotel, 845 Burdett St., at 9pm nightly in July and August. The tour lasts about 1 hour. On Sundays throughout the year, the Society offers historically focused tours of **Ross Bay Cemetery.** Tours depart at 2pm from Starbucks in the Fairfield Plaza, 1516 Fairfield Rd., across from the cemetery gate. Both tours are C$5 (US$4.25/£2.25) per person.

ECOTOURS

The 2-hour **wilderness cruise** ⋒⋒⋒ departing from the marina and ecoadventure center at **Brentwood Bay Lodge & Spa** (p. 204; ✆ **888/544-2079** or 250/652-3151), provides an extremely informative and enjoyable exploration of Finlayson Inlet, a deep fjord with a fascinating history. On the cruise it's not uncommon to spot eagles, seals, and sometimes whales. A marine biologist provides the commentary. Cost is C$60 (US$51/£27) per person; cruises are daily in summer, and only on the weekends in the winter; call for departure times.

4 Outdoor Activities

Sports Rent, 611 Discovery St. (✆ **250/385-7368;** www.sportsrentbc.com), is a great general equipment and watersports rental outlet.

BEACHES

The most popular beach is Oak Bay's **Willows Beach,** at Beach and Dalhousie roads along the esplanade. The park, playground, and snack bar make it a great place to spend the day building a sand castle. **Gyro Beach Park,** Beach Road on Cadboro Bay, is another good spot for winding down. At the **Ross Bay Beaches,** below Beacon Hill Park, you can stroll or bike along the promenade at the water's edge.

For a taste of the wild and rocky west coast, hike the oceanside trails in beautiful **East Sooke Regional Park** ⋒. Take Hwy. 14A west, turn south on Gillespie Road, and then take East Sooke Road.

Two inland lakes give you the option of swimming in fresh water. **Elk and Beaver Lake Regional Park,** on Patricia Bay Road, is 11km (6¾ miles) north of downtown Victoria; to the west is **Thetis Lake,** about 10km (6¼ miles; Hwy. 1 to exit 10 or 1a onto Old Island Hwy. 14, turn right at Six Mile Pub and follow the signs), where locals shed all their clothes but none of their civility.

BIKING

Biking is one of the best ways to get around Victoria. The 13km (8-mile) **Scenic Marine Drive bike path** ⋒⋒ begins at Dallas Road and Douglas Street, at the base of Beacon Hill Park. The paved path follows the walkway along the beaches before winding up through the residential district on Beach Drive. It eventually turns left and heads south toward downtown Victoria on Oak Bay Avenue. The **Inner Harbour pedestrian path** has a bike lane for cyclists who want to take a leisurely ride around the entire city seawall. The new **Galloping Goose Trail** (part of the Trans-Canada Trail) runs from Victoria west through Colwood and Sooke all the way up to Leechtown. If you don't want to bike the whole thing, you can park at numerous places along the way, as well as several places where the trail intersects with public transit. Contact **B.C. Transit** (✆ **250/382-6161;** www.bctransit.com) to find out which bus routes take bikes. Bikes and child trailers are available by the hour or day at **Cycle B.C. rentals,** 747 Douglas St. (year-round) or 950 Wharf St. (May–Oct; ✆ **250/885-2453;** www.cyclebc.ca). Rentals run C$7 (US$6/£3.15) per hour and C$24 (US$20/£11) per day; helmets and locks included.

BIRDING

The **Victoria Natural History Society** (www.vicnhs.bc.ca) runs regular weekend birding excursions. Their **event line** (✆ **250/479-2054**) lists upcoming outings and gives contact numbers. **Goldstream Provincial Park** (p. 230) and the village of **Malahat**—both off Highway 1 about 40 minutes north of Victoria—are filled with dozens of varieties of migratory and local birds, including eagles. **Elk and Beaver Lake Regional Park,** off Highway 17, has some rare species such as the rose-breasted grosbeak and Hutton's vireo. Ospreys also nest there. **Cowichan Bay,** off Highway 1, is the perfect place to observe ospreys, bald eagles, great egrets, and purple martins.

BOATING, CANOEING & KAYAKING

Ocean River Sports, 1437 Store St. (© **800/909-4233** or 250/381-4233; www.ocean river.com), can equip you with everything from a single or double kayak, or a canoe to life jackets, tents, and dry-storage camping gear. Rental costs for a single kayak range from C$25 (US$21/£11) per hour to C$70 (US$59/£32) per day. Multiday and weekly rates are also available. The company also offers numerous **guided tours** $\ast$ of the Gulf Islands and the B.C. west coast. For beginners, try the guided 4½-hour Explore Tour of the coast around Victoria or Sooke for C$95 (US$81/£43). Ocean River Sports also runs a guided 3-day/2-night Expedition trip to the nearby Gulf Islands for C$595 (US$506/£268).

Rowboats, kayaks, and canoes are available for hourly or daily rental from **Great Pacific Adventures,** 811 Wharf St. (© **877/733-6722** or 250/386-2277; www.great pacificadventures.com).

Blackfish Wilderness Expeditions (© **250/216-2389;** www.blackfishwilderness. com) offers a number of interesting kayak-based tours such as the kayak/boat/hike combo, where you boat to the protected waters of the Discovery Islands, hike one of the islands, and kayak to see the pods of resident killer whales that roam the waters around Victoria. Day tours start at C$70 (US$60/£31) per person.

DIVING

The coastline of **Pacific Rim National Park** is known as "the graveyard of the Pacific." Submerged in the water are dozens of 19th- and 20th-century shipwrecks and the marine life that has taken up residence in them. Underwater interpretive trails help identify what you see in the artificial reefs. If you want to take a look for yourself, contact **Great Ocean Adventures,** 1636 Cedar Hill Crossroad (© **800/414-2202** or 250/475-2202; www.greatoceanadventures.com), or the **Ogden Point Dive Centre,** 199 Dallas Rd. (© **250/380-9119;** www.divevictoria.com). Through Great Ocean Adventures, head-to-toe equipment rental costs about C$60 (US$51/£27) for 1 day, and dive trips start at C$75 (US$64/£34). The **Saanich Inlet,** about a 20-minute drive north of Victoria, is a pristine fjord considered one of the top diving areas in the world (glass sponges are a rarity found only here). Classes and underwater scuba adventures can be arranged through **Brentwood Bay Lodge & Spa** (p. 204), Canada's only luxury PADI (Professional Association of Diving Instructors) dive resort.

FISHING

Saltwater fishing's the thing out here, and unless you know the area, it's best to take a guide. **Adam's Fishing Charters** (© **250/370-2326;** www.adamsfishingcharters.com) is located on the Inner Harbour down below the Visitor Info Centre. Chartering a boat and guide starts at C$95 (US$81/£43) per hour per boat, with a minimum of 5 hours.

To fish, you need a nonresident saltwater fishing license. Licenses for saltwater fishing (including the salmon surcharge) cost C$14 (US$12/£6) for 1 day for nonresidents and C$12 (US$10/£5) for B.C. residents. Tackle shops sell licenses, have details on current restrictions, and often carry copies of the *B.C. Tidal Waters Sport Fishing Guide* and *B.C. Sport Fishing Regulations Synopsis for Non-Tidal Waters.* Independent anglers should also pick up a copy of the *B.C. Fishing Directory and Atlas.* **Robinson's Sporting Goods Ltd.,** 1307 Broad St. (© 250/385-3429), is a reliable source for information, recommendations, lures, licenses, and gear. For the latest fishing hot spots and recommendations on tackle and lures, check out **www.sportfishingbc.com**.

GOLFING

Fortunately for golfers, Victoria's Scottish heritage didn't stop at the tartan shops. The greens here are as beautiful as those at St. Andrew's, yet the fees are reasonable. The **Cedar Hill Municipal Golf Course,** 1400 Derby Rd. (© **250/595-3103;** www.golfcedarhill. com), the busiest course in Canada, is an 18-hole, par-67 public course 3km (1¾ miles) from downtown Victoria. It's open on a first-come, first-served basis; daytime greens fees are C$38 (US$32/£17) and twilight fees (after 3pm) are C$23 (US$20/£10). Golf clubs can be rented for C$15 (US$13/£7). The **Cordova Bay Golf Course,** 5333 Cordova Bay Rd. (© **250/658-4075;** www.cordovabaygolf.com), is northeast of the downtown area. Designed by Bill Robinson, the par-71, 18-hole course features 66 sand traps and some tight fairways. Greens fees are C$50 to C$79 (US$42–US$67/£22–£36) depending on day and season; twilight fees range from C$30 to C$49 (US$26–US$42/£13–£22).

The **Olympic View Golf Club,** 643 Latoria Rd. (© **250/474-3673;** www.golfbc. com/courses/olympic_view), is one of the top 35 golf courses in Canada. Amid 12 lakes and a pair of waterfalls, this 18-hole, par-72, 6,414-yard course is open daily year-round. Daytime greens fees, depending on day and season, are C$65 to C$75 (US$52–US$60/ £29–£34) and twilight fees are C$30 to C$40 (US$24–US$32/£13–£18). Power carts cost an additional C$30 (US$24/£13).

The new star of Vancouver Island golf courses, and the most expensive to play, is the 18-hole, 7,212-yard, par-72 course designed by Jack Nicklaus and his son for **Westin Bear Mountain Golf Resort & Spa,** 1376 Lynburne Place (© **888/533-2327** or 250/744-2327 tee time bookings). Golf carts (included with fee) and collared shirts (blue jeans not permitted) are mandatory on this upscale, mountaintop course that features breathtaking views and a spectacular 19th hole for recreational betting. Nonmember greens fees, depending on when you reserve and the time you play, range from C$65 to C$130 (US$55–US$110/£29–£58).

You can call **Last Minute Golf Hot Line** at © **800/684-6344** for substantial discounts and short-notice tee times. **Island Links Hot Line** at © **866/266-GOLF** acts as a booking agent for courses around Vancouver Island and will provide transportation from your hotel to the course.

HIKING

Goldstream Provincial Park (30 min. west of downtown along Hwy. 1; p. 230) is a tranquil site for a short hike through towering cedars and past clear, rushing waters.

The hour-long hike up **Mount Work** provides excellent views of the Saanich Peninsula and a good view of Finlayson Arm. The trail head is a 30- to 45-minute drive. Take Highway 17 north to Saanich, then take Highway 17A (the W. Saanich Rd.) to Wallace Drive, turn right on Willis Point Drive, and right again on the Ross-Durrance Road, looking for the parking lot on the right. Signs are posted along the way. Equally good, though more of a scramble, is the hour-plus climb up **Mount Finlayson** in

Gowland-Tod Provincial Park (take Hwy. 1 west, get off at the Millstream Rd. exit, and follow Millstream Rd. north to the very end).

The very popular **Sooke Potholes** trail wanders up beside a river to an abandoned mountain lodge. Take Highway 1A west to Colwood, then Highway 14A (the Sooke Rd.). At Sooke, turn north on Sooke River Road, and follow it to the park.

For a taste of the wild and rocky west coast, hike the oceanside trails in beautiful **East Sooke Regional Park** 𝕸𝕸. Take Hwy. 14A west, turn south on Gillespie Road, and then take East Sooke Road.

For serious backpacking, go 104km (65 miles) west of Victoria on Highway 14A to Port Renfrew and the challenging **West Coast Trail** 𝕸𝕸𝕸, extending 77km (48 miles) from Port Renfrew to Bamfield in a portion of **Pacific Rim National Park** 𝕸𝕸𝕸 (p. 281). This trail was originally established as a lifesaving trail for shipwrecked sailors. Plan a 7-day trek for the entire route; reservations are required, so call 🕿 **604/ 663-6000.** The trail is rugged and often wet, but the scenery changes from old-growth forest to magnificent secluded sand beaches, making it worth every step. You may even spot a few whales along the way. **Robinson's Outdoor Store,** 1307 Broad St. (🕿 **250/ 385-3429;** www.robinsonsoutdoors.com), is a good place to gear up before you go. At Robinson's, ask about the newer, less challenging 48km-long (30-mile) **Juan de Fuca Marine Trail** 𝕸𝕸 connecting Port Renfrew and the Jordan River.

Island Adventure Tours (🕿 **866/812-7103;** www.islandadventuretours.com) has a number of options for folks wanting to explore the outdoors. The 6-hour guided **rainforest walks** cost C$95 (US$81/£43) or a full-day hike including transportation and lunch. For the deluxe Juan de Fuca experience, sign up for a 3-day, fully catered backpacking trip along the rugged West Coast Trail for C$499 (US$424/£225).

For something less strenuous but still scenic, try the **Swan Lake Christmas Hill Nature Sanctuary,** 3873 Swan Lake Rd. (🕿 **250/479-0211;** www.swanlake.bc.ca). A floating boardwalk winds its way through this 40-hectare (99-acre) wetland past resident swans; the adjacent Nature House supplies feeding grain on request.

PARAGLIDING

Vancouver Island Paragliding (🕿 **250/886-4165;** www.viparagliding.com) offers tandem paraglide flights. The pilot steers; you hang on and enjoy the adrenaline rush. Flights last around 25 minutes. They also offer 1-day training courses that allow you to take off on your own.

SAILING

One of the most exciting ways to explore the Strait of Juan de Fuca is aboard the *Thane,* a 17m (54-ft.) sailing ship that offers **3-hour sail tours of the Strait** 𝕸𝕸 for C$60 (US$51/£27) per person. The vessel is moored in front of The Fairmont Empress. Daily summer sailings leave at 9am, 1pm, and 5pm. Guests are welcome to bring along a picnic. For information, contact the **SV *Thane*** (🕿 **877/788-4263** or 250/885-2311; www.eco-correct.com).

SKIING

Mount Washington Ski Resort, P.O. Box 3069, Courtenay, B.C. V9N 5N3 (🕿 **888/ 231-1499** or 250/338-1380, 250/338-1515 snow report; www.mtwashington.bc.ca), in the Comox Valley is British Columbia's third-largest ski area, a 5-hour drive from Victoria and open year-round (for hiking or skiing, depending on the season). A 480m (1,575-ft.) vertical drop and 50 groomed runs are serviced by four chairlifts and a beginners' tow. The terrain is popular among snowboarders and well suited to intermediate skiers. For cross-country skiers, 31km (19 miles) of track-set Nordic trails connect to Strathcona Provincial Park. Full-day rates are around C$50 (US$42/£22) for adults, C$40 (US$34/£18) for seniors and students, and C$26 (US$22/£12) for youth 7 to 12; free for kids under 7. Equipment rentals are available at the resort. Located 100km (62 miles) north of Nanaimo; take Highway 19 to exit 130.

WATERSPORTS

The **Crystal Pool & Fitness Centre,** 2275 Quadra St. (© **250/361-0732**), is Victoria's main aquatic facility. The 50m (164-ft.) lap pool; children's pool; diving pool; sauna; whirlpool; and steam, weight, and aerobics rooms are open Monday through Friday 5:30am to 11pm, Saturday 6am to 6pm, and Sunday 9am to 4pm. Drop-in admission is C$4.75 (US$4/£2.15) for adults, C$3.75 (US$3.20/£1.70) for seniors and students, and C$2.50 (US$2.10/£1.15) for children 6 to 12; free for children under 6. **Beaver Lake** in Elk and Beaver Lake Regional Park (see "Birding," above) has lifeguards on duty as well as picnicking facilities along the shore. **All Fun Recreation Park** (see "Especially for Kids," p. 232) has great waterslides.

Surfing has recently taken off on the island. The best surf is along the west coast at **China, French,** and **Mystic beaches** . To get there, take Blanshard Street north from downtown, turn left onto Highway 1 (Trans-Canada Hwy.), then after about 10km (6¼ miles), take the turnoff onto Highway 14A (Sooke Rd.). Follow Highway 14A north along the coast. The beaches are well signposted.

Windsurfers skim along outside the Inner Harbour and on Elk Lake when the breezes are right. Though French Beach, off Sooke Road on the way to Sooke Harbour, has no specific facilities, it is a popular local windsurfing spot.

WHALE-WATCHING

The waters surrounding the southern tip of Vancouver Island teem with orcas (killer whales), harbor seals, sea lions, harbor and Dall porpoises, and bald eagles. All whale-watching companies offer basically the same tour; the main difference comes in the equipment they use: Some use a 12-person Zodiac, where the jolting ride is almost as exciting as seeing the whales, whereas others take a larger, more leisurely craft. Both offer excellent platforms for seeing whales. In high season (June to Labour Day), most companies offer several trips a day. Always ask if the outfitter is a "responsible whale-watcher"—that is, doesn't go too close to disturb or harass the whales.

Seafun Safaris Whale Watching, 950 Wharf St. (© **877/360-1233** or 250/360-1200; www.seafun.com), is just one of many outfits offering whale-watching tours in Zodiacs and covered boats. Adults and kids will learn a lot from the naturalist guides, who explain the behavior and nature of the orcas, gray whales, sea lions, porpoises, cormorants, eagles, and harbor seals encountered along the way. Fares are C$99 (US$84/£45) for adults and C$69 (US$59/£31) for children.

Other reputable companies include **Prince of Whales,** 812 Wharf St. (© **888/383-4884** or 250/383-4884; www.princeofwhales.com), just below the Visitor Info Centre, and **Orca Spirit Adventures** (© **888/672-ORCA** or 250/383-8411; www.orcaspirit.com), which departs from the Coast Harbourside Hotel dock.

15

Victoria Strolls & Biking Tour

Victoria has always been a transient's town, from miners and mariners to loggers and lounge-lizards, from hard-core hippies to retired but involved investment counselors. On three occasions I've packed up and moved from Victoria myself.

—Folk Singer Valdy

Victoria's ambience is made for the wanderer, its pavements picture-perfect for perambulation—Victoria, in short, is a great place to walk, bike, in-line skate, skateboard, or scooter. The tours below work no matter what your favored form of transportation.

| WALKING TOUR 1 | THE INNER HARBOUR |

Start and Finish:	The Visitor Centre (812 Wharf St.) on the Inner Harbour.
Time:	2 hours, not including shopping, museum, and pub breaks.
Best Time:	Late afternoon, when the golden summer sunlight shines on The Fairmont Empress.
Worst Time:	Late in the evening, when the shops close and the streets empty.

Victoria was born on the Inner Harbour. When the Hudson's Bay Company's West Coast head of operations, James Douglas, happened across this sheltered inlet in 1843 while searching for a new corporate HQ, it was love at first sight. "The place appears a perfect Eden," he wrote to a friend. High praise indeed, although as Douglas was pretty deep into local real estate, his words should be taken with a wee bit of salt. His confidence in the location certainly paid off, however, for less than 20 years after Douglas set foot onshore, the native stands of Garry oak had been supplanted by small farms, the town was choked with miners and mariners, and the harbor was full of ships, many of which had circled the globe. This trip circumnavigates the Inner Harbour, showing some of its lesser-known nooks and crannies while providing an opportunity to enjoy the view as a Victorian sailor would have, quaffing a locally brewed pint from the deck of a stout Victoria pub.

We begin our tour at the:

① Victoria Visitor Centre
At 812 Wharf St., this is without a doubt one of the finest-looking visitor centers in the world—a masterful Art Deco pavilion topped with a shining white obelisk rising high above the Inner Harbour. It would be a tribute to the taste and vision of city tourism officials, except that it started out life as a gas station.

From the Visitor Centre, thread your way south through the jugglers and musicians on the causeway until you're opposite 721 Government St., where stands:

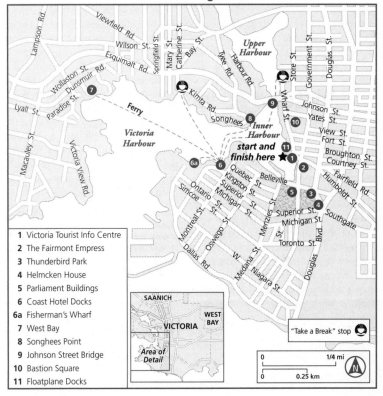

1 Victoria Tourist Info Centre
2 The Fairmont Empress
3 Thunderbird Park
4 Helmcken House
5 Parliament Buildings
6 Coast Hotel Docks
6a Fisherman's Wharf
7 West Bay
8 Songhees Point
9 Johnson Street Bridge
10 Bastion Square
11 Floatplane Docks

"Take a Break" stop

0   1/4 mi
0   0.25 km

❷ The Fairmont Empress

"There is a view, when the morning mists peel off the harbor, where the steamers tie up, of the Houses of Parliament on one hand, and a huge hotel on the other, which is an example of cunningly fitted-in waterfronts and facades worth a very long journey." Thus spoke Rudyard Kipling during a visit to the city in 1908. If he'd come only 5 years earlier, he would've been looking at a nasty, garbage-choked swamp. The causeway was then a narrow bridge over the tidal inlet, and as Victorians made a habit of pitching their refuse over the rail, the bay was, not surprisingly, a stinking cesspit of slime. In 1900, the ever-shrewd Canadian Pacific Railway made an offer to the city—we'll build a causeway and fill in the stinky bay if you let us keep the land. The city jumped at the offer. Little was expected—the land was swamp after all. But taking their cue from the good folks in Amsterdam, the CPR drove long pilings down through the muck to provide a solid foundation. And on top of that, they built The Fairmont Empress. The architect was Francis Rattenbury, and his design was masterful, complementing his own Legislature Buildings to create the view that has defined the city ever since.

Around the south side of The Fairmont Empress is a formal rose garden—worth poking your nose in for a sniff. Cut through the garden, cross over Belleville Street, and continue another half-block east to the corner of Douglas Street, where you'll find:

❸ Thunderbird Park

The park is instantly recognizable by its forest of totem poles. Even if you've overdosed on the ubiquitous 6-inch souvenir totem, take a second look at these. The original poles on this site had been collected in the early 1900s from various villages up and down the coast. Some decades later, when officials decided the severely weathered poles needed restoring, they discovered the art of native carving had eroded even more than their collection of poles. From all the thousands of carvers on the coast, only one man still carried on the craft. In 1952, Kwakiutl artist Mungo Martin set up a carving shed on the park grounds and began the work of restoration. Martin replaced or repaired all the existing poles. At the same time, he taught his son and step-grandson-in-law to carve. Seeing them at work renewed public interest in the form. Other young artists came to learn and train. Eventually, this modest training ground led to a revival of totem carving and native artistry among coastal natives.

All poles have a purpose; most tell a story. The stories associated with the poles in Thunderbird Park have unfortunately been lost, but many of the figures are easily recognized, including Thunderbird (look for the outstretched wings and curly horns on the head), Raven, Bear, and Killer Whale.

On the edge of the park is the shed where Martin carved many of the poles. Feel free to poke your head in to take a look and ask the carvers what they're up to. The artists generally welcome questions and enjoy sharing their stories.

Farther back in the park, at 610 Elliot St. Sq., stands the:

❹ Helmcken House

Dr. John Sebastian Helmcken, a surgeon with the Hudson's Bay Company, set up house here in 1852 when he married the daughter of Governor Sir James Douglas. Originally a three-room log house, the house was built by Helmcken and expanded as both the prosperity and size of the family grew. It's now the oldest house in B.C. to remain on its original site. Helmcken went on to become a statesman and helped negotiate the entry of British Columbia as a province into Canada. From June through September, the house is open daily noon to 4pm. The suggested donation for admission is C$5 (US$4/£2.25).

Walk west along Belleville past the modern-looking Carillon Tower (a gift from the Dutch people who settled in B.C.) and the not-to-be-missed Victoria Royal B.C. Museum (p. 225) and cross Government Street. You're now standing in front of 501 Belleville St. at the:

❺ Parliament Buildings

In 1892, a 25-year-old Yorkshireman arrived on the West Coast just as an architectural competition for a new Legislature Building in Victoria was announced. Francis Mawson Rattenbury had no professional credentials but was blessed with both talent and ambition. He submitted a set of drawings and, to the surprise of all, beat out 65 other entries from around the continent. A lucrative and potentially illustrious career eventually turned to ashes, however. When Rattenbury left his wife for another woman, he fell out of favor and was forced to leave Victoria. He was murdered in 1935—by his second wife and her lover, who happened to be her chauffeur.

The Parliament Buildings are open for tours 9am to 5pm. In summer, the 40-minute tours start every 20 minutes (p. 225).

Across the street, the Greek temple–style **Royal London Wax Museum** (p. 226) is another Rattenbury creation, built originally as the CPR's Steamship ticket office.

From here, ocean liners once departed for San Francisco, Sydney, and China.

From the Legislature lawn, make your way past the horse-drawn calèches parked on Menzies Street, and walk west on Belleville Street for 2 blocks to Pendray Street. The road takes a sharp right, but follow the path leading down to a waterfront walkway as it curves around Laurel Point. This headland was long the site of a stinking, fuming paint factory, so residents were delighted when it finally shut down and the luxurious Laurel Point Inn (p. 196) was erected in its place. Continuing around the pathway past the first few jetties takes you to the:

6 Coast Hotel Docks

Here is one of several ports of call for the **Victoria Harbour Ferries** (p. 233; C **250/ 708-0201**). From here, the official Frommer's route is to take the ferry all the way across the harbor to West Bay (stop 7). Along the way, are views of the Olympic Mountains to the south and possibly a seal or bald eagle for company. Alternatively, you can take a short hop out to **Fisherman's Wharf** (6A on the map on p. 241), where fresh fish is sold when in season; go directly across to Spinnakers Brewpub on the far shore; or take the ferry across to Songhees Point (stop 8) or even go directly to Canoe (see "Take a Break," after stop 9). You can even give up on your feet entirely and take the full Harbour Ferries tour.

If you stick with the program, however, the next stop is:

7 West Bay

While a pleasant little residential neighborhood with a picturesque marina, West Bay isn't anything to write home about. What is worthwhile, however, is the waterfront walkway that winds its way from here back east toward the city. The trail twists and curves through several parks, and views south through the harbor look out to the Strait of Juan de Fuca and the Olympic Mountains beyond. After about 20 minutes of walking, it may be time to:

TAKE A BREAK
Excellent beer brewed on the premises combined with an above-average patio make **Spinnakers Brewpub**, 308 Catherine St. (C 250/386-BREW; p. 213), a dangerously time-consuming port of call. For those looking for more substantial fare, the pub grub's very good and the entrees are above average. The on-site bakery makes inspired beer bread, as well as a range of more delicate goods. Open daily 11am to 11pm.

From the pub, continue along the shoreline until you see the totem pole standing at:

8 Songhees Point

The point is named after the First Nations tribe that once lived on the site. The Songhees had originally set up their village close to Fort Victoria, near the current site of Bastion Square, but relations with the Hudson's Bay Company were always strained. In 1844, a dispute over a pair of company oxen slaughtered by the Songhees was settled only after Commander Roderick Finlayson blew up the chief's house. A few years later, after a fire started in the native village, spread, and nearly burned down the fort, Finlayson told the Songhees to relocate across the Inner Harbour. They refused at first, pointing out quite rightly that as it was their land, they could live wherever they liked. They assented to the move only after Finlayson agreed to help dismantle and transport the Songhees' longhouses.

The totem pole here is called the **Spirit of Lakwammen,** presented to the city to commemorate the 1994 Commonwealth Games.

Continue on the pathway around the corner. The patio of the Delta Victoria Ocean Pointe Resort (p. 192), on your right, provides a great view of The Fairmont Empress. In summer, they show silent movies after sunset. A little farther on is the:

9 Johnson Street Bridge

The same guy who designed San Francisco's Golden Gate Bridge also designed

Victoria's Johnson Street Bridge. Alas, while the soaring Golden Gate span is justly famous for its elegance, this misshapen lump of steel and concrete is something designer Joseph Strauss would likely wish forgotten.

Cross the bridge, walk past the Esquimalt and Nanaimo (E&N) Railway station, and turn left onto Store Street. Walk 1 block north to Swift Street, turn left, walk downhill to the end of the street, and:

TAKE A BREAK

 While having a drink at **Canoe**, 450 Swift St. (© 250/361-1940; p. 213), it's hard to know who to admire more: the 19th-century engineers who built everything with brick and beam and always twice as thick as it had to be; the restorers who took this old building (once the site of the City Light Company) and turned it into a sunlit cathedral of a room; the owner, who had the vision to pay the restorers; the chef, who made the delicious plate of appetizers now quickly disappearing from your table; or the brew master, whose copper cauldrons produce such a superior brew. Try the taster option—six small glasses of different brews for about the price of a pint—and toast them all. Canoe is open daily 11am to midnight or 1am.

Salutations complete, wander back up Swift Street, turn right, and continue south down Store Street for 2 blocks, where Store Street becomes Wharf Street. Walk another 3 blocks until you reach:

⑩ Bastion Square

This pleasant public space stands on the site of the Hudson's Bay Company's original Fort Victoria. The fort was demolished in 1863 and the land sold off for development. When the B.C. government bought and renovated the Rithet Building on the southwest corner of the square, workers uncovered Fort Victoria's original water well, complete with mechanical pump. It's now in the building's lobby.

Continue south on Wharf Street another 2 blocks until you come to the pinkish Dominion Customs House. Built in 1876, it was one of the first tangible signs of British Columbia's new status as a Canadian province. The Second Empire style was meant to impart a touch of European civilization in the midst of this raw wilderness town. Take the walkway by the Customs house down to the waterline and walk out on the:

⑪ Floatplane Docks

Early in the morning these docks buzz with activity as floatplanes fly in and out on their way to and from Seattle, Vancouver, and points farther north. The docks are also the place to come to arrange diving and whale-watching tours.

Back up on Wharf Street, you're just a hop, skip, and a jump from the Visitor Centre tower, where the tour began.

WALKING TOUR 2   THE OLD TOWN & CHINATOWN

Start and Finish: The Fairmont Empress, 321 Government St.
Time: 2 hours, not including shopping, sightseeing, and eating stops.
Best Time: Any day before 6pm.
Worst Time: Any day after 6pm, when the shops close.

This tour also begins at one of Victoria's most impressive landmarks. In front of you is:

① The Fairmont Empress

At 321 Government St., this architectural delight was designed by Francis Rattenbury (see "Architectural Highlights & Historic Homes," on p. 227).

Walking north up Government Street, you'll find a number of historic buildings. British Columbia's oldest brick structure, at 901 Government St., is the:

② Windsor Hotel building

Built in 1858 as the Victoria Hotel, the building's actually a perfect metaphor for

Walking Tour 2: The Old Town & Chinatown

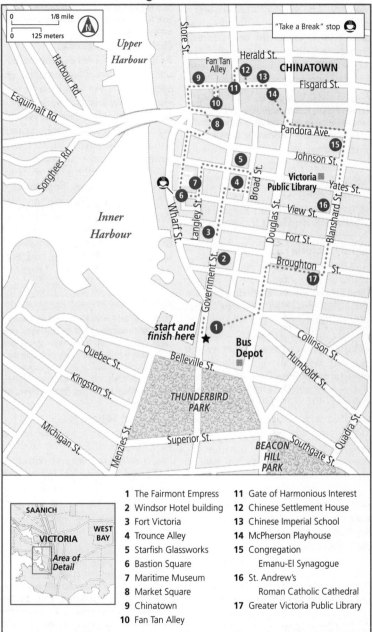

1 The Fairmont Empress	11 Gate of Harmonious Interest
2 Windsor Hotel building	12 Chinese Settlement House
3 Fort Victoria	13 Chinese Imperial School
4 Trounce Alley	14 McPherson Playhouse
5 Starfish Glassworks	15 Congregation
6 Bastion Square	Emanu-El Synagogue
7 Maritime Museum	16 St. Andrew's
8 Market Square	Roman Catholic Cathedral
9 Chinatown	17 Greater Victoria Public Library
10 Fan Tan Alley	

the city. The original structure was a robust yet stylish piece of frontier architecture, with heavy red bricks formed into graceful Romanesque arches. Then, in the 1930s, when the city began pushing the "little bit of England" shtick, the original brick was covered with stucco and fake Tudor half-timbering. Somewhere under the phony gentility, however, the robust frontier structure survives. (It's been through worse: In 1876, the hotel underwent major unexpected remodeling after the owner searched for a gas leak with a lit candle.)

On the next block, you'll find a brass sidewalk plaque at 1022 Government St., indicating the former site of:

❸ Fort Victoria

The fort was constructed in 1843 by the Hudson's Bay Company as the western headquarters of its fur-trading empire. Bound by Broughton and View streets, between Government and Wharf streets, the fort had two octagonal bastions on either side of its tall cedar picket walls. It was torn down during the 1860s gold boom to make room for more businesses. You can get an idea of its size and shape from the line of light-colored bricks—inscribed with the names of early settlers—in the sidewalk that delineates the boundaries of the original walls. The first school in British Columbia was built on this site in 1849.

Continue north 2 more blocks, just past View Street, where a little byway cuts off on the right, running 1 block to Broad Street. It's known as:

❹ Trounce Alley

This is where miners and mariners spent their extra cash on the ladies. The alley is still lit by gas lamps, hung with heraldic crests, and ablaze with flower baskets and potted shrubs. You can stroll through shops selling jewelry, fashions, and crafts, or stop for a bite to eat. Trounce Alley ends abruptly at Broad Street.

Turn left on Broad Street, walk north 1 block, turn left on Yates Street, and walk west 1 block until you come to the:

❺ Starfish Glassworks

At 630 Yates St., this ex-bank building is one of the city's finest examples of the Moderne style, but what makes it worth a visit is the gallery and workshop inside (p. 255). Set up by a couple of glass-blowing artists who couldn't get kiln time in Vancouver, the interior has been cleverly designed with the workshop on the ground floor and the gallery space on an open catwalk above. Step inside and watch the glass blowing, or wander around the gallery and admire the finished products. In summer (May 15–Sept 15), the building is open Monday through Saturday from 10am to 6pm, and Sunday from noon to 6pm. From September 16 through May 14, the gallery is closed on Tuesday.

From here, go 1 more block west on Yates. Between Government and Store streets, on the north side of the street, is a collection of mid-19th-century brick storefronts, including the former Majestic Theatre, at 564 Yates, dating from 1860. From Yates, turn left on Langley Street, and go 1 block south. Turn right on View Street and you're in:

❻ Bastion Square

This square was a bustling area with waterfront hotels, saloons, and warehouses during the late 19th century. Earlier, it had been the site of one of Fort Victoria's octagonal gun bastions. In 1963, the area was restored as a heritage square. This is a good place to:

 TAKE A BREAK
If you're in the mood for a big, healthy glass of organic juice, or some delicious vegetarian grub, stop in at **rebar**, 64 Bastion Sq. (📞 250/361-9223; p. 218), downtown Victoria's best and funkiest spot for wholesome food and drinks. It's open Monday through Thursday 8:30am to 9pm, Friday and Saturday 8:30am to 10pm, and Sunday 8:30am to 3:30pm.

The provincial courthouse and hangman's square were once located on Bastion Square, but now you'll find the:

❼ Maritime Museum

At 28 Bastion Sq. you can get a glimpse into Victoria's naval and shipping history (p. 224). The museum is housed in Victoria's original courthouse and jail, which opened in 1889.

Turn north up Commercial Alley. Cross Yates Street, and a few steps farther west, turn north again up Waddington Alley. On the other side of Johnson Street is:

❽ Market Square

This restored historic site was once a two-story complex of shipping offices and supply stores. It now contains more than 40 shops that sell everything from sports equipment and crafts to books and toys. In the summer, musicians often perform and restaurants set up outdoor seating in the large open-air court.

More than a century ago, Victoria's business was transacted in this area of winding alleys and walkways. Warehouses, mariner's hotels, and shipping offices have been carefully restored into shops, restaurants, and galleries. You'll occasionally find historic plaques explaining the function of each building before it was renovated.

Go north 1 block on Store Street, and turn right (away from the harbor) onto Fisgard Street. You're now in North America's oldest:

❾ Chinatown

Established in 1858 when the first Chinese arrived as gold seekers and railroad workers, this 6-block district (roughly between Store and Blanshard sts. and Herald St. and Pandora Ave.) fell into decline after World War I (as did many West Coast Asian communities when the U.S. and Canadian governments restricted Asian immigration). What remains is a fascinating peek into a well-hidden and exotic heritage.

On your right, halfway up the block, you'll find:

❿ Fan Tan Alley

The world's narrowest street, it's no more than 1.2m (4 ft.) wide at either end, and

expands to a little more than 1.8m (6 ft.) in the center. Through the maze of doorways (which still have their old Chinese signage) are entries to small courtyards leading to even more doorways.

During the late 1800s, this was the main entrance to "Little Canton," where the scent of legally manufactured opium wafted from the courtyards. Opium dens, gambling parlors, and brothels sprang up between the factories and bachelor rooms where male immigrants shared cramped quarters to save money.

Today, you won't find any sin for sale here—just a few little shops dealing in crafts and souvenirs. You can enter the **Chinatown Trading Company,** 551 Fisgard St., from Fisgard Street or via a back door facing Fan Tan Alley. Hidden in its back room are a couple of minimuseums cleverly displaying artifacts from old Chinatown, including the original equipment from a 19th-century Chinese gambling house.

When you're finished exploring the alley, return to Fisgard Street and continue heading east. At the corner of Government and Fisgard streets is the:

⓫ Gate of Harmonious Interest

This lavishly detailed, dragon-headed red-and-gold archway was built in 1981 to commemorate the completion—after years of deterioration—of Chinatown's revitalization by the city and the Chinese Consolidated Benevolent Association. The gate is guarded by a pair of hand-carved stone lions imported from Suzhou, China.

A half-block up at 1715 Government St. is the former location of the:

⓬ Chinese Settlement House

Newly arrived Chinese families once lived upstairs in this balconied building and made use of social services here until they were able to secure work and living quarters. The original Chinese Buddhist temple has been moved from the storefront to the second floor, but it's still open to visitors. Although admission is free, hours vary. You will have to check with temple staff to see if you may enter.

A half-block up from the Gate of Harmonious Interest at 36 Fisgard St. is the:

⑬ Chinese Imperial School (Zhongua Xuetang)

This red-and-gold, pagoda-style building with a baked-tile roof and recessed balconies was built by the Chinese Benevolent Society. In 1907, the Victoria School Board banned non-Canadian Chinese children from attending public school, and in response, the society started its own community elementary school the following year. The school is open to the public during the week, and still provides children and adults with instruction in Chinese reading and writing on weekends.

Just east of the school at 3 Centennial Sq. is the:

⑭ McPherson Playhouse

Formerly a vaudeville theater, this was the first of the vast Pantages Theatres chain (Alex Pantages went into showbiz after striking it rich in the Klondike gold fields). The building was restored in the 1960s, and is now Victoria's main performing arts center (✆ **250/386-6121**). The center is usually open during the day, although no formal tours are given; if you ask nicely, you may be allowed to take a peek inside at the ornate interior. You could also try to get tickets to a show there. *Note:* City Hall and the police department are located in the office plaza surrounding the playhouse.

When you get to the southeast corner of Centennial Square, walk east 1 more block on Pandora Avenue to Blanshard Street. At 1461 Blanshard St. (at Pandora Ave.), you'll find:

⑮ Congregation Emanu-El Synagogue

This is the oldest surviving Jewish temple on North America's west coast. Built in

1863, it has been proclaimed a national heritage site. The temple (which is not particularly impressive on the outside) is not open to the public.

Turn south on Blanshard Street, and walk 3 blocks to 740 View St., where you'll see the impressive:

⑯ St. Andrew's Roman Catholic Cathedral

Built during the 1890s, this is Victorian High Gothic at its best. The facade is 23m (75 ft.) across, the spire 53m (174 ft.) tall, and no frill, flounce, or architectural embellishment was left out of the design. Renovations in the 1980s incorporated the works of First Nations artists into the interior. Go inside and see the altar by Coast Salish carver Charles Elliot.

One block south at Fort Street is the beginning of Antique Row, which stretches 3 blocks east to Cook Street. Ignore that for the moment (or go explore and then come back), and continue 1 more block south on Blanshard. Walk across the plaza to 735 Broughton St., where you'll find the:

⑰ Greater Victoria Public Library

The attraction here is the huge skylit atrium, complete with George Norris's massive hanging artwork, *Dynamic Mobile Steel Sculpture.* Built in 1979, the library complex takes up most of the block. The library is open Monday through Saturday from 9am to 6pm (until 9pm Tues, Thurs; Sun 1–5pm Oct–Apr).

Duck out through the portal on Broughton Street, and walk west to Douglas Street, turn left and walk 1½ blocks south on Douglas until you see the entrance to the Victoria Convention Centre. Walk in and admire the indoor fountain and aviary. The Centre connects to The Fairmont Empress, which was our starting place.

BIKING TOUR   DALLAS ROAD

Start and Finish: The Fairmont Empress, 321 Government St.
Time: 2 hours, not including picnic stops, sightseeing, shopping, or food breaks.
Best Times: Clear, sunny days when the Olympic Mountains are revealed in all their glory.
Worst Times: Gray, rainy days.

Victoria cries out to be biked. The hills are modest, the traffic light and very polite, and the views incredible. When touring around by bike, you rarely have time to stop and pull out a point-by-point guide, so the descriptions offered here are shorter than for walking tours. The route is designed to take you a bit beyond what would be possible on foot, without getting into an expedition-length tour.

This tour is about 15km (9⅓ miles) long and stays on bike paths through much of its length, although some of the streets in the second half of the tour are lightly trafficked. The ride from the Dallas Road shoreline to Craigdarroch Castle involves an elevation gain of about 150m (492 ft.).

Start at **Cycle B.C. Bike Rental,** 747 Douglas St. (© **250/380-2453;** www.cyclebc.ca), behind **The Fairmont Empress** hotel. Ride south down Douglas Street to **Thunderbird Park** and have a look at the totem poles. Continue east along Belleville Street past the **Legislature** and the **Coho ferry terminal;** then go round the corner onto Kingston Street, and go left through the small park to **Fisherman's Wharf.** From here, go south along **Dallas Road,** past the helijet pad and the car-ferry docks, and stop at the entrance to the breakwater at **Ogden Point.** By this time, you should have a fabulous view of the Olympic Mountains. Park your bike and wander out along the breakwater, or stop in at the **Ogden Point Cafe,** 204 Dallas Rd., for the same view without the wind.

Continue east along the seaside bike path or on Dallas Road. Stop here and there as the urge strikes for some beach-combing. A little ways on, past Douglas Street, cross Dallas and cut north into **Beacon Hill Park** (p. 229). Stop at the petting zoo, look at the 38m-tall (125-ft.) totem pole, or just enjoy Victoria's favorite park. Exit the park by the northeast corner on Cook Street, and cycle a few blocks north into **Cook Street Village.** This is a good spot to stop for a coffee and dessert or to shop for picnic supplies at the local deli or supermarket. Head back south on Cook Street to Dallas Road; turn left and continue east a kilometer or so to **Clover Point,** a short peninsula sticking out into the Strait of Juan de Fuca. It makes a fine picnic spot. From here, head east to **Ross Bay Cemetery** (p. 228), Victoria's second oldest, where many local notables are buried, including former governor James Douglas and painter Emily Carr. From the north side of the cemetery, ride up the hill on **Stannard Street,** skirting the eastern edge of **Government House** (p. 232), the official residence of the lieutenant governor.

When you reach **Rockland Avenue,** turn right and ride a few hundred meters past the many fine homes of this elite enclave to the main entrance to Government House. Though the residence itself is closed to the public, the formal gardens are open and well worth a wander. Round back, the hillside of Garry oaks is one of the last places to see what the area's natural fauna looked like before European settlers arrived. The rose garden in front is sumptuous. Just west of the gate on Rockland Avenue, turn right onto **Joan Crescent** and ride up the small hill to opulent **Craigdarroch Castle** (p. 222), built by coal magnate Robert Dunsmuir for his wife, Joan. The castle is open for self-guided tours. From here, continue up Joan Crescent to Fort Street; turn right and go a very short way east to Yates Street; turn left and go 1 block to Fernwood Street; turn right and go 1 block north to **Pandora Street;** then turn left again and ride west down the hill. Watch for the **Christian Science church** at 1205 Pandora St. (where the street widens to include a boulevard in its center). Another 6 blocks west, and you're at **Pandora** and **Government streets,** with **Chinatown** (see stops 9–13 of Walking Tour 2, above) to your right, **Market Square** (see stop 8 of Walking Tour 2, above) to your left, and The Fairmont Empress and the bike-rental spot just a few blocks south.

16

Victoria Shopping

Victoria has dozens of little specialty shops that likely carry anything your heart desires, and because the city is built on a pedestrian scale, you can easily wander from place to place seeking out whatever treasure you're after. Nearly all of the areas listed below are within a short walk of The Fairmont Empress; for those shops located more than 6 blocks from the hotel, bus information is provided. Stores in Victoria are generally open Monday through Saturday from 10am to 6pm; some, but not many, are open on Sundays during the summer.

1 The Shopping Scene

Explorers beware: The brick-paved **Government Street promenade,** from the Inner Harbour 5 blocks north to Yates Street, is a jungle of cheap souvenir shops. There are gems in here—Irish linen, fine bone china, quality native art, and thick Cowichan sweaters—but to find these riches, you'll have to hack your way through tangled creepers of knickknacks and forbidding groves of maple-syrup bottles.

Farther north, the **Old Town district** and **Market Square** feature a fascinating blend of heritage buildings and up-to-date shops. Victoria's **Chinatown** is tiny, and since most of the city's Chinese population has moved elsewhere, it lacks some of the authenticity and vitality of Chinatowns in Vancouver or San Francisco. The area has been charmingly preserved, however, and there are a number of gallery-quality art and ceramic shops, quirky back alleys (including Canada's thinnest commercial street, Fan Tan Alley), and at least one tourist trap that knows not to take itself too seriously.

On the eastern edge of downtown, **Antique Row** is known for its high-quality British collectibles. And if you're at all interested in the native art of the Pacific Northwest, Victoria is a good place to look for pieces to add to your collection.

2 Shopping A to Z

ANTIQUES

Victoria has long had a deserved reputation for antiques—particularly those of British origin. Many of the best stores are on **Antique Row,** mentioned above. In addition to those listed below, check out **Jeffries and Co. Silversmiths,** 1026 Fort St. (© 250/383-8315); **Romanoff & Company Antiques,** 837 Fort St. (© 250/480-1543); and for furniture fans, **Charles Baird Antiques,** 1044A Fort St. (© 250/384-8809).

David Robinson Antiques   Here you'll find Oriental rugs, silver, oil paintings, brass, porcelain, and period furniture. Though it's not as large as Faith Grant's shop (see below), Robinson's pieces—especially his furniture—are particularly well chosen. 1023 Fort St. © 250/384-6425. Bus: 10 to Blanshard or Cook St.

Faith Grant's Connoisseur Shop Ltd. *(Finds)*   The farthest from downtown, this shop is also the best. The 16 rooms of this 1862 heritage building contain everything from Georgian writing desks to English flatware, not to mention fine ceramics, prints, and paintings. Furniture is especially strong here. 1156 Fort St. $\mathcal{C}$ **250/383-0121.** www.faithgrantantiques.com. Bus: 10 to Fort and Cook sts.

Vanity Fair Antiques & Collectibles *(Value)*   This large shop is fun to browse, with crystal, glassware, furniture, and lots more. If you're feeling flush, it's certainly possible to spend here, but many items can be easily snapped up without taking out a bank loan. 1044 Fort St. $\mathcal{C}$ **250/380-7274.** Bus: 10 to Blanshard or Cook St.

ART
CONTEMPORARY

Fran Willis Gallery   Soaring white walls and huge arched windows make this one of Victoria's most beautiful gallery spaces. The collection is strong in contemporary oils, mixed media, and bronzes, almost all by B.C. and Alberta artists. 1619 Store St. $\mathcal{C}$ **250/381-3422.** www.franwillis.com. Bus: 5 to Douglas and Fisgard.

Open Space   When does self-confidence start edging into pretension? This artist-run gallery and self-declared flag-bearer of the avant-garde has trod on both sides of that line since 1972. Mostly, they get it right, so the gallery is usually worth a visit. Exhibits run the full gamut, from paintings and sculpture to literary and dance performances. 510 Fort St. $\mathcal{C}$ **250/383-8833.** www.openspace.ca.

Winchester Galleries   This slightly daring gallery features contemporary oil paintings. Unlike elsewhere in town, very few wildlife paintings ever make it onto the walls. 1010 Broad St. $\mathcal{C}$ **250/386-2773.** www.winchestergalleriesltd.com.

FIRST NATIONS

Alcheringa Gallery   What began as a shop handling imports from the Antipodes has evolved into one of Victoria's truly great stores for aboriginal art connoisseurs. All the coastal tribes are represented in Alcheringa's collection, along with pieces from Papua New Guinea. The presentation is museum quality, with prices to match. 665 Fort St. $\mathcal{C}$ **250/383-8224.** www.alcheringa-gallery.com.

Hill's Native Art   Hill's is the store for established artists from up and down the B.C. coast, which means the quality is high, and so are the prices. Of course, you don't stay in business for 50 years without pleasing your drop-in customers, so Hill's has its share of dream catchers and other knickknacks. 1008 Government St. $\mathcal{C}$ **250/385-3911.** www.hillsnativeart.com.

BOOKS

Avalon Metaphysical Centre   Avalon specializes in New Age books, crystals, rune stones, body oils, and videotapes of gurus who've already trodden the path to enlightenment. 62-560 Johnson St. (in Market Sq.). $\mathcal{C}$ **250/380-1721.**

Crown Publications Inc.   In addition to dry, but informative, government publications, this store stocks an excellent selection of books covering the history, nature, and culture of the Victoria area. Keeping up with the times, digital maps are available on CD-ROM. 521 Fort St. $\mathcal{C}$ **250/386-4636.** www.crownpub.bc.ca.

Munro's Books *(Finds)*   All bookstores should look so good: a mile-high ceiling in a 1909 heritage building, complete with heavy brass lamps and murals on the walls (never mind that the building was originally a bank). The store stocks many well-chosen books—more than 35,000 titles, including an excellent selection of books about Victoria and books by local authors. The staff is friendly and very good at unearthing obscure titles. The remainder tables have some incredible deals. 1108 Government St. ✆ **888/243-2464** or 250/382-2464. www.munrobooks.com.

Russell Books (Value)   This shop offers two floors of used, new, and remaindered books. 734 Fort St. ✆ **250/361-4447**. www.russellbooks.com.

Western Canada Wilderness Committee (WCWC)   Committed to protecting Canada's endangered species and environment, the WCWC store raises funds for the cause. Choose from beautiful gift cards, posters, and souvenir T-shirts or mugs. 651 Johnson St. ✆ **250/388-9292**. www.wildernesscommittee.org.

CHINA & LINENS

Irish Linen Stores   Everything Irish since 1910: handkerchiefs, scarves, doilies, napkins, lace, and more. 1019 Government St. ✆ **250/383-6812**. www.irishlinenvictoria.com.

Sydney Reynolds   This building opened as a saloon in 1908, became a bank in 1909, was converted into a shop in 1929, and now houses a wide array of porcelains, including tea sets and Victorian dolls. 801 Government St. ✆ **250/383-3931**. www.sydneyreynolds.com.

CHINESE ARTS & CRAFTS

Chinatown Trading Company (Finds)   This unobtrusive storefront on Fisgard opens onto a veritable bazaar—three connected shops stocked with Chinese goods either useful, endearingly corny, or both. Who wouldn't want kung fu shoes or a tin pecking chicken? Browse through bamboo flutes, origami kits, useful and inexpensive Chinese kitchenware, and a few small museum displays of artifacts from Chinatown's past. Look for the sneaky back entrance off Fan Tan Alley. 551 Fisgard St. ✆ **250/381-5503**. Bus: 5 to Douglas and Fisgard sts.

CIGARS & TOBACCO

E. A. Morris Tobacconist Ltd.   This small shop maintains a century-old tradition of custom-blending pipe tobacco. You'll also find an impressive selection of cigars, including Cubans. Cuban cigars can't be brought into the United States, but a few brands like Horvath Bances duck the blockade by importing the tobacco into Canada and rolling the cigars here. 1116 Government St. ✆ **250/382-4811**.

DEPARTMENT STORE & SHOPPING MALL

The Bay Centre   The Bay Centre is named after its new anchor store, Hudson's Bay Company. Canada's oldest department store sells everything from housewares to cosmetics and the classic (and expensive) Hudson's Bay woolen point blankets. The store also has a large china and crystal department. The rest of the complex houses a full shopping mall disguised as a block of heritage buildings. Between Government and Douglas sts., off Fort and View sts. For the Bay, call ✆ **250/385-1311**. For the mall, call ✆ **250/389-2228**.

FASHION
FOR WOMEN

Breeze   This high-energy store carries a number of trendy lines such as Mexx, Powerline, and Mac+Jac. Shoes by Nine West and Steve Madden, plus stylish accessories, complete the look. 1150 Government St. ✆ **250/383-8871**.

Hughes Ltd.   This local favorite features designer fashions and trendy casual wear. 564 Yates St. ✆ **250/381-4405**. www.hughesclothing.com.

The Plum Clothing Co. This local chain features quality dressy casuals designed with the baby boomer in mind. 1298 Broad St. ℂ 250/381-5005.

FOR WOMEN & MEN

The Edinburgh Tartan Shop If there's even a drop of Celtic blood in ye, this shop can set ye up in a kilt made from your family tartan. It also stocks sweaters, blankets, tartan by the yard, and kilt pins. 909 Government St. ℂ 250/953-7788.

Still Life Originally known for its vintage clothes, Still Life has updated and moved to a contemporary style that includes fashions from Diesel, Workwear, and Toronto designer Damzels-in-distress. 551 Johnson St. ℂ 250/386-5655.

W. & J. Wilson's Clothiers Canada's oldest family-run clothing store, this shop has been owned/managed by the Wilsons since 1862. Look for sensible casuals or elegant cashmeres and leathers from British, Scottish, and other European designers. 1221 Government St. ℂ 250/383-7177.

FOR MEN

British Importers Victoria may be laid-back, but a man still needs a power suit, and this is the place to get it. Designer labels include Calvin Klein and Hugo Boss. Ties and leather jackets are also for sale. 1125 Government St. ℂ 250/386-1496.

FIRST NATIONS CRAFTS

Natives from the nearby Cowichan band are famous for their warm, durable sweaters knit with bold motifs from hand-spun raw wool. In addition to these beautiful knits, craftspeople create soft leather moccasins, moose-hide boots, ceremonial masks, sculptures carved from argillite or soapstone, baskets, bearskin rugs, and jewelry.

Cowichan Trading Company A downtown fixture for almost 50 years, Cowichan Trading follows the standard layout for its displays: junky T-shirts and gewgaws in front, Cowichan sweaters, masks, and fine silver jewelry farther in. 1328 Government St. ℂ 250/383-0321.

Quw'utsun' Cultural and Conference Centre Though a bit of a drive out of town, this store, owned/operated by the Cowichan, sells beautiful crafts and allows you to watch artisans at work. It also stocks an excellent selection of books and publications on First Nations history and lore. 200 Cowichan Way, Duncan. ℂ 250/746-8119. www.quwutsun. ca. No public transit. Take Douglas St. north, which turns into Hwy. 1 (the Trans-Canada Hwy.); remain on the Trans-Canada for about 60km (37 miles) to Duncan, then turn right onto Cowichan Way.

FOOD & WINE

Murchie's It's worth coming here just to suck up the coffee smell or sniff the many specialty teas, including the custom-made blend served at The Fairmont Empress' afternoon tea. 1110 Government St. ℂ 250/383-3112. www.murchies.com.

Rogers' Chocolates Rogers' bills itself "Quite possibly the best chocolates in the world," and with original Tiffany glass, old-fashioned counters, and free samples, this 100-year-old shrine could possibly live up to the claim. 913 Government St. ℂ 800/663-2220 or 250/384-7021. www.rogerschocolates.com.

Silk Road Aromatherapy and Tea Company *Value* Before setting up shop, the two Victoria women who run this store first trained to become tea masters in China and Taiwan. Their Victoria store on the edge of Chinatown sells a wide variety of teas, including premium loose blends and tea paraphernalia such as teapots, mugs, and kettles; they offer a full line of aromatherapy products as well. The latest addition is the spa, which offers a range of treatments at very reasonable prices; their 2-hour full facial and full-body massage at C$99 (US$84/£45) is a steal. 1624 Government St. ℂ **250/382-0006**. www. silkroadtea.com. Bus: 5 to Douglas and Fisgard sts.

The Wine Barrel   This shop sells more than 300 B.C. VQA (Vintner Quality Alliance) wines and wine accessories. It's known for carrying the largest selection of B.C. ice wines (a type of wine where grapes have to be picked when the temperature has been below 32°F/0°C for a certain amount of time) in Victoria. 644 Broughton St. ℂ **250/388-0606**. www.thewinebarrel.com.

GLASS
Starfish Glassworks *(Finds)*   The principals of this gallery-cum-workshop moved to Victoria when they couldn't get kiln time in Vancouver. They took over and renovated an ex-bank building, installing the kiln on the ground floor and the gallery on an open catwalk above, so potential customers could watch works in progress while browsing among the finished products. You can observe the artists blowing glass daily from noon to 6pm. Wannabe glass blowers can now take 1-day workshops; check their website for dates. Closed Tuesdays, September 16 through May 14. 630 Yates St. ℂ **250/388-7827**. www.starfishglass.bc.ca.

JEWELRY
Jade Tree   Here you'll find jewelry made from British Columbia jade, which is mined in northern Vancouver Island, then crafted in Victoria and China into necklaces, bracelets, and other items. 606 Humboldt St. ℂ **250/388-4326**.

MacDonald Jewelry   Ian MacDonald designs and makes all his own jewelry: diamonds cut in squares and triangles, and styles from the traditional to cutting edge. It's a great place to hunt for rings and pearls, as well as precious gems like sapphires, rubies, and emeralds. 618 View St. ℂ **250/382-4113**.

The Patch   The Island's largest provider of body jewelry has studs, rings, and other bright baubles for your nose, navel, or nipple, much of it quite creative and reasonably priced. 719 Yates St. ℂ **250/384-7070**.

OUTDOOR CLOTHES & EQUIPMENT
Ocean River Sports   This is the place to go to arrange a sea kayak tour—they'll be happy to rent (or sell) you a boat and all the gear. This is also a good spot for outdoor clothing and camping musts, such as solar-heated showers or espresso machines. 1824 Store St. ℂ **250/381-4233**. www.oceanriver.com.

Pacific Trekking   An excellent source for rain and hiking gear, this store is also good for advice on local hiking trails. 1305 Government St. ℂ **250/388-7088**.

PUBLIC MARKETS
Market Square   Constructed from the original warehouses and shipping offices built in the 1800s, this pleasant and innovative heritage reconstruction features small shops and restaurants surrounding a central courtyard, often the site of live performances in summer. 560 Johnson St. ℂ **250/386-2441**.

17

Victoria After Dark

Victoria is God's waiting room. It's the only cemetery
in the entire world with street lighting.

—a visitor from Gotham, as quoted in *Monday Magazine*

Ouch. That's harsh. More important, it's not exactly accurate. True, with retirees and civil servants making up a sizable segment of the population, Victoria is never going to set the world on fire. But the U. Vic. students, tourists, and a small but dedicated cadre of Victoria revelers form a critical mass large enough to keep a small but steady scene alive.

Monday Magazine, a weekly tabloid published on Thursdays, is the place to start. Its listings section provides comprehensive coverage of what's happening in town and is particularly good for the club scene. If you can't find *Monday* in cafes or record shops, visit it on the Web at **www. mondaymag.com**.

For information on theater, concerts, and arts events, contact the **Tourism

Victoria Visitor Centre,** 812 Wharf St. (© **800/663-3883** or 250/953-2033; www.tourismvictoria.com). You can also buy tickets for Victoria's venues from the Visitor Centre, but only in person.

Whatever you decide to do with your Victoria evenings, chances are that your destination will be close at hand: One of the great virtues of Victoria's size is that nearly all of its attractions—concert halls, pubs, dance clubs, and theaters—are no more than a 10-minute walk from The Fairmont Empress, right in the heart of the city, and easily reached by taking bus no. 5 to the Empress Hotel/Convention Centre. For those few nightlife spots a little farther out, bus information is provided throughout the chapter.

1 The Performing Arts

The **Royal Theatre,** 805 Broughton St., and the **McPherson Playhouse,** 3 Centennial Sq., share a common box office (© **888/717-6121** or 250/386-6121; www. rmts.bc.ca). The **Royal**—built in the early 1900s and renovated in the 1970s—hosts concerts by the Victoria Symphony and performances by the Pacific Opera Victoria, as well as touring dance and theater companies. The **McPherson**—built in 1914 as the first Pantages Vaudeville Theatre—is home to smaller stage plays and performances by the Victoria Operatic Society.

THEATER

Performing in an intimate playhouse that was once a church, the **Belfry Theatre Society** ★★, 1291 Gladstone St. (© **250/385-6815;** www.belfry.bc.ca; bus no. 22 to Fernwood St.), is an acclaimed theatrical group that stages four productions (usually dramatic works by contemporary Canadian playwrights) October through April, and one show in August. Tickets are C$21 to C$36 (US$18–US$31/£9–£16).

The **Intrepid Theatre Company,** 301-1205 Broad St. (© **250/383-2663;** www.intrepidtheatre.com), runs two yearly theater festivals. In spring it's the **Uno Festival of Solo Performance** ✦✦, a unique event of strictly one-person performances. Come summer, Intrepid puts on the **Victoria Fringe Festival** ✦✦. Even if you're not a theater fan—*especially* if you're not—don't miss the Fringe. More than 50 performers or small companies from around the world put on amazingly inventive plays. The festival runs from late August to early September, and performances are held at six downtown venues daily noon to midnight.

Theatre Inconnu, 1923 Fernwood (© **250/360-0234**) is Victoria's oldest alternative theater group, celebrating 20 years of performances. The actors are local and often semiprofessional, but quality is excellent and tickets are inexpensive. They stage a two-man adaptation of Charles Dickens's *A Christmas Carol* every year.

The **Langham Court Theatre,** 805 Langham Court (© **250/384-2142;** www.langhamcourttheatre.bc.ca), performs works produced by the Victoria Theatre Guild, a local amateur society dedicated to presenting a wide range of dramatic and comedic works. From downtown take bus no. 14 or 11 to Fort and Moss streets.

OPERA

The **Pacific Opera Victoria** ✦✦, 1316B Government St. (© **250/385-0222,** box office 250/386-6121; www.pov.bc.ca), presents three productions annually during the October–April season. Performances are normally at the McPherson Playhouse and Royal Theatre. The repertoire covers the classical bases, from Mozart and Rossini to Verdi and even Wagner. Tickets cost C$30 to C$110 (US$25–US$93/£13–£50).

The **Victoria Operatic Society,** 10-744 Fairview Rd. (© **250/381-1021;** www.vos.bc.ca), presents Broadway musicals and other popular fare at the McPherson Playhouse. Tickets cost C$18 to C$45 (US$15–US$38/£8–£20).

ORCHESTRAL & CHORAL MUSIC

The well-respected **Victoria Symphony Orchestra** ✦✦, 846 Broughton St. (© **250/385-9771;** www.victoriasymphony.bc.ca), kicks off its season on the first Sunday of August with Symphony Splash, a free concert performed on a barge in the Inner Harbour. Regular performances begin in September and last through May. The Orchestra performs at the Royal Theatre or the University Farquhar Auditorium. Tickets are C$14 to C$60 (US$12–US$51/£6–£27) for most concerts.

DANCE

Dance recitals and full-scale performances by local and international dance troupes such as **Danceworks** and the **Scottish Dance Society** are scheduled throughout the year. Call the **Visitor Centre** at © **250/953-2033** to find out who's performing when you're in town.

COMEDY & SPOKEN WORD

Mocambo, 1028 Blanshard (© **250/384-4468**), a coffeehouse near the public library, hosts a range of spoken-word events through the week (multimedia fusion demos, philosopher's cafes, argument for the joy of it, slam poetry), then lets loose on Saturdays with improv comedy. There is no cover.

2 Music & Dance Clubs

MUSIC FESTIVALS

Folkfest ⍟   A free multicultural celebration of song, food, and crafts, Folkfest is the largest outdoor event on Vancouver Island. It takes place late June through early July on Ship Point (the parking space below Wharf St. on the edge of the Inner Harbour). ℭ 250/388-4728. www.icafolkfest.com.

Summer in the Square   Every day at noon from early July to late August, this popular festival in downtown's Centennial Square offers free music. Each day features a different band and musical style: Monday features mostly jazz; Tuesdays offer a selection of Big-Band golden oldies; Wednesday through Saturday is potluck (show up at noon and take your chances). The festival's showstoppers are the Concerts Under the Stars held each Sunday from 7 to 9:30pm; the series features some 15 local bands over the 6-week length of the festival. Centennial Sq. ℭ 250/361-0388.

Victoria Jazz Society/Jazz Fest International ⍟   The Jazz Society is a good place to call any time of year to find out what's happening; it runs a hotline listing jazz events throughout the year. Its raison d'être, however, is **Jazz Fest International,** held from late June to early July. The more progressive of Victoria's two summer jazz fests, this one offers a range of styles from Cuban, salsa, and world beat to fusion and acid jazz. Many free concerts are given in the Market Square courtyard; others are held in live-music venues around the city. This organization also puts on the excellent **Blues Bash** on Labour Day weekend on an outdoor stage in Victoria's Inner Harbour. ℭ 888/671-2112 or 250/388-4423. www.vicjazz.bc.ca.

LIVE MUSIC

Swans Pub (see review under "Bars & Pubs," below) presents a live band every night.

Hermann's Jazz Club   This venue cultivates a community center feel, which is definitely and defiantly *not* chic. Still, the reasonable cover charge gets you in for some good old-time jazz and Dixieland. Open Thursday through Saturday at 8pm, Sunday at 4:30pm. 753 View St. ℭ 250/388-9166. www.hermannsjazz.com. Cover C$5–C$10 (US$4.25–US$8/£2.25–£4.50).

Legends ⍟   Legends is one of the best places to hear live music in Victoria. At this pop-music palace, you'll encounter some hopping international bands, covering the gamut from Afro-pop and blues to R&B and zydeco. 919 Douglas St. ℭ 250/383-7137. www.legendsnightclub.com. Cover C$6 (US$5/£2.50) or more depending on the band Thurs–Sat.

Lucky Bar   This long, low, cavernous space has a pleasantly grungy feel to it. DJs spin house and trance on the weekends, with bands often showing up earlier in the week. 517 Yates St. ℭ 250/382-5825. www.luckybar.ca. Cover hovers around C$5 (US$4.25/£2.25), bigger shows up to C$20 (US$17/£9).

Steamers ⍟   One of the best places to catch live music on the cheap, Steamers features live music 7 nights a week. Once a strip bar, this long, narrow downtown spot got a new interior and was reborn as the city's premium blues bar. "Blues" here isn't taken too literally: acts often stray into the realms of zydeco, Celtic, and world beat. Mondays present an open-stage acoustic jam (no cover). 570 Yates St. ℭ 250/381-4340. www.steamerspub.ca. Cover free–C$5 (US$4.25/£2.25).

The Upstairs Lounge   Victoria's newest hot spot for live music sits overtop Darcy's Wharf Street Pub (see below) on the edge of Bastion Square. The Upstairs has space, good sightlines, and a crowd of attractive Victoria locals who come for touring bands, DJ'd house and Top 40. 15 Bastion Sq. ℰ **250/385-5483.** Cover about C$6 (US$5/£2.50), bigger shows up to C$12 (US$10/£5).

DANCE CLUBS

Most places are open Monday through Saturday until 2am, and Sunday until midnight. Drinks run from C$4 to C$8 (US$4.25–US$7/£1.80–£3.60).

The One Lounge   Open Thursday to Saturday, this club spins Top 40 and dance tracks for a late-20s to early-30s crowd. The format (1970s and 1980s retro) depends on the night of the week. 1318 Broad St. ℰ **250/384-3557.** Cover C$5 (US$4.25/£2.25) on weekends.

The Red Jacket   Opened in 2004, Red Jacket quickly became *the* hoppin' hot spot thanks to Caramel @ The Red Jacket, a Friday night bash featuring some of Victoria's finest urban DJ talent. 751 View St. ℰ **250/384-2582.**

Sugar   Groove the night away under an old-fashioned disco ball. Open Thursday through Saturday only; lineups start at 10pm so come early. DJs spin mostly hip-hop, house, and Top 40 tunes. 858 Yates St. ℰ **250/920-9950.** Cover Fri–Sat C$3–C$6 (US$2.50– US$5/£1.35–£2.70).

3 Lounges, Bars & Pubs
LOUNGES

Bengal Lounge ℱ   The Bengal is one of the last outposts of the old empire—a Raffles or a Harry's Bar—except the martinis are ice-cold and jazz plays in the background (and on weekends, live in the foreground). The couches are huge and covered in leather thick enough to stop an elephant gun. The cocktail list is extensive. The combination has lately attracted the young and elegant lounge-lizard crowd. 721 Government St., in The Fairmont Empress. ℰ **250/384-8111.**

Med Grill@Mosaic ℱ   Bistro by day, this cool, contemporary space turns into a martini spot at night (happy hour nightly 9–10pm), when DJs spin mellow sounds. Everything's reasonably priced and pretty. 1063 Fort St. ℰ **250/381-3417.**

The Reef   This Caribbean restaurant transforms into a funky reggae lounge when the sun has faded away. Features include great martinis and good tunes, and a DJ now and again. 533 Yates St. ℰ **250/388-5375.** www.thereefrestaurant.com.

BARS & PUBS

Big Bad John's   Victoria's first, favorite, and only hillbilly bar is a low, dark warren of a place, with thick gunk on the walls, inches of discarded peanut shells on the plank floor, and a crowd of drunk and happy rowdies. 919 Douglas St., in the Strathcona Hotel. ℰ **250/383-7137.**

Gambling

At the **Great Canadian Casino,** 1708 Old Island Hwy. (ℰ **250/391-0311;** www.gc gaming.com), in the View Royal neighborhood, there are no floor shows, no alcohol, no dancing girls in glittering bikinis—just a casual and slightly genteel casino. Games include blackjack, roulette, sic bo, red dog (diamond dog), and Caribbean stud poker. It's open daily noon to 3am. Contact the casino for complimentary shuttle service from downtown Victoria.

Canoe ☆ If it's a nice night, head for this fabulous outdoor patio overlooking the Upper Harbour. The beer is brewed on the premises (try the taster option—six small glasses of different brews for more or less the price of a pint). The century-old brick and beam building is a joy to look at, and the food is fun and hearty. 450 Swift St. ℂ 250/361-1940. www.canoebrewpub.com.

Darcy's Wharf Street Pub   Eating anywhere on Wharf Street would be a foolish newbie move, but drinking? That's another story. This large, bright, harborfront pub features a range of fine brews, pool tables, occasional live bands, and a lovely view of the sunset. The crowd is young and lively. 1127 Wharf St. ℂ 250/380-1322. www.darcyspub.ca.

Spinnakers Brewpub ☆ One of the best brewpubs in town, Spinnakers did it first and did it well. Overlooking Victoria Harbour on the west side of the Songhees Point Development, Spinnakers' view of the harbor and Legislature is fabulous. On sunny days it's worth coming here for the view alone. At other times (all times in fact), the brewed-on-the-premises ales, lagers, and stouts are uniformly excellent and the pub grub is always good. An on-site bakery sells various beer breads. The weekends often feature a band. There are also dartboards and pool tables. 308 Catherine St. ℂ 250/386-2739. www.spinnakers.com. Bus: 24 to Songhees Rd.

The Sticky Wicket   This is yet another pub in the Strathcona Hotel (see Big Bad John's, above)—but the Wicket is a standout. The beautiful wood interior—including dividers, glass, and a long teak bar—spent many years in Dublin before being shipped here to Victoria, making it about as original an Irish bar as you're likely to find. Elevators can whip you from deepest Dublin up three floors to the mini-Malibu on the outdoor patio balcony, complete with beach volleyball. 919 Douglas St., in the Strathcona Hotel. ℂ 250/383-7137.

Swans Pub ☆ Few drinking spots are more intriguing—or more enjoyable—than Swans. The intrigue comes from the founding owner's vast Pacific Northwest and First Nations art collection. The enjoyment comes from the room itself, on the ground floor of a beautifully converted 1913 feed warehouse across from the Johnson Street Bridge. The beer here is brewed on-site and delicious. There's live entertainment every night. 506 Pandora Ave., in Swans Hotel. ℂ 250/361-3310.

4 Gay & Lesbian Bars

Victoria's entertainment options for the gay and lesbian community are few. A good resource for local contacts can be found online at **www.gayvictoria.ca**.

Hush   This straight-friendly space (crowd is about fifty-fifty) features top-end touring DJs spinning house, trance, and disco house. Open Wednesday to Sunday. 1325 Government St. ℂ 250/385-0566. Cover on weekends C$5 (US$4.25/£2.25).

Prism Lounge   Drag shows, karaoke, techno, Top 40—something different every night. 642 Johnson St. (entrance on Broad St.). ℂ 250/388-0505. www.prismlounge.com.

18

Side Trips: The Best of British Columbia

Set on the very edge of a great wilderness, southwestern British Columbia is the gateway to experiences and places found nowhere else on earth. In Whistler, 2 hours by car northeast of Vancouver, the skiing and mountainbiking are truly spectacular, and the place has become a year-round mecca for recreation that goes from extreme to sublime. Over on the west coast of Vancouver Island, about a 4½-hour drive from Victoria, you'll find a world of mysterious maritime beauty at Pacific Rim National Park Reserve of Canada, a temperate coastal rainforest with crashing surf, old-growth giants, soaring bald eagles, and a resort town named Tofino—all the ingredients to make an ecotourist's dreams come true.

1 Whistler Blackcomb: One of North America's Premier Ski Resorts ★★★

128km (80 miles) N of Vancouver

The premier ski resort in North America, according to *Ski* and *Snow Country* magazines, **Whistler Blackcomb** has more vertical runs, lifts, and varied ski terrain than any other ski resort on the continent. Winter sports rule from December through April: Downhill, backcountry, cross-country and heli-skiing, snowboarding, sledding, and sleigh riding are just the tip of the iceberg.

In the off season, Whistler is also becoming a mecca for mountainbiking, with a world-class mountainbike park to match its world-class skiing. If you're not a fan of biking, you can spend your summer days in Whistler rafting, hiking, golfing, and horseback riding. Or, for some wonderful low-tech, ecofriendly fun, try zipping across Fitzsimmons Creek on Ziptrek (p. 279) and exploring the sublimely beautiful coastal rainforest hidden between Whistler and Blackcomb mountains.

The focus for all this action is **Whistler Village.** Sophisticated, international, and overwhelmingly youthful, this resort community is so new that at first glance it might strike you as a bit like Disneyland, or a huge mall with hotels (what the retail industry calls a "lifestyle center"). Back in the 1970s, a few visionary planners made the decision to build a resort town and set about creating a carefully planned infrastructure and aesthetic. The results are impressive—a compact resort arranged around a strollable, ski-able, and completely carless village street lined with upscale shopping, great restaurants, lots of pubs and cafes with outdoor patios, and plenty of plazas. What was sacrificed in this drive to become the perfectly planned community was space for the odd, the funky, the quaint, and the nonconforming. It's just too new and too affluent (at least in the winter; in the summer mountainbiking season it becomes more family oriented). When word went out that the 2010 Winter Olympics would be held here, real estate prices skyrocketed and more luxury hotels went up.

The resort is divided into Whistler Village (where you get the gondola for Whistler Mountain) and the Upper Village (where you get the gondola for Blackcomb Mountain); it takes about 5 minutes to walk between them. At some of the hotels, you can ski from the front entrance directly to the gondolas. Prices for hotels jump considerably during the high season from December through April, and that's also—not surprisingly—when Whistler is at its most seductive, blanketed with snow and twinkling with lights. July, August, and September are the best months for summer recreation on the mountains. During the shoulder seasons, May and June and October and November, you can expect rain—the area is, after all, a coastal rainforest.

The towns north of Whistler, **Pemberton** and **Mount Currie,** are refreshment stops for touring cyclists and hikers, and the gateway to the icy alpine waters of **Birkenhead Lake Provincial Park** (p. 271) and the majestic **Cayoosh Valley,** which winds through the glacier-topped mountains to the Cariboo town of Lillooet.

ESSENTIALS

GETTING THERE   By Bus   The **Whistler Express,** 8695 Barnard St., Vancouver (© **877/317-7788** or 604/266-5386; www.perimeterbus.com), operates bus service from Vancouver International Airport to the Whistler Bus Loop, as well as drop-off service at many of the hotels. In summer, there are seven daily departures; in winter, there are nine. The trip takes about 2½ to 3 hours; one-way fares are C$67 (US$57/£30) adults, C$45 (US$38/£20) for children 5 to 11 years of age and free for children under 5. Reservations are required year-round.

Snowbus (www.snowbus.ca) is a luxury coach featuring hosts, movies, snacks, drinks, and a hot breakfast option for early-morning departures from Vancouver during the winter ski season. They can also arrange lift tickets and rentals. One-way adult fare is C$21 (US$18/£9). **Whistler Direct Shuttle** (www.whistlerdirectshuttle.com) operates a deluxe highway coach service between Vancouver and Whistler. The service is by reservation only and is licensed to pick up at all downtown Vancouver hotels. Adult one-way fare is C$49 (US$42/£22).

Greyhound, Pacific Central Station, 1150 Station St., Vancouver (© **800/661-8747** or 604/662-8074; www.greyhound.ca), operates daily bus service (six trips a day 5:30am–5:30pm) from the Vancouver airport or downtown bus depot to the Whistler Bus Loop. The trip takes about 2½ hours; round-trip fares are C$38 (US$32/£17) for adults, C$19 (US$16/£9) for children 5 to 12, and free for children under 5.

By Car   Whistler is about a 2-hour drive from Vancouver along **Highway 99,** also called the **Sea-to-Sky Highway.** The drive is spectacular, winding first along the edge of Howe Sound before climbing through the mountains. In preparation for the 2010 Winter Olympics, the highway is being given a complete overhaul; you can find out about construction work and potential delays at www.seatoskyimprovements.ca, or by calling © **877/474-3399** (toll-free in Canada) or 604/660-1008. Parking is free for day skiers and visitors in Whistler. Most hotels in Whistler Village and Upper Village charge about C$20 (US$17/£9) for underground parking.

By Plane   Howe Sound Seaplanes (© **866/882-3252;** www.howesoundseaplanes.com) offers two daily flights from Victoria to the Whistler area. Passengers fly from Victoria's Inner Harbour via the Vancouver Airport to Squamish, located 30 minutes south of Whistler, where a courtesy shuttle transfers them to Whistler. The flight from

Whistler Valley

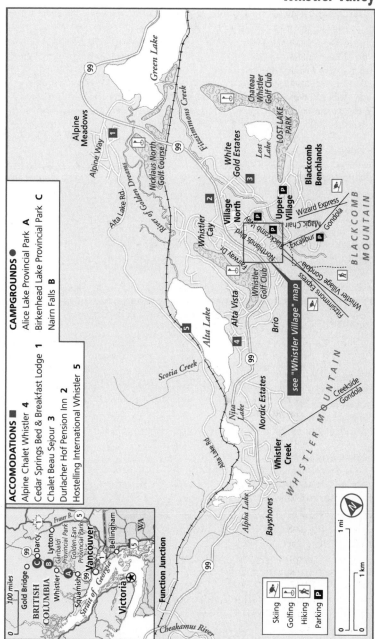

ACCOMODATIONS ■

Alpine Chalet Whistler **4**
Cedar Springs Bed & Breakfast Lodge **1**
Chalet Beau Sejour **3**
Durlacher Hof Pension Inn **2**
Hostelling International Whistler **5**

CAMPGROUNDS ●

Alice Lake Provincial Park **A**
Birkenhead Lake Provincial Park **C**
Nairn Falls **B**

see "Whistler Village" map

Skiing
Golfing
Hiking
Parking **P**

Whistler Village

ACCOMMODATIONS ■
Adara Whistler Hotel **14**
Delta Whistler Village Suites **19**
The Fairmont Chateau Whistler **2**
Four Seasons Resort Whistler **1**
Pan Pacific Whistler Mountainside **4**
Pan Pacific Whistler Village Centre **11**
Summit Lodge & Spa **22**
The Westin Resort & Spa Whistler **6**

DINING ◆
Araxi **12**
Bearfoot Bistro **17**
Caramba! Restaurant **9**
Ciao Thyme Bistro and B. B. K.'s Pub **3**
Citta Bistro **16**
Dubh Linn Gate Irish Lounge/Pub **4**
Hy's Steakhouse **20**
Ingrid's Village Café **13**
Quattro **23**
Rimrock Cafe and Oyster Bar **24**
Whistler BrewHouse **7**

NIGHTLIFE ▼
Boot Pub **24**
Buffalo Bills **15**
Dubh Linn Gate Irish Lounge/Pub **4**
Garfinkel's **10**
Maxx Fish **13**
Savage Beagle **12**
Tommy Africa's **12**
Whistler BrewHouse **7**

OTHER ATTRACTIONS ●
Maurice Young Millenium Place **8**
Whistler Conference Center **18**
Whistler Museum & Archives Society **21**
Whilster Village Gondola **5**

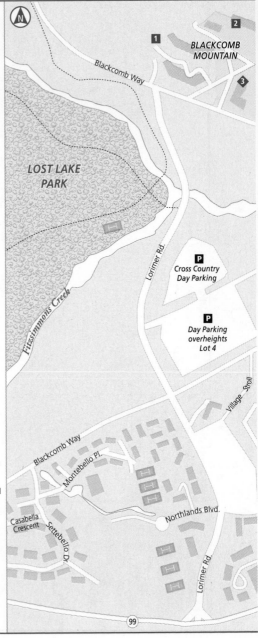

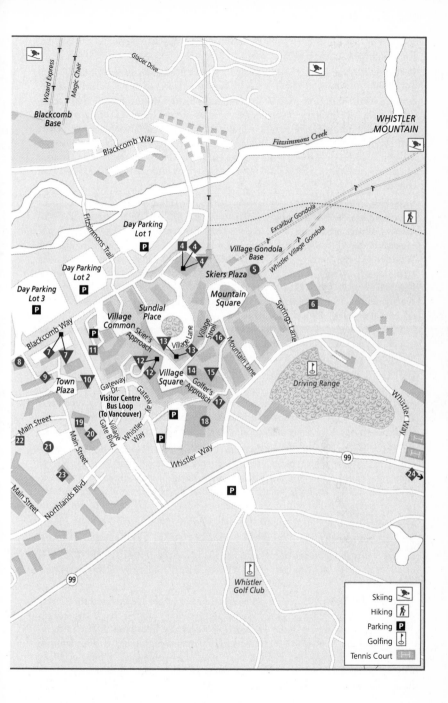

Victoria to Vancouver is 35 minutes and from Vancouver to Squamish 30 minutes. Fares begin at C$149 (US$127/£67).

By Train   Between May 1 and October 16, **Rocky Mountaineer Vacations** (© 877/ 460-3200 or 604/606-7245; www.rockymountaineer.com) offers daily service between North Vancouver and Whistler on the **Whistler Mountaineer** ★★★, a refurbished train with a vintage observation car. Trains depart North Vancouver at 8:30am (transportation to the train station is provided by most Vancouver hotels) and arrive at 11:30am; departure time from Whistler is 3pm, arriving back in North Vancouver at 6pm. Breakfast is served on the way up, and a light meal on the return. Standard round-trip fares are C$199 (US$169/£90) for adults and C$109 (US$93/£49) for children ages 2 to 11.

VISITOR INFORMATION   The **Whistler Visitor Info Centre,** 201-4230 Gateway Dr., off Village Gate Boulevard from Highway 99 (© 877/991-9988 or 604/935-3357; www.whistlerchamber.com), is open daily from 8:30am (Fri–Sat 9am–6:30pm), and can answer questions about the area, as well as help you find accommodations. **Tourism Whistler Activity Centre** (© 877/991-9988 or 604/938-2769; www.tourismwhistler. com), located in front of the TELUS Conference Centre near the Whistler gondola, is open daily 9am to 5pm (11am–7pm on Sat), and can assist you with ski-lift and other activity tickets and information, plus last-minute accommodations bookings. For **hotel reservations,** call © 800/WHISTLER.

Whistler.com (© 877/932-0606; www.whistler.com), a locally based call center, can answer all your questions and help you book hotels and activities. Another good website for general information is **www.whistlerblackcomb.com**.

GETTING AROUND   Compact and pedestrian-oriented, Whistler Village has signed trails and pathways linking hotels, shops, and restaurants with the gondolas up to Whistler and Blackcomb mountains. If you're staying in the Village, you can park and leave your car for the duration of your stay. The walk between Whistler Mountain (Whistler Village) and Blackcomb Mountain (Upper Village) takes about 5 minutes.

By Bus   Whistler and Valley Express (WAVE) (© 604/932-4020; www.bus online.ca), a year-round public transit service, runs from the Gondola Transit Exchange to the neighboring districts of Nester's Village, Alpine Meadows, and Emerald Estates. Service from the Village to Village North and Upper Village accommodations is free; other routes, one-way fares are C$1.50 (US$1.25/70p) for adults, C$1.25 (US$1.05/55p) for seniors and students, and free for children under 5.

By Cab   Sea-to-Sky Taxi (© 800/203-5322 or 604/932-3333) operates 24 hours.

By Car   Rental cars are available from **Avis,** 4315 Northlands Blvd. (© 800/879-2847 or 604/932-1236), and **Budget,** 4005 Whistler Way (© 800/299-3199 or 604/493-4122).

SPECIAL EVENTS   Downhill **ski competitions** are held December through May. Contact Tourism Whistler (see "Visitor Information," above) for event listings. Mountainbikers compete in the **24 Hours of Adrenalin bike races** in September.

Cornucopia (© 604/932-3434; www.whistlercornucopia.com) is Whistler's premier wine-and-food festival. Held in November, the opening gala showcases 50 top wineries from the Pacific region. Other events include a celebrity chef competition, food and wine seminars, and wine tastings.

WHERE TO STAY

The first and biggest decision to make is whether to stay in or out of Whistler Village. Staying in the Village, you can forget about your car for the duration of your visit and walk along paved pathways from hotel to ski lift to restaurant to pub. Staying outside the Village, you'll have a short drive to the parking lots on the perimeter of Whistler Village (many hotels outside the Village offer shuttle service). Accommodations within the Village are top quality, while outside the Village affords a bit more variety, including some fine European-style inns.

Whistler Central Reservations (© **800/944-7853;** www.tourismwhistler.com) can book a wide range of accommodations in the Whistler area, and provide a customized package with lift tickets and transportation from and to Vancouver.

To get the best rates on the hotels listed below, check the hotel's website to see if special packages are available or promotions are going on. In some cases, you can nab incredible ski/hotel packages. During the winter ski season hotel rates are considerably higher than during the shoulder and summer seasons.

IN THE VILLAGE

Adara Whistler Hotel ⟨★★⟩   Whistler's newest hotel, and its first member of Small Luxury Hotels of the World, opened in June 2007 right in the center of the village. Adara offers its guests a stylish alternative to Whistler's more traditional lodge-style hotels. It uses all the traditional Whistler "ingredients" (stone and wood), but in a more playful manner. The guest rooms come in four configurations (including a loft studio) with furnishings that highlight British Columbia's best contemporary design elements. The bathrooms in the larger units are like spas.

4122 Village Green, Whistler, B.C. V0N 1B4. © 866/502-3272 or 250/248-5194. www.adarahotel.com. 41 units. C$229–C$639 (US$195–US$543/£103–£288) double. AE, MC, V. Underground valet parking C$25 (US$121/£11). **Amenities:** Restaurant; heated outdoor pool (seasonal); spa; sauna; ski and bike rental; executive-level rooms. *In room:* A/C, TV/DVD w/pay movies, Wi-Fi, kitchen, minibar, coffeemaker, hair dryer, safe.

Delta Whistler Village Suites ⟨★⟩ ⟨*Kids*⟩   Just minutes from all the major attractions in Whistler, the Delta offers a variety of comfortable, unpretentious, one- and two-bedroom suites with gas fireplaces, balconies, living rooms, fully equipped kitchens, and washer-dryers. They have standard double rooms as well. The beds are firm and comfortable, and the bathrooms are more than adequate. You won't find the fine finishes and furnishings of a luxury hotel, but you will get great service and the use of a large heated pool with three Jacuzzis. **Hy's Steakhouse** (p. 273) is in the same building. The hotel welcomes children and has special kids' programs.

4308 Main St., Whistler, B.C. V0N 1B4. © 888/299-3987 or 604/905-3987. Fax 604/938-6335. www.deltahotels. com. 207 units. May–Dec 15 C$99–C$199 (US$84–US$169/£45–£90) double, C$129–C$399 (US$110–US$339/£58–£180) suite; Dec 16–Apr C$129–C$399 (US$110–US$339/£58–£180) double, C$199–C$999 (US$169–US$849/£90–£450) suite. AE, MC, V. Underground valet parking C$24 (US$20/£11). **Amenities:** Restaurant; heated outdoor pool; health club; spa; indoor and outdoor Jacuzzis; sauna; ski and bike rental; children's programs; concierge; business center; 24-hr. room service; babysitting; laundry service; same-day dry cleaning; executive-level rooms; rooms for those w/limited mobility. *In room:* A/C, TV w/pay movies, Wi-Fi, kitchen, minibar, coffeemaker, hair dryer, safe, fireplace (in suites).

The Fairmont Chateau Whistler ⟨★★⟩   The Chateau Whistler in the Upper Village at the foot of Blackcomb Mountain is absolutely enormous. The rooms and suites are quite large (the Mountain Suites, in fact, are huge), very quiet, and have good-size bathrooms with a separate soaker tub and shower. Guests have use of the heated outdoor pool and Jacuzzis, which look out over the base of the ski hill. Massive wooden beams, double-sided stone fireplaces, and an on-site spa help create an elegant country-retreat ambience, but the decor looks oddly dowdy. Wildflower is the hotel's fine-dining restaurant; Portobello a restaurant for more casual fare.

4599 Chateau Blvd., Whistler, B.C. V0N 1B4. © 800/606-8244 or 604/938-8000. Fax 604/938-2291. www.fairmont. com. 550 units. Spring–fall C$159–C$549 (US$135–US$467/£72–£247) double, C$249–C$1,849 (US$212–US$1,572/£112–£932) suite; winter C$599–C$949 (US$509–US$807/£270–£427) double, C$749–C$3,099 (US$637–US$2,634/£337–£1,395) suite. AE, MC, V. Underground valet parking C$28 (US$24/£14). **Amenities:** 4 restaurants; bar; 2 heated outdoor pools; 3 tennis courts; health club; spa; Jacuzzi; children's programs; concierge; tour desk; business center; shopping arcade; 24-hr. room service; in-room massage; babysitting; coin laundry; laundry service; same-day dry cleaning; nonsmoking rooms; concierge-level rooms; rooms for those w/limited mobility. *In room:* A/C, TV w/pay movies, high-speed Internet, minibar, coffeemaker, hair dryer, iron, safe.

Four Seasons Resort Whistler ✹✹✹   If you want the best, this is it. In the Upper Village, near the Fairmont Chateau, the Four Seasons has set a new standard for luxury and service in Whistler. The guest rooms, suites, and town houses are the largest in Whistler. All feature beautifully detailed wood-trimmed interiors, gas fireplaces, and views of the mountains, forest, valley, pool, or courtyard from step-out balconies. The decor is an updated version of a 1920s grand mountain lodge. The beds are fitted with Frette sheets. You won't find larger or more luxurious bathrooms anywhere in Whistler; each one has a deep soaker tub, a separate glass-enclosed shower, and two sinks. Every amenity you can think of is available here, including valet ski service.

4591 Blackcomb Way, Whistler, B.C. V0N 1B4. © 888/935-2460 or 604/935-3400. Fax 604/935-3455. www.fourseasons. com. 273 units. Summer–fall C$245–C$465 (US$208–US$395/£110–£209) double, C$540–C$3,100 (US$459–US$2,635/£459–£1,395) suite; winter C$395–C$1,095 (US$336–US$931/£178–£493) double, C$895–C$4,000 (US$761–US$3,900/£402–£1,800) suite. AE, DC, MC, V. Underground valet parking C$30 (US$25/£13). **Amenities:** Restaurant; bar; heated outdoor pool; health club; spa; Jacuzzi; sauna; children's programs; concierge; tour desk; business center; 24-hr. room service; in-room massage; babysitting; laundry service; same-day dry cleaning; nonsmoking rooms; executive-level rooms; rooms for those w/limited mobility. *In room:* A/C, TV w/pay movies, high-speed Internet, DVD/CD player, minibar, coffeemaker, hair dryer, iron, safe, fireplace.

Pan Pacific Whistler Mountainside ✹✹   The Pan Pacific's furnishings and appointments are really attractive, and the location, overlooking the Whistler gondola and ski slopes, puts this hotel right in the center of the action. You can literally ski out the door straight to the gondola. The look here is contemporary lodge-style, sophisticated, and very comfortable, with lots of warm wood in the rooms. Every suite has a fully equipped kitchenette and balcony. The studio suites with fold-down Murphy beds are the smallest units available; the one- and two-bedroom suites are quite roomy. One of the best features is the huge heated outdoor pool and Jacuzzi deck overlooking the snowy slopes. The hotel's **Dubh Linn Gate Irish Lounge/Pub** (p. 272) is a popular après-ski rendezvous point.

The new **Pan Pacific Whistler Village Centre,** 4299 Blackcomb Way (© **888/ 966-5574** or 604/966-5575; www.panpacificwhistler.com), which opened in 2005 and is run by the same company as the Whistler Mountainside, is an all-suite, boutique hotel with fine amenities and a village location. Spring-fall rates for a one-bedroom suite are C$179 to C$429 (US$152–US$365/£81–£193); winter rates for a one-bedroom suite are C$249 to C$999 (US$212–US$849/£112–£450).

4320 Sundial Crescent, Whistler, B.C. V0N 1B4. © 888/905-9995 or 604/905-2999. Fax 604/905-2995. www.panpacific. com. 121 units. Spring–fall C$129–C$329 (US$110–US$280/£58–£148) studio, C$169–C$529 (US$144–US$450/£76–£238) suite; winter C$199–C$849 (US$169–US$722/£90–£382) studio, C$299–C$1,499 (US$254–US$1,274/£135–£675) suite. AE, MC, V. Underground valet parking C$20 (US$17/£9). **Amenities:** Restaurant; pub; heated outdoor pool;

fitness center; Jacuzzi; steam room; concierge; limited room service; laundry service; rooms for those w/limited mobility. *In room:* A/C, TV, dataport, kitchen, minibar, fridge, coffeemaker, hair dryer, iron, safe.

Summit Lodge & Spa 🐦🐦
Peace and harmony reign at this classy boutique hotel located just a short stroll from the slopes and featuring a unique, full-service spa. Essence of bergamot and grapefruit wafts through the lobby, hallways, and rooms, all of which are suites with kitchenettes, fireplaces, and balconies. All the units showcase granite countertops, custom-designed cherrywood furnishings, original artwork, and oversize beds with down-filled duvets and pillows. The bathrooms are very nice and feature soaker tubs. Among the complimentary services are a yoga program and hot chocolate every evening; you can also borrow portable Zen waterfalls and tranquillity rock/sand gardens. The hotel's new dining spot, Elements Urban Tapas Lounge, offers upscale tapas, fresh seafood, infused martinis, and rare wines. The hotel's on-site Taman Sari Royal Heritage Spa features traditional Javanese spa treatments.

4359 Main St., Whistler, B.C. V0N 1B4. (℗ **888/913-8811** or 604/932-2778. Fax 604/932-2716. www.summitlodge. com. 81 units. C$119–C$450 (US$101–US$382/£54–£202) double; C$179–C$650 (US$152–US$552/£81–£252) suite. AE, MC, V. Underground valet parking C$20 (US$17/£9). **Amenities:** Restaurant; heated outdoor pool; full-service spa; Jacuzzi; concierge; ski shuttle; babysitting; Wi-Fi; laptop computer rental; rooms for those w/limited mobility. *In room:* A/C, TV, Internet, kitchenette, minibar, fridge, coffeemaker, hair dryer, iron, safe, microwave.

The Westin Resort & Spa Whistler 🐦★★
Though a latecomer to the Whistler hotel scene, The Westin Resort managed to snap up the best piece of property in town by squeezing itself onto the mountainside beside the main ski run into the Village. The Whistler gondola is within a few hundred yards of its doorstep. Built in 2000, the two-tower hotel has the outstanding service and luxury-level amenities Westin is known for (and like all Westins, it's now completely nonsmoking). It's a handsome property, with contemporary Western decor that includes lots of granite and cedar finishes. All 419 generously sized suites include upscale kitchens, gas fireplaces, and most have balconies. The bathrooms are roomy, with separate bathtubs and showers in most units. Some rooms in the back have lovely mountain views, but you can hear distant traffic noise from Highway 99, so ask about this when booking. Little luxuries include ski valet, boot-warming services, and the full-service spa, Avello, one of the best in Canada, offering more than 75 treatments. There's also an award-winning restaurant, Aubergine Grille, for fine dining.

4090 Whistler Way, Whistler, B.C. V0N 1B4. (℗ **888/634-5577** or 604/905-5000. Fax 604/905-5640. www.westin whistler.net. 419 units. Low season C$459–C$539 (US$390–US$458/£207–£243) junior suite, C$509–C$639 (US$433–US$543/£229–£288) suite; high season C$899–C$1,199 (US$764–US$1,019/£405–£540) junior suite, C$1,099–C$1,949 (US$934–US$1,656/£495–£877) suite. Children 17 and under stay free in parent's room. AE, DC, DISC, MC, V. Underground valet parking C$25 (US$23/£11). **Amenities:** 2 restaurants; bar; outdoor pool; health club; spa; indoor and outdoor whirlpool; sauna; children's program available; concierge; business center; shopping arcade; salon; 24-hr. room service; babysitting; laundry service; dry cleaning. *In room:* TV w/pay movies, high-speed Internet, Wi-Fi, kitchen, coffeemaker, hair dryer, iron, safe.

OUTSIDE THE VILLAGE
Alpine Chalet Whistler 🐦
This elegant newcomer was built to the exact specifications of a Czech couple who took up a second career as innkeepers. The common room is a dream, with comfy chairs and a big fireplace. The adjoining dining area is flooded with natural light from the overhead skylights. Rooms are named after trees and come in essentially two configurations: Standard rooms are comfortable but not huge, with two twins or a king-size bed, bathrooms with heated floors, and a functional tub/shower combo. Signature rooms are larger, with vaulted ceilings, the same

bed combinations but with Italian linen, as well as a gas fireplace and comfy leather armchairs. Several of these rooms also have pocket balconies, though with views of nothing much. Breakfasts are a top-quality feast.

3012 Alpine Crescent, Whistler, B.C. V0N 1B3. (✆) **800/736-9967** or 604/935-3003. Fax 604/935-3008. www. alpinechaletwhistler.com. 8 units. C$139–C$259 (US$118–US$220/£63–£117) double. Rates include full breakfast. MC, V. Free parking. Take Hwy. 99 about 2km (1¼ miles) past Whistler Creekside (before Whistler Village), turn left onto Hillcrest Dr., then a quick right onto Alpine Crescent; the chalet is on the left side about a block away. **Amenities:** Hot tub; small steam room; nonsmoking lodge; drying room; ski and bike storage. *In room:* TV, high-speed Internet.

Cedar Springs Bed & Breakfast Lodge *(Kids)*   This is one of Whistler's few B&Bs that welcomes children. Guests at this charming lodge choose from king-, queen-, or twin-size beds in comfortably modern surroundings. The largest room (no. 4) features a fireplace and balcony, though the bathroom is shower only. Room no. 8 has a queen-size bed, two single futons, and a big soaker tub, while room no. 7 has two queen-size and a shower only. The guest sitting room has a fireplace, TV, VCR, and video library; a sauna and hot tub on the sun deck (overlooking the gardens) fill out the list of amenities. An excellent breakfast is served by the fireplace in the dining room, and guests are welcome to enjoy afternoon tea. A complimentary shuttle service takes you to and from the ski lifts.

8106 Cedar Springs Rd., Whistler, B.C. V0N 1B8. (✆) **800/727-7547** or 604/938-8007. Fax 604/938-8023. www. whistlerbb.com. 8 units, 6 with private bathroom (5 with shower only). Winter C$85–C$285 (US$72–US$242/£38–£109) double; summer C$85–C$289 (US$72–US$246/£38–£130) double. Rates include full breakfast. AE, MC, V. Take Hwy. 99 north toward Pemberton 4km (2½ miles) past Whistler Village; turn left onto Alpine Way, go a block to Rainbow Dr., and turn left; go a block to Camino St. and turn left; the lodge is a block down at the corner of Camino and Cedar Springs Rd. Free parking. **Amenities:** Jacuzzi; sauna; bike rental; game room; courtesy car to ski slopes; nonsmoking lodge. *In room:* Hair dryer, no phone.

Chalet Beau Sejour *(Value)*   The standout feature of the Beau Sejour is a large common room with a fireplace and a fine view of Whistler Mountain and the valley. The medium-size rooms are comfortable and clean, with two single beds that can be joined together to make a king-size. Of the four units, one is a self-contained suite with a queen-size bed and its own fireplace and full kitchen, although all units provide the best value you're likely to find in a Whistler B&B. The back patio has a large hot tub for guests' use. The B&B is on a public bus route, and located only about a 15-minute walk from the Village via pedestrian paths. Guests are provided with lockers at the base of Whistler for the duration of their stay, plus a shuttle to/from the Chalet on their first/last day (so you can drop off/pick up your ski gear).

7414 Ambassador Crescent, Whistler, B.C. V0N 1B0. (✆) **604/938-4966.** Fax 604/938-6296. www.beausejour whistler.com. 4 units, shower only. Summer C$95–C$120 (US$81–US$102/£43–£54) double; winter C$120–C$165 (US$102–US$140/£54–£74) double. Rates include full breakfast. AE, MC, V. No children under 12. Take Hwy. 99 north toward Pemberton about 2km (1¼ miles) past Whistler Village; turn right onto Nancy Green Dr., go over the creek and 3 blocks to Ambassador Crescent, and turn right. Free parking. **Amenities:** Large hot tub; nonsmoking lodge. *In room:* No phone.

Durlacher Hof Pension Inn *(★ Finds)*   This lovely inn has an Austrian feel and a wonderfully sociable atmosphere. Both are the result of the exceptional care and service shown by owners Peter and Erika Durlacher. The guest rooms in this two-story chalet-style property vary in size from comfortable to spacious, and come with goose-down duvets and Ralph Lauren linens on extralong twin- or queen-size beds, and private bathrooms (some with jetted tubs) with deluxe toiletries. The private balconies give way to incredible mountain views. Better still is the downstairs lounge, with a

welcoming fireplace and complementary après-ski appetizers baked by innkeeper Erika, who also provides a substantial gourmet breakfast.

7055 Nesters Rd., Whistler, B.C. V0N 1B7. © 877/932-1924 or 604/932-1924. Fax 604/938-1980. www.durlacherhof. com. 8 units. Summer C$99–C$299 (US$84–US$254/£45–£135) double; winter C$129–C$299 (US$110–US$254/£58–£135) double. Extra person C$35 (US$28/£16). Rates include full breakfast and afternoon tea. MC, V. Free parking. Take Hwy. 99 about .8km (½ mile) north of Whistler Village to Nester's Rd.; turn left and the inn is immediately on the right. **Amenities:** Jacuzzi; sauna; laundry service; dry cleaning; nonsmoking lodge; ski and bike storage; 1 room for those w/limited mobility. *In room:* Hair dryer, no phone.

Hostelling International Whistler *(Value* One of the few inexpensive spots in Whistler, this hostel also happens to have a great location on the south edge of Alta Lake, with a dining room, deck, and lawn overlooking the lake to Whistler Mountain. Inside this pleasant hostel is a lounge with a wood-burning stove, a common kitchen, a piano, Ping-Pong tables, and a sauna, as well as a drying room for ski gear and storage for bikes, boards, and skis. In the summer, guests have use of a barbecue, canoe, and rowboat. As with all hostels, most rooms and facilities are shared, but some private rooms are available. Book by September at the latest for the winter ski season.

5678 Alta Lake Rd., Whistler, B.C. V0N 1B5. © 604/932-5492. Fax 604/932-4687. www.hihostels.ca. 32 beds in 4- to 8-bed dorms. C$20–C$60 (US$17–US$51/£9–£27) IYHA members, C$24–C$68 (US$20–US$58/£11–£31) non-members; annual adult membership C$35 (US$28/£16). MC, V. Free parking. The turnoff for Alta Lake Rd. is before the main village, to the left of Hwy. 99. **Amenities:** Sauna; watersports equipment; bike rental.

CAMPGROUNDS

You can reserve spots for the campgrounds listed here through **Discover Camping** (© **800/689-9025;** www.discovercamping.ca). Reservation fees are uniformly C$6.40 (US$5/£2.90) per night with a maximum of C$19 (US$16/£9) for 3 nights. South of Whistler on the Sea-to-Sky corridor is the very popular **Alice Lake Provincial Park.** Free hot showers, flush toilets, and a sani-station are among the available facilities. Hiking trails, picnic areas, sandy beaches, swimming areas, and fishing spots are also on the grounds. Twenty-seven kilometers (17 miles) north of Whistler, the well-maintained campground at **Nairn Falls** on Highway 99 is more adult oriented, with pit toilets, pumped well water, fire pits and firewood, but no showers. Its proximity to the roaring Green River and the town of Pemberton makes it appealing to many hikers, and the sound of the river is sweeter than any lullaby. The 85 campsites at **Birkenhead Lake Provincial Park,** off Portage Road, Birken, fill up quickly in summer. Boat launches, great fishing, and well-maintained tent and RV sites make the park an angler's paradise and one of the province's top 10 camping destinations. Facilities include fire pits, firewood, pumped well water, and pit toilets. Please note that many provincial parks now charge a day-use parking fee of C$3 to C$5 (US$2.60–US$4/£1.35–£2.25) per vehicle; you may also encounter a C$2 (US$1.70/£1) charge for using the sani-station.

WHERE TO DINE

Whistler literally overflows with dining choices. A stroll through the Village will take you past 25 or 30 restaurants. Some serve overpriced resort food, but a number of them stand out for either atmosphere or the quality of their meals. For those willing to spend a bit more, Whistler has some outstanding fine-dining options.

On the Village Square, **Ingrid's Village Cafe** (© **604/932-7000**), open daily 7am to 6pm, is a local favorite for quality and price; it's been around for over 20 years, making it one of Whistler's oldest businesses. A large bowl of Ingrid's daily soup costs

C$4.50 (US$3.80/£2), a veggie burger, C$6.50 (US$5.50/£3). Right across from Ingrid's, **Citta Bistro** (© 604/932-4177) is a favorite dining and nightspot, open daily 9am to 1am. It serves thin-crust pizzas, gourmet burgers, and various appetizers. Besides having good food and good prices (main courses are C$7–C$15/US$6–US$13/£3.15–£7), it has terrace seating perfect for people-watching.

For good beer and stick-to-your-ribs grub, try the family-friendly **Whistler Brew-House,** 4355 Blackcomb Way (© 604/905-2739; www.drinkfreshbeer.com), located just over the creek in Upper Village. It's open Sunday through Thursday from 11:30am to midnight, and Friday and Saturday from 11:30am to 1am. Main courses in the less expensive pub run from C$10 to C$18 (US$8–US$16/£4.50–£8); in the restaurant, where prime rib is a featured specialty, prices are C$18 to C$38 (US$15–US$32/£8–£17). There's a special kids' menu, too. Equally fun indoor dining can be had at the **Dubh Linn Gate Irish Lounge/Pub** (© 604/905-4047) in the Pan Pacific hotel (p. 268). The Gate offers solid pub grub and the atmosphere of the Emerald Isle. Open Monday through Saturday 7am to 1am, Sundays 7am to midnight; main courses cost C$11 to C$18 (US$9–US$15/£5–£8).

Araxi ✸✸✸ PACIFIC NORTHWEST   If you're looking for sublime food and an atmosphere of relaxed but sophisticated elegance, Araxi has no peers. The haute spot of Whistler cuisine, Araxi has been voted "Best Restaurant in Whistler" by *Vancouver* magazine for 9 consecutive years. The menu is nominally Italian but with a Pacific Northwest bent that emphasizes fresh regional products. The seafood is extraordinary, with appetizers such as fresh oysters and Dungeness crab soufflé. Meat eaters should try the superlative foie gras parfait; vegetarians can choose from starters such as buffalo mozzarella with beets salad. When it comes to main courses, Araxi's wonderful possibilities might include a scallop and prawn fettuccine (unlike anything you've ever tasted), roasted garlic-crusted halibut, or lamb. Many dishes are available as small plates. Araxi's wine list is an awe-inspiring 27 pages long, 12,000 bottles strong, with numerous exceptional vintages (many of them from B.C.) and—for those without unlimited wealth—one of the best selections of wines by the glass around. Dinner is served in a warm, woody, beautifully designed space that looks out on the main village street; they also have an outdoor patio.

4222 Village Sq. © 604/932-4540. www.araxi.com. Reservations recommended. Main courses C$29–C$42 (US$25–US$36/£13–£19). AE, MC, V. Mon–Fri 11am–2pm and 5–11pm; Sat–Sun 10:30am–2pm and 5–11pm.

Bearfoot Bistro ✸✸ FRENCH   What began as a fairly simple bistro has become Whistler's most reliable French restaurant. The kitchen procures the finest wild and cultivated products, and almost everything is prepared "a la minute" and in such a manner as to emphasize the quality of the ingredients without over-complication. Diners create their own tasting menus from selections that change daily. For an appetizer, you might choose white truffle fettuccine with prosciutto and champagne cream, and your main course might be wild striped bass and king crab with lemon confit. The wine list at Bearfoot Bistro is outstanding, and a sommelier can help you with wine pairings. For the proper experience, allot at least 2 hours to dine here.

4121 Village Green. © 604/932-3433. www.bearfootbistro.com. Reservations essential. Tasting menus C$98–C$135 (US$83–US$115/£44–£61). AE, MC, V. Daily 5–10pm.

Caramba! Restaurant *Kids* MEDITERRANEAN   The food here won't win any awards, but Caramba! remains a good spot for casual dining; parents can bring their kids and not feel like they're "eating down." The nominally Mediterranean menu is something of an anomaly when it comes to culinary influences. Try the pasta, free-range chicken, or roasted pork loin. If you're into sharing, order a pizza or two and a plate of sliced prosciutto and bullfighter's toast (toasted Spanish bread with herbs).

12-4314 Main St., Town Plaza. © 604/938-1879. Main courses C$11–C$18 (US$9–US$15/£5–£8). AE, MC, V. Daily 11:30am–10:30pm.

Ciao Thyme Bistro and B. B. K.'s Pub ⚓ *Finds* *Kids* CASUAL/PACIFIC NORTH-WEST This popular spot in the Upper Village is a favorite with locals and a dream come true for visitors who want to eat well on a limited budget. The space is small, and the lines can be long (reserve if you're coming for dinner), but the fresh, delicious food is worth any wait you may endure. The bistro is a great spot for breakfast (until 3pm), lunch, or dinner, serving a menu reaching from free-range egg omelets to duck leg confit. The special kids' menu features standards like grilled cheese sandwiches and pasta. The menu is the same in both the bistro and the nonsmoking pub next door.

4573 Chateau Blvd., Upper Village. © 604/932-7051. Main courses C$11–C$23 (US$9–US$19/£5–£10). AE, DC, MC, V. Daily 8am–4pm and 6–10pm.

Hy's Steakhouse ⚓ NORTH AMERICAN This is the place to go if you're hungering for a big slab of roast beef with garlic mashed potatoes or a juicy steak (Hy's is famous for the quality of its beef). The menu also has seafood and even a vegetarian dish of grilled vegetables.

In the Delta Whistler Village Suites (p. 267), 4308 Main St. © 604/905-5555. Main courses C$30–C$40 (US$25–US$34/£13–£18). AE, DC, MC, V. Oct and May–June daily 8am–3pm; July–Sept and Nov–Apr daily 8am–3pm and 5–10pm.

Quattro ⚓⚓ ITALIAN Quattro is in the Village, but it's a little off the beaten path. The room is warm and slightly quirky, while the food is fairly simple (fresh ingredients in uncomplicated seasonings), but satisfyingly well done. Though menus change regularly, typical appetizers include fresh minestrone with pesto, while main courses include a variety of great pastas (if you can't decide, order the *pazza a pezzi* and sample all five), as well as daily specials such as saltimbocca (veal scaloppine with sage and prosciutto in a butter sauce). The wine list is extraordinary, with a few token vintages from B.C. and California, but a heart and soul residing in Italy.

4319 Main St. © 604/905-4844. www.quattrorestaurants.com. Reservations recommended. Main courses C$21–C$39 (US$18–US$33/£10–£18). AE, MC, V. Daily 5:30–11pm. Closed Mon–Tues mid-Apr to June.

Rimrock Cafe and Oyster Bar ⚓⚓ SEAFOOD Rimrock is like a Viking hall of old, with a long, narrow room, high ceiling, and a great stone fireplace. It's not the atmosphere, however, that draws folks in, it's the food. The first order of business should be a plate of oysters. The chef serves them up in half a dozen ways, from raw with champagne to "cooked in hell" (broiled with fresh chiles). The signature Rimrock oyster is broiled with béchamel sauce and smoked salmon. Entrees are seafood oriented. Look for wild sockeye salmon with lobster mashed potatoes, and sea bass pan-fried in an almond-ginger crust. The accompanying wine list has a number of fine vintages from B.C., California, New Zealand, and Australia.

2117 Whistler Rd. © 877/932-5589 or 604/932-5565. www.rimrockwhistler.com. Reservations recommended. Main courses C$24–C$40 (US$20–US$34/£11–£18). AE, MC, V. Daily 6–11:30pm, but call ahead in the low season (May–June and Sept–Nov) as hours may change.

WHAT TO SEE & DO OUTDOORS: WHISTLER'S RAISON D'ETRE

Whistler and Blackcomb Mountains ⭐⭐⭐ *Kids*   Both mountain resorts are operated by Intrawest, so your pass gives you access to both ski areas. Whistler is generally considered better for beginners and middle-range skiers, while steeper Blackcomb is geared to the experienced. (By 2009, a new gondola—the longest in the world—will link the two mountains.) **Whistler Mountain** has 1,502m (4,928 ft.) of vertical (and more than 100 marked) runs serviced by a high-speed gondola and eight high-speed chairlifts, plus four other lifts and tows. Helicopter service from the top of the mountain provides access to another 100-plus runs on nearby glaciers. The peak has cafeterias, gift shops, and a restaurant. **Blackcomb Mountain** has 1,584m (5,197 ft.) of vertical and more than 100 marked runs serviced by nine high-speed chairlifts, plus three other lifts and tows. The cafeteria, restaurant, and gift shop aren't far from the peak. Both mountains also have bowls and glade skiing, with Blackcomb Mountain offering glacier skiing well into August. A family-friendly Tube Park, located at Base II on Blackcomb, offers a 385m (1,263-ft.) run with six lanes, accessed by a carpet-style lift. *Note:* You can save about 20% on your lift tickets by booking online.

4545 Blackcomb Way, Whistler, B.C. V0N 1B4. ⓒ **800/766-0449** in North America, or 0800/587-1743 in the U.K.; snow report 604/687-7507 in Vancouver, 604/932-4211 in Whistler. www.whistlerblackcomb.com. Winter lift tickets C$48 (US$41/£22) adults, C$38 (US$32/£17) seniors and youths 13–18, C$24 (US$21/£11) children 7–12, free for children 6 and under. A variety of multiday passes are available. Tube park per hour C$13 (US$11/£6) adults, C$10 (US$8/£4.50) children. Lifts open daily 8:30am–3:30pm (until 4:30pm mid-Mar until the end of season, depending on weather and conditions).

DIFFERENT SLOPES FOR DIFFERENT FOLKS: THE LOWDOWN ON SKIING IN WHISTLER

Whistler Blackcomb offers **ski lessons** and **ski guides** for all levels and interests. For skiers looking to try snowboarding, a rental package and a half-day lesson is a particularly attractive option. Phone **Guest Relations** at ⓒ **604/932-3434** for details.

You can **rent ski and snowboard gear** at the base of both Whistler and Blackcomb Villages just prior to purchasing your lift pass. No appointment is necessary (or accepted), and the system is first-come, first-served. Arrive at 8am, and you'll be on the gondola by 8:15. Arrive at 8:30am, and you won't be up until 9:15 at the earliest.

Summit Ski (ⓒ **604/932-6225;** www.summitsport.com), at various locations including the Delta Whistler Resort and Market Pavilion, rents high-performance and regular skis, snowboards, telemark and cross-country skis, and snowshoes.

BACKCOUNTRY SKIING   The **Spearhead Traverse,** which starts at Whistler and finishes at Blackcomb, is a well-marked backcountry route that has become extremely popular in the past few years.

Moments Après Ski

"Après ski" refers to that delicious hour after a hard day on the slopes, when you sit back with a cold or hot drink and nurse the sore spots in your muscles. On the Whistler side, the many loud and kicky beer bars will be in your face the moment your skis cease to schuss. On the Blackcomb side, **Merlin's Bar** (ⓒ **604/938-7735**) is almost as obvious and equally young and lubricated. However, the **Mallard Bar** 𝄞 (ⓒ **604/938-8000**), inside The Fairmont Chateau Whistler (p. 267), is one of the most civilized après-ski bars on earth.

Garibaldi Provincial Park (© 604/898-3678) maintains marked backcountry trails at **Diamond Head, Singing Pass,** and **Cheakamus Lake.** These are ungroomed and unpatrolled rugged trails, and you have to be at least an intermediate skier and bring (and know how to use) appropriate clothing and avalanche gear. Several access points to the trails are along Highway 99 between Squamish and Whistler. If you're not sure of yourself off-*piste,* hire a guide through **Whistler Alpine Guides Bureau** (© 604/938-9242; www.whistlerguides.com) or **Whistler Cross Country Ski and Hike** (© 888/771-2382; www.whistlerski-hike.com).

CROSS-COUNTRY SKIING   Well-marked, fully groomed cross-country trails run throughout the area. The 30km (19 miles) of easy-to-very-difficult marked trails at **Lost Lake** start a block away from the Blackcomb Mountain parking lot. These trails are groomed for track skiing and ski-skating, are patrolled by Whistler employees, and are at their best from mid-December to mid-March. Passes are C$15 (US$13/£7) per day; a 1-hour cross-country lesson including pass and equipment rental runs about C$65 (US$55/£29), and can be booked at the same station where you buy your trail pass. For more information, contact **Lost Lake Cross Country Connection** (© 604/ 905-0071; www.crosscountryconnection.bc.ca). The **Valley Trail System** in the village becomes a well-marked cross-country ski trail during winter.

HELI-SKIING   For intermediate and advanced skiers who can't get enough fresh powder or vertical on the regular slopes, there's always heli-skiing. **Whistler Heli-Skiing** (© 888/847-7669 or 604/932-4105; www.whistlerheliskiing.com) offers a three-run day, with 2,400 to 3,000m (7,874–9,843 ft.) of vertical helicopter lift, for C$695 (US$591/£313) per person. A four-run day for expert skiers and riders only, with 3,000 to 3,600m (9,843–11,811 ft.) of vertical helicopter lift, is also available.

OTHER WINTER PURSUITS

SLEIGHING & DOG SLEDDING   For a horse-drawn sleigh ride, contact **Blackcomb Horsedrawn Sleigh Rides,** 103-4338 Main St. (© 604/932-7631; www. blackcombsleighrides.com). In winter, tours go out every evening and cost C$45 (US$38/£20) for adults and C$25 (US$22/£11) for children under 12. Other options include daylight and dinner sleigh rides.

From mid-December through March, **Cougar Mountain Adventures** (© 888/ 297-2222; www.cougarmountain.ca) and **Whistler Blackcomb** (© 888/403-4727; www.whistlerblackcomb.com) offer dog-sled rides. A backcountry dog-sled tour costs C$298 (US$253/£134) for one or two people.

SNOWMOBILING & ATVs   Year-round combination ATV and snowmobile tours of the Whistler Mountain trails are offered by **Canadian Snowmobile Adventures Ltd.,** Carleton Lodge, 4290 Mountain Sq., Whistler Village (© 604/938-1616; www.canadian snowmobile.com). All tours are weather and snow conditions permitting. Exploring the Fitzsimmons Creek watershed, a 2-hour tour, costs C$119 (US$101/£54) for a driver and C$89 (US$76/£40) for a passenger. Drivers on both the snowmobile and the ATV must have a valid driver's license. A 2-hour Mountain Safari on Blackcomb Mountain costs C$159 (US$135/£61) for a driver and C$119 (US$101/£54) for a passenger.

Blackcomb Snowmobile (© 604/932-8484; www.blackcombsnowmobile.com) offers a variety of guided snowmobile tours, including family tours on Blackcomb Mountain. A 2-hour tour costs C$119 (US$101/£54) for one adult, C$178 (US$151/£80) for two adults, and half-price for children.

SNOWSHOEING Snowshoeing is the world's easiest and most environmentally friendly form of snow-comotion; it requires none of the training and motor skills of skiing or boarding, and it's quiet, so it lets you appreciate nature in a different way. You can wear your own shoes or boots, provided they're warm and waterproof, strap on your snowshoes, and off you go. Rentals are available at the ski-and-board rental companies listed above. One of the best rental and trail companies is **Lost Lake Cross Country Connection** (℗ 604/905-0071; www.crosscountryconnection.bc.ca), which rents snowshoes for C$6 (US$5/£2.70).

Cougar Mountain Adventures (℗ 888/297-2222; www.cougarmountain.ca) has guided tours to the Cougar Mountain area at C$49 (US$42/£22) for 2 hours.

SUMMER PURSUITS

CANOEING & KAYAKING The 3-hour River of Golden Dreams Kayak & Canoe Tour is a great way for novices, intermediates, and experts to get acquainted with the beautiful stretch of slow-moving glacial water running between Green Lake and Alta Lake behind the village of Whistler. Contact the **Whistler Activity and Information Centre** (℗ 877/991-9988) for information. Packages begin at C$35 (US$30/£16) per person, unguided, and include all gear and return transportation to the village center. The Whistler Activity and Information Centre also offers lessons and clinics, as well as sailboat and windsurfing rentals.

FISHING Everything from rainbow trout to coho salmon attracts anglers from around the world to the area's many glacier-fed lakes and rivers and to **Birkenhead Lake Provincial Park,** 67km (42 miles) north of Pemberton.

Whistler River Adventures (℗ 888/932-3532 or 604/932-3532; www.whistler river.com), offers half- and full-day catch-and-release fishing trips in the surrounding glacial rivers. Rates are C$240 (US$204/£108) per person for a full day, based on two people, which includes all fishing gear, round-trip transport to/from the Whistler Village Bus Loop, and a snack or lunch. A 1-day fishing license is an additional C$20 (US$17/£9).

GOLFING Robert Trent Jones, Jr.'s **Chateau Whistler Golf Club,** at the base of Blackcomb Mountain (℗ 604/938-2092, or pro shop 604/938-2095; www. whistler.com), is an 18-hole, par-72 course. With an elevation gain of more than 120m (394 ft.), this course traverses mountain ledges and crosses cascading creeks. A panoramic view of the Coast Mountains unfolds midcourse. Greens fees range from C$125 to C$195 (US$106–US$166/£56–£88), including power-cart rental.

A multiple-award-winning golf course, **Nicklaus North at Whistler** (℗ 604/938-9898; www.golfwhistler.com) is a 5-minute drive north of the Village on the shores of Green Lake. The par-71 course's mountain views are spectacular. It's only the second Canadian course designed by Nicklaus, and, of all the courses he's designed worldwide, the only one to bear his name. Greens fees are C$37 to C$185 (US$17–US$157/£17–£83).

Whistler Golf Club (℗ 800/376-1777 or 604/932-4544; www.golfwhistler.com), designed by Arnold Palmer, features nine lakes, two creeks, and magnificent vistas. Having recently undergone a C$2-million (US$1.7-million/£900,900) renovation, this 18-hole, par-72 course offers a driving range, putting green, sand bunker, and pitching area. Greens fees are C$59 to C$159 (US$50–US$135/£27–£72).

A-1 Last Minute Golf Hotline (℗ 800/684-6344 or 604/878-1833) can arrange a next-day, last-minute tee time at Whistler golf courses and elsewhere in B.C. at more than 30 courses. Savings can be as much as 40%. No membership is necessary. Call between 3 and 9pm for the next day or before noon for the same day. The hotline also arranges group and advanced bookings (as much as a year ahead).

HIKING   Numerous easy hiking trails can be found in and around Whistler. Besides taking a lift up to Whistler and Blackcomb mountains' high mountain trails (you can somewhat easily hike to the foot of a glacier) during summer, you have a number of other choices.

Lost Lake Trail starts at the northern end of the Day Skier Parking Lot at Blackcomb Mountain. The lake is less than a mile from the entry. The 30km (19 miles) of marked trails that wind around creeks, beaver dams, blueberry patches, and lush cedar groves are ideal for biking, cross-country skiing, or just strolling and picnicking. The **Valley Trail System** is a well-marked paved trail that connects parts of Whistler. The trail starts on the west side of Highway 99 adjacent to the Whistler Golf Course and winds through quiet residential areas as well as golf courses and parks.

Garibaldi Provincial Park's **Singing Pass Trail** is a 4-hour hike of moderate difficulty. The fun way is to take the Whistler Mountain gondola to the top and walk down the well-marked path that ends on an access road in the Village. Winding down from above the tree line, the trail takes you through stunted alpine forest into Fitzsimmons Valley. Along Highway 99 between Squamish and Whistler are several access points into the park.

Nairn Falls Provincial Park ★★ is about 33km (21 miles) north of Whistler on Highway 99. This provincial park features a mile-long trail that leads you to a stupendous view of the glacial Green River as it plunges 59m (194 ft.) over a rocky cliff into a narrow gorge on its way downstream. You will also spy an incredible view of Mount Currie peeking over the treetops.

On Highway 99 north of Mount Currie, **Joffre Lakes Provincial Park** has an intermediate-level hike that leads past several brilliant blue glacial lakes up to the very foot of a glacier. The **Ancient Cedars** area of Cougar Mountain is an awe-inspiring grove of towering cedars and Douglas firs. (Some of the trees are more than 1,000 years old and measure 3m/9¾ ft. in diameter.)

Guided nature hikes provide an excellent opportunity to learn more about the ecology of the region. Contact the **Whistler Activity and Information Centre** (© 877/ **991-9988** or 604/938-2769; www.tourismwhistler.com) for guided hikes and interpretive tours. Two- to 3-hour nature walks start at C$35 (US$28/£16).

HORSEBACK RIDING   **Whistler River Adventures** (© 888/932-3532 or 604/ 932-3532; www.whistlerriver.com) offers 2-hour trail rides along the Green River, through the forest, and across the Pemberton Valley from its 4-hectare (10-acre) riverside facility in nearby Pemberton, a 35-minute drive north of Whistler. The 2-hour ride costs C$60 (US$51/£27); longer rides can be arranged.

JET BOATING   **Whistler River Adventures,** Whistler Mountain Village Gondola Base (© **888/932-3532** or 604/932-3532; www.whistlerriver.com), takes guests up the Green River just below Nairn Falls, where moose, deer, and bear sightings are common in the canyon. Later in the season, tours go up the Lillooet River past ancient petroglyphs, fishing sites, and the tiny native village of Skookumchuck. Tours range from C$99 to C$145 (US$84–US$123/£45–£65).

MOUNTAINBIKING   A rumor is afloat that within 5 years, mountainbiking at Whistler will be bigger than skiing. **Whistler Mountain Bike Park** ★★★ (℃ 866/ 218-9688; www.whistlerblackcomb.com/bike) offers some of the best mountainbiking trails, skill centers, and jump parks in the world. When the snow melts and skiing is over, the slope is reconfigured for biking—with 48km (30 miles) of marked trails, open daily mid-May to mid-October from 10am to 5pm (until 8pm Sat; additional late openings June–July). The variety of trails can accommodate almost all ages and experience levels. Depending on the season, single-day ticket prices with gondola are C$47 (US$40/£21) for adults, C$41 (US$35/£18) for seniors and youths 13 to 18, and C$25 (US$21/£11) for children 10 to 12. *Note:* Children 12 and under are not permitted in the bike park unless accompanied by a parent.

You can rent the best mountainbikes (C$69/US$59/£31 for 4 hr.) and body armor (C$20/US$17/£9) right next to the bike park. **Lost Lake Cross Country Connection** (℃ 604/905-0071; www.crosscountryconnection.bc.ca) offers bike rentals and guided tours for levels from beginner to expert.

RAFTING   Whistler River Adventures (℃ 888/932-3532 or 604/932-3532; www. whistlerriver.com) offers 2-hour, 4-hour, and full-day round-trip rafting runs down the Green, Birkenhead, Elaho, and Squamish rivers. They include equipment and ground transportation for C$69 to C$109 (US$59–US$93/£31–£49) for a 2- to 4-hour tour, or C$154 (US$131/£69) for a full day on the Elaho and Squamish rivers. Children are welcome as long as they can hold on by themselves and weigh a minimum of 90 pounds. Novices are taken to the Green River on a half-day trip, where small rapids and snowcapped mountain views are the highlights. Experts are transported to the Elaho River or Squamish River for full-day, Class 4 excitement. May through August, trips depart daily. The full-day trip includes a salmon barbecue lunch.

For first-timers, **Wedge Rafting,** Carleton Lodge, Whistler Village (℃ 604/932-7171; www.wedgerafting.com), offers a Green River, Birkenhead River, and Cheakamus River tour. For the Green River trip, about 2½ hours, the shuttle picks up rafters in Whistler and takes them to the wilderness launch area for briefing and equipping. It's an exciting hour or more on the icy rapids. After the run, rafters can relax at the outfitter's log lodge with a snack and soda before being shuttled back into town. Tours cost C$69 (US$59/ £27), with up to three daily departures. The Birkenhead River tour takes about 4 hours and costs C$89 (US$75/£40). Discounts are available for youths 10 to 16; however, they must weigh at least 90 pounds.

Located in the gorgeous Squamish valley, **Sun Wolf Outdoor Centre** (℃ 877/806-8046; www.sunwolf.net) has summer rafting trips on the Elaho River and winter eagle viewing trips on the Cheakamus and Squamish rivers. Full-day summer rafting trips cost C$149 (US$127/£67) per person, and the winter eagle trips cost C$99 (US$84/ £45) per person.

ROCK CLIMBING   The Great Wall, 4340 Sundial Crescent (℃ 604/905-7625; www.greatwallclimbing.com), has a year-round indoor climbing center and summer outdoor climbing wall, as well as guided climbs and instruction. The indoor center is on the lower level of the Westbrook Hotel at the base of Whistler. The outdoor center is in the Blackcomb Upper Village near the Wizard Chair. A day pass is C$16 (US$14/£7).

TENNIS   The **Whistler Racquet & Golf Resort,** 4500 Northland Blvd. (℃ 604/ 932-1991; www.whistlertennis.com), has three covered courts, seven outdoor courts,

Zipping with Ziptrek ★★★

One of the newest and most exciting year-round adventures is offered by **Ziptrek Ecotours** (① **604/935-0001**; www.ziptrek.com). On guided 2½-hour tours, you're taken through Whistler's ancient temperate rainforest on a network of five zipline rides joined by canopy bridges, boardwalks, and trails. Along the way, you're harnessed into a safety contraption that lets you whiz out on cables suspended hundreds of feet above glacier-fed Fitzsimmons Creek. It sounds hair-raising, but it's completely safe for all ages and abilities, and you'll never forget the experience. Individual Ziptrekkers must be over 6 years old and weigh between 65 and 275 pounds; children can ride tandem with one of the guides. Choose from two five-line tours (one new as of 2006), or you can do a 10-line zip all the way back to Whistler for C$149 (US$127/£67). The sales desk is located in the Carleton Lodge right across from the Whistler Village Gondolas. The five-line tour costs C$98 (US$83/£44) for adults, C$78 (US$66/£35) for seniors over 65 and children 14 and under. If you don't want to zip, consider the **Treetrek,** which explores the rare and ancient temperate rainforest along a network of suspension bridges, boardwalks, and treetop viewing platforms.

and a practice cage, all open to drop-in visitors. Indoor courts are C$32 (US$27/£14) per hour, outdoor courts C$16 (US$14/£7) per hour. Adult and junior tennis camps are offered in summer. Camp prices run C$300 to C$370 (US$255–US$314/£135–£166) for a 3-day adult camp. Kids' camps cost C$48 (US$41/£22) per day drop-in, or C$198 (US$168/£89) for a week. Book early, as these camps fill up quickly.

The **Mountain Spa & Tennis Club,** Delta Whistler Resort, Whistler Village (① **604/938-2044**), and the **Chateau Whistler Resort,** Fairmont Chateau Whistler Hotel, Upper Village (① **604/938-8000**), also offer courts to drop-in players. Prices run about C$20 (US$17/£9) per hour per court; racquet rentals are available for C$5 (US$4/£2.25) per hour.

Free public courts (① **604/935-7529**) are located at Myrtle Public School, Alpha Lake Park, Meadow Park, Millar's Pond, Brio, Blackcomb Benchlands, White Gold, and Emerald Park.

INDOOR PURSUITS

For **performing arts,** from classical and choral to folk and blues, check out the **Maurice Young Millennium Place (My Place)** (① **604/935-8414;** www.myplacewhistler.org).

A MUSEUM To learn more about Whistler, visit the **Whistler Museum & Archives Society,** 4329 Main St., off Northlands Boulevard (① **604/932-2019;** www.whistlermuseum.com). The museum exhibits reveal the life and culture of the First Nations tribes that have lived in the lush Whistler and Pemberton valleys for thousands of years. There are also re-creations of the village's early settlement by British immigrants during the late 1800s and early 1900s. The museum is open daily from 10am to 4pm in July and August, and Thursday through Sunday 10am to 4pm

September through June (Thurs until 8pm year-round). Admission is C$5 (US$4/
£2.25) for adults, C$4 (US$3.40/£1.80) for seniors and students, C$3 (US$2.50/
£1.35) for children 7 to 18, and free for children 6 and under.

SHOPPING   The **Whistler Marketplace** (in the center of Whistler Village) and the
area surrounding the **Blackcomb Mountain lift** brim with clothing, jewelry, crafts,
specialty, and equipment shops that are generally open daily from 10am to 6pm.
Horstman Trading Company (② 604/938-7725), next to The Fairmont Chateau
Whistler, carries casual wear, from swimwear and footwear to polar-fleece vests and
nylon jacket shells. **Escape Route** (② 604/938-3228), at Whistler Marketplace and
Crystal Lodge, has a great line of outdoor clothing and equipment.

For some of the finer things in life, visit the **Whistler Village Art Gallery** (② 604/
938-3001; www.whistlerart.com) and **Adele Campbell Gallery** (② 604/938-0887;
www.adelecampbell.com). Their collections include fine art, sculpture, and glass. **Keir
Fine Jewelry,** Village Gate House (② 604/932-2944; www.keirfinejewellery.com),
sells Italian gold, Swiss watches, and handmade Canadian jewelry. For a list and map
of all the galleries in town, as well as information on events, contact the **Whistler
Community Arts Council** (② 604/935-8419; www.whistlerartscouncil.com).

SPAS   The **Taman Sari Royal Heritage Spa** (② 888/913-8811; www.tamansarispa.
com), one of the newest in town, offers an unusual array of Javanese and European
spa treatments. The Westin's **Avello** (② 877/935-3444; www.whistlerspa.com) has a
variety of signature treatments, including hot rock, Chinese, and Satago massage. The
Spa at Chateau Whistler Resort (② 604/938-2086) provides massage therapy, skin
care, and body wraps.

Whistler Body Wrap, 210 St. Andrews House (② 604/932-4710; www.whistler
bodywrap.com), next to the Keg in the Village, can nurture you with an array of services, such as shiatsu massage, facials, pedicures or manicures, and aromatherapy. If
something didn't quite go right on the slopes or on the trails, **Whistler Physiother-
apy** specializes in sports therapy. There are two locations: 339-4370 Lorimer Rd., at
Marketplace (② 604/932-4001; www.whistlerphysio.com), and 202-2011 Innsbruck
Dr., next to Boston Pizza in Creekside (② 604/938-9001).

ESPECIALLY FOR KIDS

Near the base of the mountains, Whistler Village and the Upper Village sponsor daily
activities for kids of all ages. Mountainbike races, an in-line skating park, trapeze,
trampoline, and wall-climbing lessons, summer skiing, snowboarding, snowshoeing,
bungee jumping, and a first-run multiplex movie theater are just a few of the choices.

Based at Blackcomb Mountain, the **Dave Murray Summer Ski and Snowboard
Camp** (② 604/932-5765; www.skiandsnowboard.com) is North America's longest-
running summer ski camp. Junior programs cost C$2,095 (US$1,780/£943) for 8
days, or C$1,095 (US$931/£492) for a 5-day package; both available from mid-June
to mid-July. Packages include food, lodging (day-camp packages without the hotel are
also available), lift passes, and tennis, trapeze, and mountainbiking options. Days are
spent skiing, boarding, or free-riding on the excellent-terrain parks and half-pipes.
This camp accommodates a range of abilities from beginners to champion-level skiers
and riders; the age group is 10 to 18 years. The comprehensive instruction and adult
supervision at this activity-oriented camp are excellent.

WHISTLER AFTER DARK

For a town of just 10,000, Whistler has a pretty good nightlife scene. Of course, it *is* considered the preeminent ski resort in North America, and attracts millions of year-round visitors. Bands touring through Vancouver regularly make the trip up the Sea-to-Sky Highway; some even make Whistler their Canadian debut. Concert listings can be found in *Pique,* a free local paper available at cafes and food stores.

Tommy Africa's (© 604/932-6090; www.tommyafricas.com), beneath the Pharmasave at the entrance to the Main Village, and the dark and cavernous **Maxx Fish** (© 604/932-1904; www.maxxfish.moonfruit.com), in the Village Square below the Amsterdam Cafe, cater to the 18- to-22-year-old crowd: lots of beat and not much light. The crowd at **Garfinkel's** (© 604/932-2323; www.garfswhistler.com), at the entrance to Village North, is similar, though the cutoff age can reach as high as 27. The **Boot Pub** (© 604/932-3338), on Nancy Green Drive, just off Highway 99, advertises itself as Whistler's living room and more than lives up to its billing: Throngs of young Australian ski-lift operators cram the space, bouncing to the band or DJ and spilling draft beer all over the floor. **Buffalo Bills** (© 604/932-6613; www.buffalo bills.ca), across from the Whistler Gondola, and the **Savage Beagle** (© 604/938-3337), in the Village Square, cater to the 30-something crowd. Bills is bigger, with a pool table, video ski machine, a small dance floor, and music straight from the 1980s. The Beagle has a fabulous selection of beer and bar drinks, with a pub upstairs and a house-oriented dance floor below.

If all you want to do is savor a beer and swap ski stories, try the **Whistler Brew-House** (© 604/905-2739; www.markjamesgroup.com) in the Upper Village, or the fun and very Irish **Dubh Linn Gate Irish Lounge/Pub** (© 604/905-4047) in the Pan Pacific Whistler Mountainside hotel (p. 268).

2 Ucluelet, Tofino & Pacific Rim National Park Reserve of Canada (Long Beach Section) ✦✦✦

Ucluelet is 292km (181 miles) NE of Victoria; Tofino is 316km (196 miles) NE of Victoria.

The west coast of Vancouver Island is a magnificent area of old-growth forests, stunning fjords, rocky coastline, and long sandy beaches. And though **Pacific Rim National Park Reserve of Canada** ✦✦✦ was established in 1971 as Canada's first marine park, it wasn't until 1991 that it really became significant in the consciousness of people outside the area. That was when thousands of environmentalists from across the province and around the world gathered to protest and blockade the clear-cutting of old-growth forests on Meares Island in Clayoquot Sound. When footage of the protests ran on the evening news, people who saw the unspoiled beauty of this coastal landscape for the first time were moved to come experience it firsthand. Tourism in the area has never looked back, and because of its importance as a pristine marine environment, Clayoquot Sound was designated a UNESCO Marine Biosphere Reserve in 2000.

The three main areas to visit are **Ucluelet, Tofino,** and the **Long Beach section** of Pacific Rim National Park. Tofino and Ucluelet are small towns on the northern and southern edges of a peninsula about halfway up the western shore of Vancouver Island, with the Long Beach section of the park between them. From Victoria, the trip by car—along a highway considered one of the top three scenic drives in Canada—takes about 4½ hours and includes such highlights as massive old-growth trees (Cathedral

Grove), an enormous mountain lake (Kennedy Lake), snow-covered peaks, and brief stretches of oceanside highway.

The park receives about one million visitors a year, most of them June through August. In those high-season months, traffic between Ucluelet and Tofino becomes an all-day jam, beaches are crammed with international vacationers, and every restaurant, hotel room, and B&B is full. Thick fog that doesn't burn off until midafternoon is typical in August. As locals will tell you, September and October are actually the best times to visit, and coming out for winter storm-watching is increasingly popular. This is a coastal rainforest area, so be prepared for rain no matter which season you visit.

The town of **Ucluelet** (pronounced you-*clue*-let, meaning "safe harbor" in the local Nuu-chah-nulth dialect) sits on the southern end of the peninsula, on the edge of Barkley Sound. It's the first town you come to if you're driving across the island from Victoria. Back when fishing was the dominant local industry, Ucluelet was the primary town on the peninsula. When tourism began to take over, Tofino became more popular (it's better developed). Ucluelet, gorgeously situated, only has about 2,100 permanent year-round residents; in the summer, however, its population jumps tenfold. Like Tofino, it's a small coastal town with mostly new houses and businesses, so don't expect a quaint old fishing village.

At the far northern tip of the peninsula, about a 25-minute drive from Ucluelet, **Tofino** (pop. 1,800) sits on beautiful Clayoquot Sound, and is the center of the West Coast's growing ecotourism business. Hikers and beachcombers come to Tofino simply for the scenery—few landscapes in the Pacific Northwest are more majestically diverse, with the Island Mountains rising to the east of island-studded Clayoquot (pronounced *clay*-oh-quot) Sound, and the thundering-surf beaches of the Pacific just to the west. The town, with its ecotour and fishing outfitters, a growing number of restaurants, and new beachfront lodges, provides all the ingredients necessary for a memorable getaway. Meares Island, where you can walk among giant old-growth trees, is a 10-minute boat ride from Tofino.

Long Beach, part of the Pacific Rim National Park group, stretches between Tofino and Ucluelet. The beach is more than 30km (19 miles) long, broken here and there by rocky headlands and bordered by groves of cedar and Sitka spruce. The rocky, fish-rich coastline is popular with countless species of birds and marine life—bald eagles routinely nest in the vicinity, and between March and May as many as 20,000 Pacific gray whales pass the shore as they migrate north to their summer feeding grounds in the Arctic Circle. Tofino has also become a mecca for surfers and surf-kayakers.

ESSENTIALS
To get to Vancouver Island, see "Getting to Victoria," p. 29.

No Water in the Rainforest
The town of Tofino, cashing in on its status as a resort mecca, is in the midst of a building boom that is bringing more and more people to this part of the island. Can the town's infrastructure handle ever greater numbers of tourists and year-round residents? That was the question in August 2006 when, at the height of the summer tourist season, Tofino was suddenly faced with a water shortage, and resorts had to severely curtail their water usage. It was a sad and ironic dilemma for a coastal town that sits in a temperate rainforest.

Pacific Rim National Park Reserve

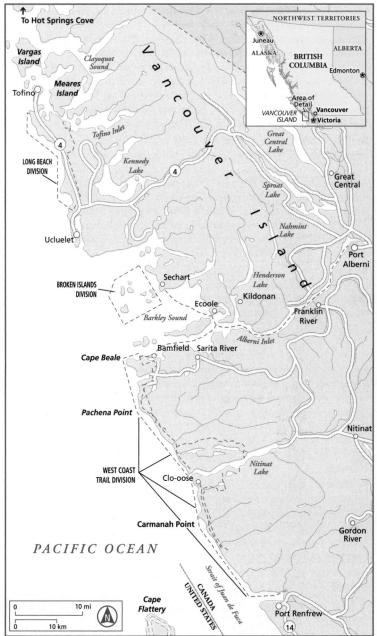

To Hot Springs Cove

NORTHWEST TERRITORIES

Juneau

ALASKA

BRITISH COLUMBIA

ALBERTA

Edmonton

Area of Detail

VANCOUVER ISLAND

Vancouver

Victoria

Vargas Island

Clayoquot Sound

Vancouver Island

Meares Island

Tofino

Tofino Inlet

4

LONG BEACH DIVISION

Kennedy Lake

4

Great Central Lake

Sproat Lake

Great Central

Ucluelet

Nahmint Lake

Port Alberni

BROKEN ISLANDS DIVISION

Sechart

Henderson Lake

Kildonan

Ecoole

Barkley Sound

Franklin River

Bamfield   Sarita River

Alberni Inlet

Cape Beale

Pachena Point

Nitinat

WEST COAST TRAIL DIVISION

Clo-oose

Nitinat Lake

Carmanah Point

Gordon River

PACIFIC OCEAN

Cape Flattery

Strait of Juan de Fuca

CANADA
UNITED STATES

Port Renfrew

14

| 0 | 10 mi |
| 0 | 10 km |

N

GETTING THERE   By Boat   A 4½-hour ride aboard the Alberni Marine Transportation passenger ferry **MV *Lady Rose*** ✿✿ (✆ **250/723-8313;** www.ladyrose marine.com) takes you from Port Alberni through Alberni Inlet to Ucluelet, making brief stops along the way to deliver mail and packages to solitary cabin dwellers along the coast and to let off or pick up kayakers bound for the Broken Islands Group. This is a wonderful way to see portions of Vancouver Island aboard a heritage vessel; the round-trip takes 11 hours. The *Lady Rose* departs at 8am Monday through Friday from June to late September (Tues, Thurs, and Sat the rest of the year) from Alberni Harbour Quay's Angle Street. The round-trip fare to Ucluelet is C$64 (US$54/£29).

By Bus   Tofino Bus (✆ **866/986-3466** or 250/725-2871; www.tofinobus.com) operates regular daily bus service between Victoria, Nanaimo, Port Alberni, and Tofino/ Ucluelet. The 5½-hour trip, departing Victoria at 7:30am daily and arriving in Tofino at 1:55pm, costs C$60 (US$51/£27) one-way. From mid-March to mid-September, there are additional departures from Victoria (including from Victoria Airport). More expensive but quicker (5 hr.) is **Pacific Rim Navigators** (✆ **800/697-1114** or 250/ 954-8702; www.pacificrimnavigators.ca), which does pickups in Victoria, Nanaimo, or Comox, and then drops you off at your door in Tofino/Ucluelet. Transportation is in a luxury SUV and costs C$85 (US$72/£38) per hour for up to six people.

By Car   Once you are on Vancouver Island, the same scenic, easy-to-follow route takes you to Ucluelet, Long Beach, and Tofino. Considered one of the top scenic drives in Canada, the paved route, mostly two lanes, gets twisty toward the end, and takes about 4 to 4½ hours from Victoria. From Victoria, take Highway 1 north along the Saanich Peninsula to Nanaimo, where you take the Island Highway (Hwy. 19) north for 52km (32 miles). Just beyond the town of Parksville, turn west on Highway 4, which leads past **Cathedral Grove** ✿✿★—worth a stop to see the old-growth inland forest—to the midisland town of Port Alberni (about 38km/24 miles west). Highway 4 continues west, past giant Kennedy Lake, and reaches the Pacific Ocean just north of Ucluelet (103km/64 miles west of Port Alberni). Highway 4, also called Pacific Rim Highway, then turns north, passing through the Long Beach section of Pacific Rim National Park, to Tofino (34km/21 miles north of Ucluelet). If you arrive on Vancouver Island by ferry, you can rent a car on Vancouver Island from **Budget** (✆ **888/ 368-7368**), which offers customer pickup at all the ferry terminals in Victoria and Nanaimo.

By Plane   Tofino's airport is tiny (only small planes can land) and the airline companies serving it change frequently. At press time, **Orca Airways** (✆ **888/359-6722;** www.flyorcaair.com) was the only company providing daily service between Vancouver and Tofino. The flight takes 55 minutes. You can fly between Vancouver and Nanaimo Airport on **Air Canada** (✆ **888/247-2262;** www.aircanada.com).

VISITOR INFORMATION   The **Pacific Rim Visitor Centre** (✆ **250/726-4600;** www.pacificrimvisitor.ca), at the junction of Highway 4 and Ucluelet, serves as a general information gateway for Ucluelet, Tofino, Port Alberni, and Banfield. Pick up information on area accommodations and attractions, and buy a **day-use park pass** (C$7/US$6/£3.15 adults, C$6/US$5/£2.70 seniors, C$3.50/US$3/£1.60 youth 6–16, C$18/US$15/£8 family/group per day), which you'll need if you want to visit the beaches and park at any of Pacific Rim's official parking lots (passes can also be purchased with credit cards only from machines at the parking lots). The Visitor Centre is open daily 10am to 5pm (9am–7pm July–Aug; 10am–4pm Oct–Mar).

The **Ucluelet Visitor Info Centre** (℃ **250/726-4600;** www.uclueletinfo.com), in town on Main Street, is open daily June through September from 9am to 5pm. The **Tofino Visitor Info Centre** (℃ **250/725-3414;** www.tofinobc.org), 380 Campbell St. in Tofino, is open the same hours. For information on the park itself, stop in at the **Long Beach Unit of Pacific Rim National Park Reserve of Canada** (℃ **250/726-4701**), north of Ucluelet (take the Wickaninnish Interpretive Centre exit from Hwy. 4). This park office, with a spectacular location above Wickaninnish Beach, is home to the **Wickaninnish Interpretive Centre** and a scenically stunning restaurant (see "Where to Dine," under "Tofino," below). The center is open daily from mid-March through mid-October from 10am to 6pm. A good all-purpose website is **www. gotofino.com**.

SPECIAL EVENTS   About 20,000 whales migrate past this section of Vancouver Island annually. During the third and last week of March, the **Pacific Rim Whale Festival** (℃ **250/726-4641** or 250/726-7742; www.pacificrimwhalefestival.org) is held in Tofino and Ucluelet. The **Edge to Edge Marathon** in June is a distance run between Tofino and Ucluelet through Pacific Rim National Park; contact **Ucluelet Chamber of Commerce** for details (℃ **250/726-4641;** www.uclueletinfo.com).

UCLUELET

Ucluelet enjoys a beautiful location on a sheltered harbor. You can choose from a number of fine B&Bs and cabin accommodations, but Ucluelet has yet to develop the same range of restaurants and activities as Tofino. If you want to stay in a seaside resort or lodge, head for Tofino.

WHERE TO STAY

If you're backpacking and want budget hostel accommodations or a place to pitch a tent, try **Ucluelet Oceanfront Hostel,** 2081 Peninsula Road, Ucluelet, B.C. V0R 3A0 (℃ **888/434-6060** or 250/726-7416; www.cnnbackpackers.com). The hostel, on its own private beach, provides free linen, use of a kitchen and lounge, Internet, and kayak and bike rentals. Rates are C$65 (US$55/£24) for a private room, C$25 (US$21/£11) for a single dorm bed. Campers seeking a family-friendly campground close to the park can reserve a spot at **Ucluelet Campground** (℃ **250/726-4355;** www.uclueletcampground.com), located at the edge of the village. The 125 campsites range from no service to full service; prices range from C$20 to C$38 (US$17–US$32/£9–£17).

Pacific Rim Motel *Kids*   Ucluelet has more upscale places to stay, but if you're looking for a clean, simple, inexpensive motel room, this is a good place to know about. The motel overlooks the harbor and offers one- and two-bedroom units, some with kitchenettes, a couple with full kitchens. The rooms are plain, the property well-maintained and well run, and you're close to the wild Pacific Trail. They can help you arrange whale-watching or fishing tours.

1755 Peninsula Rd., Ucluelet, B.C. V0R 3A0. ℃ **800/810-0031.** www.pacificrimmotel.com. 55 units. C$85–C$150 (US$72–US$127/£38–£67) double. MC, V.

WHERE TO DINE

Matterson Teahouse and Garden   ECLECTIC/PACIFIC NORTHWEST Located on Ucluelet's main street, this is a good spot for lunch; sandwiches, salads, and a great seafood chowder are served in the two front rooms of a small frame house.

On a nice summer day, you have the option of sitting on the shady porch or the sunny back deck. The Teahouse also serves dinner, with seafood always on the menu along with other eclectic offerings.

1682 Peninsula Rd. ⓒ 250/725-2200. Reservations recommended for dinner in summer. Soup and sandwiches C$5–C$8 (US$4–US$7/£2.25–£3.60); lunch and dinner C$17–C$25 (US$14–US$21/£8–£11). MC, V. Daily 7:30am–8pm; winter weekends 9am–8pm.

ACTIVITIES

Fishing is still the big outdoor activity in Ucluelet, and salmon is still the most sought-after catch. Charter companies that can take you out include **Island West Resort** (ⓒ **250/726-1515;** www.islandwestresort.com), **Castaway Charters** (ⓒ **250/720-7970;** www.castawaycharter.com), and **Long Beach Charters** (ⓒ **877/726-2878** or 250/726-3474; www.longbeachcharters.com).

The recently completed **Wild Pacific Trail** ✸✸✸ skirts the rugged coastline with fabulous views of the Pacific and the Broken Islands; bald eagles nest along parts of the trail. For an easy and fabulously **scenic walk,** take the 2.7km (1.7-mile) stretch from Peninsula Road in Ucluelet to the lighthouse. On this 30- to 45-minute hike along a gravel-paved trail, the path winds as close as possible to the ocean's edge, passing surge channels and huge rock formations. Check out **www.wildpacifictrail.com** for more information on walks and access points.

For **kayaking,** contact **Majestic Ocean Kayaking** (ⓒ **800/889-7644;** www. oceankayaking.com) about their half-day harbor trips, full-day paddles to Barkley Sound or the Broken Islands, and weeklong adventures in Clayoquot Sound.

Long Beach Nature Tours ✸✸ (ⓒ **250/726-7099;** www.oceansedge.bc.ca), run by retired Pacific Rim Park chief naturalist Bill McIntyre, does **guided beach, rainforest, and storm walks** that explain the ecology and wildlife of the area.

TOFINO

The center of the environmental protest against industrial logging—and the center of the ecotourism business ever since—**Tofino** was, and to some extent remains, a schizophrenic kind of town. Until very recently, about half of the town was composed of ecotourism outfitters, nature lovers, and activists, while the other half was loggers and fishermen. Conflict was common in the early years, but gradually the two sides learned how to get along—more important than ever, now that a million visitors a year come to experience the area's natural wonders. Recently, the balance has definitely swung in favor of the ecopreservationists, who seek to manage growth and preserve the diverse habitats in a sustainable manner. But the town faces big pressures now that it's been "discovered" and has become such a popular destination.

WHERE TO STAY

Tofino sits at the tip of Long Beach peninsula. One paved road—Highway 4—runs along the spine of the peninsula from Ucluelet up through Pacific Rim National Park to Tofino. The big resort hotels are all located on their own private roads, each of which has a name and connects to Highway 4. Big signs on Highway 4 advise drivers of the location of these private access roads, which will help you find your way to your hotel.

Brimar Bed and Breakfast ✸   The location, right on Chesterman Beach, is what makes this place special. From your room, you can step out onto the sand and start exploring the wild Pacific. All three nonsmoking rooms have antique furnishings and lots of natural light. The upstairs Loft room features a queen-size bed, a bathroom with claw-foot tub and separate shower, and a bay window with a seat—and view of the ocean. The small Moonrise room has a queen-size sleigh bed and its own private bathroom across the hall. The larger, brighter Sunset room has a king-size bed and bathroom with shower. Breakfast and common areas look out over the ocean.

1375 Thornberg Crescent, Tofino, B.C. V0R 2Z0. ✆ **800/714-9373** or 250/725-3410. Fax 250/725-3410. www.brimarbb. com. 3 units. C$110–C$200 (US$93–US$170/£49–£90) double. Rates include breakfast. AE, MC, V. Stay on Hwy. 4 going north through Pacific Rim National Park until you pass the turnoff for the Pacific Sands Resort; take the next left on Chesterman Beach Rd., and proceed to the fork in the road. Take Thornburg Crescent (the left fork), and follow it to the end. No pets. No children under 12. *In room:* TV, no phone.

The Inn at Tough City
Right in town, overlooking Clayoquot Sound, this is Tofino's nicest and quirkiest small inn. Built in 1996 from salvaged and recycled material, it's filled with antiques, stained glass, and bric-a-brac. Several of the spacious rooms feature soaker tubs, fireplaces, or both. Rooms at the back enjoy views over the Sound and Tofino harbor. Three rooms on the main floor are wheelchair accessible. The sushi restaurant on the Inn's main floor is open for dinner only.

350 Main St., P.O. Box 8, Tofino, B.C. V0R 2Z0. ✆ **877/725-2021** or 250/725-2021. Fax 250/725-2088. www.tough city.com. 8 units. C$99–C$229 (US$84–US$195/£46–£103) double. MC, V. Drive into town and you'll see it on your right—it's impossible to miss. **Amenities:** Restaurant; laundry service; nonsmoking rooms; 3 rooms for those w/limited mobility. *In room:* TV.

Long Beach Lodge Resort ★★
Opened in 2003, this luxurious beachfront resort perched on the edge of Cox Bay, 3.2km (2 miles) south of Tofino, was built to resemble a grand West Coast–style home. The lodge has a cedar board-and-shingle exterior and a central great room (with bar and restaurant) with a massive granite fireplace and stunning ocean views. The guest rooms are luxuriously comfortable, some with fireplaces, balconies, and soaker tubs; all have marvelous beds and fine linens. Each of the 20 two-bedroom cottages, located in the forest and without ocean views, features a ground-floor master bedroom and bathroom with soaker tub and separate shower, a sitting area with gas fireplace, dining area, fully equipped kitchen, private hot tub, and a second bedroom and bathroom upstairs. The dining room serves fresh regional cuisine with a hint of Asian influence.

1441 Pacific Rim Hwy., P.O. Box 897, Tofino, B.C. V0R 2Z0. ✆ **877/844-7873** or 250/725-2442. Fax 250/725-2402. www.longbeachlodgeresort.com. 61 units. C$289–C$399 (US$246–US$339/£130–£180) double; C$569 (US$484/£256) suite; C$299–C$469 (US$254–US$399/£134–£211) cabin. Rates include continental breakfast. AE, DC, MC, V. At the Pacific Rim Hwy. junction, turn right (north), and travel through Pacific Rim National Park; watch for lodge sign on the left after you exit the park. **Amenities:** Restaurant; lounge. *In room:* TV, DVD/CD player, high-speed Internet, fridge, coffeemaker, hair dryer, iron, fireplace (in some rooms), Jacuzzi (in some rooms).

Middle Beach Lodge ★★ (Kids)
This beautiful resort complex is on a headland overlooking the Pacific, and features Middle Beach Lodge at the Beach, for adult guests only, and Middle Beach Lodge at the Headlands, a lodge and cabins suitable for families. The centerpiece of the first and smaller of the lodges is a large but rustically cozy common room with big windows that look out over crashing waves. Accommodations here are simple lodge rooms (26 of them) with private bathrooms and balconies, and no phone or TV. The 38 rooms and suites in the second lodge have more of the standard amenities, and nearby are 19 cabins designed for one to six people, with decks, kitchenettes, and wood-burning fireplaces, some with soaker tubs or outside Jacuzzis. This is a very comfortable, unpretentious place with a good restaurant, lots of nooks and crannies, and wonderful views of the ocean and beaches.

P.O. Box 100, Tofino, B.C. V0R 2Z0. ☎ 866/725-2900 or 250/725-2900. Fax 250/725-2901. www.middlebeach.com. 64 units, 19 cabins. Lodge rooms C$110–C$350 (US$93–US$257/£50–£158) double; C$300–C$450 (US$255–US$382/£135–£202) cabin. Rates include continental breakfast. AE, MC, V. **Amenities:** Exercise room; laundry service. *In room:* TV/VCR, kitchenette, coffeemaker, no phone/TV in Middle Beach Lodge at the Beach rooms.

Whalers on the Point Guesthouse *(Kids)*   Located at the foot of Main Street in "downtown" Tofino, right beside Clayoquot Sound, this 1990s building is part of the Hosteling International network of backpackers' hostels. It's clean and inexpensive, and everything in Tofino is within walking distance. As in other HI properties, you can rent a shared dorm room (four to six beds in a room), a private double room, or a larger family room. Rooms H to K, and N to Q are the best—all have views of Clayoquot Sound. There's an outdoor patio with a barbecue and a steam sauna.

81 West St., P.O. Box 296, Tofino, B.C. V0R 2Z0. ☎ 250/725-3443. Fax 250/725-3463. www.tofinohostel.com. 3 units. C$22–C$27 (US$19–US$23/£10–£12) dorm room; C$50–C$85 (US$42–US$72/£22–£38) double. Nonmembers pay slightly higher rates. MC, V. At the foot of Main St. in downtown Tofino. **Amenities:** Kitchen, TV/game room, coin-op laundry, sauna. *In room:* No phone.

The Wickaninnish Inn *(★★★)*   A five-star Relais & Château property, the Wickaninnish sets the standard for all high-end accommodations in the area; it's the most beautifully designed and built of all the Long Beach resorts, and the place to stay if you're looking for absolutely the best of everything. From the two buildings, no matter which room you book, you'll wake to a magnificent view of the untamed Pacific. The inn sits on a rocky promontory, surrounded by an old-growth spruce and cedar rainforest and the sands of Chesterman Beach. Don't be surprised if a bald eagle flies past your window. All rooms in the original cedar, stone, and glass lodge feature handcrafted furniture, richly printed textiles, and local artwork, as well as a fireplace, soaker tub, and private balcony. The Wic's new wing features deluxe rooms or suites with more space, more light, and a higher price. The superfriendly staff can arrange ecotours to Meares Island or Hot Springs Cove, whale-watching, golfing, fishing, and diving packages. On-site is also an Aveda spa. **The Pointe Restaurant** (p. 289) and On-the-Rocks Bar serve three meals daily with an oceanfront view; this is the most accomplished restaurant in the area, and certainly the most beautiful.

Osprey Lane at Chesterman Beach, P.O. Box 250, Tofino, B.C. V0R 2Z0. ☎ 800/333-4604 or 250/725-3100. Fax 250/725-3110. www.wickinn.com. 75 units. C$300–C$660 (US$255–US$561/£135–£306) double. AE, DC, MC, V. Drive 5km (3 miles) south of Tofino toward Chesterman Beach to Osprey Lane. **Amenities:** Restaurant; bar; spa; concierge; in-room massage; babysitting; rooms for those w/limited mobility. *In room:* TV, high-speed Internet, minibar, raingear, coffeemaker, hair dryer, iron.

CAMPGROUNDS

The 94 campsites on the bluff at **Green Point** *(★★)* are maintained by Pacific Rim National Park. Reservations are required in high season as the grounds are full every day in July and August, and the average wait for a site is 1 to 2 days. To make a reservation, call ☎ **877/RESERVE,** or go online at **www.pccamping.ca.** The cost is C$21 (US$18/£9) per night. You're rewarded with a magnificent ocean view, pit toilets, fire pits, pumped well water, and free firewood, but no showers or hookups. The campground is closed October through February.

   Bella Pacifica Resort & Campground, P.O. Box 413, Tofino, B.C. V0R 2Z0, 3km (1¾ miles) south of Tofino on the Pacific Rim Highway (☎ **250/725-3400;** www.bellapacifica.com), is privately owned. March through November, it has 165 campsites from which you can walk to Mackenzie Beach or take the resort's private nature trails to Templar Beach. Flush toilets, hot showers, water, laundry, ice, fire pits, firewood, and full and partial hookups are available. Rates are C$21 to C$46 (US$18–US$39/£9–£18) per two-person campsite. Reserve at least a month in advance for a summer weekend.

WHERE TO DINE

Tofino is gaining a reputation for fine dining, with new restaurants opening every year, but it's also a laid-back place where you can grab a bite with the locals. If you're looking for a cup of coffee and a snack (or want to check your e-mail), it's hard to beat **Tuff Beans,** 151 4th St. (© 250/725-4246), located at the entrance to town. Open daily from 7am to 9pm, the cafe also serves breakfast and lunch, with main courses running C$7 to C$9 (US$6–US$8/£3.15–£4). You can rent two computers with high-speed Internet access for a nominal fee. The **Common Loaf Bakeshop,** 180 1st St. (© 250/725-3915), open 8am to 9pm, is locally famous as a gathering place for the community. Located at the "far" end of town, the Loaf does baked goods really well and serves a healthy lunch and dinner for C$4 to C$8 (US$3.40–US$7/£1.80–£3.60). For the best handmade chocolates and gelato on the west coast, visit **Chocolate Tofino,** 1180 Pacific Rim Hwy. (© 250/725-2526; www.chocolatetofino.com), about 3.3km (2 miles) south of town at the Live to Surf location next to Groovy Movies.

The Pointe Restaurant ★★★ PACIFIC NORTHWEST   Perched on the water's edge in The Wickaninnish Inn at Chesterman Beach, The Pointe offers a memorable dining experience and a 280-degree view of the roaring Pacific. The Relais & Château chef deliciously interprets Pacific Northwest cuisine with an array of top West Coast ingredients, including Dungeness crab, lamb, and rabbit. Order the daily tasting menu, a progression of four courses priced at C$75 (US$64/£34), C$120 (US$102/£54) with wine pairings. The menu changes daily, but a recent offering included potato and watercress velouté with butter-poached side stripe prawn, and warm peach cake and ice cream. The wine list is drawn from the best B.C. has to offer.

In The Wickaninnish Inn (p. 288), Osprey Lane at Chesterman Beach. © 250/725-3100. Reservations required. Main courses C$32–C$40 (US$27–US$34/£14–£18). MC, V. Daily 8am–2:30pm, 2–5pm (snacks), and 5–9:30pm.

The RainCoast Cafe ★ FUSION/PACIFIC NORTHWEST   This tiny restaurant has developed a reputation for some of the best—and best-value—meals in town. The decor is calm and simple, the atmosphere cozy and casually romantic, and the food prepared with an Asian twist. Mainstays include a signature dish of organic Muscovy duck breast with blackberry sauce, and pad thai noodles with shrimp. The menu has fresh daily specials and vegetarian choices; a tapas menu is served during the occasional live music night.

120 4th St. © 250/725-2215. Main courses C$17–C$32 (US$14–US$27/£8–£12). AE, MC, V. Reservations recommended. Daily 5:30–10pm (9pm in winter).

The Schooner ★★ SEAFOOD/PACIFIC NORTHWEST   Established in 1949, The Schooner is the most venerable of Tofino restaurants and also one of the best for fresh seafood. The restaurant has two dining areas, one on the second floor with big windows looking out toward Clayoquot Sound. If you love fresh oysters, start with the "six pack," fresh shucked and served over ice with Tabasco and lemon. The classic signature dish here, served for more than 3 decades, is the Mates Plate, which includes fresh seafood from Clayoquot Sound (charbroiled salmon and halibut, grilled oysters, and garlic sautéed prawns and scallops). Lamb, chicken, and pasta dishes are also available, but I'd stick with the seafood. A good wine list and wonderful desserts complement the menu.

331 Campbell St. © **250/725-3444**. Main courses C$19–C$39 (US$16–US$33/£9–£18). AE, MC, V. Reservations recommended for dinner. Mon–Sat 9–11:30am, noon–3pm, and 5–9pm; Sun 9am–12:30pm, 1–3pm, and 5–9pm.

Sobo 🌀 ECLECTIC PACIFIC NORTHWEST   Located in Tofino Botanical Gardens, Sobo started life as a food truck and became so popular that it expanded into a sit-down restaurant. The truck is still there, and once you taste the famous fish tacos made with wild salmon and halibut topped with fresh-fruit salsa, you'll know why locals line up here every day. Sobo is short for "sophisticated bohemian," which is how chef Lisa Ahier describes her cooking: She's interested in street food and tastes from all over the world. You can enjoy your meal at picnic tables next to the truck or take it into the restaurant, where dinner is served 5 nights a week. The dinner menu includes seafood tapas, soups, salads, and complete meals with offerings such as pan-roasted pancetta-and-sage-crusted pork loin and anise-and-garlic-roasted chicken.

1184 Pacific Rim Hwy. (Tofino Botanical Gardens turnoff). © **250/725-4265**. www.sobo.ca. Truck lunch and snacks C$5–C$8 (US$4.25–US$7/£2.25–£3.60); restaurant main courses C$20–C$26 (US$17–US$22/£9–£12). MC, V. Truck daily summer 11am–5pm; restaurant dinner 5–9pm. Closed Mon in winter, Jan, and last 2 weeks of Dec.

Wickaninnish Restaurant PACIFIC NORTHWEST   This restaurant, inside the Wickaninnish Interpretive Centre, is notable for the incredible ocean views from its wall of glass windows. It's a good lunch spot, with lots of fresh seafood on the menu, plus soups, salads, sandwiches, and fresh daily specials. Main courses include roasted chicken and baked salmon.

In the Wickaninnish Interpretive Centre (p. 285), north of Ucluelet off Hwy. 4 (take Wickaninnish Centre exit). © **250/726-7706**. Reservations recommended in summer. Main courses C$18–C$29 (US$15–US$25/£8–£13). MC, V. Daily mid-Mar to Oct 11am–9pm (until 10pm in summer).

WHAT TO SEE & DO

For a good, overall introduction to the unique ecology of this area, stop by the **Raincoast Interpretive Center,** 451 Main St. (© **250/725-2560;** www.tofinores.com). Open daily in summer from noon to 5pm, this center features exhibits on local flora, fauna, and history, and often has guest speakers and slide shows relating to the area; off-season hours vary, so call ahead. **Wickaninnish Interpretive Center,** described under "Visitor Information," earlier in this chapter, has exhibits on coastal life and stunning views over Wickaninnish Beach.

BIRDING   The Tofino/Ucluelet area is directly in the path of the Pacific Flyway, and attracts tens of thousands of birds and wildfowl; it's also home to bald eagles. The area celebrates its rich birdlife with the annual **Flying Geese & Shorebird Festival** every April and May. During those months, large flocks of migrating birds fill the skies and estuaries along Barkley Sound and Clayoquot Sound. Avid aviophiles should contact **Just Birding** (© **250/725-8018;** www.justbirding.com), run by keen birders who can show you the best bird spots on shore (very early in the morning) or on the open ocean. **Bird & Breakfast,** P.O. Box 990, Tofino, B.C. V0R 2Z0 (© **250/725-2570**), is a newly opened (June 2007) bed-and-breakfast run in conjunction with Just Birding. Perfect for birders, it's located adjacent to the walking trail in the Tofino Mudflat Conservation Area, right in the middle of the second biggest shorebird pit stop this side of North America. April, May, and early June, sees literally thousands of shorebirds of all species fly by in their annual migration.

FIRST NATIONS TOURISM   Clayoquot Sound is the traditional home of the Nuu-chah-nulth peoples, some of whom have recently gone into the cultural and ecotourism business. **Tla-ook Cultural Adventures** ✸✸✸ (📞 **877/942-2663** or 250/725-2656; www.tlaook.com) run three different tours: a 6-hour Cluptl-Chas **(canoeing and salmon barbecue)** Adventure (C$140/US$119/£63), in which participants paddle ancient fishing grounds and clam beds, explore the rainforest, hear traditional stories, and feast on fresh local salmon; a 2½-hour **Inlet Paddle** (C$44/US$37/£20), in which participants paddle the local waters and learn about historical sites and local wildlife; and a 4-hour **Meares Island Tour** ✸✸✸ (C$64/US$54/£29), which explores the ancient rainforest on Meares Island and offers insight into the trees, plants, and animals that make it their home. All tours are led by First Nations guides and often use traditional Nuu-chah-nulth canoes. These are among the most informative and memorable eco-tours on Vancouver Island.

FISHING   Sport fishing for salmon, steelhead, rainbow trout, Dolly Varden char, halibut, cod, and snapper is excellent off the west coast of Vancouver Island. Long Beach is also great for bottom fishing. To fish here, you need a nonresident saltwater or freshwater license. Tackle shops sell licenses, have information on current restrictions, and often carry copies of *B.C. Tidal Waters Sport Fishing Guide* and *B.C. Sport Fishing Regulations Synopsis for Non-Tidal Waters.* Independent anglers should also pick up a copy of the *B.C. Fishing Directory and Atlas.*

   Jay's Clayoquot Ventures, Box 652, 564 Campbell St., Tofino (📞 **888/534-7432** or 250/725-2313; www.tofinofishing.com), offers half- and full-day fishing charters (saltwater and fresh) throughout the Clayoquot Sound area.

GOLF   Year-round golf is available at **Long Beach Golf Course** (📞 **250/725-3332;** www.longbeachgolfcourse.com), one of the most challenging—and scenic—9-hole champion courses in British Columbia; guest rate is C$20 (US$18/£9).

GUIDED NATURE HIKES   Owned and operated by Bill McIntyre, former chief naturalist of Pacific Rim National Park, **Long Beach Nature Tours** ✸✸ (📞 **250/726-7099;** www.oceansedge.bc.ca), offers guided beach walks, storm-watching, land-based whale-watching, and rainforest tours customized to suit your needs. **Raincoast Interpretive Center,** 451 Main St. (📞 **250/725-2560;** www.tofinores.com), offers guided 1-hour and longer rainforest and shore walks for a suggested donation of C$5 (US$4/£2.25).

HIKING   The 11km (6.8-mile) stretch of rocky headlands, sand, and surf along the **Long Beach Headlands Trail** is the most accessible section of the Pacific Rim National Park system, incorporating Long Beach, the West Coast Trail, and the Broken Islands Group. Take the Wickaninnish Interpretive Centre exit on Highway 4.

   In and around **Long Beach,** numerous marked trails .8 to 3.3km-long (.5–2 miles) meander through the thick, temperate rainforest edging the shore. The 3.3km (2-mile) **Gold Mine Trail** near Florencia Bay still has a few artifacts from the days when a gold-mining operation flourished amid the trees. The partially boardwalked **South Beach Trail** (less than 1.6km/1mile) leads through the moss-draped rainforest onto small quiet coves and rocky tidal pools of Lismer Beach and South Beach.

   For a truly memorable walk, take the 3.3m (2-mile) **Big Cedar Trail** ✸✸✸ through the dense rainforest on Meares Island in Clayoquot Sound. The best and most memorable way to experience Meares Island is to canoe over and enjoy a guided walk with Tla-ook Cultural Adventures (see "First Nations Tourism," above). Built in 1993 to protect the old-growth temperate rainforest, the boardwalked trail is maintained by the Tla-o-qui-aht First Nations band, and has a long staircase leading up to the Hanging Garden Tree, the province's fourth-largest western red cedar.

HOT SPRINGS COVE A natural, coastal hot springs about 67km (42 miles) north of Tofino, and accessible only by water makes a wonderful day trip from Tofino. Take a chartered boat, sail, canoe, or kayak up Clayoquot Sound to enjoy swimming in the steaming pools and bracing waterfalls. A number of kayak outfitters and boat charters offer trips to the springs (see "Whale-Watching & Bear-Watching," below).

INDOOR PURSUITS Browse the excellent selection at **Wildside Booksellers,** 320 Main St. (© **250/725-4222**), in the same building as the Tofino Sea Kayaking Company. Or tour some of the 20 **galleries.** The Tourist Info Centre has a pamphlet with a map and contact info for all of them. Standouts include **Sandstone Jewellery and Gifts** ♠, at the corner of Campbell and 2nd streets (© **250/725-4482**), and the **Reflecting Spirit Gallery,** 411 Campbell St. at 3rd Street (© **250/725-2472**).

Just outside of town, the 5-hectare (12-acre) **Tofino Botanical Gardens** ♠, 1084 Pacific Rim Hwy. (© **250/725-1220;** www.tofinobotanicalgardens.com), features a landscaped walking garden with native and exotic plants from rainforests of the world, as well as outdoor sculptures and small pavilions for sitting and contemplating the surroundings; they also sponsor special workshops and naturalist programs. It's open daily from 9am to dusk; admission is C$10 (US$8/£4.50). You can combine a trip to the gardens with a fabulous fish taco from Sobo (see p. 290).

KAYAKING Perhaps the quintessential Clayoquot experience, and certainly one of the most fun, is to slip into a kayak and paddle out into the calm waters of the sound. For beginners, half-day tours to Meares Island (usually with the chance to do a little hiking) are an especially good bet. For rentals, lessons, and tours, try **Tofino Sea Kayaking Company,** 320 Main St. (© **800/863-8664** or 250/725-4222; www.tofino-kayaking. com); **Pacific Kayak,** 606 Campbell St., at **Jamie's Adventure Centre** (© **250/725-3232;** www.jamies.com); or **Remote Passages Sea Kayaking,** 71 Wharf St. (© **800/ 666-9833** or 250/725-3330; www.remotepassages.com). Kayaking packages range from 4-hour paddles around Meares Island to weeklong paddling and camping expeditions. Instruction by experienced guides makes even your first kayaking experience a comfortable, safe, and enjoyable one. Single kayak rental averages around C$40 (US$34/£18) per day.

STORM-WATCHING Watching the winter storms behind big glass windows has become very popular in Tofino. For a slight twist on this, try the outdoor storm-watching tours offered by the **Long Beach Nature Tour Co.** (© **250/726-7099;** www. oceansedge.bc.ca). Owner Bill McIntyre used to be chief naturalist of Pacific Rim National Park, and can explain how storms work and where to stand so you can get close without getting swept away.

SURFING The wild Pacific coast is known as one of the best surfing destinations in Canada, and most surfers work in the tourism industry around Tofino, spending all their free time in the water. To try this exciting and exhilarating sport, call **Live to Surf,** 1180 Pacific Rim Hwy. (© **250/725-4464;** www.livetosurf.com). Lessons start at C$55 (US$47/£25) without gear. Live to Surf also rents boards at C$25 (US$21/£11) and wet suits (don't even think about going in without one) at C$20 (US$17/£9). Another option is **Pacific Surf School,** 444 Campbell St. (© **888/777-9961;** www.pacificsurf school.com); or try the all-female surfing school, **Surf Sister** (© **877/724-7873;** www. surfsister.com).

Moments Two Trips of a Lifetime

These two trips are within striking distance of Vancouver or Victoria and can't be done anywhere else on earth.

SAILING THE GREAT BEAR RAINFOREST 🐾🐾🐾 About halfway up the coast of British Columbia, is the Great Bear Rainforest—an area accessible only by boat. The lush landscape, the largest expanse of intact temperate rainforest left on the planet, encompasses fjords, rivers, streams, and waterfalls; the forest is filled with old growth hemlock and cedar forests, and shelters the rare white spirit bear, as well as grizzlies and wolves. In 2006 a landmark agreement between First Nations tribes, environmentalists, timber companies, and the Canadian government designated the Great Bear Rainforest a protected habitat, thus preserving its unique splendor for ages to come.

With 3 decades of sailing experience in the region, Tom Ellison and his wife, Jen, run **Ocean Light II Adventures** (© **604/328-5339;** www.ocean light2.bc.ca), the only company to offer trips to this magical part of the world on a 21m (70-ft.) sailboat. Skipper Tom Ellison is extremely knowledgeable and takes great delight in exploring the waters and coastline looking for whales, dolphins, and grizzlies. Trips between 6 and 9 days cover just the rainforest, while 14-day trips include stops along the coast, all the way down to Vancouver. Prices range from C$2,800 to C$4,400 (US$1,647–US$3,760/£1,272–£2,000). All include excellent home-cooked meals and comfortable, but not luxurious, accommodations aboard the *Ocean Light.*

HORSE TREKKING THE CHILCOTIN PLATEAU 🐾🐾 The high plateau country of the B.C. interior has some of the most impressive scenery around. Soaring peaks rise above deep valleys, and mountain meadows are alive with flowers that bloom for just a few weeks in high summer. In British Columbia, one guide company is granted exclusive rights to run tours through particular sections of wilderness. The territories are typically 5,000 sq. km (1,931 sq. miles) of high-country wilderness, where you won't meet another horse team. One of the guide-outfitters closest to Vancouver is **Chilcotin Holidays Guest Ranch,** Gun Creek Road, Gold Bridge (© **250/238-2274;** www.chilcotin holidays.com), in the Chilcotin Mountains north of Whistler. Their trips, running from 4 to 13 days and costing C$900 to C$3,500 (US$765–US$2,975/ £405–£1,575), inevitably involve encounters with wildflowers, bighorn sheep, grizzly bears, and wolves.

WHALE-WATCHING & BEAR-WATCHING A number of outfitters conduct tours through this region, which is inhabited by gray whales, bald eagles, black bears, porpoises, orcas, seals, and sea lions. One of the oldest, **Jamie's Whaling Station,** 606 Campbell St. (© **800/667-9913** or 250/725-3919; www.jamies.com), uses a glass-bottomed 20m (64-ft.) power cruiser as well as a fleet of Zodiacs for tours to watch the gray whales March through October. A combined Hot Springs Cove and whale-watching trip is offered year-round. Three-hour bear-watching trips are normally scheduled around low tides when the bruins forage for seafood on the mudflats. Fares (for this and other companies) generally start at around C$79 (US$68/£36) per person; customized trips can run as high as C$200 (US$170/£90) per person for a full day. For an interesting combination, try the Sea-to-Sky tour, a 5-hour trip with a boat ride, a hike through the rainforest to the hot springs, and a return to Tofino by floatplane, at the cost of C$165 (US$140/£74) for adults.

Remote Passages, Meares Landing, 71 Wharf St. (© **800/666-9833** or 250/725-3330; www.remotepassages.com), runs 2½-hour-long whale-watching tours in Clayoquot Sound on Zodiac boats, daily March through November. Fares are C$79 (US$68/£36) for adults and C$59 (US$50/£27) for children under 12. The company also conducts a 7-hour combination whale-watching and hot springs trip at C$110 (US$93/£49) for adults and C$89 (US$76/£40) for children under 12. Reservations are recommended.

Index

See also Accommodations and Restaurant indexes, below.

The Raven and the Bear
(Vancouver), 167
The Raven and the First Men
(Vancouver), 123
The Red Jacket (Victoria), 259
The Red Room (Vancouver),
179
The Reef (Victoria), 259
Remembrance Day, 24
Remote Passages, 294
Reo Rafting (Vancouver), 141
Restaurants. *See also* Restau-
rants Index
Tofino, 289–290
Ucluelet, 285–286
Vancouver, 83–108
best, 13–14, 83–84
Victoria, 209–220
best, 14, 209–210
Restrooms, Vancouver, 62
Revue Stage (Vancouver), 172
Richard's on Richards (Vancou-
ver), 179
Richmond (Vancouver), 114
Richmond Nature Park
(Vancouver), 142
Richmond Night Market
(Vancouver), 162
The Richmond Oval (Vancou-
ver), 2
Robert Burns's birthday, 25
Robinson's Outdoor Store
(Victoria), 238
Robinson's Sporting Goods Ltd.
(Victoria), 237
Robson Square (Vancouver),
23, 126, 149
Robson Street (Vancouver),
109, 146, 159
Rock climbing, Whistler, 278
Rockwood Adventures (Vancou-
ver), 137
Rocky Mountaineer Vacations,
266
Roedde House (Vancouver),
146
Rogers' Chocolates (Victoria),
254
Romanoff & Company Antiques
(Victoria), 251
Roots Canada (Vancouver), 164
Ross Bay (Victoria), 186, 229
Ross Bay Beaches (Victoria),
235
Ross Bay Cemetery (Victoria),
228–229, 249
The Roundhouse (Vancouver),
155
The Roxy (Vancouver), 174

Royal B.C. Museum (Victoria),
225–226, 232
Royal Caribbean, 28
Royal London Wax Museum
(Victoria), 226–227, 242
Royal Theatre (Victoria), 256
Royal Victoria Marathon, 26
Running, Vancouver, 143–144
Running Room (Vancouver),
139
Russell Books (Victoria), 253

Saanich Inlet, 236
Safety, 35
Sailing
Vancouver, 139
Victoria, 238
St. Andrew's Roman Catholic
Cathedral (Victoria), 248
St. James Anglican Church
(Vancouver), 154
St. Paul's Episcopal Church
(Vancouver), 148
Salmon
Steveston Salmon Festival, 22
Vancouver area, 128, 142
shopping, 165, 166
Victoria area, 230
Salmon Village (Vancouver),
166
Salvatore Ferragamo (Vancou-
ver), 163
Sam Kee Building (Vancouver),
153
SATH (Society for Accessible
Travel & Hospitality), 36
Scenic Marine Drive bike path
(Victoria), 235
Science World at Telus World of
Science (Vancouver), 123,
130
Scotiabank Dance Centre
(Vancouver), 173
Scottish Dance Society
(Victoria), 257
Scuba diving, Victoria, 236
SeaBus (Vancouver), 58
Seafun Safaris Whale Watching
(Victoria), 239
Seasons, 19–20
Sea-to-Sky Highway (Highway
99), 3, 142
Whistler Blackcomb, 262
Seawall, Stanley Park (Vancou-
ver), 139
Seawall around Stanley Park
(Vancouver), 116, 117, 126,
136

Second Beach (Vancouver),
117, 130, 134, 140
Second Suit for Men & Women
(Vancouver), 163
Senior travel, 37
Seymour Golf and Country
Club (Vancouver), 138
Shanghai Alley (Vancouver),
153
The Shark Club Bar and Grill
(Vancouver), 176
Shaughnessy (Vancouver),
113–114
Shaughnessy Golf and Country
Club (Vancouver), 138
Shine (Vancouver), 179
Ships and ferries. *See* Boat
travel and cruises
Shoes, Vancouver, 168
Shopping, 159–170
Victoria, 251–255
Whistler Blackcomb, 280
Sights and attractions
Vancouver, 109–144
Victoria, 221–239
Silk Road Aromatherapy and
Tea Company (Victoria),
254–255
Silk Road Art Trading Co.
(Vancouver), 153, 161
Sinclair Centre (Vancouver),
167
Singing Pass Trail, 277
Sins of the City Walking Tour
(Vancouver), 119–120
Skiing
Mt. Washington, 238–239
Vancouver area, 139–140
Whistler, 274
Skoah (Vancouver), 163
SkyRide gondola (Vancouver),
125
SkyTrain (Vancouver), 58
Sleighing, 275
Smoking, 62
Snowbus, 262
Snow Goose Festival (Vancou-
ver), 142
Snowmobiling, 275
Snowshoeing, 276
Soccer, Vancouver, 144
Sonar (Vancouver), 179
Songhees Point (Victoria), 243
Sooke Potholes trail, 238
South Beach Trail, 291
South China Seas Trading Com-
pany (Vancouver), 164
Space Centre, H. R. MacMillan
(Vancouver), 120, 122, 158

ACCOMMODATIONS— VANCOUVER

RESTAURANTS— VICTORIA

RESTAURANTS— OTHER AREAS

There's a parking lot where my ocean view should be.

 À la place de la vue sur l'océan, me voilà avec une vue sur un parking.

 Anstatt Meerblick habe ich Sicht auf einen Parkplatz.

 Al posto della vista sull'oceano c'è un parcheggio.

 No tengo vista al mar porque hay un parque de estacionamiento.

 Há um parque de estacionamento onde deveria estar a minha vista do oceano.

 Ett parkeringsområde har byggts på den plats där min utsikt över oceanen borde vara.

Er ligt een parkeerterrein waar mijn zee-uitzicht zou moeten zijn.

هنالك موقف للسيارات مكان ما وجب ان يكون المنظر الخلاب المطل على المحيط .

眼前に広がる紺碧の海・・・じゃない。窓の外は駐車場！

停车场的位置应该是我的海景所在。

I'm fluent in pig latin.

Hotel mishaps aren't bound by geography.
Neither is our Guarantee. It covers your entire travel experience, including the price. So if you don't get the ocean view you booked, we'll work with our travel partners to make it right, right away. See www.travelocity.com/guarantee for details.